In Pursuit of Meaning

Vol. 1: Religion

In Pursuit of Meaning
Collected Studies of Baruch A. Levine

Volume 1: Religion

BARUCH A. LEVINE

Edited by
ANDREW D. GROSS

Winona Lake, Indiana
EISENBRAUNS
2011

Printed in the United States of America

www.eisenbrauns.com

Library of Congress Cataloging-in-Publication Data

Levine, Baruch A.
In pursuit of meaning : collected studies of Baruch A. Levine / edited by Andrew Gross.
v. cm.
Includes bibliographical references and index.
ISBN 978-1-57506-206-8 (hardback; 2-vol. set : alk. paper) — ISBN 978-1-57506-207-5 (hardback; vol. 1 : alk. paper) — ISBN 978-1-57506-208-2 (hardback; vol. 2 : alk. paper)
1. Bible. O.T.—Criticism, interpretation, etc. 2. Sacrifice—Biblical teaching. 3. Ugarit (Extinct city)—Religious life and customs. 4. Inscriptions, Aramaic—Jordan—Dayr ʿAlla, Tall. 5. Canaanites—Religion. 6. Balaam (Biblical figure). 7. Temple scroll. 8. Cosmography. 9. Hebrew language—Lexicography. 10. Hebrew language—Grammar. I. Gross, Andrew. II. Title.
BS1171.3.L48 2011
221.9—dc22
2010045563

The paper used in this publication meets the minimum requirements of the American National Standard for Information Sciences—Permanence of Paper for Printed Library Materials, ANSI Z39.48-1984.⊗™

To my wife,
Corinne
A "support-group" of one.

Table of Contents
Volume I: Religion

D. Religious Themes

Preface

The fifty-one articles collected in these volumes represent the diverse contributions Prof. Levine has made to the study of the Hebrew Bible, the Ancient Near East, and Early Judaism. While brief addenda have been added in a few places, the articles otherwise appear here unchanged with regard to their contents. Each article was re-typeset, and then carefully edited in order to clean up any typographical errors that had occurred in the original publications. Whenever an article cites another article included in this collection, we have added a cross-reference enclosed within braces in the following format: {*VOL 1, PP. 45–54*}. For each article, we have included the original publication information in the first footnote (where we also acknowledge permission for republication).

When we began this project, it quickly became apparent that there is no single blueprint for how one publishes a collection of *kleine Schriften*. Besides the abovementioned addenda, we resisted the temptation to update any of the contents and opted to let each piece stand as a reflection of the author's thinking at the time of publication. We also decided against reformatting the articles to conform to a single style sheet, though we did make some minor adjustments where we deemed it appropriate (e.g., endnotes were converted to footnotes; British-style usage of quotation marks was replaced with American usage; references to forthcoming works were updated to include the full publication information, etc.).

I am honored to have been asked to help Prof. Levine shepherd this project though. Having learned a great deal from him as his student, it is both humbling and reassuring to realize that he has a great deal more wisdom yet to share.

Andrew D. Gross
Assistant Professor of Semitic Languages
The Catholic University of America
Washington, D.C.

Introduction

It is an accepted practice for senior scholars to publish volumes of their collected writings. This is especially true of those who, like myself, have most often presented their findings in the form of separate articles, rather than as complete books. For the most part, my publications have appeared in conference volumes, *Festschriften*, and a variety of journals. In an effort to render such works more accessible, and to call attention to their central themes, I have selected fifty-one of my articles that have appeared since 1963 for inclusion in the present collection.

I am most grateful to Jim Eisenbraun for welcoming this project, and for his invaluable guidance in carrying it to fruition. My former student, Andrew Gross, undertook to edit the materials, and to prepare the manuscript for publication. He is not only to be credited with exceptional technical skills, and praised for his assiduous commitment to task, but also to be recognized for his scholarly insights. I was fortunate to be able to turn to him for assistance.

Looking back, and reviewing my writings, I realize what it is that I have been seeking all along. I have been in pursuit of meaning, employing scholarly methods, primarily philology and semantics, to the exegesis of ancient Near Eastern texts, preserved in several languages, principally the Hebrew Bible. I regard language as the key to meaning. This conclusion would appear to be self-evident, and yet, philology is often sidelined in favor of engaging larger frameworks. Most of all, I challenge the notion that we already know the meaning of the words and clauses central to the texts under investigation, and may proceed directly to other considerations without first re-examining the smaller units. Again and again, that policy has resulted in flawed interpretation, and in missed opportunities for learning. This is not to say that scholars should stop at the smaller units, and, indeed, the tendency to do so has been largely responsible for the reaction against Semitic philology so noticeable since the latter part of the 20th century. It is our challenge to move outward from focal points to the circumference, from text to context, from content to structure.

Scholars approach their primary sources with certain questions in mind, and special interests to be addressed. In my case, the religion of the ancient Israelites and their neighbors has attracted most of my attention, and accounts for the largest group of studies included in the present collection. The order in which these studies are presented, and their groupings, were intended to reflect the primary research objective that informed them, while recognizing that most studies will involve the application of more than one method. I have not grouped the studies according to language or societal provenience, nor have I separated discussions of biblical religion from those which deal with Ugaritic religion, for example. This is because I subscribe to the idea of a cultural continuum in the ancient

Near East, which means, simply stated, that the Semitic languages are more alike than they are different from each other; that the religions of the region were more alike than they were different, and that we can identify common patterns of culture. To be sure, we note the phenomenon of *Eigendbegrifflichkeit*, (a term often used by Benno Landsberger), the autonomous character of individual societies and their core concepts, their special character. Yet, what is special can only be revealed through comparison.

As the years passed, my interests expanded to law and society, and to ancient history. As of late, it has become important in scholarly circles to clarify the difference between the historian and the textual scholar, especially in the biblical field. The textual scholar seeks to understand what the texts mean (or as we now hear, "*how* the texts mean"), whereas the historian seeks to reconstruct what happened, how life was lived. The two approaches overlap, and scholars employing either of them will inevitably utilize many of the same sources, but in different ways. Clearly, I belong with those textual scholars who are interested in history, but whose primary objective is to understand what texts, and other kinds of sources, are saying; to parse the narrative. Where I overlap most clearly with the historian of Near Eastern antiquity is in the area of contextual interpretation, a class of methods aimed at identifying for whom our sources speak, at locating the *Sitz-im-Leben* of their authors, compilers, and preservers. The search for original context is best pursued in comparative scope, with attention to the larger region of the Near East.

As I review the collected articles, I can recall the factors that originally generated them. In some cases, I was exploring specific subjects related to the two commentary projects that occupied my attention for about twenty-five years, the commentary on Leviticus in the *JPS Torah Commentary* (1989), and the *Anchor Bible Commentary* on Numbers, Volume 1 (1993), and Volume 2 (2000). My engagement with these projects was gradual, and a good number of the studies collected here paved the way, by targeting specific problems raised by the biblical texts. These include the poetic passages in Numbers (e.g. the Balaam Orations), and specific rituals in Leviticus, such as the celebration of the festivals. In other cases, new discoveries attracted my attention, some of which also related to the larger projects. The salient examples are my several articles on the Deir 'Alla inscriptions which mention the name of Balaam, thereby connecting with the so-called Balaam Pericope of Numbers 22–24.

I actually know how I became interested in biblical cultic studies in the first place. Early on, I undertook a study of a group of Ugaritic ritual texts, which had not received commensurate scholarly attention at the time, only to realize that they could be better understood by comparing them with biblical ritual texts, with which they shared cognate cultic terminology and similar textual forms. I was so fascinated by the significance of Ugaritic for biblical studies, that I made a U-turn, and began to utilize Ugaritic evidence for the explication of biblical texts! In 1974, my first monograph, *In the Presence of the Lord* (Leiden: E. J. Brill) appeared, where I presented a preliminary analysis of the biblical sacrificial system.

There is inevitably a chance element in every scholar's publication history. I refer to invitations to contribute and participate. I had always been interested in Aramaic, but it was an invitation by my colleague, Jacob Neusner, to contribute an Appendix to the 5th volume of his classic work, *A History of the Jews of Babylonia* (Leiden: E.J.Brill, 1970), on the Aramaic magical bowls, that stimulated me to pursue Aramaic studies in a lasting way. Generally, invitations to participate in conferences and professional meetings, and to contribute to Jubilee Volumes, have played a role in setting my agenda. Finally, my teaching curriculum over the years, first at Brandeis University (1962–1969) and then at New York University (1969–2000) stimulated creativity, with many scholarly problems coming up for discussion, not only in graduate, but in undergraduate classes, as well. I have been privileged to instruct gifted students, who have tested the limits of my knowledge and comprehension. The persistent need to answer questions posed by students, and to explicate the subjects of instruction, has been stimulating, as have the intellectual demands posed by directing Doctoral dissertations. Both Brandeis University and New York University supported my research endeavors generously. As I review the list of articles, I realize how important was the role of the library of the École Biblique in Jerusalem, over the years.

The post World War II period saw a surge of scholarly activity, making it possible for me to study and consult with great masters and learned colleagues, here and abroad, especially in Israel. There was something magical about that period of time, when many European scholars came to live in America, and when the Israeli academy was being enriched by immigrant Europeans, and also by emergent, home-grown Israelis. Biblical archeology was in full bloom, Assyriology was expanding, research in Ugaritic was advancing, with new discoveries of texts, and scholars were strengthening their hold on Northwest-Semitic and Aramaic sources. The study of ancient Near Eastern history was being transformed. It was not long until the European centers revived, generating new contacts across the ocean. In a single generation, I could consult with Benjamin Mazar, Abraham Malamat and Hayim Tadmor in Jerusalem, with Thorkild Jacobsen at Harvard, with my former teacher, H.L.Ginsberg in New York, and with Franz Rosenthal and William Hallo at Yale. I could study Aramaic and Syriac with Yehezkel Kutscher, and discuss almost any subject with Jonas Greenfield. I could participate in the Biblical Colloquium every year. All of this was in addition to the formal instruction that I received (see further). I believe that I was born at the right time!

There is a background to my publication history, namely, my "situation in life" prior to 1962, when I received my Doctorate. I come from the Jewish tradition of Torah study, mentored by my first Hebrew teacher, my father, Benjamin Levine ("May his light enlighten us"). My brother, Joseph, and I were taught at an early age that learning was God's program for humankind, and that learning never ends! My environment was both religious and secular from my youth, and I never experienced intellectual or emotional conflict on that account. Together with my father, my mother, Helen Kaplan Levine, rejected the then prevalent notion that a child could only master one language at a time, and they affirmed our devotion as a family to the Jewish heritage. During my teens, I concurrently studied Hebrew Bible and Modern Hebrew literature with a private teacher, and Talmud at a famous Yeshivah. At the Jewish Theological Seminary (1951–55) I studied Hebrew Bible with H. Louis Ginsberg and Talmud with Saul Lieberman, and pursued a full curriculum of Judaic studies. At Brandeis University (1959–62) I studied with Cyrus H. Gordon, who taught me that the Hebrew Bible was "an open book," inviting new methods of comparative study. All three overwhelmed me, but at the same time, encouraged me. Then, I started writing!

Baruch A. Levine
Skirball Professor Emeritus,
of Bible and Ancient Near Eastern Studies
New York University

Abbreviations

References to Assyriological publications follow the abbreviations lists in *CAD* and *AHw*. Note also that some individual articles include their own abbreviations list.

AASOR	*Annual of the American Schools of Oriental Research*
AB	Anchor Bible
ABD	D. N. Freedman (ed.), *Anchor Bible Dictionary* (6 vols.; New York: Doubleday, 1992).
AHw	W. von Soden, *Akkadisches Handwörterbuch* (3 vols.; Wiesbaden: Harrasowitz, 1965–1981)
AJSL	*American Journal of Semitic Languages and Literatures*
ANET	J. B. Pritchard (ed.), *Ancient Near Eastern Texts Relating to the Old Testament* (3rd edition; Princeton University Press, 1969)
AOAT	Alter Orient und Altes Testament
AOS	American Oriental Series
AP	A. E. Cowley, *Aramaic Papyri of the Fifth Century B.C.* (Oxford: Clarendon Press, 1923)
BASOR	*Bulletin of the American Schools of Oriental Research*
CAD	*The Assyrian Dictionary of the Oriental Institute of the University of Chicago* (Chicago: The Oriental Institute, 1956–)
CCPA	*A Corpus of Christian Palestinian Aramaic*, C. Müller-Kessler and M. Sokoloff (5 vols.; Groningen: Styx Publications, 1997–).
CHANE	Culture and History of the Ancient Near East
DJD	Discoveries in the Judaean Desert (of Jordan)
DSA	Abraham Tal, *A Dictionary of Samaritan Aramaic* (2 vols.; Leiden: Brill, 2000)
DNWSI	J. Hoftijzer and K. Jongeling, *Dictionary of the North-west Semitic Inscriptions* (2 vols.; Leiden: E. J. Brill, 1995)
DUL	G. del Olmo Lete and J. Sanmartín, *A Dictionary of the Ugaritic Language in the Alphabetic Tradition* (2 vols.; Leiden: Brill, 2003)
EA	J. A. Knudtzon, *Die El-Amarna Tafeln* (2 vols.; Leipzig: J. C. Hinrichs, 1908–15)
GKC	*Gesenius' Hebrew Grammar, as edited and enlarged by the late E. Kautzsch.* 2nd English ed., rev. in accordance with the 28th German ed. (1909) by A. E. Cowley (Oxford: Clarendon Press; New York: Oxford University Press, 1910)
HALAT	L. Koehler and W. Baumgartner, *Hebräisches und Aramäisches Lexikon zum Alten Testament* (5 vols.; Leiden: E.J. Brill, 1967–1990)
HAR	*Hebrew Annual Review*
HdO	Handbuch der Orientalistik
HTR	*Harvard Theological Review*
HUCA	*Hebrew Union College Annual*
IEJ	*Israel Exploration Journal*
JANES	*Journal of the Ancient Near Eastern Society* (*of Columbia University*)

JAOS	*Journal of the American Oriental Society*
JBL	*Journal of Biblical Literature*
JCS	*Journal of Cuneiform Studies*
JDS	Judean Desert Studies
JNES	*Journal of Near Eastern Studies*
JSOTSup	Journal for the Study of the Old Testament. Supplement series
KBL	L. Koehler and W. Baumgartner, *Lexicon in Veteris Testamenti Libros* (2 vols.; Leiden: E. J. Brill, 1953)
KTU	M. Dietrich, O. Loretz, and J. Sanmartín, *The Cuneiform Alphabetic Texts from Ugarit, Ras Ibn Hani and Other Places* (*KTU* 2nd ed.) (Münster: Ugarit-Verlag, 1995)
LS	C. Brockelmann, *Lexicon Syriacum* (2nd edition; Halle: M. Niemeyer, 1928; reprint: Hildesheim: Georg Olms, 1966)
NEB	New English Bible
NJPS	New Jewish Publication Society Version (*Tanakh: The Holy Scriptures, The New JPS Translation According to the Traditional Hebrew Text* [Philadelphia: Jewish Publication Society, 1985])
PIHANS	Publications de l'Institut historique et archeologique neerlandais de Stamboul
RB	*Revue Biblique*
SAA	State Archives of Assyria
ScrHier	Scripta Hierosolymitana
TAD	B. Porten and A. Yardeni, *Textbook of Aramaic Documents from Ancient Egypt* (4 vols.; Jerusalem: The Hebrew University, 1986–1999).
UF	*Ugarit-Forschungen*
VTSup	Supplements to Vetus Testamentum
ZA	*Zeitschrift für Assyriologie*
ZAW	*Zeitschrift für die alttestamentliche Wissenschaft*
ZDPV	*Zeitschrift des deutschen Palästina-Vereins*

A. History of Religions

Assyrian Ideology and Israelite Monotheism*

Few subjects in the field of biblical and ancient Near Eastern studies have elicited as much attention in recent decades as the origin and development of Israelite-biblical monotheism. One needs more than the fingers of both hands to list the many collections of articles and individual monographs that treat this threshold in the history of religions. Attention shifts in the search for precursors from ancient Egypt to Mesopotamia, and in the West Semitic sphere, to Ugarit and the Middle Euphrates. It will be the burden of the present discussion, while providing requisite background, to focus on the Neo-Assyrian factor in the ongoing development of Israelite monotheism, rather than on the search for its ultimate origin, which may be beyond reach in the present state of knowledge.

More precisely, I will propose that the policies and campaigns of the Sargonids, especially of Sennacherib, who made Nineveh his political capital, elicited an Israelite response that directly impacted the God-idea. That response is most immediately expressed in the prophecies of First Isaiah of Jerusalem, Sennacherib's contemporary. It was the threat to the survival of Judah and Jerusalem, emanating from Assyria, which called forth an enhanced God-idea. That idea evolved into universal monotheism, and in effect, enabled the people of Israel to survive exile and domination by successive world empires. In such terms, universal monotheism is to be seen as a religious response to empire, an enduring world-view founded on the proposition that all power exercised by humans, no matter how grandiose, is transient, and ultimately subservient to a divine plan for the whole earth, for all nations.

Mythic, Thematic, and Socio-Political Approaches to Israelite Monotheism

If we are to achieve greater clarity as to the true character of Israelite monotheism, it will be necessary to liberate ourselves from the dominance of certain methodologies that have held sway. One often encounters the view that the roots of monotheism go back far in human experience, to very ancient notions of

---

* Originally published in D. Colon and A. George (eds.), *NINEVEH: Papers of the XLIXe Rencontre Assyriologique Internationale* (London 7–11 July, 2003) (London: British School of Archaeology in Iraq (Gertrude Bell Memorial) with the aid of the MBI Foundation, 2005), Vol. 2, pp. 411–427 (= *Iraq* 67 [2005]). Reprinted with permission from the British Institute for the Study of Iraq.

This article is the written version of the paper originally scheduled to conclude the final session of the XLIXe Rencontre Assyriologique Internationale. In the event, the report of Col. Bogdanos was much longer than expected and left no time for Professor Levine to speak. It is a pleasure to right that wrong at last by publishing Professor Levine's paper here. Eds.

a unified cosmos under the rule of a supreme, creator god. This essentially mythological approach has much to contribute to our understanding of monotheism, to be sure, but it can also be misleading. It fails to distinguish between what H. W. F. Saggs, in his monograph *The Encounter with the Divine in Mesopotamia and Israel*, calls the "divine in creation" and the "divine in history" (Saggs 1978:30–92). The notion of the "cosmos as a state", to use Thorkild Jacobsen's phrase (1946, and cf. Jacobsen 1963), is a dynamic projection of human existence on earth. It expands in rhythm with the broadening of human social and political horizons—from a celestial city-state, governed by a divine council, to a kingdom of deities, to a cosmic empire. Innovations in configuring the god-idea did not originate in such mythic projections, however. They are rather a function of the "divine in history", where we find that political entities and leadership roles are projected onto or reflected in the god-idea, ultimately of a world empire ruled over by an imperial king.

In considering such developments, we must bear in mind that long periods of time elapsed until the cosmic, celestial horizon, already experienced by humans at an early period, was translated into a socio-political awareness of interconnected human societies, inhabiting far-flung regions of the known world. In fact, such a global horizon is a feature of the Neo-Assyrian period, exemplified by the many lands that are encompassed by the "Sargon Geography", a *mappa mundi* recently re-edited and discussed by Wayne Horowitz (1998:67–95). The implications of its measured distances and relative locations have been discussed by Mario Liverani (2001). It was the very expansion of the Neo-Assyrian Empire that broadened the horizon of identification of many peoples of the ancient Near East, the Israelites among them.

Here is some of what Mario Liverani has to say about imperial kingship in the context of Assyrian ideology:

> A king is not legitimate because of the approval of god Aššur; a king, while he rules in Assyria is always legitimate, and his legitimacy is expressed in religious terms. In a broader sense, the divine approval is not the cause of the legitimacy of the action, it is clearly its *expressed form*. Therefore it would be incorrect to speak of the Assyrian king as "non-absolutist" in so far as he acts in the name and stead of the god Aššur, since Aššur is precisely the hypostasis of the Assyrian kingship (Liverani 1979:301).

We can say the same regarding kingship in ancient Israel, even though some biblical scholars resist comparative insights because of their theological implications. As examples, the profiles of ideal kingship set forth in Isaiah 9:5–6 and 11:1–10, whether or not they refer in the first instance to Hezekiah, express the very hypostasis of which Liverani speaks. The attributes of the ideal king, his wise counsel and judgment, and his capacity to resolve conflicts peacefully rather than by use of military force, are said to have been endowed by the God of Israel. It would be more accurate to invert this statement: Yahweh is the ideal king, by virtue of the fact that kingship serves as the model for configuring the

God-idea. Anticipating the discussion to follow, it is interesting to note that in one of the Assyrian prophecies, which Simo Parpola entitles "Prophecies for the Crown Prince Aššurbanipal", the kings of the lands come to Aššurbanipal to seek arbitration of their disputes. Parpola notes the comparison with the visions of world peace in Isaiah 2//Micah 4 (Parpola 1997:38, ll. 8–13).

This observation leads directly to the second methodological caveat, and to further consideration of Simo Parpola's recent studies. As is true of most students of the rise of monotheism in ancient Israel, Parpola focuses on thematic and conceptual similarities among religions, using phenomenological models, albeit with new evidence and deepened insight. He regards the ascendancy of the cult of Aššur during the Neo-Assyrian period as having had a direct bearing on the development of Israelite monotheism, an approach now further elaborated in his introduction to the volume of Assyrian prophecies (Parpola 1997:xiii–cviii). Parpola draws his evidence primarily from religious documents in configuring the god Aššur as head of the Assyrian pantheon. It is his view that Aššur came to embody all of the gods, beyond synthesizing all of their attributes, and he explores the relevance of this process for understanding the development of Israelite monotheism.

Although it is valid to conclude that Aššur eclipsed the other gods of the Assyrian pantheon as the Neo-Assyrian period progressed, it is not accurate to state that references to other gods in treaties, oaths and rituals, and in royal inscriptions and correspondence came to an end (on this, and related issues raised by Parpola's interpretation of Assyrian religion, see Porter 2000 and Weippert 2002). In a more fundamental respect, it is doubtful whether any amount of thematic or theological analysis of divine functions and attributes, however penetrating, can fully explain either the ascendancy of the god Aššur in Assyria, or of Yahweh in ancient Israel. Such analysis, as helpful as it is in describing phenomena, cannot explain why these divine "personalities", if one may use the term, emerged at specific times and locales, under particular circumstances. For this we require an understanding of the ideological dimensions of political history.

The importance of political documents as sources for the study of religion was brought home by a study of religious and legal concepts in the parity treaty between Ramesses II and Ḫattušili III. That study was undertaken in the mid-1990s in collaboration with my colleague at New York University, the Egyptologist Ogden Goelet (Goelet and Levine 1998). The Egyptian-Hittite treaty drew attention to political documents, especially those that speak for major ancient Near Eastern powers, as informative sources for the study of religion. It provided a clear illustration of how religious ideas, including conceptions of the gods, can be understood as responses to changing political realities. A critical edition of both versions of the treaty by Elmar Edel appeared posthumously (Edel 1997).

The treaty projects a bipolar world-order in which power is to be shared by Egypt and Hatti under their respective rulers on earth, and in heaven by the chief deity of each party, the sun-god representing Egypt and the weather-god representing the Hittites. Such two-dimensional parity pervades both the introductory section of the treaty and the paired line-up of divine witnesses to its enactment at the conclusion. In ideological translation, the treaty mirrored the political realities of the mid-thirteenth century B.C.E., pursuant to the historic impasse at the battle of Kadesh on the Orontes, where Egyptian power had been checked to a critical degree.

What is most interesting is that the treaty breaks with traditional claims of invincibility, especially prominent in the Egyptian sources, and instead of asserting that the chief god of one or the other power had guaranteed victory to his chosen king, sanctioned the resulting *status quo*, a *détente* of sorts, as having been divinely ordained from time immemorial. We encounter brotherly language reminiscent of earlier correspondence pertaining to royal marriages between Egypt and other powers, and such treaty language is subsequently cited in the Ramesside correspondence.

In religious terms, no one deity was perceived at the time as ruling over both Egypt and Hatti, just as, in reality, no one earthly empire enjoyed unrivalled power. A careful study of the Egyptian term *p3 nṯr*, "the god", and its Akkadian parallel, DINGIR-*lì*, occurring only once in the introduction to the treaty, led us to conclude that this terminology did not refer to a single, omnipotent deity, but either to some impersonal notion of divinity, or more likely, to the deity of reference, in immediate context. On this and other subjects related to the often adduced Egyptian precursors of Israelite monotheism, the reader is referred to the work by Erik Hornung (1982) on Egyptian conceptions of the divine. For its part, the Ramesside treaty captured a moment in the history of religious ideas, a message of earthly and cosmic peace, pronounced subsequent to the Amarna period, and just preceding the critical twelfth century B.C.E. The title of our 1998 study began: "Making Peace in Heaven and on Earth".

Studying this remarkable parity treaty left me with an afterthought that soon became an urgent question: If the Egyptian-Hittite treaty spoke for a bipolar world order, how would political documents that spoke for a unipolar world power express divine sanctions? Would they not proclaim the global supremacy of the unrivalled chief god of the imperial pantheon of the sole world-empire? With the historical context of classical, biblical prophecy in mind, I turned to the Neo-Assyrian annals and royal inscriptions of the eighth to seventh centuries B.C.E., from Tiglath-Pileser III, through Sargon II, to Sennacherib and beyond. In line with earlier Assyrian traditions, such documents speak of expansive conquests, and project a world dominated by the king of Assyria on earth and by the god Aššur in heaven. During this period, the ancient mandate of the Assyrian kings to expand their territory, to tread where no previous king had been before, was achieved in large measure, persistent rebellions and challenges to Assyrian hegemony notwithstanding.

The growing pre-eminence of the god Aššur at the expense of Marduk, the venerated patron deity of Babylon, can be correlated precisely with Sennacherib's aggressive policy toward Babylonia. What is more, the Assyrian claim to world supremacy and the exaltation of Aššur were most emphatic at the very time that Jerusalem and Judah were in the greatest danger. It is fascinating to contemplate that Sennacherib, that most celebrated servant of Aššur, may have inadvertently played a major role in assuring the enduring worship of Yahweh, the God of Israel!

I hypothesized that the critical political events of the Sargonid period, and the ideology that was generated by them, would have elicited an Israelite response, which was to go beyond the situation of the moment and have a lasting effect on Israelite religion. It is better to speak of response than of influence; in truth, response may be the clearest form of influence. This observation is directly relevant, because the Hebrew Bible, which fails to provide explicit evidence of stages in the development of Israelite religion, and contains no political documents in original form, nevertheless preserves distinctive, if not unique paradigms of response literature. As regards the present discussion, such responses are associated with the role of First Isaiah in counseling Judean kings against rebellion and anti-Assyrian alliances. The prophetic counsel, expressed overtly in the historiography of 2 Kings 18–20//Isaiah 36–9, is encoded in those sections of Isaiah 1–39 that can be reliably identified as Isaianic, thereby requiring us to decode the prophetic message. If properly understood, Isaiah's prophecies reveal how those who spoke for a beleaguered and conquered people reacted to the overwhelming impact of Assyrian conquest, and more generally, to the persistent threats of imperial power. In these orations, among the most beautiful examples of ancient Hebrew poetry, we hear the voice of the defeated trying to make sense of their desperate situation. Thus, Mario Liverani once again, in his discussion of the function of the imperialist ideology in times of conquest:

> At the moment of the impact there obviously takes place a struggle between ideologies; each providing its own audience with the explanation of what is happening: as there is an ideological justification for the victory, there can be an ideological justification for defeat and subjugation. When we possess sources from conquered countries, as in the case of Israel, the comparison is possible and rather enlightening (Liverani 1979:300).

We have clear indications that biblical authors of the period, foremost among them First Isaiah, not only knew what the Sargonid kings were about, but were also familiar with the particular style and idiom of Neo-Assyrian documents of the period. That they were clearly informed of Neo-Assyrian ideology, or propaganda, if you wish, is further indicated by their efforts to skew it to their own purposes. Thus, Peter Machinist (1983) identifies a series of specific idioms and motifs common to First Isaiah and the Neo-Assyrian sources, drawing many of his examples from the annals of Sargon II. In an ideological mode, Mordechai Cogan (1974:9–15) focuses on motifs such as divine abandonment, which figure in both biblical and Assyrian rationalizations of defeat, both of one's own forces and of those of the enemy. John Brinkman (1983) greatly clarifies this phenomenon by analyzing Esarhaddon's reflections on the causes of Babylon's downfall. In biblical prophecy, these rationalizations were enhanced, supplying causes for the displeasure of the God of Israel. Attributions of culpability ranged from religious to social and moral offenses, from idolatry to injustice and corruption, from religious hypocrisy to mistreatment of the poor and weak.

Thus far, I have published a preliminary Hebrew study on this subject (Levine 2003). A further elaboration of it in German, translated from lectures I delivered at several German universities in October 2001, has also appeared in a collection of studies on the subject of monotheism, entitled *Der eine Gott und die Götter* (Levine 2003a). This is my third effort, in which there will be inevitable repetition, but also a new emphasis on the cult of Aššur.

As already stated, it is my contention that in the Judean society of First Isaiah's time, the immediacy and inescapable force of the Assyrian threat demanded a God-idea broad enough to measure up to empire. First Isaiah expounded just such a concept for the first time in biblical literature. He preached that international events, albeit catastrophic, were going according to the plan of the God of Israel for the whole earth. Powerful Assyria, with its boastful king, was nothing more than an instrument of punishment, a rod of rage wielded by the God of Israel against his own people.

The sparing of Jerusalem from destruction by Sennacherib in 701 B.C.E., regarded in Hebrew Scripture as miraculous, served as a powerful sign that the God of Israel controlled the fortunes of the Assyrians. Remember the refrain of the Assyrian royal annals: *i-na e-muq* ^{d}*Aš-šur* EN-*ia* "By the strength of Aššur, my lord" (Frahm 1997:51, l. 9 *et passim*). If it is Aššur who empowers the Assyrian empire, only a Yahweh more powerful still could rescue even a remnant of Israel.

From Henotheism to Monotheism: The Expanding Horizon of Israelite Religion

Before attempting to interpret First Isaiah's conception of God, it would be well to step back for a moment, and to ask how religious thinking in Jerusalem and Judah arrived at this point of development. We have already identified several methodologies, indicating that it is the sociopolitical approach that affords the clearest insights into the development of Israelite monotheism, because the most appropriate model for configuring universal monotheism is world-empire. If it is accurate to say that concepts of the divine expand in response to an expanding horizon of identification, we can identify at least two overlapping phases in the expanding Israelite horizon, the regional and the global. A disproportionate amount of attention has been devoted to the former, and too little to the latter!

The regional phase, which began earlier and overlapped with the global, is associated with the emergence of the Israelite societies and the founding of two monarchies in Canaan. It involves confrontations with Canaanites and Philistines, and with neighboring peoples—Ammonites, Moabites, Edomites and Midianites. I would include encounters with the expanding Aramean kingdom in Syria and the less bellicose Phoenician city-states. All of these entities shared an overarching West Semitic pantheon, known in earlier forms from Ugaritic myth and ritual, where El and the younger Baal, and Ashtoret and Asherah, and Dagon, and some other divinities, realized in various manifestations, held sway. At the same time, we note the presence of national gods Kemosh of the Moabites, for instance, and Yahweh of the Israelites.

The "central concern" (once again, a locution favored by Thorkild Jacobsen) of the Yahwistic leadership in this context was to demonstrate that it was Yahweh, the tribal-national god of the Israelites, not some other deity, such as El or Baal, who had granted his people sovereignty in Canaan and victory over neighboring foes. The religious agenda was directed at advancing henotheistic Yahwism. The Israelites are told in Exodus 6 that El, who was worshipped by their patriarchs, is only a manifestation of Yahweh: Yahweh by another name. It was really Yahweh who brought them out of Egypt.

The Egyptian saga, which projects a war of gods between Yahweh and the mighty gods of Egypt, is part of the henotheistic phase. Some would dispute this classification because, as a world power, Egypt was a recurring variable in relations between Northern Israel and Judah, and the Mesopotamian empires. However, the saga of liberation from Egyptian bondage more properly belongs with the conquest-settlement traditions, and is very different in tone from the chronicles of 2 Kings, and from prophetic reactions to the Neo-Assyrian threat, as will become evident in the discussion to follow. The Egyptian saga served to inform Israelites, in a manner perhaps more epic than historical, how they came to live in Canaan in the first place.

The national agenda is epitomized in the narratives of the book of Judges, which may have been composed as far back as the eighth or ninth century B.C.E. Thus, Gideon is reassured that Yahweh, not Baal and his Asherah, will bring him victory over the Midianites (Judges 6). We are told that Gideon had heard of Yahweh and his wondrous deeds at the Exodus, but had yet to be persuaded that Yahweh was with him in his current battles. Similarly, in Judges 11 we find Jephthah telling the Ammonites that what Kemosh (apparently on loan from the Moabites) had granted them is theirs, but what Yahweh had granted Israel is theirs. In seeking to explain how exclusive Yahwism ultimately predominated in Judah in the near-exilic period, the best I can come up with is this: The fervor of the national movement led to the progressive paring-away of gods and goddesses, and the exaltation of the national God, Yahweh (Levine 1996).

In the same polemical spirit, Elijah at the Muḥraqa of the Carmel range demands that the people, living in an area of mixed Phoenician and Israelite demography, choose between Baal and Yahweh (1 Kings 18). That message is conveyed in tales that condemn the policy of the Northern Israelite king, Ahab, of the ninth century B.C.E. If we want to know why El was synthesized and Baal rejected by the same Yahwists, we shall not find the answer in the respective attributes of these two deities. As we now know from Ugaritic mythology, both were beneficent heaven gods. The answer lies in the fact that Baal worship presented a real and present threat to the spread of Yahwism early on, especially in the Northern Kingdom, whereas El worship apparently did not. In fact, the only early polemic against El worship, as manifested in the bull cult, is to be found in some veiled references in Hosea (8:4–5, 10:5) to heterodox practices among the Transjordanian Israelites of Gilead.

It must be conceded that there are certain aspects of the rejection of polytheism, evident in early Israelite religion, which I am at a loss to explain fully. It seems that we are confronted by a culture that we do not fully understand, a mentality that was averse to goddesses and emphatically aniconic. Trygve Mettinger (1979), Saul Olyan (1988), Morton Smith (1971), and Mark Smith (1991, 2001) have further clarified these aspects of religious life in ancient Israel. More recently, there is the study by Bernhard Lang (2003), entitled "Die Jahwe-allein-Bewegung", which takes its cue from the label coined by Morton Smith, "The Yahweh-Alone" party. For his part, Olyan deals with the cult of Asherah, and Mettinger discusses current views on iconography and the ban on cult images. Morton Smith has attempted to chart the internal tension between the strict Yahwists and those endorsing a more traditional and less exclusive cultic policy. Mark Smith has contributed a regional overview, with strong emphasis on the Ugaritic sources. In sum, although we now possess a greater understanding of what happened in ancient Israel, and how it happened, we still cannot fully explain why religious thinking took the course that it did.

Perhaps we can achieve greater clarity about why the global horizon emerged in ancient Israel when it did. It begins to be felt when the security of Judah and Northern Israel became increasingly affected by the western campaigns of the Assyrian Empire, situated as these kingdoms were in the crosscurrent with Egypt. We see early signs of this expanded horizon in the prophecies of Hosea and Amos. Yahwistic henotheism was fast becoming untenable, as the Neo-Assyrian threat produced a crisis of faith, along with more practical dangers. The global horizon reaches its apex in First Isaiah, who talks most noticeably about Israel's fate and the destiny of empires. In a sense, that conversation was to continue indefinitely throughout Jewish history, as the people of Israel, inside its land and outside of it, lived under successive imperial regimes—Babylonian, Persian, Seleucid, Roman, and so on. It was not too long until prophecy, an historically oriented genre, gave way to apocalyptic, which spoke of the end of history and a new world to come.

It is my sense that the most significant breakthrough in the development of Israelite monotheism was not the exclusionary break-away of Israelite henotheism from its counterparts in the region, but rather its vital response to Assyrian imperialism. The exclusive worship of Yahweh, the Israelite national God, though surely basic to Israelite monotheism, represents only one phase in the process. Monotheism became universal only at the point when Yahweh was declared to be the sole sovereign over all nations. In this respect, the statement of the Decalogue, "You shall have no other gods (אלהים אחרים) in my presence", is best taken as henotheistic, not strictly as monotheistic, as it has been understood in both the Jewish and Christian traditions.

Assyria and Judah: The Historical Background

The historical review could begin at any one of several points during the Sargonid period, but the most critical time to be examined for present purposes is the reign of Sennacherib (705–681), viewed against the background of Sargon II, his predecessor. Mario Liverani and Hayim Tadmor, foremost among many, have not only clarified the events of this period but have developed methodologies for dealing with the ideological underpinnings of Assyrian imperialism. John Brinkman has contributed a penetrating treatment of the view from Babylonia. Coming to this area of inquiry from biblical and West Semitic studies, I have drawn extensively on the findings of these and other scholars. For purposes of the present discussion, a general historical outline of the immediate situation in Judah prior to the Assyrian blockade of Jerusalem in 701 will suffice.

During the first years of his reign, which began in 705 after the death of Sargon II in battle in Cilicia, Sennacherib embarked on major campaigns, first to Babylonia and then to Judah and the west, after rebellions had broken out in both quarters. Merodach-Baladan II, a veteran fomenter of insurrections in Babylonia, was in contact with Hezekiah, king of Judah in Jerusalem, so that we have at the very least, a triangulated situation if not an outright alliance (Brinkman 1964, 1973, 1984:45–83). The Egyptian forces that came to Hezekiah's aid were defeated, and Sennacherib's army arrived at the gates of Jerusalem in 701, after the Assyrian capture of Lachish. According to both the annals of Sennacherib's third campaign and the biblical account in 2 Kings, notwithstanding their differences, Sennacherib did not destroy Jerusalem or annex Judah. After devastating the area, he accepted heavy tribute from Hezekiah. Some biblical scholars and political historians, including A. Kirk Grayson (1992), have considered it probable that there was a second Assyrian campaign against Judah later in Sennacherib's reign, after his destruction of Babylon in 689. It was then, according to this view, that the Nubian Pharaoh, Tarhaqa, led an army into Palestine (2 Kings 19:9–13). There is no Assyrian evidence for a second campaign, and it is likely that such a reconstruction of events is harmonistic, and not historical.

As for Sennacherib, he took his time in solving the Babylonian problem to his satisfaction (although it did not remain solved!), and after successive campaigns and changes in Babylonian administration, he destroyed the city and its temples, foremost among them Esagila in 689 (Brinkman 1973). He was murdered by one of his sons in Nineveh in 681, an event that did not go unnoticed in the Hebrew Bible. Note the typological telescoping of events in 2 Kings 19:36–7. In v. 36 we are told that Sennacherib returned to Nineveh, an event that presumably occurred *ca* 701, and in the very next verse we read that he was murdered, an event that we know occurred twenty years later. In the mind of the biblical historiographer, divine justice was on fast-forward!

Throughout the better part of the second half of the eighth century B.C.E., Isaiah had counseled against rebellion and anti-Assyrian alliances. The so-called "Syro-Ephraimite" coalition against Assyria had led to the annexation of the Northern Kingdom and the deportation of much of its population (Cazelles

1992). However we frame the events of the period between the fall of Samaria and the death of Sargon, from *ca* 720 to 705, involving Hezekiah either more or less in anti-Assyrian activity, it is clear that after Sargon's death in 705 Hezekiah committed the serious error of going against the prophet's counsel. He ceased to pay tribute, and in an effort to exercise hegemony in the south, deposed the Philistine ruler of Ekron, Padi (Naʿaman 1994). The name Padi has now been attested in a royal dedicatory inscription from Tell Miqneh-Ekron (Gitin *et al.* 1997).

Tadmor (1986) goes into considerable detail to emphasize the international scope of the political and military situation at the unusual death of Sargon II, the first king in Assyrian history to die in battle, whose body was never retrieved, and who was left unburied. These events undoubtedly sent shock-waves throughout the empire, and the fact that Sennacherib waited four years before launching his campaign to Judah and the west suggests hesitation on his part about undertaking this venture at all. It may not have been entirely unreasonable for Hezekiah and others in the west, far from the Assyrian heartland, to calculate that rebellion would succeed. Hezekiah's final decision to submit to the Assyrian yoke saved the day, and if we accept the basic record of events as presented by the authors and redactors of 2 Kings 18–20//Isaiah 36–9, that decision was obedient to First Isaiah's counsel. Jerusalem was spared, which was a powerful sign of divine providence.

The end-result of Sennacherib's military ventures in Judah was unexpected, for it was not Assyrian policy to leave the capital of an insurrectionist kingdom standing on its tell. There have been diverse explanations as to why Sennacherib spared Jerusalem, none of them conclusive. Eva von Dassow (by written communication) speculates that Padi, the Philistine ruler of Ekron, may have served as Hezekiah's bargaining chip. Sennacherib may have been content to restore his own hegemony in Philistia by securing Padi's release and reinstatement, to collect tribute, and to leave a submissive Hezekiah in Jerusalem. In any event, both Hezekiah and Jerusalem survived!

The Book of Kings presents a highly unfavorable view of the long reign of Manasseh that is conditioned by a particular religious outlook, focusing on his heterodoxy. He was in reality an effective king under the precarious circumstances. Israel Finkelstein (1994) has summarized in considerable detail the sketchy archeological record of the seventh century B.C.E. prior to the reign of Josiah, and concludes that under Manasseh the kingdom of Judah continued to exist, albeit with a seriously reduced population and the loss of the fertile Shephelah. Nevertheless, Jerusalem remained the capital of Judah throughout the seventh century, though its area and population density during the middle part of the century are not known for certain. Manasseh continued to pay tribute to the Assyrians, but perhaps not as much as was formerly thought. Actually, Judah began an economic revival, attributable in large measure to activity in the Beer-Sheba area on the Arabian trade routes. Finkelstein suggests that this effort was actively encouraged by the Assyrians for their own purposes. There is reference to Manasseh's construction projects in 2 Chron 33:14, which may preserve historical information.

In retrospect, it is sobering to realize that had Jerusalem not been spared in 701, Judah would have undoubtedly met the same fate as Northern Israel twenty years earlier, and that would have marked the end of the Israelites as a people. Even in the midst of loss, many Judeans may have been heartened by Isaiah's assurances of survival.

Assyrian Ideology

In his recent essay "World Dominion: The Expanding Horizon of the Assyrian Empire", Hayim Tadmor (1999) takes us back to the reign of Tukulti-Ninurta I (1244–1208). An annual royal ritual, edited by K. F. Müller (1937), reports that the priest of Aššur placed a scepter in the hand of the king and commanded him, "With your just scepter, extend your land!" Assyrian kings also received weapons with which to carry out this mandate. Curiously, I discussed the very same ritual about thirty years ago in my early studies of the biblical priestly cult, explaining the Hebrew term *šelāmîm* as a cognate of Akkadian *šulmānu*, an Assyrian temple offering which figured prominently in the Assyrian royal ritual (Levine 1974:29–32). Now my interest in this text lies not in ritual itself, but in the nexus of cult and kingship.

Tadmor immediately shifts forward in time to about six hundred years later, when a similar expansionist command is issued to Aššurbanipal. Tadmor proceeds to discuss the notion of "heroic priority", the duty of a king to tread where none of his predecessors had ventured, to extend the land of Aššur. We thus observe an ideological continuity, beginning even before Tukulti-Ninurta I and reaching down to the last Assyrian kings of the seventh century B.C.E., endorsing military expansion and exalting the god Aššur as its divine standard bearer. The claim that history repeats itself has no better demonstration than that provided by a comparison of the reigns of Tukulti-Ninurta I and Sennacherib. Both Machinist (1976), in his study of the Tukulti-Ninurta epic, and Tadmor take particular note of the seal from Babylon mentioned in one of Sennacherib's inscriptions. It had been seized as booty by Tukulti-Ninurta I and somehow found its way back to Babylon, only to be retrieved once again by Sennacherib from the spoils of Babylon. The obverse of the inscription reads in part, "I, Sennacherib, King of Assyria, after six hundred years, conquered Babylon, and from the wealth of Babylon, I retrieved it" (Luckenbill 1924:93, d ll. 5–7). This recollection is a fascinating example of how memory functions in historical writing, as traditional justification. It also directs our attention to an important cultic-political correlation between (a) Sennacherib's Babylonian policy, which marked a departure from that of Sargon II, and from almost all of his predecessors, and (b) the consequent rise in status of Aššur at the expense of Marduk, the venerated patron deity of Babylon, as will be discussed presently.

In retrospect, as Tadmor explains, Sennacherib did not excel at "heroic priority", as had Tiglath-Pileser III and Sargon II. He inherited an empire rather than creating one through expansion, and his third campaign to Judah and the west was actually exceptional. Sennacherib rather focused on the center, on subduing Babylonia and having Assyria take its place as the heart of empire. Tadmor (1989) explains how the militant policy of Sennacherib toward Babylonia was registered and expressed in texts related to the cult of Aššur, and in epic and royal inscriptions, all of which signaled changes in Assyrian religion. A valuable treatment of texts relevant to what is often termed the theological reform of Sennacherib is provided in concise form, with critical analysis, by Eckart Frahm in his recent work, *Einleitung in die Sanherib-Inschriften* (1997:220–9), under the headings "Reformtheologisch inspirierte Texte mit Bezug zum Gott Aššur" and "Die 'Sünde Sargons' und ein verwandter Text". These sections are followed by a thematic discussion entitled "Exkurs: Die Inschriften als Quellen für Sanheribs Religionspolitik" (Frahm 1997:282–8), where Frahm speaks of the "'Persönlichkeit' Aššurs".

Beginning in the reign of Sargon II we find, in texts coming mainly from the old Assyrian capital of Aššur, the name of the god Aššur written as AN.ŠÁR. Tadmor has analyzed in depth the significant import of this spelling, in several of his studies. AN.ŠÁR is the name of a Babylonian cosmogonic deity, and this rendering of the name of Aššur identifies AN.ŠÁR with the similarly sounding Assyrian god. Initially, this identification might have served the pro-Babylonian Sargon II in making the god Aššur more acceptably "Babylonian", but later, in the reign of Sennacherib, it served to indicate that Aššur-AN.ŠÁR, not Marduk, ruled Babylon, just as Assyria ruled in reality. Significantly, the writing AN.ŠÁR is found in this period only at in the city of Aššur, whereas in texts from Nineveh the traditional writing is used. Added to this is the titulary of Sennacherib from Aššur, naming this king as the one who fashioned the statue of AN.ŠÁR (see further below). This important cultic event can be dated to the period between 704 and 700. After the destruction of Babylon in 689, additional symbolic acts reinforced the demotion of Marduk: The titulary of Aššur becomes grander, and the *bīt akīti ša ṣēri* at Aššur is renovated and dedicated to Aššur-AN.ŠÁR. Dust from the destroyed Babylon is placed there, and additional accoutrements are shipped to Aššur from Babylon. It is the god Aššur who vanquishes Tiamat in the Assyrian version of Enuma Eliš, not Marduk, and Sennacherib rides together with the god Aššur in his divine chariot!

Another way of assessing change is to study the enhancement of the god Aššur's epithets, if we may call them that, in tandem with the variants in the titulary of Sennacherib. We are fortunate in having a study of Sennacherib's titulary by Mario Liverani (1981), who contrasts the developing Nineveh versions with the static Aššur version. The Aššur version, from the final years of Sennacherib's reign, is focused on the king's building projects and related activities honoring the gods, especially Aššur, whereas the Nineveh version "morphs", and becomes grander in rhythm with his heroic campaigns and conquests during his reign. The result of this analysis yields a long list of status indicators, which can be classified in various ways. Sennacherib is empowered by Aššur, head of the gods, who granted him unrivalled kingship and invincible weapons, and caused powerful princes to fear his military advance. He has dominion over vast territories, over the four quarters, from the upper sea to the lower sea, and can traverse the earth with no interference. All of the black-headed men fall at his feet in submission. We also encounter epithets that express royal virtues—love of justice, what Liverani calls "pietistic pastoral titles", qualities that enhanced the king's favor in the sight of the gods.

As for the god Aššur, we can further pinpoint his divine "personality", and Sennacherib's special relationship to him, by reference to the Tablet of Destinies (*tuppi šīmāti*), Text B, in the British Museum, a fascinating text interpreted by Andrew George (1986), and based on a join made by Wilfred Lambert. It depicts Sennacherib as the cultically devoted king who did so much to honor Aššur, and who humbles himself before him, praying to him for further blessings, most of all for the continuation of his dynasty: *išid* ^{gi}[^{š}*k*]*ussî-iá kima šadî*^{i} *li-kun a-na* u_4*-mi r*[*e-qu-ti*] "Let the base of my throne be secure as a mountain for long days to come" (l. 20).

But more than this, the tablet assigns unusual status to the god Aššur himself, making him, not Marduk, the deity who holds in his hand the Tablet of Destinies. Aššur's image was most likely depicted on a seal imprinted on the tablet. It should be mentioned, however, that already in the final years of Sennacherib's reign we observe a conciliatory attitude toward Babylonia and Marduk, which prevails during the reign of Esarhaddon, when the window of about twenty years into Aššur's exaltation over Marduk closes.

First Isaiah and Monotheism

In the discussion to follow, many biblical passages, some of them quite extensive, will be presented in adapted translations, informed by the New Jewish Translation (NJPS), and for Isaiah 1–39, specifically, by the renderings of G. B. Gray (1912). How a biblical verse or passage is translated impacts our understanding of the larger issues. With due respect, I have found no single translation that is fully acceptable in every case, and have adopted the practice of introducing my own translations of cited biblical texts, and even of extra-biblical sources where deemed necessary.

Before treating selected passages from First Isaiah on the subject of monotheism, it would clarify matters if we prefaced some comment on the status of the pertinent historiographic passages in 2 Kings 18–20//Isaiah 36–9. Those texts are composite, and show signs of later authorship and, at points, of redaction by the Deuteronomist. Nevertheless, they have been impacted by the prophetic ideology, whether or not they are directly dependent on First Isaiah's prophecies, and at points resonate clearly with the diction of the Neo-Assyrian sources. Thus, Chaim Cohen (1979) has analyzed what he refers to as "Neo-Assyrian elements" in the first Rabshaqeh speech. Although these biblical sources provide information valuable for reconstructing the events of 701 B.C.E., they do not have the same historical valence as do prophecies that can be reliably attributed to First Isaiah. Thus it is that poetry often sheds more light on history than chronicles do!

This said, it remains difficult, nonetheless, to assign precise dates to those texts within the canon of Isaiah 1–39 that are regarded by most biblical scholars as the genuine writings of First Isaiah. The prophecies are not arranged in chronological sequence, and the captions, where we have them, are not necessarily reliable. In a recent study entitled "Historical Information in Isaiah 1–39", Anton Schoors (1979) guides us through a frustrating maze of theories on the composition of every part of Isaiah 1–39. I must emphasize, however, that my hypothesis that First Isaiah was responding to Assyrian claims of supremacy of an ideological nature can be validated in a general way at various times during the reigns of Tiglath-Pileser III, Sargon II and Sennacherib. It is just that the early years of Sennacherib are especially focused, and ideologically magnetic, and it would be preferable to find a more precise historical location for First Isaiah's principal response, if possible. For example, it is likely that Isaiah 1 was composed soon after 701, not earlier than that. The give-away comes in vv. 8–9:

> The daughter of Zion remains as a hut in a vineyard,
> As a lean-to in a cucumber patch, as a besieged town.
> Had not Yahweh of Hosts left us the sparsest remnant,
> We would have become like Sodom,
> We would have resembled Gomorrah!

The accompanying description of conditions in Judah that is conveyed in Isaiah 1 surely fits the aftermath of Sennacherib's invasion. The whole land is devastated, towns have gone up in flames, and the populace is wounded beyond healing. The point of Isaiah's tirade against Jerusalem is that even after being rescued from mighty Assyria, and in the face of so much suffering, Jerusalem and its officialdom remain corrupt, and ironically deserve to be compared to Sodom and Gomorrah! Jerusalem can only regain its eminence through repentance and the formation of a just society, not through profuse temple worship alone. Isaiah 1 condemns the failure of Jerusalem's leaders and its society to heed Yahweh's teachings, and regards their inability to see the meaning of recent events as extreme stupidity. All of their suffering had come upon them to start with because they had abandoned the Holy One of Israel, in whom they should have trusted. They should have heeded the counsel of the prophet Isaiah who spoke in the name of the God of Israel; now they have another chance.

The monotheistic message of First Isaiah is most clearly expressed in two texts that can also be dated to the period immediately following 701, namely Isaiah 10:5–19 and 14:24–7. The translations will be followed by brief commentary, leaving purely textual problems to be addressed in the footnotes.

1) Isaiah 10:5–15. Assyria is a punitive instrument of Yahweh's anger.

> 5. "Ah, Assyria, rod of my rage!

He is an arm-staff of my wrath.[1]
6. I drive him against an ungodly nation,
I command him against a people who provoke me.
To take spoils and seize booty,
And to subject it to trampling, like the mire of the streets.
7. But he does not perceive it thus, nor does his mind so comprehend;
For it is in his heart to destroy, to terminate nations, more than a few!"
8. For he thinks:
"After all, my captains are all (former) kings!
9. Was Calno any different from Carchemish?[2]
Or Hamath from Arpad, or Samaria from Damascus?
10. Just as my power overtook the idolatrous kingdoms,
(and their images exceeded those of Jerusalem and Samaria!)
11. Verily, just as I did to Samaria and her idols,
So will I do to Jerusalem and her images".
12. But when my Lord has carried out his program on Mount Zion and in Jerusalem, he will (then) visit punishment upon the fruits of the king of Assyria's pride, and on his colossal arrogance.
13. For he thought:
"By the might of my (own) arm have I done it;
And by my skill, for I am discerning.
I removed the boundaries of peoples;
I beat down their rulers, and led vast populations into exile.[3]

---

[1] The Masoretic text presents difficulties. ומטה הוא בידם זעמי, literally: "It is a staff in their arm, my wrath". This would mean that Yahweh's wrath was a staff in the arm of Assyria, which differs from what was said in the first stich. This is, after all, an important statement, and we would have expected the more symmetrical parallelism: שבט אפי "rod of my rage" // מטה זעמי "staff of my wrath". What, then, is to be made of the unusual syntax, with intervening בידם "in their arm"? Conceivably, the final *mem* is enclitic: -ביד מ, and not a pronominal suffix, so that the parallel of שבט was intended to be מטה (ב)יד "staff-in-arm; arm staff". The staff is wielded by extending one's arm (Exodus 7:19, 8:13). Emphatic הוא "he/it is" merely breaks the construct formation. This would yield, literally: "And a staff-in-arm/arm staff, he (= Assyria) is, of my wrath".

[2] On the toponym in Amos 6:2 written כלנה, see Tadmor (1994:58, comment on 11′), where information is provided on the toponym Kinalia, occurring in the inscriptions of Tiglath-Pileser III, and earlier written Kunulua, the capital of Unqi (Tell Tainat). It has been identified by J. D. Hawkins and Nadav Naʿaman with Kullani, conquered by Tiglath-Pileser III in 738. The metathesis: KNL > KLN resulted from the transcription of the Neo-Hittite place name into Semitic. Nonetheless, Tadmor reports the occurrence of the form כלנה in an Aramaic inscription from Tell Tainat.

[3] In the history of exegesis, Hebrew ועתודיהם (*Qere*; ועתידיהם *Kethib*) has been taken in several ways. The most frequent rendering is "their treasures, stores". The conqueror plunders or destroys what has been laid away for the future. This is a forced rendering, because the root *ʿ-t-d* means "to stand, be ready", and in certain Aramaic dialects the Pael, with causative force, means "to erect, prepare, make ready" (Hoftijzer and Jongeling 1995:897 s.v. *ʿtd*$_1$). This is how certain forms of this root appropriated the sense of

14. I was able to seize, as (from) a nest, the wealth of peoples;
And just as one gathers abandoned eggs,
So did I rein in the whole earth.
And no one so much as flapped a wing, or opened a mouth to chirp!"
15. Should the axe boast over the one who hews with it?
Should the saw lord it over the one wielding it?
As though the rod can wave the one who raises it;
As though a staff can lift (a man) not of wood!
16. Therefore, the Sovereign, Yahweh of Hosts,
Will drive leanness into his corpulence,
So that under his great body there shall be a burning like that of fire,
<18b–c: Destroying frame and flesh, until he wastes away,
Like one deteriorating from illness,>
17. The Light of Israel shall be (that) fire, and his Holy One (that) flame.
It shall burn and consume his thorns and his thistles in a single day;
<18a. Along with the great mass of his scrub, and his garden land.>
19. And the trees that remain of his scrub shall be so few in number,
So that a mere youth would know how to record them!

Commentary. Isaiah 10:5–19 has received extensive attention from biblical commentators, many of whom question the integrity of this prophecy. It is not my intention to discuss its composition here because, aside from the juxtaposition of part of v. 18 indicated in the translation, I see no reason not to treat it as an organic whole. The first part of the prophecy (vv. 5–11) clearly postdates 721 B.C.E., because, in his boasting, the unnamed king of Assyria refers explicitly to the capture of Samaria (v. 11). The question is, by how many years? It is probable that in listing conquered capitals in the west, this prophecy is telescoping the exploits of several Assyrian kings, beginning with Tiglath-Pileser III, continuing with Sargon II, and concluding with Sennacherib, who would be the king most likely to have threatened Jerusalem. The closest we come to this tone of voice is in Amos 6:2, within an earlier prophecy on the fall of Samaria, capital of Northern Israel:

Traverse Calneh and observe,

"future" (cf. Deut 32:35, Esther 3:14, 8:13). Some, including the Medieval Jewish commentary Isaiah of Trani (Cohen 1996:83 s.v. Isa 10:13), have taken this locution to mean "chieftains", those who stand at the head of the flock, citing Isaiah 14:9, where עתודי ארץ "the chieftains of the earth" is parallel with מלכי גוים "the kings of the nations". Hebrew עתוד means "mature he-goat, ram" (Gen 31:10, 12), so-called because he "mounts" females in mating. In the biblical mentality, leadership roles are often expressed figuratively, having been appropriated from the pastoral economy. The overall sense of the verse is that the conqueror removes boundaries, subdues leaders, and exiles large populations (literally: "inhabitants"). A third possibility is that the Hebrew is to be rendered "their fortifications", a connotation suggested by the meaning "to stand". It is often said of Assyrian conquerors that they lay waste to towns and fortifications. The orthography of Hebrew כ[א]ביר is unusual, but the meaning is clear: "many, multitude".

Proceed from there to Greater Hamath,
Then descend to Gath of the Philistines.
Are (you) better than those kingdoms;
Is your territory larger than theirs?

There is, therefore, a typology of boastfulness in prophetic literature, and it continues through Isaiah 10:13–15, where the Assyrian conqueror boasts of altering boundaries, deporting populations, and reining in the whole earth, acquiring its wealth like one gathering abandoned eggs from a nest. All of this reminds us of the Neo-Assyrian annals, as noted by any number of scholars. The prophecy concludes in Isaiah 10:16–19 with a prediction of Assyria's downfall, the punishment for the hubris of its kings, and the retribution for its cruel history of oppression. Like Isaiah 1, such a prediction would have enjoyed very little credibility in the years preceding the Assyrian blockade of 701 by Sennacherib's forces, but it might have had dramatic impact after the sparing of Jerusalem, which was a powerful sign of divine providence.

Isaiah's doctrine is that the People of Israel are being punished by their God at the hand of Assyria. This is, at the heart of it, a traditional Israelite ideology for explaining defeat. We know, of course, that it is not at all limited to biblical writers. It has been shown that Assyrian ideologists at times placed the blame for the defeat of their enemies on the enemies themselves, and we encounter in the Assyrian sources what has been called the "motif of abandonment", whereby patron deities abandon their own sacred cities, as Marduk was said to have abandoned Babylon (Cogan 1974:9–15, Tadmor 1986). Closer to home, Mesha, king of Moab in the mid-ninth century B.C.E. similarly explains his loss of territory to Northern Israel as the punishment imposed by Kemosh. The national god of the Moabites had become enraged at his own land, handing it over to the enemy, in that case, Northern Israel (Dearman and Mattingly 1992).

What makes Isaiah 10:5–19 so remarkable within biblical literature is its global horizon. We read that Yahweh, the national God of Israel, a small and powerless people, is using Assyria, the global empire, as a punitive tool against his own people. In effect, the Israelite response has risen to the dimensions of the triumphal claims of the Assyrians. Yahweh controls the Assyrian Empire, and it is he who has granted the kings of Assyria their many victories and conquests. In my sequencing of the biblical sources, First Isaiah is the first to state the matter in such terms. None of the early narratives, neither the Yahwist nor the Elohist of Torah literature, looks at history this way, and none of the other eighth-century prophets went as far as Isaiah in articulating this global perspective. It is only later that we find resonance of this ideology, as in Deuteronomy 4, especially v. 35: "It has been clearly demonstrated to you that Yahweh, he is the (true) God; there is no other besides him".

Now, Isaiah does not mention the god Aššur, or any other Assyrian god for that matter. Isaiah employs the Hebrew אשור, which refers to the unnamed king of Assyria (explicitly מלך אשור in Isaiah 10:12a, and in 7:17, 8:4 etc.) and to Assyria, the land and/or its people, and the empire. Conceivably, the triad—(a)

Aššur the city, (b) Aššur the land and empire, (c) Aššur the god—might allow us to detect in Isaiah's exclamation, הוי אשור "Ah, Assyria", a veiled allusion to the deity with that name. However, Isaiah would not openly acknowledge the existence, much less the power of the head of the Assyrian pantheon! He does not project a battle of gods between Yahweh and Aššur, as the authors of the Egyptian saga do between Yahweh and the gods of Egypt. Yahweh is not Aššur's adversary or counterpart, he is the only true God. For First Isaiah there were no "other gods", to cite the Decalogue, only idols, and omens and magic. In Isaiah 8:19–21 Isaiah mocks those who have recourse to various forms of divination, making oracular inquiry of their dead would-be gods on behalf of the living. Granted, in Isaiah 14 the unnamed king of the *māšāl* (most probably Sargon II) is said to have pretensions of celestial exaltation, of dwelling at the side of El with the West Semitic pantheon atop Mt Zaphon. But that is just more of the same hubris that we observe in Isaiah 10, put into the mouth of a foreign king. For Isaiah, it is all the king of Assyria's doing, in accordance with Yahweh's plan. He is an instrument of Yahweh, carrying out his commands.

In the Assyrian inscriptions, kings not only boast of their own conquests, as Isaiah accuses them of doing, but, as we would expect, dutifully credit their gods with their victories. In Assyrian eyes, this recognition of divine power on the part of their kings may have made their boasts more acceptable. But Isaiah cannot see things this way. Rather, he rationalizes the eventual downfall of the Assyrian king by seeing it as a consequence of his hubris, in the same spirit that Israelite kings are warned against boastfulness in Deuteronomy 17, the so-called "law of the king". The boasting of the Assyrian king forces the hand of Yahweh, who is sovereign over all nations, to intervene on Israel's behalf, because Yahweh will never countenance such arrogation of power. Come to think of it, the bias evident in Isaiah's taunt actually points to an important feature of response literature: Those who respond internalize; they factor-in their own ideological culture, at times inverting the propaganda of the other.

2) Isaiah 14:24–7. Yahweh takes an oath that he will destroy Assyria and release Judah from its yoke.

Yahweh of Hosts has taken an oath, saying:

> As I have devised, so has it happened;
> As I have planned, so has it come about.
> To break Assyria in my land;
> To trample him on my mountains.
> His yoke shall be removed from him,
> And his tributary burden removed from their back.
> This is the plan (העצה) devised for all the earth,
> And this is the arm outstretched over all the nations.
> For Yahweh of the heavenly hosts had devised it, who can foil it?
> And his outstretched arm—who can stay it?

Commentary. This brief passage is an explicit statement of Isaiah's monotheism. It was undoubtedly composed soon after 701, for the same reasons already adduced with respect to Isaiah 1 and 10:5–19. Reference to an oath taken by Yahweh, God of Israel, is highly suggestive against the background of Neo-Assyrian loyalty oaths imposed on vassals (Tadmor 1982). It parallels the divine sanctions characteristic of treaties, according to which the gods guarantee protection to those who fulfill their treaty obligations. Another tell-tale resonance is the reference to the yoke of Assyria and to payment of tribute. In his annals, Sennacherib states that Hezekiah did not submit to his yoke, for which he was severely penalized by the imposition of heavy tribute (*mandattu*; Luckenbill 1924:32–4, ll. 18–49; Frahm 1997:54–5, ll. 49–58).

Of course, things did not turn out as well as promised; the Assyrian yoke was not removed from Judah during the reign of Manasseh. And yet, the improbable turn of events by which Jerusalem survived the Assyrian threat surely lent credence to Isaiah's assurance that Yahweh controlled the destiny of Assyria, and that matters had been going according to his plan for all the earth. First Isaiah introduces a grand idea that came to dominate religious thought in ancient Israel, although it was often resisted. The God of Israel rules over empires and their kings and determines their fate according to his plan for all the earth. He commands his people Israel to submit to his designated imperial agents. Because Hezekiah heeded Isaiah and finally submitted to Sennacherib of Nineveh, Jerusalem was spared.

Yahweh's Supremacy over Empires: An Enduring Ideology

First Isaiah's doctrine that the God of Israel used imperial kings as his agents took hold in prophetic circles, and informed Jeremiah's teachings about a century later in the Neo-Babylonian period. One of the ways of affirming its presence is to trace those passages in Jeremiah where Nebuchadnezzar II, the Babylonian conqueror, is called "my servant" by the prophet, speaking in the name of Yahweh. The Babylonian king is called עבדי "my servant" in Jeremiah 25:8–14, in the prophecy of seventy years. Jeremiah states that the God of Israel will give his servant, the king of Babylonia, dominion over many nations. Those who resist will suffer the consequences for seventy years, at which time Babylonia will receive its own delayed punishment from Yahweh. One of those nations that resisted was Judah.

The same theme is presented even more dramatically in a prophecy addressed to several nearby nations, in addition to Zedekiah's Judah, in Jeremiah 27: Whoever fails to submit to Nebuchadnezzar king of Babylonia, "my servant", will suffer war and its terrible consequences. The kings addressed are cautioned not to heed those false prophets and diviners who counsel rebellion. Zedekiah, king of Judah, and the priests and people are specifically admonished in these terms, and told that their only hope for survival is to submit. Nebuchadnezzar is called "my servant" a final time in a prophecy of his destruction of

Egypt and its temples in Jeremiah 43:10, indicating that Jeremiah's doctrine was not applicable only to Israel; it was a world-view.

Between Jeremiah 25 and 27, chapter 26 reports on the trial of Jeremiah for treason, after the prophet had predicted that the Temple and the city of Jerusalem would be destroyed, as Shiloh had been. In the course of the trial, some of the elders reminded the people assembled that Micah of Moreshet Gat had similarly predicted the destruction of Jerusalem in the time of Hezekiah, but instead of condemning him to death, Hezekiah heeded Micah, entreated God, and Jerusalem was spared. We have no record that Micah actually counseled Hezekiah in this manner, although Micah 4:11–12 states that the nations who had come to despoil Zion failed to comprehend Yahweh's long-term design—עצתו "his plan". This diction resonates clearly with First Isaiah. Unfortunately, this time around, Israel did not heed the prophet's words, and Jerusalem was destroyed.

First Isaiah labels conquering Assyria "rod of my rage", and in Jeremiah the God of Israel calls Nebuchadnezzar II, who defeated the Assyrians, "my servant". Both kings devastated Israel, but both were, nevertheless, agents carrying out the God of Israel's international plan. In the later words of Deutero-Isaiah 45, Cyrus the Great, founder of the universal Achemenid empire and conqueror of Babylon, is called, in addition to עבדי "my servant" and רעי "my shepherd", also משיחו "his anointed one". He is viewed as a redeemer, charged by the God of Israel to restore his people and rebuild his temple in Jerusalem (see further below). But the principle is the same: Empires rise and fall, but it is Yahweh of Hosts who grants kings their transient power and retains possession of true kingship. Verses 1–5 read as follows:

Isaiah 45:1–5. Yahweh and Cyrus

> Thus said Yahweh to his anointed one, to Cyrus,
> Whose right arm I have grasped;
> Subduing nations before him, undoing the girded loins of kings;
> Opening doors before him, allowing no gates to remain barred.
> I march (אלך) in advance of you, and level (*Qere*: אישר) all of the hills.
> I shatter (אשבר) doors of bronze, and cut down (אגדע) iron bars.
> I will give you treasures buried in darkness, the caches of hidden places.
> So that you may know that it is I, Yahweh,
> Who calls you by your name, the God of Israel.
> I have called you by your name;
> I entitle you (אכנך) though you do not acknowledge me.
> I am Yahweh, and there is no other!
> Except for me—there is no divinity!
> I empower you (אאזרך) though you do not acknowledge me.

Commentary. The translation given here reflects a particular view of the use of tenses in the prophecy. The six Hebrew verbs in the imperfect tense are taken as present progressives. They describe what is happening, or has been happening, rather than predicting what will occur in the future. There is only one inverted perfect, Hebrew ונתתי "I will give" (v. 3), and one inverted future ואקרא "I have called" (v. 4). Yahweh has already called Cyrus by name, a way of saying that he has empowered Cyrus to have dominion over many kings and nations. Yahweh will, pursuant to Cyrus' conquests, grant him untold treasures. This prophecy reflects the situation obtaining during the years following Cyrus' conquest of Babylonia and his exercise of hegemony over Babylonia's former territories, and probably constitutes, in its own way, a fairly immediate response to the Cyrus Edict of 538 B.C.E. One can deduce as much from Isaiah 44:26–8, which immediately precedes this prophecy. Yahweh instructs Cyrus, there called רעי "my shepherd", to rebuild Jerusalem and its temple.

On the first level, Isaiah 45:1–5 reinforces what had been said in First Isaiah and in Jeremiah. The conquests of Cyrus, including the conquest of Judah and Jerusalem from the Neo-Babylonians, are in accordance with Yahweh's plan. There is, however, something new that is conveyed by the title משיח "anointed one" that was not conveyed by the term עבד "servant", applied to Nebuchadnezzar, or by reference to the Assyrian king as a "rod of rage". Judah's legitimate king is not a scion of the House of David, but rather Cyrus the Great, whose capital is in far-off Persia. This doctrine, most recently discussed by Lisbeth Fried (2004:179–83), was to have far-reaching consequences, and was not readily accepted by those who hoped for the restoration of the Davidic dynasty.

Hayim Tadmor (1999a) has shed new light on this question, by showing how seriously the prophecy of seventy years, enunciated by Jeremiah, was taken by many of the returning Judean exiles. Their delay in rebuilding the temple, decried by the prophet in the second year of Darius I, may be explained by their strict adherence to the time-frame of seventy years. In their minds, the time specified by Jeremiah had not yet come, as they are quoted in Haggai 1:2: "The appointed time has not yet come, the appointed time for the Temple of Yahweh to be built!" Underlying their resistance may have been an unwillingness to acknowledge a foreign ruler as their legitimate king. That is, of course, the role explicitly envisioned for Cyrus by Deutero-Isaiah (44:28). As Tadmor explains, a compromise was reached by which Zerubbabel, governor of Judea, a scion of the House of David, was commissioned to rebuild the temple, and a recalculation of the seventy-year time frame was devised to justify avoiding further delay.

The deliberations of the returning exiles indicate that the sovereignty of Yahweh over imperial kings, a concept introduced by First Isaiah in response to the Assyrian threat, continued to function as an operative political ideology in the early post-exilic period. By that time, the last of the Hebrew prophets, Deutero-Isaiah and Trito-Isaiah, Haggai, Zechariah and Malachi, had achieved a long-term, almost apocalyptic view of history, an awareness that empires are transient. Assyria had fallen to Babylonia, and not long after, Babylonia fell to Persia. The gods of Assyria and Babylonia had also fallen.

As for Israel, its "remnant" had returned to Zion under an imperial charter, the Temple of Jerusalem was being rebuilt, and Judean society was being reconstituted in the homeland. The "divine in creation" and the "divine in history", the cosmic and the terrestrial, had been brought into harmony, as the plan of the

God of Israel for the whole earth proceeded to unfold. In the words of a late Psalm (113:3–4):

> From the rising of the sun to its setting,
> The name of Yahweh be praised!
> For Yahweh is supreme over all nations;
> His glorious presence is above the heavens.

Acknowledgements

I am grateful to several scholars who generously shared their knowledge with me at various stages in the progress of this study: Simo Parpola, for his understanding of monotheism in its Assyrian context, Barbara Porter, for her detailed critique of an earlier draft, and most recently Hayim Tadmor, for his valuable insights on the subject of Assyrian ideology. The opportunity to address scholarly audiences was also of great assistance.

References

Brinkman, J. A.
1964 Merodach-Baladan II. Pages 6–53 in *Studies Presented to A. Leo Oppenheim*, ed. R. D. Biggs *et al*. Chicago: University of Chicago Press.

Brinkman, J. A.
1973 Sennacherib's Babylonian Problem. *JCS* 25:89–95.
1983 Through a Glass Darkly: Esarhaddon's Retrospects on the Downfall of Babylon. *JAOS* 103:35–42.
1984 *Prelude to Empire: Babylonian Society and Politics, 747–626 B.C.* (Occasional Publications of the Babylonian Fund 7). Philadelphia: University Museum.

Cogan, M.
1974 *Imperialism and Religion: Assyria, Judah, and Israel in the Eighth and Seventh Centuries B.C.E.* (Society of Biblical Literature Monograph Series 19). Missoula, MT: Scholars Press.

Cazelles, H.
1992 Syro-Ephraimite War. *ABD* 6:282–5.

Cohen, Ch.
1979 Neo-Assyrian Elements in the First Speech of the Biblical Rab-Saqe. *Israel Oriental Studies* 9:32–47.

Cohen, M. (ed.)
1996 *Mikraʾot Gedolot 'HaKeter': Isaiah* (in Hebrew). Ramat-Gan: Bar Ilan University.

von Dassow, Eva
2003 By written communication.

Dearman, J. A. and G. L. Mattingly
1992 Mesha Stele. *ABD* 4:708–9.

Edel, E.
1997 *Der Vertrag zwischen Ramses II. von Ägypten und Ḫattušili III. von Hatti*. Berlin: Gebr. Mann.

Finkelstein, I.
1994 The Archaeology of the Days of Manasseh. Pages 169–187 in *Scripture and Other Artifacts: Essays on the Bible and Archaeology in Honor of Philip J. King*, ed. M. D. Coogan *et al.* Louisville, KY: Westminster/John Knox Press.

Frahm, Eckart
1997 *Einleitung in die Sanherib-Inschriften*. Archiv für Orientforschung Beiheft 26. Vienna: Institut fur Orientalistik der Universität Wien.

Fried, Lisbeth S.
2004 *The Priest and the Great King*. Winona Lake, IN: Eisenbrauns.

George, A. R.
1986 Sennacherib and the Tablet of Destinies. *Iraq* 48:133–46.

Gitin, S. *et al.*
1997 A Royal Dedicatory Inscription from Ekron. *IEJ* 47:1–16.

Goelet, O. and B. A. Levine
1998 Making Peace in Heaven and on Earth: Religious and Legal Aspects of the Treaty between Rameses II and Ḫattušili III. Pages 252–99 in *Boundaries of the Ancient Near Eastern World*, ed. M. Lubetsky *et al.* JSOTSup 273. Sheffield: Sheffield Academic Press.

Gray, G. B.
1912 *The Book of Isaiah, I–XXXIX*, International Critical Commentary. Edinburgh: T. & T. Clark.

Grayson, A. K.
1992 Sennacherib. *ABD* 5:1088–9.

Hoftijzer, J. and K. Jongeling (eds.)
1995 *Dictionary of the North-West Semitic Inscriptions*. Leiden: E. J. Brill.

Hornung, E.
1982 *Conceptions of God in Ancient Egypt: The One and the Many*, trans. J. Baines. Ithaca, NY: Cornell University Press.

Horowitz, W.
1998 *Mesopotamian Cosmic Geography*. Winona Lake, IN: Eisenbrauns.

Jacobsen, Th.
1946 Mesopotamia: The Cosmos as a State, the Function of the State, the Good Life. Pages 125–219 in *The Intellectual Adventure of Ancient Man*, ed. H. Frankfort *et al.* Chicago: University of Chicago Press.

Jacobsen, Th.
1963 Ancient Mesopotamian Religion: The Central Concerns. Pages 473–84 in *Cuneiform Studies and the History of Civilization*. Proceedings of the

American Philosophical Society 107. Philadelphia: American Philosophical Society.

Lang, B.
2003 Die Jahwe-allein-Bewegung: Neue Erwägungen über die Anfänge des biblischen Monotheismus. Pages 97–110 in *Der eine Gott und die Götter: Polytheismus und Monotheismus in antiken Israel*, ed. M. Oeming, K. Schmid. Zurich: Theologischer Verlag.

Levine, Baruch A.
1974 *In the Presence of the Lord: A Study of Cult and Some Cultic Terms in Ancient Israel*. Studies in Judaism in Late Antiquity 5. Leiden: E. J. Brill.
1996 "What's in a name?" The Onomasticon of the Biblical Record and the Religious Beliefs of Israelites (in Hebrew). *Eretz-Israel* 25 (Joseph Aviram Volume): 202–9.
2003 "Ah, Assyria, Rod of My Rage" (Isa 10:5): Biblical Monotheism as Seen in an International Political Perspective: A Prolegomenon (in Hebrew). *Eretz-Israel* 27 (Hayim and Miriam Tadmor Volume): 136–42.
2003a "Weihe, Aššur, Rute meines Zorns!" Der biblische Monotheismus als Antwort auf die neue politische Realität des assyrischen Weltreiches. Pages 77–96 in *Der eine Gott und die Götter*, ed. M. Oeming, K. Schmid. Zurich: Theologischer Verlag Zurich.

Liverani, M.
1979 The Ideology of the Assyrian Empire. Pages 297–317 in *Power and Propaganda: A Symposium on Ancient Empires*, ed. M. T. Larsen. Mesopotamia 7. Copenhagen: Akademisk Forlag.
1981 Critique of Variants and the Titulary of Sennacherib. Pages 225–57 in *Assyrian Royal Inscriptions: New Horizons in Literary, Ideological and Historical Analysis*, ed. F. M. Fales. Orientis Antiqui Collectio 17. Rome: Istituto per l'Oriente.
2001 The Sargon Geography and the Late Assyrian Mensuration of the Earth. *State Archives of Assyria Bulletin* 13:57–85.

Luckenbill, D. D.
1924 *The Annals of Sennacherib*. Chicago: University of Chicago Press.

Machinist, P.
1976 Literature as Politics: The Tukulti-Ninurta Epic and the Bible. *Catholic Biblical Quarterly* 38:455–82.
1983 Assyria and its Image in the First Isaiah. *JAOS* 103:719–37.

Mettinger, T.
1979 The Veto on Images and the Aniconic God in Ancient Israel. Pages 15–29 in *Religious Symbols and their Functions*, ed. H. Biezais. Stockholm: Almquist & Wicksell International.

Müller, Karl Fr.
1937 *Das assyrische Ritual*, Teil I: *Texte zum assyrischen Königsritual*. Mitteilungen der vorderasiatisch-ägyptischen Gesellschaft 41/3. Leipzig: J. C. Hinrichs.

Naʿaman, N.
1994 Hezekiah and the Kings of Assyria. *Tel Aviv* 21:235–254.

Olyan, S.
1988 *Asherah and the Cult of Yahweh in Israel.* Society of Biblical Literature Monograph Series 34. Atlanta: Scholars Press.

Parpola, S.
1997 *Assyrian Prophecies*. SAA 9. Helsinki: Helsinki University Press.

Porter, B. N.
2000 The Anxiety of Multiplicity: Concepts of Divinity as One and Many in Ancient Assyria. Pages 211–71 in *One God or Many? Concepts of Divinity in the Ancient World*, ed. B. N. Porter. Bethesda, MD: CDL Press.

Saggs, H. W. F.
1978 *The Encounter with the Divine in Mesopotamia and Israel.* London: Athlone Press.

Schoors, A.
1997 Historical Information in Isaiah 1–39. Pages 75–93 in *Studies in the Book of Isaiah* (Fs Willem A. M. Beuken), ed. J. van Ruiten, M. Vervenne. Leuven: Leuven University Press.

Smith, Mark S.
1991 *The Early History of God.* San Francisco: Harper and Row.
2001 *The Origins of Biblical Monotheism.* Oxford: Oxford University Press.

Smith, Morton
1971 *Palestinian Parties and Politics that Shaped the Old Testament.* New York: Columbia University Press.

Tadmor, H.
1981 History and Ideology in the Assyrian Royal Inscriptions. Pages 13–33 in *Assyrian Royal Inscriptions: New Horizons in Literary, Ideological and Historical Analysis*, ed. F. M. Fales. Orientis Antiqui Collectio 17. Rome: Istituto per l'Oriente.
1982 Treaty and Oath in the Ancient Near East: A Historian's Approach. Pages 127–52 in *Humanizing America's Iconic Book: Society of Biblical Literature Centennial Addresses 1980*, ed. G. M Tucker, D. A. Knight. Chico, CA: Scholar's Press.
1986 Sennacherib's Campaign in Judah (Hebrew). *Zion* 50:66–80.
1989 The Sin of Sargon and Sennacherib's Last Will, Part II: The Historical Background. *State Archives of Assyria Bulletin* 3:25–32.
1994 *The Inscriptions of Tiglath-Pileser III, King of Assyria.* Jerusalem: Israel Academy of Sciences and Humanities.
1999 World Dominion: The Expanding Horizon of the Assyrian Empire. Pages 55–62 in *Landscapes: Territories, Frontiers and Horizons in the Ancient Near East*, ed. L. Milano *et al.* (RAI 44, 1997). Padua: Sargon srl.
1999a "The Appointed Time Has Not Yet Arrived": The Historical Background of Haggai 1:2. Pages 401–8 in *Ki Baruch Hu: Ancient Near Eastern, Bib-*

lical, and Judaic Studies in Honor of Baruch A. Levine, ed. R. Chazan *et al.* Winona Lake, IN: Eisenbrauns.

Weippert, M.

1972 "Heiliger Krieg" in Israel und Assyrien. *ZAW* 84:460–93.

2002 "König, fürchte dich nicht!" Assyrische Prophetie in 7. Jahrhundert v. Chr. *Orientalia* 71:1–54.

The Next Phase in Jewish Religion: The Land of Israel as Sacred Space*

In the ancient Near East of biblical times, one worshiped within sacred space and repaired to sacred precincts to perform other acts of religious significance. The operative premise in the concept of sacred space is that the "where" is a factor as important, if not more important, than the "what," "who," or "how." Actually, the "where" is often a prior condition governing the efficacy of the acts themselves. Simply put, the same act that is performed effectively in a designated, sacred space is not efficacious if performed outside of it.

Specifying that sacrificial worship must take place in sacred space is a way of saying that it must take place in the presence of the deity (or deities) in order to be efficacious. The consecration of space is realized by bringing the deity close to the human community and, ultimately, by bringing the human community close to the deity. So it has been that religious communities have promulgated set policies on sacred space, carefully instructing their members as to where worship is proper, and where it will be efficacious. In this respect, the Hebrew Bible is no exception, although identifying biblical statements of cultic policy requires methodical study.

It is clear in hindsight that since late antiquity, the monotheistic religions—Judaism, Christianity, and Islam—have differed significantly in their respective attitudes toward sacred space. Of the three, the religious civilization of Diaspora Jews has, ever since the destruction of the Second Temple of Jerusalem, placed the least emphasis on the function of sacred space. Of course, Jewish prayers speak dramatically of an earlier, ancient period, and of more blessed circumstances when the Temple stood in Jerusalem, and they express the eschatology of redemption that will bring with it cultic restoration. Such memories and hopes have had little to do, however, with the ongoing experience of Jewish religiosity in the Diaspora. In the traditional synagogue there is no cult of purity and no consecrated priesthood; any adult, male Jew may officiate.

---

* Originally published in Mordechai Cogan, Barry L. Eichler, and Jeffrey H. Tigay (eds.), *Tehillah le-Moshe: Biblical and Judaic Studies in Honor of Moshe Greenberg* (Winona Lake, IN: Eisenbrauns, 1997), pp. 245–257. Reprinted with permission from Eisenbrauns.

Author's note: Aspects of this study were discussed in an address inaugurating the Skirball Chair in Bible and Ancient Near Eastern Studies at New York University, in December, 1992.

To understand how this basic change came about requires studying a series of ancient decisions on religious policy by various waves of Israelite, and later, Jewish leaders. When the First Temple of Jerusalem was destroyed, prophets, priests, and civic leaders of the exilic communities faced real choices regarding the character of worship in foreign lands and subsequently, in Judea and Jerusalem restored. It is not to be taken for granted that they would opt to discontinue sacrificial worship of the God of Israel in Babylonia or elsewhere outside of Jerusalem. By the time the cult of the Second Temple of Jerusalem came to an end in the first Christian century, alternative forms of worship had greatly developed in Jewish religion.

One Temple and a Single Altar: Deuteronomic Doctrine and the Edict of Josiah

This discussion begins in the monarchic period of biblical history and focuses on the historical relationship between two biblical sources: (1) the edicts of Josiah recorded in 2 Kings 22–23, aimed at terminating the *bāmôt* "cult-platforms" and at centralizing all cultic worship of the God of Israel in the Temple of Jerusalem (these are dated by the biblical record to ca. 622 B.C.E.); (2) the legislation and doctrinal statements of Deuteronomy 12–18 on the restriction of all cultic activity to one, central temple, whose location is left unspecified. The essential connection between these two sources has been explored extensively but with varying conclusions since the beginnings of modern biblical research.[1]

The motivations and objectives of the movement to restrict sacred space, on which the Hebrew Bible reports, require renewed study, as do the important phenomenological factors associated with them. For now, it will suffice to examine aspects of the history of the movement. In my earlier review of H. L. Ginsberg's monograph *The Israelian Heritage of Judaism* (1982), I accepted the proposition that the policy restricting sacred space to a single, central temple is expressed, at least as a hidden agenda, in Hosea's strong opposition to the proliferation of royally-sponsored altars and cult places in Northern Israel.[2] This opposition was voiced during the period preceding the Assyrian invasion, in the mid-eighth century B.C.E. It is likely that the delegitimation of *mĕqômôt* "cult-sites" (the Northern Israelite term) ordained in Deuteronomy was not voiced for

---

[1] See R. Altmann, "Josiah," *ABD* 3:1015–18. The reader is directed to two chapters in *The Age of the Monarchies: Political History*, vol. 4/1: *World History of the Jewish People* (Jerusalem: Massada, 1979); H. Reviv, "The History of Judah from Hezekiah to Josiah" (chapter 9), 193–204, notes: pp. 344–48; and A. Malamat, "The Last Years of the Kingdom of Judah" (chapter 10), 205– 21, notes: pp. 349–53. A bold reappraisal of the period of Josiah is provided by N. Naʾaman, "The Kingdom of Judah under Josiah," *Tel Aviv* 18 (1991) 3–71, particularly the section entitled: "Summary: Josiah in Historiography and in Historical Reality," 55–59.

[2] H. L. Ginsberg, *The Israelian Heritage of Judaism* (New York, 1982); B. A. Levine, "Review of Ginsberg," *AJS Review* 12 (1987) 143–57. {*VOL 1, PP. 101–12*}

the first time in Judah of the mid-to-late-seventh century, when we read in the book of Kings that the *bāmôt* "high places" were regarded as illegitimate, but rather at an earlier period and quite possibly in Northern Israel.

Religious ferment in Northern Israel in the mid-eighth century B.C.E. might explain Hezekiah's attempt to eliminate the *bāmôt* in Jerusalem and Judah at the end of the eighth century B.C.E. His policy, though probably abortive and surely short lived, would have constituted a response to Northern Israelite prophetic teaching. In and of itself, the historicity of the report of Hezekiah's effort to remove the *bāmôt*, preserved in 2 Kgs 18:4 and following, would be in doubt were it not for the speech subsequently attributed to the Assyrian Rabshakeh in 2 Kgs 18:19–35. Therein, the Assyrian commander taunted the citizens of Jerusalem on the subject of this very policy:

> And should you say to me: "Upon the LORD our God we rely"—Is He not the [very] one whose *bāmôt* and altars Hezekiah eliminated, saying to Judah and Jerusalem: "Before this altar alone shall you bow down, in Jerusalem"?

Expressed as part of a propagandistic statement and appealing to traditional notions of sacred space, the reference to Hezekiah's reform in 2 Kgs 18:22 sounds genuine and should not be taken merely as part of a noticeable tendency, *post hoc*, to credit otherwise virtuous kings with additional claims to religious correctness. In this light, we can also regard 2 Kgs 18:4 as a genuine report after all.

The radical shift of religious doctrine reflected in Deuteronomy 12–18 can be documented by comparing this source with Exod 20:19–23, the prologue to the Book of the Covenant, which should be regarded as an earlier statement. It is probable that both Exod 20:19–23 and Deuteronomy 12–18 are of Northern Israelite provenance, so that differentiating between their respective provisions can help to trace religious development within Northern Israel itself. The terms of reference employed in Exod 20:19–23 require careful elucidation:

> The LORD said to Moses: So shall you say to the Israelite people: You saw that from the very heavens I spoke with you. Do not fashion alongside Me gods of silver, nor fashion for yourselves gods of gold. Fashion for Me an altar of earth, and offer upon it your burnt offerings and your sacred gifts of greeting, your flocks and your large cattle; in every cult-place where I will pronounce My name (*bekol hammāqôm ʾašer ʾazkîr ʾet šemî*) I will come to you and grant you blessings. And should you fashion for Me a stone altar, do not construct it of hewn stone, for by wielding your sword upon such you have rendered it unfit.

As a construction, *bekol hammāqôm* is unique in Scripture, but *kol hammāqôm*, minus the preposition, is elsewhere attested; thus, Deut 11:24: "Wherever (*kol hammāqôm*) your foot treads shall belong to you." This is resonated in Josh 1:3 as *kol māqôm*, without the definite article, showing that both constructions may share the same meaning.

I have translated the term *māqôm* as "cult-place", which represents a specialized usage of a more general term. In Biblical Hebrew, *māqôm* is a highly nuanced term of reference, and serves as the *Leitmotif* of Jacob's theophany at Bethel (Genesis 28), also a Northern Israelite source. One immediately associates the statements of Jeremiah (7:12), concerning Shiloh in Northern Israel where *bayit* "temple" and *māqôm* "cult-place" are equated:

> Just go to My "cult-place" (*ʾel meqômî*) that is at Shiloh, where I formerly had my name installed (*ʾašer šikkantî ʾet šemî*), and see what I have done to it because of the wrongdoing of my people, Israel.

Continuing in Jer 7:14, we read:

> I shall do to the temple (*bayit*) over which My name is called (*ʾašer niqrāʾ semî ʿālâw*) and to the cult-place (*welammāqôm*) that I have granted to you and to your ancestors what I did to Shiloh.

Exod 20:19–23 speaks of multiple, legitimate cult-sites, such as were in operation throughout the land of Israel at certain periods of preexilic history. This brief code of cultic practice insists only that such installations be constructed properly, and that the rites performed at them and the clergy officiating at them be proper. Although the Exodus statement is not explicit in prescribing these cultic regulations for Israel's governance in the Promised Land, rather than the wilderness, this undoubtedly should be assumed.

It is this very system of multiple cult-sites that is renounced in Deuteronomy 12 and following. Thus, instead of formulaic *bekol hammāqôm* "in whichever cult-place", we read in Deut 12:13–14 of a restrictive doctrine, expressed in the very same language:

> Be careful not to offer your burnt offerings at whichever cult-place you see fit (*bekol māqôm ʾašer tirʾeh*). Rather in the cult-site (*bammāqôm*) that the LORD will select in one of your tribal territories, there shall you offer your burnt offerings….

Or, earlier, in Deut 12:5:

> Rather to the cult-place (*ʾel hammāqôm*) that the LORD your God will select from all of your tribal territories to inscribe His name there (*laśûm ʾet šemô šām*); you shall seek out his dwelling place and come there.

I take Exod 20:19–23 to represent the policy current in Northern Israel during the ninth-to-early-eighth centuries B.C.E., or even earlier; in other words, the pre-Deuteronomic cultic doctrine. If Ginsberg is correct, this doctrine was questioned in the Northern Kingdom later in the eighth century B.C.E., and a new policy was advocated, one aimed at restricting sacred space. It is core-Deuteronomy that formulates this new policy, one that was never implemented in Northern Israel, as far as we know.

After the fall of Samaria, writings and teachings from the temples and schools of Northern Israel were transmitted to Jerusalem and Judah. It was in this way that core-Deuteronomy, or parts of it, reached Jerusalem during the reign of Hezekiah, who actively endorsed the new doctrine of cult centralization and attempted to implement it. When he was followed by Manasseh, a king known for his heterodoxy, the Deuteronomic doctrine was abandoned, reemerging in Judah only in the mid-to-late-seventh century. Ultimately, it was a version of this doctrine that informed Josiah's edict.

The originally unspecified site within the Northern Kingdom, probably intended as Shechem-Gerizim originally, was now reidentified as Jerusalem and its Temple. This reinterpretation is presupposed in any number of biblical sources, most notably in the deuteronomistic excurses of 1 Kgs 8:16–21, 11:29–39, 14:21–24, and most likely in Ps 78:67–72. In all of these sources, the verb *bāḥar* "to choose, select" is pivotal and resonates with deuteronomic diction.

Ginsberg provides a clue regarding the way this localization of the Northern Israelite doctrine was rationalized.[3] It may have been taught that since the Temple of Jerusalem was first erected by Solomon, son of David, a Judean, and since it had survived the downfall of Northern Israel, it was blessed and indeed represented "the cult-place that the LORD will choose."

2 Kings 22–23 emphatically endorse the restriction of sacred space ordained in Deuteronomy once we recognize that the venue chosen by God has become Jerusalem, the Judean capital. But 2 Kings 23 in particular shows considerable evidence of redactional activity, and this condition complicates the task of the historian. I take a more critical view than Ginsberg or even than Cogan and Tadmor in this instance and consider 2 Kgs 23:24–27, which assesses Josiah's activities as the fulfillment of "teaching" (*tôrâ*), to be composed of exilic and possibly postexilic interpolations.[4]

Source-critical analysis allows us to read interpolations in 2 Kings 23 as evidence for the acceptance of Josiah's reforms by the exilic leadership and by the restored, postexilic community and brings into relief at least two sets of historical viewpoints: we have, first of all, a fairly contemporary record of Josiah's actual reforms in 2 Kings 23, and, in the second instance, we have, most notably in 2 Kgs 23:24–27, evidence of the later endorsement of these reforms.

Let us examine 2 Kgs 23:24–27 in particular detail:

> (24) And further, Josiah removed (*biʿēr*) the necromancers and mediums, the idols and the fetishes—all the detestable objects that were to be seen in the land of Judah and Jerusalem. Thus he fulfilled the terms of the teaching (*hattôrâ*) recorded in the scroll that the priest Hilkiah had found in the Temple of the LORD.
>
> (25) [And the likes of him (= Josiah) there never was before him; a king who turned back to the LORD (*ʾašer šāb ʾel YHWH*) with

[3] See Ginsberg, *Israelian Heritage*, 34–38.

[4] See *ibid.*, 39–54; M. Cogan and H. Tadmor, "The Reign of Josiah: The Great Reform," *II Kings* (AB 11; New York: Doubleday, 1988) 277–302. Naʾaman, "Kingdom of Judah," 55–59.

> all his heart and with all his being, and with all his resources (*bekol lebābô ûbekol napšô ûbekol meʾōdô*), according to all of the teaching of Moses (*kekol tôrat Môšeh*). And after him—the likes of him never arose again!]
>
> (26) However, the LORD did not turn back (*lōʾ šāb*) from His awesome wrath which blazed up against Judah because of all the things Menasseh had done to anger Him.
>
> (27) The LORD said: I will also banish Judah from My presence, as I banished Israel; and I will reject the city of Jerusalem that I chose, and the Temple of which I declared: "My name shall abide there."

The redactional analysis of this passage should proceed in two phases: We should first present indications of the interpolation of vv. 24–27 within 2 Kings 23 and then, turning to v. 25 itself, show how it digresses from v. 24, which precedes it, and from vv. 26–27, which follow it.

2 Kgs 23:23 concludes the description of the celebration of the paschal sacrifice in Jerusalem, a major enactment of Josiah. 2 Kgs 23:28 and following resume the ongoing report of Josiah's activities. Within 2 Kings 23, adverbial *wegam* "and also, further" occurs twice, in v. 19 and now, in v. 24. In both instances it most likely introduces an interpolation. Verse 19 extends Josiah's iconoclastic activities to the towns of Samaria, taking a cue from the reference to a prophet from Samaria in the preceding verse, v. 18. In v. 24, adverbial *wegam* introduces further iconoclastic activities by Josiah in Jerusalem and Judah. It is worth noting, however, that whereas 2 Kgs 23:21 tells how Josiah proclaimed celebration of the paschal sacrifice in Jerusalem in compliance with "what was written on this scroll of the covenant" (*kakkātûb ʿal sēper habberît hazzeh*), v. 24 speaks of "the terms of the teaching that were written on the scroll" (*dibrê hattôrâ hakketûbîm ʿal hassēper*). The language has clearly changed. Subsequently, vv. 26–27 add the dire qualification that, notwithstanding Josiah's devoted efforts, the LORD "did not turn back (*lōʾ šāb*) from his great wrath" and brought about the destruction and exile. Verses 26–27 thus proceed logically from v. 24.

The language of v. 24 and of vv. 26–27 is picked up and amplified in v. 25, where we read that Josiah acted "according to all the teaching of Moses" (*kekol tôrat Môseh*), a distinctly postexilic designation. This designation (like the kindred *besēper tôrat Môseh* "in the scroll of Moses' teaching") is characteristic of postexilic biblical statements (Mal 3:22; Neh 8:1; Dan 9:11, 13; Ezra 3:2, 7:6; and 2 Chr 23:18, 30:1, 16) and of late glosses in Joshua (8:31–32, 23:6).

What is perhaps most telling is that v. 26 says of the LORD that "He did not turn back" (*lōʾ šāb*) from His wrath, and in v. 25 it is said of Josiah that he did, in fact, "turn back to the LORD" (*šāb ʾel YHWH*), wholeheartedly. The interpolated v. 25 is "braided" into the fabric of vv. 24 and 26–27 by echoing their language.

In effect, the passage including 2 Kgs 23:24, 26–27 endorses Josiah's reforms, adding further detail to his iconoclastic activities. At the same time, it concedes, with the awareness of hindsight, that even Josiah's iconoclasm and his restoration of cultic purity did not save Judah and Jerusalem from God's wrath over the sins of Manasseh. 2 Kgs 23:25, ensconced within this passage, may represent an even later gloss, parenthetically extolling Josiah as a repentant king. Read historically, the interpolations in 2 Kgs 23:24 [25] 26–27 anticipate the acceptance of Josiah's restriction of sacred space to the Temple of Jerusalem by the exilic community in Babylonia, who, quite significantly, understood that restriction to apply to them. Ultimately, this doctrine was endorsed by the restored Judean community under Persian rule.

Further Responses to the Edict of Josiah

It is difficult to assess the effectiveness of Josiah's edict during the period between 622 B.C.E. and the final destruction of 586 B.C.E., and opinions vary as to the extent of its enforcement and acceptance in this time frame when the situation in Judah was rapidly deteriorating. Yohanan Aharoni thought he had found evidence at Arad of the enforcement of Josiah's edicts aimed at the termination of local and regional cult-places.[5] Stratum VII at Arad, dating from the latter years of Manasseh (ca. 687–642 B.C.E.) and into the reign of Josiah (ca. 640–609 B.C.E.), was destroyed at the end of the seventh century. Aharoni is of the view that this destruction occurred in the process of enforcing Josiah's edict. Stratum VI, of the period from Jehoiakin to Zedekiah (from 608–586 B.C.E.), was destroyed at the time of the fall of Jerusalem early in the sixth century B.C.E.

Now, the sanctuary at Arad was part of a royal, military installation on the southern Judean border, and there is every reason to conclude that it had served as a proper, Yahwistic sanctuary ever since its initial construction in the tenth century on the site of an earlier, twelfth-to-eleventh-century B.C.E. *bāmâ*. The measurements of the altar and orientation of the sanctuary further express its legitimacy. Throughout this period, the sanctuary contained at least one, perhaps two cultic stelae (*maṣṣēbôt*), and sacrifices were offered to the God of Israel on its main altar.

Did the destruction of stratum VII at Arad result from the implementation of royal edicts, or was it also the result of attacks by foreign forces? Whether correct or not, Aharoni's interpretation of the archaeological evidence at least focuses on the likelihood that the movement to restrict sacrificial worship to the Temple of Jerusalem had as one of its objectives the elimination of sacrificial worship at such sites as Arad.

It has been argued, however, that even if there was an initial enforcement of Josiah's edict at royally sponsored cult-places like Arad, it is far from evident

---

[5] See M. Aharoni, "Arad: The Israelite Citadels," in *The New Encyclopaedia of Archaeological Excavations in the Holy Land* (ed. E. Stern; Jerusalem: Israel Exploration Society, 1993) 1.81–87; A. F. Rainey, "Arad in the Latter Days of the Judean Monarchy," *Cathedra* 42 (1986) 16–25 [Heb.].

that such enforcement extended to many local and regional cult-places, which may not have been under direct, royal administration. Furthermore, there is the possibility of a relapse after the untimely death of Josiah, a reversion to previous practice in the last decades of Judean sovereignty. The prophetic tirades of Jeremiah and Ezekiel are replete with condemnations of all sorts of heterodoxy associated with cult-places, even with the Temple of Jerusalem itself. The realism of these prophetic statements, has, however, been heatedly debated. It must be conceded that at the present time we cannot determine how effective Josiah's edict was in the near-exilic period.

Of considerable significance, therefore, are the policies adopted by the exilic communities in Egypt and Babylonian on the matter of sacred space. What do we know of such decisions and of their long-range effect on the character of Jewish worship?[6] We know of two Jewish temples in Egypt, separated by time, and of radically diverse character. The Elephantine Jewish temple, where a sacrificial cult was practiced, operated throughout most of the fifth century B.C.E. under Persian rule, after which it was destroyed. There is no evidence that it had any impact on Egyptian Jewry of later times, although continuity from the Persian to the Hellenistic periods should not be summarily discounted. Contemporary leaders of the Jewish mercenary community at Elephantine were in contact with Jerusalem and its priesthood. We know that these Jews observed the Sabbath and the Passover festival at the very least, although their religious orientation shows evidence of syncretism. Since it is not known exactly when this temple was founded and by whom, it is uncertain whether its founders would have known of Josiah's edict in the first place.[7]

The Onias temple in Leontopolis was erected ca. 160 B.C.E., after Onias IV had fled to Egypt. Its origin can be traced to a rift in the ranks of the Jerusalem priesthood and attributed to the initiative of a leading priest of Jerusalem seeking to reestablish himself in the Egyptian Jewish diaspora. The Onias temple was modeled after the Temple of Jerusalem, and Zadokite priests officiated at its sacrificial cult, for which there is archaeological evidence. The Jewish community of Leontopolis maintained fairly close relations with Jerusalem. Even the later rulings of the Mishnah, *m. Menāḥ.* 13:10, do not condemn the Jewish cult of Leontopolis as illegitimate in all respects. Considering that the Onias temple lasted for more than 200 years, until 73 C.E., when it was torn down by order of

[6] For a view that has deeply influenced scholarship, see Y. Kaufmann, *Toledot Haʾemunah Ha-Yisraʾelit* (Jerusalem: Bialik, 1955) 1.81–112 and 2.268–75 [Heb.]. Also see M. Greenberg, "Religion: Stability and Ferment," in *The Age of the Monarchies: Religion and Culture*, vol. 4/2: *World History of the Jewish People* (Jerusalem: Massada, 1979) 79–123, notes pp. 297–303.

[7] For a recent review, see B. Porten, "Elephantine Papyri," *ABD* 2:445–55.

Vespasian, one would have to conclude that during the Hellenistic Period there was receptivity within Egyptian Jewry to a sacrificial cult.[8]

These two, differing Jewish temples of Egypt, both with active sacrificial cults, could be regarded as evidence that the Deuteronomic doctrine expressed in Josiah's edict had not been given uniform endorsement. This would be true, however, only if we were to conclude that Josiah's edict initially envisioned Diaspora communities and was not directed solely at the kings and people of the kingdom of Judah within the land of Israel. It seems, however, that neither core Deuteronomy, nor what we would regard as primary sources in 2 Kings shows concern with policy outside the land, in what were to become exilic communities. In fact, the dire prophecy interpreted by the prophetess Huldah (2 Kgs 22:16–20) speaks explicitly about the destruction to come "upon this place" (*ʿal hammāqôm hazzeh*), never mentioning exile or deportation as such. This suggests that those who subsequently understood the restrictions as prohibiting the sacrificial worship of the God of Israel in the lands of exile and whose views we see reflected in the interpolations of 2 Kgs 23:24–27 were applying this doctrine to their own situations, interpreting it to mean that no place on the face of the earth is sacred except the site of the Temple in Jerusalem. Consequently, at a time when no Temple stood in Jerusalem, as was the reality from 586 until 516 B.C.E., there would be no opportunity to persist in the sacrificial worship of the God of Israel elsewhere, either within the land of Israel or outside of it.

It would be of great value to have evidence of policy-making by the Jewish community in Babylonia during the actual period of the exile. It was Shalom Spiegel who first directed my attention to Ezekiel 20, which he viewed as a cryptic record of Ezekiel's instruction to the elders of the exilic community not to build altars or offer sacrifice in exile. A similar interpretation of the inquiry of the elders and of the substance of Ezekiel's oracle had been put forward by M. Friedmann in the late-nineteenth century, and it was subsequently adopted with modifications by several other scholars.[9]

With the exception of probable interpolations, Ezekiel 20 is dated to 591 B.C.E., several years after the first deportations under Jehoiachin.

We read in Ezek 20:1–3 that the elders of the exilic community in Babylonia approached the prophet to seek oracular guidance but were rebuffed. They were told that they would receive no response from God, leaving unspecified what the subject of their inquiry was to begin with. The prophet is simply instructed to indict the people for their abominations, an act conveyed by the verb

---

[8] On Onias IV and the Jewish temple at Leontopolis, see U. Rapaport, "Onias (Person)," *ABD* 5:23–24; and A. Shalit, "Onias, Temple of," *Encyclopaedia Judaica* 12:1404–5. The main source of our limited knowledge is Josephus *Ant.* 13.62–72.

[9] See M. Friedmann (Meir Ish-Shalom), *Hassiyyun, That Is, A Commentary on the Prophecy of Ezekiel, Chapter 20* (Vienna, 1888) [Heb.]; A. Menes, "Tempel und Synagoge," *ZAW* 50 (1932) 268–76; J. A. Bewer, "Beiträge zur Exegese des Buches Ezechiel," *ZAW* 63 (1952) 193–201.

šāpaṭ in v. 3. We would have to infer the subject of the elders' inquiry from the content of the elaborate prophecies that follow, in Ezek 20:4–44.

The main question is whether Ezekiel 20 is talking about the specific problem of sacrificial worship in Babylonia, against the background of the Josianic reform, or in more general terms about the potential attraction of the Judean exiles to idolatrous cults they would encounter there and the resulting abandonment of God's commandments. After all, it is a theme of admonition and prophecy, most notably of the Deuteronomic school, that in exile the people of Israel will worship foreign gods (Deut 4:25–28; 28:36, 63–64; Jer 16:13). In fact, reference in Ezek 20:32 to worship of "wood and stone" (*ʿēṣ wāʾeben*) in the lands of exile is particularly reminiscent of similar characterizations of idolatry (2 Kgs 19:18; Isa 37:19; Jer 2:27, 3:9).

Moshe Greenberg is of the view that once the inquiry of the elders, as reported in Ezek 20:1–3, had been rebuffed categorically, it would be illogical to regard the oracle (or oracles) contained in the rest of chapter 20 as responsive to the subject of the original inquiry, whatever it was.[10]

Greenberg explains the dynamics of inquiry and response by referring to Ezekiel 14, which also begins with an inquiry by the elders of Israel that is repeatedly rebuffed. There, the prophet explicitly clarifies why the community could not be afforded the oracular services of the prophet and would receive no response to their inquiries from God. Israelites who flaunted their fetishes could hardly expect divine guidance! So too in Ezekiel 20, the refusal of God to respond to the inquiries of the exilic community is followed by a denunciation of *gillûlîm* "fetishes" and *šiqqûṣîm* "detestable things".

The situation in Ezekiel 20 is somewhat special, nonetheless. I would follow Moshe Greenberg in regard to Ezek 20:4–26, 30–31, which I consider to be the primary oracle, but I would insist that in contrast, Ezek 20:27–29 represents an interpolation and that it contains an explicit reference to *bāmâ* worship in Ezek 20:29a. Furthermore, the oracle that follows and that is contained in Ezek 20:32–44, allows for the interpretation that the issue of sacrificial worship in Babylonia was on the prophet's mind. Whether by the author of Ezek 20:1–26, 30–31, or by a different hand, Ezek 20:32–44 may be understood as a commentary on the primary oracle.

Let us first take up the interpolation of Ezek 20:27–29, which can be shown to refer to the issue of the *bāmôt*:

> By this, as well, your fathers affronted Me and committed trespass against Me. When I brought them to the land I had sworn to give them, and they saw any high hill and any leafy tree, they slaughtered their sacrifices there and presented their angering offerings (*kaʿas*

---

[10] See M. Greenberg, *Ezekiel 1–20* (AB 22; New York: Doubleday, 1983) 360–88 on Ezekiel 20; and *ibid.*, 155–57 for a comment on Ezek 7:26; *ibid.*, "Structure and Themes," 251–55 on Ezekiel 14. Also see W. Zimmerli, *Ezekiel 1* (trans. R. Clements; Hermeneia; Philadelphia: Fortress, 1979) 399–418.

> *qorbānām*) there; there they produced their pleasing odors and poured out their libations. Then I said to them: What is this *bāmâ* which you visit? [It's name has been called *Bā-mâ* until this very day.]

The first observation to be made about Ezek 20:27–29 is that the rhetoric of condemnation has changed. There is no explicit reference to idolatry, to *gillûlîm* "fetishes", for instance. The operative category is *maʿal*, a term known best in priestly literature, where it connotes sacrilege. Furthermore, Ezek 20:29a explicitly denounces the fathers of the exiles, the Judeans of near-exilic times, for building cult-platforms and in that way offending God. This recalls 2 Kgs 17:11, where we read:

> They offered sacrifices there, on all [kinds of] *bāmôt*, like the Gentiles whom YHWH had driven out from before them, and they did evil things to anger YHWH (*lehakʿîs ʾet YHWH*).

Use of the *Hiphil hikʿîs* recalls the unique locution *kaʿas qorbānām* "their angering offerings" in Ezek 20:28. It would make sense, therefore, to interpret the probable interpolation in Ezek 20:27–29 as expressing a viewpoint on the *bāmâ* question similar to that of the redactor (or one of the redactors) of Kings.

It is difficult to determine the comprehensive agenda of Ezek 20:32–44. Ezek 20:32, the opening statement of the second oracle, recalls 2 Kgs 17:11 in its reference to what the Gentiles do in the course of their worship of foreign gods. What the exiles are considering doing and what the author of the second oracle is telling them will never be countenanced is to act like the Gentiles! Can we be more specific as to what this tendency was perceived to mean?

Reference to the worship of objects of wood and stone begins in the near-exilic period as a derisive way of characterizing idolatry (2 Kgs 19:18; Isa 37:19; and Jer 2:27, 3:9). In Ezek 20:32, the idiom in question has been altered to *lešārēt ʿēṣ wāʾeben*, using a verb of ambiguous connotation that may mean both "to worship" and "to minister to" wood and stone, rather than *ʿābad*, which decidedly connotes worship. But the general intent may have remained the same. It can be argued that Ezek 30:32–44 is simply speaking of idolatry in exile, comparable to the idolatry for which the Israelites of the wilderness period were punished in their time (Ezek 20:36), and that this passage is not addressing the issue of sacrifice in exile at all.

And yet some modulation may have occurred. It may be the intent of the author of Ezek 20:32–44 to compare sacrifice at *bāmôt* in Babylonia to idolatry. What we may have in Ezek 20:32–44 and in the Deuteronomistic excurses in 1 and 2 Kings is the modulation of traditional denunciations of idolatry and their application to the new doctrine of cult-centralization. With this application, later authors were saying, in effect, that the worship of the God of Israel at *bāmôt* was henceforth tantamount to idolatry. If correctly analyzed, this would represent a major example of innerbiblical exegesis.

Ezek 20:39–40 is formulated as if in response to a question:

> As for you, O House of Israel, thus said the LORD, YHWH: Go, every one of you, and worship his fetishes, and continue [to do so], if you will not obey Me; but do not profane My holy name any more with your idolatrous gifts. For only on My holy mountain, on the lofty mountain of Israel—declares the LORD, YHWH; there, in the land, the entire House of Israel, all of it, shall worship Me. There I will accept them and there I will take note of your contributions and the choicest offerings of all your sacred things.

Would it be reading too much into this prophecy to say that the issue informing it is the unacceptability of sacrificial worship in the lands of exile, awaiting restoration to the land of Israel? The contrast between the thrice-emphasized *šām* "there", namely, on God's mountain, and the exilic venue would support this reading. One could say that on the authority of Ezek 20:27–29, 32–44, sacrificial worship of the God of Israel was illicit in Babylonia.

The Restoration to Zion and Religious Fulfillment: A Hypothetical Reflection

The restoration of the Temple in Jerusalem was indispensable to the program of national repatriation. We can hypothesize that if religious fulfillment had been possible in the Diaspora, if the leadership of the exilic community in Babylonia had decided to erect Jewish temples there, sacred sites where the sacrificial worship of the God of Israel would have been legitimate, the drive toward a return to Zion would have been considerably weakened. Prophecies of the end of exile might have gone largely unheeded. This is to suggest that the decision to limit sacred space to the Temple of Jerusalem, taken in the near-exilic period for a particular set of contemporary reasons, gained new poignancy during the exile, when it was interpreted by at least some leaders of the exilic community in Babylonia to apply, as well, to foreign lands.

The elaborate repertoire of biblical ideas current during the near-exilic and exilic periods assumes a curious configuration. Alongside prophetic notions of universalism, which held that the loss of one's land did not mean the defeat or demise of one's God, the restriction of sacred space to the Temple of Jerusalem left the Babylonian community religiously deprived. Alongside the liberation of religion from territory, a departure in the history of religious ideas that enabled the communities of the Diaspora to retain an identity, the prophecies of restoration attained greater acceptance by holding forth the prospect of religious fulfillment. The restriction of sacred space to the Temple of Jerusalem ultimately stimulated alternative forms of worship, while at the same time withholding cultic sanctity from foreign spaces. In turn, this tension virtually necessitated that an exiled people would remain linked to its homeland.

For almost twenty centuries most of the Jewish people have been living out their religious life without sacred space. Even those small groups of Jews who have inhabited the Holy Land down through the centuries and the dribbling of arriving pilgrims had a very limited experience of sacred space. Not only were ancient buildings in ruin and consecrated sites abandoned, but the people of Israel were distant from its land. After all, the sanctification of space is realized by vital communities, acting out of a need and a want to experience *qirbat ʾelōhîm* "the nearness of God" (Isa 58:2). As the sages put it in their laconic succinctness: "If there are no flocks, there is no Shepherd."

In our own day, both the Jewish society of modern Israel, representing about 30% of world Jewry, and the rest of the Jewish people face a new opportunity and a new challenge. There are indications that the next phase in Jewish religion will be characterized by the return of sacred space, albeit in ways modulated by new concepts of sanctity and by new modes of religious expression. The land of Israel has been rebuilt by fellow Jews. It is they who lend sanctity to its space; they are the flocks who assure that the Shepherd is near.

B. Sources on Religion

Ugaritic Descriptive Rituals*

Certain Ugaritic texts are classified as religious or ritual. These are of several types including lists of gods and sanctuaries, contributions and offerings to the gods, and the texts of recited rituals. Three of these texts (*Ugaritic Manual*, 1, 3, and 9) show marked peculiarities in their formulation, and employ a pair of terms, *dqt* and *gdlt*, which, except for several fragmentary texts (33, 42, 44) do not occur elsewhere either in Ugaritic or biblical sources. These three texts consist principally of offerings to various deities in the Ugaritic pantheon. A duplicate of text 3 (henceforth 3b) was published by Miss A. Herdner in 1956. It is in certain respects more nearly complete than the earlier known text 3, and adds considerably to our understanding of the contents.[1]

Texts 1, 3 (3b), and 9 differ in form from other Ugaritic religious texts, such as texts 2 and 5. The latter are semi-poetic, and employ characteristic features of epic style. Like "The Birth of the Gods" (text 52), texts 2 and 5 are liturgies meant for recitation and perhaps dramatization as a part of religious rites. Texts 1, 3 (3b), and 9, on the other hand, give no evidence of containing the certa verba actually accompanying rituals.

These texts also differ from the prescriptive type of rituals which set down the manner in which rites were to be performed. Only a few verbs occur in these texts; they are in the *yqtl* formation.[2] They are best taken as the usual narrative tense rather than the jussive or subjunctive, and will be so translated. These texts are descriptions of what transpired on special cultic occasions—the sequence of sacrifices to the various gods, and the rites which accompanied them. In compo-

---

* Originally published in *JCS* 17 (1963), pp. 105–111. Reprinted with permission from the American Schools of Oriental Research.

I am indebted to my teacher, Prof. H. L. Ginsberg, for his helpful critique of this study, and to Prof. W. Hallo for his assistance with the Mesopotamian material.

[1] Editio princeps: Ch. Virolleaud, *Syria* 10 (1929), pls. 41, 43 and 47. Literature: E. Dhorme, *RB* 40 (1931), pp. 32–56. R. Dussaud, *Syria* 20 (1931), pp. 66–77 (text 1). H. L. Ginsberg, *The Ugarit Texts* (Hebrew) (1936), pp. 111–119. C. H. Gordon, *Ugaritic Manual*, texts 1, 3, and 9, grammar, and glossary (1955); *Ugaritic Literature* (1949), pp. 107–115. A. Herdner, *Syria*, 33 (1956) pp. 104–112 (duplicate of text 3). References to Ugaritic texts are according to the numeration of the *Ugaritic Manual* (1955), unless otherwise indicated.

[2] *Ugaritic Manual*, grammar, nos. 9.2 and 9.7.

sition they are "formulaic" rather than prosaic, employing the same formulas repeatedly to record the quantities and types of sacrifices and rites.[3]

Texts 1, 3 (3b), and 9 represent a specific type of Ugaritic texts. Text 3 is the most elaborate of the group, and may therefore serve as a starting-point for our study. The reconstruction of the first six lines of 3b is made possible by the perusal of text 3:[4]

1 *[byr]ḫ[.r]išyn.bym.ḥdṯ*
2 *[šmtr].uṯkl.lil.šlmm*
3 *b[ṯlṯt].ᶜšrt.yrtḥṣ.mlk*
4 *br[r.]ba[r]bᶜt.ᶜšrt.riš*
5 *arg[— wṯn.]šm.lbᶜlt*
6 *bhtm.ᶜṣ[rm.lin]šilm*

Lines 3–4a contain a clause, missing from the earlier known duplicate, which mentions the rite of ablution. In the clause *yrtḥṣ mlk br*[*r*] the word *yrtḥṣ* means "he washes himself." On the basis of this reading we discover the same clause in text 9:10 where the word *yrtḥl* is to be read *yrtḥṣ*, as was correctly anticipated by Gordon.[5] Both texts therefore include the act of washing, which at Ugarit, as elsewhere, played a role in sacrificial rites. Thus Kret, prior to offering sacrifices on the wall, is commanded to wash his hands and arms (Kret, 62ff.). ᶜAnat washes herself as part of a sacrificial rite (6:18-19).[6]

The subject of the clause, *mlk*, refers to the king, or an official called "king", rather than offering the name of a deity. Unlike the poetic and semi-poetic texts, text 3 (3b) would not be likely to describe the acts of divine beings, but rather, those of the actual cultic personnel who were observed in the performance of the rites.[7] The word *brr* is to be taken as the active participle (*bârir*) in the sense of "purifier", as suggested by Herdner. It serves as an epithet of *mlk*. *Mlk brr* is a title, which means "the king, the purifier." It corresponds to the title of a biblical priest: *hakkôhēn hameṭahēr* "the priest, the purifier" (Lev. 14:11). The epithet *brr* can occur independently of *mlk* as in 3b:7–8: — *mlk*, *yṯb brr* "the king, the purifier sits/responds." It occurs again in the fairly certain restorations further on in the text: *brr r*[*gm yṯṯb bṯdṯ*] (3b:49) and [*rgm yṯṯb*] *brr bšbᶜ* (3b:50–51). These restorations are based on 3:45; 46–47, where the words *rgm yṯṯb* "he brings back a word" actually occur.[8] In the context of religious rites this idiom indicates a recitation of a ritual nature. The notion that "responding" means "ritual recitation" is evident in the biblical usage of the verb *ᶜnh* (normally "to an-

[3] The term "formulaic" was suggested by Prof. Gordon, who used it previously in connection with the epistolary texts (*ibid.*, grammar, no. 13. 97 and note 2).

[4] Restoration and commentary in Herdner, *op. cit.*

[5] *Ugaritic Manual*, glossary, no. 1854; *Ugaritic Literature*, p. 114.

[6] Cf. 129:20; II ᶜAnat:32; Lev. 16:14.

[7] On the meanings of *mlk*, see *Ugaritic Manual*, glossary, no. 1119.

[8] Cf. *rgm ṯṯb* in an epistle to the queen (89:14).

swer, reply") in the more technical sense of reciting the text of a ritual.[9] The clause *brr rgm yṯṯb bṯdṯ* (*bšbʿ*) therefore means "the purifier delivers a recitation on the sixth (seventh)."

To what do these ordinal numbers (*bṯdṯ*, *bšbʿ*) refer? It was previously supposed that in text 3 there was a sequence of days of the month on which rites were performed. Thus, according to the copy known first *bṯlṯt* (3:3), *barbʿt* (3:4), *b.ḫmš* (3:38), *bṯdṯ* (3:45), and *bšbʿ* (3:47) represented the sequence of the third, fourth, fifth, sixth, and seventh days of the month. This view is no longer tenable in the light of 3b:3–4 which mentions the thirteenth and fourteenth days of the month instead of the third and fourth days as in text 3. If the ordinals "on the sixth/seventh", occurring further on in the text, referred to days of the month, we would have the rites of the thirteenth and fourteenth days followed by those of the sixth and seventh days. In a text which covers the period from one New Moon to the next, it is reasonable to expect chronological order.

These ordinals might indicate that at the sixth (or seventh) time an act was performed, a recitation was inserted. The complete clause *brr rgm yṯṯb bṯdṯ* (*bšbʿ*) would mean "The purifier delivers a recitation on the sixth (or seventh) performance." It is normal for rituals to be interrupted by recitations or dramatizations at certain points in the proceedings. In poetic and semi-poetic texts we occasionally find instructions to the officiant: *wṯb lmspr* "and return to the narration" (2:27; 51:V:104; I Aqhat, side after line 169). In text 2 it is quite clear that these instructions indicate a prior break in the recitation of the service for the performance of some ritual act. The concluding words of the preceding section are: *hn ʿr* "behold, the ass/city" (2:26). Since the preceding lines speak of carrying the offerings to the gods, it is probable that here *ʿr* refers to "ass", a beast of burden, rather than to "city." The attention of the congregation is being directed to the beast that was to carry their offerings to the temple. In text 2 the recitation of the service was interrupted for the conveying of the offerings. In text 3 (3b) the rites are interrupted at several points for the recitation of a service of unspecified contents. Significantly, the recitations come at intervals leading up to the seventh performance of the rites.[10]

---

[9] Cf. Deut. 21:7; 26:5; 27:14.

[10] Cf. the seven sprinklings of blood in Lev. 8:11; 16:14. The notion of an act performed a specific number of times is characteristic of this text. We have *pamt šbʿ klbh* "seven times as he wishes" (3:52, cf. 5:26) and *ṯn lʿšrm pamt* "twenty-two times" (3:43—restorations in 3b:46–47, and see *Ugaritic Manual*, grammar, no. 7.60). In Tannaitic sources we have instances of sacrificial rites being interrupted by recitation. In *Mishnah, Yomah* there is a description of the sending off of the scapegoat on the Day of Atonement, the very service prescribed in Lev. 16. There were recitations at certain points, including the confessions of the High Priest (*Yomah* 4:2; 6:2), the counting of the seven sprinklings of blood (5:3, 4), and the reading of the Pentateuchal portion (7:1). Such recitations were also apart of the sacrificial rites of the Day of Atonement described in *Mishnah, Tamid.* At a particular point in the sacrificial service, the officiants descended to "the chamber of cut stone" and recited certain blessings and selections from Scripture,

The text of 3b yields the following register of cultic occasions:

The New Moon of the month *rišyn* "First of the Wine" (3b:1–2).
— Peace offerings to El (*lil šlmm*) and other sacrifices.[11]
The thirteenth day of the month (3b:3–4a).
— Ablutions.
The fourteenth day of the month (3b:4b–6).
— Offerings of sheep and fowl to "The Lady of the Houses" and to *inš ilm*(?), as well as other sacrifices.[12]
The New Moon (month unnamed) (3b:52–53).
— Sacrifices, including sheep.

(beginning of new section in the text)
The fourteenth day of the month *ši* (name incomplete) (3b:54–57).
— Ablutions, perhaps followed by sacrifices.

These two sections of text 3b (1–53; 54–57) cover a period of more than one month and constitute a list of dates on which rites were performed, including detailed records of the sacrifices that were brought to each deity. The third section of 3b (58–61), although fragmentary, appears to be a record of offerings brought by various persons, some of whom are designated as *bn X* (*bn aup*, *bn gda*). This manner of designating personnel is frequently found in economic and administrative texts.[13]

Of the three texts, text 9 reveals most about its exact character. Line 1 has *slḫ npš* "forgiveness of soul" and line 11 mentions an unspecified date in the month of Tishri: *yrḫ 2 tšrt* (Tašrītu); a month of considerable importance in Mesopotamian religions,[14] and the month in which the Israelite Day of Atonement occurred. In 9:10, where ablutions are mentioned, it would be reasonable to expect the date on which they were performed, as in 3b:3–4a; 54–55. Following Herdner, 9:10 is to be restored: [*bar*]*bᶜt* (or [*bš*]*bᶜt*).ᶜ[*š*]*rt yrtḥṣ mlk.brr* "on the fourteenth (or seventeenth) day, the king, the purifier washes himself."

It is from text 1, the most completely preserved of the three, that we learn most about the composition and formulation of these texts, and receive impor-

---

including the Ten Commandments (*Tamid*, end of 4; 5:1). Further on in the service, at the point when the High Priest was ascending the steps of the Temple, a blessing was recited (7:2). Finally, at the offering of the libation, the Levites provided music, and at each break in the music there was a blast of the shofar and genuflections (7:3).

[11] Cf. *ym ḥdṯ* (3b:1, 52) with Mesopotamian *um arḫu* (U$_4$-U$_4$-SAR) (Landsberger, *Der kultische Kalender der Babylonier und Assyrer*, p. 105, par. 1, and note 1). Cf. biblical *yôm haḥôdeš* (1 Sam. 20:34; Ezek. 46:1).

[12] *rišarg*(*mn*) (?) "First of the tribute/purple" (cf. Herdner, *op. cit.*, on lines 5–6) could be a month name on the model of *rišyn* (3b:1), but the sequence of thirteenth-fourteenth days makes this unlikely. Also note that in entering a date, the month name precedes the date (cf. 3b:1, 52–53, 54).

[13] See Levine, *JBL* 82, pp. 211–212.

[14] See R. Labat, *Hémérologies et Ménologies d'Assur*, pp. 112–124; 169–181 and S. Langdon, *Babylonian Menologies*, pp. 6–7; 97–109.

tant clues for determining the meaning of the terms *dqt* and *gdlt*, and for establishing affinities between these texts and other Ugaritic and biblical sources. We observe in text 1 four formulas employed in listing objects of sacrifice:

> 1. *Item — name of deity* (a genitive construction, with the name of the deity in the genitive): *alp wš ilhm* "a bull and a male of the flock for the gods" (1:5).[15]
>
> 2. *Name of deity — item*: *ršp š* "Rešep, a male of the flock" (1:7). The formula: *name* (of a person, city, etc.) — *item* is used in the economic texts.[16]
>
> 3. *Item — to* (*name of*) *deity* (with the preposition *l*): *alp š lil* "a bull, a male of the flock to El" (1:2). This formula occurs in religious texts.[17]
>
> 4. *Item — type of sacrifice* (a genitive construction with the name of the type of sacrifice in the genitive): *dqt šrp wšlmm* "a female of the flock for the burnt offering and peace offering" (1:4). This formula occurs in other religious texts and in biblical sources.[18]

The foregoing analysis fixes the identification of *dqt* and *gdlt* as sacrificial animals, because the pair of terms *dqt*/*gdlt* replaces the pair *alp*/*š*. Thus, alongside *alp wš ilhm* (1:5) we have *gdlt ilhm* (1:3), and corresponding to *ršp š* (1:7) we have, for example, *ym gdlt* (1:13).

Now that we have established that in texts 1, 3 (3b), and 9 *dqt* and *gdlt* represent sacrificial animals, what types of animals do the terms themselves designate? Since these two pairs of terms occur side by side, they cannot designate the same objects. The feminine form of *dqt* and *gdlt* suggests that these pairs of terms are employed to differentiate animals on the basis of sex, a matter of importance in the cult. If, then, we take *dqt* and *gdlt* as referring to female animals, and accordingly take *š* and *alp* as referring to male animals, the result is a special system of terminology which differentiates animals on the basis of

---

[15] For the presence of *w* in the construct, cf. 5:6–7; *alp wṯlṯ ṣin šlm*[*m*], and for *w* in the genitive cf. 1:4: *dqt šrp wšlmm.*

[16] Cf. text 321.

[17] Cf. 23:4: *š lʿṯtr*[*t*] "a male of the flock to Asirat." Prof. S. Talmon called to my attention a probable vestigial usage of this formula in the Bible: *haśśāʿîr laʿazāʾzēl* "the goat to Azazel" (Lev. 16:26), originally the name of a deity. Formulas whose purpose it was to record to which deity offerings were brought would have little function in a monotheistic text.

[18] Cf. 5:6–7: *alp wṯlṯ ṣin šlm*[*m*] "a head of large cattle and 3 small cattle for the peace offering," and Lev. 4:8: *par haḥaṭṭāʾt* "the bull for the sin offering." This formula occurs in ancient temple records from Mesopotamia which enumerate contributions of animals received for special sacrifices. See L. Legrain, *Le temps des rois d'Ur*, No. 323:6: UDU-GI(G)-KAM "sheep of the night (offering)" (also quoted in Landsberger, *Der kultische Kalender*, p. 32 under 6). There are also examples of this formula in the lexical texts; see Landsberger, *MSL* VIII/1, HAR-*ra* = *ḫubullu* XIII, line 124: udu-ŠUK(ni-ni-im) dINNIN = *immer taklīmi* "a sheep for the *taklīmu* offering."

class (whether small or large) and sex. We may translate these four terms as follows:

š "a male of the flock (ram or he-goat)."
dqt "a female of the flock (ewe or she-goat)."
alp "a male of the herd (bull)."
gdlt "a female of the herd (cow)."[19]

---

[19] If *gdlm* (3:17) is correct (thus Dhorme, Gordon) it would mean "bulls", but see Ginsberg, *op. cit.*, p. 114, and Herdner, *op. cit.* for more probable reading, *gdlt*.

It must be noted, with respect to the situation in Ugaritic sources, that the terms "small cattle" and "flocks" include two genera: *ovis* "sheep" and *capra* "goat" (more accurately: *ovis vignei platyura* "fat-tailed sheep", and *capra hircus mambria* "member goat"). In Ugaritic the following, apart from *š*, *ṣin*, and *dqt*, are included in this group: *imr* "sheep"(?), *ṯat* "ewe", *ḫprt* "spring lamb", *annḫ*(?) || *gdy* "kid" (of the goat), *ṣpr* "goat", *ll*ʾ "'goat" (see *Ugaritic Manual*, glossary) . The terms "large cattle " and "herd" include, in fact, only one species, *bos taurus*. In Ugaritic the following, besides *alp* and *gdlt*, are in this group: *ṯwr* (*ṯr*) "bull", *ibr* "steer"(?), *ʿgl* "young bull", *arḫ* "cow", *prt* "cow", *ʿglt* "young cow" (cf. M. Held *apud MSL* X III/1, p. 65, note 2) and *ypt* "cow' (?) (cf. *Ugaritic Manual* glossary, no. 849). The term *mr*ʾ (*mra*, *mria*) does not designate a separate species in Ugaritic, but merely means "fatling" (cf. Akk. *marû*, and see note 26), and it is also questionable if it means "buffalo" in biblical sources (*pace* J. Felix, *The Fauna of the Bible* (Hebrew), p. 20). When undomesticated animals are used for sacrifice, they are not subsumed under the category of *ṣin* or *alpm*. Thus, in text 62:18–29 we have, in addition to *ṣin* "small cattle" (line 22) and *alpm* "large cattle" (line 20), *aylm* "deer" (line 24), *yʿlm* "ibex" (a kind of wild goats) (line 26), [*y*]*ḥmrm* "antelopes" (line 28 — restoration by Ginsberg, *op. cit.*, p. 58) and *rumm* "wild oxen" (Hebrew *rʾēm*, of the species *bos primigenius*, rather than "buffalo" (pace Gordon, *Ugaritic Manual*, glossary, no. 1732) since one passage speaks of its goring (49:VI:17–18) as the Bible speaks of the goring of the *rʾēm* (Deut. 33:17).

The fact that we are dealing with two genera of small cattle and only one species of large cattle injects a complication into our suggested interpretation. The terms *alp* and *gdlt* were meant to specify only the class and sex of the animal, like *dqt* and *š* which include two genera without differentiation; but, in fact, they also tell us the species of the thus designated animals by the process of elimination, since only one species can be intended by *alp*, and therefore *gdlt*.

Our interpretation has not been anticipated. Dussaud does not take *dqt* as the designation of an animal. Dhorme's interpretation recognizes that *š*/*alp* refer to male animals and *dqt*/*gdlt* to females. He correctly translates *alp* "boeuf" and *gdlt* "génisse", but in the case of small cattle, where there are two genera, his translations reveal that he understood meanings different from what we are suggesting. He renders *š* "agneau" and *dqt* "brébis", the male and female of the sheep genus. He gives a second meaning for *dqt*: "menu bétail", and identifies this term with Late Hebrew *behēmāh daqqāh*, which includes both sexes of small cattle. Gordon, followed by Herdner, translates *š*/*alp* "a head of small/large cattle" and *dqt*/*gdlt* "small/large beast." Ginsberg (*op. cit.*, p. 111) correctly questions Dhorme's interpretation of *dqt* as "menu bétail" (= Late Hebrew *behēmāh daqqāh*), for, if *dqt* in Ugaritic had the sense of the Late Hebrew term, which includes both genera and

The etymology of *dqt* does not oppose this interpretation. In Semitic languages the root *dqq* seems to have two distinct connotations: (1) "thin, fine" (in Early Aramaic, Empire Aramaic, Phoenician, and Biblical Hebrew). (2) "small (child), small." These latter meanings are attested for *daqqu* (and related forms) in Old Akkadian, Old Babylonian, Standard Babylonian, and in certain dialects of Aramaic (in the Targum, Rabbah Midrashim, and the Palestinian Talmud) where *deqāqāh* means" small child", and *daqqîq* (cf. "Babylonian" *daqqiqu*) means "small." In Late Hebrew the adjectival form *daqq* (fem. *daqqāh*) at times means "thin, fine", reflecting biblical usage, but more often means "small." What is more, in Late Hebrew *daqqāh* in the sense of "small" occurs in a pair of terms, (*behēmāh*) *daqqāh* "a head of small cattle" and (*behēmāh*) *gassāh* "a head of large cattle" which correspond to Ugaritic *dqt* and *gdlt*, Ugaritic *gdlt* being replaced in Late Hebrew by the semantic equivalent *gassāh.*[20]

Nevertheless, our interpretation of *dqt* and *gdlt* poses several problems. The terms *š* and *alp* appear to have a more inclusive meaning elsewhere in Ugaritic. Thus, *alpm* and *ṣin* constitute a pair in Ugaritic (5:6–7; 51:VI:40) just as they do in biblical sources (Ps. 8:8), which indicates that *alp* does not refer specifically to "a male of the herd," but to "a head of large cattle" generally. It is the counterpart of *ṣin*, which is a term that normally includes all small cattle. In the case of *š* (*šuʾu*), although an exact definition is not possible from Ugaritic sources, there is no indication that, elsewhere in Ugaritic, this term is limited to male

---

sexes of small cattle, this meaning would be accurately represented elsewhere in Ugaritic by *š* (and *gdlt* by *alp*). We are attempting to preserve the identification of *dqt* — *daqqāh*, despite the variance in meaning, by explicating the pattern of variation which accounts for the generalization of the meaning of *dqt*, and by showing that *š* and *alp* were also subject to variations in meaning (see further). It is also true, however, that more than one term can exist for the same animal. This is due in part to the difference in the lexicons of the epics and other texts (see note 28) and partly because these terms often indicate distinctions in age, in the bearing of young, etc., which are not evident to us. *Dqt* has no equivalent in Ugaritic, but there is a biblical equivalent: *neqēbāh min haṣṣôn* "a female of the flock" (Lev. 5:6), defined in the same verse exactly as we have defined *dqt* in these texts: "a ewe or a she-goat." Because, in fact, only one species of large cattle is involved, *gdlt* has the same meaning as *arḫ* "cow", and probably *prt* "cow" (cf. Akk. *pu-ur-tu* in *MSL* VIII/1, p. 65 and Ginsberg, *op. cit.*, p. 111). *Alp*, in these texts, is possibly equivalent to *ṯwr* (*ṯr*).

[20] Jean-Hoftijzer, *Dictionnaire*, s.v. *daqq*. Koehler-Baumgartner, *Lexicon*, s.v. *daqq*. *CAD*, s.v. *daqqu* and *daqīqu*. Jastrow, *Dictionary* s.v. *daqq*, *daqqîq*, *deqaqah*. Kasofsky, *Thesaurus Mishnae* and *Thesaurus Tosephthae* (Hebrew), s.v. *daqq* (fem. *daqqāh*). Also note *ḥayyāh daqqāh* "a small beast" (*M. Baba Bathra* 9:3) and *ʿôp haddaq* "small fowl" (*M. Ḥullin* 3:1). *Daqqāh* also occurs with *behēmāh* understood (*M. Shabbath* 24:2, *passim.*). Some Aramaic usages of *daqq* in the sense of "small" can be accounted for as translations from Late Hebrew (cf. *Lev. Rabbah*, ed. Margulies, section 27, p. 622, line 4: *beʿîr daqqîq* "a head of small cattle").

animals. A comparison of biblical *śeh* would lead us to infer that Ugaritic *š* also includes both sexes of sheep and goats (Ex. 12:5; Lev. 22:28).

Similarly, the Late Hebrew meaning of (*behēmāh*) *daqqāh* differs from our interpretation of Ugaritic *dqt* in that it is used to designate "a head of small cattle" regardless of sex, whereas we have taken Ugaritic *dqt* to be a term which precisely differentiates small cattle on the basis of their sex.

These problems emerge from the complexity of the terminology used to classify domestic animals, and from the frequent variations in meaning to which the names of animals (and groups of animals) are subject. An analysis of this terminology reveals that four systems are employed in Ugaritic sources, each fulfilling a particular requirement of classification:

> 1. Classification according to class, irrespective of whether small or large cattle. An example is the collective *ṣin* "small cattle" (and normally *alp* "a head of large cattle").[21]
>
> 2. Classification according to class and sex. Examples are the terms *dqt/gdlt* and *š/alp* in texts 1, 3 (3b), and 9 as we have interpreted them.
>
> 3. Classification according to class and species (or genus) regardless of sex. In Ugaritic we have no term which definitely fits into this system, since the sources are too vague to allow for an exact definition of such terms as *imr* (*immeru*) "sheep" (?) or *llʾ* (*lalū*) "goat" (?). Conceivably they could refer to males of one genus, to both sexes of the genus, or, in the case of *imr* to both sexes of sheep and goats.[22] Biblical examples of this classification are *ʿēz* (*enzu*), which often definitely means "goat (m. and f.)", and *kebeś*, which often means "sheep (m. and f.)."[23]
>
> 4. Classification according to class, species (or genus), and sex. There are quite a few of this type. An example is *ṯat* "ewe."

In Mesopotamian, Ugaritic, and biblical sources we observe that many names of animals (or groups of animals) do not belong exclusively to one or the other system, but may function in several systems, depending on the particular requirements of classification imposed by the texts themselves.

In the case of *š* and *alp* we can observe significant variations in meaning. In some Mesopotamian sources *alpu* (GUD) means "bull" in contradistinction to *arḫu* (ÁB), and other terms, which mean "cow."[24] Yet in still other Mesopotamian sources *alpē* (GU_4.MEŠ) and *ṣēnē* occur as a pair, just as in Ugaritic and biblical sources, and *alpē* means "large cattle" without specification of sex, the

---

[21] Note that, in 1 Sam. 25:2, *ṣôn* does not include "goats."

[22] Cf. *CAD I/J*, s.v. *immeru*.

[23] See note 27.

[24] Landsberger, *MSL*, VIII/1, HAR-*ra* = *ḫubullu* XIII, line 280: GUD = *alpi*, and line 333: ÁB = *arḫu*. Also see discussion, p. 61ff.

counterpart of *ṣēnē* "small cattle."[25] It is therefore reasonable to suggest that the same variation exists in Ugaritic itself. Normally, *alp* means "a head of large cattle" with no sex indicated, but in texts 1, 3 (3b), and 9, where the particular requirements of the cult necessitated a system of classification that specified not only the class of the animal but also its sex, *alp* retains its more limited sense of "bull", and serves as a counterpart of *gdlt* "cow."

As regards *š* (*šuʾu*) the evidence is not nearly so conclusive. The most that can be said is that, in a commonplace clause, occurring with slight variations in a number of documents from the period of Sargon II, *šuʾu* interchanges with UDU.NITÁ ("sheep-male").[26] This suggests that *šuʾu* might also have had the specific meaning of "ram." If this is so, we have variations in the meaning of *šuʾu* somewhat similar to those we have observed in the case of *alp*. At one end of the series we have the possibility that *šuʾu* has the limited meaning of "ram," and at the other end, the evidence from Biblical Hebrew that *śeh* means "a head of small cattle" generally. Somewhere between the two extremes is the meaning suggested for *š* in these ritual texts. Despite the absence of conclusive evidence, we may provisionally suggest that normally *š* in Ugaritic includes more than just the males of the flock, but that the particular requirements of these ritual texts dictated a more limited meaning for *š*.[27]

---

[25] D. D. Luckenbill, *The Annals of Sennacherib, Oriental Institute Prism Inscription*, Col. III, line 26: GUD.MEŠ (= *alpē* pl.) *ù ṣi-e-ni* "cattle and sheep" (p. 182). Cf. the same variation in the meaning of *ṯwr* (*ṯr*), Hebrew *šôr*. In Biblical Hebrew *šôr* can mean specifically "bull" (Ex. 21:29), or "a head of large cattle" generally (Lev. 22:27, 28). In Ugaritic *ṯwr* (*ṯr*) probably refers only to the male (cf. its use as an epithet of El in 49:IV:34, etc.).

[26] Cf. Delitzsch, *Ass. Handwörterbuch*, s.v. *šuʾu*. Deimel, *Šumerisches Lexicon* (Teil II, p. 990, No. 57) lists *šuʾu* as interchanging with UDU.NITÁ ("sheep-male"). This is based on a comparison of the Nimrud Inscription (H. Winckler, *Keilschrifttexte Sargons*, II, pl. 48, line 19) with the Annals of Sargon (A.G. Lie, *The Inscriptions of Sargon II, King of Assyria*, Part I, The Annals, p. 58, line 386). Both texts come from the same period and the passages compared both speak of offerings. In the Annals the passage in which *šuʾu* occurs is restored from the Display Inscription (Winckler, *op. cit.*, p. 36, pl. 30, No. 76, line 168). This passage is repeated a number of times. It reads: *gu-maḫ-ḫi bit-ru-ti šu-ʾe-e ma-ru-ti kurkē*MUSEN.MEŠ *paspasē*MUSEN.MEŠ *šummē is-ḫi-it nūnē*MEŠ "fat bulls, fattened sheep, fowl, ducks(?), *šummu* plants, and strings of fish." In the Nimrud Inscription l. 19 we read: *gu-maḫ-ḫi* GAL.MEŠ UDU.NITÁ.MEŠ *ma-ru-ti* "large bulls, fattened sheep (m.)." See also *CAD G*, s.v. *gumāḫu*; furthermore D. D. Luckenbill, *Ancient Records of Assyria and Babylonia* II, p. 73 (Nimrud Inscription), p. 19 (Annals of Sargon), p. 38 (Display Inscription). For a reason that is not clear Deimel equals UDU.NITÁ of the Boğazköy texts (e.g., KBo V, No. 7 rev. 30; Hitt. Laws §59) with *šuʾu*.

[27] Cf. biblical *ʿēz* (Akk. *enzu*) which may mean "goat" in general (Lev. 1:10) or specifically "she-goat" in contradistinction to *tayiš* (Akk. *daššu*) which, in biblical sources, designates the "male goat" (Gen. 32:15). The same variation is attested in Mesopotamia where ÙZ (i.e. *enzu*) may be used in a list to designate "she goat" and in the total of the same list may include "he-goat" (MÁŠ = *urīṣu*):

The problem of Late Hebrew (*behēmāh*) *daqqāh* can be treated in the same way. In the Ugaritic ritual texts a system of classification was needed that specified the sex of the animal as well as its class, and consequently a term meaning "small", in the feminine gender, was used to designate "a female of the flock." In Tannaitic sources where, more often than not, questions of law centered around the class of the animal and not its sex, this term was used descriptively with *behēmāh* (itself feminine in gender) to specify only the class of the animal.

In the light of this analysis it is clear that not only does the lexicon of the epics differ from that of other types of Ugaritic texts, as is noted by Held,[28] but that the same terms are used differently according to the demands of various types of texts. The terms *dqt* and *gdlt* are peculiar to texts 1, 3 (3b), and 9 (and fragments of the same type). These terms were probably created specially for this type of text. The terms *š* and *alp*, on the other hand, occur both in the epics and in other types of texts, where they appear to have a constant meaning. It is only in these formulaic rituals that we observe a variation toward a more limited connotation. This is further indication, apart from considerations already noted, that texts 1, 3 (3b), and 9 differ not only from the epics, but from other types of economic, epistolary, and administrative texts as well. They represent a distinct type of Ugaritic document.

---

x ÙZ.HI.A "x she-goats"
x MÁŠ.DU "x he-goats"
x ÙZ.HI.A "x goats (generic)"

(see *CAD E*, s.v. *enzu*). Similarly, in Biblical Hebrew, *kebeś* can mean "sheep" generally (Lev. 1:10) or specifically the male, as evidenced by *kibśāh* (Lev. 5:6) for the female.

[28] M. Held, *JAOS* 79, p. 174 with notes 95–107.

The Descriptive Tabernacle Texts of the Pentateuch*

Exodus 35–39, Leviticus 8–9, and Numbers 7 are descriptive accounts of the construction of the ark and tabernacle, their consecration, and the initiation of the priestly cult. Our method in studying these texts will be form-critical in that we are interested primarily in the types of textual materials utilized by the writers of the Pentateuch and not in the various documentary sources which are adduced for the Pentateuch. The descriptive tabernacle texts bear affinities to other records preserved in the Bible, and also to extra-biblical archival material from many parts of the ancient Near East, principally Mesopotamia. In analyzing these tabernacle accounts we will be attempting to identify the forms, or types, which they represent. Such analysis cannot normally yield an exact date for the texts under consideration, but it can afford insight into the process of the composition of the Pentateuch and into the origins of its institutions.

I. Exodus 35–39

Exodus 35–39 is in large part the description of the fashioning of the tabernacle, its vessels, and the priestly vestments. This section presents a critical problem because of the fact that the arrangement of its contents differs from the organization of the same material in a prior section of Exodus, chapters 25–31, where the tabernacle project is ordained in a series of instructions addressed by God to Moses. In the prescriptive section (particularly 25:10–27:19) the instructions concerning the tabernacle begin with the interior vessels of the sanctuary—the ark, table, and lampstand (25:10–40), proceed to specify the features of the tent structure itself (26:1–37) and conclude by delineating the parts of the tabernacle complex which are outside the tent, i.e. the altar of burnt offerings and the courtyard where it was to be located (27:1–19). In the descriptive section (particularly 36:8–38:31) the text begins with the tent structure (36:8–38), continues by describing the cultic vessels—the ark, table, lampstand, the altars of incense and burnt offerings, and the laver (37:1–38:8), and concludes with the description of the outer courtyard (38:9–20).

The order of the instructions in 25:10–27:19 has been correctly explained in terms of the relative importance of various parts of the tabernacle. The ark was the central object of the cult and the instructions begin, therefore, with the speci-

---

* Originally published in *JAOS* 85 (1965), pp. 307–318. Reprinted with permission from the American Oriental Society.

fications of its construction.[1] Chapters 30–31 remain problematic. Certain items seem to be misplaced, and matters extraneous to the tabernacle project are included. The arrangement of the material in chapters 35–39 is systematic. The structure is projected first, then its furnishings, and finally the courtyard around it.

We have the view of von Rad, followed in its essentials by Noth, that chapters 35–39 are a slavish copy of the prior instructions, in which the material was adapted and rearranged so as to harmonize the several strata present in chapters 25–31. The systematic arrangement characteristic of chapters 35–39 is taken as evidence of an artificial reworking of more original materials, whereas the very lack of order in parts of chapters 25–31 indicates actual literary development. Cassuto, proceeding from an entirely different set of critical assumptions, explains the differing arrangements as chiastic. The author simply switched the order for literary effect. In 25–27:19 the order is: ark-tabernacle, and in 35–39: tabernacle-ark.[2]

We do not dispute the literary dependence of chapters 35–39 on certain sections of chapters 25–31. On the one hand, chapters 25–27 give evidence of originality and coherence. The section is unified by the recurrent theme that Moses was shown the "pattern" (*tabnît*) of the tabernacle by God while he was on the mountain (25:9, 40, 26:30, 37:8).[3] This theme relates to the ancient typology of the earthly sanctuary as the replica of the heavenly abode of the gods.[4] On the other hand, chapters 35–39 reveal literary dependence on chapters 25–31. The provisions of chapter 28, prescribing the sacred vestments, are slightly abbreviated in the descriptive version of 39:2–31. Likewise, the contents of chapters 30–31, included in the descriptive section, are divested of all but pure description, and contain no dicta regarding the cultic use of the objects presented. There is only passing reference to the "oil of anointing" and the incense (37:29) which would presuppose that specific data existed about these ingredients. Furthermore, chapters 35–39 clearly utilize material from chapters 25–31 interpretively. Thus, 38:25–28 reflects the blending of two traditions found in chapters 25–31. There it is stated that the silver to be contributed to the tabernacle project (25:3) was paid in the form of the poll-tax of a half-shekel (30:13).[5]

---

[1] M. Noth, *Exodus*, (*The Old Testament Library*), trans. by J. S. Bowden, (1962), pp. 202–203. U. Cassuto, *A Commentary on the Book of Exodus*, (Hebrew), (1953), p. 228.

[2] G. von Rad, *Die Priesterschrift im Hexateuch, Beiträge zur Wissenschaft von alten und neuen Testament*, 65, (1934), pp. 58, 68–70. Noth, *op. cit.*, pp. 274–280. Cassuto, *op. cit.*, pp. 323f. Also see M. Noth, *Leviticus: The Old Testament Library*, (1965), pp. 68–82.

[3] See von Rad, *op. cit.*, p. 58, and F. M. Cross, *The Biblical Archaeologist Reader* I, (1961), p. 220.

[4] See Cassuto, *op. cit.*, pp. 223–224 and W. L. Moran, *Analecta Biblica*, 12, (1959), pp. 257–265 for new light on this typology in Mesopotamian sources.

[5] Exod. 38:25–26 seems to anticipate the total of the census recorded in Num. 2:32, but the tradition of the six hundred thousand is also known from other sources (Exod.

We do question whether the above analysis conveys the complete literary reality which underlies the composition of the descriptive account in chapters 35–39. It is generally reasonable to posit that rigid order and system indicate artificiality, and that natural literary development would take a less systematic course. On the other hand, ancient scribes and authors, in committing their material to writing, adhered devotedly to accepted forms. Just as the analysis of the forms employed in poetry, narrative, and legal texts has proved fundamental to their appreciation, here, too, it is necessary to determine whether the composition of the descriptive account has anything to contribute to our understanding of its contents and provenience.

One type of biblical account that achieved a specific form is the palace record describing architectural and artistic projects. The most elaborate example of such records in the Bible, if not in the literature of the entire ancient Near East, is the description of the construction of Solomon's temple and royal buildings (1 Kings 6–7). It is generally considered to be an authentic document based on actual archival records.[6] A comparison of 1 Kings 6–8 with Exodus 35–39 reveals that in both accounts the description begins with the outer structure. 1 Kings 6:1–10 describes the exterior of the temple. Verse 2 gives the length, breadth, and height of the building and verse 3 provides the same dimensions for the portico. In the section describing the royal buildings we observe the same pattern (1 Kings 7:1–12). Verse 2 presents the dimensions of the House of the Cedars of Lebanon, and verse 6, in its description of the Hall of Columns, first gives its length and breadth. It is to be noted that in the brief Aramaic excerpt of the Persian royal edict authorizing the building of Zerubabel's temple (Ezra 6:3–5) the exterior dimensions of the building are given first, in much the same terms as were used in the 1 Kings record.[7]

In the purely descriptive parts of Exodus 35–39 dealing with the sanctuary and its vessels (36:8–38:20), the account also begins by delineating the dimensions of the tent structure, its strips of cloth, its covering of goat's hair, and its frames of wood (36:8–38). The orientation of the record, both in 1 Kings and in Exodus, is from the exterior structure inward, to its furnishings.

Thus, in the 1 Kings account, after presenting an elaborate view of the interior walls of the building (1 Kings 6:14–36), an aspect of description not applicable in the case of a tent structure, the text continues with a description of the

12:37). Exod. 38:8 mentions "the mirrors of the women who performed tasks" which were used in fashioning the copper laver and its stand. There is no mention of this in 25–31. Such women are known from 1 Sam. 2:22, and the term *ṣbʾ* "to perform cultic service" is applied to the Levites in Num. 4:23, 8:24.

[6] J. A. Montgomery and H. S. Gehman, *Kings, The International Critical Commentary*, (1951), pp. 37–38, 142. Also J. A. Montgomery, *JBL* 53, (1934) pp. 51–52.

[7] Cf. the Aramaic terms in Ezra 6:3–5 with the Hebrew terms in 1 Kings 6:2–9, etc: *rûmēh* = *qômātô* "its height," *petāyēh* = *roḥbô* "its breadth," and *nidbāk* = *yaṣîʿa* (Kethib *yṣwʿ*) "a layer of stones."

interior vessels and appointments of the temple (1 Kings 7:15–46).[8] Likewise, in Exodus 35–39, after the features of the tent structure itself had been recorded, we are provided the details concerning the vessels which were to be housed in the tabernacle complex (Exodus 37:1–38:8).

Several other similarities in the presentation of the material in both Exodus and 1 Kings reinforce the observation that we are here dealing with a specific genre. Where an outer courtyard is projected, it is described at the end of the record.[9] In both accounts the passages which introduce the craftsmen precede the actual descriptions of the projects they undertook and characterize the craftsmen in the same terms.[10] Both accounts end with a clause recording, in commonplace formularies, the satisfactory completion of the work.[11] The 1 Kings account is more detailed in this respect. It specifies the amount of time taken by the project (1 Kings 7:1) and includes a regnal date (6:1), which would not be applicable in the Exodus account.

Still another indication of the archival character of Exodus 35–39 is the list of totals in 38:24–30, which records the expenditures of gold, silver, and copper received from contributions for the fashioning of certain tabernacle fixtures[12] as shown in Table 1.

TABLE 1

BIBLICAL VERSE	METALS	QUANTITY	EXPENDITURE
Ex 38:24	gold	29 talents + 730 shekels (sanctuary weight)	Unspecified
Ex 38:25	silver	100 talents + 1,775 shekels (sanctuary weight)[13]	
38:27–28			100 sockets @ 1 talent + hooks made of 1,775 silver shekels

[8] See Cross, *op. cit.*, pp. 217–221 for a discussion of the construction of the tabernacle. In 1 Kings 6:15f., the interior of the walls is paneled with "cedar planks" (*ṣalᶜôt ʾarāzîm*) which covered the entire wall, whereas the desert tabernacle had "frames" (*qerāšîm*) which did not cover the entire sides of the tent and were light enough to be transported (Exod. 26:15–25, 36:20–30). The relevance of Ugaritic *qršm*, discussed by Cross, *op. cit.*, p. 220, was earlier noted by Cassuto, *op. cit.*, p. 224.

[9] Cf. 1 Kings 7:12 and Exod. 38:9–20.

[10] Cf. 1 Kings 7:13–15 and Exod. 35:30–36:1. Both Hiram and Bezalel are characterized as possessing three attributes: "skill, ability, and knowledge" (*ḥokmāh*, *tebûnāh*, and *daᶜat*).

[11] Cf. 1 Kings 6:37–38 and Exod. 39:32, 40:17.

[12] The totals are listed in the order of descending value. Cf. the brief list of totals in Ezra 1:9–11.

[13] Exod. 38:26 provides the basis for reckoning the total amount of silver contributed. ½ shekel × 603,550 (no. of male Israelites 20–50 years of age) = 100 talents + 1775 shekels. See R. B. Y. Scott, *Biblical Archaeologist* 22, (1959), pp. 32–33.

38:29	copper	70 talents + 2,400 shekels (sanctuary weight)	
38:30			1) hooks for a) entrance to the tent, b) altar vessels 2) sockets for a) courtyard and gate, b) tent pegs.

In terms of composition, therefore, Exodus 35–39, in its descriptive portions, is a document patterned after archival records. It follows the logic of architectural conceptualization in the arrangement of its material and employs traditional methods of accounting.

Just as the comparison of Exodus 35–39 with 1 Kings 6–7 proves fruitful in identifying the character of the Pentateuch account, so does the contrasting of the two sources point to significant aspects of the tabernacle texts. There is an element present in Exodus 35–39 which is absent from the 1 Kings account: the priestly orientation. As Montgomery has noted, the 1 Kings account of Solomon's projects is presented entirely as a royal enterprise. It lacks the inspirational dimension so prominent in the Ezekiel visions (chapter 40f.), in the Exodus accounts, and in the Gudea inscriptions.[14]

Two notions are basic to the priestly outlook: 1) Every detail of the early Israelite cult was specifically ordained by God through direct communication to Moses, the leader of the people. 2) The ancient Israelites demonstrated their obedience to God by carrying out his commands with precision and dispatch. The mere presence of the descriptive record makes this second notion clear, but further emphasis was deemed necessary, and consequently the descriptive record itself was adapted by means of two literary devices: 1) the prescriptive introduction, which ordains the activity, in this instance for the second time (Exodus 35:4–19), and 2) the compliance formula "as/which the LORD commanded Moses" (*kaʾᵃšer/ʾᵃšer ṣiwwāh YHWH ʾet Môšeh*) and its variants (35:4, 29, 36:1, 38:22, 39:1, 5, 7, etc.). These devices are also employed elsewhere in the priestly writings to incorporate early archival and legal material into the overall Pentateuch narrative.[15] In the case of Exodus 35–39, the prescriptive introduction and the compliance formula reinforce the effects of the descriptive account by linking it to its prescriptive antecedents. In other cases, where prior prescriptions do not occur, the prescriptive introduction provides the ideological basis for the record which follows upon it.

---

[14] Montgomery-Gehman, *op. cit.*, p. 152.

[15] Cf. 1) The census in Num. 25:19–26:51: a) prescriptive introduction (25:19–26:4a), b) archival record (26:4b–51), and c) the compliance formula (26:4a). 2) The census in Num. l: a) prescriptive introduction (1:1–19), (b) archival record (1:20–54), and c) the compliance formula (1:19, 54). 3) Legal-cultic material: prescriptive introductions in Lev. 17:1–2, Num. 30:2.

II. Leviticus 8–9

With this background, we can now turn to two other descriptive tabernacle texts, Leviticus 8 and 9. It will be more expedient to treat Leviticus 9 first since it is free of certain problems involved in the analysis of Leviticus 8 which will be discussed subsequently. Leviticus 9 describes the rites of the eighth day of the ordination of the priests on which occasion Aaron, the High Priest, initiated the sacrificial cult on the tabernacle altar of burnt offerings. The chapter follows the pattern noted above: 1) prescriptive introduction (vv. 1–7), 2) descriptive ritual text (vv. 8–24), and 3) the compliance formula (vv. 6, 7, 10, and 21, according to 34 manuscripts).

The descriptive ritual text (9:8–24) is narrative in style and bears distinctive features. It uses the Hipʿîl stem of the root *mṣʾ* in the technical sense of "passing on, handing over," a usage not attested elsewhere in the Bible.[16] There is also the usage of *yāṣaq dām* "to pour our blood" (v. 9), otherwise attested only in Leviticus 8:15.[17]

Leviticus 8 follows the same pattern as Leviticus 9. Verses 1–5 are a prescriptive introduction, verses 6–36 contain a narrative descriptive account, and the compliance formula recurs at regular intervals (vv. 5, 9, 13, *etc*.). Leviticus 8 actually portrays two distinct, but combined rituals: 1) the sanctification of the tabernacle and its vessels, and of the High Priest, Aaron, by the rite of unction with the "oil of anointing" (vv. 7–12), and 2) the ordination of Aaron and his sons in their priestly office by means of sacrificial rites and a seven-day period of incubation (vv. 13–36). The rite of ordination followed directly upon the sanctification, and the priests underwent ablutions before the sanctification rites commenced (v. 6). The two rites are further joined by the use of a mixture of the "oil of anointing" and the blood from the altar, which is sprinkled on the garments of the ordained priests (v. 30), and by the use of the term "sanctify" (*qiddēš*), which occurs in both sections of Leviticus 8 (vv. 10, 11, 12, and 30).

The status of Leviticus 8 is complicated by the fact that it appears to be the fulfillment of rites previously ordained in the book of Exodus,[18] and yet it does not bear the same clear relationship to its alleged prescriptive antecedents as did Exodus 35–39 to chapters 25–28, 30–31.

---

[16] Cf. vs. 12, 13, 18: *himṣîʾû, wayyamṣîʾû.*

[17] The verb used elsewhere in Leviticus to denote the same action (i.e. pouring out blood at the base of the altar) is *špk*. (Cf. Lev. 4:7, 18, 25, etc.).

[18] The Exodus passages which supposedly ordain the rites described in Lev. 8 are: 1) Exod. 28:1, 41—commanding the ordination of Aaron and his sons as priests and their investiture; 2) Exod. 29:1–37—commanding the unction of Aaron, and the ordination of the priesthood in a rite to last seven days; 3) Exod. 30:22–33—prescribing the concoction of the "oil of anointing" and its use in sanctifying the tabernacle and the priesthood by the rite of unction; 4) Exod. 40:9–15—ordaining the sanctification of the tabernacle and priests by unction, and their ordination.

Although our identification of Leviticus 8 as a narrative descriptive ritual, akin to Leviticus 9, would not be invalidated even if Leviticus 8 were in fact the reflex of the Exodus prescriptions, it is necessary to analyze it in depth in order to clarify its relationship to the traditions of Exodus, since it gives evidence of being an original source.

In Leviticus 8:7–12, Aaron, the High Priest, is viewed as the bearer of a distinct office, not as a priest who is *primus inter pares*. The vestments in which he is garbed (vv. 7–9) are worn only by him. Aaron is anointed in the same manner as the tabernacle and its vessels, and the term "to anoint" (*mšḥ*), used in connection with both Aaron and the tabernacle, is not used anywhere in the ordination rites (vv. 13–36). In Leviticus 8:7–12 we are presented with a coordinate typology which embraces both sanctuary and High Priest. The High Priest is a sacred vessel and is consecrated as such.

This conception of the High Priest corresponds to the legal definition of his status in the book of Leviticus (21:10–15). He may not leave the sanctuary because he is distinguished by unction with the "oil of anointing" and by his unique right to don the sacred vestments. His special status emerges from the entire structure of the priestly cult according to which only the High Priest may minister inside the tent of meeting, before the ark, whereas ordinary priests may officiate only outside the tent.[19]

Exodus 29:1–37 would correspond to this picture of the special role of the High Priest as regards his unique unction (Exodus 29:7), but it does not view that unction as part of the sanctification of the tabernacle and its vessels, as is the case in Leviticus 8, but as an act connected with ordination. The other Exodus passages which speak of the sanctification of the tabernacle and the priests (Exodus 30:22–33, 40:9–15, etc.) prescribe unction for all of the priests. Nowhere in Exodus do we find the same conceptual framework which characterizes Leviticus 8.

We must conclude, therefore, that the Exodus passages which prescribe unction for both Aaron and his sons represent a tradition different from that of Leviticus. This difference in cultic traditions between Leviticus and Exodus is not restricted to the rite of unction. In another instance a rite specified for the High Priest in the book of Leviticus includes, in its Exodus version, all of the priests. In Leviticus 24:1–4 Aaron alone is commanded to kindle lights inside the tent of meeting. A parallel of that passage occurs in Exodus 27:20–21 where both Aaron and his sons are to perform this rite.[20]

---

[19] This is conclusively demonstrated by M. Haran, "The Complex of Ritual Acts Performed inside the Tabernacle," in *Studies in the Bible*, ed. Ch. Rabin, ScrHier 8, (1961), pp. 273–302, (especially p. 274, note 4, 275, note 5, and 277–278, note 9).

[20] This is an alternative to Haran's explanation (*ibid.* pp. 277–278, note 9) that the occurrence of the word *ûbānāyw* "and his sons" in Exod. 27:21 is an erroneous insertion. This observation does not affect Haran's thesis that activities inside the tent of meeting are reserved for the High Priest according to the basic priestly tradition. That tradition has

It is hardly likely that Leviticus 8:7–12, which agrees fundamentally with Leviticus traditions, is based on the Exodus passages which ordain unction for all priests. Nor can Exodus 29:1–37 be the source of Leviticus 8:13–36. Exodus 29 generally gives evidence of being based on other texts.[21] The regular offerings ordained in verses 38–41 are probably based on Numbers 28:3–8, where they are in context, and are repeated here with accretions. In like manner, verses 1–37 are probably based on Leviticus 8:13–36 and were inserted here in association with Exodus 28:2 which prescribes the fashioning of the sacred vestments. The purpose was to specify the use to which these vestments would be put, just as the regular offerings (vv. 38–41) are associated with 28:1. The limitation of unction to the High Priest (29:7) indicates that Exodus 29 is a later addition to the Exodus tabernacle texts and was not affected by the normative Exodus traditions which provided unction for all priests. It was apparently deemed necessary to include several aspects of the cult in the original prescriptions concerning the tabernacle project by providing prescriptive antecedents in Exodus for the ordination of the priests and the daily offerings.[22] On the basis of this analysis, Leviticus 8 emerges as an original narrative descriptive ritual, a partner to Leviticus 9.

Our search for analogues to Leviticus 8 and 9 has not been entirely successful. In its underlying circumstances, Leviticus 9 resembles the dedication of Solomon's temple described in 1 Kings 8. The people assemble at the locale of the ceremonies (Lev. 9:5/1 Kgs 8:1–5). Sacrifices are offered (Lev. 9:8–21/1 Kgs 8:5b, 62–64). The officiant blesses the people with hands raised (Lev. 9:22–23/1 Kgs 8:22, 55). The glory of God is revealed to the whole people assembled at the sanctification of a cultic edifice (Lev. 9:23b/1 Kgs 8:10–11).[23]

---

simply been affected by the outlook of the book of Exodus, and a passage most likely original to Lev. 24:1–4 (*contra* Haran) has been altered in its Exodus version.

[21] According to 29:26–28, Moses is to consecrate the "breast" (*ḥazeh*), his "portion" (*mānāh*) as officiant, together with the "thigh" (*šôq*, not mentioned as his *mānāh*), thus making them the regular portions of Aaron and his sons from the Israelite sacrifices. This presupposes the provisions of Lev. 7:31–34 which designate both the breast and thigh portions as the "regular portion" (*ḥôq*) of the priests. In contrast to Exod. 29:26–28, Lev. 8:29 merely states that Moses, as officiant on that occasion, received the breast portion as his *mānāh*, and it makes no attempt to go beyond the immediate rites of ordination and to link Moses' *mānāh* with the regular provisions of the priestly cult.

[22] Cf. Noth's suggestion (*op. cit.*, pp. 282–283) that chapter 40 may represent an attempt to include in Exodus the completion of the entire tabernacle project by anticipating the actual cultic use of the tabernacle altar and vessels. The revelation of divine glory in the cloud (vv. 34–38) would seem to anticipate Num. 9:15f. A similar notion is expressed by the medieval commentator Nachmanides: "For thus it is the manner of Scripture in every instance to complete a matter it has begun to discuss." See R. Haim Shevel, *Moses b. Nachman: Commentaries on the Torah*, (Hebrew), vol. 2, Jerusalem, (1960), s.v. Lev. 8:1, p. 38.

[23] Also cf. 2 Sam. 6:1–6a, 12b–18, and Neh. 8–10.

And yet there is a distinct difference in style and tone between Leviticus 9 and the 1 Kings account. This difference manifests itself in the detailed delineation of specific ritual acts which characterizes the Leviticus ritual. In Leviticus it is the detail of the ritual which is emphasized, whereas in the 1 Kings account it is the general character of the event which is stressed. 1 Kings 8 enumerates in archival fashion how many animals were slaughtered and recounts the sequence of events in the ceremony without, however, elaborating the manner in which specific rites were performed.[24]

Detailed descriptions of rituals, similar in composition to Leviticus 8 and 9 are to be found in Ugaritic, Assyrian, and Hittite.[25] Certain types of ritual texts in these languages describe the proper procedure for the performance of specific ritual acts. The descriptions they contain are not stated in prescriptive form, however, but in the style of running accounts, written as though by one who has witnessed the performance of the ritual, and is recording what he saw.[26] The Ugaritic descriptive rituals employ the *yqṭl* formation of the verb with narrative force to describe contemporaneous action, and include lists of the animals of-

---

[24] A fundamental distinction is intended between descriptive and prescriptive ritual texts, and for that reason, the prescriptive rituals in the Pentateuch which emphasize detail (Lev. 1–7, 10f., Deut. 21:1–9, 26:1–15; cf. also Ezek 43:18–27), are not being taken into account in our form-critical analysis. Two types of descriptive rituals can be identified: 1) the narrative descriptive rituals, as we have classified Lev. 8 and 9, and 2) the formulaic descriptive ritual represented by Num. 7:12–88.

[25] The Ugaritic descriptive rituals were studied by this author in *JCS* 17, (1963), pp. 105–111. {*VOL 1, PP. 45–54*}. For examples in Assyrian see Karl Fr. Müller, *Texte zum Assyrischen Königsritual, MVAG* 41, (1937), Teil 1 (dated by Müller in the reign of Tukulti-Ninurta I). W. von Soden, "Aus einem Ersatzopferritual für den assyrischen Hof," *ZA*, n.F. 11, (1939), pp. 42–61 (dated in the reign of Assarhaddon). For examples in Hittite see A. Goetze, *ANET*, (1955), pp. 346–361, and *The Hittite Ritual of Tunnawi, AOS* 14, (1938). E. Sturtevant, "The Ritual of Anniwiyanis", *A Hittite Chrestomathy*, (1915), p. 107f. R. Jestin, "Texte Religieux Hittite," *Revue d'Assyriologie* 34, (1937), pp. 45–58. E. C. Kingsbury has published an Old Babylonian ritual from Larsa (*HUCA* 24, (1963), pp. 1–28), which should be classified as an example of the descriptive ritual in primitive form. It is formulaic, and contains no finite verbs, only verbal nouns. What differentiates it from an ordinary temple record is its coherence, in which respect it resembles *UET* III, no. 270 (see note 42). It covers a period of at least seven days, and systematically presents rituals performed at specific times of the day and night. It is one-dimensional (see note 35), and includes lists of objects of sacrifice.

[26] On the extra-temporal sense of the Assyrian present tense in ritual texts, see W. von Soden, *Grundriss der Akkadischen Grammatik*, (1952), p. 102 (§78, 6, d). For the provenience of the present tense (*mi*-conjugation) in Hittite, see E. Sturtevant and E. A. Hahn, *A Comparative Grammar of the Hittite Language* I, (1951), pp. 118–119, 139. Contrast the use of verbs in direct address, and 3rd presents, with the force of jussives in Akkadian (F. Thureau-Dangin, *Rituels Accadiens*, p. 10f., and cf. A. Sachs, *ANET*, pp. 331–345). Imperatives are widely used in Hittite prescriptive rituals (E. Sturtevant, *A Hittite Chrestomathy*, p. 148f.).

fered on a series of cultic occasions. The Ugaritic texts are more formulaic than narrative. The Assyrian descriptive rituals employ, for the most part, verbs in the present tense to convey the sense of customary action not limited to any point in time. Some of the Assyrian texts also include lists of animals and objects of value offered to the gods. The several examples noted pertain to the investment of power in the king or his substitute. Like Leviticus 8 and 9 they describe the symbols of office and record the sacrifices celebrating the assumption of preeminent sacral status. The Hittite descriptive rituals noted here deal with purification and sacrificial rites and employ verbs in the present tense (the *mi*-conjugation) to convey the customary sense noted in the Assyrian present tense, and are more completely narrative than either the Ugaritic or Assyrian examples.[27]

Leviticus 8 and 9 differ from this form, although they reflect the same emphasis on detail. Leviticus 8 and 9 do not present what is being witnessed nor do they describe what is customarily enacted. They narrate an account of what was performed on one occasion in the past. The purpose of the writer of Leviticus 8 and 9 differed from that of the Ugaritic, Assyrian and Hittite writers, and it is this difference in intent which accounts for the difference in form.[28] In this instance, the non-biblical writers intended to preserve accurate reports of rituals which could serve as guides, or manuals, for correct cultic practice. The writer of Leviticus 8 and 9 sought to preserve a record concerning the origins of the Israelite cult. He adapted descriptive accounts of the ordination of the priesthood and the initiation of the tabernacle cult so as to integrate them into his ongoing narrative of ancient Israelite history, just as he did with the accounts of the construction of the tabernacle (Exodus 35–39) and the dedication of the tabernacle altar (Numbers 7).

This historicizing tendency and its resulting narrativization of documentary and archival material is not peculiar to the Pentateuch writer. It characterizes the treatment of ritual in the Bible generally. Except for brief descriptions of ritual

---

[27] In form and content, the most suggestive modern parallels to the ancient descriptive rituals are the simultaneous narrations of ceremonial events provided by radio and television commentators, who describe in detail what is occurring. Examples are the funerals of the late President Kennedy and Prime Minister Churchill, or a midnight mass on Christmas Eve, seen on television. If such verbal descriptions were committed to writing, we would have the same form of texts as the ancient rituals of which we are speaking.

[28] Had the writer of Lev. 8 and 9 intended to provide an eye-witness account, he could have written in the manner of the reports of dreams and visions (Gen. 37:6–9, 40:9–11, 41:2–7, Isa. 6:1–4, Ezek. 1, etc.). Note that the demonstrative *hinnēh* is used to convey a sense of immediacy and physical presence, often before participles. Imperfects can be employed to portray contemporaneous action, with the added nuance of customary, extra-temporal action, conveyed in parallel fashion by the Akkadian present. The point is that, despite the limitations of biblical Hebrew, which has no present tense, the reason for the use of verbs in the perfect and consecutive tenses in Lev. 8 and 9 is typological, not linguistic. Also see B. Mazar, *JNES* 10, (1951), pp. 265–267.

acts in poetic passages ritual content in the Bible is always treated either as a divine command presented prescriptively, or as an event presented in narrative form.[29] It is only in post-biblical Jewish sources that one finds counterparts to the Ugaritic, Assyrian, and Hittite descriptive rituals. The Mishnah employs the participle (turned present tense) to describe what is the proper procedure in the same manner that the non-biblical rituals, noted here, use the present tense.[30] The concern of the Mishnaic writer was, like his non-Israelite predecessors', to establish standard procedures and promote obedience to the details of ritual obligation. In biblical sources this purpose was achieved solely by prescription, perhaps because the details of ritual were regarded as originating in specific communications from God. To the Tannaitic writer the details of ritual were certainly considered to have divine sanction, but the Rabbinic outlook on ritual had been affected by the notion of tradition, and obligatory rites were exposited descriptively, as were legal duties generally.

It is our suggestion that Leviticus 8 and 9 were originally reports of ritual occasions, similar to the Ugaritic, Assyrian, and Hittite descriptive rituals discussed above, and that they were subsequently adapted into narrative, historical accounts.

III. Numbers 7

Numbers 7 records that the princes of the twelve tribes of Israel donated wagons and oxen for transporting the portable sanctuary and that, at the dedication of the tabernacle altar, they made offerings of silver and golden vessels filled with fine flour and incense, and sacrificial animals. It is the list of these dedicatory offerings (vv. 12–88) which will concern us primarily.

The system of enumeration employed in the list of offerings is a distinctive feature of the record. In ancient Near Eastern sources enumeration is normally accomplished in two ways: 1) by ideographic numerals, and 2) by non-ideographic numerals, i.e. words. Both methods are very ancient and their use seems to be regulated by the character of the texts themselves. Literary texts tend more toward non-ideographic numerals, and archival texts tend to employ ideographs.

There is evidence of a distinctive Northwest Semitic system of ideographic enumeration according to which the numeral follows the item enumerated rather

---

[29] Some poetic descriptions of ritual acts, employing the imperfect form of the verb for the most part, are: Isa. 40:19–20 (the fashioning of an idol), Hos. 4:13–14, Ps. 42:5f., 107:21–22. For a comprehensive survey of ritual texts in the Bible, see R. J. Thompson, *Penitence and Sacrifice in Early Israel outside the Levitical Code*, (1963).

[30] The best examples of Mishnaic descriptive rituals are to be found in the tractate *Tamid* which, in a sense, is simply one continuous descriptive ritual text. Also see *Yomah*, and *Berakhoth*, I. The Mishnah also employs simple perfects and compound perfects (*hāyāh* + the participle) in its descriptions. For a comparison of Ugaritic and Mishnaic descriptive rituals, see B. Levine, *op. cit.*, p. 106, note 10. {*VOL 1, P. 47F.*}

than preceding it. Instead of listing a number of animals as, for example, "5 sheep," the entry will read: "sheep, 5."[31]

In the Bible there are no ideographic numerals, but it is probable that in some instances we have before us archival texts which originally employed ideographic numerals subsequently transposed into words. It would be reasonable to see this background reality in those texts which correlate with the Northwest Semitic system of ideographic enumeration (item-quantity) although they actually use words instead of ideographs in our received text.[32]

Examination will reveal that this system is used with almost complete consistency in Numbers 7:12–88. Although this is not proved from entries of commodities in the quantity of one, the several animals contributed for "sacrifices of well-being" are always entered as: "bulls, 2/rams, 5/yearling lambs, 5."[33] This same method is also evident in the calendar of festivals in Numbers 28–30.[34] It is but one indication of the archival character of Numbers 7:12–88.

The list of totals (vv. 84–88) is basic to understanding the archival record on which Numbers 7:12–88 is based. Totals for six standard items are listed in the following order: 1) silver bowls, 2) silver basins, 3) gold ladles, 4) herd animals for burnt offerings, 5) goats for sin offerings, 6) herd animals for sacrifices of well-being. The order in which these totals are listed is identical with the consistent order in which the items themselves are entered in each of the twelve sections of the account. This would be logically explained if the writer had before him an account of six columns, each concluding with a total, and each containing entries for one of the six standard commodities.

We have numerous records in this format from Mesopotamia beginning in the Old Babylonian period and continuing in use through Neo-Babylonian times. Such records are variously termed "tabular" or "two-dimensional," the latter

---

[31] In Aramaic and Phoenician: Cowley, *AP*, nos. 22, 24, 35–36, 50, 55, 61, 63, 73, 81, 83. Kraeling, *BMAP*, nos. 14, 16, verso, e. Cooke, *NSI*, nos. 66, 77, 147. M. Pallottino, *The Illustrated London News*, 13 February, (1965), pp. 22–25. G. Garbini, *Oriens Antiquus* IV, (1965), p. 33f. Cf. M. Ventris and J. Chadwick, *Documents in Mycenaean Greek*, wherein the ideographic numeral also follows the item enumerated in administrative accounts, just as in the Northwest Semitic texts; see p. 180, no. 50, etc. In Ugaritic: C. H. Gordon, *Ugaritic Textbook*, Roma, (1965), nos. 81–82, 113–115, 149–150, 170, 301, 307, 324, 400, 1046, 2016, 2074, 2087, 2106, 2117, and especially nos. 2039 and 2096–2097.

[32] The clearest example is Jos. 12:9–24, a check-list of cities subdued during the conquest of Canaan: "King of X. city, 1/King of Y. city, 1." etc. Also cf. Gen. 46:15, 22, 26–27; Jos. 15:32, 36, 42, etc., 18:28, 19:6–7, 15, etc., 21:1, 6–7, etc.; Ezra 1:10–11, 8:35; 1 Chron. 6:46–48, 7:40, etc., 12:24–37, 15:5–10, 23:8, 10, 12, etc., 25:9–31; 2 Chron. 2:9, 3:8, 10, etc., 4 (*passim*), 17:11, 14, 35:7–8.

[33] Num. 7:17, etc. In the totals (vv. 87f.) we have two entries that do not fit this system: "12 bulls" and "24 bulls" instead of "bulls, 12" and "bulls, 24."

[34] Cf. Num. 28:11, etc.: "bulls of the herd, 2 ... yearling lambs, 7, without blemish." Also see 29:13, 17, etc.

being a more accurate term. As "two-dimensional" implies, such accounts were meant to be read both horizontally and vertically and resemble graphs in use today.[35]

We will represent Numbers 7:12–88 graphically as a two-dimensional account, although it is not certain that this is the only possible model for the Pentateuch account. Prior to Old Babylonian (or possibly late Neo-Sumerian) times the Neo-Sumerian scribes had adapted the one-dimensional account so as to allow for the inclusion of more complex data in a single record and such modified one-dimensional accounts were often divided into sections and included lists of totals placed at the end of the account, much in the manner of Numbers 7:12–88. The two-dimensional graph which follows is therefore presented provisionally, and both types of Mesopotamian records will be considered in our discussion.[36]

[35] The term "two-dimensional" is used by William W. Hallo, *JCS* 18, (1964), p. 61, note 29, and literature cited. The origin of this format is still under study. The following is a partial list of edited two-dimensional accounts: Old Babylonian: W. F. Leemans, *Legal and Economic Records from the Kingdom of Larsa*, (*SLB* I, 2), (1954), nos. 52–55. *Legal and Administrative Documents of the Time of Hammurabi and Samsuiluna* (*mainly from Lagaba*), (*SLB* I, 3), (1960), nos. 75–76, 80–83, 88, 90, 98, etc. Cassite: H. Torczyner, *Altbabylonische Tempelrechnungen* (*Denkschriften der Kaiserlichen Akademie der Wissenschaften in Wien*) 55, II, (1913). Neo-Babylonian: M. San-Nicolò, *Orientalia* 18, (1949), pp. 304–305, 20 (1951), pp. 130–131, 23 (1954), pp. 363–364. *OLZ*, suppl. vol. II (1908), pp. 24–25 (from Sippar).

[36] In our graphic representation *šq* = *šeqel haqqôdeš* "sanctuary weight."

TABLE 2

(*yom*) "day"	(*hammaqrîb*) the offering prince	silver bowls 130šq@	silver basins 70šq@	golden ladles 10šq@	(herd animals) for burnt offerings			goats for sin-offerings	herd animals for the sacrifice of well-being				(*zeh qôrban*) "This is the offering of —"
		filled with fine flour		filled with incense	bull	ram	yearling lambs		bulls	rams	he-goats	yearling lambs	
I	Nahshon son of Amminadab of Judah	1	1	1	1	1	1	1	2	5	5	5	Nahshon son of Amminadab of Judah
II	Nethanel son of Zuar of Issachar	1	1	1	1	1	1	1	2	5	5	5	Nethanel son of Zuar of Issachar
III	Eliab son of Helon of Zebulun	1	1	1	1	1	1	1	2	5	5	5	Eliab son of Helon of Zebulun
IV	Elizur son of Shedeur of Reuben	1	1	1	1	1	1	1	2	5	5	5	Elizur son of Shedeur of Reuben
V	Shelumiel son of Zuri-shaddai of Simeon	1	1	1	1	1	1	1	2	5	5	5	Shelumiel son of Zuri-shaddai of Simeon
VI	Eliasaph son of Deuel of Gad	1	1	1	1	1	1	1	2	5	5	5	Eliasaph son of Deuel of Gad
VII	Elishama son of Ammihud of Ephraim	1	1	1	1	1	1	1	2	5	5	5	Elishama son of Ammihud of Ephraim
VIII	Gamaliel son of Pedahzur of Manasseh	1	1	1	1	1	1	1	2	5	5	5	Gamaliel son of Pedahzur of Manasseh
IX	Abidan son of Gideoni of Benjamin	1	1	1	1	1	1	1	2	5	5	5	Abidan son of Gideoni of Benjamin

X	Ahiezer son of Ammishaddai of Dan	1	1	1	1	1	1	1	2	5	5	5	Ahiezer son of Ammi-shad dai of Dan
XI	Pagiel son of Ochran of Asher	1	1	1	1	1	1	1	2	5	5	5	Pagiel son of Ochran of Asher
XII	Ahira son of Enan of Naphtali	1	1	1	1	1	1	1	2	5	5	5	Ahira son of Enan of Naphtali
	“total” (*kôl*)	12 total silver: 2400 šq	12 total gold: 120 šq	12	12	12	12	12	24	60	60	60	“This was the dedica-tion of the altar after it had been anointed.”

Comments:

1. In many of the two-dimensional accounts, the last vertical column has the Sumerian heading MU.BI.IM "is its name", often the name of the person receiving the goods listed in the account, or, on the contrary, the one disbursing them.[78] As is shown in the graph, this corresponds to the second occurrence of the name of the contributing prince at the end of each section in Numbers 7:12–88 which appears to be mere repetition. More likely it is the earlier occurrence of the name of the prince at the beginning of each section which has been added as part of the narrativization of the record.

2. We have already mentioned the order of the totals in verses 84–88. Two-dimensional accounts often have totals at the end of each column.[79] Sumerian ŠU.NIGIN (or PAB) = Akkadian *napḫaru* = Hebrew *kôl* "total."[80]

3. Specification of the standard of weights and measures is a typical feature of archival accounts, both one- and two-dimensional. This was necessary because the composition of the units varied. The standard was often inserted almost parenthetically in the heading of the account, or of one its columns.[81] This specification of the standard occurs in Numbers 7:12–88 and elsewhere in biblical archival texts.[82]

---

[78] Cf. examples in Leemans, *SLB* I, 2, nos. 52–55 and Torczyner, *op. cit.*, pp. 16–17, 19, 21, etc. Also note the heading LÚ "man, person" in *SLB* I, 3, no. 80. MU.BI.IM can also indicate the classification under which the goods, disbursed or received, were filed. Professional titles can also head the last vertical column. Cf. Torczyner, p. 34 (*BE* XIV:99a): *nāqidu* "shepherd" and *ḫa-za-an-nu* "chief magistrate," etc. The last vertical column can also have a heading which identifies the character of the listings it contains. See *Orientalia* 18, (1949), p. 304 (*YBT* VI:130) with the heading: *a-mir-tum makkur* [d]*Ištar u* [d]*Na-na-a*, "inspection (of) the goods of Ištar and Nanâ." Often, in one dimensional accounts containing several sections, the name of the person ordering the goods or receiving them comes at the end each section.

[79] Examples in Torczyner, *op. cit.*, pp. 58–59, etc.

[80] See note 32, and also Jos. 21:26, 39, Ezra 2:64.

[81] Cf. Torczyner, *op. cit.*, p. 60 (*BE* XIV:104), a simple one-dimensional record: *ḫimētu* [giš]BÁN 6 *qa šattu X*, "butter (the BÁN = 6 *qa*) for the year X." Also see *ibid.*, p. 58 (*BE* XIV:136) in the headings of the first three columns of a two-dimensional account:

(Col. I)	(Col. II)	(Col. III)
šeum	*šamaššammu*	*ḫimētu*
[giš]BÁN 10 *qa*	[giš]BÁN 10 *qa*	[giš]BÁN 10 *qa*
"barley (the BÁN = 10 *qa*)"	"sesame (the BÁN = 10 *qa*)"	"butter (the BÁN = 10 *qa*)."

Also cf. *ibid.*, pp. 4f. and 15 (*BE* XIV:18) for the specification BÁN.GAL, "the large BÁN," in contrast to the regular standard.

[82] See Num. 7:13, 19, etc.: *bešeqel haqqôdeš*, "according to the sanctuary weight." Exod. 30:13: *ʿeśrîm gērāh haššeqel*, "twenty *gērāh* to the shekel." Also Lev. 27:25, Num. 3:47, 18:16. On the *ʾēpāh* see Exod. 16:36, Deut. 25:14. Ezek. 45:10–15 is a list of

4. The uniformity of the types and quantities of the commodities entered in Numbers 7:12–88 initially conveys the impression of artificiality. A study of ritual texts, both biblical and extra-biblical, will show, however, that a high degree of uniformity is characteristic of cultic offerings.[83] In biblical ritual there is the notion of the "rule" (*mišpāṭ*), a set amount or portion, which in itself dictates standard quantities for certain offerings.[84] Against this background, the uniformity evident in Number 7:12–88 is not a sign of artificiality, but rather assigns to this list a definite archival character.

5. The degree of narrativization in Numbers 7:12–88 is very slight. (Verse 11 provides a general narrative introduction.) The offerings of the first day begin with the introductory clause "The one who presented his offering was" (*wayyehî hammaqrîb*; v. 12). The second section is more economical: "On the second day X. made his offering" (*bayyôm haššēnî hiqrîb*; v. 18). From that point on there are only nominal clauses which designate rather than narrate.

In its priestly context, Numbers 7 is correctly interpreted as a record of religious acts of devotion. The princes voluntarily contributed to the needs of the tabernacle and to the dedicatory rites of the tabernacle altar, thus affirming that the tribal society bore allegiance to the sanctuary, and that the leaders of all the people participated in the establishment and maintenance of the cult. This, too, reflects the actual religious climate of the ancient Near East. Behind the priestly context of Numbers 7 lies the archival record itself, which, in its simplest terms, is an account of sanctuary income resembling numerous similar accounts from Mesopotamia.

We have already noted that the calendar of festivals in Numbers 28–30 resembles Numbers 7:12–88 in several of its compositional features. The provisions of Numbers 28–30 exhibit the same uniformity in the quantities and types of sacrifices which is typical of cultic practice as recorded in temple accounts, and which characterizes Numbers 7:12–88. In both texts we have essentially the

---

weights and measures. See Torczyner *op. cit.*, pp. 4–7 and R. B. Y. Scott, *op. cit.*, for a discussion of standards.

[83] The meal offering of "fine flour with meal mixed in" always consists of two "tenth parts" (*ʿeśrônîm*) when accompanying the sacrifice of a small animal (Lev. 23:13, 17; 24:5) and of three *ʿeśrônîm* for a large animal (Num. 28:9, 12, 20, 29; 29:3, 9, 14). Note the fairly standard number of animals prescribed for the burnt offerings on various festivals: 1) 2 bulls, 1 ram, and 7 yearling lambs are prescribed for a) the New Moon (Num. 28:11), b) the seven days of Passover (Num. 28:19), c) Pentecost (28:27); 2) 1 bull, 1 ram, and 7 yearling lambs for the burnt offerings on a) the New Year (Num. 29:2), and b) the Day of Atonement (29:8). In a ritual text now under study by the author (L. Legrain, *Ur Excavation Texts III*, no. 270) from the Isin-Larsa period which lists offerings brought on a series of cultic occasions, a high degree of uniformity is evident in the quantities and types of commodities used as offerings. Even the order in which commodities are listed is identical in several cases.

[84] Num. 29:18, 21, etc.

same situation: a series of cultic occasions on which offerings were brought. Both texts are primarily enumerative, and both employ the same Northwest Semitic system of enumeration. Numbers 28–30 also suggests the same accounting formats which we saw reflected in Numbers 7:12–88. The difference is that whereas Numbers 7:12–88 describes what was offered, Numbers 28–30 prescribes what is to be offered.

We must consider the possibility that Numbers 7:12–88 and Numbers 28–30 represent respectively two steps in the process of adapting archival material in the priestly writings. In Numbers 7:12–88 that material is in a form closer to the original temple record, whereas in Numbers 28–30 the material has been restated as prescription. That is to say that data taken from actual temple records was incorporated into ritual prescriptions. This suggestion does not dispute the notion that the prescriptions of Numbers 28–30 were understood as divine ordinances in the manner stated. It is reasonable to suppose that cultic practice, with all of its rigid specifications, was ordered by spokesmen of the deity. We are also aware that prescriptive rituals represent a type of text as ancient as temple records and that, historically, it is not necessary to posit that all ritual prescriptions are based on temple records. Because of the striking affinities between the two texts, the descriptive and the prescriptive, it is reasonable, in this instance, to suppose that temple records, similar in form to Numbers 7:12–88, were the sources for the detailed sacrificial offerings prescribed in the calendar of festivals. Whether it is reasonable to posit a similar origin for other prescriptive rituals in the Pentateuch is a matter requiring further investigation."[85]

[85] The author wishes to thank Profs. Moshe Greenberg, William W. Hallo, and Thorkild Jacobsen, with whom he discussed this study, and who offered valuable suggestions.

The Descriptive Ritual Texts from Ugarit: Some Formal and Functional Features of the *Genre*[*]

The term "descriptive ritual" was first proposed as a way of identifying what was, in the early 1960's, a small group of texts and fragments from Ugarit, containing unusual formulas, and employing terms of reference largely unknown from other types of material written in alphabetic cuneiform.[1] Since that time, many new finds from Ugarit, and from Ras Ibn-Hani in the vicinity of Ugarit, have lent substance to the identity of this *genre*. It is now possible to classify, on the basis of formal criteria, more than forty examples—in Ugaritic, Hurrian, and in mixtures of the two languages—as descriptive rituals. This classification is valid whether or not one is entirely satisfied with the adjective "descriptive," which has been problematic since the outset (see further below).

These ritual texts have not received as much scholarly attention as has been showered on other types of texts, especially Ugaritic poetry. And yet the realization is growing that they are an indispensable source of knowledge about the operative cult at Ugarit, despite perplexing problems of interpretation.[2]

In a volume of studies dedicated to David Noel Freedman, who has enriched our formal understanding of ancient Near Eastern poetry in particular, and of literary creativity generally, it is certainly appropriate to engage the problem of *engenresment* with respect to the descriptive rituals in alphabetic cuneiform.[3]

Preliminary to a complete edition of the descriptive rituals, now in preparation, it might be of value to re-examine certain features of their structure and

---

[*] Originally published in Carol L. Meyers and Michael O'Connor (eds.), *The Word of the Lord Shall Go Forth: Essays in Honor of David Noel Freedman in Celebration of His Sixtieth Birthday* (Winona Lake, IN: Eisenbrauns, 1983), pp. 467–75. Reprinted with permission from Eisenbrauns.

[1] See Levine 1963 and 1965. See also Levine and Hallo 1967 for a discussion of the descriptive character of temple records in the ancient Near East and the historical implications of this type of archival material. Also see Levine 1974:8–9 for further comment on some Ugaritic descriptive rituals.

[2] See the recent monograph by J.-M. de Tarragon (1980) which utilizes extensive data furnished by the ritual texts and my review of de Tarragon's study, Levine 1981.

[3] All textual references and citations are from KTU (= Dietrich, Loretz, and Sanmartín 1976). This was considered convenient since KTU is the first publication to incorporate the more recently discovered texts, along with those previously available, in a systematic way. For Ras Ibn-Hani, see Bordreuil and Caquot 1979.

archival character, showing just how these texts cohere as a *genre*, and how they relate to other types of preserved materials.

The descriptive rituals from Ugarit and from Ras Ibn-Hani are written in alphabetic cuneiform, mostly in the Ugaritic language, but also in Hurrian, and even in mixtures of both languages. As Laroche has shown in his valuable study of the Hurrian texts from Ugarit, the Hurrian rituals, and Hurrian sections of rituals, parallel their Ugaritic counterparts in most aspects of composition and formulation.[4]

In terms of content, the descriptive ritual records or describes a coherent rite, or more often, a complex of rites. It provides detailed information on the following subjects: 1) sacrificial offerings to specific deities, 2) dates, occasions, and sites where rites are performed, 3) ritual acts, such as purifications and processionals, which compose overall celebrations, and 4) officiants, quite often the king, who had a significant role in the cult.

This definition may be sharpened by showing how the descriptive ritual differs, strictly speaking, from the administrative list or temple record. The descriptive ritual purports to describe a coherent rite or complex of rites, and this is its organizing principle. What it describes is unified by time-frames and centers around certain localities. In its totality, the descriptive ritual includes at least most of what constituted the rite(s) as a whole, after which it is entitled or designated. This distinction may be illustrated by reference to KTU 1.104, a text of the contrasting, administrative list type. Entitled *iršt*, "requisition,"[5] this text lists several commodities as "used up" (*d ykl*) and "delivered" (*ytn*) to various cult sites on particular occasions.[6] It does not, however, record the overall rituals to which it is related functionally, and it cannot be said to "describe" the performance of a temple ritual as such.

A similar case is represented by KTU 1.91, a text entitled *yn d ykl b dbḥ mlk*, "Wine that is 'used up' in the sacral celebration[7] by the king." This record pertains to a single commodity, wine of several varieties, to be supplied for a series of elaborate occasions. In fact, two of these occasions are known from another ritual text, KTU 1.148. Thus *dbḥ ṣpn*, "The sacral celebration in honor

---

[4] See Laroche 1968:497–99.

[5] See Herdner (1978:39), who translates in a more religious or personal sense. Ugaritic *iršt* and the cognate verb *arš* can, of course, have many specific connotations, but it seems that administrative and legal contexts are primary. This primacy also emerges among the Akkadian usages of *erēšu* A and nominal *erištu*; see *CAD*, s.v. *erištu*. It is a fairly widespread phenomenon to have cultic and religious terminology that originates in the administrative vocabulary, and it is crucial, in interpreting temple records, not to read piety into the accounting system!

[6] In KTU 1.104 see line 3 for *d ykl*, and note forms of the verb *ytn* in line 12 and line 16, where *tpnn* is erroneously written for *ttnn*.

[7] Ugaritic *dbḥ* (substantive) in titles of elaborate rituals should be understood in a generic sense, as designating the overall celebration. On the etymology of *dbḥ*, Hebrew *zebaḥ*, see Levine (1974:115f.); see Xella (1979) on KTU 1.91 as a whole.

of *Ṣapān*" (line 3), is a rite described in KTU 1.148 lines 1f.; this phrase is actually the main title of the text as a whole. Also related to KTU 1.148 is the reference in line 10 of KTU 1.91 (cf. KTU 1.148 lines 18f.).

> *k tʿrb ʿṯtrt šd bt mlk*
> As "ʿAthtart of the Field' enters the temple of Mulku.

Administrative records such as KTU 1.91 and 1.104 thus have a direct bearing on the compilation of the descriptive rituals, and they shed light on the relationship between the temple record *per se* and the more coherent structure of the descriptive ritual. The temple records were, in reality, the sources upon which the scribes drew for their data.

KTU 1.91 is suggestive in yet another way. Most of KTU 1.148 deals with sacrifices of animals and fowl, but lines 18–22 list other commodities as well, including oil and spices, honey, etc. Now, parts of this section are difficult to understand and there are sizable breaks; it is conceivable that *yn*, "wine," might have been listed originally and not been preserved. It is more likely, however, that KTU 1.91, in this instance, provides information relevant to one of the occasions described by KTU 1.148, *but not included in that text*. This method is reminiscent of certain priestly codes in the Pentateuch of the Hebrew Bible which are limited to ancillary commodities, such as wine for libations, spices, etc.[8] If this analysis of the relationship between KTU 1.91 and 1.148, as examples, is correct, we may suggest that the descriptive rituals focused on the major components of the coherent rites—largely but not exclusively on animal sacrifices—but did not exhaust all of the accompanying ritual acts involved.

It is now relevant to discuss the adjective "descriptive" which I have used to characterize these and similar ritual texts in Hebrew and other languages. This characterization has met with the objection that such texts were clearly intended to serve as manuals for priests and other officiants, and that they had, consequently, more of a *prescriptive* than a *descriptive* function. This objection actually confuses *form* with *function*. The adjective "descriptive" is meant primarily to reflect the formulation and detailed structure of these texts, not their operative function.

An ambiguity exists regarding the formulation of the ritual texts, one which derives ultimately from the alphabetic cuneiform writing system itself. In the case of strong verbs, it is impossible to determine from the orthography whether *yqtl* forms are *indicative* or *modal* in force. For example, the recurrent clause *yrtḥṣ mlk brr* could be translated in either of two ways: a) "The king, the purifier (?), *washes* himself," or b) "The king, the purifier (?), *shall wash* himself." In my earlier studies, I opted for the former alternative, taking such *yqtl* forms as indicatives. This interpretation has seemed to be borne out by the growing num-

---

[8] As an example, see Num 15:1–16, which specifies the ingredients used for the grain-offering (Hebrew *minḥa*), and the libation (Hebrew *nesek*). These offerings normally accompanied the major sacrifices.

ber of verbal clauses appearing in these texts wherein *yqtl* forms are preceded by adverbial indicators, for example, *id ydbḥ mlk*, "When the king performs a sacral celebration" (KTU 1.41 line 50).[9]

In the light of more recent discoveries, one could argue that modal forms occur in the ritual texts, thus demonstrating that they are not consistently descriptive. For example, in KTU 1.119 lines 13–14 we read *l ydbḥ mlk*, "Let the king perform a sacral celebration." What are we to conclude from this occurrence, which will inevitably be replicated in further discoveries? Actually it illustrates the process by which descriptive rituals gradually appropriate prescriptive formulations as their functional role comes to determine their formal structure to an ever greater extent. There appears to be only one case of a modal form in this text, which, for the rest, lists sacrifices in pretty much the usual manner. The fact that, in this instance, the *yqtl* form of the verb is introduced by *l* (= *lû*) strongly implies that where modal force was intended, it was clearly indicated, and that elsewhere, *yqtl* forms were intended to have indicative force.

It seems that KTU 1.119 represents a transitional form, helping us to trace a development from a) archival records, to b) descriptions of coherent rites, to c) prescriptions, and actual codes. That development was the context in which the contrast was originally drawn between "descriptive" and "prescriptive" rituals; special reference was made to the *archival* derivation of the priestly codes of the Pentateuch in the Hebrew Bible. Such a development is not inevitably chronological, although there is evidence to suggest that the temple record is the oldest source of information on the operation of temple cults in the ancient Near East.

The relationship between form and function, relevant to the descriptive rituals, can be approached in another way. There can be little doubt that these texts, though formulated descriptively, were virtually canonical or, at the least, fixed in structure and formulation. This is indicated, first of all, by the retrieval of duplicates, as, for instance, KTU 1.41 and 1.87, and by the overlapping of, for example, KTU 1.46 and 1.109. What is more, a close comparison of KTU 1.46 and 1.109 reveals a clear instance of scribal variation, and a probable instance of a copyist's error.

---

[9] Cf. the same clause in KTU 1.115 line 1. Also note the following examples of temporal clauses: a) KTU 1.43 line 1: *k tʿrb ʿṯtrt ḫr*, "As *ʿAthtart Ḫr* enters"; b) KTU 1.90 line 1: *id yph mlk*, "When the king 'sees'" (cf. KTU 1.151 line 12); c) KTU 1.91 line 10: *k tʿrb ʿṯtrt šd*, "When 'Athtart of the Field' enters," and in line 11: *k tʿrbn ršpm*, "When the Reshep-gods enter," and in line 14: *k tdd bʿlt bhtm*, "When 'Baalat of the Temples' marches (in the processional)."

On the sense of the verb *ndd*, see Xella (1979:834); cf. Psalm 42:5: *kîʾeʿebōr bassāk ʾeddaddēm* (*read: ʾeddad-ma*) *ʿad-bêt ʾĕlōhîm*, "as I pass in the processional, I march toward the Temple of God." (I remember hearing H. L. Ginsberg suggest that Massoretic *ʾddm* reflects a 1st person singular imperfect of the verb *nādad*, with enclitic *mem*). Perhaps cf. Psalm 68:13.

Similar verbal clauses in the Ras Ibn-Hani texts are: 1) Hani 77/2B: *id ydbḥ mlk* (lines 1, 3); 2) Hani 77/10B: *id yph mlk* (lines 1, 8). See Bordreuil and Caquot (1979).

A) KTU 1.46, lines 10f.

10) *[b ar]bʿt ʿ[š]rt yrtḥṣ mlk brr*
11) *[b ym ml]at y[qln] ṯn alpm yrḫ . . ʿšrt*
12) *[l bʿl ṣ]pn d[q]tm w[yn]t qrt*
13) *[w mtntm š] l rm[š] kbd w š*
14) *[l šlm]* etc.

B) KTU 1.109, line 1f.

1) *b arbʿt ʿšr[t]*
2) *yrtḥṣ mlk b[rr]*
3) *b ym mlat*
4) *tqln alpm*
5) *yrḫ ʿšrt l bʿ[l ṣpn]*
6) *dqtm w ynt qr[t]*
7) *w mtntm š l rmš*
8) *w kbd w š l šlm* etc.

When the two copies are compared, one notes that in KTU 1.46 line 11, we have *y[qln]*, as restored, followed by *ṯn alpm yrḫ*, literally, "They shall 'fall,' two male heads of large cattle, (before) *Yariḫ*." Note that KTU 1.109 line 4 has *tqln alpm yrḫ*, with the dual form of the noun, and the 3rd person plural imperfect with *t*-preformative, instead of *y*-preformative. This is a clear scribal variant.

The probable copyist's error concerns the word *ʿšrt* in KTU 1.46 line 11 (// 1.109 line 5). This word, which means "ten," cannot indicate the number of large cattle offered to *bʿl ṣpn* because such an interpretation would upset the formulation of the sacrifices, which follows:

l bʿl ṣpn dqtm w ynt qrt w mtntm
š l rmš
w kbd w š l šlm, etc.

For Baal-Ṣāpān — 2 female head of small cattle and a domestic dove (?) and two gifts (?);
A male head of small cattle for Remeš;
And a liver, and a male head of small cattle for Šalām, etc.

If we look at KTU 1.46, with its longer lines, we can surmise that the word *ʿšrt* was erroneously copied from the line above, from the day-formula *b arbʿt ʿšrt*, "on the fourteenth day." Note the brief space left before this word in line 11 of KTU 1.46, which does not show up on KTU 1.109 line 5. If this word is an error, it was undoubtedly copied from KTU 1.46 into 1.109 and not *vice versa*, since in the latter tablet the shorter lines created a greater distance between the day-formula and the subsequent *ʿšrt*, making the error less likely.

When we compare KTU 1.41 with the duplicate KTU 1.87 we see a different situation. In KTU 1.41, lines 1–49 are almost identical with 1.87 lines 1–53. But, here, too, there is a slight variation, hardly significant in terms of meaning, but informative in terms of scribal practice.

A) KTU 1.41 lines 17–19

17) [*w b urm lb*]
18) *rmṣt ilhm* [*bʿlm dṯt w*]
19) *ksm ṯlṯm* [*mlu*]

B) KTU 1.87 lines 19–21

19) *w b urm l*[*b rmṣt ilhm*]
20) *bʿlm w mlu* [*dṯt w ksm*]
21) *ṯlṯm*

The adjective *mlu* is simply located at different syntactic points in the two copies, as can be learned from KTU 1.39 lines 9–10, where the order is the same as that in KTU 1.41 lines 9–10.

More important, perhaps, is the fact that in KTU 1.41 a brief descriptive ritual, opening with a verbal clause, has been appended to or combined with the larger description (lines 50–55), whereas in 1.87, we find two *addenda*, 1) a brief descriptive ritual, opening with a day formula (lines 54–57), and 2) a list of persons, according to the *bn X* formula (lines 58–61).[10] This means that scribes could combine different ritual texts for preservation in the temple archives.

The fixed structure of the descriptive rituals is also demonstrated by the order in which deities, the recipients of the sacrificial offerings, are listed. Virolleaud long ago noted that the divine name *kṯr* could be restored in KTU 1.39 line 14, on the basis of the list of gods in KTU 1.102, because the order in 1.39 lines 13–19 was identical with that in 1.102 obverse.[11] Now, one can add the same correspondence between the order of deities in KTU 1.148 lines 1ff. and that in the list of gods KTU 1.118 lines 1ff. There were several lists of deities, which were variously utilized by scribes in compiling the descriptive rituals.

The characterization of the descriptive rituals as non-poetic, which is valid generally, also requires further comment and some qualification. First of all, there are several ritual texts which actually contain poetic excerpts. In KTU 1.119, discussed above in another connection, we find a hymn to Baal (lines 24–36). This is topically logical, because the text had been describing rites performed on various occasions in the temple of Baal of Ugarit. A brief poetic excerpt also occurs in KTU 1.43 lines 22–26; it relates to the appearance of the king before the gods. Finally, in KTU 1.148 there is a Hurrian section, which, although not fully interpreted, seems to be a hymn (lines 13–17).[12]

[10] On the anonymous *bn X* formula for listing names, see Levine 1962.

[11] See Virolleaud 1968:594.

[12] See Laroche 1968:517. Also note, in KTU 1.43 lines 7–8, a trace of poetic parallelism:

šbʿ pamt l ilm
šb[ʿ] *l kṯr*

The relationship between on the one hand the descriptive rituals and on the other hymns and liturgical recitations is further demonstrated by recurrent references in the descriptive ritual texts to poetic recitations. The most frequent formula is *rgm yṯṯb*, "He responds with a recitation," or variations of the same. Usually this introductory formula is followed by the identifying first lines of the intended liturgical recitation or hymn:

ṣbu špš ḥl ym
ʿrb špš w ḥl mlk

"The going-forth of Shapsh (= the East),
"And the rampart of Yamm;
"The setting of Shapsh (= the West),
"And the rampart of Mulku."[13]

Often, this couplet is abbreviated, after the introductory formula; in other instances, it appears, in full or abbreviated, without any formulaic introduction! Similarly, in KTU 1.106 line 15f., we find another reference to a poetic recitation:

w šr yšr šr (= *ʿšr*) *pamt l pn mlk:*
"ptḥ yd mlk!"

And he truly recites (= sings) ten times before Mulku:
"Open (your) hand, O Mulku!"[14]

This excerpt is reminiscent of KTU 1.112 line 20:

wrgm yṯṯb w qdš yšr

And he responds with a recitation,
And he sings in the sanctuary (?).

These references to well-known liturgical poems suggest that the descriptive rituals belong to the widespread tradition of the *Ritualtafel*, a type of canonical text, best known from the magical literature of Mesopotamia, which specifies details of praxis, while making reference, at special points, to known recitations of a magical or ritual character.

There are two observations that can be made about another structural feature of the descriptive rituals, i.e., chronological designations. One pertains to different times of the twenty-four day cycle, and the other to the practice of recapitulation, whereby the text may revert to earlier days in the month in order to specify additional rituals.

Seven times to the gods;
Seven — to Kothar.

[13] This is my proposed translation, argued for in Levine (1981).

[14] Biblical hymnody offers numerous expressions of the notion that "opening the hand" is as much a sign of divine blessing and the granting of abundance as it is of human generosity. See Pss 104:28; 145:16, and, on the human level, Deut 15:8, 11.

The former subject relates to the enigmatic sub-title *w b urm*, which occurs several times in some of the more elaborate rituals. Most interpreters have taken *urm* as reflecting *ʾur*, "fire," and have suggested that it indicates the manner in which the sacrifices which follow it were to be disposed of.[15] And yet in KTU 1.39 we have an uninterrupted sequence of *w b urm* and *w l ll* (cf. line 8 with line 12). The meaning of Ugaritic *ll* is established independently as "evening, night." In KTU 1.132 we find *l pn ll* "before evening/night" (line 22), and *pn ll*, with the same meaning, later on (line 25). The structure of KTU 1.132 is quite clear. On the nineteenth day of an unnamed month, a complex of rituals was performed, which involved the offering of certain sacrifices (lines 1–16). Subsequently, on the same day, before evening, two birds were to be offered (lines 16–17). This sequence is repeated further on in the text: line 22 records that on the third day (*b ṯlṯ*) certain sacrifices were offered, and further *pn ll* another ritual took place in addition (lines 35–36).

This suggests that in the sequence *w b urm / w l ll*, the word *urm* should yield a meaning such as "day, morning," or the like. Indeed Akkadian supplies a probable cognate: *urru*(*m*), "light, the brightness of day," etc., is related to *urra*(*m*), a form with adverbial force "in the morning, in day-time." This form frequently occurs in the idiom *urram šēram*, "morning and evening," and it is also used in contrast to *mūšu*(*m*), "night." We could, therefore, read *b urm* as *be urrima*, "in the light of day," referring, perhaps, to the morning, in contrast to *w l ll* "and in the evening/night."[16] This interpretation also makes sense out of KTU 1.119 lines 12–13:

> *b ṯmnt ʿšrt ibʿlt alp l mgdl bʿl ugrt b urm*
>
> On the eighteenth of *ibʿlt*, a male head of large cattle to the watchtower of Baal of Ugarit, in the morning.

As for the custom of recapitulation, we had best return for a moment to KTU 1.132, where we just noted that the text opens with a reference to the nineteenth of the month and then reverts to rites performed on the third day of the month. A close examination of several of the more complex rituals reveals that such recapitulation was a fairly common practice among the scribes at Ugarit. Thus KTU 1.41 (// 1.87) begins with the New Moon, and proceeds to the thirteenth and fourteenth of the month. Later on in the text (lines 37–38) we read of rites performed on the fifth day of the month, and in line 45, on the sixth day. In line 47, we read of a recitation scheduled for the seventh of the month. Finally, in line 48 we again find a reference to the New Moon. This final reference may, of course, indicate the New Moon of the following month, but this is unlikely. In any event, we see how this text focuses on major features of the ritual complex,

---

[15] Thus, for instance, de Moor 1970:115 and note 21, and also Dietrich-Loretz-Sanmartín 1975:142.

[16] See *AHw* s.v. *urra*(*m*) and *urru*(*m*).

carrying us up to the middle of the month, and then reverts to earlier days of the month.

It is likely that this recapitulation reflects a change of locale, because it is introduced as follows: *w bt bʿlt btm rmm w ʿly mdbḥt* "And (in) the temple of Baalat of the Exalted Temples: And for the ascent onto the altar(s)."[17] This, of course, also leaves open the possibility that the reversion to earlier days of the month had something to do with a shift to another category of sacrificial offerings. In KTU 1.132, where we also noted a recapitulation, it is difficult to explain it as clearly. In another text, KTU 1.119, the text begins with the seventh day of *ibʿlt*, and proceeds to the seventeenth and eighteenth days of the month. But later on, in line 20, a new sequence is begun, referring to the fourth, fifth, and seventh days of the month. The preceding lines of the text are broken, and do not allow us to speculate on the reason for the reversion.

As new finds become available for study, it will be possible to venture resolutions to other enigmatic terms and formulas occurring in the descriptive ritual texts. What we have learned thus far is that this *genre* allowed for considerable adaptation in its structure and content, and that it bore a direct, functional relationship to other *genres* of texts, especially to the hymns and poetic recitations of the Ugaritic cult. The ritual texts were essentially descriptive in style, but functionally speaking were quasi-canonical models, or manuals for the operation of the temple cults at Ugarit and vicinity. Copies were made of the same text and deposited. The deities were listed according to several accepted or canonical lists of the pantheon.

As a whole this *genre* exhibits a high degree of tradition and conventionality, so that it should be possible, bit by bit, to arrive at a proper apparatus for the study and analysis of the descriptive rituals.

References

Bordreuil, P. and A. Caquot

1979 Les Textes en cunéiformes alphabétiques découverts en 1977 à Ibn Hani. *Syria* 56:295–315.

Dietrich, M., O. Loretz, and J. Sanmartín

1975 Die Texteinheiten in *RS* 1.2 = *CTA* 32 and *RS* 17.100 = *CTA* Appendice I. *Ugarit Forschungen* 7:141–46.

Herdner, A.

1978 Nouveaux Textes Alphabétiques de Ras Shamra — XXIVe Campagne, 1961. Pp. 1–78 in *Ugaritica VII*. Paris: Geuthner.

[17] On the spelling *btm*, instead of *bhtm* (or *bwtm*), see KTU 1.48 line 3. For a discussion of what is known from the ritual texts about this goddess, see de Tarragon 1980:163ff.

Laroche, E.

1968 Documents en langue hourrite provenant de Ras Shamra. Pp. 447–544 in *Ugaritica V*. Paris: Geuthner.

Levine, B. A.

1962 The Netînîm. *JBL* 82:207–12.

1963 Ugaritic Descriptive Rituals. *JCS* 17:105–11. {*VOL 1, PP. 45–54*}

1965 The Descriptive Tabernacle Texts of the Pentateuch. *JAOS* 85:307–18. {*VOL 1, PP. 55–72*}

1974 *In the Presence of Lord*. Leiden: E. J. Brill.

1981 Review de Tarragon 1980. *RB* 88:245–50.

Levine, B. A. and W. W. Hallo

1967 Offerings to the Temple Gates at Ur. *HUCA* 38:17–58.

de Moor, J. C.

1970 The Peace Offering in Ugarit and Israel. Pp. 113–17 in *Schrift en Uitleg W. H. Gispen*. Kampen.

de Tarragon, J.-M.

1980 *Le Culte à Ugarit*. Cahiers de la Revue Biblique 19. Paris: Geuthner.

Virolleaud, Ch.

1968 Les Nouveaux Textes Mythologiques et Liturgiques de Ras Shamra. Pp. 544–604 in *Ugaritica V*. Paris: Geuthner.

Xella, P.

1979 *KTU* 1.91 (*RS* 19.15) Ei Sacrifici del Re. *UF* 11:833–38.

Toward an Institutional Overview of Public Ritual at Ugarit*

The sustained effort to interpret the ritual texts from Ugarit,[1] initially late in coming, has reached an unprecedented level with the recent publication of Dennis Pardee's encyclopedic edition, *Les Textes Rituels*.[2] He has made it possible to engage the corpus of ritual texts *en masse*, providing greatly improved readings, and extensive commentary on all available examples of this *genre*. Now that the lexical problems have been mastered to a considerable degree through careful collation and the application of new technology, and now that the literature has been reviewed, the focus must shift to philological and exegetical issues. Major disagreements persist as to the meaning of the cultic vocabulary, and regarding the structure and composition of the ritual texts. This situation is due primarily to intrinsic factors, not to scholarly shortcomings. The repertoire remains limited, and there is much that the texts, themselves, fail to reveal.

The recent dictionary of del Olmo Lete and Sanmartín (*DUL*),[3] as valuable as it is for the comprehensive data it provides, exposes just how problematic Ugaritic lexicography is at the present time. It would be a serious error to presume that we adequately understand the ritual texts, and it is to Pardee's credit that he avoids this noticeable tendency, and carefully argues positions other than his own. In contrast, the recent *Handbook of Ugaritic Studies*,[4] although it contributes valuable treatments of many aspects of Ugaritic history, culture, language, literature, politics and economy, is, in my view, less cogent when it comes to cult and religion. Of obvious concern in the present context is the contribution of Paolo Merla and Paolo Xella's in chapter seven ("The Ugaritic Cul-

---

* Originally published in Jean-Marc Michaud (ed.), *Le royaume d'Ougarit de la Crète à l'Euphrate: Nouveaux axes de recherche, Actes du Congrès International de Sherbrooke 2005* (Proche-Orient et Littérature Ougaritique 2; Sherbrooke, QE: Éditions GGC; FaTEP Université de Sherbrooke; LÉSA, Collège de France, 2007), pp. 357–380. Reprinted with permission from Éditions GGC.

[1] Acknowledgements: I am grateful to Professor Jean-Marc Michaud of the University of Sherbrooke for his kind invitation to participate in the international conference on Ugaritic studies in July, 2005, the first of its scope since 1979. This piece is dedicated to the memory of my masterful teacher, Cyrus H. Gordon.

[2] Pardee 2000.

[3] Del Olmo Lete and Sanmartín 2003.

[4] Watson and Wyatt 1999.

tic Texts") entitled "The Rituals."[5] I did not expect to encounter the following introductory statement:

> With the increase in our knowledge of the religion and sacrificial system of centres such as Ebla, Emar, as well as Mari (with the requisite changes), it is necessary to get away from the usual and repeated references to the Bible in order to reconstruct the religious tradition peculiar to Syria, the consistency and essential continuity of which are perceptible.[6]

Fortunately, such ideological tendencies do not dominate the investigation of the Ugaritic ritual texts. Scholars continue to integrate comparative evidence from the larger region for what it contributes to our understanding of Ugaritic religion, and they do so to great advantage. One wonders how far scholarship would have progressed in decoding the Ugaritic ritual texts without access to the kinds of information provided by the Hebrew Bible.

The present investigation is made up of three case studies, two of which deal with issues already raised in previous studies, most notably in a collaborative effort with Jean-Michel de Tarragon.[7] These are (1) the meaning of Ugaritic *b urm* (*KTU* 1.39:8, *et passim*), and (2) the interpretation of a recurrent passage which I have interpreted as a poetic recitation, but which has been taken by most scholars to refer to the cultic status of the king. The third case study breaks new ground for me, and deals with processionals that brought divine images into the royal palace. A certain degree of repetition will be required by way of background, but discussion will move quickly to new considerations.

The Institutional Approach

In his monograph *Le culte à Ougarit*,[8] Jean-Michel de Tarragon pursued a primarily institutional approach, arranging his discussion along functional lines, with chapters on the cultic calendar, offerings and rites, cultic personnel, and the like. He also devoted considerable attention to the cultic vocabulary. What he has to say about the significant cultic role of the king is subsumed, for the most part, under his treatment of the calendar of celebrations, highlighting those events in which the king participated. In his "*Conclusions*,"[9] Pardee likewise proceeds along institutional lines, especially in his many appendices, where we find extensive data on the venues and time-frames applicable to sacrificial rites. Pardee is often able to match specific offerings with particular deities and cultic events in the process. An institutional approach focuses on four, interrelated dimensions of the ritual texts:

---

[5] *Ibid*, pp. 287–304.

[6] *Ibid*, p. 290.

[7] Levine and de Tarragon 1993.

[8] de Tarragon 1980.

[9] Pardee 2000, 2:898–1090.

1) WHO – the identification of celebrants and cultic personnel

As has been noted by de Tarragon and others, even the term *khn* "priest" does not appear in the ritual texts themselves. It is not that we lack information about the administrative role of priests at Ugarit, or that we are unable to project their probable cultic functions. It is just that such information comes from other sources, such as epistles and personnel lists, and from the Akkadian texts at Ugarit.

It is from such sources that we learn about the fellowship of the priesthood, *dr khnm* "the priestly circle", about the chief priest, *rb khnm*, and about priests called *qdšm* "sacred persons". A term discussed at length by de Tarragon is *inš ilm*, "the personnel of the gods". They are listed as divine recipients of offerings, not as temple staff. Nevertheless, de Tarragon is correct in suggesting that certain titles given to participants in celestial liturgies were appropriated from the temple administration. As an example, we read in the poetic texts of *ʿrbm* a class of priests, literally "the enterers" (Akkadian *erib bīti* "one allowed entry into the temple"—*CAD E*, 290–293; *DUL* 181, s.v *ʿrb II*). These are listed together with *ṯnnm*, a military term also appearing in the syllabic texts, and whose function is uncertain (*DUL* 922–923, s.v. *ṯnn*). Thus it is that the register of temple personnel expands when we include projections of temple roles found in the celestial liturgies, as depicted in the poetic texts.

When speaking of WHO, the role of the king comes to the fore, and one of the case-studies to be discussed here will address aspects of the royal role in the cult, and functions that impact the relationship between temple and palace at Ugarit.

2) WHAT - the character of cultic rites and their attendant purifications at Ugarit

Although we know a great deal about the substance of cultic activity at Ugarit, the performance of certain cultic acts remains unclear. One of the case-studies will address a problem having to do with recitations, wherein the king is the reciter.

3) WHEN – the schedule and timing of cultic events

Generally speaking, we have annual rites, those performed on stated days of the month, clustering around the New Moon and the full moon at the middle of the month, in Ugaritic: *ym mlat* "the day of the full moon". We also have indications of sacred times of the day. Another of the case-studies will deal with this last time-frame.

4) WHERE – the identification of cultic venues

Of all questions, this is perhaps the most challenging. It arises when we attempt to describe processionals, wherein statues of the gods were brought into the royal palace. This subject will be addressed in the third case study.

1: Divisions of the Day: KTU *1.39 as a Case in Point*

It would be of value to outline *KTU* 1.39, a major ritual text, as a way of introducing a possible division of the day, Ugaritic *b urm*, whose meaning has been in dispute.

Lines 1–8: A series of sacrifices, variously termed *ṯ*ʿ "benefaction", *šrp* "burnt offering", and *šlmm* "sacred gifts of greeting".
Lines 8–10:

> *w b urm.* [*l*]*b*
> *rmṣt. ilhm. b*ʿ*lm. dṯt. w kśm. ḫmš*
> ʿ[*š*]*rh. mlun. šnpt. ḫṣth.*

Pardee:[10]

> et dans les flammes le coeur (comme offrande) rôtie (pour) les ʾIlāhūma (et pour) les Baʿalūma; (céréale)-*dṯt* et emmer, (comme offrande) quinze (pots) pleins (de chaque denrée?) (aussi pour les ʾIlāhūma et les Baʿalūma?). (Comme) sacrifice de présentation, la-moitié de cela (aussi pour les ʾIlāhūma et les Baʿalūma?).

Levine:

> And in the brightness/heat (of day), inside the convening room of the ʾIlāhūma and the Baʿalūma—goblets and chalices, fifteen, filled, (as) a presentation offering, half of it.

Lines 10–11: More offerings, apparently *šrp*, but not labeled as such.
Line 12:

> *w l ll. špš pgr. w ṯrmnm. bt mlk*
>
> And at night, Šapšu-Pagri and Ṯarummannūma (being) in the royal palace.

Lines 13–19: More offerings, unspecified.

The text of lines 8–10 recurs with some variations in *KTU* 1.41//1.87, and in several other texts, in part or in full. A major problem in its interpretation concerns the meaning of Ugaritic *w b urm*, and as a corollary, the meaning of *w lb rmṣt* (or: *w l b rmṣt*), which immediately follows. Does Ugaritic *b urm* mean (a) "in the flames", (thus Pardee and most others), or (b) "in the brightness of day, midday" (thus Levine). If (a) is correct, then we would expect *lb rmṣt* to connote a kind of sacrifice, and the suggested meaning is "a heart as a roasted offering". This indicates an open hearth, or an appurtenance like a brazier, in which flames burned. If (b) is correct, *lb rmṣt* might still designate a kind of offering, but it could just as well designate a venue, to be rendered "inside the *rmṣt*".

---

[10] Pardee 2000, 1:18.

The argument in favor of taking Ugaritic *b urm* as indicating a time-frame during the day can be improved over previous attempts. The main event in official cults throughout the ancient Near East occurred at dawn, or soon after. There is one additional time of the day registered in *KTU* 1.39, 12, and in some other texts, that cannot be disputed, namely, *w l ll* (alternatively *l pn ll* / *pn ll*) "at eventide, before nightfall." In my view, there is yet another time of the day indicated, namely *b urm* (*beʾuri-ma*), a singular form with enclitic *mēm* "in the brightness/heat (of day)", appearing in recurrences of this passage. As of now, *KTU* 1.39 is the only ritual text that attests both *b urm* and *w l ll*.

Akkadian *urru*(*m*) "morning, day-time" is better for comparison than the idiom *urram šeram*, calqued in Ugaritic as *šḥr ʿlmt* "from dawn and forever" (*KTU* 3.5:15; *DUL* 612–613, s.v. *šḥr*), which is less precise. Akkadian *urru*(*m*) contrasts with *mūšu*(*m*) "night", just as in *KTU* 1:39 Ugaritic *ur* contrasts with Ugaritic *ll* (*CAD M*/II, 291–295, especially 294, mng. c "day and night"). In Ugaritic, the word for "light" and the verb "to shine" are usually vocalized *ar*, once as *ir*, thus: *lbšt b ir* "clothed in light" (*KTU* 1.13:25), indicating that vocalization is fluid, not phonemic. So, why not take *ur to* mean "light" yielding the translation of *w b urm* as "in the light of day, in the brightness of day"? In Biblical Hebrew, the word for "light" is vocalized *ʾôr*, and for "heat, fire" *ʾûr*, but both forms derive from the same root, the difference being merely contextual.

It is also possible to translate *b urm* "in the heat (of day)", to be compared with Biblical Hebrew *ḥōm hayyôm* which bears this meaning (Gen 18:1, 1 Sam 11:11), or *ḥōm haššemeš* "the heat of the sun" (1 Sam 11:9), a time near midday. It is also interesting that new sequences of sacrifices begin after both *b urm* and *w l ll*, further suggesting that these are time indicators that bracket the day. Both burnt offerings *šrp* and *šlmm* offerings precede this particular entry, and are labeled in the usual manner.

If *b urm* designates a time during the day, how shall we explain *lb rmṣt*, which follows directly? Pardee takes *lb* to mean "heart", designating a sacrifice consisting of the heart of an animal. This is possible, of course, seeing as there were at Ugarit sacrifices consisting of the liver (*kbd*), the nose or face (*ap*), and the breast (*npš*). So, why not sacrifices of animal hearts? More problematic as regards the prevailing interpretation is taking *rmṣt* to mean "a roasted offering". The word *rmṣt* cannot be an adjective modifying *lb* because it is feminine in form. Pardee parses it as a gerund, as if to mean "by roasting", positing a Ugaritic verb *r-m-ṣ* "to burn". Pardee and others cite an Arabic cognate *ramaḍa*, with a *ḍod*, "to become intensely heated"—as by the sun, or by being placed on hot stones, or on hot sand. This verb can be used to connote the roasting of meat, and the Arabic *ḍod* would be realized in Ugaritic as a *ṣadē* (Lane 1980:1156–57). We also note rare Late Hebrew/Jewish Aramaic *remeṣ, rimṣāʾ* "burnt wood, ashes" (Levy 1963 4:455–456). *CAD R*, 126 lists for Akkadian *ramāṣu* only one lexical entry of uncertain meaning, quite possibly an error. Pardee has support for understanding this passage to refer to a sacrifice of an animal heart "in the flames", as "an offering by roasting", for the ʾIlāhūma and Baʿalūma. In his translation, the passage would then go on to record additional offerings, presumably for the same deities.

Although possible, this interpretation is far from certain, notwithstanding its wide acceptance. I would leave the description of what the offering consisted of to the latter part of the passage, where, indeed, we have a listing of goblets and cups (or: "of grain and emmer", if you will), presented as *šnpt*, a term cognate with Hebrew *tenûpāh* "presentation offering". However, to parse the entry as Pardee does requires a lot of "filling-in", and leaves question marks. I prefer to translate *w lb rmṣt ilhm bᶜlm* "and inside the *rmṣt* of the ʾIlāhūma and Baᶜalūma", namely, inside the chamber where the offerings were presented. In such terms, we can read *w lb* "and inside", taking *lb* as adverbial (cf. Akkadian *libbi*) or assuming a cluster of prepositions: *l* + *b* "within". Either way, cf. *KTU* 1.46:9: *l b* / *lb btm* "inside the temples" and *KTU* 1.115:3, 11: *w l b* / *lb bt* "and inside the temple". This leaves the word *rmṣt* in need of clarification.

The conditioned sound shift *b*<>*m*, from original **rbṣt* to *rmṣt*, under pressure from prepositional *beth*, would explain the unusual form *rmṣt*. Ugaritic attests a form, *trbṣ*, variant *trbṣt* "resting place, sitting room" (*KTU* 1.14.II:4; *KTU* 1.14.III:37; *DUL* 877). This locution is also attested in syllabic texts from Ugarit as a synonym of *bītu* "house". Thus: É-*tu*$_4$ *: ta-ar-bá-ṣi* (*apud* Huehnergard 1987:176, s.v. *RBṢ*), to which cf. Akkadian *tarbāṣu*, Hebrew *rēbeṣ*, *marbēṣ* (*AHw* 1327–1328; *HALAT* 1102, 597).

In *KTU* 1.119:13, we find an unusual entry, one of uncertain reading: Pardee[11] restores: [*u*] *urm u šnpt*, translating: "le sacrifice «de flammes» et le sacrifice de presentation." He suggests that the unclear letter could be either *u* or *d*, noticing three verticals and no sign of bottom horizontals. Others have read *b urm*, since the letter *b* exhibits two verticals, which is quite similar, and because *b urm* is the well attested combination. Actually, any one of the three readings would work as well for my interpretation as it would for the alternative.

In summary: The passage under discussion is problematic, no matter how we approach it. My interpretation requires a conditioned sound shift, whereas Pardee's introduces an unusual kind of burnt offering. Specifically, the meaning "in the brightness/heat (of day)" is supported philologically every bit as well as the meaning "in the flames". The problems are far from being settled and cannot be settled, if truth be told, until more evidence is forthcoming.

2: Liturgical Recitations in the Ritual Texts

From the start,[12] I have been interested in recitations as a special feature of ritual performance. In *KTU* 1.119 we have an actual prayer addressed to Baᶜlu, protector of the kingdom of Ugarit. *KTU* 1.161, except for its caption, consists entirely of a recited liturgy. The king (or another officiant) ordains that repeated

---

[11] Pardee 2000, 2:662–666.

[12] Levine 1963.

sacrifices be offered, but the text does not record their actual performance. *KTU* 1.40 consists of a series of recitations, based on what is preserved of it. At one point, we have the announcement *hn ʿr* "Here is the ass" and at others, *hn š* "here is the sheep". After *hn ʿr* there is an instruction at the beginning of the next section of the liturgy that reads: *w ṯb l mspr* "Now return to the narration". This is unusual, because normally, ritual acts are interrupted by recitations, not recitations by ritual acts. Nevertheless, the pattern of alternation between ritual performance and recitation is once again affirmed.

The usual formula for indicating a recitation contains two elements: the noun *rgm* "word, message, recitation", plus the Šapʿēl of the verb *t-w-b*, e.g. *yṯṯb* "He responds, recites", producing a formula such as *rgm yṯṯb* "He declaims a recitation, he responds with a recitation". At times, we merely have a finite form of the verb *r-g-m* "to speak, proclaim". The subject is usually the king, but this may vary. Such formulas undoubtedly derive from epistolography, where they signify the reply to a communication. Also attested is the verb *š-y-r* "to chant" and *d-y-n* "to proclaim".

It is my view that the Ugaritic texts register the catch-lines of known texts, parts of the actual *rgm* (*rigmu*), so to speak. This conclusion proceeds from structure and composition. One expects that a statement to the effect that the king "recites" would be followed directly by the words that were recited! Just such a sequence occurs in *KTU* 1.106:15–17:

w šr yšr
<ʿ>šr. pamt. l pn
mlk. ptḥ yd. mlk

And he verily chants ten times in the presence of 'the King' (= ʾIlu)
[or: "the king"]: "Open the hand, oh King" (= ʾIlu) [or: the king]!"

However we take the word *mlk*, whether as the king of Ugarit, or as the god Ilu, whose epithet is *mlk* (see further), it is clear that the actual text of the entreaty begins with the words: *ptḥ yd* "Open the hand!" These words are either the catch-line of a known text that was chanted, or the entire chant. Does this not suggest, in turn, that what follows the notice *rgm yṯṯb* "He responds with a recitation" would likewise represent the opening words of a known text?

In its fullest form, the proverbial statement reads as follows (*Locus classicus*: *KTU* 1.41:46–47 // *KTU* 1.87:50–51. Restorations are based on parallels and are fairly certain).

rgm. yṯ[ṯ] [b. mlk. brr]
b. [šb]ʿ. ṣbu. [š]p
š. w ḥl. ym. ʿrb [.] šp[š]
w ḥl mlk

Pardee:[13]

> [Le roi, (étant pur),] rép[ét]era la parole. Le [sept]ième (jour de la fête), quand le soleil se lève, ce sera jour libre (d'obligations cultu-relles); quand le sole[il] se couche, le roi [sera libre (d'obligations cultuelles).]

Levine:

> He responds with a recitation, the pure king, on the seventh day:
> "From the rising of Šapšu to the rampart of Yammu,
> "From the setting of Šapšu to the rampart of 'the King' (= ʾIlu)"

Also note a similar passage in *KTU* 1.41:52–53, parsed as I read it:

> *pamt. šbʿ. k lbh*
> *yr[gm] ml[k.] ṣbu. špš. w ḥl. mlk*

Pardee:[14]

> sept fois. Selon (ce qui est dans) son coeur le roi pa[rl]era, Quand le soleil se lève, le roi sera libre (d'obligations cultuelles).

Levine:

> Seven times, agreeably, the king declaims:
> "From the rising of Šapšu to the rampart of 'the king' (= ʾIlu)."

In this latter instance, the catch-line is abbreviated, producing an *inclusio*. It begins with the first component of the full version, and proceeds directly to the last component. In other passages and texts we find additional abbreviations, variously framed (e.g. *KTU* 1.106:23–24, 32–33; 1.86:22; for syllabic texts, Huehnergard 1987:52 (no. 32.3), 177, s.v. ?RGM).

It is my understanding that this is a poetic couplet, usually but not always chiastic in structure. My interpretation has not been accepted, and even de Tarragon and I, in our collaborative study of *KTU* 1.41,[15] were unable to agree on the meaning of this passage. The prevailing view, represented by Pardee, understands the statement under discussion as registering the changing ritual status of the king (Ugaritic *mlk* = "king") and the status of certain days (Ugaritic *ym* = "day"). It would be well to offer a fuller critique of that view than I have provided in previous studies.

A crucial word is *ḥl*, which Pardee and some others take as a cognate of the Akkadian adjective *ellu* "pure" from the verb *elēlu* "to become pure". This verbal root is realized in West Semitic with *ḥēt*, as in the D-stem Ugaritic construction *ḥll ydm* "the purification of the hands" (*KTU* 1.115:6.). Now, the Akkadian verb *elēlu*, and adjectival *ellu*, appropriate extended meanings such as: "to be free of debt; free of claims; noble, free"—as opposed to being a slave (*CAD E*, 102–106, s.v. *ellu*, especially 105, s.v. mng. 3: "free (of claims), noble". This

[13] Pardee 2000, 1:151.

[14] *Ibid.*

[15] Levine and de Tarragon 1993.

semantic range is shared by other terms that denote purity, such as Akkadian *zakû* (Aramaic *d-k-y*) and *ebēbu*, and Hebrew *nāqî.* On this basis, the Ugaritic formula *w ḥl mlk* would mean "The king is free (of cultic obligations)", just as *w ḥl ym* would mean "The day is free".

This interpretation poses several difficulties. Whereas, in immediate context, the seventh day would become "free" at sunrise, the king would not be declared "free" until sunset, which is odd. Then, too, the Akkadian evidence reflects a socio-legal semantic range, not a cultic one. In a cultic context, Akkadian *ellu* would most probably mean "pure", not "free". Others relate Ugaritic *ḥl* to Biblical Hebrew *ḥōl* "impure, unholy, profane", from a root *ḥ-l-l* "to be desecrated, impure", D-stem *ḥillēl* "to desecrate, defile". This verb is distinct from the homonym that connotes purification, and in my view, is not attested in Ugaritic.

In Late Hebrew, it is appropriate to classify a day as *ḥōl,* by which is meant that it is not a festival day. In biblical usage, this classification usually pertains to what is unfit for sacrifice. Ironically, *ḥl* as "free" might work for the king, or other officiant, but would we say that a day is free of obligations? In contrast, *ḥl* as "profane" might work for describing a day (as in Late Hebrew), but would not be appropriate for characterizing the status of the king on a particular day.

How, then, do I understand this couplet? As already indicated, I see it as part of the *rgm* (*rigmu*) "recitation", more precisely, the opening lines of a known recitation.

Note the following points:

1) Ugaritic *ṣbu špš* – *ʿrb špš*, and the counterparts in Akkadian and Hebrew, indicate poles of time (sunrise – sunset), but also serve as directional contrasts in nature (east-west). Ugaritic *ṣbu špš* is an alternative to *ṣat špš* "east" which, in turn, contrasts in parallelism with *ḫp ym* "the shore of the sea / of Yammu" in the west (*KTU* 1.3.II:7–8). As directional indicators, these ancient Near Eastern formulas are cosmic merisms for the expanse between one horizon to the other, and they often occur in statements attesting to the sovereignty of gods over the expanse of creation, or the rule of kings over the inhabited world.

2) The word *ḥl* is once again pivotal. There is a Ugaritic word *ḥl* (= *ḥīlu*), from the root *ḥ-w-l* "to encircle, turn about" parallel with *ǵr* "mountain" which means "circuit, surrounding rampart, fortress, region". Thus, *KTU* 1.16.I:6ff.

> For you, oh father, weeps the mount (*ǵr*) of Baʿlu;
> Ṣapanu, the sacred rampart (*ḥlm qdš*),
> Nanaya (Anti-Casius), the mighty rampart (*ḥlm adr*).

What is more, syllabic Ugaritic *ḥīlu* occurs in town names within the kingdom of Ugarit (*DUL* 359–360, s.v. *ḥl* (*III*)). Furthermore, the place name *ḥl y*[*m*] can probably be restored in *KTU* 4.68:40. Van Soldt[16] lists a town on the western slope of the Anti-Casius, in the northwest corner of the kingdom, named Ḥilu.

[16] van Soldt 2005:173.

However, this noun has nothing to do with the notion of "strength". It is the form of the structure, or of the natural formation that accounts for its meaning. Ugaritic *ḥīlu* appears to function like Akkadian *dūru* in place names, reflecting the notion of encirclement (*CAD D*, 102–107, s.v. *dūru* A). In Biblical Hebrew, the combination *ḥêl yām* "sea wall" is actually attested; it describes the Egyptian town of No-Amon on the Nile, protected by a wall of water (Nah 3:8).

3) That *mlk* is an epithet of Ilu is best illustrated by *KTU* 1.2.III:4–8:

Then indeed he (=Yammu) set his face
Toward Ilu at the confluence of the rivers,
Within the spring of the two oceans,
He arrived at the roofed dwelling of Ilu,
He entered the beamed house of 'the King' (=Ilu),
The eternal father.

There is an additional source that may help to justify my structural analysis of the proverbial couplet, and it has been saved for last. Reference is to *KTU* 1.119:22–25:

w b šbᶜ. tdn mḥllm.
ᶜrb. špš w ḥl. m[l]k.
hn. šmn. šlm bᶜl.
mtk. mlk[m.] rišyt
k ǵr ᶜz. tǵ[r]km.
[q]rd ḥmytkm…

And on the seventh day the musicians proclaim:
"From the setting of Šapšu to the rampart of 'the King' (= ʾIlu).
Behold! Oil of wellbeing, oh Baᶜlu;
A royal libation of first quality.
Whenever a fierce (foe) attacks your gates,
A strong warrior your walls,…"

This appears to be the only instance, according to my understanding, where the catch-line immediately precedes a second, or continuing recitation. In *KTU* 1.119, we actually have three phases of recitation: (1) the proverbial couplet, (2) the declaration of an offering to Baᶜlu, and (3) an entreaty to Baᶜlu for protection against attack. It is unclear whether they were meant to flow into each other, or whether there were stops intervening, and more text to the first two recitations.

In contrast, the prevailing interpretation projects a specific regimen affecting the king's shifting ritual status, and the scheduling of his duties. What we know is that on many occasions the king performs ablutions on the day preceding the date of the cultic event in which he is due to participate. For example: If *ym mlat* "the day of the full moon" falls on the fourteenth of the month, his ablutions will be performed on the thirteenth, and if on the fifteenth day, his ablutions would be performed on the fourteenth. There are cases where one could see a nexus of (a) preparatory ablutions by the king and (b) the release of the king from cultic obligations on the following day. Thus, the brief entry in *KTU* 1.87:54–57, reconstructed by Pardee[17] as follows.

> 54) *b yrḫ. š*[… ..*b arbʿt. ʿš*
> 55) *rt. yr*[*tḥṣ. m l k. brr*
> 56) *ʿlm. š. š r p l* [-] -. *ʿrb. šp*
> 57) *š. w ḥ* [*l*] [. *m*] *l k*

Pardee:

> Au mois Š-[…, au qu]atorze (du mois), [le r]oi se lavera (avec pour-résultat d'être) pur. Au (jour) suivant, (un) bélier (comme) ho[locauste](pour) Ilu (?). Quand le soleil se couche, [le r]oi sera libre (d'obligations cultuelles).

The same nexus possibly occurs in *KTU* 1.106:25–28, where we read that the king undergoes ablutions, and then, at night, the throne is prepared, and more sacrifices are offered. Read in this manner, it would indeed seem that just as the king undergoes purification in advance of his cultic performance, so is he released at sunset of the following day, when his tasks are over. However, this reading requires us to understand Ugaritic *ʿlm* (= *ʿalāma*) to mean "the following day" as suggested by J. Tropper[18] and adopted by Pardee. Ugaritic *ʿlm* is adverbial: *ʿl* + *m* (enclitic *mēm*), and means "in addition, then, afterwards". To assign to Ugaritc *ʿlm* the specific meaning "the following day" in all of its occurrences in the ritual texts, as Pardee does, is arbitrary.

I would translate the relevant entry in *KTU* 1.87:56 simply as follows: "In addition—a head of small cattle as a burnt offering to Ilu(?)" Or, in *KTU* 1.106:28: "Then, provisions are brought out." As already noted, there are instances where it would make little sense to translate *ʿlm* as "the following day." For example: in *KTU* 1.41:6–9, a broken passage, the king is portrayed as enthroned, and about to preside over an important annual celebration. When the text continues: with *ʿlm,* it is more likely that it is introducing a rite to be performed on that very occasion, rather than on the morrow. What sense would it make to record that the king is free of cultic obligations in *medias res*, and in *KTU* 1.119—just before an offering is announced, and the text of a prayer recited?

If the Ugaritic ritual texts had expressed their themes as effusively as the biblical Psalms, my proposed reading might have gained greater acceptance: Thus, Ps 113:3:

> From the rising of the sun all the way to its setting, the name of Yahweh receives praise.

The biblical resonance of the well-known ancient Near Eastern merism emphasizes that throughout the expanse between the eastern and western horizons Yahweh is worshipped as supreme. In the Ugaritic rituals, there is no compara-

---

[17] Pardee 2000, 1:470.
[18] Tropper 2000:332.

ble referent for the same merism, so that the relevance of the cosmic, or global perspective to the performance of sacrifices is left unexplained.

In previous studies, I have attempted to deal with this problem by supposing that reference to the eastern and western horizons expressed a perception of Ugarit's location, and coastal topography.[19] A person standing atop the acropolis near the temple of Baᶜlu, or on the roof of the temple, would be overlooking the sea, personified as Yammu, as he gazed at the western horizon. If he turned around, he would literally be oriented to the eastern horizon, to the mountains where Ilu resided. The sense of the couplet, though not fully expressed, would be that Baᶜlu, having defeated Yammu, rules over heaven, earth and sea, and protects Ugarit and its seafaring merchants. This theme would be appropriate for a refrain of praise.

3: Processionals Entering the Royal Palace (bt mlk)

Identifying the specific venues of cultic events at Ugarit is not a simple task, and Pardee is not to be faulted for leaving many questions unresolved. It is also a challenge to correlate data provided by the ritual texts with the archaeological and architectural finds uncovered by Marguerite Yon, Jean Margueron, and their associates; in a sense that is the ultimate task if we are to identify cultic venues. In a number of texts, we are explicitly informed that the rites recorded took place in *bt bᶜl ugrt* "the temple of Baᶜlu of Ugarit". Reference is to the principal temple at Ugarit of the period. Some ritual texts fail to specify in any way where the relevant rites took place. In other cases, such as in *KTU* 1.41, an elaborate ritual text, we find additional venues, such as: *bt il*, *bt ilt*, and *bt bᶜlt btm rmm*. These designations are open to interpretation. They may indicate that the unifying principle of this ritual text is the cultic occasion, or occasions, that it records, not the venue, so that it would record rites performed in separate locations, but all related to the same cultic event. These *bt*-structures might represent smaller sanctuaries situated around the town of Ugarit, and which are indicated architecturally, such as the so-called rhyton temple.[20] Alternatively, Ugaritic *bt* may, in certain contexts, designate "chapel" so that everything recorded in a ritual text took place in the same, overall temple, but in different chapels, or installations within it, such as *mdgl* "tower," *urbt* "aperture", *ǵr*, "cave", and *mdbḥt* "altars".

This brings us to the designation *bt mlk*, which recurs in the ritual texts. All through the years, I have equivocated over its meaning, vacillating between "royal chapel" and "temple of Milku/Mulku", because I could not conceive that public sacrificial activity, especially altar sacrifices, would take place in the royal palace. Such activities take place in temples, and if reference was to a royal

[19] Levine and de Tarragon 1993:106–110.

[20] Yon 2006:78–83.

chapel located within the palace complex at Ugarit, that locale would have been identified more precisely.

What I failed to understand was that no sacrifices were ever reported as actually being performed in the palace! For the most part, the relevant texts record processionals, with the operative verb being *ʿ-r-b* "to enter". When we read that a god or goddess "enters" *bt mlk*, it means that a statue of that deity was brought into the palace in a processional. This awareness has led me to conclude that all references to *bt mlk* indeed refer to the royal palace complex at Ugarit, as Pardee and others have maintained all along. It is unclear, however, whether the same problem which occupied me has figured in the thinking of other scholars, or whether they would necessarily agree with my interpretation of those ritual texts which attest the term *bt mlk*. It would be well, therefore, to review all attestations of *bt mlk* in the ritual texts in immediate context before speculating as to the implications of the rendering "royal palace".

I begin with *KTU* 1.43:1–3:

> *k tʿrb. ʿṯtrt. ḫr. g*[*b*] *bt mlk*
> *ʿšr. ʿšr. b* [*mṯ*]*bt ilm kbkbm*
>
> When ʿAṯtartu-Ḫurri enters the inner area of the royal palace,
> A banquet is prepared at the seats of the astral divinities.

Subsequently, in lines 9–10 we read:

> *ʿlm tʿrbn gṯrm bt mlk*
>
> Afterwards, the Gaṯarūma enter the royal palace.

Finally, at the conclusion of the text, in lines 23–26 we read:

> *mlk. ylk. lqḥ* [.] *ilm.*
> *aṯr. ilm. ylk. pʿnm.*
> *mlk. pʿnm. yl*[*k.*]
> *šbʿ. pamt. l klhm*
>
> The king goes to bring the gods;
> After (= in pursuit of) the gods he walks on foot;
> The king goes on foot;
> Seven times, for all of them.

This ritual text informs us of several important matters associated with processionals. When ʿAṯtartu-Ḫurri enters the royal palace, a banquet is held at a certain location within the palace, most likely in a throne room or banquet hall, where the "seats" of the astral divinities were placed. Soon after (not on "the following day!"), the Gaṯarūma enter the royal palace in a second processional. The concluding passage, expressed in poetic form, tells of the king's particular role in these events. He bears the task of going to the temple to get the statues of the gods and of bringing them to the palace. In effect, just as the chief god in heaven invites other gods to a feast in his palace, which in the celestial context is by definition a temple, so the earthly king invites gods to his palace where a feast is prepared in their honor. What is described for this celebration might indicate the practice followed on other occasions, as well. It would be interesting to explore why certain deities are mentioned in connection with processionals, and not others.

There is, however, a further dimension to what is described in *KTU* 1.43. Following each of the two, recorded processionals, and in synch with them, other forms of celebration take place. The question is where that happened, and what such activity consisted of. Following upon the first processional, lines 3–7 list *trmt* "a levied offering" (perhaps cf. Hebrew *terûmah*), consisting of golden garments, but also of small and large cattle. Similarly, following upon the second processional, lines 10–16 (where the text is broken) list offerings of gold and silver ingots, but also of animals, and of parts of them. If only precious metals and garments had been listed, we could say that these were donated in connection with the processional, with no actual sacrificial activity involved. However, since animals are also mentioned, we must opt for one of two interpretations, in order to sustain the principle that no actual sacrificial activity took place in the palace: (a) The animals were donated "to, for" (= prepositional *lamed*) various deities by the palace, but sacrificed in the temple. (b) All that is listed was disposed of in the temple, concurrent with the processional that was being enacted in the palace.

In other cases, it is quite evident that the scenes projected in a single text shift between palace and temple. Thus, in *KTU* 1.39:12 we find the statement: *w l ll. špš pgr. w trmnm bt mlk* "And before nightfall, Šapšu-Pagri and Ṯarummannūma (being) in the royal palace." This statement interrupts, as it were, a long list of offerings, all but the last one being identified without prepositional *lamed*. Here we may conclude that as the processional was being enacted in the palace, sacrifices were being offered concurrently in the temple. The same is indicated by *KTU* 1.91:7: *pdry. bt. mlk* "Pidray (being) in the royal palace". That text is an inventory of wine needed for several celebrations, including *dbḥ ṣpn* "the cultic celebration in honor of Ṣapanu", *dbḥ mlk* "the royal celebration," and *dbḥ bʿl* "the celebration in honor of Baʿlu". The text is severely damaged, and ends with a total (Ugaritic *tgmr*) of wine requisitioned by, or delivered to the temple. It is in the course of registering this commodity that *KTU* 1.91 reports that a statue of Pidray was in the royal palace.

Further on, in *KTU* 1.91:10–11, also referring to the celebration in honor of Ṣapānu, we read:

> *k tʿrb. ʿṯtrt. šd. bt* [. *m*]*lk*
> *k tʿrbn. ršpm. bt. mlk*
>
> When ʿAṯtartu-Šadi enters the royal palace.
> When the Rašapūma enter the royal palace.

The text then briefly registers rites of uncertain meaning, apparently also offered in the temple. Finally, *KTU* 1.91:14–15 records further movement, although it is not entirely clear where such movement took place:

dbḥ. bˁl[ERASURE] *k. tdd. bˁlt. bhtm*
b. ǵb. ršp. ṣbi

The celebration in honor of Baˁlu [...] when Baˁalatu Bahatīma moves in the *ǵb* of Rašap-Ṣabi.

Ugaritic *ǵb* is of uncertain etymology. If it means "sacrificial pit" then what is being described took place in the temple, whereas if it denotes something else, perhaps a structure or chamber, then the movement in question could have taken place in the royal palace, according to my view.

There is another reference to *bt mlk* that warrants scrutiny at this point, namely, *KTU* 1.41:19–24 (as reconstructed on the basis of *KTU* 1.87):

w mˁrb d yqḥ [.] *bt mlk*

In a previous study this had been translated: "And the pledge that he (= the king) brings to the royal chapel". Now I would translate: "And the offering of entry that the royal palace brings (or: that is brought by the royal palace)." The subject of the verb *l-q-ḥ* is, therefore, the royal palace; which is not the destination of the offerings. The offerings were delivered to the temple. The king is enthroned in the temple, presiding over an annual celebration, and the text proceeds to list his donated gifts.

This leads us directly to *KTU* 1.148:18:

k tˁrb ˁṯtrt. šd bt. mlk

When ˁAṯtartu-Šadi enters the royal palace.

This is the opening line of a demarcated section of the text (lines 18–22) that proceeds to list vestments, as well as perfumed oil and containers of honey, that were donated to the temple by the king on the occasion. It was presumably a part of the large celebration in honor of Ṣapānu (*dbḥ ṣpn*), which is the caption of *KTU* 1.148. It implies no sacrificial activity inside the palace.

To summarize: It is possible to sustain the principle that no sacrificial activity took place in the royal palace, which is what *bt mlk* always means. Some texts project scene-shifts between palace and temple, and still others describe rites occurring in more than one sacred venue. The public cult at Ugarit was sponsored by "the palace", which is to say, by the king. The king actively participated in the temple cult, as well as hosting the gods in his palace at banquets. Processionals led divine images into the palace on such occasions. At times, the ritual texts possibly refer to other, named sanctuaries in the town of Ugarit, as well as to specific installations within the major temple, itself. There is little to suggest that what the Ugaritic ritual texts describe was restricted to the king and his court. Nor is there information regarding private worship at Ugarit, though *KTU* 1.80, as sketchy as it is, may describe ritual activity by a private individual, carried out at a sanctuary, as Pardee suggests.

Conclusion

It is unwarranted to suppose that a comprehensive model of the public cult at Ugarit can be generated in the present state of knowledge. The institutional approach is, however, the most productive way of pursuing this objective, because it focuses on function and context, and can help to elucidate the phenomenology of worship. Meanwhile, further study of the cultic vocabulary, and analysis of textual structure must proceed vigorously. The urge to "get past" philology must be resisted, and accepted interpretations questioned. The publication of additional ritual texts is imminent, and at the very least, their appearance will enhance the repertoire, and hopefully settle some of the enigmas that still affect interpretation.

Bibliography

Huehnergard, J.
1987 *Ugaritic Vocabulary in Syllabic Transcription.* HSS 32. Atlanta: Scholars Press.

Lane, E. W.
1980 *An Arabic-English Lexicon.* 8 vols. Beirut: Librairie du Liban (Reprint of London, 1863).

Levine, B. A.
1963 Ugaritic Descriptive Rituals. *JCS* 17:105–111. {*VOL 1, PP. 45–54*}

Levine, B. A. and J.-M. de Tarragon
1993 The King Proclaims the Day: Ugaritic Rites for the Vintage (*KTU* 1.41//1.87). *RB* 100:76–115.

Levy, J.
1963 *Wörterbuch über die Talmudim und Midraschim.* 4 vols. Darmstadt: Wissenschaftliche Buchgesellschaft.

Merlo, P. and P. Xella
1999 The Ugaritic Cultic Texts: The Rituals. Pages 287–304 in Watson and Wyatt 1999.

del Olmo Lete, G. and J. Sanmartín
2003 *A Dictionary of the Ugaritic Language in the Alphabetic Tradition.* 2 vols. HdO 67. Leiden: Brill.

Pardee, D.
2000 *Les textes rituels*. Fascicules 1 et 2. Ras Shamra-Ougarit 12. Paris: Éditions Recherche sur les civilisations.

van Soldt, W.
2005 *The Topography of the City-State of Ugarit.* AOAT 324. Münster: Ugarit-Verlag.

de Tarragon, J.-M.
1980 *Le culte à Ugarit: d'après les textes de la pratique en cunéiformes alphabétiques*. Cahiers de la Revue Biblique 19. Paris: Gabalda.

Tropper, J.
2000 *Ugaritische Grammatik*. AOAT 273. Münster: Ugarit-Verlag.

Watson, W.G.E. and N. Wyatt
1999 *Handbook of Ugaritic Studies*. Leiden; Boston; Köln: Brill.

Yon, M.
2006 *The City of Ugarit at Tell Ras Shamra*. Winona Lake: Eisenbrauns.

Review of *The Israelian Heritage of Judaism*[*]

H. Louis Ginsberg. *The Israelian Heritage of Judaism*. New York Jewish Theological Seminary of America, 1982. 145 pp.

H. L. Ginsberg's recent monograph is perhaps the most seminal study of the Deuteronomic question since Julius Wellhausen's *History of Israel*, Volume 1, first published in 1878, a work which in its time revolutionized biblical research.[1] No two works could be more dissimilar, however, either in style or method. Wellhausen wrote expansively, seeking to demonstrate a comprehensive theory of religious development in ancient Israel. He worked with historical models derived from other disciplines. Ginsberg, on the other hand, writes more in the manner of a theoretical mathematician, providing us with a series of equations, laconically stated, and accompanied by only brief comments.

Ginsberg focuses on a limited number of key biblical passages, and subjects these to a type of exegesis which he himself has perfected and refined more than any other modern scholar. His method rests on the analysis of *diction*, which allows him to trace literary provenance. Ultimately, Ginsberg's potential for conclusive demonstration is greater than was Wellhausen's, because he bases his conclusions on biblical Hebrew expression, on the evidence of language, rather than on a theoretical model. Ironically, what has remained valid in Wellhausen's own reconstruction is his interpretation of certain specific biblical texts, whereas his overall historical reconstruction has been shown to be problematic in basic respects.

In the present study, Ginsberg argues that "proto-Deuteronomy" (a term designating those sections of the book which we have reason to consider primary) originated in the northern Israelite kingdom of the mid- to late-eighth century B.C.E., in the period prior to the downfall of northern Israel. Ginsberg coined the term "Israelian" to convey this geosocial context. In the course of the monograph, he also exposes the Israelian origin of other biblical writings—chapters 6–7 of Micah, parts of the Book of Proverbs, and certain Psalms. The cumulative effect of his discussions is to provide a more balanced view of literary creativity and religious development during the eighth century B.C.E. We become

---

[*] Originally published in *AJS Review* 12 (1987), pp. 143–57. Reprinted with permission from Cambridge University Press.

[1] The original German title was *Geschichte Israels*. In 1883, Wellhausen published a second, revised edition under the title *Prolegomena zur Geschichte Israels*, which has become the standard reference work (English trans., *Prolegomena to the History of Israel* [Cleveland and New York: Meridian Books, 1961]).

aware of positive responses to the problems of northern Israelite society, coming from within that society itself. Ginsberg's effort corrects for the "bad press" received by the northern Israelite kingdom in much of biblical literature.

Foremost among the Israelian responses are the teachings preserved in Deuteronomy. Ginsberg argues that the doctrine restricting all sacrifice and cultic activity to one legitimate temple first emerged in northern Israel and was then transmitted to Jerusalem and Judah. It eventually impacted seventh-century Judah, as well as the postexilic Judean community restored. By positioning proto-Deuteronomy in northern Israel of the eighth century B.C.E. instead of in seventh-century Judah, as most scholars had concluded, Ginsberg also places the priestly component within Torah literature (known as P) in literary-historical perspective.[2] He shows that, with surprisingly few exceptions, priestly legislation represents a set of accommodations to the Deuteronomic program, especially as regards the changing character of the annual pilgrimage festivals.

I

Undoubtedly, the best way to underscore the importance of Ginsberg's contribution would be to clarify the centrality of the Deuteronomic question itself, in both historical and phenomenological terms. Essentially, what we call the Deuteronomic question concerns patterns of worship and the delimiting of sacred space. In the Near East, as elsewhere in the ancient world, the sanctity of space lay at the heart of religious experience. A primary function of institutionalized religions was, therefore, to determine *where* one could legitimately worship. In antiquity, worship inevitably involved sacrifice, for prayer, by itself, was regarded as insufficient.

It was generally held that sacrifice was efficacious only at sacred sites. To put it another way: sacrifice worked only at sites where divine beings were thought to be present, or to which they could be invited. When we read of the initiation of sacrificial worship at a site previously unknown for its sanctity (at least, as the Bible states the matter), we find that worshippers would invoke the deity by name. The resultant appearance of the deity, the theophany, served to confirm the sanctity of the site. Ritual activity and magical means were aimed at consecrating space—the ground itself, as well as the related structures, artifacts, and *matériel*, extending to the personnel operating in sacred space. Decisions relevant to the locus of worship and celebration determined, to a considerable degree, the manifest character of a given religion. One would surely expect to find in the Hebrew Bible statements of policy on the matter of sacred space; and indeed we do.

---

[2] Perhaps the best representative discussion of the Deuteronomic question is to be found in M. Weinfeld, *Deuteronomy and the Deuteronomic School* (Oxford, 1972). Ginsberg's monograph will, however, require serious modification of Weinfeld's treatment.

Exodus 20:19–23 tells us what certain "Israelian" spokesmen of the ninth or perhaps early eighth century B.C.E. thought about sacred space. The stated policy is as follows: Israelites may offer sacrifices to the God of Israel at any *māqôm* ("cult-place") in the land where God permits His name to be invoked. He permits this where certain specific conditions are met; namely, idolatrous worship is emphatically forbidden, the altar is constructed in a specific manner, and the priests conduct themselves decorously. The God of Israel will "arrive" at a proper *māqôm* in response to invocation, and will grant blessings to His worshippers. There is no limit on the number of such cult-places.

This relatively early statement, appearing almost directly after the Decalogue, and immediately before the laws of the Book of the Covenant, correlates with the most reliable biblical traditions on religion and worship. The Patriarchs, as we read about them in the earliest narratives of Genesis, erected altars all over the land, and offered sacrifices upon them, invoking God's name and experiencing theophanies in sacred space. Jacob's experiences at Beth-El, as related in the northern Israelite narrative of Gen. 28:12–22, provide a good example.

Judges of Israel acted in the same way, and even Solomon offered sacrifices regularly on the great *bāmāh* at Gibeon before the Temple was built in Jerusalem (1 Kings 3). Elijah sacrificed on a Yahwistic altar somewhere in the Carmel range (1 Kings 18), just as Samuel had, before him, at any number of cult-places located along his circuit.[3] Archaeological excavations have unearthed Israelite cult-places all over the land, literally from tell-Dan to tell-Beer-Sheva, dating from the period of the monarchies, and even prior to that time at such sites as Shiloh, in the Ephraimite hills.

Although we find conflicting traditions in biblical literature, it would seem that Exodus 20:19–23 accords with official policy up to and until the historical period covered by approximately the last ten chapters of Second Kings; which is to say, until near the close of the eighth century B.C.E., when Hezekiah was king over Judah and Jerusalem.

The normal pattern in biblical Israel, according to law, policy, and custom, was one of multiple cult-places of varying magnitude and complexity, functioning on a local, regional, and even a national basis. Every town of any size would normally have a cult-place of some sort nearby, either an altar or a *bāmāh*. There were places for worship located on the main roads and in border areas, often attached to military or administrative outposts. The sanctuaries at Arad and Beer-Sheva were representative of this system.

This system is specifically renounced in Deuteronomy, chapters 12 and 14–17, where a different doctrine altogether is expounded. If Exodus 20:19–23 permits worship at any proper *māqôm* in the land, Deuteronomy explicitly forbids this. All cultic activity is to be restricted to one *māqôm*, whose location will be determined by God. All that we are told is that this *māqôm* would stand in

---

[3] A fairly elaborate description of such a cult-installation is found in 1 Samuel 9.

one of the tribal territories. The restriction covers festival celebrations and the remittance of tithes, votives, and firstlings.

In literary context, Deuteronomy 12, which is the principal statement of policy, addresses the Israelites of Moses' time, as they prepared to cross the Jordan into Canaan. The chapter opens with the command to destroy all existing pagan cult-places in Canaan, where the native inhabitants of the land worshiped, together with their attendant artifacts. The one legitimate *māqôm* was to be newly constructed, not produced from an earlier structure. As the chapter unfolds, however, the Israelites are told not to persist in their own erstwhile pattern of offering sacrifice at various cult-places. The justification of that policy (the one followed before entry into the land) was that a people on the move, who had not as yet arrived at a secure haven, might require many places of worship. Once settled, however, Israelites were to utilize only one, newly erected sanctuary in the Promised Land.

Deuteronomy 12 continues with regulations concerning the slaughter of animals. Since all sacrificing would be restricted to a single sanctuary, the act of slaughtering animals, when performed elsewhere, could have no sacral significance whatsoever. No cult of purity would be involved, nor any altar used. Instead of being dashed on the altar, as was the practice with sacrificial blood, such blood was to be spilled on the ground and covered over. Among other things, this change in the phenomenology of slaughtering would eliminate the need for priests and other cult-practitioners throughout the land. Indeed, chapter 12 proceeds to exhort Israelites to be generous to the Levites, who would presumably join the ranks of the unemployed!

Chapter 12 of Deuteronomy ends with an admonition to avoid forms of worship practiced by the indigenous Canaanites. Deut. 14:22–27 extends the laws of chapter 12 to tithes and firstlings, and 15:19–23 restates the law as regards firstlings. Chapter 16 emphasizes the requirement that the annual pilgrimage festivals take place exclusively at the central *māqôm*, including even the paschal sacrifice. In chapter 17 we read that the High Court would be located at the central *māqôm*, as well.

The point to be made about Deuteronomy 12, in particular, is that it purports to speak only of idolatry. The polarity it generates is between worship of the God of Israel and pagan worship, and this is part of a widespread tendency in biblical literature to brand improper worship of the God of Israel as tantamount to idolatry. This tendency masks several different forms of heterodoxy, some purportedly representing the worship of the God of Israel, but which were objectionable in the view of biblical spokesmen.

But the reference in chapter 12 of Deuteronomy to the earlier pattern of worship among the Israelites, who themselves used multiple cult-places, is a giveaway! It alludes to reality, and suggests that the issue actually being addressed is the policy governing worship of the God of Israel, not simply the eradication of idolatry, on which every official tradition agreed. Deuteronomy is ostensibly blind to the actual history of worship in ancient Israel. It imposes its doctrine on the entering Israelites, whereas, in historical perspective, what it states clashes with a background experience of local and regional worship of the God of Israel, in the Promised Land itself. Its message confronts a longstanding, customary pattern, formerly thought to be proper and in accordance with God's will.

Here is not the place to deal with traditional attempts to resolve the Deuteronomic disagreement with patterns of worship recorded in biblical books canonically subsequent to Deuteronomy, and which were believed to pertain to subsequent periods of biblical history. Understandably, later Jewish interpreters sought to demonstrate the overall consistency of the biblical record. The offerings of Samuel and Elijah, recorded in the books of Samuel and Kings, were taken to be sporadic and unusual measures, and not representative of normal patterns of worship in the premonarchic and monarchic periods.

In utter contrast to the traditionalist view, modern critical scholars eagerly seized on what they correctly regarded as a significant, documented shift in religious policy, inevitably connected in some way to the edicts of Josiah, king of Judah, recorded in 2 Kings 22–23, and dated ca. 622 B.C.E. This shift in policy surely accounts for the repeated proverbial condemnations of the *bāmôt* editorially implanted into the text of Kings.[4]

While the Temple in Jerusalem was under renovation, a priest discovered an old document, which was brought to Josiah and read in his presence. Upon hearing its contents, Josiah rent his garments, and sought clarification from the prophetess Huldah. She confirmed the authenticity of the document, and interpreted its contents to mean that Jerusalem and the Temple would be destroyed, and the people sent into exile. God had been angered by the widespread idolatry.

From the measures which Josiah undertook in response to the discovered document, we may infer something of its specific contents. He destroyed, or at least put out of commission, cult-places all over the land. He singled out for particular attention the cult-center at Beth-El and its adjoining necropolis, and the Tophet outside of Jerusalem. He killed off pagan priests, and ordered Israelite priests to report to Jerusalem, thereby terminating their operations elsewhere. Of particular interest was his directive proclaiming celebration of the paschal sacrifice in the Temple of Jerusalem, something that had never before occurred.

Against this background, we may now formulate what we have been referring to as the Deuteronomic question. We do so in several phases:

1. What is the *historical* relationship between the legislation of Deuteronomy and the edicts of Josiah? Are both sources referring to the same religious movement, and if so, how?

2. Is the tale told in 2 Kings about an old document discovered in the Temple to be taken at face value? Are we to conclude that the objection to existing cult-places had, indeed, emerged at an earlier period, but had been ignored or opposed during the long reign of Manasseh, throughout most of the seventh cen-

---

[4] For examples see 1 Kings 22:44, 2 Kings 12:14, 14:4, 15:4, 35, etc.

tury B.C.E.? Or is this tale legendary, merely intended to lend sanction to what was, in reality, a reform of worship and of the priesthood initiated by Josiah himself, and actually a product of religious ferment in the Judah of the mid- to late seventh century B.C.E.?

3. How are we, in either case, to interpret the efforts of Hezekiah, who had also sought to eliminate existing cult-places, as reported in 2 Kings 18:3–5, 22? These efforts would have taken place soon after the fall of the northern Israelite kingdom, in the late eighth century.

II

Ginsberg does justice to all phases of the Deuteronomic question as we have just formulated it. How he does so requires us to read Hosea with new eyes, and to register its diction more precisely than we have been doing.

A cursory reading of Hosea in tandem with Deuteronomy would hardly endorse Ginsberg's claim that the Deuteronomic program originally constituted a response to Hosean prophecies. There is little overall similarity between the two works. And yet, Ginsberg has identified three examples of corresponding diction which are so distinctive in biblical writings of the ninth to eighth century B.C.E. that we may theorize that the author (or authors) of proto-Deuteronomy most likely would not have derived such diction from any source other than the books of Hosea, which are collections of Israelian writings. (As a matter of fact, Ginsberg posits two Hoseas: chapters 1–3, written in the ninth century, and chapters 4–14, of the eighth century.)

The theory that dictional correspondences indicate shared literary provenance rests on the reality that in ancient societies writers and scribes learned their techniques of composing narratives and chronicles, as well as poems, and legal and ritual codes from relatively few teachers. The successive exponents of specific teachings were usually associated with the same, ongoing institutions, and worked in the same schools, or circles, so that they would expectedly employ the same diction as their mentors and precursors had.

In Hosea 2:10 we read that the LORD, in His kindness, had provided the Israelites with *dāgān*, *tîrôš*, and *yiṣhār*, "grain, wine, and oil," in that order (cf. further in Hos. 2:24). In Deut. 12:17, part of the basic exposition of the Deuteronomic program, we read that Israelites are required to remit tithes of *dāgān*, *tîrôš*, and *yiṣhār*, in that order, to the LORD, at the one central *māqôm*. This is repeated in Deut. 14:23 and 18:4.

What was, in the first instance, a merism became a cliché in the writings of the Deuteronomist (Deut. 7:13, 11:14, 28:51). Independently, two of the three components of the merism, *dāgān* and *tîrôš*, occur as a pair in Gen. 27:28, 37, in the work of the Elohist of northern Israel; and in Hos. 7:14 and 9:1, somewhat adapted. The fact that, according to Ginsberg, chapters 1–3 of Hosea derive from the ninth century B.C.E. adds significance to the dictional correspondence between Hosea and Deuteronomy, because it brings us back to the northern Israelite society of an even earlier period.

What we have is, therefore, Israelian diction par excellence, and we can trace the further transmission of the same merism in Judean literature and into postexilic times, even as far as the recently discovered Temple Scroll. The other two examples of diction discussed by Ginsberg are equally compelling.

But diction alone cannot make the case that proto-Deuteronomy is an Israelian creation of the period between 740 and 725 B.C.E. Ginsberg consequently discusses examples of Deuteronomic legislation which he regards as responses, at least in part, to Hosean prophecies. It is the interaction of diction, theme, and law which ultimately clinches the argument.

Ginsberg cites two examples of Hosean influence. One seemingly has nothing directly to do with the religious doctrine of Deuteronomy, but we shall learn that, in a curious way, it does! In Hos. 10:13–15, the prophet condemns reliance on chariotry and professional warriors, as part of his antiwar policy. Deut. 20:1–9, part of the law of warfare, and Deut. 17:16–17, part of the law of the king, echo this Hosean theme.

More immediately pertinent to the argument is Ginsberg's suggestion that Hos. 8:11–14 was the impetus behind Deut. 12:8–18. Here is how Ginsberg explains this point:

> The centralization of the cult which is required by Deut. 12:8–18 is surely, at least in part, a response to the denunciation cum threat of Hos. 8:11–14: "For Ephraim has multiplied altars—for guilt; his altars have redounded to his guilt; (12) The principles (?) of the instruction I wrote for him have been treated as something alien. (13) They have *slaughtered* victims to no purpose (?)—only for *meat* to *eat*. YHWH has *not* been appeased by them. Behold, He will remember their iniquity and punish their sins: back to Egypt with them! (14) Since Israel has forgotten his Maker while building temples... I will send down fire on his cities and it shall devour his fortresses." The Deuteronomist evidently reasoned: if a multiplicity of altars and temples will lead to exile and devastation, the catastrophe may be averted by reducing the number of temples to one, so that people may not rely on them as a means of obtaining absolution. That this passage in Hosea was a factor in giving rise to the law in Deut. 12, is confirmed by the recurrence in the latter of the phrase we have italicized in the former: *yzbḥw bśr wyʾlkw* (Hos. 8:13) *tzbḥ wʾklt bśr* (Deut. 12:15) [p. 21].

Surely, this matter warrants added discussion, because it is pivotal to the entire attribution of an Israelian provenance to proto-Deuteronomy. We begin with Ginsberg's keen observation that Hos. 8:11–14 and Deut. 12:15 are linked by shared and highly distinctive diction. As a matter of fact, no other biblical passage contains, in a single clause, these three ingredients: the verb *ʾāḵal*, "eat," the verb *zābḥah*, "to slaughter," and the noun *bāśār*, "meat." But this is more than a technical correspondence. The theme of feasting on meat is basic to Deuteronomy 12, which repeatedly states that in the new order of worship, feasting on meat will have no sacral significance. Whereas Hosea regards as regrettable the practice of reducing the sacrificing of animals to mere feasting on meat, with no worshipful intent, Deuteronomy ordains that henceforth, the slaughter of animals outside the one legitimate *māqôm* will, ironically, be nothing more than feasting on meat.

So much for diction and its allusiveness. The real question is whether the Deuteronomic program is a logical response to Hosean prophecies. Is the reduction of sacred space to one legitimate cult-place a reasonable response to what Hosea was opposing in the northern Israelite society of the mid- to late eighth century B.C.E.?

All of Hosea 8 expresses the prophet's observation that Israel has abandoned "what is good," as verse 3 puts it. As a consequence of its disloyalty, northern Israel will be destroyed by an enemy. The people had betrayed *berît* and *tôrāh*, and their worship of God had been hypocritical. They seek ritual atonement as a mask for their transgressions. They appoint kings unacceptable to the LORD, and spend their wealth on idols, a prime example being the Bull of Samaria.

This brings us to vv. 11–14, which Ginsberg cites in particular. It is a case of "the more the worse!" The prophet posits a correlation between the proliferation of altars and temples and the guilt of the people. Those who endow temples and erect altars are the very ones who have forgotten God. The more cult-places, therefore, the greater the affront to God and the more severe the degeneration of society. The same quantitative correlation is expressed in Hos. 4:7, with reference to priests: "The more numerous they (=the priests) have become, the more so have they offended Me. I will turn their prestige into disgrace!"

The theme of Hosea 8 is carried forward in Hos. 10:1–8, which adds vehemence to the prophetic denunciation of an expanded cultic establishment under royal sponsorship. The passage is extremely difficult to interpret with assurance, but it holds forth potential insights into the thrust of Hosea's policy on cult and worship.

> Israel is a ravaged vine,
> And his fruit resembles him!
> When his fruit abounded,
> He had built abundant altars!
> When his land enjoyed plenty,
> He had erected stelae aplenty!
> But because *his devotion failed*,
> He now faces ruin![5]

---

[5] I prefer to see the botanical metaphor as moving quickly to the people of Israel. NJPS translates: "Now that his *boughs are broken up*," etc. This rendering takes its cue from 2 Sam. 18:14, where *bĕlēḇ hāʾēlāh* means "in the *thick growth* of the terebinth." The verb *ḥālaq* is taken in the usual sense of "dividing, splitting off, or the like." The translation given here posits a second root in biblical Hebrew: *ḥālaq*, cognate to Akkadian *ḫalāqu*, "to disappear, vanish, to become missing or lost, to perish" (see *CAD Ḫ*, 36f.).

So now he himself will pull down his altars,
He will smash his own stelae!
For now they claim: "We have no king!
We did not fear the LORD,
So what can the king do to us?"
Agreements were concluded with false oaths,
And covenants enacted,
And justice broke out like poisonous weeds
In the furrows of the field!
The residents of Samaria fear for the calf of Beît-ʾĀwen,
Its populace mourns over its glory,
That has departed from it.[6]
It, too, will be transported to Assyria,
As tribute to an imperial king.
Ephraim shall be shamed,
Israel shall be failed by its own policy!
Samaria's monarchy is dissolving,
Like foam upon the water!
The high-places of ʾĀwen shall be ruined,
The guilt of Israel!
Thorns and thistles shall overrun her altars,
They shall say to the mountains: "Cover us!"
To the hills: "Slide over us!"

Hosea might have preferred no cult at all to what he had observed in northern Israel. The cult establishment was a major part of the problem, because its influence contradicted the true objectives of religious life. It represented what we might call "state religion." Joash and Jeroboam II, kings of northern Israel, exploited the popular penchant for worship and celebration, and the strongly felt need for expiation and divine forgiveness. The royal establishment endowed numerous altars and cult places, and royally appointed priests undoubtedly assumed control over existing traditional cult-places so that everywhere, royal policy would be sanctioned by the institutions of religion. This strategy is brought home by the sharp interchange between the prophet Amos and Amaziah, the priest of Beth-El, preserved in chapter 7 of Amos.

Chapters 8 and 10 of Hosea inform us that royal policies had proved disastrous, both in domestic and international terms. The people were beginning to defy their king. They were tearing down the lavish symbols of royal policy, the

---

This root is probably attested elsewhere in biblical Hebrew, unbeknown to most (cf. the niphal form in Gen. 14:15, as an example). The sense here is that the metaphor, having shifted from the vine to the people, speaks of their loss of "heart," namely, their loss of devotion or loyalty. For this sense of Hebrew *lēḇ*, see usage in Num. 32:7, 9; 2 Sam. 15:13; 1 Kings 12:27, etc.

[6] Hebrew *ʾāwen*, "iniquity," represents a pejorative alteration of the toponymic *Beît-ʾĒl*, "House of God," to *Beît-ʾĀen*, or just *ʾĀwen*, for the actual town of Beth-El. See Hosea 4:15, 5:8, in addition to our passage.

altars and stelae. They reasoned, *a fortiori*, that once they had offended God and suffered His wrath, they had little to fear from a discredited king!

In Hosea 8 and 10 we observe a subtle blending of the religious and the sociopolitical as themes of prophetic denunciation. Most assuredly, there was something seriously wrong with current modes of worship and with religious attitudes, but there was more to the problem than heterodoxy and hypocrisy.

Hosea and Amos refer by name to a number of cult-centers, undoubtedly royally sponsored, which were operative in the northern Israel of the eighth century B.C.E. They mention Beth-El, of course, as well as Dan, Gilead (Jabesh Gilead?), Gilgal, Samaria, and Shechem. They also refer to *mizbāḥôt*, "altars," and this is significant, as we have seen in the case of Hosea 8:11.[7]

Now, Isaiah of Jerusalem, who also objected to lavishing wealth on idols (Isa. 2:7–8), refers only once to the problematic of such altars. This is as part of an oracle on the downfall of the Kingdom of Damascus (Isa. 17:1–11), in which the prophet predicts for the Arameans the same misfortune that was about to befall *the northern kingdom of Israel*!

The point is that the phenomenon of altars was a distinctive feature of religious life in northern Israel, and it is only when he is characterizing the situation in *northern* Israel that Isaiah refers to it specifically. In fact, a good case could be made for concluding that Isaiah of Jerusalem spoke somewhat like a northerner when his subject was the religious disloyalty of northern Israelite society. One need only compare Hosea 14:4b with Isaiah 17:8!

The target of Hosea's critique is the domination of religious life by the kings of northern Israel. In these terms, we can appreciate Ginsberg's attention to the thematic link between Hosea's reference to chariotry and professional soldiers, on the one hand, and the laws of Deuteronomy 17 and 20, regarding the duties of the king and warfare, on the other. Is it coincidental that Hosea 8:1 accuses the House of *Israel* (for that is how Ginsberg reads this verse) of transgressing the covenant, while Deut. 17:2 speaks of an Israelite who advocates doing the same, with both texts employing the fairly rare formula, *ʿāḇar bĕrît*?[8]

Given the emphasis in chapters 8 and 10 of Hosea on *bĕrît*, *mišpāṭ*, "justice," and *tôrāh* "instruction," is it coincidental that Deuteronomy 17 calls for the establishment of a High Court in the projected central *māqôm*, where *tôrāh*

---

[7] See Hosea 8:11, 10:1–2, 8, 12:2, Amos 3:14. The quantitative correlation reappears later in Jer. 11:13, 17:1, and the problem of numerous altars informs Ezekiel 6, for instance, and is addressed in Kings and Deuteronomistic literature generally.

[8] The Masoretic text of v. 1 has *bêt YHWH*, "House of the LORD," but NJPS, informed by Ginsberg, suggests that an emendation would yield *bêt Yisrāʾēl*, "House of Israel." It was Ginsberg who surmised that biblical manuscripts may have registered only a *yod* (in our case, *bêt y*-), not the entire word, so that an ancient copyist might have misread the intent. See the article by Ginsberg, "Hosea," in *Encyclopaedia Judaica*, vol. 8, cols. 1010f. For the formula *ʿāḇar bĕrît*, "to transgress the covenant," see Hosea 6:7, and also Jos. 7:15, 23:16, Judg. 2:20, which are Deuteronomistic in tone.

and *mišpāṭ* would, it was hoped, be dispensed faithfully? Ginsberg notes the theme of royal arrogance shared by Deut. 8:12–15, 17:20, and Hosea 13:5–6.

We find in Hosea and Deuteronomy shared themes associated with the monarchy, in addition to distinctive dictional links between the two sources. The structure of Deuteronomy 17 seems almost to be dictated, or conditioned, perhaps, by Hosea's agenda. It begins by condemning an Israelite who worships other gods, and proceeds to ordain a High Court in the central temple, so as to promote justice in the land. It continues to warn of the danger presented by a king who becomes haughty and profligate, and requires kings to study the book of God's teachings diligently.

The prophecies of Hosea prompt us to regard the Deuteronomic restriction of cultic activity to one central sanctuary as part of a larger, more comprehensive program. We must not miss the point of Deuteronomy 12 that the one legitimate *māqôm* for sacrifice and celebration will *not* stand in the royal capital; that its location will *not* be determined either by the monarchy or by any traditional institutions. It will be located where God determines, "in one of your tribal territories." This is Deuteronomy's way of saying that the central temple would be taken out of the hands of the royal administration, and that the High Court would also be independent.

The beautiful oracle preserved in Hosea 14:2–9 affords us a mirror-image of the Hosean critique of northern Israelite society. When Israel repents, and "returns" to the LORD, what will then be its national policy?

Israel will not enter into unwise treaties, nor place its reliance on Assyria. Nor will it rely on chariotry, an allusion to relations with Egypt. Israel will no longer worship idols, but will look to the LORD for help. For His part, the LORD will bless Israel bountifully. The most significant statement comes in v. 2b:

> Say to Him: "You absolve all sinfulness,
> And accept good acts.
> We shall substitute for bulls,
> The [pledge] of our lips!"

In context, this is not, I submit, a suggestion that prayer may replace sacrifice as a mode of worship, as the later Jewish tradition has interpreted this passage, followed by some modern scholars. Rather, the statement emphasizes that a pledge of loyalty to the LORD is more efficacious than sacrificing bulls! Such a pledge might be expressed in the very words of this oracle, the words of vv. 3b–4 and 9. All who are wise and intelligent (*ḥāḵām*, *nāḇôn*) realize that this is what the LORD truly desires from His people. Once again, diction suggests a link between Hosea and Deuteronomy.[9]

---

[9] Note this diction in Gen. 41:33, 39, which represents northern Israelite writing (the work of the Elohist), and in Deuteronomistic sources such as Deut. 4:6, 1 Kings 3:12, Jer. 9:11.

III

Most of Ginsberg's monograph actually deals with the transmission of proto-Deuteronomy into Judah, and with assessing its eventual impact there. Ginsberg's reconstruction of the development of the annual festivals is a major breakthrough in itself. His treatment of the Josianic edicts is incisive. He explains how Hezekiah, in his own time, was motivated by the doctrine of proto-Deuteronomy, and how, in a later generation, Josiah revived this doctrine, and ordered major changes in religious life, adapted to the Judean situation of the late seventh century B.C.E.

The Addenda which Ginsberg provides attest to his magnificent obsession with philology and exegesis, and further elucidate the relationship between the priestly source of the Torah and the Book of Ezekiel.

The purpose of this review essay was to attempt an explanation of Ginsberg's "equations," as I called them at the outset. My understanding of them may differ from what Ginsberg himself had in mind, but I have tried to convey, at least, what one student has learned from his teacher. More study of royal policy as it affected religious life in the northern kingdom of Israel during the eighth century B.C.E. is certainly required. Nevertheless, I am prepared to accept Ginsberg's principal hypothesis: Originally, the program stated in Deuteronomy 12 constituted a response to the situation which obtained in the northern Israel of the mid- to late eighth century B.C.E., before the Assyrian invasion.

A word should be said, in conclusion, about the long-term effects of the restriction of sacred space ordered by Josiah, less than half a century before the final destruction of the First Temple of Jerusalem, an edict ultimately based on the doctrine of proto-Deuteronomy.

To understand the relevance of Josiah's edicts for the Judean exiles in Babylonia, one should read Ezekiel 20 closely. The single, legitimate temple in Jerusalem was relevant to the hope of national restoration to the Land of Israel. An exiled people whose religious fulfillment depended on access to Jerusalem would be less likely to abandon its hope of return!

The Jewish communities of the Diaspora were to establish alternative types of religious institutions, such as synagogues; but with relatively few exceptions, these communities were to consider sacrificial worship improper in the lands of exile. After all, they had been taught that the God of Israel had ordered their ancestors, as they were about to enter Canaan, to limit worship and celebration to the single *māqôm* which He would select as the unique locus of His earthly presence. To Judeans, this meant the site of the Temple in Jerusalem.

Leviticus: Its Literary History and Location in Biblical Literature*

The entire book of Leviticus is most probably composed of priestly literature. Attempts to find traces of the ubiquitous Deuteronomist in Leviticus have been less than convincing, and proceed from the questionable assumption that writers of the Deuteronomistic "school" were the final redactors of Torah literature. It is more likely that priestly writers were the last to contribute to the text of the Torah, and to edit it. We may gather as much from a series of priestly addenda appearing in the final chapters of Deuteronomy. We first encounter the priestly passage in Deut 31:23–30 that introduces Moses' poetic oration, האזינו "Give ear!" (Deut 32:1–43) which, even if not fully priestly, was certainly edited by priests. Then comes a priestly postscript to that very poem, in Deut 32:48–52. Finally, there are the concluding verses of the entire book of Deuteronomy (34:6–12), which bear all the earmarks of priestly diction. This means, in effect, that the task of tracing the formation and redaction of Leviticus is part of the larger endeavor of reconstructing the transmission of priestly writings in the Torah, with a spin-off in the book of Joshua.

Since the beginnings of modern biblical research, the literary history of the Torah has been a subject of controversy between the traditionalists and the modernists within both Christian and Jewish scholarship, as well as among diverse modernists from both confessions, and critical scholars who would not regard themselves as religiously affiliated, at all. The discussion to follow is primarily intended to summarize my own views and methodology, within a publication where others are presenting diverse views. The basic positions taken here have been argued in detail in my publications, with progressive refinements and modifications, and the reader will be directed to the relevant literature in due course. These studies contain extensive bibliographies for reference. The challenge of preparing the present discussion has stimulated some new observations on my part.

The issues involved in tracing the formation of Torah literature ought to be engaged in two complementary ways: (1) Through inner-biblical investigation. This would include the identification of the Pentateuchal "sources," and their alignment in chronological sequence, so as to approximate the dates, or periods of their compilation, and the *Sitz im Leben* of their respective authors. It would

---

* Originally published in Rolf Rendtorff and Robert A. Kugler (eds.), *The Book of Leviticus: Composition and Reception* (VTSup 93; Formation and Interpretation of Old Testament Literature 3; Brill, 2006), pp. 11–23. Reprinted with permission from Brill.

also involve tracing the development of biblical institutions and practices, in the case of priestly literature—the festivals, celebrations, and purifications characteristic of the cult; the roles of the clergy, the nature of sacred space, and much more. (2) Through comparative investigation. This would involve examining comparative evidence bearing on the language, structure, and substantive content of the Torah sources, all of which would help to fix their historical and cultural context. It would also include historical inquiry into the situation of the Israelite-Jewish people at various periods, into its socio-political status and cultural character.

In my view, it is unlikely that inner-biblical evidence alone, as enlightening as it may be, can enable us to reconstruct the formation of priestly literature, in particular. This is because Torah literature has been variously analyzed in terms of its distinctive language and themes, and the relationship of the *Priesterschrift* to the other sources, and there is no clear way to demonstrate the conclusiveness of any one reconstruction over the others. Biblical texts provide no colophons, and efforts to date them can only produce a relative chronology, at best. Ultimately, it is on the basis of comparative evidence that we may succeed in locating this textual material in a more or less definitive historical setting, because such external information, though limited, is available in its original form, and can often be dated, and its provenance identified quite precisely. The argument, based on inner-biblical considerations, as to whether the *Priesterschrift* is pre-exilic or post-exilic, has become stale, and it is time to look to comparative indications for resolution.

Inner-Biblical Considerations

At the present time, source criticism is hardly at the center of biblical research, with major attention being given rather to the study of the Hebrew Bible as literature. In recent years, historicism as a method of biblical study has come under attack by the so-called "minimalists," and the resulting ferment has inevitably affected efforts in the area of source criticism, which shares with historicism the objective of tracing the chronology of the biblical record. The emphasis on literary approaches has also dampened interest in philology and exegesis, directing scholarly focus to larger textual units in the quest for structural insights. It should be conceded that source-criticism had become progressively atomistic, breaking down discrete texts into ever more minute units, and positing numerous sub-sections. At the same time, the beginnings of a synthesis between archaeological discovery and textual interpretation are now clearly visible. This process has a long way to go before producing coherent results, and what is more, the dearth of written records among the archaeological finds from Bible lands severely restricts our ability to relate material culture to texts.

And yet, we should not be too quick to dismiss the importance of source criticism, if this method is pursued intelligently and applied to the literary history of Leviticus, and of priestly literature, as a whole. With penetrating insight, Julius Wellhausen effectively fixed the order of the Torah sources as (1) J and E

(= Jahwist and Elohist), the oldest Torah sources, (2) D (= Deuteronomy), and P (= *Priesterschrift*). He and other scholars of his time were very detailed in their analysis, but for the purposes of the present discussion, it will be sufficient to limit ourselves to the relationship between D and P. Wellhausen correctly understood that the requirements of Leviticus 17, the Prologue to the Holiness Code (= H), were inevitably based on the doctrine of cult centralization put forth in Deuteronomy, chapters 12 and 16. The rule that all sacrifices must be offered at the altar standing at the opening of the Tent of Meeting makes sense only if we assume that the authors of Leviticus 17 were endorsing, in a retrojection of the wilderness period that portrays a tent-like, portable Tabernacle, the Deuteronomic doctrine of cult centralization, in reality aimed at outlawing the many permanent cult installations of ancient Israel.[1] A close reading of Leviticus 17, with its reference to pouring out the blood of hunted animals, leads to the conclusion that it is a veritable reflex of Deuteronomy 12. Wellhausen went much further, however, in stressing that the entire regimen of worship and celebration as prescribed in P was based on the concept of a unique altar and sanctuary. Focusing on the Tabernacle traditions of Exodus 25–Leviticus 9, he notes: "The assumption that worship is restricted to one single centre runs everywhere throughout the entire document."[2]

The more recent studies by H. L. Ginsberg on the harvest festivals of biblical Israel, and on the early transmission of core-Deuteronomy to Judah from northern Israel, serve to corroborate Wellhausen's basic insight.[3] The deferral of the pilgrimage festival of First Fruits to a date seven weeks after the offering of the first sheaf during the Pesaḥ-מצות festival, as ordained in Leviticus 23 (assigned to H, in its primary form), seems surely to be a response to the festival legislation of Deuteronomy 16. Once all sacrificial activity was restricted to a central temple, the long pilgrimage that was required of one if he were to be present at the sacrifice would be most inconvenient at the beginning of the spring, grain harvest. It is this new situation that explains the deferral legislated in Deuteronomy 16, and endorsed by priestly law in Leviticus 23. In Ginsberg's reconstruction, the Deuteronomic movement toward cult centralization, first proposed in northern Israel and encouraged by the prophecies of Hosea, was revived in Judah late in the reign of the heterodox king, Manasseh, and subsequently adopted by Josiah, king of Judah, as a practical program of cultic reform (2 Kings 22–23).

---

[1] J. Wellhausen, *Prolegomena to the History of Ancient Israel* (1878; repr., Cleveland: World Publishing, 1965) 34–38.

[2] Wellhausen, *Prolegomena*, 34.

[3] H. L. Ginsberg, *The Israelian Heritage of Judaism* (New York: Jewish Theological Seminary of America, 1982) 55–83.

In contrast, the Herculean attempt of Yehezkel Kaufmann[4] to reverse the order of the two sources, dating P before D, runs into serious problems, especially if we accept the northern-Israelite hypothesis, according to Ginsberg. The first objection is raised by an analysis of language and diction. It is a curious fact that early attempts, by the likes of S. R. Driver,[5] for instance, to establish the textual limits of the *Priesterschrift* primarily on the basis of distinctive language, have held their ground, and are, with a few minor exceptions, acceptable even today. Notwithstanding all of the refinements in our knowledge of Biblical Hebrew, it remains clear that priestly writings show evidence of lateness relative to the other sources. This can now be argued on a comparative basis, as will be clarified further on. How, then, are we to explain that texts which read so much like post-exilic biblical writings, like Ezra-Nehemiah and Chronicles, are allegedly to be assigned to a relatively early period? Specifically, some have pointed to the reign of Hezekiah, in the late eighth to early seventh centuries B.C.E., who is credited with having attempted to eliminate the local and regional high-places (במות, 2 Kgs 18:3–4, 22). However, the notion that early priestly texts were regarded as being so esoteric as not to be promulgated until a much later period, and then pervasively reformulated in the diction of later writings, is highly questionable.

If the precedence of D is accepted, and if the movement toward cult centralization it propounds was revived in Judah only in the mid-to-late seventh century B.C.E., then the earliest strata of the *Priesterschrift* would have been composed in the near-exilic period, or, as is more likely, subsequent to that time, during the exile or after the waves of return following 538 B.C.E., when the Cyrus edict was issued. When we examine the evidence of Ezekiel, especially of chapters 40–48, on the performance of the Jerusalem cult we are prompted to doubt that the author(s) of Ezekiel had very much of the *Priesterschrift* before them. This issue becomes more poignant when we apply source critical analysis to Ezekiel 40–48, in particular, and find that these chapters contain major interpolations, bringing us well into the exilic period, at the earliest. If we conclude, as we do, that Ezekiel 40–48 preceded the composition of at least most of the *Priesterschrift*, then we are well into the exile, more probably in post-exilic Jerusalem and Judea. Although it is possible that parts of the *Priesterschrift* were composed in Babylonia, it is more likely that such creativity occurred in the restored Jewish community, with the Temple of Jerusalem as its central institution. It has already been noted by many scholars that the daily burnt offering (עלת תמיד) of the evening, ordained in Exodus 29 and Numbers 28–29, is not mentioned in Ezekiel 40–48, or in Kings, for that matter, which knows only one daily burnt offering brought in the morning (2 Kgs 16:15). It is also suggestive

[4] Y. Kaufmann, *The Religion of Israel from Its Beginnings to the Babylonian Exile* (trans. and ed. M. Greenberg; Chicago: University of Chicago Press, 1960).

[5] S. R. Driver, *Introduction to the Literature of the Old Testament* (Edinburgh: T&T Clark, 1894) 118–50.

that the notion of "release" (דרור), employed in Jeremiah 34 with reference to the manumission of slaves when the Chaldeans were at the gates of Jerusalem, becomes in Isa 61:1 a way of expressing the release of the Judeans after fifty years of exile. This could be what lies behind the theme of the Jubilee year so prominent in Leviticus 25 and 27. It is also worth noting that the verb גאל "to redeem, restore," so central to the exilic visions of national return to the homeland in Deutero- (and Trito-)Isaiah (Isa 41:14; 43:1, 14; 44:22–24; 47:4; 48:17, 20; 49:7, 26; 51:10; 54:5, 8; 59:20; 60:16; 62:12; 63:4, 9) is prominent in Leviticus 25, where the subject at hand is redemption of family land lost through default of debt. We must concede, however, that the author of Ezek 46:17, part of a late interpolation in Ezekiel 40–48, who refers to "the year of release" (שנת הדרור) as a known institution relevant to land tenure, may have had Leviticus 25 and 27 before him.[6]

This last caveat leads us directly to a consideration of a rather clear stratification within the *Priesterschrift*, itself, between what has become known as the Holiness Code (= H), and the rest of this source. Generally speaking, the Holiness Code is contained in Leviticus 17–27, minus its accretions, wherein the theme of קדוש "holy" is prominent. Notwithstanding the recent attempts to argue that H is largely redactional, and therefore subsequent to the core of the *Priesterschrift* it is more likely that H represents the primary stratum of the *Priesterschrift*. This can be shown by an analysis of a core section of H, the festival calendar of Leviticus 23. Within that chapter we observe a series of interpolations which significantly alter the character of the rites involved.

Representing H, Leviticus 23 had originally prescribed a sequence of display offerings, beginning with the first sheaf (עמר) of new barley grain brought at some point during the Pesaḥ festival (Lev 23:9–11, 14), and concluding with two further display offerings of new wheat seven Sabbaths later (Lev 23:15–17, 20–22). The mode of display offerings, or of presentation, expressed by the verb הניף "to raise," and the noun תנופה "raised offering," represents an early, typically Near Eastern type of sacrifice. It is this mode which we observe in the offering of first fruits as prescribed in Deuteronomy 26, for instance, where the operative verb is הניח "to set down, present." However, presentation as a mode of sacrifice lost ground in ancient Israel to the burnt altar offering, and to similarly disposed rites, so that even certain display offerings, themselves, were adapted to the ascendant mode. In synch with this development in cultic practice, Lev 23:12–13 and 18–20 were interpolated by a later priestly writer so as to bring the festival rites of Leviticus 23 into conformity with what had become the prevailing pattern, a pattern evident, for example, in the sacrificial prescriptions of Leviticus 1–7. These verses add the requirement of an עלה, and a burnt grain offer-

[6] B. A. Levine, "Late Language in the Priestly Source: Some Literary and Historical Observations," in U. O. Schmelz, P. Glikson, and S. DellaPergola (eds.), *Proceedings of the 8th World Congress of Jewish Studies* (1981) (Jerusalem: Hebrew University, 1983) 69–82.

ing (מנחה) at the beginning of the seven-week period, and of an even more elaborate combination of burnt altar sacrifices, including libations, at the end of that period.[7]

This source-critical analysis argues for the primacy of H in the *Priesterschrift*, showing that the rites as prescribed in H, representing the earlier mode, were adapted to the later mode, which became normal thereafter. When we encounter the קדוש theme in such redactional verses as Lev 11:44–45, at the end of the dietary code, it is likely that we have the work of an even later priestly writer, expressing himself in the idiom of the Holiness Code. In late priestly writings, we note a widespread tendency toward anachronism, and the blending of early and late traditions.

It is important to emphasize that the *Priesterschrift* contains both ritual texts and legislation, on the one hand, and narratives, on the other, and even preserves a poetic, or liturgical excerpt or two (Num 6:24–26, the priestly benediction; Num 10:35–36, the song of the ark). Priestly law and ritual cannot be studied in detachment from priestly narrative. True, the primary reality underlying the priestly Torah texts was undoubtedly the cult, itself, with its sacred spaces, edifices and appurtenances, and its sanctified clergy; its rites of sacrifice, celebration, and purification, and its appointed times—Sabbaths and festivals and other sacred occasions. More generally, priestly law presents a coherent program for the constitution of Israelite-Jewish society in which cult and celebration, and the personnel and institutions pertaining to them, were to play a central role. In turn, this program was sanctioned by a recasting of Israelite origins and early history in the priestly narratives of Genesis and Exodus.

These narratives share the distinctive priestly vocabulary. Thus, Leviticus 25 and 27, in discussing the legalities of land tenure, define the status of land in Canaan as אחזה "acquired land," and the status of the Israelites who possess it as that of גרים ותושבים "resident aliens, tenants." Compare these categories with the priestly narrative of Genesis 23, where we read that Abraham, self-defined as גר ותושב, purchases a grave site as an אחזה. Or, with Genesis 34, an account of negotiations on rights of residence with the Canaanites of Shechem, where the denominative האחז "to acquire the right of אחזה" is used. In Genesis 47 we find similar terminology in recounting Pharaoh's grant of land in Egypt to the clan of Jacob. As a further example, Lev 25:30 stipulates that urban real estate sold under duress may be redeemed only up to a year after the sale, and if not redeemed within that period of time becomes the permanent possession of the purchaser. This legal status is expressed by the verb קום "to become legally valid," an Aramaistic connotation also present in Gen 23:17, where it conveys that Ephron's field and the cave located within it have, indeed, become Abraham's property. Such distinctive diction suggests a purposeful literary program intended to offer

[7] B. A. Levine, *Leviticus* (JPS Torah Commentary; Philadelphia: Jewish Publication Society, 1989) 153–63.

an alternative version of Israelite origins in Canaan to that presented in JE and D.

More can be said about the place of Leviticus, and of the *Priesterschrift* within Torah literature, but the above discussion will suffice to clarify the view that Leviticus is subsequent to core-Deuteronomy, and even to the additions of the Deuteronomist. Within Leviticus, itself, we can distinguish between the Holiness Code, and later priestly ritual and law by tracing the adaptation of certain presentational sacrifices to the ascendant mode of the burnt altar offering.

Comparative Considerations

We ought not to conclude from what has been said up to this point that all of the priestly rites and laws of the Torah were introduced, or originated in late biblical times. Even Wellhausen in his day realized that very ancient practices were preserved in the *Priesterschrift*, itself a product of a later age. We now possess comparative evidence indicating that burnt offerings like the עלה, and sacred meals like the שלמים are known from Ugaritic rituals, dating from the Late Bronze Age, where burnt offerings go by the name of *šrp* and sacred meals by the same name as in the biblical cult, namely, *šlmm*. In the Ebla texts of the late third millennium B.C.E. there is mention of burnt offerings known as *sarapati.*[8] Although such offerings are described in earlier biblical texts, the elaborate ritual structure of Leviticus (and of Numbers), shows substantial development beyond what had been formerly introduced into practice. Whereas it is true that very ancient rites and legal practices often persisted over long periods of time (e.g. the law of release [דרור, Lev 25:10], and that which prohibits irretrievable sale [לצמתת, Lev 25:23]), it is from innovations, not from survivals, that we learn how relatively late certain patterns were.

In some respects, distinctive vocabulary and diction are inner-biblical features, as we have seen. And yet, they also provide comparative evidence on the dating and provenance of the *Priesterschrift*, and of Leviticus, in particular. This is because we now possess extra-biblical evidence on language that can be dated rather closely. Attention has already been called to the nuances of the verb קום "to arise, stand," which, in Aramaic legal parlance of the Persian period, means "to be legally valid, binding." These very nuances predominate in Numbers 30, the chapter on vows, where we also encounter the Aramaic term אסר "binding agreement," now attested in the Aramaic papyri from Wadi Daliyeh of the fourth century B.C.E.[9]

The *Priesterschrift*'s distinctive term for the Israelite community, and for its representative assemblies, namely, עדה (Lev 4:15, 19:2, *et passim*), is attested in

---

[8] B. A. Levine and J.-M. de Tarragon "The King Proclaims the Day: Ugaritic Rites for the Vintage (*KTU* 1.41//1.97)," *RB* 100 (1993) 76–115.

[9] B. A. Levine, *Numbers 21–36* (AB 4A; New York: Doubleday, 2000) 425–41.

the Elephantine Aramaic papyri of the fifth century B.C.E.[10] The unit of three tribes called דגל in Numbers 2 and 10 is identical with Aramaic דגל, דגלא, used to designate the Persian military unit in the Elephantine papyri, a designation also attested at contemporary Saqqara, in Egypt. What is more, it has turned up at Arad, in Aramaic ostraca of the Persian period, which is closer to home.[11]

The significance of such terms as עדה and דגל is much more than linguistic, however. The case of דגל suggests that what is projected in Numbers as the Israelite encampment of the wilderness period is really a mirror-image of the Persian system of military colonies on the borders of the empire. The case of עדה is a bit more subtle. It directs our attention to Persian administration in the Babylonian cities, where the local assembly, called *puḫru*, in Akkadian, exercised considerable power. Now, Hebrew/Aramaic עדה is a semantic equivalent of Akkadian *puḫru*; it may even be a calque of it, for all we know.

Another informative term is Hebrew נשיא, "chieftain," an early tribal office (Exod 22:27), revived and modulated by the priestly writers, beginning with Ezekiel. It, too, leads us to comparative considerations. In Ezra 1:8, Sheshbazzar is called הנשיא ליהודה "the נשיא for Judea." We read that he was given the temple vessels seized by Nebuchadnezzar by the Persian authorities, and, indeed, in Ezra 5:14 we are told that the very same Sheshbazzar was appointed פחה "governor." This equivalence suggests that the same official whom the Persians called פחה, using an Aramaic form of the Akkadian title, *bēl piḫati* "governor," was called נשיא by the Judeans, and that the priestly writers had, in fact, internalized a feature of Persian administration. The title פחה appears frequently in the Aramaic Elephantine papyri, and on Palestinian coins of the Persian period. More recently, it has turned up in the Samaria papyri of the fourth century B.C.E.[12]

This very equation: פחה = נשיא may lie behind the expanded role of the נשיא envisioned in Ezekiel 40–48, and would explain why David, whom God calls עבדי "my servant," is given the title נשיא in Ezek 34:24, 37:25. The political organization of the Persian period may also explain the fact that the Hivite ruler of Shechem is called נשיא הארץ "the governor of the land" in Gen 34:2, within a priestly text, and why the so-called Hittite ruler of Hebron calls Abraham נשיא אלהים "a governor favored by God," in Genesis 23, another priestly text.

Methodologically, it is research into the political, religious, and institutional history of cities and provinces under Persian imperial administration that may ultimately reveal the *Sitz im Leben* of priestly literature. Information similar to what the Aramaic papyri from Persian Egypt provide is to be found in Late-Babylonian sources, and in records from other locations. The central role ascribed to the priesthood and the functions of the Jerusalem temple projected in

---

[10] B. A. Levine, *Leviticus*, 22; *idem*, *Numbers 1–21* (AB 4; New York: Doubleday, 1993) 130–31, 411–13.

[11] Levine, *Numbers 1–21*, 142–50.

[12] *DNWSI*, 904.

Leviticus 25–27 accord well with what is known of Persian administration elsewhere. A give-away of post-exilic provenance is the exceptional provision of Lev 25:47 enjoining clan relatives to redeem land lost through forfeiture to non-Israelites. This would be realistic in the post-exilic period, as it reflects the problems of a mixed population such as existed in Jerusalem and Judea, and the coastal areas during the Persian period. Generally, there is much in common between Leviticus 25 and 27 and Nehemiah 5, a chronicle of life under Persian administration. The comparative approach to the literary history of the *Priesterschrift* is only in its beginnings, and will undoubtedly benefit greatly from recent interest in the history of the Persian Empire. In summary, comparative indications, when combined with inner-biblical considerations point to the Persian period as a time of priestly creativity in law, ritual and narrative.

The Composition of Leviticus and its Location

Once we acknowledge that the Holiness Code (H), contained within Leviticus 17–27, is the primary stratum of Leviticus we may proceed to an internal analysis of this major section of the book. Allowing for the usual prescriptive introductions and summary postscripts, we may identify the following as basic components of H: (1) Leviticus 17, the Prologue to the Holiness Code. Although there is evidence of internal redaction in Leviticus 17, as indicated by repetition and shifts in language, the principal thrusts of the chapter, namely, the idea of a single altar, and the emphatic statement of the blood *tabu* express the policy of H on proper sacrifice, a policy impacted by Deuteronomy. (2) Leviticus 18, the rules of incest, which define the limits of the nuclear family, and the prohibition of certain other sexual unions. The provisions of Lev 18:6–23 are undoubtedly primary vis-à-vis Leviticus 20, which restates the subject. (3) Leviticus 19, the basic teachings of the Holiness Code, commanding the Israelites to be קדושים "holy." (4) Leviticus 21, special rules governing the Israelite priesthood, including disqualifying blemishes. (5) Leviticus 22, a collection of regulations affecting the priesthood, including the priestly entitlements and the requirements of ritual purity. Also included are rules regarding sacrificial animals. It is unlikely, however, that all of this material belongs with the Holiness Code. (6) Leviticus 23, a calendar of annual festivals which shows considerable internal redaction. It has already been noted that some of the required sacrificial rites, originally presentational in their performance, have been accommodated to the ascendant mode of burnt altar offerings. We also note two versions of the rites celebrating the autumn harvest festival and the addition of a Sabbath law at the beginning of the chapter. What is singular in Leviticus 23 is the emphasis on the Sabbath as defining the week, a theme expanded in Leviticus 25 and 27, where we read of periods of seven years' duration, even of seven-times-seven. (7) Lev 24:15–23, an early collection of laws resembling the Book of the Covenant of Exodus in its formulation. (8) Leviticus 25, and its supplement, Leviticus 27, laws of land tenure, debt and indenture, the Sabbatical year and the Jubilee, and the funding of the sanctuary.

It would seem that (a) Leviticus 20, (b) unidentified parts of Leviticus 22, (c) certain insertions in Leviticus 23, (d) most of Leviticus 24, and (e) Lev 26:3–46, the Epilogue to the Holiness Code, all represent later strata. What we have in Leviticus 17–27 is, therefore, a blending of H and later strands of P, all expressive of priestly concerns, and addressed for the most part to the Israelite people. It is worth mentioning that Leviticus 24:11–14 provide a narrative introduction to a previously unmentioned law governing blasphemy, as if to say that the relevant law was occasioned by an actual incident. We note the same literary device in Num 9:6–8, and 15:33–36. The only truly prosaic contribution to Leviticus is to be found in the Epilogue to the Holiness Code, Lev 26:3–26. This binary admonition to the people of Israel resembles a blessing-curse section of a treaty, and in some respects recalls the similar admonition of Deuteronomy 28. It reflects the progressive, ever deepening despair of the Judeans in the Babylonian exile, but ends with the divine promise that the God of Israel will remember his covenant with the Patriarchs, and remember the desolate land, as well.[13]

The former part of Leviticus, chapters 1–16, pertains more specifically to the priesthood. An exception is Leviticus 11, the dietary code, which expands on Deuteronomy 14. Although these dietary regulations applied to all Israelites, the priests were the ones charged with instructing the people in their proper observance. For the rest, Leviticus 1–7 outline the various classes of sacrificial rites, whereas Leviticus 8–10 record the installation of the Aaronide priesthood, and the initiation of sacrificial worship in the Tabernacle. Leviticus 8–10 contain narrative elements, and this is particularly true of Leviticus 10. There is an obvious logic to this sequence, whereby the various types of sacrifices are first set forth, and then the initiation of the cult is recorded. Turning to purification, Leviticus 11–16 lay out the role of the priesthood in purifying afflicted Israelites. The priests are to instruct the Israelites in avoiding improper foods (Leviticus 11), and they undertake to maintain the purity of afflicted individual Israelites, and of the Sanctuary itself.

Although Leviticus is located between Exodus and Numbers, there are clear indications that most of the material included in the Tabernacle texts of Exodus 25–40 is subsequent to Leviticus, and that there is a clear link between Exodus 25–40 and the Tabernacle traditions of Numbers 1:1–10:28.

Most probably, it was a basic thrust of the priestly agenda to link the Tabernacle project to the Sinai theophany, and to embed Leviticus in the ongoing chronology of the wilderness period. In that traditional, priestly chronology, all that is recorded in the book of Leviticus took up one month's time. Thus, Exod 40:17 records that the Tabernacle was erected on the first day of the first month of the second year after the Exodus. Leviticus then sets forth the cultic regimen of the Tabernacle, most often called אהל מועד "the Tent of Meeting," and of its clergy. Numbers 1:1 is dated on the first day of the second month of the same year, when the ordering of the Israelite encampment around the Tabernacle

[13] Levine, *Leviticus*, 275–81.

commenced with a census. We may assume that the Leviticus material was encased in a subsequently composed rubric, which began in Exodus 25 and concluded in Num 10:28, when the encampment set forth on the march. In Leviticus there is no movement.

Review Article: The Deir ᶜAlla Plaster Inscriptions*

The Deir ᶜAlla texts record the first attestation of Balaam's name in the pre-exilic period, outside the Bible. The two "Combinations" provided in this volume comprise a myth about a disaster that occurred in the land, and relate how in this situation Balaam, son of Beor, functioned in the role of a diviner. A new edition of both of the two "Combinations" is presented here, with translation and commentary. The study concludes with a discussion of major themes in the Deir ᶜAlla texts.[1]

The inscriptions discovered at Deir ᶜAlla in the Jordan Valley by a Dutch expedition in 1967 have now been published in a lavish volume, consisting of three, principal sections: 1) A report on the archeological and historical background of the site by several scholars, including the excavator, H. Franken. 2) A detailed paleographic analysis by G. van der Kooij, and 3) An edition of the inscriptions, with translation, commentary, and general discussion by J. Hoftijzer.

The plaster fragments are in a poor state of preservation, and it did not help matters that the plates were done in color. Black and white would have been preferable. Precise readings are, therefore, difficult to come by. The date of the inscription remains somewhat uncertain, but a date around the end of the eighth or the beginning of the seventh century B.C.E. would appear to be near the mark.

The language of the Deir ᶜAlla inscriptions shows affinities to that of the Zakur, Arslan Tash and Mesha texts. There are clear affinities to Biblical Hebrew as well as Aramaic. Certain conditioned sound-shifts characteristic of Aramaic occur regularly, as do words typical of Aramaic. On the other hand, the *waw*-consecutive is employed with some frequency, and at points, the text reads curiously like Biblical Hebrew. Whether one can call this language Aramaic is really a question of definitions.

Plaster writing is fast emerging as a significant factor in Holy Land archeology; witness the recently discovered plaster inscriptions from Kuntillet ᶜAjrud, a site south of Kadesh Barnea, dating a century or more earlier than the Deir

---

* Originally published in *JAOS* 101 (1981), pp. 195–205. Reprinted with permission from the American Oriental Society.

[1] This is a review article of: *Aramaic Texts from Deir ᶜAlla*, ed. by J. Hoftijzer and G. van der Kooij, with contributions by V. R. Mehra, J. Voskuil, J. A. Mosk; preface by A. A. H. de Boer, Leiden, 1976. Pp. 324 and plates.

ʿAlla inscriptions.[2] Both discoveries lend realism to the commandment of Deuteronomy 27:2f., and suggest that it would be practical to look for additional plaster inscriptions in the arid climates of the Negev, Aravah, Sinai, and Dead Sea regions.

A. Caquot and A. Lemaire have restudied the inscriptions, and have provided valuable new readings.[3] I am also indebted to P. Kyle McCarter for providing me with a manuscript of his forthcoming study covering a part of the inscriptions, in advance of publication.[4] Jo Ann Carlton has afforded me the benefit of her examination of the texts, thus clarifying certain doubtful readings and interpretations.[5]

The editors have provided us with two major Combinations and with numerous fragments. The Combinations were pieced together from fragments that had fallen to the ground, and it seems that the fragments which have become the first Combination were found some distance from those which comprise the second. Exactly how these two Combinations relate to each other is not certain, therefore, and this question is especially important for the interpretation of the second Combination. Anticipating the commentary and discussion to follow, it might be helpful at this point to present an opening statement, conveying my basic understanding of the two Combinations.

Combination I relates that Balaam, son of Beor, is visited at night by gods, who communicate to him an ominous message. Balaam gathers his comrades and informs them as follows: certain gods convened a council, and commanded a goddess, whose name is unfortunately not preserved, to cover the heavens with dense cloud, thus producing darkness. Balaam proceeds to interpret this omen by depicting the disaster which it predicts. There will be trouble and distress!

At this point, it is unclear whether the description of the disaster merely continues, or whether a new theme is being introduced. The interpretation proposed here sees an attempt on Balaam's part to free the goddess from subservience to the will of the inimical council. He does this through execrations and other forms of magic. It is logical to assume that Balaam succeeded, and that for this reason his exploits were preserved on the wall of a sanctuary.

As for the identity of the goddess placed under the edict, the only clue is the composite divine name *šgr wʿštr*, occurring near the end of Combination I; and

---

[2] See Z. Meshel, C. Meyers, "The Name of God in the Wilderness of Zin," *Biblical Archeologist* 39 (1976), 6–10.

[3] A. Caquot, A. Lemaire, "Les Textes Arameens de Deir ʿAlla," *Syria* 44 (1977), 189–208. Also see J. A. Fitzmyer, *Catholic Biblical Quarterly* 10 (1978), 93–95.

[4] P. Kyle McCarter, "The Balaam Texts from Deir ʿAllā: The First Combination," *BASOR* 239 (1980), 49–60.

[5] Jo Ann Carlton is completing a PhD dissertation (Harvard University), entitled: "Studies in the Plaster Texts from Tell Deir ʿAlla," and in the course of preparation, personally examined the Deir ʿAlla plaster inscriptions in Amman, Jordan.

that name should also be restored in two places earlier on in the text. This is the goddess about whom Combination I speaks.

The first readable passage in Combination II relates that El built an eternal home, a netherworld. In language reminiscent of the Sheol literature of the Bible and of Mesopotamian myths of the netherworld; we read of kings, of eternal repose, and of the moaning of the dead. Someone unnamed is addressed in the second person and referred to in the third person. He is told that his counsel will no longer be sought, and that his powers no longer function. It is probable that this addressee is none other than Balaam himself. This, then, would provide the link between the Combinations: for interfering in the affairs of the gods, Balaam was consigned to Sheol, and condemned.

This study will be organized in the following manner: Each Combination will be presented in transcription and translation, in a plotted format, designed to place the phrasing in clear perspective, and to position the *lacunae*.[6] Each combination will be followed by a running commentary. The study will then conclude with a discussion of certain major themes relevant to the interpretation of the Deir ʿAlla texts.

COMBINATION I *Transcription.*	COMBINATION I *Translation.*
1) *[zh s]ṗṙ [blʿ]ṁ [br bʿ]r.*	1) [This is the inscrip]tion of [Bala]am [son of Be]or.
2) *ʾš. hzh. ʾlhn. hʾ*	2) He was a divine seer.
3) *wyʾtw. ʾlwh. ʾlhn. blylḣ.*	3) And the gods came to him at night,
4) *[/]. / [2]kmṧʾ ʾl.*	4) [*And they spoke to*] him according to the vision of El,
5) *ẇyʾmrw. /[blʿ]m. br bʿr.*	5) And they said to [Bala]am, son of Beor:
6) *kh ypʿl [ ]ʾ. ʾḥrʾh.*	6) "This will the [ ] do in the future.
7) *ʾš. lr[ʾh š]ṁʿt. / [3]*	7) No man has s[een what you have he]ard,"
8) *wyqm. blʿm. mn. mḥr*[7]	8) And Balaam arose on the morrow,
9) *[ ]ṫ . ymṅ. [ ]h.*	9) [ ]? days [ ].
10) *wlyṁ [ ]*	10) And on the [ ] day [ ].
11) *wbk /[4]h. ybkh.*	11) And he truly wept!
12) *wyʿl . ʿmh. ʾlẇh.*	12) And his people came into him,
13) *[wyʾmrw] l̇blʿm br bʿr*	13) [And they said] to Balaam, son of Beor:

[6] In the transcription, a slash (/), followed by a bracketed number, in the upper register [ ] indicates the line divisions, as amended by Caquot-Lemaire. (See note 7). Word-dividers will appear in the transcription only when legible, initially, and will not be inserted in restorations. Translations of biblical passages are the responsibility of this author. A dot above a transcribed letter (ẋ) indicates an uncertain, or unclear reading.

[7] The text of lines 8–18 (lines 3–5 in Caquot-Lemaire) have been reconstructed according to the suggestion by Caquot-Lemaire that fragments VIII:d and XII:c belong in this place. Jo Ann Carlton corroborated the location of these fragments, and McCarter also adopted this insertion. Caquot-Lemaire have also adopted a juxtaposition here which yields better sense, but which results in having a total of 17, instead of 19 lines in Combination I.

14) *lm.tṣm.* [*wlm*] *tbkh.*	14) "Why do you fast? Why do you weep?"
15) *wyʾ* / [5]*mr. lhn.*	15) And he said to them:
16) *š*[*b*]*w. ʾḥwkm. mh. .šḋ*[*yn pʿlw*]	16) "Be seated, and I will show you what the Sha[dday-gods have done]
17) *wlkw. rʾw. pʿl̇t. ʾl*[*h*]*n.*	17) And go, behold the workings of the gods!
18) *ʾl*[*h*]*n ʾtyḥdw.* / [6]	18) The gods have joined forces,
19) *wnṣbw. šdyn. mwʿd.*	19) And the Shadday-gods have established a council.
20) *wʾ* [*m*]*rw. lš*[*gr wʿštr*]	20) And they have said to Sha[gar-Weʿishtar]:
21) *tpry. skry. šmyn. bʿb*	21) 'Sew up, cover up the heavens with dense cloud,
22) *ky. šm. ḥšk. wʾl. n*/[7]*gh.*	22) So that darkness, and no brilliance will be there;
23) *ʿlm. wʾl sṁṙ*	23) Concealment, and not bristling light(?)
24) *ky.thby. ḥt*	24) That you may instill dread,
25) [*wr*]*b. ḥšk.*	25) [and much] darkness.
26) *wʾl. thgy. ʿd. ʿlm.*	26) And never raise your voice again!'
27) *ky. ss ʿgr. ḥr* / [8]*pt. ṅšr.*	27) For the swift [and] crane will shriek insult to the eagle,
28) *wql̇. rḥṁn. yʿnh.*	28) And the voice of vultures will resound.
29) [ ]*ny*	29) [ ]
30) *nḥṣ. wṣṙh.*	30) Distress and trouble!
31) *ʾprḥy. ʾnph. drr. nšrt.* /	31) The chicks of the heron, sparrow and cluster of eagles,
32) [9]*ywn. wṣpr.* [ ]*yn. ẇ*[	32) Pigeons and birds of [ ], [ ] and [ ]
33) [ ] *mṭh*	33) [ ] a rod,
34) *bʾšr. rḥln. yybl. ḥṭr.*	34) Where there are ewes, there shall be brought the staff.
35) *ʾrṅbn. ʾk̇l̇w.* /[10][*y*]*ḥḋ*	35) Hares—feed together!
36) *ḥpš*[*y*]	36) Free[ly]
37) [ ] *štyw. ḥmr. wqbʿn.*	37) [ ] drink, asses and hyenas!
38) *šmʿw. mwsr. gry. š*/[11][*gr wʿštr*]	38) Hear the admonition, adversaries of Sha[gar-Weʿishtar]!
39) [ ]	39) [ ]
40) *lḥkmn. yqḥk. wʿnyh.*	40) To skilled diviners you shall be taken, and an oracle,
41) *rgḥt. mr. wk̇hnh.* /	41) A perfumer of myrrh, and a priestess;
42) [12][ ]	42) [ ]
43) [ ] *l̇ṅšʾ. ʾzr. qrn.*	43) [ ]. to one wearing a belt of foes(?)
44) *ḥšb. ḥšb. wḥšḃ.*	44) One augurer after another, and yet another!
45) *ḥ* /[13][*šb*]	45) One augurer[ ]
46) [ ]	46) [ ]
47) *ẇšmʿw. ḥršṅ. mn. ṙḥq.*/	47) And give heed to incantations from afar!
48) [14][ ]	48) [ ]
49) [ ]	49) [ ]
50) *ẇkl . ḥzw. qqn.*	50) And all beheld acts of constraint.
51) *šgr. wʿštr. l* /[15][ ]	51) Shagar Weʿishtar did not[ ].
52) [ ]	52) [ ]
53) [ ] *lnmr. ḥnyṣ.*	53) The piglet [*drove out*?] the leopard,
54) *hqrqt. ḃn*/ [16][ ]	54) The [ ] caused the young of the [ ] to flee,

55) [ ] *mšn. ʾżṙn.*	55) [ ]two girded warriors(?)
56) *wʿyn* [ ]	56) And [ ]beheld [ ]
(Final line unpreserved)	

Commentary, Combination I:

Lines 1–8: This opening section provides a title, characterizes Balaam as a seer, and reports on the predictive communication he received from the gods. In line 1, the restoration echoes frequent superscriptions in the Hebrew Bible, and contemporary epigraphy. In line 2, consonantal *hʾ* is taken as a demonstrative, ending a clause. The fact, noted by McCarter, that the red ink, used in certain parts of the inscriptions for magical effect, terminates after the word *ʾlhn* must be weighed against syntax. Cf. *ʾîš ṣārûʿa hûʾ* "A leprous person is he" (Lev. 13:44), or: *ʾîš hāʾelôhîm hûʾ* "The man of God is he" (1 Kings 13:26, and cf. Zech. 13:5).[8] The spelling *ʾlwh* is a variant of *ʿlwh*, reflecting the interplay of *ʿal* and *ʾel* in certain strata of Hebrew and Aramaic.

Line 4: The reading: *kmšʾ* "according to the vision of -" resulted from a suggestion by É. Puech (by oral communication), that the reading: *kml*[*y*]*ʾ ʾl* "according to these words," was difficult. He doubted the *Lamed*, and saw no room on the plaster for an additional letter, before the final *ʾaleph*. If correct, our reading would eliminate the unique attestation, presumably, of the Aramaistic determined plural affix: *-yʾ*, in the Deir ʿAlla inscriptions.

Line 6 is difficult because of the *lacuna* after the word *ypʿl*. Caquot-Lemaire, followed by McCarter, did better than Hoftijzer in translating: "*postérité*" (cf. Hebrew *hālʾāh* "farther"). In line 7, prefixed *lamed* connotes negation, its frequent function in these texts. McCarter's restoration: *šm*]*ʿt* is persuasive. The sense is that no man has seen the like of what is to happen. This is a frequent hyperbole in biblical literature.[9] The characterization of Balaam as *ḥzh*, Hebrew *ḥôzeh*, is significant, since he is never explicitly given that title in the Bible.

Lines 9–17: This section relates what happened after Balaam was visited by the gods. Amid weeping and fasting, he assembles his comrades, and discloses to them what the gods had informed him. McCarter, noting that the *qoph* of presumed *ʾlqh* (thus Hoftijzer, Caquot-Lemaire) was written oddly, wisely abandoned the idea that a personal name occurred here. Although one would expect: *wyʿl ʾlwh ʿmh* instead of: *wyʿl ʿmh ʾlwh*, this interpretation has the virtue of biblical associations. Num 22:5 mentions Balaam's *ʿamm* "kinsmen."

In line 16, we are to read: *šd*[*yn* (McCarter). Just as in lines 18–19 the actors are *šdyn* and *ʾlhn*, the same is true here. At the end of line 16, I accept McCarter's restoration: [*pʿlw*]. This is reminiscent of Num. 23:23: *mah pāʿal ʾēl* "What El (= God) plans to do."

What does consonantal *šdyn* mean? Given the orthography of the Deir ʿAlla inscriptions, there are two possibilities: a) A dual of *šēd* "demon," parallel with *ʾelôhîm* in Deut.

---

[8] The beginning of the inscription is written in red ink, up to and including the word *ʾlhn*, in line 2. In lines 2–3, the words: *ypʿl* [ ]*ʾ ʾš lr*[*ʾh š*]*mʿt* are, as far as they are legible, also written in red. Cf. Combination II, line 47, and the first words in line 48. Because of the poor state of preservation, I doubt if one can draw precise interpretive conclusions from what remains visible of the red ink.

[9] Cf. Isa. 64:3, 66:8, and also Deut. 4:32–33, 7:19, 10:21, etc.

32:17, or b) A pluralized form, previously unattested, of *šadday*, whatever that word means. A preference for the latter is indicated by references to *šadday* in the biblical oracles (Num. 24:4, 16). It is clear, in either case, that inimical beings are intended.[10]

Lines 18–26: This section contains the substance of the communication transmitted by Balaam. A syntactic observation is in place here: Previous treatments have consistently assumed that consonantal *ky*, following the words *ʿb* (line 21) and *smr* (line 23) represents the 2nd pronominal suffix, feminine, on the Aramaic model. Hence, one would translate: "With *your* dense cloud," etc. The fact that there are no word-dividers between *ʿb* and *ky*, or *smr* and *ky* does not require us to join *ky* to the letters which precede it. The feminine suffix *-ky* is nowhere else attested in these inscriptions, as preserved. On the other hand, conjunctive *ky* is clearly attested in line 27, where it begins a clause. I prefer, therefore, to see a stylistic pattern:

Line 22: *ky šm ḥšk wʾl ngh*
Line 24: *ky thby ḥt*
Line 27: *ky ss ʿgr ḥrpt nšr*

As will be shown, this analysis seriously affects the interpretation of line 40.

To return to the contents of this section, *nṣbw* in line 19 is better taken as a *Pael*. There is a sequence of action and result: the gods first join forces, and then convene a council. In line 21, the verb *s-k-r* connotes the shutting off of the wells of the deep in Gen. 8:20. On the interplay of *ʿb* "dense cloud," *ḥšk* "darkness," and *ngh* "brilliance," see 2 Sam. 22:12–13 // Ps. 18:12–13, Isa. 60:19.

In line 23, both key words are badly preserved. McCarter ingeniously suggests rendering *smr* "bristling light." This fits the context, and the contrasting parallelism of lines 22–23, although this meaning is not actually attested. If correct, the reading *ʿlm* suggests Hebrew *ʿălûm* "hidden [deeds]" in Ps. 90:3, and *Niphal* forms connoting concealment. In line 24, *ḥt* is best taken as "dread" (Gen. 9:2, Job 41:25).[11] The idiom "to instill dread," with the equivalent Hebrew verb *n-t-n* also occurs (Exod. 26:17, 32:23–32, *passim*). In line 26, consonantal *hgh* means: "to utter a sound," rather than: "to remove" (McCarter). That vocable actually means: "to extract," as in Prov. 25:4.[12]

The central problem in this section is identifying the goddess addressed in line 20, and later referred to in line 38. In both places, we can read the first letter of the name as *shin*. Now, the full name is legible in line 51: *šgr wʿštr*. Methodologically, this should be

---

[10] Hoftijzer's reference to a pluralized form, *šdyn* in the *Kethib* of Job 19:29 is probably incorrect. The passage is difficult to start with. Tur-Sinai reads: *šādîn* "acts of destruction," which fits the immediate context. (See N. H. Tur-Sinai, *The Book of Job*, Jerusalem, 1957, 307–308). A pluralized form is possible, of course, probably on the model of plural gentilics in Aramaic. Cf. the *Qere yehûdāyîn* in Dan. 3:12. The hypostasis of *šadday*, whatever it means, is suggested by several biblical theophoric names: *ʿammîšadday* 1:12, etc.); *ṣûrîšadday* (Num. 1:6, etc.); and *šedêʾur* Num. 1:5, etc.).

[11] Both McCarter and Carlton read *ʿlm*, but interpret this word as *ʿôlām*/*ʿālam* "forever," or the like.

[12] In Biblical Hebrew, the verb *hāgāh* sometimes conveys an adverse utterance (Isa. 59:3, Ps. 2:1, 38:13, Job 27:4, Prov. 24:2). If this root is related to nominal *hagîg*, a geminate form (Ps. 5:2, 39:4), then a cognate relationship with Akkadian *agāgu* "to be angry" is also possible (See *CAD A*/I, 139, s.v. *agāgu*).

the cue for any reconstructions in the earlier lines of the inscription. As Hoftijzer notes, this composite divine name evokes the biblical cliché: *šegar ʾalāpêkā weʿašterôt ṣôʾnekā* "the issue of your herds and the fertility of your flocks" (Deut. 7:13, 28:4, 18, 51, and cf. Exod. 13:12). Hoftijzer calls attention to the Punic personal name: *ʿbdšgr* "worshipper of Shagar".[13] This attests the hypostasis of *šgr*. In the Deuteronomic cliché we observe the de-hypostasis of *ʿaštôret* to yield the more generalized meaning: "fertility," whereas here we see the hypostasis of *šqr*. The masculinized form *ʿštr* is admittedly surprising in a West Semitic inscription, but it is impossible that the male aspect, Moabite *ʿštr*, Ugaritic *ʿṯtr*, etc., is intended, since the terms of reference are clearly feminine. What we have is a goddess whose composite name synthesizes an astral aspect with one of fertility on earth.

Lines 27–37: In this section, it is Balaam who is speaking. He now continues his oration by describing what will happen when the heavens are covered by dense clouds. In effect, he interprets the omen, projecting a scene of alarm and disruption. The overall context is established by the words *nḥṣ wṣrh* "distress and trouble," in line 30. Eagles and vultures, and birds making shrill sounds, are employed as a motif for dramatizing the devastation to come.

In line 27, it is probable that two birds, *ss* (Hebrew *sûs* or *sîs*) "swift" and *ʿgr* (Hebrew *ʿāgûr*) "crane" are intended, despite the absence of conjunctive *waw* (cf. Ps. 38:4). This allows us to take *ḥrpt* as a plural participle, feminine, Hebrew: *ḥôrepôt*. These two birds are known for the shrill sounds they make in flight (Isa. 38:14, Jer. 8:7). The *Qal* of *ḥ-r-p* connotes "reviling" in Ps. 119:42, Prov. 27:11, and we have the interplay of *ḥārap* and *ʿānāh* "to respond," as we have here. The portrayal is actually realistic. Birds shriek at each other, which, in human perception, might mean defiance. The gathering of vultures signals imminent death. This is all a projection of what is to come, not a report on what had already occurred, or is occurring.

Line 29 undoubtedly contained the names of more birds. There is a certain logic in seeking the names of still more birds or animals in line 30, but the fact is that no one had identified birds named *nḥṣ* or *ṣrh*. The obvious meaning should not be resisted. Lines 31–34 are problematic because of the lacuna in line 33, where a verb, parallel in meaning to *y-b-l* occurred, along with something parallel to *rḥln* "ewes." In any event, we have the parallelism of *mṭh* and *ḥṭr* "rod, staff." The form *yybl* would seem to be conjugated on the Phoenician model (*Yiphil*, 3rd masc. sing. imperfect, with stative force).

Hoftijzer was on the right track in speaking of the rod of punishment, known from biblical imagery, but he was perhaps overly theological. Here, the text projects the beating and scattering of herds and flocks as a wrathful act of the gods, as well as the abandonment of grazing areas to wild animals. This is what the omen means.

In line 35, I restore [*y*]*ḥd*. The sense of line 36f. is that wild animals will eat and drink freely where once there was grazing. Consonantal *ḥpš*[*y* yields an adverbial sense, cf. Hebrew *ḥopšî*.

Lines 38–56: Line 38 is best understood as introducing a new theme: Balaam begins his attempt to free Shagar-Weʿishtar from the power of the council. He calls out to the gods.

---

[13] Hoftijzer (page 273, note 5) cites F. L. Benz, *Personal Names in the Phoenician and Punic Inscriptions*, Rome, 1972, 163. I am indebted to R. Tomback for collating the relevant texts from Carthage. Hoftijzer's reference to a Ugaritic deity *šgr* is, however, uncertain. (See J.-M. de Tarragon, *Le Culte à Ugarit*, Paris, 1980, 172.)

They are *gry š[gr wʿštr]* "the adversaries of Shagar-Weʿishtar." Nominal *gār*, from the root *g-r-h* is cognate to Akkadian *gērû* (or *gārû*) "enemy,"[14] (Hoftijzer).

In line 40, the verbal form *yqḥk* has been consistently understood as a reflex of *ḍḥk* "to laugh, mock." The idea is that a reversal, or overturning of the normal order has occurred, whereby a poor woman (*ʿnyh*) mocks wise men, just as small birds revile ferocious vultures. I doubt, however, whether there is anything abnormal about small birds shrieking at large ones! The form *yqḥk* could derive from the verb *l-q-ḥ* (see Combination II, line 31). If one accepts the analysis of the particle *ky* proposed above (see comments to lines 18–26), to the effect that it is not the feminine pronominal suffix, then there is no reason why *ygḥk* here cannot be rendered: "He/One shall take you (feminine)," the object being the goddess, Shagar-Weʿishtar, herself. In the effort to free her, Balaam takes the goddess to skilled magical practitioners, a list of which immediately follows: *khnh* "priestess," *rqḥt mr* "a perfumer of myrrh," and *ʿnyh* "an oracle." Here, Hoftijzer's discussion is most informative. Referring to A. Malamat, he cites Akkadian *āpilu*, feminine *āpiltu*, from the verb *apālu* "to respond," the semantic equivalent of Hebrew *ʿānāh.*[15]

This leaves the term *ḥkmn*, and further on, the term *ḥšb*. In Isa. 3:3, *ḥakam ḥarāšîm* "one skilled in incantations," is parallel to *nebôn laḥaš* "one expert in spells." In Exod. 7:11, *ḥakāmîm* is synonymous with *mekaššepîm* "sorcerers," and in Gen. 41:8 with *ḥarṭummîm* "magicians." (Also cf. Isa. 19:11, and see comments to line 47, below). I maintain the *ḥšb* (= Hebrew *ḥošēb*) also designates a magical practitioner. Perhaps "augurer" is appropriate. The basic connotation would be to calculate omens.[16] The sequence of three may have distributive force. Cf. *ʾeben wāʾeben, ʾêpāh wĕʾêpāh* "two kinds of weights; two kinds of measures."

In summary: The goddess is taken to various magical practitioners. In line 42, *nšʾ ʾzr* is the last in the list, translated: "girded warrior." Consonantal *qrn* is problematic. It could mean "horn," which suggests the horned crowns in representations of divine figures. It is unlikely, however, that *ʾzr* means crown, although a relationship to *zēr* "diadem" is possible. The alternative, adopted in the translation, is to take *qrn* as deriving from *ḍ-r-r*, in Hebrew *ṣ-r-r*, and in Aramaic as *ʿ-r-r*, yielding Deir ʿAlla *q-r-r*. Thus, *qrn* would be a plural participle, masculine. The sense would be: "foes," (cf. Dan. 4:16).

In line 47 the meaning "deaf persons" for *ḥršn* is rejected in favor of *ḥarāšîn* "incantations" (Isa. 3:3). In later Aramaic texts, *ḥarš-* is a frequent term for "incantation."[17] In line 50–51f., we are told, at least implicitly, that Balaam's efforts were effective. In line 51, prefixed *lamed*, just before the *lacuna*, connotes negation. Shagar-Weʿishtar "did not" do something. Therefore, line 49 refers to the unfortunate effects (*qqn*) of Balaam's actions on the adversaries of the goddess, and not to anything she, herself, suffered.

---

[14] See *CAD G*, 62f., s.v. *gērû* (substantive).

[15] See Hoftijzer (page 212, and notes 79–82), and *CAD A*/II, 155f., s.v. *apālu* A, especially mng. 2, and *ibid.*, 170, s.v. *āpilu*, mng. 1. Also see Micah 3:7: *maʿanēh ʾelôhîm* "a divine response." (Also cf. 1 Kings 18:24f., Prov. 16:1).

[16] It may be relevant that Akkadian *šutābulu*, a form of the verb *abālu* "to bring," means "to think, ponder," but also: "to mix ingredients, calculate (ominous features)." See *CAD A*/I, 27, s.v. *abālu* A, mng. 10, *šutābulu.*

[17] See J. Levy, *Wörterbuch über die Talmudim und Midraschim*, Darmstadt, 1963, 2:119 s.v. *ḥārāš*, and *ḥaršāʾ*, and cf. Syriac *ḥeraš* and related forms in *LS* 259. Possibly cf. Akkadian *ḫarāšu* A, mng. 2 in *CAD Ḫ*, 95.

As a result of victory over the council of the gods, the devastation that had come over the land was terminated, and salutary conditions restored. This is the force of what has been preserved in lines 53–54. The wild animals are driven out of the grazing areas by domesticated animals, like the piglet. This is a reversal: in the portrayal of panic and alarm, domesticated animals are scattered. Now, the wild animals are driven out. Consonantal *hqrqt* is the 3rd feminine singular, perfect, of the *Haphel*. Line 55 preserves only two words: *mšn ʾzrn* (Hebrew *mišnēh ʾēzôrîn*), "double belt, two belts," or: "two girded warriors," referring to *nšʾ ʾzr* "girded warrior," in line 43, above. In line 56, the verb *ʿ-y-n* is a denominative from *ʿayin*, meaning: "to see," frequent in Ugaritic. The *hapax ʿôyēn* (*Qere*) in 1 Sam. 18:9 means: "to regard in an angry, or inimical manner."

COMBINATION II *Transcription*	COMBINATION II *Translation*
(The transcription begins with what has been restored as the final word in line 5)	
1) [*ddn*] / [6]*yrwy. ʾl.*	1) El [satisfies] himself with lovemaking.
2) *wyʿbd ʾl. byt. ʿlmn.*	2) And El built an eternal home.
3) by[t]	3) A house [ ],
4) [byt] /	4) [A house]
5) [7]*byt. lyʿl. hlk.*	5) A house where no traveler enters,
6) *wlyʿl. ḥtn. šm.*	6) Nor does a bridegroom enter there.
7) [byt ?]	7) [A house]
8) [ ]	8) [ ]
9) [ ] / [8] *rmh. mn. gdš.*	9) [ ] as wormrot from a grassy grave.
10) *mn. pḥzy. bny. ʾš.*	10) From the reckless affairs of men,
11) *wrnn. šqy.* [*bny ʾdm*?]	11) And from the lustful desires [of people]
12) [ ] / [9]*ly*	12) [ ] to me?
13) *hlʿṣh. bk. lytʿs.*	13) If it is for counsel, no one will consult you!
14) *ʾw lmlkh. lytmlk.*	14) Or for his advice, no one will take counsel!
15) *yšbr* [ ]	15) He breaks ?[
16) [ ] /	16) [ ]
17) [10][*m*]*n. ṁšk̇b.mtksn. lbš*	17) From the bed, they cover themselves with a wrap.
18) *ḥd ḣn. tšnʾn.*	18) One—behold, you hate him! ?
19) *yʾnš. hn. t*[ ]	19) He will become mortally ill, behold, you [ ]
20)[ ]	20) [ ]
21)[ ] /[11] *ʾšṁ*	21) [ ] punishment.
22) [*rmh*] *tḥt. rʾšk.*	22) [And wormrot] under you head.
23) *tšk̇b. mškby. ʿlmyk.*	23) You shall lie on your eternal bed,
24) *lḥlq. l*[ ]	24) To pass away to [ ]
25) [ ] /	25) [ ]
26) [12] *ʾḋ*[ ]*k* [ ]*ṭr kl*[ ]h blbbm	26) [ ] all [ ] in their heart.
27) *nʾnḥ. nqr. blbḃh.*	27) The corpse moans in his heart!
28) *nʾnḥ* [ ]	28) He moans [ ]
29) [ ] / [13]*bt*	29) [ ] a daughter(?)
30) *šmh. mlkn. yḥzw.* [*l*]*ḃl̇*[*ʿm*?]	30) There, kings shall behold Bal[aam?].
31) *lyš. bm yqḥ. mwt. ʿl. rḥm.*	31) There is no compassion when Death seizes an infant!

32) *wʿl* [ ]	32) And an infant [ ]
33) [14]*ʿl* [ ] *r*[ ]*ṫ*	33) An infant [ ]
34) *šmh kb*[ ]*h yk̇ṅ.*	34) There [ ] shall endure.
35) *lbb. nqr. šhh.*	35) The heart of the corpse is desolate,
36) *ky. ʾth. l*[*šʾl*]	36) As he approaches [Sheol].
37) [ ] /	37) [ ]
38) [15]*lqṣh. š*[*ʾl*]*ʾh*	38) To the edge of She[ol].
39) *wzl. ṁġdr. ṭš*[ ]	39) And the shadow of the hedge.
40) *šʾlt. mlk. ssh.*	40) The quest of a king becomes his "moth,"
41) *wš*[*ʾ*]*l*[*t*]	41) And the quest of [ ]
42) [ ] / [16] *h*	42) [ ]
43) [ ] *ẇ* [ ] *ḥzn.*	43) [ ] and [ ] seers.
44) *rḥq*[*t*] *mk. šʾltk.*	44) Your quest has become distant from you!
45) *lm* [ ]	45) Why[ ]
46) [ ] /	46) [ ]
47) [17] *ldʿt. spr. dbr. lʿmḣ.*	47) To know how to deliver an oracle to his people.
48) *ʿl. lšn. lk. nšpṭ.*	48) You have been condemned for what you have said,
49) *wmlqb. ʾmr.*	49) And banned from pronouncing words of execration.
(The last four lines are too fragmentary for plotting).	

Commentary, Combination II:

The plotted transcription begins at the end of line 5, according to Hoftijzer's original delineation. There are some comments to be made about lines 3–5, which read as follows:

> 03) *rn. ʾkl* [
> 04) *ʿlmh. rwy. ddn. k* [
> 05) *lh. lm nqr. wmdr. kl. rṭb.* [

The parallelism of *ʾkl* "to eat," and *rwy* "to be sated" is attested in Jer. 46:10. The idiom *rwy ddn*, Hebrew *rāwāh dôdîm* "to satisfy one's self with lovemaking" occurs in Prov. 7:18. The first word in line 04 might be *ʿalmāh* "young woman," the object of the lovemaking. The morphology of *rwy* is Aramaic, to be vocalized *rewê*, and represents either a 3rd perfect masculine singular, or an imperative. In line 1 of the plotted format, *yirwê* is 3rd masculine singular, imperfect. Both forms are *Qal*/*Peal*.

In line 05, above, the word *nqr* means "corpse." It is a key word in Combination II, to be discussed in the comments to lines 26–39. The words: *wmdr kl rṭb*, if the reading is correct, might be rendered: "a slope that was all damp." The noun *mdr* relates to Late Aramaic *midrāʾ* to Late Hebrew *midrôn* meaning "slope," and probably to Akkadian *midru.*[18] This fits in with the descriptions of the grave later on in this combination.

We can now turn to the plotted format.

Lines 1–11: In line 2, the term *byt ʿlmn* occurs as *bêt ʿôlām* in Eccl. 12:5, and frequently in post-biblical Jewish literature, as noted extensively by Hoftijzer.[19] He need not have

---

[18] See Levy, *op. cit.*, 3:33, s.v. *midrāʾ*, and *midrôn*, and *CAD M*/II, 48, s.v. *midru* C.

[19] See E. Ben-Yehudah, *Dictionary and Thesaurus of the Hebrew Language* (Hebrew), New York, 1960, 1:36, s.v. *bayit*.

concluded, however, that a plural, i.e. "cemeteries." was intended. Conceptually, what is plural is *ᶜlmn*, not *byt*. Plural *ᶜlmn* projects more than one *ᶜôlām*, or aeon of time. It spans eternity, all the aeons. This also applies to the plural *ᶜlmyk* "your eternity," in line 23. Hoftijzer notes that this may be the first occurrence on record of the term *byt ᶜlmn*.

Stylistically, we have in lines 3–5, and possibly for several more lines, a series of characterizations, each beginning with the word *byt* "a house." Cf. Deut. 8:7–9, where, in a series of similar characterizations of Canaan, each clause begins with the word *ʾereṣ* "land" (also cf. Deut. 11:11–12). In lines 5–6, Hebrew *hēlek* in the sense of "traveler" is a *hapax* in 1 Sam. 12:4. In line 9, *rmh* "wormrot" is a word often associated with the grave. The meaning of *gdš* (Hebrew *gādîš*) as "grave" was established by Hoftijzer, who noted the parallelism of *gādîš* and *qebārôt* "graves" in Job 21:32, cf., also, Arabic *jadaṯun* "grave".

In lines 10–11f., I must depart from previous attempts to make sense out of *pḥzy bny ʾš*, and the incomplete *šqy* [. This couplet describes conditions in the netherworld. Hebrew *paḥaz* means "recklessness, instability", in Gen. 49:4. (Cf. participial *pôḥēz* "shiftless" in Jud. 9:4, Zeph. 3:4, as well as abstract *paḥazût* in Job. 23:32.) Curiously, a synonymous sense is conveyed by *šôqê hāʾîš* "the lustful desires of men" (Ps. 147:10). Hebrew *šôq-* is to be related to the nominal form *tešûqāh* "desire" (Gen. 3:16, 4:7, Song 7:11), from the root *š-w-q*. In the netherworld, one is without human passions.

Lines 12(or 13)–15: The plotting is extremely approximate here. It seems that in line 12 or 13 a sub-theme is introduced: The one addressed is told that he has been denied his powers as an advisor (Hoftijzer). The verb *m-l-k* in the *Niphal* of Late Hebrew, and the *Ithpeel* of Aramaic means: "to take counsel."[20] As regards line 15, it is not certain whether the sub-theme of the preceding lines continues, or whether the text reverts to its main subject, a description of the netherworld. Consonantal *yšbr* may derive from *š-b-r* "to break, be broken," or, given the sound-shifts attested at Deir ᶜAlla, it could derive from *ś/s-b-r* "to examine, intend, think, etc" (Neh. 2:13, 15).[21] This would link up with notions of "advice" and "counsel" in the preceding lines.

In line 17, the description of Sheol continues. Here, Caquot-Lemaire elicited better readings. Consonantal *mtksn* is taken as a *Hithpael*. The best that could be done with Caquot-Lemaire's *mšgb* "fort" is to suggest *mškb* "bed." The *gimel*, in their reading, is uncertain, in any case, and in view of the importance of the "bed," and the verb *š-k-b* "to lie" in this text, this suggestion seemed logical. (See below, in lines 22–23).

In lines 18–19, the suggested translation is, of course, highly conjectural. Consonantal *yʾnš*, is related to forms of the verb *ʾ-n-š* "to be mortally ill, wounded" in 2 Sam. 12:5, Jer. 17:9, etc. The *taw* just before the *lacuna* probably represents the 2nd person imperfect preformative of a verbal form. In line 22, the restoration *rmh* "wormrot" is self evident. In line 24, *lhlq* is an infinitival form, with prefixed *lamed*. It is cognate to Akkadian *ḫalāqu* "to pass away, depart." Cf. Hebrew *ḥālaq* in Hos. 10:2: *ḥālaq libbam* "their heart has departed."[22]

Lines 26–39: This section speaks primarily of the corpse, *nqr*. Line 26 is in parallelism with line 27. Caquot-Lemaire correctly relate *nqr* to Hebrew *nēṣer*, but they identified the

[20] See Levy, *op. cit.*, 3:126, s.v. *mālak*, mng. 2.

[21] See Levy, *op. cit.*, 3:470, s.v. *sebar*, mng. 2.

[22] See *CAD Ḫ*, 36, s.v. *ḫalāqu*.

wrong vocable! It is not *nēṣer* "shoot" (Isa. 11:1, 60:21), but *nēṣer* "corpse." Thus, we read in Isa. 14:19: *kenēṣer nitʿāb* "like loathsome carrion," which is parallel to *kepeger mubbās* "like a trampled corpse." In this verse, *nēṣer* is to be related to post-biblical *nēṣel* "putrefying flesh, or blood."[23] It is, after all, the corpse that moans, and is desolate (see below, in line 35f.).

In lines 27–28, we again have the repetition of the same word for emphasis: *nʾnḥ* "He moans." At the end of line 30, Caquot-Lemaire tentatively read: *bl??*. The writing is hardly legible, and no theory of interpretation regarding Combination II should rest on such tentative, albeit tantalizing possibilities. The case for identifying Balaam as the *nqr* "corpse" can be made independently.

Lines 31–34: These lines probably refer to infant mortality. In line 31, the first word is analyzed as: *l* + *yš* "there is not," cf. Hebrew *lôʾ yēš* in Job 9:37, and Aramaic *lāʾ ʾîtay*. Hoftijzer's suggestion that *bm yqḥ* is equivalent to Hebrew *bemô yiqqaḥ* "while he takes, seizes," is plausible. It appears that we have here a personification of Mot, god of death and the netherworld.

Lines 35–39: This section speaks of the anguish of the corpse in Sheol. The verb *š-h-y* is a variant of Hebrew *š-ʾ-h* "to lie waste, be desolate" (Isa. 6:11, Nah. 1:5. etc.).[24] On the strength of line 38, where we have: *lgṣh š*[*ʾl*] "to the edge of Sheol," I have restored *l*[*šʾl*] in line 36, as well. In line 39, the suggestion *mgdr* pictures a fence, or hedge around Sheol. (Cf. Hebrew *gādēr*).

Lines 40–49: This section returns to the theme, introduced in lines 13–14, of the denial of powers to the one addressed. In line 40, *ssh* could mean: "his horse" (Hoftijzer), but, given the context, perhaps *ssh* can be related to the *hapax sās* "moth," in Isa. 51:8. The sense is that the desires even of kings come to naught with their death. In line 44, *mk* "from you" is a variant of *mnk* > *mmk*, on the model of the plural, *mikkem*, etc. in Hebrew. In line 47, we have what is the second stich of a couplet. The one addressed is told that he will not have the skill to interpret oracles to his people. In context, *dbr*, Hebrew *dābār* is to be taken technically, as: "oracle" (Jer. 18:18, etc.). The idiom *ʿl lšn* uses the preposition *ʿl* (= *ʿal*) to mean: "on account of" (cf. Jer. 6:19, 9:11, 12, etc. and Amos 1:3, *passim*, Ps. 5:8, 119:36, Job 16:7).

Especially suggestive in identifying the one addressed in Combination II, is line 49. The verb *q-b-h* "to curse," is associated with Balaam (Num. 23:7–8, *passim*).[25] He is also said to be: *šômēʿa ʾimrê ʾēl* "The hearer of El's (= God's) words" (Num. 24:4, 16).

---

[23] See *The Prophets* (*Neviʾim*), Philadelphia, 1978, 382, and note *i*, to Isa. 14:19, and Levy, *op. cit.*, 3:430, s.v. *nāṣāl*. I am indebted to Prof. S. Iwry, who is currently investigating this subject, for calling my attention to the distinctive usage of *nēṣer* in Isa. 14:19.

[24] As a matter of fact, the verb *š-ʾ-h* may be the derivation of *šeʾôl* "place of desolation," on the model of *karnel*, from *karm-*, and *ʿarāpel*, from the plural stem *ʿarāp-*. See L. Koehler, W. Baumgartner, *Lexicon in Veteris Testamenti Libros*, Leiden, 1958, 935, s.v. *šʾh* I.

[25] The clustering of prepositional elements as in the construction: *w-m-l-q-h* occurs in early Phoenician, and recurs in Late Hebrew. See B. A. Levine, *Survivals of Ancient Canaanite in the Mishnah*, unpublished PhD dissertation, Brandeis University, 1962, 4, and 63, note 6.

MAJOR THEMES IN THE DEIR ʿALLA INSCRIPTIONS. Around the beginning of the seventh century B.C.E., or slightly earlier, inhabitants of the Jordan Valley knew the identity of Balaam, son of Beor, and made him the subject of preserved writings. Their language shows affinities to both Aramaic and Hebrew. For the first time, Balaam's name occurs in an extra-biblical source of the pre-exilic period of biblical history. What is more, Balaam's activities are portrayed in a style and manner reminiscent of biblical poetry and historical narrative. Here, some central themes will be explored, in comparative perspective, as a first step toward resolving the complex cultural and historical problems evoked by the Deir ʿAlla inscriptions.

1) *Descriptions of the Netherworld.* The netherworld fashioned by El, and conditions within it, are described in Combination II. These suggest comparison with both biblical and Mesopotamian literature. At Deir ʿAlla, the netherworld is called *byt* (Combination II, line 2f.). It seems that there were several sequential statements, each beginning with the word *byt*.

In what E. A. Speiser called the "Semitic" version of the myth known as "The Descent of Ishtar," the netherworld is also called *bītu* "house":

> To the dark house, the abode of Irka[la],
> To the house which none leave who have entered it,
> To the road from which there is no way back,
> To the house wherein the entrants are bereft of li[ght].

In biblical poetry, Sheol is likewise called a house (Job 30:23):

> I know that you will hand me over to death,
> To the house where all mortal men gather (*bêt môʿēd lekol ḥay*).[26]

A similar image is evoked in Isa. 14:18:

> All the kings of nations
> Were laid, every one, in honor,
> Each in his own house (*ʾîš bebêtô*)

Combination II suggests still other comparisons with biblical descriptions of Sheol. Consider line 23: *tškb mškby ʿlmyk* "You shall lie on your eternal bed."

The Hebrew verb *š-k-b*, apart from frequently connoting burial, is especially relevant to descriptions of Sheol. Some of this material was cited by Hoftijzer. In Isa. 57:2, "the righteous dead" rest on their beds (*miškebôtām*). In a prediction of Tyre's downfall, Ezekiel (32:25) refers to the bed (*miškāb*) of the slain.

In line 22, the restoration: [*rmh*] *tḥt rʾšk* "wormrot is under your head," is based on Isa. 14:11: *taḥtêkā yuṣṣaʿ rimmāh* "wormrot is to be set as your bed."

---

[26] See E. A. Speiser, "The Descent of Ishtar," in J. B. Pritchard, *Ancient Near Eastern Texts*, 3rd ed., Princeton, 1969, 107, lines 3–7. Also see, *ibid.*, 509, col. 1, line 49f., in the additions to the myth of Nergal and Ereshkigal, translated by A. K. Grayson, where the same passage occurs.

The notion of eternal repose conveyed by the word *ʿlm* has already been noted in the comments to line 2. In most of biblical literature, *ʿôlām*, plural *ʿôlāmîm* refer to the progression of life on earth, not to what occurs after death. And yet, this theme is not entirely absent (Ps. 49:11–12):

> For one sees wise men die,
> Together the fool and boorish man perish,
> And leave their wealth to others.
> Their grave is their home forever (*leʿôlām*).[27]

In a mixed metaphor, predicting the sinking of Tyre into the depths of the sea, Ezekiel (26:20) utilized Sheol imagery in a similar way:

> Then I will bring you down,
> With those who descend to the pit.
> To the people of time immemorial (*ʿam ʿôlām*).

There are further echoes of this theme in Ezek. 27:36, 28:19. In Jer. 51:39 we read of *šenat ʿôlām* "eternal sleep," and in Ps. 143:3 of *mētê ʿôlām* "the eternal dead." (Also cf. Jonah 2:7, Lament. 3:6).

2) *The Goddess Shagar-Weʿishtar, the Council, and the Omen of Darkness.* Lines 21–36 of Combination I tell what the gods (*ʾlhn*) revealed to Balaam at night, and then proceed to describe, in Balaam's words, the predictable consequences of the action taken by the council of gods (*mwʿd*). There are actually four "actors" in this mythological plot: a) The gods who visit Balaam, b) The council of gods, consisting of *ʾlhn* and *šdyn*, c) The goddess Shagar-Weʿishtar, and d) Balaam, himself.

The gods who disclose to Balaam the scheme of the council are friendly, whereas the beings who comprise the council must be seen as inimical. Given what is known of the politics of pantheons and divine councils in the ancient Near East, it is entirely possible that the friendly *ʾlhn* who forewarn Balaam were also members of the council, or had been at one time, but who, out of concern for the goddess and the land, leaked out the council's plan in advance.

The council has been amply discussed by Hoftijzer and McCarter. The precise identification of the *šdyn*, tentatively translated as: "Shadday-gods," remains elusive.[28] On the other hand, the omen, itself, is clear enough, when viewed against the background of the extensive omen literature of the ancient Near East, mostly of Mesopotamian provenance. In the collection *Enūma-Anu-Enlil*, taken mostly from Neo-Bab. sources, clouds often play an ominous role, especially, though not exclusively, in the Adad omens, as is only to be expected. The obscuring of the heavens, conveyed by forms of the Akkadian verb *adāru*

---

[27] In Ps. 49:12 read: *qibrām* "their grave," not *qirbām*, as in the Massoretic text. Cf. the translation in the NEB.

[28] For some of the problems involved, see M. D. Cassuto, "*ʾĒl Šadday*" (Hebrew), in *Encyclopaedia Biblica*, vol. 1, Jerusalem, 1955, 290–292.

"to become obscured," is often involved in the calculation of omens. Such darkening, or obscurity, could occur either at night, or during the day. There were, of course, many variables to be considered, such as the position, shape, and color of clouds, as well the date of the month when they were observed. These factors, in turn, had to be correlated with the positions of relevant heavenly bodies at certain times. It is accurate to say, however, that a darkened sky qualified as an evil omen.[29]

The information provided in lines 21–26 of Combination I is what one would find in the protasis of an omen text, i.e., the observable celestial situation. The information provided in lines 27–37 is what one would find in the apodosis, i.e., the interpretation of the omen; what could be predicted on the basis of it. In effect, Balaam interprets the omen for his listeners. The darkened skies mean that a disaster will occur.

The reference to *ngh* (Hebrew *nôgah*) "brilliance" is highly suggestive.[30] There will be no *ngh*! Based on biblical usage, one prefers to envisage a darkened night sky (cf. 2 Sam. 22:29 // Psa. 18:29, Isa. 4:5, 9:1, 13:10, etc.), and yet, *nôgah* can also refer to the light of day (Isa. 60:1–3, Amos 5:20). It would be overly pedantic to insist on one or the other interpretation, exclusively. Although the obscuring of the heavens is not an eclipse, technically speaking, there are indications, in the omen literature, that such a celestial situation was associated with eclipses. At the very least, this created anxiety as to whether an eclipse had gone unobserved. There is also the possibility, raised by Hoftijzer, that a flood or rainstorm was predicted.

Leaving open several possibilities as to the realistic import of the omen transmitted by Balaam, the real difficulty lies in the dynamics of the plot. How do we explain why Shagar-Weᶜishtar was ordered to produce this celestial situation? Perhaps there is a clue in the composite name Shagar-Weᶜishtar, itself. The component *šgr* expresses fertility, of the flocks and herds. The component *ᶜštr* reflects the astral synthesis of Ishtar-Venus. There surely must be some special

---

[29] I am informed that a complete edition of *Enūma-Anu-Enlil* is in preparation. Existing materials are inadequate. See Ch. Virolleaud, *L'Astrologie Chaldéenne*, Paris, 1905–1912, issued in fascicules. Clouds figure prominently in the following Adad omens: Nos. 22, 27, 30, 36, Suppl. nos. 59, 63–68. Illustrative passages are cited and referred to in *CAD A*/I, 104, s.v. *adāru* A, mng. 2; *CAD A*/II, 229, s.v. *arāmu* mng. 1, d: "to cover the sky, or heavenly body, said of clouds"; *CAD E*, 302, s.v. *erpetu* "cloud," and, *ibid.*, 279, s.v. *erēpu* "to become dusky, dark." See the brief discussion in A. L. Oppenheim, *Ancient Mesopotamia*, Chicago, 1964, 225. See also E. Reiner and D. Pingree, *The Venus Tablet of Ammiṣaduqa*, Undena Publications, Malibu, 1975.

Perhaps a single, complete omen statement will illustrate the possibilities for comparison: *šum-ma* GÍG *a-dir* GIG.ME *u* NAM.ÚŠ.ME *ina* KUR GÁL.MEŠ "If the night is obscured, there will be diseases and pestilences in the land" (Adad, no. 35, line 48).

[30] It should be mentioned that in post-biblical Jewish literature, (*kôkab*) *nôgah* serves as the Hebrew name of Venus. See L. Ginzberg, *Legends of the Jews*, Philadelphia, 1947, 5:29, note 80.

significance to the fact that the very goddess associated with astral brilliance is commanded to produce celestial darkness! Presumably, the light of Ishtar would also be obscured by the clouds darkening the heavens.

As is often the case in myth, no reason or cause is provided for the edict of the council, or for the selection of this particular goddess. The only clue is the statement of the council: "And never raise your voice again!" (Combination I, line 26). Perhaps Shagar-Weᶜishtar had offended the gods in some way, and this was their way of punishing her. No background on the status of this goddess at Deir ᶜAlla is available. It is likely that she was revered by the inhabitants, and may have been the protectress of the land.

The Deir ᶜAlla myth may be understood as a variation on the theme of the Sumero-Akkadian myth known as "The Descent of Ishtar," to which reference has already been made. Ishtar demands entry into the netherworld, for no given reason. She is allowed to enter, but is then incarcerated. Until she is freed by heavenly gods acting on her behalf, all fertility ceases on earth. This seems to be the underlying dynamic of the Deir ᶜAlla myth, as well. Just as the incarceration of the fertility goddess is a way of explaining the absence of fertility, the blotting out of heavenly light is a way of explaining a natural disaster. The protective goddess of the Jordan Valley peoples, who shines in heaven and guarantees the increment of their flocks and herds, is coerced into producing a situation which bodes disaster for the land.

What is Balaam's role? He attempts to reverse the situation brought about by the council, by means of their edict. He uses his craft to extricate the goddess from her subservience to the power of the council. By restoring her to her position as guardian of the land, Balaam is acting to terminate the disaster. Should he fail, suffering would continue.

The praxis seems to be of a mixed kind, combining the craft of the *āšipu*, who exorcizes demons, pronounces curses, and fortifies his clients by prophylactic and apotropaic means, with that of the *bārû*, who interprets omens, and makes divinatory predictions. In the magical literature of Mesopotamia, these two functionaries are usually considered distinct from each other, but in the variegated culture of Deir ᶜAlla we should not be surprised to see them enmeshed. Thus, Balaam consults a priestess and a perfumer, as well as pronouncers of spells and powerful warriors, in his effort to save the goddess; but he also transmits omens. The functioning of the biblical Balaam is actually not too different.

The biblical traditions are, of course, the work of Israelite writers, who convey their negative view of divination. At Deir ᶜAlla we perceive the arts of the diviner through the eyes of those who take omens seriously. There are still other differences. In the biblical traditions, divine power is providential toward the would-be targets of Balaam's power, the Israelites. At Deir ᶜAlla, Balaam acts to protect his people against divine powers which are destructive. In the biblical tradition, Balaam is powerless to oppose Yahweh's edicts, whereas at Deir ᶜAlla, he attempts to contravene the edict of the gods. All that the gods could do was to punish Balaam, after the fact. Thus, the biblical tradition epitomizes Yahweh's supremacy, and Balaam's use of divination is ineffectual (Num. 24:1). Of interest is the fact that both the early biblical traditions and the Deir ʿAlla inscriptions assume a laudatory view of Balaam.

Perhaps it is the theme of celestial darkness which links the diction of the Deir ʿAlla texts most dramatically to biblical literature, especially as it combines with descriptions of panic and desolation on earth. There are two biblical passages that so closely parallel the diction of Deir ʿAlla that they require no commentary. Hoftijzer referred to particulars expressed in them, and, in a more general way, observed that biblical predictions of divine punishment were relevant to an understanding of the Deir ʿAlla myth. Consider the following:

a) *Zeph. 1:14–17* (with deletions):

> The great day of the Lord is approaching ...
> That day shall be a day of wrath,
> A day of trouble and distress (*ṣārāh umeṣûqāh*) ...
> A day of darkness and deep gloom (*ḥôšek waʾapēlāh*),
> A day of dense clouds (*ʿānān waʿarāpel*),
> A day of hornblasts and alarms -

b) *Ezekiel 32:3–8* (with deletions):

> Thus said the Lord, God:
> I will cast my net over you...
> I will cause all the birds of the sky to settle upon you.
> I will cause the beasts of all the earth to batten on you.
> I will cover the sky, and darken its stars;
> I will cover the sun with clouds,
> And the moon shall not give its light.
> All the lights that shine in the sky, I will darken above you;
> And I will bring darkness upon your land...[31]

---

[31] I am indebted to Profs. M. Astour, J. Naveh, E. Puech and D. Pingree for discussing aspects of this study with me. Prof. S. Kaufman read the manuscript, and was kind enough to refer to it in his forthcoming review of this volume, which I was able to consult in advance of publication. Prof. W. W. Hallo read the manuscript, and offered valuable suggestions.

The Balaam Inscription from Deir ʿAlla: Historical Aspects*

The recent discovery of inscribed plaster fragments fallen onto the floor within the walls of the Iron Age temple at Deir ʿAlla, has caused a curious sensation: on these fragments a literary composition is preserved in which the name of Balaam son of Beor (written: *blʿm br bʿr*) is repeatedly mentioned. He is designated a divine seer (*ḥzh ʾlhn*). This fact alone, quite apart from the intriguing character of the text as a whole, enhances the realism of biblical poetry and historiography. An epic figure known only from the Hebrew Bible (and from post-biblical interpretive literature) was, in fact, renowned in the Jordan Valley during the pre-exilic biblical period at a site just north of the lower Jabbok (Zerqa), some 12 km north-northeast of its juncture with the Jordan. This area, known in the Bible as the Valley of Succoth (Psalms 60:8, 108:89), is not all that remote from the Plains of Moab, the site of Balaam's encounter with the Israelites, which biblical historiography assigns to an earlier period.

The discovery of the Deir ʿAlla fragments has raised the question of just how the biblical Balaam saga and the Balaam text from Deir ʿAlla are related to one another, for surely a relationship exists. It is this awareness of connection that is basic to the field we call biblical archaeology, and to the comparative method in the study of ancient civilizations.

The study of the Balaam text from Deir ʿAlla is affected by four principal types of evidence: historical, archaeological, epigraphic and biblical. In each class of evidence we encounter difficulties of interpretation, and suffer, at the present time, from grossly inadequate information. In fact, this is perhaps the most uncertain time to venture historical hypotheses regarding the Balaam text! The pottery from Phase M, H.J. Franken's designation for the level in which the plaster fragments were found, has not yet been published. Thus, his assertion that the ceramic assemblage characteristic of Phase M is distinct from that found west of the Jordan during the same period cannot as yet be evaluated.[1]

---

* Originally published in A. Biran (ed.), *Biblical Archaeology Today* (Jerusalem: Israel Exploration Society, 1985), pp. 326–339. Reprinted with permission from the Israel Exploration Society.

[1] J. Hoftijzer and G. van der Kooij, eds., *Aramaic Texts from Deir ʿAlla* (Leiden, 1976). See H.J. Franken, "Archaeological Evidence Relating to the Interpretation of the Text," *ibid.*, especially his comments on the pottery on pp. 11–12. See also, H.J. Franken and M.M. Ibrahim, "Two Seasons of Excavation at Tell Deir ʿAlla," *Annual of the Department of Antiquities, Jordan* 2 (1977–78): 57–10, with a note by J. Hoftijzer; M. Ibrahim, J. Sauer, K. Yassine, "The East Jordan Valley Survey, 1975," *BASOR* 222 (1976):

The stratigraphy of Tell Deir ᶜAlla is far from clear, due to natural conditions, and to the limited excavations carried out. Work has been resumed under G. van der Kooij, who accomplished the palaeographic study of the inscription for the 1976 publication, and a Jordanian archaeologist, M. Ibrahim. The present excavations are concentrated on the higher levels of the mound, and thus promise to provide us with information about the strata most relevant to the Balaam text. We are awaiting publication of the report of J.B. Pritchard's excavations at nearby Tell es-Saᶜidiyeh, and that of Mohammed Kh. Yassine, at Tell el-Mazār. One hopes that additional plaster inscriptions may be uncovered at one or another of these sites. Within the near future we should, in any event, know much more about the material culture of the immediate area.

Historically, we know less about life in Gilead during the eighth and seventh centuries B.C.E. than we do, on the basis of Egyptian, Assyrian and Aramean sources, about the preceding centuries, and the same imbalance characterizes the biblical record. Finally, the state of the fragments has made their reading an uncertain enterprise, and even the alignment of the fragments has proved to be precarious. Palaeographic analysis has yielded diverse dates, and disagreement persists even on the language of the text. An extensive literature has arisen on the subject of the Balaam text, and the divergence of views expressed only further reinforces our uncertainties regarding its proper interpretation.

In historical terms, the primary question confronting us is whether the Balaam text was a product of the period *prior* to the Assyrian subjugation of Gilead, a series of events probably extending from 734 to 721 B.C.E. under Tiglath-Pileser III and Sargon, or whether it was a product of the period *subsequent* to these pivotal events. The Assyrian campaigns must be regarded as a watershed in any attempt to ascertain whose temple it was at Deir ᶜAlla that had the Balaam text inscribed within its rooms; to know for whom this text speaks, and by whom it was authored. In the wake of the Assyrian campaigns there were mass deportations of the inhabitants of Gilead, and the demography of the Valley of Succoth changed radically. Before the Assyrian campaigns the population was probably predominantly Israelite, although direct evidence bearing on this conclusion is admittedly sparse. Settlement patterns are often complex, and the population may well have been mixed. On the other hand, it is quite clear that after the Assyrian deportations there is less likelihood that the population of the area was predominantly Israelite, and consequently, it is less likely that our text would have been the work of Israelite authors.

I prefer to outline my hypothesis on the historical provenience of the Balaam text at this point, so that the discussion to follow may be accepted as an attempt to deal with specific historical problems.

I submit that the Balaam text may well preserve a literary composition antedating the Assyrian subjugation of Gilead. Palaeographic analysis allows for

41–66. An interesting attempt to synthesize the biblical record with external evidence is provided by O. Ottosson, *Gilead: Tradition and History* (Lund, 1969).

this conclusion, though it by no means compels its acceptance. I further submit, with greater assurance, that the language of the Balaam text from Deir ʿAlla is *not* Aramaic, as we know it from the eighth and seventh centuries B.C.E., but rather a regional language. Whatever limited features of the language that point us in the direction of Old Aramaic can be explained either as originally dialectal, or as the result of language contact with Aramaic, introduced into the area by Arameans. Nothing in the Deir ʿAlla language suggests that the Balaam text is culturally remote from contemporaneous Hebrew, Moabite or Ammonite creativity.

In literary form and with respect to its themes and diction, the Balaam text bears striking affinities to biblical literature, and of course, to the biblical Balaam saga itself; to the point of suggesting that the biblical saga is of Transjordanian origin! There is also a great similarity between "Combination II" of the Balaam text (according to Hoftijzer's delineation) and the Sheol oracle of Isaiah 14. Many such similarities are documented in my earlier study, where I stopped short of attempting to explain these affinities in literary-historical terms.[2]

It is possible that the Balaam text from Deir ʿAlla speaks for the predominantly Israelite population of Gilead before the Assyrian subjugation. When further evidence becomes available this hypothesis will be tested, but for the moment it should not be excluded, *a priori*, simply because of the context of the text itself. This is a polytheistic text, of a mythological character, in which the Syro-Canaanite deity El is prominent, and in which a goddess, Shagar weʿIshtar, plays a role. It is my assessment, nonetheless, that Israelite culture was more pervasive in the pre-exilic period than was Israelite monotheism, and that the existence of non-Yahwistic, Israelite temples in Judah, in northern Israel or in Transjordan (which was at various periods incorporated within the northern Israelite kingdom) should not be denied, in principle or in fact. Judging from the content of the Balaam text, one may conclude that the Iron Age temple at Deir ʿAlla was an El temple.

Having prefaced these general remarks, I may now begin a more detailed analysis of the text in historical perspective.

It would be well to engage the language question at this point. The Aramaic label that was affixed to the Deir ʿAlla text has, in my opinion, impeded a proper historical and cultural assessment of its provenience.

In Phase M at Deir ʿAlla, four brief Aramaic inscriptions were found. One of them, on a clay jar, reads: *zy ś/šrʿʾ*, "belonging to X," attesting the Aramaic relative pronoun. The same name appears on the handle of a stone jar. A third inscription preserves a partial abecedary and the fourth is too fragmentary to be intelligible. Both Franken and Hoftijzer, as well as others it seems, have assumed a direct connection between these Aramaic inscriptions and the language

[2] B.A. Levine, "The Deir ʿAlla Plaster Inscriptions," *JAOS* 101 (1981): 196–205. {*VOL 1, PP. 125–41*}

of the literary Balaam text.[3] This assumption is unsound methodologically. One would only expect to find Aramaic administrative notations at a site governed by Arameans, or at a later time by Assyrians, if that proved to be the case. The name *ś/šrʿʾ* is not likely a divine name, as Franken and Hoftijzer suggest, but rather an official name. It does not occur in the Balaam text, nor should it logically be restored there as the name of a goddess. There is no warrant for adducing the presence of these Aramaic administrative notations as evidence for the language of the Balaam text.

As uncertain readings are reexamined, it becomes evident that there are fewer clear indications of Aramaic factors in the Deir ʿAlla language. An instructive example occurs near the beginning of "Combination I." Once, a preferred reading was: *kmlyʾ ʾl*, "according to these words," the sense being that the "gods" (*ʾlhn*) spoke to Balaam. Just as my study was going to press, I benefited from a suggestion by É. Puech that *kmśʾ ʾl* should be read "according to the revelation of El." Later, I learned that A. Rofé had suggested the same reading, and now I find that the Weipperts have adopted it as well, and it is gaining wider acceptance.[4] In terms of linguistic assignment, the effect of this reading has been to eliminate the only putative attestation of the Aramaic post-positive determination in the Balaam text!

An example of another type illustrates how the Aramaic label may condition the mind of the exegete, and lead one to seek validation for an undemonstrated conclusion. According to my understanding of the text, the second feminine suffix, *-ky*, which is suggestive of Old Aramaic and of later dialects, but surely not an unequivocal indication of such, does not actually occur in the Balaam text. There are three attestations of *ky*, in close succession, and I prefer to take all of them as the particle *ky*, "for" or "that," and as initiating discrete clauses:

1. *ky šm ḥsk wʾl ngh*, "So that darkness and no brilliance will be there."
2. *ky thby ḥtt*, "That you may instill dread!"
3. *ky ss ʿgr ḥrpt nšr*, "For the swift [and] crane will shriek insult to the eagle."

As far as I can determine, the only phonetic feature of the Deir ʿAlla language that is common to Old Aramaic is the representation of the phoneme *Ḍod* as *Qoph*, rather than as a *Ṣade* or *ʿAyin*, as is normal in the Canaanite languages. Thus, we have the verbal form *hqrqt*, "She put to flight," late in "Combination I," and probably a few more examples. Most important is the word *nqr*, which occurs three times in "Combination II." It means "corpse, the dead," and is cog-

[3] For comments on these Aramaic notations, see Hoftijzer and van der Kooij, *Aramaic Texts* (note 1), pp. 15, 267f., 274f., and 285f.

[4] Cf. A. Rofé, *The Book of Balaam* (Jerusalem, 1979), p. 61, s.v. line 2 (Hebrew); H. and M. Weippert, "Die Bileam-Inschrift von Tell Der ʿAlla," *ZDPV* 98 (1982): 77–103, especially 83, s.v. line 2. Now see J. Hackett, *The Balaam Text from Deir ʿAlla* (Scholars Press, 1984), p. 25, line 2, and commentary, and p. 33.

nate to the Hebrew *hapax nēṣer* in Isaiah 14:19, unrelated to נצר, "shoot." Deir ʿAlla *nqr* and Hebrew נצר of Isaiah 14:19 may be derived from a root *nḍl* (or *nḍr*), given the Syriac form *neṣlāʾ*, "carrion." In this connection, J. Naveh has overstated his case for claiming that no such sound-shift is attested in the Balaam text.[5]

What does the occurrence of this sound-shift, usually regarded as critical in the differentiation of Old Aramaic from the Canaanite languages of the eighth and seventh centuries B.C.E., truly indicate? It is, in my judgment, an error to base the linguistic assignment of the Balaam text solely on one criterion. We should evaluate the overall linguistic character of a given text. Similarly, the probable occurrence of Ethpeʿel forms (such as *lytmlk*, "He will not consult") is not conclusive in morphological terms. Nor does a text become Aramaic because it uses a number of verbs uncharacteristic of the Canaanite languages and known mostly from Aramaic, such as *ʿbd*, "to do, make" (Aramaic connotation), *qrq*, "to flee," *ʿll*, "to enter," and the verb *ḥwy*," to show, tell." The form *ḥad*, "one," is not a clear indication of Aramaic, and as Naveh has pointed out, *br* (instead of *bn*), "son," occurs only in the name of Balaam, and no more makes this text Aramaic than does the name *klmw br ḥy*(ʾ) ("Kilamuwa son of Ḥayya," render a Phoenician text from Samal Aramaic![6]

On balance, what is most revealing about the language of the Balaam text is its dominant syntax, which is based on the consecutive tense, with the *Waw* of succession, as W. Moran calls it (or the *Waw* conversive, if you will). This tense system is not at home in Aramaic. It does no good to cite the several occurrences of the consecutive tense in the inscription of Zakur of Hamath, dated to the end of the ninth or the beginning of the eighth century B.C.E., as evidence for the currency of this tense system in Aramaic. If anything, the occurrence of this tense in the Zakur inscription reflects the earlier, native culture of the kingdom of Hamath, prior to its Aramaization, when the language of the area was a form of Canaanite (or northwest Semitic, if you will), coexisting with a form of Hittite. Indeed, the Zakur inscription is a salient example of the expansion of the Aramaic language, but not, in and of itself, a paradigm of Old Aramaic![7]

Although the Deir ʿAlla language exhibits some phonetic and morphological peculiarities when compared to Hebrew, Moabite and Ammonite, as well as Phoenician, it is much closer to the Canaanite group than it is to Old Aramaic, as

[5] Cf. J. Naveh, *IEJ* 29 (1979): 133–136, which is a review of Hoftijzer and van der Kooij, *Aramaic Texts* (see note 1). Also see Levine, "The Deir ʿAlla Inscriptions" (note 2), p. 200, s.v. lines 27, 35; and p. 201, s.v. line 05 {*VOL 1, PP. 133F.*}. See also Hackett, *The Balaam Text* (note 4), Ch. IV: The Dialect, pp. 109–124.

[6] The occurrence of Aramaic *bar*, "son," is explained in this manner by Naveh, *IEJ* (note 5), p. 136, as an official representation of the name of the seer perceived as an Aramean.

[7] See discussion of this question by J. Hoftijzer, in Hoftijzer and van der Kooij, *Aramaic Texts* (see note 1), p. 296, n. 23.

preserved in the Sefire inscriptions, for example. Historically, this analysis, if correct, is quite significant because it endorses the conclusion that the Balaam text is a native literary creation of the immediate region, not one imported from Syria or elsewhere.

A word about palaeography is now in order. Scholars such as van der Kooij, Naveh, Cross and now Puech have utilized palaeographic criteria in dating the Balaam text and, to the extent that script has a bearing on language and cultural provenience, to determine whose text this was. The script derives from the Aramaic script group. Cross, and now Puech, suggest that it exhibits characteristics of Ammonite script.[8]

This discussion has only indirect bearing on the language question, because script and language are different phenomena. At a site such as Deir ʿAlla, so close to Ammonite territory, one might expect Ammonite scribes to be at work, just as one would expect to find Aramean scribes at this site, which was at certain periods under Aramean administration. It is not unknown for one group or people to employ the script of another, for political or sociological reasons. The determining factors in ascertaining the cultural provenience of a given literary text are language and diction, in addition to specific content, of course.

The value of palaeographic analysis for dating a given script must also be stated cautiously. Van der Kooij subjected the script to painstaking analysis, character by character, even describing the movement of the nib used to write on the plaster in forming each character. He does not relate to any historical event, such as the Assyrian campaigns, but provides a qualified date of 700 B.C.E., give or take twenty-five years, as is customary. Naveh dates the script to around the middle of the eighth century B.C.E., perhaps a bit earlier, and Puech now suggests a date of ca. 725 B.C.E., plus or minus twenty-five years, favoring a pre-Assyrian provenience. Cross fixed a date of ca. 700 B.C.E., and has verbally stated that the Balaam text postdated the Assyrian campaigns, and that he does not consider it an Israelite creation.[9]

Palaeographic analysis alone cannot answer the most pressing historical questions regarding the Balaam text, certainly not in the present state of the overall evidence. At best, it can project sequences, differentiate between lapi-

---

[8] See the careful treatment of the script by G. van der Kooij in Hoftijzer and van der Kooij, *Aramaic Texts* (see note 1), pp. 23–170. This study includes a detailed description of the method of writing used at Deir ʿAlla. In addition to Naveh's review of 1979 and his early analysis of the script in *IEJ* 17 (1967): 256–258, we have two statements by F.M. Cross Jr., "Epigraphic Notes on the Amman Citadel Inscription," *BASOR* 193 (1969): 13–19, especially p. 14, n. 2, where he tends to agree with Naveh's early dating in the eighth century B.C.E. with reservations, and "Notes on the Ammonite Inscription from Tell Siran," *BASOR* 212 (1973): 12–15, where he alters his view. Also see É. Puech, "L'Inscription de la Statue d'Amman et la Paléographie Ammonite," *RB* 92 (1985): 5–24.

[9] Cf. the remarks in É. Puech, "Response – l'Inscription sur plâtre de Tell Deir ʿAlla, *Biblical Archaeology Today* (Jerusalem, 1985), pp. 354–365; and by F.M. Cross Jr., *ibid.*, p. 369.

dary and cursive scripts and their respective rates of change and development, and trace the emergence of new forms, geographically.

I have already referred to the tentative state of the archaeological evidence. On the basis of what is presently known (April 1984), it seems that Phase M at Deir ᶜAlla though it may have survived the Assyrian campaigns by a brief span, is primarily a pre-Assyrian phase and most probably not one initiated after 721 B.C.E. This seems to be Franken's conclusion, although his discussion is difficult to follow on this point.[10] The radio-carbon testing of a charred grain sample from Phase M yielded a date of ca. 800 B.C.E., plus or minus seventy years, with a 66% probability.[11] According to Franken, the lower limit of Phase M is ca. 650 B.C.E., because it was at about that time that wheel-turned pottery, absent from Phase M, was introduced to the area. The pottery changed between Phases M and N, according to Franken, and there may even have been an intermediate M–to–N phase. This matter will undoubtedly be clarified by the current excavations at the site. It is quite possible that the Ammonites did not move into the area until quite late in the seventh century B.C.E., and not very soon after the Assyrian subjugation of the area, as has been supposed.

What is at stake in this discussion is a clear indication of the demography of the Valley of Succoth at the time the Balaam text appeared on the inner walls of the Deir ᶜAlla temple. There were two radical changes in the demography of the immediate area, one at the end of the Late Bronze Age (ca. 1200 B.C.E.) and the other as a consequence of the Assyrian deportations, occurring near the end of the eighth century B.C.E.

The Late Bronze Age culture of the lower Jabbok is called Canaanite for lack of a more precise term. We know that Egypt was interested in the area, as evidenced by the scarab of Taossert found at Deir ᶜAlla, dating to the thirteenth century B.C.E.[12] The Late Bronze Age II temple at Deir ᶜAlla was destroyed ca. 1200 B.C.E. — exactly how is not presently known. Construction at Deir ᶜAlla was resumed early in the twelfth century. Clear historical information about the Valley of Succoth begins to appear only late in the tenth century B.C.E. I prefer, pending the publication of the Late Bronze Age II pottery and the Iron Age material, not to discuss in detail what has been reported about the finds of the early Iron Age at Deir ᶜAlla. We are told that, after a brief Israelite period, there was an extended period characterized by Philistine-type pottery, perhaps of local manufacture. Then followed the period of the United Monarchy.

Very soon after the breakup of the United Monarchy, Jeroboam I fortified Penuel (1 Kings 12:25). Very shortly thereafter, early in the last quarter of the tenth century B.C.E., Shishak overran the Valley of Succoth, and his stele at Kar-

---

[10] See the discussion by Franken, in Hoftijzer and van der Kooij, *Aramaic Texts* (note 1), pp. 12f.

[11] *Ibid.*, p. 16 under "Note."

[12] See J. Yoyotte, "Un Souvenir du 'Pharaon' Taossert en Jordanie," *VT* 12 (1962): 464f.

nak, so effectively illuminated by Mazar, mentions no less than six sites in the area: Adam, a site named Kadesh, Penuel, Succoth, Mahanaim and Zaphon. Whether Deir ʿAlla is indeed ancient Succoth, or some other mound a few kilometers away, is not yet certain and matters little for the present discussion.[13]

At the time of Shishak's campaign, the Valley of Succoth was a fertile, densely populated area fed by the waters of the Jabbok as they poured down into the Jordan. In effect, Shishak went out of his way to reach this area, undoubtedly so as to reassert Egyptian interests here, and perhaps as punishment imposed on Jeroboam who had in some way displeased the Egyptians, after having found refuge in Egypt during the last days of Solomon. According to the latest information available to me, there is as yet no evidence of a Shishak destruction-level at Deir ʿAlla, but such evidence has turned up at Nimrin, a site south of Deir ʿAlla in the direction of Jericho and the Dead Sea. Further excavations may clarify this matter considerably.[14]

As Mazar emphasizes, the importance of the Valley of Succoth declined sharply after Shishak's campaign, and we have very little information about the area in the biblical record. The focus of international attention shifted to Ashtaroth in the Bashan and to Ramoth Gilead, both important stations on the international route linking up with the King's Highway and proceeding northward to Damascus.

With interruptions and setbacks, Aramean expansion, beginning in the early ninth century B.C.E. under Ben-Hadad II and continuing until near the end of the century under Hazael, eventually encompassed all of Gilead. At the end of the ninth century the campaigns of Adad-Nirari III weakened Aram-Damascus considerably, and for a time Israelite hegemony was reasserted under Joash and Jeroboam II. But sometime before the campaigns of Tiglath-Pileser III, Rezin, the Aramean king, probably regained control of Transjordan. We do not know how extensive the Aramean presence was in the Valley of Succoth during this period, but the discovery of the Aramaic administrative notations in Phase M at Deir ʿAlla indicates at least an official presence, if we are correct in dating Phase M prior to the Assyrian subjugation of Gilead.

H. Tadmor has meticulously summarized what is known of the effects of the Assyrian subjugation in Bashan and Gilead, showing that the forces of Tiglath-Pileser III reached all the way south to Moab. There were mass deportations from Gilead and Galilee.[15]

In the period prior to the Assyrian campaigns we have some evidence of a strong Israelite factor in the population of Gilead. Possibly as many as four kings of northern Israel were Gileadites! Pekah son of Remaliah was a Gileadite

---

[13] See B. Mazar, "Shishak's Campaign to Eretz-Israel," in *Canaan and Israel: Historical Essays* (Jerusalem, 1974), pp. 234–244, especially 236–237. (Hebrew)

[14] Nimrin is perhaps biblical בית נמרה (Numbers 32:3, 36, Joshua 13:27).

[15] See H. Tadmor, *Encyclopaedia Biblica*, vol. VIII (Jerusalem, 1982), s.v. *Tiglat-Pilʾeser*, pp. 415f., especially 423f. (Hebrew).

and came to power with the assistance of a group of important Gileadites (2 Kings 15:25). It is also probable that Menahem son of Gadi (that is, a resident of the territory of Gad) was a Gileadite, which would make his son, Pekahiah, a Gileadite as well (2 Kings 15:14–17, 23). Come to think of it, Shallum son of Jabesh (2 Kings 15:13) must have been a Gileadite, from Jabesh of Gilead.[16] We would thus have a sequence of four kings in northern Israel who were Gileadites, from Shallum to Pekah, ruling from 748/47 to 733/32 B.C.E. Without overstating the implications of this political reality, it is safe to say that even during periods of Aramean hegemony in Transjordan, Gilead was part of the political configuration of the northern Israelite kingdom.

In summary, a date prior to the Assyrian campaigns for the Deir ʿAlla plasters would not be incompatible with the evidence currently available. At the present time, pending further evidence, the strongest argument for a Transjordan-Israelite provenience, as against a non-Israelite provenience, is the character of the Balaam text itself, especially its close affinity to certain biblical literary traditions. It is this complex of affinities which can be explored productively at the present time, always with an eye to historical questions but in a manner that does not presuppose as certain one set of historical conclusions. We turn now to the literary-historical provenience of the Balaam text from Deir ʿAlla.

In the light of a restoration proposed independently by both G. Hamilton and É. Puech, and pursuant to my earlier interpretation, we may now read, near the beginning of "Combination I," the following:

> (*wyḥz mḥzh*) *kmśʾ ʾl*, "He [Balaam] beheld a vision according to the revelation of El."

This reading, with its specific reference to the deity El, links the two "Combinations" of the Balaam text to one another more firmly than was previously possible. Near the beginning of "Combination II" we read:

> (*ddn*) *yrwy ʾl wyʿbd ʾl byt ʿlmn*, El sates himself with lovemaking; then El fashioned a netherworld.

El emerges as the dominant deity in the Balaam text, one who shows compassion by revealing to Balaam, through his divine messengers, the imminence of disaster. Subsequently, El provides a proper burial and residence for the rejected, though heroic seer, Balaam. The exact relationship of the goddess Shagar weʿIshtar to El is not explicit; but El is clearly concerned with her fate.

All this means that the Iron Age temple at Deir ʿAlla was most probably an El temple. This should hardly surprise us, either during the eighth or the seventh century B.C.E. in the Valley of Succoth, whatever the demography of the region. El is by far the most frequent element in the Ammonite theophoric onomasticon,

[16] The name of the town is יב(י)ש in 1 Samuel 11:1, 3, *passim*; in 1 Samuel 31:12, etc.

as known primarily from the seventh century B.C.E.[17] Biblical traditions inform us that El was specifically associated with the Valley of Succoth in earlier centuries. This is most clearly epitomized in the Genesis narratives, which relate that Jacob became *Yisrael* at Penuel (Genesis 32:25–32)! This narrative qualifies as a *hieros logos* of Penuel, much in the same way that Genesis 28:10–22 represent a *hieros logos* of Bethel. The *Sitz-im-Leben* of the Penuel episode is most logically the period prior to Shishak's invasion, although in its present form it is probably a later composition.

The entire complex of El traditions associated with the Patriarchs is topically relevant to the present discussion, but is far too involved to be dealt with here in any detail. Suffice it to say that in contrast to Baal, who was utterly rejected in monotheistic circles early in the monarchic period, the last persons properly to be given Baalistic names being Saul's sons, El was generally welcomed, and the attitude toward El remained positive. El was synthesized or fused with Yahweh, the God of Israel. Some of the Genesis traditions betray an awareness that the Patriarchs (or, to put it less traditionally, the earliest Israelites) were devoted to El. This hindsight is not expressed with any disapproval, as evidenced by the startling statement in Exodus 6:2–4.

In the Balaam text from Deir ʿAlla, El is the proper name of a deity and certainly not a common noun, or a way of referring to the God of Israel!

The classification of the Iron Age temple at Deir ʿAlla as an El temple leads one to conclusions of both historical and literary relevance. In historical perspective, it means that there was more than one pattern to cult practice and religious life in pre-exilic Israel. Yahwistic temples and cult sites could be "polluted" by the introduction of pagan rites or the like, and this situation is repeatedly called to our attention by biblical prophets and historiographers. There was another pattern whereby temples and cult sites dedicated to pagan gods coexisted with Yahwistic ones. There was a Baal temple in (or outside of) Samaria, which was put out of commission by Jehu (2 Kings 10:18f.) and subsequently, after Athaliah's backsliding, by the priests under Jehoiada (2 Kings 11:17f.).

As for Gilead, we know that there was a temple of Yahweh in Nebo around the middle of the ninth century B.C.E. Mesha tells us that, upon conquering Nebo, then an Israelite stronghold, he dragged "the vessels of Yahweh" before Ashtar-Kemosh, at his capital of Dibon.[18] The presence of an El temple in Gilead during the eighth century B.C.E. does not mean that Israelite monotheism

---

[17] See K.P. Jackson, *The Ammonite Language of the Iron Age* (Scholars Press, 1983), pp. 95f., and his study, "Ammonite Personal Names in the Context of the West Semitic Onomasticon," in *The Word of the Lord Shall Go Forth. Essays in Honor of D.N. Freedman* (Philadelphia, 1983), pp. 507–521.

[18] See H. Donner and W. Röllig, *Kanaanäische und Aramäische Inschriften*, vol. I (Wiesbaden, 1962), p. 33, no. 181, lines 17–18, as restored: *wʾqḥ mšm ʾ*[*t k*]*ly YHWH*, "I took from there [Nebo] the vessels of Yahweh," etc.

was not established there, but only that it coexisted, in this case, with an autochthonous El cult of probable great antiquity.

The northern Israelite prophet of the eighth century B.C.E., Hosea, twice speaks of Gilead in his denunciations of improper worship and societal wickedness. Both passages are somewhat cryptic but, if studied in depth, may prove to be relevant to our discussion. Our starting point is Hosea 6:4. Continuing with deletions until verse 10, we read the text as follows:

4. What can I do for you Ephraim,
What can I do for you, *Israel*,
When your goodness is like morning clouds,
Like dew early gone? ...
6. For I desire goodness, not sacrifice,
Obedience to God, rather than burnt offerings!
7. But they, in *Adam* have transgressed the covenant,
There they have been false to Me.
8. Gilead is a city of evildoers, Tracked up with blood!
9. The gang of priests is
Like the *ambuscade* of bandits
Who murder on the road to Shechem,
For they have encouraged depravity.
10. *At Beth Shean* I have seen
A horrible thing:
Ephraim has fornicated there,
Israel has defiled himself![19]

Hosea is condemning the undue emphasis on cult and worship to the utter disregard for "steadfast love," a theme frequent in biblical prophecy, and in which sexual depravity, even if not actual, serves as a poignant way of expressing Israel's infidelity. What is significant is the fact that Hosea, like other prophets, targets certain towns as focal points of iniquity. He includes sites on both sides of the Jordan, starting with Adam and Gilead, projected as a town not a region (perhaps intending Jabesh-Gilead), and going on to encompass two major sites west of the Jordan, Shechem and Beth-Shean.

---

[19] H.L. Ginsberg has suggested that in transmission of Hosea from northern Israel to Judah, archetypal *Yod*s, originally standing for ישראל, were misunderstood as referring to יהודה. This explains the proposed reading ישראל, "Israel," in v. 4. See H.L. Ginsberg, "Hosea, Book of," *Encyclopaedia Judaica* 8:1015. For this reading, and for the reading בית-שאן instead of בית-ישראל in v. 10, see *The Prophets* (Jewish Publication Society of America: New York, 1978), to Hosea 6:4f., and notes, pp. 774–775. For the reading באדם, "in Adam," instead of Masoretic כאדם, "to a man," see E. Sellin, "Die Geschichtliche Orientierung der Prophetie des Hosea," *Neue kirchliche Zeitschrift* 36 (1925): 607–658, especially 624–625. In v. 9, Masoretic וכחכי probably misrepresents a form of the verb חבא, "to conceal," as suggested by Sellin and others. Cf. H. Tadmor, "The Historical Background of Hosea's Prophecies," in *Y. Kaufmann Jubilee Volume*, ed. M. Haran (Jerusalem, 1962), pp. 84–88.

The geographic scope reflected in this list of places points to ancient realities affecting economy, trade and culture. *En route* from central Gilead to the Mediterranean, one could cross the Jordan at Adam. The route branched off west of the Jordan, northward to Beth-Shean, then westward to Megiddo, where it linked up with the "Via Maria." Another branch of the same route continued in a westerly direction to a point between Shechem and Tirzah, also linking up with the "Via Maria," either by way of Samaria or Dothan. Beth-Shean was also a station on the route from Jabesh-Gilead, which extended from the King's Highway in Transjordan to the "Via Maria." At various points, these routes exploited rifts in the northern mountains.[20]

Hosea 11 tells the same story, albeit in much less detail. In verse 11 we read:

> As for Gilead, it is worthless,
> And to no purpose have they
> Been sacrificing oxen in Gilgal.
> The altars of these are also
> Like stone heaps upon a plowed field.

It is not our purpose to suggest that Hosea is necessarily referring to the pattern of pagan worship we have proposed as applicable to an El temple at Deir ʿAlla, during the eighth century B.C.E. It is sufficient, in terms of our argument, to note that he is speaking of an Israelite society in the Gilead of his time, and that, in so doing, he perceives a societal configuration on both sides of the Jordan that is parallel with the political configuration discernible in the history of the northern Israelite monarchy during the same period.

Our literary analysis begins with the observation that the closest biblical parallels to the Balaam text from Deir ʿAlla are, as one would expect, the biblical Balaam oracles and the narrative saga. I am not speaking merely of topical parallels but of close affinities in diction. This prompts me to suggest the existence of an El repertoire, emanating from centers of the El cult, upon which biblical writers drew for their materials. Some of chose centers were in Transjordan, and this would explain how a complex of traditions and oracles about Balaam, originating at sites such as Deir ʿAlla, found its way into biblical literature. Monotheistic writers fused El with Yahweh, by using אל in parallelism with יהוה, or with such terms as אלהים/אלה. Often אל was used as a common noun or as an epithet of Yahweh. It is difficult, of course, to ascertain where in the Hebrew Bible אל was intended by the ancient writers to designate a deity, Syro-Canaanite El. It is, however, precisely in those biblical poetic passages most similar in diction to the Balaam text from Deir ʿAlla that this is most likely the case! Let us begin with the Sheol oracle of Isaiah 14, which I have compared to "Combination II" of the Balaam text.

---

[20] See Y. Aharoni and M. Avi-Yonah, *The Macmillan Bible Atlas* (New York, 1968), map no. 10, p. 17.

There are salient dictional affinities for comparison: Isaiah 14:19 refers to "the wrap of the slain" (לובש הרוגים), while "Combination II" has (*mn*) *mškb mtksn lbš*, "From the bed, they cover themselves with a wrap." Further compare Isaiah 14:11: "Your covering is the worm" (ומכסיך תולעת). Isaiah 14:18 states "They all repose in honor, each in his own 'house'" (כלם שכבו בכבוד), while "Combination II" has *tškb mškby ʿlmyk*, "you will repose on your eternal bed."

A remarkable parallel is provided by the term נצר, "carrion, corpse" in Isaiah 14:19 "You have been cast from your grave like loathsome carrion" (ואתה השלכתה מקברך כנצר תצב). In "Combination II," the term *nqr*, as it is expressed in the phonetic system of the Deir ʿAlla language, occurs three times. Two of the occurrences appear in clear contexts:

1. *nʾnḥ nqr blbbh*, "The corpse moans in his heart."
2. *lbb nqr šhh*, "The heart of the corpse is desolate."

These affinities would suggest that the two compositions derive from the same repertoire, and indeed the Sheol oracle of Isaiah 14 is El literature! Long ago M.D. Cassuto speculated that the term אל in Isaiah 14:13–14, in the boastful speech of the pagan king, was not a common noun referring to the God of Israel, but a reference to the well-known Syro-Canaanite deity, El.[21] The passage reads:

I will ascend to the heavens;
I will set my throne above the stars of *El* (ממעל לכוכבי-אל);
I will mount the back of a dense cloud;
I will be comparable to Elyon (אדמה לעליון)!

In contrast to words attributed to a pagan king, the tone of the Balaam oracles is passionately monotheistic. The biblical poets sing a paean of praise to Yahweh, and carefully synthesize El with Yahweh. In the first instance, this is shown through poetic parallelism (Numbers 23:8):

How can I curse what אל has not cursed?
How can I condemn what Yahweh (יהוה) has not damned?

Nonetheless, the derivation of the Balaam oracles from an El repertoire glares through the Yahwistic fusion. In citing the following verses, I render the Hebrew אל as *El* in italics, to show that one could just as well read these verses (Numbers 23:19) as referring to the deity, El:

El is not a person that he would deceive,
No mortal man, that he would retract.

And Numbers 23:22 and 24:8:

El, who freed them from Egypt,

---

[21] See M. D. Cassuto, *Encyclopaedia Biblica*, vol. I (1955), pp. 283–284, s.v. אל, p. 2 (Hebrew). Also see O. Eissfeldt, "El and Yahweh," *Journal of Semitic Studies* 1 (1956): 25–37.

> Has horns like a wild ox!

And Numbers 23:24:

> It is promptly told to Jacob,
> To Israel—what *El* has done.

The third and fourth oracles open with a statement about Balaam himself (Numbers 24:3–4):

> The oration of Balaam, son of Beor
> The oration of the man whose vision is clear;
> The oration of one who hears *El*'s oracles,
> Who beholds the vision of Shaddai—
> Prostrate, but with eyes wide open!

In the opening statement of the fourth oracle, the following words are added (Numbers 24:15–46):

> Who possesses knowledge of Elyon

In addition to the El theme, there are other links between the biblical Balaam saga and the Deir ʿAlla text. In both, divine beings "come" to Balaam at night, and in both he beholds visions and relates to others what has been disclosed to him. He tells what the gods are doing, conveyed by the verb פעל/*pʿl*. In both, Shaddai or Shaddai-gods play a role.

Apart from the sources being discussed here because of their direct bearing on the Balaam text from Deir ʿAlla, there are other inroads of the El repertoire in biblical literature. One example, of a later period, is the book of Job which, exclusive of the prologue and epilogue, may well be of Transjordanian origin. One also recalls the opening lines of Psalm 19:

> The heavens relate the glory of *El*;
> The firmament tells of his handiwork.

Although the biblical Balaam oracles may antedate the version of the Balaam text from Deir ʿAlla, the latter has the advantage of showing us an example of El literature as it was, unaffected by the Yahwistic monotheism of the biblical writers. Given the history of Transjordan as it has been outlined here, one may suppose that contacts across the Jordan, in both directions, were normal throughout the tenth to the late eighth centuries B.C.E., allowing for continuous cultural interaction. Biblical writers drew on native, Transjordanian traditions, and it is probable that Transjordanian writers, no less skilled and artistic—whether Israelite or not—were affected by literary movements west of the Jordan, primarily in northern Israel.

Bible scholars will now be required to focus attention on the Transjordanian factor in biblical literature, just as we have been seeking to identify Judean and north Israelite factors. The discovery of the inscribed plaster fragments at Deir ʿAlla has initiated a new era in Bible scholarship, as well as in the study of the ancient cultures of Transjordan. It is hoped that increased archaeological activity on the soil of ancient Transjordan, especially in the Zerqa Valley, will provide valuable materials for study to all students of Near Eastern antiquity.[22]

[22] I am grateful to Profs. H.L. Ginsberg and B. Mazar for the pleasure of discussing this study with them. Prof. Sauer was kind enough to share with me his extensive knowledge of the archaeological history of ancient Transjordan.

The Plaster Inscriptions from Deir ʿAlla: General Interpretation*

This study is the third effort on my part to investigate the inscriptions from Deir ʿAlla. In the brief span of time since their publication, these inscriptions have stimulated a considerable literature from which we have all learned a great deal.

My first study was a commentary of sorts, whereas the second was an attempt to establish *Sitz-im-Leben*.[1] In the first study I proposed relating the themes of the Deir ʿAlla inscriptions to Syro-Mesopotamian myths and omens, particularly sources pertaining to the Ishtar-Venus astral synthesis. In my view, the goddess addressed in Combination I is Shagar-we-Ishtar, a name written out fully in line 14 of Combination I. In the second Combination, I saw traces of the netherworld descriptions known from such compositions as "The Descent of Ishtar." All of this is in addition to the plentiful affinities to biblical literature.

In my second piece I proposed that the Deir ʿAlla inscriptions belonged to an El *repertoire*, a body of literary creativity originally composed at various centers of El worship on both sides of the Jordan; in biblical Israel, as well as in Gilead of Transjordan. Excellent examples of such works are preserved in the Hebrew Bible, including the Balaam orations of the book of Numbers, where El has been synthesized with Yahweh, the God of Israel. I went so far as to suggest that these inscriptions might speak for Israelites in Transjordan who were El worshippers, and as such, similar to those who were the targets of Hosea's denunciations. It seems quite possible to me that some of the El literature preserved in the Hebrew Bible, especially in the Balaam orations, had actually originated in Transjordan. We can all probably agree that the Deir ʿAlla inscriptions mandate a re-evaluation of the cultural climate in Transjordan during the tenth-to-eighth centuries B.C.E. The style and diction of the Deir ʿAlla texts indicate a high level of literary creativity, by any contemporary standards.

Since these earlier studies appeared, basic questions relevant to the plaster inscriptions from Deir ʿAlla have been focused more sharply. There is, first of all, the question of provenance: Are these compositions regional in origin, hav-

---

* Originally published in J. Hoftijzer and G. van der Kooij (eds.), *The Balaam Text from Deir ʿAlla Re-Evaluated: Proceedings of the International Symposium Held at Leiden, 21–24 August 1989* (Leiden: E. J. Brill, 1991), pp. 58–72. Reprinted with permission from Brill.

[1] B. A. Levine, "The Deir ʿAlla Plaster Inscriptions," *JAOS* 101, 1981, 195–205 {*VOL 1, PP. 125–41*}. *Idem*, "The Balaam Inscription: Historical Aspects," *Biblical Archaeology Today*, Jerusalem: Israel Exploration Society, 1985, 326–339 {*VOL 1, PP. 143–57*}.

ing been composed in Gilead, or in nearby areas; or are they foreign in origin, having been imported into central Transjordan from Syria, or elsewhere? In other words, do the plaster inscriptions represent native culture, or not? In a larger sense, this is the significance of the language question, although language and cultural provenance do not precisely overlap.

Questions of dating have also occupied considerable attention, with scholarly opinion, generally supported by archaeological data, now opting for a time earlier in the eighth century B.C.E. than was initially thought. The political situation in Gilead, and in Transjordan generally, has come in for considerable attention, as well as the relative valence of the ruling, Aramean administration versus the regional population in determining the cultural climate of the area.

The present address is my response to the invitation to offer some further thoughts in the area of General Interpretation. I cannot guarantee that it will be possible to eschew details of the texts, to avoid reference to language, or to maintain my distance from all biblical associations, subjects to be discussed by others. And yet, it should be possible to revise some of my earlier impressions on the general, interpretational level.[2]

Permit me to propose two methodological caveats: Some of the readings suggested by different investigators should be regarded as open options; they often result from the process of elimination. Such options at times lack real significance, and need not be debated heatedly, and at any rate, cannot be verified palaeographically. We must guard against basing too much on uncertain readings, while at the same time using plausible suggestions prudently. The second point to be made pertains to the poetic, or "parallelistic" quality of these texts. I have, of course, corrected the format I initially presented wherever new information relevant to the positioning and spacing of the inscribed fragments has so indicated. And yet, I find the parallelistic alignment highly suggestive and I recommend it to others.

I intend to discuss combinations I and II in tandem, and then deal with the relationship between them. I am intrigued by Émile Puech's suggestion that where we again encounter red ink, in line 17 of Combination II, we may have the beginning of a new unit, possibly setting forth the functions of the diviner, in the form of a manual.

As I see it, Combination I is comprised of four identifiable sections:

---

[2] See primarily the contributions of André Lemaire, "L'Inscription de Balaam trouvée a Deir ᶜAlla: Epigraphie" In *Biblical Archaeology Today*, 313–325, and that of Émile Puech, "Response – l'Inscription sur plâtre de Tell Deir ᶜAlla," *ibid.* 354–365. Also see by Puech "Le texte 'ammonite' de Deir ᶜAlla; Les admonitions de Balaam," *La Vie de la Parole, Mélanges Grelot*, Paris: 1986, 12–30. Further see S. A. Kaufman, "The Classification of the North-West Semitic Dialects of the Biblical Period," etc. *Proceedings, Ninth World Congress of Jewish Studies*, Jerusalem, 1988, *Panel Sessions*: *Hebrew and Aramaic*, 41–57.

1) *Lines 1–5*: the introduction of Balaam; the report of his visitation by gods who reveal to him a vision uttered by El. There follows a rhetorical dialogue between Balaam and his associates in which he announces what has been disclosed to him.

2) *Lines 5 (end)–7*: What Balaam saw and heard from El's messengers. Some gods and Shadday-beings convened a council (*mwᶜd* = *moᶜēd*) and issued a decree against a goddess, who, by my interpretation, is Shagar-we-Ishtar, whose name is written out fully in line 14. She is ordered to produce celestial darkness by covering the heavens with dense cloud. She is told never to raise her voice again.

3) *Lines 7 (near end)–10*: A depiction of desolation and wilderness, with birds shrieking and wild animals feeding freely. The implication is that where domestic animals had formerly been tended, wild animals now reign.

4) *Lines 10 (near end)–16*: Beginning with the words: *šmᶜw mwsr* "Heed admonition!", this poorly preserved section almost defies interpretation. We will defer any attempt to identify its meaning until first engaging the better preserved, three sections which precede it in Combination I.

I lack a new contribution to each and every section of Combination I. As a matter of interpretation, I now intend to agree with those who find in Section 3 an uninterrupted list of birds and animals, and reluctantly surrender the tempting but less likely reading *nḥṣ wṣrh* "distress and trouble" for the more likely *bny nṣṣ wṣdh* "young falcons and the owl."

Following is my proposed rendition of Section 2, about which I will have the most to say in the context of Combination I:

tpry skry šmyn bᶜb
ky šm ḥšk wʾl ngh
ᶜṭm wʾl smṙ
ky thby ḥt[t bᶜ]b ḥšk
wʾl thgy ᶜd ᶜlm

"Sew up, block up the heavens with dense cloud,
So that darkness be there, not brilliance;
Darkness and not bristling (?):
That you may instill dread, in the density of darkness,
And may you never raise your voice again!"

May I call your attention to the recent publication by E. Reiner and D. Pingree of parts of the Babylonian omen series, *Enuma Anu Enlil* (*EAE*).[3] When we examine the protases and apodoses, and the terms of reference recurring in these omen texts, representative of an Old Babylonian tradition, but undoubtedly the

[3] E. Reiner in collaboration with D. Pingree, *Babylonian Planetary Omens*, part 1: *Enūma Anu Enlil Tablet 63, The Venus Tablet of Ammiṣaduqa*; and part 2: *Enūma Anu Enlil, Tablets 50–51*. Bibliotheca Mesopotamica 2; Malibu, CA: Undena, 1975 and 1981.

work of early, first millennium scribes in their preserved form, we gain insight into the ominous diction of this section of Combination I.

First, a word about the visibility, or shining of stars, in general: Contrast the following entries:

a) (*EAE* 50–51: III:15–16):

> MUL.MEŠ *nam-ru ana* IM ZI.GA
> MUL.MEŠ SAR.MEŠ-*ḫu ana* ZI IM
>
> "Bright stars are for the rising of wind;
> Scintillating stars (*napḫū*) are for the rising of wind."

b) (*EAE* 50–51: III:18):

> MUL.MEŠ DUL.LA *ana* IM.ŠUB.BA
>
> "Veiled stars (*katmū*) are for the abating of wind."

Rising wind (*tību*) signals rain, which is a good forecast. (cf., *EAE* 50–51: IV:10–11, 13). The Akkadian verb *katāmu* is suggestive, because it variously refers to veiling, or covering by means of a garment, as well as to covering the sky with dust, smoke, or fog (*CAD K*, s.v.). This wide range of meanings for Akkadian *katāmu* may clarify usage of the verb *t-p-r* "to sew" in the Deir ʿAlla text. After all, we read in Hebrew poetry of the heavens depicted as a tent-flap, and as thin cloth. Thus, Isa. 40:22:

> *hannôṭeh kaddôq šāmâyim*
> *wayyimtāḥēm kāʾôhel lāšāḇet*
>
> "Who spread out the heavens like gauze,
> Stretched them out like a tent for dwelling."

Or Pss. 104:2:

> *ʿôṭeh ʾôr kaśśalmāh*
> *nôṭeh šāmâyim kayyĕrîʿāh*
>
> "You wrapped yourself in light like a garment,
> Spread out the heavens like a tent-flap."

Yet another Akkadian verb of interest is *arāmu* "to stretch, or place a membrane, skin, or layer of metal over an object." The following protases are instructive:

a) *Ištar* 9:4, and duplicates:

> [*šumma*] *Ištar ina pan šatti ši-ši-tam ár-mat*
>
> "If in the spring of the year, Ishtar is *covered* by a 'membrane'"

b) *Adad* 112:14:7:

> *šumma erpetu ṣalimtu elât šamê i-rim*

"If a black cloud covers the upper sky"[4]

A third Akkadian verb that is suggestive for the interpretation of our text is *adāru* "to obscure," usually occurring in the stative, in the omen texts. Cf., *EAE* 50–51: II:7c:

> ^{d}*Dil-bat ina* ITI.APIN *a-dir*
>
> "Venus in month VIII is obscured."

It is significant that in Akkadian, derived forms of the verb *adāru*, such as *adirtu*, for instance, mean both "darkness" and "misfortune, calamity."

The point to be made is that Mesopotamian omen literature uses comparable diction to that of the Deir ʿAlla inscriptions, and to that of the Hebrew Bible, in describing celestial phenomena. We are warranted in concluding, in literary terms, that the diction of omen literature of various sorts resonates in the Deir ʿAlla inscriptions, and helps us to establish their meaning.

At some risk, I would like to comment on the still uncertain reading *sṁṙ* in line 7, which by virtue of its parallel position should, I think, constitute an antonym to *ʿṭm*, and consequently, should connote "light", in some sense. The reading *ʿṭm* is pretty well accepted, though the interpretation of this vocable is still being debated. A relationship to Akkadian *eṭû* (adj.) "dark' (and related forms) is surely logical, but it is less certain how to explain the final *mem* of *ʿṭm*. Others derive *ʿṭm* from other roots, while agreeing on the meaning "darkness."

Now, if the reading *sṁṙ* is viable, then this vocable may be related to Hebrew-Aramaic *s-m-r* (cf., *ṣ-m-r*), "to bristle, stand up like hairs, nails, etc." (Pss. 119:20, Job 4:15, and in Late Hebrew). It may be relevant that Sumerian MUL.MUL "stars" at times refers to the Pleiades, and has the Akkadian value *zappu* "the Bristle", in that context.[5] The point is that visible features of heavenly bodies can be referred to as "bristling."

While I am discussing the diction of celestial omens, I would like to call attention to a series of consecutive entries in *EAE* 50–51, IV:6–7 regarding the astral "profile" we might say, of Ishtar-Venus. I do not fully understand these entries but I sense their relevance:

> MUL.UŠ A.KE$_{x}$ *ana* NAM.BAD MÈ ŠUB.BA
> ^{d}*Dil-bat ina* ^{d}UTU.SU.A IGI-*ma zik-rat*
> MUL.SAL.A.KE$_{x}$ *ana* NAM.SAL.TUK *ana* US.MES *ul-lu-di*
> ^{d}*Dil-bat ina* ^{d}UTU.E IGI-*ma sin-ni-šat*
>
> "The Star of Men is for pestilence.
> Venus is seen in the West—she is male.
> The Star of Women is for taking a wife [...] for giving birth to males.
> Venus is seen in the East—she is female."

---

[4] *Apud CAD A*/II, 229, s.v. *arāmu*, 1, d.

[5] See *CAD Z*, 49f., s.v. *zappu*.

These statements express the Ishtar-Venus astral synthesis whereby the aspect of fertility associated with Ishtar is fused with the aspect of celestial brilliance. Ishtar-Venus is hermaphroditic, and her female aspect is that of fertility, whereas the male aspect is negative, "anti-life," so to speak.

I see no dichotomy, therefore, between Ishtar as depicted in "The Descent of Ishtar," whose incarceration in the netherworld, and absence bring all human and animal fertility to a halt on the one hand, and the astral phenomenology, on the other. The fusion expressed in the omens clarifies the composite, divine name *šgr wʿštr*, as it was originally explained by Prof. Hoftijzer, as expressing the hypostasis of fertility conveyed by the verb *š-g-r* "to issue, give birth."

Usage of the noun *ḥt*[*t*] (or: *ḥt* = Hebrew *ḥāt*) "dread" in the Deir ʿAlla texts correlates well with the biblical diction, as we read in Jer. 10:2:

ûmēʾôtôt haššāmâyim ʾal tēḥātû
kîy yēḥattu haggôyîm mēhēmāh

"And do not be in dread of the celestial omens,
Let the nations be in dread of them!"

The above analysis of Section 2 raises the question of the professional roles attributed to Balaam in Combination I. In Syro-Mesopotamian magical literature, such roles are more clearly designated by official titles and classifications, although inevitable overlapping of functions, and the common utilization of practices are also evident there.

Whereas the vision of celestial darkness, as it is expressed, recalls the functions of the biblical *mĕʿônēn* "cloud-observer," a term often occurring together with *qôsēm* "diviner," (actually used with reference to Balaam in Jos. 13:22; cf., Deut. 18:10, 14), Balaam's relationship, both to the gods and to his listeners makes him a veritable *ḥôzeh*, a function also mingled with that of the *qôsēm* in biblical literature, as we read in Micah 3:6–7:

lākēn lâylāh lāḵem mēḥāzôn
wāḥḥăšēkāh lākem miqqesem
ûḇāʾāh hāššemeš ʿal hannĕḇîʾîm
wĕqādar ʿălêyhem hayyôm

"It shall be night for you without visions
And darkness for you without divination.
The sun shall set over the prophets,
And daytime shall be darkened for them."[6]

What I find poignant here is the suggestion that false prophets rely on a starlit sky and celestial omens, and that they will be sorely disappointed!

Reference to the verb *ḥ-z-h* brings me back to line 1 of Combination I, in section 1 of my outline. I continue to insist that the title *ḥzh* (=*ḥôzeh*) occurs there, and find difficulty with assuming a relative clause *ʾš ḥzh ʾlhn* for indepen-

[6] I have taken liberty with the Masoretic pointing, to render the reading smoother.

dent reasons. Taking *hʾ* as an exclamation before a verb in the consecutive tense, *wyʾtw*, strikes me as jarring, stylistically. The problem of where the red ink ends has, I have been informed, been solved by measuring the lengths of those lines wherein it appears. The red ink, it seems, reaches to precisely one-half of the length of the line, and resumes right below, extending over the second half of the second line. It may have no syntactic implications at all. Although we have in Exod. 24:11b: *wayyeḥĕzû ʾet haʾĕlôhîm* "They beheld God" (cf., *ibid.*, vs. 10), the diction of Deir ʿAlla suggests that the object of *ḥ-z-h* is *mḥzh* "vision," as we read in line 1: [*w*]*yḥz mḥzh* "He beheld a vision" (cf., Num. 24:3, 16). I prefer, therefore, to sustain the titulary here, and I have already documented the emphatic syntax required to generate: *ʾš ḥzh ʾlhn hʾ* "He is a divine seer" (cf., Lev. 13:44, 1 Kings 13:26, Zech. 13:5). I should also mention that *mśʾ* (= Hebrew *maśśāʾ* "forensic vision") serves as the direct object of the verb *ḥ-z-h* in biblical diction (Hab. 1:1, Lament. 2:14).

To continue the discussion of roles, it is clear that Balaam is principally a *ḥôzeh* in the Deir ʿAlla text by virtue of the fact (a fact obtaining whether or not we can agree on the syntax of line 1), that he beheld and heard divine visions. These visions, in addition to informing him of the "actions" (*pʿlt*) of the divine *mwʿd*, also included a depiction of celestial darkness strongly reminiscent of Syro-Mesopotamian celestial omens, some specifically relevant to Ishtar-Venus herself. Whereas we might say that omens appear as automatic, impersonal and objective, the spirit of Balaam's visions expresses divine will and authority. This raises a question endemic to the relation between astrology and religion, namely, the role of the gods (or of God), in determining the position of the stars and the other heavenly bodies. In biblical literature this question was finally answered in Isa. chapter 40, a product of exilic times. But the power of gods, individually and collectively, to assign the heavenly bodies to various positions, and to darken them by eclipse and by means of clouds, was hardly an exclusively monotheistic notion!

Second 3 in my outline of Combination I appears to me to be part of Balaam's transmission, and in the context of omen literature, functions as an apodosis of sorts. Celestial darkness, as a punishment for some acts by the goddess Shagar-we-Ishtar, means that there will be desolation in the land. This situation is predicted, or projected, somewhat symbolically, somewhat realistically. At the very beginning of the effort to interpret Deir ʿAlla, Prof. Hoftijzer had already cited the extensive biblical sources on the role of birds and wild animals in descriptions of disaster and desolation. I merely follow his lead in this matter.

My understanding of lines 1–10 (near end) of Combination I, what I have charted as Sections 1–3, may be summarized as follows: The *ʾlhn* who appear to Balaam were sent by El to warn Balaam's people of impending disaster. The prediction is expressed as an edict pronounced by a divine council (*mwʿd*) over the goddess, Shagar-we-Ishtar who has acted against some of the gods and who is being punished. Her punishment, projected in terms similar to the protases and apodoses of Syro-Mesopotamian celestial omens, some pertaining to Ishtar, herself, equates darkness with desolation. The goddess is not permitted to shine. On earth this condition is dramatized by reference to the frenzied movements and shrieking of birds and the abandonment of grazing land to wild animals.

Before attempting to relate Section 4 to these first three sections of Combination I, permit me to comment that it should not surprise us when we encounter reflections, or versions of Syro-Mesopotamian genres in West Semitic languages such as Aramaic, Hebrew and regional dialects of various sorts. Long ago, W. F. Albright noted a passage from the Neo-Assyrian *utukkê limnūtī* magical series, translated almost literally in an inscription from Arslan-Tash, composed in a West Semitic dialect.[7] In Ugaritic we have West Semitic renditions of *šumma izbu* omens.[8] There should be no problem, historically or culturally, in concluding that magical sources from the classical omen literature of Babylonia would be known in some form to eighth century B.C.E. writers on either side of the Jordan.

Now, let us turn to the last section of my outline, which I see as beginning in line 10 with the words: *šmʿw mwsr gry š*[*gr wʿštr*] (*pace*, Puech and others, who divide the text in different ways). How shall we read this statement? To me, there is a symmetry between this statement, and the one in line 13, below: *wšmʿw ḥršn mn rḥq*, which I translate: "Hear incantations from afar!" I therefore translate the former, opening statement "Heed admonition!" At this point, a real difference in possible interpretations arises, one which could affect our overall understanding of how Section 4 relates to the first three sections of Combination I, as I have outlined them.

a) "Heed the admonition *of the adversaries* of Shagar-we-Ishtar."

b) "Heed admonition, *oh adversaries* of Shagar-we-Ishtar!"

Option (a) bids the listeners obey the admonitions of the enemies of the goddess, whom I take to be the gods and Shadday-beings of the inimical *mwʿd*. The adversaries would be the admonishers! Option (b) makes someone else the admonisher, and bids the enemies of the goddess obey the admonition.

Who is the speaker? To me, it makes better sense to regard Balaam as the speaker, and to posit that his oration simply continued. Balaam would be doing what he is best known for in biblical tradition—he would be pronouncing execrations, if my reading of line 13 is deemed preferable to a reference to the deaf (*ḥēršîn*). This model suggests that Balaam is attacking the adversaries of the goddess. After all, he is severely distressed to hear that an edict has been issued against her. He is depicted in Section 1 as empathizing strongly with "his people" (*ʿmh*) and eager to warn them of impending disaster. It would be in character for him to attempt to defend his people by rescuing their goddess.

I wish I could be more certain of the contents of Section 4. In line 14 we read clearly *wkl ḥzw qqn* which likely means: "And all beheld acts of oppression." But I question the syntactic analysis which makes the goddess, whose

---

[7] See W. F. Albright, *BASOR* 76, 1939, 5–11.

[8] See the contributions of A. Herdner, "Nouveaux Textes alphabétiques de Ras Shamra" in *Ugaritica* VII, Paris, 1978, "Présages" pp. 44–63.

name appears fully, the object of a possessive construction: "And all beheld the oppression *of* Shagar-we-Ishtar." The author of the Deir ʿAlla texts knew how to express the masculine plural construct in normal ways. More likely, the name *šgr wʿštr* begins a new clause in line 14, relating something about the goddess, herself.

All I can offer is the observation that cultic and magical activities are being carried on in Section 4. In line 11, we have two professional titles: *rqḥt mr* "perfumer(s) of myrrh," and *khnh* "priestess." Nobody disputes *khnh*, and I prefer a title, rather than an active participle for *rqḥt* (cf., Hebrew *hāraqqāḥ* in Neh. 3:8, and feminine plural *raqqāḥôt* in 1 Sam. 8:13). Much less obvious are such possible terms as *ḥkmn* "skilled practitioners," *ʿnyh* "oracle" (rather than "poor woman") and *ḥšb* "craftsman," whether *nśʾ zr qrn* means "bearer of an offering in a horn," or: "bearer of a horned belt," is, of course, uncertain, as is the sense of *mšn ʾzrn* nearer the end of the section.

Some have argued that in ancient Near Eastern myth, magic diviners could not take on the gods, or act against them, and that Balaam would not be given an heroic role of this kind in the Deir ʿAlla inscriptions. What we have here is something more complex: El, the supreme god of the Deir ʿAlla inscriptions, acts to warn the people, through Balaam, of impending disaster. That disaster was decreed by a *mwʿd* or other gods. There is, therefore, conflict among the gods, themselves, and in championing the cause of the goddess Shagar-we-Ishtar, Balaam is aligning himself with El and his messengers against the inimical gods of the *mwʿd*.

Let us now turn to Combination II.

I would like to pursue the suggestion I first made, that *nqr* in the second Combination means "corpse," based on a comparison with Isa. 14:19: *kěnēṣer niṯʿāb* "like abhorrent carrion," parallel in sequence to *kěpeger mûḇās* "like a trampled corpse." I once mentioned a cognate Aramaic-Syriac vocable *nēṣlāʾ*. JoAnn Hackett questioned my interpretation by noting that in Aramaic, the postulated phoneme *ḍod*, required to produce the Deir ʿAlla term *nqr*, would not be represented by *ṣadē* in the Aramaic dialects. Upon further examination, I discovered that lexicographers had, indeed, confused the situation, and that Aramaic *nēṣlāʾ* was actually a variant of another verb *n-z-l* "to flow, run," and was irrelevant to my discussion. It turns out that all of the relevant forms I have considered are Hebrew, where postulated *ḍod* is often realized as *ṣadē*, after all.

A note in the New Jewish Version of Isa. 14:19 refers the reader to post-exilic *nēṣel* "putrefying flesh, or blood," as justification for not rendering *nēṣer* as "offshoot," by extension "scion, offspring" (cf., Isa. 11:1) Context alone would recommend positing two vocables:

> 1) *nēṣer* I "offshoot," cognate to the Arabic verb *naḍara* "to be verdant, to shine, grow."

> 2) *nēṣer* II "carrion, dead flesh," a phonetic variant of post-biblical Hebrew *neṣel*, and cognate to the Arabic verb *naḍala* "to pull back, tear off," as is said of "drawing a sword or selecting an arrow from the quiver"; "to extract."[9]

Let us examine the Late Hebrew form, *nēṣel*, also written *nāṣāl*. In Mishnah, *Nazir* 7:2 (also *ʾAhilot* 2:1). This word appears in a clear context:

> "Over which sorts of impurity is the Nazirite required to shave (Num. 6:8f.)? Over a corpse, over the equivalent of an olive from a corpse, over the equivalent of an olive of *nēṣel* and over a large, ladle-full of bloodied soil."

The law of Numbers 6 provides that if a Nazirite accidently comes into contact with a corpse during the term of his vow, he must begin all over again, shave and bathe, etc. What constitutes a sufficient substance to interrupt his votive term? Not only a corpse or a part of one, we are told, but also *nēṣel* and bloodied soil. The Talmud of Jerusalem, *ad loc.*, *Nazir* 9:2 explains *nēṣel* as follows: "What is a *nēṣel*? Flesh from a corpse which has become *detached* (Hebrew *šenuttaq*) and [bloody] liquid that has congealed."

There are, in fact additional Late Hebrew forms derived from the root *n-ṣ-l*. There is a feminine form *nĕṣûlāh* "refuse, what is cast off" (cf., Maimonides, *Code*, *Terumot* 11:13: "The waste-product (*nĕṣôlet*) of rotten parts of priestly gifts.")

But, we need not venture so far because I identify another biblical form akin to *nēṣer* of Isa. 14:19, and refer you to Isa. 49:6:

> *wayyôʾmer: nāqēl mihyôṯĕḵā lî ʿebed lĕhāqîm ʾet šiḇṭê Yisrāʾēl ûnĕṣirê* (Qere: *ûnĕṣûrê*) *Yiśrāʾēl lĕhāšîb*
> "Is it of so little import that you act as my servant, to reconstitute the tribes of Israel, and to bring back the *cast-offs* of Israel?"

Usually, *nĕṣîrê/nĕṣûrê* has been derived from the verb *n-ṣ-r* "to guard," and this verse has been interpreted with reference to prisoners and captives. Some have suggested, and I agree, that we actually have a vocable deriving from the same root as *nēṣer* "carrion, corpse." The unifying factor is that of "detachment," said of dead, putrefying flesh, and of abandoned, or exiled human beings. The context of the servant passage certainly suggests this because in the continuation, Israel is characterized as follows: *liḇzôh-nepeš limĕṯôʿāb gôy*—"to the despised person, to the abhorred nation." Here, the cast-off is *mĕṯôʿāb*, whereas in Isa. 14:19, carrion is *nitʿāb*!

---

[9] See Ibn Manzur, *Lisān al-ʿarab* Beirut, 1956 v. 2 p. 663, s.v. *Naḍala*. Stem V, *tanaḍḍala* means: "[to remove] a sword from its scabbard," and the same meaning is attested for the dialectal variant *tanaṣṣala*. Stem V also has the extended connotation "to get out of something," as to get out of a sin or evil deed. I am indebted to my colleague at New York University, Prof. Michael Carter, for directing me to this reference.

I prefer this interpretation to concluding that *nqr* means "descendant," and/or that Combination II depicts child sacrifice. The affinities to Isaiah, chapter 14, are in my opinion, compelling, as is the similarity of diction between our text and "The Descent of Ishtar." This persuades me that in Combination II we have a corpse languishing in Sheol; more precisely in a necropolis, or netherworld (*byt ʿlmn*) built by El, himself.

The question now poses itself as to whether Combination II follows topically upon Combination I, or to put it another way: Are both Combinations speaking of Balaam, or of the same prediction?

I am grateful to André Lemaire and to Émile Puech for their painstaking attempts to resolve this question by reconstructing the physical position of the fallen plaster fragments within the structure at Deir ʿAlla where they were discovered.

According to Lemaire, Combinations I and II were written on plastered surfaces lateral to each other, and for this reason, as well as for others based on content, we need not conclude that the two Combinations are topically related to each other. According to Puech and others, the two Combinations stood above and below each other, more precisely—Combination II was below Combination I, in the same column, and was sequential to Combination I.[10]

These discussions have re-opened the overall question of the relationship between the two Combinations.

We would do well to re-examine the readable content of Combination II. I find only two clues to an oracular function, and the pronouncement of execrations that might suggest that the corpse of Combination II (or the scion, for that matter) is, indeed, Balaam. At the present time, the name of Balaam cannot be read with any assurance in Combination II, and there is no readable clause or group of words where this name is required, or where its absence can be assumed. The two clues I find are as follows:

1) in line 9 I read:

> *hlʿṣh bk lytʿṣ*
> *ʾw lmlkh lytmlk*

I originally translated as follows, and I see no problems with this translation now:

> "If it is for counsel, no one will consult you!
> Or for his advice, no one will take counsel!"

2) The second clue comes in line 17:

> *ldʿt spr dbr lʿmh*
> *ʿl lšn lk n/mšpṭ*

---

[10] A. Lemaire, "La disposition originelle des Inscriptions sur Plâtre de Deir ʿAlla", *Studi Epigrafici e Linguistici* 3, 1986, 79–93. Also see É. Puech, "Admonitions de Balaam", etc. *Le Monde de la Bible*, 46, 1986, 36–38.

wmlqb ʾmr

"—To know how to transmit an oracle to his people,
You have been judged for your speech,
And [banned] from pronouncing words of execration."

The sense may be that someone has been deprived of the gifts of the diviner, thus reinforcing the suggested meaning of line 13, as pertaining to one such as Balaam. If, however, Puech is correct that line 17 begins a new unit, this passage would lose its relevance for defining the relationship between Combinations I and II. We would then be left solely with the statement in line 13, which could just as well be understood as part of the generally moribund description of the netherworld, where the dead never sense emotion or perform any useful function!

I now seriously doubt that Combination II is topically sequential to Combination I, which is to say that it should be understood as recounting the assignment of Balaam to Sheol as punishment for his actions performed in Combination I; or that the contents of Combination II relate to the goddess punished by the *mwᶜd*, or to celestial darkness and desolation. I agree with the analysis of Puech, and with my own original hunch, that the introductory statements of Combination I functioned as the general title of all that followed, in our two Combinations, as well as in what might have been intended for other sections. What we have in the plaster inscriptions is a collection of Balaam's orations, the *spr* of Balaam, son of Beor, who was a divine seer (*ḥzh ʾlhn*). It is not entirely clear how much of what Combination I says about Balaam is part of the overall introduction to the *spr*. A conservative view would be that only the initial statement served as the title: (*zh*/*ysry*) *spr blᶜm br bᶜr ʾš ḥzh ʾlhn hʾ* "This is/ the admonition of the *recorded collection* of Balaam son of Beor; he is the divine seer!" As is true of biblical collections of prophecies attributed to a single prophet, separate orations may cover a range of subjects. In our case, Combination I preserves one prophecy, and Combination II another, in which the netherworld is depicted in language reminiscent of Isaiah, ch. 14.

There is, however, indication of what may turn out to be a further relationship between the two combinations, and I have already alluded to it: The real link is expressed by the presence of El, and by descriptions of his acts, as found in both Combinations. In Combination I, it is El's *maśśāʾ* "forensic vision" that is revealed to Balaam, and in Combination II, it is El who, after sating himself with lovemaking, builds a netherworld which is then depicted so dramatically. The two combinations (and possibly additional inscriptions) belonged near each other in the structure at Deir ᶜAlla, whatever its precise function was, because they were part of the El *repertoire* of Deir ᶜAlla. El is a deity who shows concern for human beings; the preparation of a proper Sheol is also an act of concern! For me, this proposed literary provenance represents the most suggestive aspect of General Interpretation to have emerged.

The Temple Scroll: Aspects of its Historical Provenance and Literary Character*

Late in 1977, the Hebrew edition of *The Temple Scroll* (*Megillat Hammiqdāš*) by Professor Yigael Yadin appeared in three volumes: Vol. I, *Introduction*; Vol. II, *Text and Commentary*; and Vol. III, *Plates and Texts*, with a *Supplement* containing additional plates (Yadin 1977).[1] An English version is in preparation. Since the latter is being planned as a precise rendition of the Hebrew edition, with only minor modifications, I considered it advantageous to begin work immediately on a study of the Scroll, based on the Hebrew edition, for submission to an American journal. I reasoned that whatever I discuss would remain relevant once the English version appeared. In this way, information concerning the Scroll's overall character could be transmitted promptly, and certain problems arising from it could be engaged at the outset.

What follows here is a preliminary study. It will necessarily leave many important areas of interest unexplored and will touch upon others only in passing. Principal attention will be given to the question of historical provenance, which cuts across the Scroll's variegated contents, and also to aspects of its literary character. Problems of language and orthography, together with questions relating to the detailed temple plan and the cultic prescriptions set forth in the Scroll, will be touched upon only tangentially, since their full investigation must await further study. The main purpose here is to focus attention on some of the interpretive problems basic to a general understanding of the Scroll as an ancient document.

---

* Originally published in *BASOR* 232 (1978), pp. 5–23. Reprinted with permission from the American Schools of Oriental Research.

[1] Citations from the Hebrew text of the Scroll will indicate column and line. Page references to the Hebrew edition will be kept to a minimum, since the pagination of the forthcoming English edition will undoubtedly be different. When provided, such citations will indicate volume and page (for example, II:45, etc.). The general point of reference will be the column and line of the text in Vol. II. Yadin's running commentary consistently refers the reader to pertinent topical discussions in Vol. I. Note that all translations into English from the Hebrew text of the Scroll itself, as well as from biblical and all other non-English sources (including Yadin's Hebrew discussion), are by this author, who assumes full responsibility for them.

Introduction

It would be superfluous to go into detail concerning data soon to be summarized and tabulated in the English edition, and yet it is essential to provide some basic facts about the Scroll itself and Yadin's treatment of it.

The Scroll is written on a very thin parchment, with a sharp instrument. As preserved, it consists of 19 parchment strips, most of which contain three or four columns. The total number of preserved columns is 65, beginning with col. 2. The preserved text breaks off at the end of col. 66, with indications that there was an additional column. Columns 2–5 were written by a different scribe, who probably also wrote col. 1. The upper parts of the parchments are considerably damaged, a fact which often makes it difficult to establish the continuity from one column to the next. In cols. 6–48 and 61–66 there were originally 22 lines, and in cols. 49–60 there were 28 lines. Columns 1–5 may have also contained 22 lines each. The preserved length of the Scroll is 8.148 m.

The script of the presently published copy is characterized by Yadin as typically Herodian. It seems that the copyist of cols. 2–5 used a more "progressive" Herodian script than did the copyist of the rest of the columns.

In 1967, Yadin found some unpublished fragments from Qumran Cave 4 in the Rockefeller Museum. He was able to identify them as coming from two or three other copies of the Scroll. Photographs of these fragments are reproduced in the *Supplement* to Vol. III, nos. 35*–40*, by permission of the late Roland de Vaux.

One group of these fragments, numbered *Rockefeller* 43.366, exhibits a different script. In the opinion of Yadin and N. Avigad, to whom these fragments were shown, this script resembled that of the Isaiah A and Deuteronomy scrolls from Qumran Cave 4, which had been assigned to the middle-Hasmonean period.[2] On the basis of this paleographic assessment, Yadin concluded that the Scroll was in existence as early as the end of the second pre-Christian century or thereabouts. The fact that fragments of other copies of the Scroll were actually found at Qumran makes it certain that this document was part of that ancient library. The present copy was, of course, obtained from a dealer.

Anticipating conclusions regarding the pseudepigraphic character of the Scroll to be presented below, I must express serious doubt that one of the fragments in the group numbered, *Rockefeller* 43.366, truly represents an excerpt from the Scroll (see fragment no. 1, on pl. 40 of the *Supplement* to Vol. III). This fragment contains an introductory formula:

> And Yahweh spoke to Moses saying: Command the Israelites saying:

It also contains a postscript, taken from Lev 23:44, which reads:

---

[2] This script has been discussed by N. Avigad (1958) and by F. M. Cross, Jr. (1965). Yadin provides a detailed chart (1977:I:17, fig. 1) which compares the script of *Rockefeller* 43.366 with the later Herodian scripts.

> So Moses declared the set times (*môᶜădîm*) of Yahweh to the Israelites.

Yadin suggests utilizing lines 3–8 of this fragment, where the above statements occur, to fill a *lacuna* at the beginning of col. 11 of the Scroll. It is not entirely clear whether he meant that this fragment should actually be inserted at that point, or whether he merely found its contents suggestive of what might have been written there originally. In any event, the continuity that would result is not entirely convincing. Furthermore, the fact that in this fragment Yahweh speaks to Moses brings it into conflict with the outlook of the entire Scroll, where Moses' name is never mentioned, and for a specific reason: The words of the Scroll are represented as God's own words, and the role of Moses as the teacher of God's word to Israel has been meticulously eliminated. Thus, many of Deuteronomy's *dicta* have actually been altered so that Yahweh is no longer referred to in the third person but becomes the speaker, or first-person referent.

It is inconceivable that the Scroll contained any passages naming Moses. I therefore suggest that fragment no. 1 be detached from the group numbered *Rockefeller* 43.366 and given a different catalogue designation. It goes without saying, therefore, that this fragment cannot be utilized to shed light on the lacuna at the beginning of col. 11 of the Scroll.

Briefly the contents of the Scroll may be outlined as follows. After an introductory exhortation to remain loyal to the covenant (col. 2), the Scroll proceeds to ordain the construction of a temple to Yahweh, whose dimensions and various structures are then delineated, including those cultic appurtenances which were to be located inside the temple proper (cols. 3:1–13:10). These columns are poorly preserved. Columns 13:10–30:3(?) contain the Scroll's major prescriptions on the investiture of the priesthood, the observance of the festivals, modes of sacrifice, and the like. From col. 30:3(?) to 45:7 we encounter prescriptions pertaining to the courtyards of the temple complex, its gates, installations, and appurtenances. There is also information on the assignment of personnel to certain areas of the temple complex. Finally, cols. 45:7 to 66 (the end of the preserved Scroll) provide extensive ordinances on the subject of cultic purity, along with other requirements only tangentially related to the specific theme of the Scroll. Included are aspects of testimony, norms of justice, and the like. This material was probably included so as to enhance the overall tone of the Scroll as a pseudepigraphic Torah.

Yadin's edition reflects a Herculean effort of preservation and interpretation. Only a decade after the first retrieval of this lengthy and poorly preserved scroll, an edition has seen the light of day. The photographs are of very good quality, considering the poor condition of the parchments. There is very little conjecture in Yadin's readings, and he has done an amazing job of eliciting legibility from the parchments. The suggested restorations fall into the two usual categories: some are verifiable from parallel passages or from biblical sources on a similar theme, others from joins of fragments from other copies of the scroll or from mirror images. Some restorations, however, are more conjectural.

For this reason, I question the wisdom of including at the end of Vol. II a separately printed "Restored Version." Even though it is presented most conservatively, it may be given more weight by readers than it warrants.

Perhaps Yadin's most valuable contributions to a proper understanding of the Scroll are his detailed illustrations of the temple plan and its various components. These appear with a step-by-step reconstruction of the plan from the text. What has resulted is a feat of graphic skill and conceptual acumen.

The Question of Provenance and the Calendar

The question of the Scroll's possibly sectarian provenance is basic to its overall interpretation. Yadin argues at great length that the Scroll belongs to the corpus of writings particular to the Qumran sect, which he identifies with the Essenes. In his view, the Scroll expresses the Qumran sect's distinctive outlook on such matters as ritual purity and the cult, much in the same way as do the codes and manuals from Qumran, the War Scroll, and the Thanksgiving Scroll on other subjects of vital concern to the sect. This hypothesis is fundamental to his entire interpretation, and it directly affects many of the specific determinations made in the running commentary to the text. At times, Yadin's reasoning seems to be circular, as he imposes on the textual evidence an undemonstrated hypothesis, lending it the status of a prior conclusion.

Before taking up the question as to whether or not the Scroll is "sectarian," a working definition of sectarianism is required. A text may be designated sectarian if it originated with, or was adopted by, an identifiable group whose members cut themselves off from the prevailing religious community. Now when one surveys "the ancient library of Qumran" (to borrow a title from F. M. Cross, Jr. 1961) a distinction must be made between at least two categories of writings: (a) writings which specifically refer to a group by name and/or characterize its particular outlook and speak of its opposition to other groups; and (b) writings preserved by a sect and considered important by it, but which did not come into being for the express purpose of conveying the sect's doctrinaire point of view. A sect preserving such writings obviously felt a particular affinity toward them, but such writings were not sectarian in the strict sense. A complete breakdown of the Qumran library is not possible here, but a contrast can be drawn: In the category of strictly sectarian writings one would place the *sĕrākîm*, the War Scroll, Thanksgiving Scroll, and most likely a text such as the Sabbath liturgy edited by Strugnell (1960). (The Zadokite Document is a special problem, as we shall see.) In the latter category of preserved writings one would place the biblical scrolls: the versions, text of Jubilees, Enoch, Ben-Sira, and probably the Qumran psalms. In my opinion, the Scroll belongs in this latter category, not in the former.[3]

---

[3] Smith (1960–61:347ff.) makes a somewhat similar point about the diversity of literary materials found at Qumran.

One may, of course, proceed from a broader definition of sectarianism, as well as recognize the probability that more than one sect was operative at any one time. Much of what has been discovered thus far in Palestine from the final, two pre-Christian centuries seems to be divergent, or restricted to limited circles, as was the case with the book of Jubilees. For all we know, this judgment may be distorted, because it is based, after all, largely on what we know about the character of Jewish religious life in earlier and later periods, not from the contemporary period. It is clear, nevertheless, that the Scroll's author was especially familiar with the traditions of Jubilees and with the legal content of the Zadokite Document, in particular. These affinities must be weighed against similarities in language and content between the Scroll and the later Rabbinic literature, on the one hand, and against elements of continuity with central biblical traditions on the other.

One of Yadin's principal arguments in favor of identifying the Scroll as one of the writings of the Qumran sect, strictly speaking, is his contention that the calendar which underlies the scheduling of "set-times" (*môᶜădîm*), as ordained in the Scroll, is the sectarian calendar of the Qumran sect, common to it and to the traditions of Jubilees. If it could be demonstrated that this distinctive calendar accounts for the specific scheduling of the Scroll's sacred occasions, one would, indeed, be inclined to argue for sectarian provenance (but see below). If, on the other hand, it can be shown that the Scroll's *môᶜădîm* do not necessarily presuppose the Qumran calendar, then serious doubt would be raised concerning the alleged sectarian provenance of the Scroll.

The crux of the calendric problem pertains to the date intended for the offering of the *ᶜômer*, "sheaf," of new barley, an occasion which in the Scroll is termed *yôm hānēp hāᶜômer* and *yôm hănîpat hāᶜômer*, "the day of presenting the sheaf" (cols. 11:10; 18:10).[4] As in the biblical prescriptions of Lev 23:9–21, so in the Scroll's provisions no calendar date is stipulated for this celebration or for the Pentecost. Rather, information is provided on the basis of which one was to compute the respective dates of these celebrations. Now, whereas Leviticus 23 limits itself to the initial presentation of the barley sheaf and to the Pentecost, 50 days later, the Scroll extends the *môᶜădîm* subsequent to the Pentecost, which was likewise the occasion for presenting the sheaf of wheat. These two occasions are *môᶜēd hattîrôš*, "the set-time of the wine," and *môᶜēd hayyiṣhār*, "the set-time of the oil." Neither of these occasions is specifically mentioned in the Bible.

The problem of dating the Pentecost (and hence of any occasions subsequent to it) on the 49-day cycle derives from an ambiguity already present in Lev 23:11 and 15a. There it is specified that the initial presentation of the barley

---

[4] Milgrom (1972) corrects the longstanding misinterpretation of the term *tĕnûpāh* (usually rendered "wave offering") by explaining that the *Hipᶜil* form *hēnîp* really means "to raise, lift up." Hence *tĕnûpāh* means "that which is raised up" (cf. Hebrew *tĕrûmāh*). The translation given "to present," is intended as functional, not literal.

sheaf is to take place on "the day after the 'sabbath'" (*mimmoḥŏrat haššabbāt*). What does the Hebrew term *šabbāt* mean in verses 11 and 15a? What does it mean subsequently in verses 15b and 16 of the same chapter? Until such questions can be answered the term *šabbāt* should be rendered 'sabbath' (in single quotes) for greater clarity.

The relevant passages are as follows:

> (a) Lev 23:11:
>
> And he (the priest) shall present (*wĕhēnīp*) the sheaf before Yahweh for acceptance on your behalf; on the day after the 'sabbath' (*mimmoḥŏrat haššabbāt*) the priest shall present it.
>
> (b) Lev 23:15–16:
>
> (15a) And from the day on which you bring the sheaf for the presentation offering (*ʿômer hattĕnûpāh*)—the day after the 'sabbath' (*mimmoḥŏrat haššabbāt*)—(15b) you shall count off seven 'sabbaths' (*šebaʿ šabbātôt*). They shall be complete; (16) you must count until the day after the seventh 'sabbath' (*ʿad mimmoḥŏrat haššabbāt haššĕbîʿît*) 50 days; then you shall bring an offering of new grain to Yahweh.

The ambiguities present in the above verses have served as the nexus for continuing disputes within Jewry, along both hermeneutic and sectarian lines, well into the Middle Ages. These disputes are echoed in Talmudic sources as well as in the Medieval Jewish commentaries. Even primary exegesis immediately requires definitions for the term *šabbāt* in Lev 23:9–21. In these verses, does it ever actually mean "the Sabbath day," i.e., Saturday?

By way of background, it is important to explain that the calendar projected in Jubilees and theorized in 1 Enoch provided for a year containing twelve 30-day months, with four additional days each year, one added each quarter, making a total of 364 days in the year. According to this system, the first day of Passover (the 15th of Nisan) would always fall on a Wednesday, and the same was true for the Day of Memorial (the first of Tishri) and the first day of Sukkoth (the 15th of Tishri). To those operating on this system, the formula *mimmoḥŏrat haššabbāt* in Lev 23:11 and 15a must have been literally taken to refer to the first Sunday after the seven days of Passover, the 26th of Nisan. This is because Jubilees (16:4) gives the date of the Pentecost as the 15th of Sivan, which is the 50th day after the 26th of Nisan.

As for the definition of the term *šabbāt* in verses 15b–16, this same system would require it to mean "a week ending on the Sabbath," a Sunday-to-Saturday week, not merely a unit of seven days. Conceivably, it also could have been taken to mean "the Sabbath day," because, in fact, seven Sabbath days would transpire between the initial presentation of the barley sheaf and the Pentecost. This would not have to be so according to Rabbinic interpretation, known to us from later sources, according to which *šabbāt* in Lev 23:11 and 15a was interpreted to mean "a day of rest," i.e., the holy convocation of the first day of Passover, on which labor was forbidden (cf. Lev 23:7). According to Rabbinic tradition, the barley sheaf was to be offered on the 16th of Nisan, and the Pentecost occurred on the 6th of Sivan. Since the Rabbinic month was lunar, the lengths of successive months would vary, and as a result, festivals might fall on different days of the week from year to year.

Now it is fairly well established that the calendar projected in Jubilees was used by the Qumran sect, or at least known to it. An insertion in one of the Qumran psalms, which has become known as "David's Composition," states clearly that the year consists of 52 Sabbaths and 364 days. Other sources list 26 two-week periods of service (*mišmārôt*) for the priests, which predicates a year of 52 weeks.[5] Yadin further notes that a fragment from Qumran Cave 4, cited by Milik, gives the 22nd of Elul as the date for "the set-time of the oil" (*môᶜēd haššemen*), another name for what the Scroll calls *môᶜēd hayyiṣhār*. Now it is significant that the 22nd of Elul comes at the end of three cycles of 49 days each, commencing on the 26th of Nisan![6]

Is there explicit evidence that the Scroll's author followed the above-described calendar? Yadin answers in the affirmative. He bases his view primarily on the specific wording of the Scroll's formulations for the *môᶜădîm*, which commence with the presentation of the barley sheaf, and continue through three consecutive cycles of 49 days each. He also stresses the fact that the Scroll prescribes some of the same nonbiblical *môᶜădîm* as are known from other Qumran texts, as well as from later sectarian writings.

It would be well, therefore, to examine the precise wording of the relevant passages in the Scroll:

> (a) Col. 18:10–13:
>
> You shall count off seven complete 'sabbaths' (*šebaᶜ šabbātôt tĕmîmôt*), from the day on which you bring the sheaf for the presentation offering. You shall count until the day after the seventh 'sabbath' (*ᶜad mimmoḥŏrat haššabbāt haššĕbîᶜît*). 50 days.
>
> (b) Col. 19:11–13:
>
> You shall count off, from the day on which you bring the offering of new grain to Yahweh, the bread of the new grain, seven weeks (*šibᶜāh šābûᶜôt*); seven complete 'sabbaths' (*šebaᶜ šabbātôt tĕmîmôt*)

---

[5] This and related problems have been extensively discussed by A. Jaubert in two related studies (1953; 1957). Also see Talmon (1958) for further insights into the historical implications of the Qumran calendar. Summaries are provided by Licht (1970) and Fitzmyer (1975). Aside from Jubilees 16:4, cf. also I Enoch, chapters 72–78, and Jubilees 6:29–30. Ankori (1959) provides an incisive discussion of the prolonged history of the dispute between the Karaites and the Rabbinites on the matter of the calendar (see 269ff., "Upholding the Calendar"; 292ff., "Calendar Feuds"; and 394ff., "Refuting Solar Calendation"). Now see Milik (1976), for additional discussion.

[6] Milik (1957:25). The text reads as follows: *bᶜśrm/wšnym/bw mwᶜd/hšmn*, "on the 22nd day of it (i.e., the 6th month) is the set-time of oil."

there shall be; until the day after the seventh 'sabbath' (*ʿad mimmoḥŏrat haššabbāt haššĕbîʿît*) you shall count 50 days.

(c) Col. 21:12–14:

You shall count, from this day, seven weeks, seven times (*šibʿāh šābûʿôt šebaʿ pĕʿāmîm*). nine and forty days, seven complete 'sabbaths' (*šebaʿ šabbātôt tĕmîmôt*); until the day after the seventh 'sabbath' (*ʿad mimmoḥŏrat haššabbāt haššĕbîʿît*) you shall count 50 days.

The wording in *b* and *c* above becomes progressively more expansive, whereas *a* remains a closer paraphrase of Lev 23:15–16, with the syntactic awkwardness of the biblical original merely smoothed out. In *b* and *c*, which refer to occasions not ordained in the Torah, the Scroll's author harmonized the language of Leviticus 23 with Deut 16:9 by interpolating the words *šibʿāh šābûʿôt*, "seven weeks." In *c* he even added words of his own, *šebaʿ pĕʿāmîm*, "seven times."

What is the cumulative effect of the interpolation from Deut 16:9 and the addition? In Hebrew usage, biblical and postbiblical, the term *šābûʿa* never specifically connotes anything but a unit of seven, whether days or years.[7] Taken by itself, Deut 16:9, which uses only the term *šābûʿa* and not *šabbāt* to designate a week, could not be interpreted to mean seven Sunday-to-Saturday weeks. Certainly *šebaʿ pĕʿāmîm*, "seven times," does nothing to identify which day from Sunday to Saturday is to be considered "day one."

It is, therefore, difficult to understand just how Yadin is able to conclude on the basis of the three cited formulations in the Scroll that its author is speaking of seven weeks, each beginning on a Sunday and ending on a Saturday, and that consequently the Scroll's calendar began its cycles from the 26th of Nisan, a Sunday. One could just as well argue that the Scroll's author utilized Deut 16:9 to remove the ambiguity endemic to Lev 23:9–21 by making it clear that he understood *šabbāt* to mean *šābûʿa* and that "seven 'sabbaths'" merely meant seven × seven days, i.e., *šebaʿ pĕʿāmîm*, "seven times."

In this connection, it is also significant that the Scroll's author omitted the words *mimmoḥŏrat haššabbāt*, "the day after the 'sabbath'," in his version of Lev 23:15a and that he never employs this formula in any of his subsequent prescriptions for the *môʿădîm*. It is curious that at least one modern scholar (Ginsberg 1978) has suggested that both in Lev 23:11 and in 15a the words *mimmoḥŏrat haššabbāt* are a gloss, stimulated by verse 16. In verse 16, the complete formula occurs, *ʿad mimmoḥŏrat haššabbāt haššĕbîʿît*, "until the day after the seventh week." The antecedent is *šabbatôt*, "weeks," in verse 15b. In verses 11 and 15a, *mimmoḥŏrat haššabbāt* represents an adumbration of the original

[7] The term *šābûʿa* is relatively rare in biblical Hebrew usage. In Lev 12:5 the dual *šĕbûʿaîm* must, by context, designate a period of 14 days, reckoned from whatever day the impurity in question actually commenced. For later Hebrew usage see Ben-Yehudah (1960).

phrase, in which the word *šabbāt* is taken out of context and made to refer to a certain day, not a week. On this basis the *ʾetnāḥ* should be moved back one word, and the verse should read:

> *wĕhenîp ʾet hāʿômer lipnê YHWH;*
> *lirṣônkem yĕnîpennû hakkôhēn*
>
> And he shall present the sheaf before Yahweh; the priest shall present it for acceptance on your behalf (cf. Lev 19:5b).

As regards verse 15a, the words *mimmoḥŏrat haššabbāt* would simply be deleted, as they are in the Scroll's version of that verse.

If the words *mimmoḥŏrat haššabbāt* in verses 11 and 15a are a gloss, they represent a very ancient gloss, already known to the author of Josh 5:10–11, who engaged in exegesis of his own. Josh 5:10–11 read as follows:

> And the Israelites encamped at Gilgal and performed the paschal sacrifice on the 14th day of the month in the plains of Jericho. And they ate of the crop of the land on the day after the "*pesaḥ*" (*mimmoḥŏrat happesaḥ*)—unleavened bread (*maṣṣôt*) and parched grain (*qālî*) on that very day (*bĕʿeṣem hayyôm hazzeh*).

Now the language of the passage in Joshua clearly echoes that of Lev 23:9–21. Thus Lev 23:14 mentions that until the barley sheaf is offered no bread (*leḥem*) or parched grain (*qālî*) may be eaten and it even uses the same phrase, *ʿeṣem hayyôm hazzeh*, "that very day." It is significant that Josh 5:11 substitutes the word *pesaḥ* for *šabbāt* and speaks of eating the new crop on the day after the "*pesaḥ*." Now Medieval Jewish commentators argued over the question as to whether *happesaḥ* in Josh 5:11 referred to the sacrifice of the 14th of Nisan, so that the day after would be the 15th; or whether it referred to the first day of the festival proper, the 15th of Nisan, so that the day after would be the 16th of the month. In no way could the reference be specifically to a Sunday, either during or after the seven days of Passover.[8]

The point is that the Scroll's author must have had the words *mimmoḥŏrat haššabbāt* in his Torah text, if this was the version already known to the author of Josh 5:10–11. Whereas the author of Josh 5:10–11 made it clear that he understood *šabbāt* in Lev 23:11 and 15a as referring in some manner to the Passover and not in the sense of "the Sabbath day," the Scroll's author, in presenting his code for the expanded *môʿădîm*, solved the ambiguity by deleting the problematic construction *mimmoḥŏrat haššabbāt* entirely from his version of Lev 23:15a and by using Deuteronomic and original terminology to indicate that in verse 16 *šabbāt* merely meant a unit of seven days. If, however, he had agreed that the initial presentation of the barley sheaf was to take place on the first Sunday after the seven days of Passover according to the sectarian calendar, i.e., on

---

[8] See, for example, the prolonged discussion by Nachmanides, in his commentary to the Torah, *ad loc.* Lev 23:11.

the 26th of Nisan, he should have been strongly motivated to *retain* the critical words *mimmoḥŏrat haššabbāt* in his version of Lev 23:15a.

Yadin explains that omission of the words *mimmoḥŏrat haššabbāt* from the Scroll's version of Lev 23:15–16 is understandable because, as he puts it, "This matter had already been established in the prescriptions concerning the day of presenting the [barley] sheaf" (1977:I:85). The problem is that lines 1–3 of col. 18, where the initial prescription governing that occasion is to be expected, are almost entirely missing. Conceivably, if these lines had been preserved we might have found the critical words we are seeking. It is curious, nevertheless, that these words, *mimmoḥŏrat haššabbāt*, which are the ones that actually make the point about initiating the counting on a Sunday, are nowhere to be found in any of the Scroll's preserved formulations. In later periods, those Jewish sects who disputed the Rabbinic calendar, such as the Karaites, justified their divergence by insisting on the literal interpretation of the word *šabbāt* in Lev 23:11 and 15a, and yet the Scroll's author, who is alleged to be an advocate of the Qumran-Jubilees calendar, failed to avail himself of three perfect opportunities to make the same point!

All that we know, therefore, is that the liturgical calendar of the Scroll shared certain nonbiblical "set-times" with the Qumran sect. We have no way of knowing, however, how limited or how widespread such celebrations were at the time. Yadin expands the scope of the argument by citing later evidence, notably a polemical word written in Judeo-Arabic by Saadiah Gaon against the Karaites. In it Saadiah refers to a certain Judah the Alexandrian, whose identity and dates are still uncertain. This Judah knew of the "set-times" common to the Qumran sect and Jubilees and to the Scroll. Since the Hebrew names of these occasions were retained in the Judeo-Arabic text of Saadiah, it is possible to compare them precisely with the earlier evidence.

The relevant passage reads:

> And as for Judah the Alexandrian, he says that just as there are 50 days between the "first fruits" of barley (*bikkûrê śĕʿôrîm*) and the "first fruits" of wheat (*bikkûrê ḥiṭṭîm*), in the same way there are 50 days between the "first fruits" of wheat and the "first fruits" of wine (*bikkûrê tîrôš*); and it will be … at the end of the month of Tammuz. And there are also 50 days between the "first fruits" of wine and the "first fruits" of oil (*bikkûrê yiṣhār*), and the offering of oil (*qorban šemen*) will be on the 20th of Elul.[9]

There have been various speculations as to who was actually responsible for those precise calculations, Saadiah himself or Judah the Alexandrian, but in any event they present certain difficulties apart from the minor discrepancy of two

[9] On Judah the Alexandrian's statement, see Hirschfeld (1904). Some had thought that this person was none other than Philo Judaeus, but this possibility has pretty much been dismissed. The polemical tract by Saadiah Gaon is entitled Kitāb al-Tamyîz, first published by Hirschfeld from the Cairo Genizah.

days in Elul. If we work back from the 20th of Elul according to the Qumran-Jubilees calendar, we end up with a sequence in which all of the "set-times" fall on a Friday, the first being on Friday, the 24th of Nisan. That would only be true, however, if we count the fiftieth day after each 49-day cycle as the first day of the following cycle. Otherwise we end up with a sequence, from Elul back to Nisan, of "set-times" which fall successively on Friday, Thursday, Wednesday, and Tuesday. Either way, whatever happened to the notion that the "set-times" fell on Sundays? We must conclude either that the calendar used in these computations reported by Saadiah was one which had months of varying lengths, or that the notion of Sunday as the day of the week for the presentation of the barley sheaf, and hence for all subsequent *môᶜădîm*, played no role at all. From the fact that Judah the Alexandrian is quoted as saying that the "first fruits" of wine falls at the end of Tammuz, it may be that he was operating on a calendar of 30-day months, since such a calendar would have that festival fall on the 30th of Tammuz.

It should be clear by now that we are dealing with several variables: (a) the length of the month and the year; (b) the specific *môᶜădîm* to be celebrated; and (c) the reconciliation of a particular calendric system with biblical statements governing the festivals. The point to be made is that those celebrating the same sacred occasions did not necessarily operate on the same calendric system.

These considerations lead us to a broader question regarding the relationship between exegesis and hermeneutic, on the one hand, and sectarianism, however we define it, on the other. Did calendric disputes within Jewish communities result from disagreements as to the correct meaning of the biblical *dicta*? Did the Boethusians, for instance, reject the 16th of Nisan as the date for the initial presentation of the barley sheaf because they disagreed about the meaning of Lev 23:11 and 15a?

Historically, the reverse was probably more often the case: For any of several reasons, a sect decided to adopt a divergent calendar, or to persist in its use against the main trend of Jewish religious life. If compelled to reconcile this divergence with Mosaic law or to seek sanction in the Torah, the sect would produce the required hermeneutic.

Explicit hermeneutic was not the method used by early Jewish pseudepigraphy, however. In contrast to the authors of avowedly original works, the early pseudepigraphists communicated their point of view more subtly, by means of selectivity (see below). In Jubilees, where we find an elaborate projection of a special calendar, there is no visible attempt to reconcile that calendar with Scripture. In "David's Composition" the description of the year is introduced on a pretext. Since the psalm required one to praise God every day of the year, the "year" was defined according to a special system.

Against this background, the avoidance by the Scroll's author of any reference (so far as we know) to the words *mimmoḥŏrat haššabbāt* should mean one of two things: (a) the author, knowing that the accepted or traditional interpretation pointed to the 16th of Nisan, omitted these words so as to avoid their usual legal implications; (b) the author omitted *mimmoḥŏrat haššabbāt* because these are the words which allowed for the conclusion that the counting period was to commence on a Sunday and, consequently, that the *môʿădîm* were all to occur on Sundays. Such a conclusion would, of course, suit the advocates of the Qumran-Jubilees calendar admirably!

Let us, then, summarize the evidence on the question of the calendar.

(a) There is some correspondence between the *môʿădîm* prescribed in the Scroll and those otherwise known at Qumran. Specifically, a fragment from Qumran Cave 4 mentions "the set-time of oil" as occurring on the 22nd of Elul.

(b) Some later Jewish sectarian sources evidence a knowledge of the same *môʿădîm* as are set forth in the Scroll.

(c) The specific formulation of the Scroll's prescriptions for the "set-times" is ambiguous and by no means compels us to conclude that the Scroll's author was operating on the Qumran-Jubilees calendar. All that is certain is that he is going further than the Torah in ordaining two additional *môʿădîm*, each at the end of a 49-day cycle.

(d) Finally, there is a logical *caveat* to be observed when attempting to argue for a particular sectarian provenance on the basis of calendric systems. Even if one had explicit evidence that the Scroll's author was operating on the Qumran-Jubilees calendar, the precise provenance of the Scroll would have to be established independently. After all, the book of Jubilees and the Qumran sect shared the same calendric tradition, and yet it is not being suggested that the book of Jubilees is one of the writings of the Qumran sect, strictly speaking. In fact, the evidence of Jubilees, when taken together with that from Qumran, clearly demonstrates that the calendar in question was not limited to one single sect, but rather was current in several related, but separate contemporary circles.

Purity Regulations and Sectarian Provenance

At various points, Yadin compares specific codes set forth in the Scroll with similar provisions found in other texts discovered at Qumran or known to have been extant there. Many of these comparisons pertain to the purity of persons or to family law, aspects of which were normally subsumed under the category of purity. Yadin lays great stress on those of the shared features which run counter to the dominant pattern of Jewish religious law as it later developed but which also correlate with what is known of sectarian law during later periods of Jewish history. In this way, a cumulative impression is created that the Scroll fits into a recurring or persistent sectarian tradition. This is, of course, only an impression, because little is actually known about Jewish religious law in the period contemporary with the Scroll.

There is yet another *caveat* affecting Yadin's legal comparisons: They center predominantly around the Zadokite Document. (The same is true, by the way, with respect to the linguistic and terminological parallels which he adduces elsewhere in his discussion.) There seems to be a particular affinity between the Scroll and the Zadokite Document which is not generally shared by the other acknowledged writings of the Qumran sect. Instead of assuming that such comparisons with the Zadokite Document reinforce the Qumranic provenance of the Scroll, perhaps we ought to assume that neither the Scroll nor the Zadokite Document was authored by the same group which produced the *sĕrākîm*, the Thanksgiving Scroll, and others. This possibility needs to be explored in a separate investigation.

With these reservations in mind, let us examine three important legal comparisons discussed by Yadin.

The most precise of these comparisons pertains to the ban on marriage with nieces. Col. 66:15–17 of the Scroll reads as follows:

> Let no man marry the daughter of his brother or the daughter of his sister, for it is an abomination.

This corresponds to what is stated in the Zadokite Document, V:7–11:

> They each take the daughter of his brother and the daughter of his sister. But Moses said: "Do not approach your mother's sister, for she is your mother's flesh" (cf. Lev 18:12, 20:19). Although the law governing incest with relatives is addressed to the males, females are equally bound by it; and if a brother's daughter were to uncover the nakedness of her father's brother, she would be considered his "flesh."

The Zadokite Document derives the ban on marriage with nieces hermeneutically and states it polemically, whereas the Scroll merely appends it innocently to its list of incest prohibitions in its version of Leviticus chapters 18 and 20, in true pseudepigraphical fashion. Otherwise the two statements bear the identical legal import.

The subject of marriage with nieces was studied by S. Krauss (1913) and commented upon more recently by C. Rabin (1957). At various periods in Jewish history the prohibition against marriages with nieces was endorsed by the Samaritans, the Falashas, and the Karaites. What is more, it found its way into the law of the early Christian church and was adopted by Islam. We lack information about the situation during the periods of the Scroll and the Zadokite Document. Krauss, following Geiger, assumed that the Rabbinic view (Mishnah, *Nĕdārîm* 8:7, 9:10; Babylonian Talmud, *Yebāmôt* 62b), which encouraged marriage with the daughter of one's sister in particular, sought to reform an early Pharisaic prohibition against such marriages. It was assumed that the exhortatory tone of the later Rabbinic statements was directed against accepted tradition. It is questionable, however, whether one can deduce so much from the Rabbinic and later evidence. The Rabbinic and post-Rabbinic statements were probably responses to divergence on the part of contemporary groups—Christians, and later, Karaites, etc.[10] Furthermore, if the Zadokite Document and the Scroll,

---

[10] Lieberman 1973:276, s.v. lines 8–9, provides a comprehensive survey of the relevant Rabbinic and post-Rabbinic sources, as well as critical literature, *à propos* the statement in Tosefta, *Qiddûšîn* 1:4.

each in its own way, legislated against a practice, there must have been some group, or groups, who followed that practice.

For all we know, therefore, the ban recorded in the Scroll and the Zadokite Document was directed against the early Pharisees, who might have formulated their more permissive view at an early stage. It could also just as well have been directed against the Sadducees and upper classes. Krauss notes at least one case of marriage with a niece in the Herodian family. Thus Joseph, the uncle of Herod the Great, married Herod's sister, Salome, who was his niece, the daughter of his brother Antipater.[11]

The question to be asked, when we encounter such precise correspondence between two documents, is this: Was the definition of incest the kind of issue that would most likely be drawn between only one sect and the rest of the Jewish community; and, if two documents exhibit the same ban, can they be presumed to have originated with the same sect? It is also possible, of course, that the matter of incest constituted an issue of broad socio-religious implications, as it did in later periods, and that any number of groups might have differed on this subject.

This question leads us directly to the second of Yadin's legal comparisons with the Zadokite Document, which will be discussed here. After Deut 17:14f., the Scroll, in col. 56:12f., makes the following statement as part of its code of conduct for Israelite kings:

> He (the king) may not marry a wife from any of the daughters of the gentiles, but only from his father's household may he take himself a wife, from the family of his father. Furthermore, he may not take another wife in addition to her; for she, alone, shall remain with him all the days of her life. But if she dies, he may marry another, from his father's household, from his family.

To this Yadin compares the statement of the Zadokite Document, IV:20–V:5. The text categorizes the several cardinal sins of the evildoers:

> In matters of sexual misconduct (*zĕnût*)—by taking two wives in their lifetimes (i.e., in the lifetime of either wife). But the fundamental principle of creation is: "Male and female did He create them" (Gen 1:27). And those who entered the ark came in pairs of two (cf. Gen 7:9). And concerning the "chief" (*nāśîʾ*) it is written: "He shall not take many wives" (Deut 17:17).

It is evident that the respective authors were acquainted with the same essential interpretation of Deut 17:17, according to which more than one wife was too "many." We may assume that those who shared this interpretation shared a general attitude toward marriage. One should not, therefore, belabor the point that in the Scroll monogamy is presented as part of the code of the king, whereas in the Zadokite Document it is a requirement for all Jews. Conceivably, if the

[11] See the chart in Schürer (1891), Appendix VIII, entitled "The House of Herod."

incest code of the Scroll, as preserved, did not break off at the end of col. 66, we might have found in col. 67 a statement on monogamy.

The point is that here, as in the case of the definition of incest, we are dealing with a major factor in societal organization—in this instance, even more clearly so. It is likely that many circles within Jewry during the Greco-Roman period objected to polygamy, in theory as well as practice. Monogamy was, after all, the common practice for Palestinian Jewry, and for parts of the diaspora as well.[12]

The third of Yadin's legal comparisons with the Zadokite Document is particularly significant in its implications. Long before the publication of the Scroll, Yadin regularly emphasized in lectures and preliminary statements the special importance of purity regulations for ascertaining the historical provenance of the Scroll. Now in the publication he repeatedly points to the tendency toward stringency in matters of purity, as this tendency affects the temple, Jerusalem, the priests, and even ordinary Jews, in support of his view that the Scroll voices the particular outlook of the Qumran sect. He sees a trend toward asceticism in sexual relations, which in his opinion tallies with what is known from other sources about the Essenes. He considers these tendencies as contrary to the normative Rabbinic tradition which, he says, tended progressively to ease its stand, interpreting biblical injunctions on matters of purity in such a way as to limit their application, rather than intensifying it or extending it further.

It should be emphasized at the outset that the development of purity legislation in ancient Judaism is much more complex than Yadin assumes. He cites several related statements by G. Alon (1957) as a preamble to his discussion of this subject. In their original context, perhaps Alon's statements would not appear as simplistic as they do standing alone as a brief capsulization of a vast subject. Jacob Neusner (1974–) has recently completed a multivolume study of the order *Ṭohŏrôt* of the Mishnah, in which he reveals the diverse tendencies at work during the protracted development of Rabbinic law in this area. In many respects, the Sages exhibited great creativity in extending certain aspects of biblical cultic law from the domain of priest and temple to the Jewish home and family. Around often sparse biblical *dicta*, they fashioned an elaborate system of private ritual. To characterize the normative Rabbinic tradition as consistently opting for "contraction" as against "expansion," as Alon does, fails to account for the growth of Rabbinic law governing purity, in matters of diet as well as marital relations, a system which became a cornerstone of historical Judaism.

There is another complicated problem with respect to the Scroll: how to account for its preoccupation with temple and cult, in the light of the suspended relationship to the Jerusalem temple cult which is evident in the acknowledged writings of the Qumran sect.

---

[12] Baron (1952) surveys the relevant evidence. Information from Palestine about what he terms "Monogamous Tendencies" is more abundant than that known about the diaspora.

Of critical importance for understanding the Scroll's ordinances governing purity is the term *ʿîr hammiqdāš*. It is previously attested only in the Zadokite Document, XII:1–2. To a great extent, Yadin's emphatic attempt to argue for the Qumranic, sectarian provenance of the Scroll depends on whether or not he is correct in taking the term *ʿîr hammiqdāš* as a designation for the entire walled city of Jerusalem. In my opinion, it refers only to the temple complex itself, and it is best translated "Temple City," a rendering suggested by such known designations as "Vatican City" and "*Cité de l'Université*," etc.

An examination of the relevant passages reveals that the Scroll's author carefully differentiated between two terms which appear to be similar in meaning but are not: *ʿîr hammiqdāš*, "Temple City" (col. 45:11, 16–17); and *ʿîr miqdāšî*, "the city of My temple," i.e., Jerusalem (col. 47:9, 13).

Let us examine the term *ʿîr hammiqdāš* within the context of col. 45, where we encounter three significant passages:

> (a) If a man has a nocturnal emission *he may not enter any part of the temple* (*lôʾ yābôʾ ʾel kol hammiqdāš*) until he completes three days and launders his clothing. And he must bathe on the first day, and on the third day both launder his clothing and bathe. Then, after the sun sets, *he may enter the temple* (*yābôʾ ʾel hammiqdāš*). And let them not enter *my temple* (*miqdāšî*) with their "menstrual" impurity, and defile it (lines 7–10).
>
> (b) If a man lies with his wife, experiencing an emission of semen, he may not enter any part of "Temple City" (*lôʾ yābôʾ ʾel kol ʿîr hammiqdāš*), where I cause my name to dwell, for three days (lines 11–12).
>
> (c) No blinded man may enter *it* (i.e., *ʿîr hammiqdāš*) all their (!) days, so as not to defile the city in which I dwell; for I am Yahweh, who dwells amidst the Israelites forever. Any man who becomes pure from his flux (*zôb*) shall count off seven days in his state of purity, and shall launder his clothing on the seventh day, and bathe his whole body in living water. Afterwards, *he may enter "Temple City"* (*ʾaḥḥar yābôʾ ʾel ʿîr hammiqdāš*). Furthermore, no person impure by reason of contact with a dead body (*ṭāmēʾ lammēt*) may enter into *it* (i.e., *ʿîr hammiqdāš*) until they (!) have become pure, and no leper(?) (*meṣôrāʿ*) or diseased person may enter into it until they (!) have become pure, etc. (lines 12–18).

The ordinance of *b* above corresponds to what is stated in the Zadokite Document, XII:1–2:

> Let no man lie with a woman in "Temple City" (*bĕʿîr hammiqdāš*), thus defiling "Temple City" (*ʿîr hammiqdāš*) with their "menstruation" (*bĕniddātām*).

A comparison of *a* and *b* above shows that they are parallel. The basis for the ban on entry is the same, i.e., the emission of semen.

In *a* we read: *lôʾ yābôʾ ʾel kol hammiqdāš*
He may not enter any part *of the temple.*
In *b* we read: *lôʾ yābôʾ ʾel kol ʿîr hammiqdāš*
He may not enter any part *of "Temple City."*

It is clear that both formulas bear the same legal import and that in effect *kol ʿîr hammiqdāš* = *kol hammiqdāš*, the whole temple complex.

One cannot argue that the sphere of prohibited entry is widened in the provisions of *b* above, because a woman is directly involved in the emission of semen. There is no law prohibiting the actual presence of women in *ʿîr hammiqdāš*, according to the Scroll. The only prohibition is intercourse, and hence cohabitation, because such lead to the emission of semen. Usage of the term *niddāh*, "menstruation," is not literal, either in the Scroll or the Zadokite Document, and does not imply the presence of a woman. This is evident from the fact that in *a* above the Scroll uses this same term with reference to sorts of impurity which have nothing to do with women.

One could argue, however, that reference to "the city in which I dwell" and "where I cause My name to dwell" in *b* and *c* above suggests that *ʿîr hammiqdāš* designates the whole city of Jerusalem. These "Deuteronomisms" hardly determine the technical force of the proximate terminology, as is evidenced by the fact that in *b* above one such *cliché* is followed by the statement "for I am Yahweh, who dwells *in the midst of the Israelites* forever." Usage here is dramatic, not technical. The same is true in col. 47, to be discussed presently.

When one contrasts the terms of reference in col. 45 with those of col. 47 (especially lines 3–18), the distinction between the terms *ʿîr hammiqdāš* of col. 45 and *ʿîr miqdāšî* of col. 47 becomes quite clear:

> And the city (*wĕhāʿîr*) which I do sanctify by causing *My name and temple to dwell in it* shall be holy and pure from any defiling substance, by means of which persons become impure, and whatever enters into it shall be pure (lines 3–6).

The text then proceeds to list such commodities as oil, wine, and food, and—most critical for understanding the real nature of these provisions—skins of animals, even pure ones, slaughtered in other cities. The precise wording is significant:

> They shall not bring into *it* (i.e., *hāʿîr*, "the city") skins even of pure animals which they slaughter *in their cities* (*bĕtôk ʿārêhemmāh*)—they shall not bring into *it.* For *in their cities* (*kî bĕʿārêhemmāh*) they are accustomed to performing work with them and using them for all their needs. Consequently, *they must not bring them into the city of my temple* (*wĕʾel ʿîr miqdāšî lôʾ yābîʾû*). For their state of purity corresponds only to the purity of their flesh. And you shall not defile *the city where I cause My name and My temple to dwell.* For only skins of animals which they slaughter in the temple—in these they may bring their wine, their oil, and all their food *to the city of My temple* (*lĕʿîr miqdāšî*), that they may not contaminate My

> temple with the skins *of their unfit slain offerings* (*zibḥê piggûlêhemmāh*) which they slaughter *in the midst of their land* (*bĕtôk ʾarṣāmāh*).
>
> And you shall not consider any of *your cities to be as pure as my city*. For as is the purity of the flesh, in that degree are the skins pure. If you slaughter it in My temple, it shall be adequately pure for My temple; but if you slaughter it in *your cities* it shall be pure enough for *your cities*. But all that requires *the purity of the temple* (*ṭohôrat hammiqdāš*) you must bring in skins of the temple, that you may not defile *My temple and My city* (*ʾet miqdāšî wĕʿîrî*) with the skins *of your unfit flesh* (*piggûlêkemmāh*), the city in whose midst I dwell (lines 7–18).

This long passage is dominated by a single polarity: "My city" versus "your cities" or "their cities." The prohibitions set forth here clearly apply to the whole city of Jerusalem. The designation *ʿîr miqdāšî*, "the city of My temple," is synonymous with *ʿîrî*, "My city," whereas in col. 45 the designation *ʿîr hammiqdāš* refers only to the temple complex itself. The two terms ought not to be confused.

This column (col. 47) is a contemporary statement, emphatic in tone, and it represents what Yadin calls "additional Torah," i.e., textual content not directly based on a biblical source (see further below). The Scroll's author took his cue from the polemics of Deuteronomy, primarily chapters 12 and 16. There all sacrifice is limited to one, unnamed "cult-site" (*māqôm*) which, in the Judean tradition, was identified as Jerusalem. The words of 1 Kgs 8:16 must have been in the author's mind:

> Since the day when I brought My people, Israel, out of Egypt, I have not chosen a city (*ʿîr*) from all the tribal territories of Israel for building a temple, so that My name may be there, etc.

Against this biblical background, the Scroll's author ordained that skins from animals, even pure ones, slaughtered in other towns may not be used as containers for conveying wine, oil, and foodstuffs into Jerusalem. The term *piggûl* is used in characterizing the flesh of animals slaughtered outside Jerusalem. This term originally applied to the flesh of *šelāmîm* offerings not consumed in due time (Lev 7:16–18; 19:5–7), but it also appropriated more extended meanings in Isaiah (65:4) and Ezekiel (4:14), where it refers to meat unfit for consumption for a variety of reasons.[13] It is in this extended sense that the Scroll's author uses *piggûl* in col. 47, and in col. 52:16–19, where he terms meat from blemished animals *bĕšār piggûl*. Such meat may be eaten only a distance of more than 30 *rîs* from the temple.[14]

---

[13] Levine (1971) discusses usage of the term *piggûl*, pl. *piggûlîm*.

[14] See comments by Milik (1962:187–88), where it is explained that *rîs* (perhaps *rês*) is to be identified with the Roman *stadium* (Gk. *stádion*). The word is derived by Milik and others from Persian *aspres*, Pahlevi *aspras*. It is now attested in an Aramaic temple description.

The evidence from col. 52:13–15 makes it clear that the concern with animals slaughtered outside Jerusalem is with the unique status of the temple cult of Jerusalem. There we read:

> You shall not slaughter a head of large cattle, or a sheep or goat, that are pure, in all of your gates, within proximity of a three days' journey to My temple. Rather, inside My temple shall you slaughter it, making of it a burnt offering or a *šelāmîm* offering, etc.

The Deuteronomic dispensation (Deut 12:21; cf. Deut 14:24; and in the Scroll, col. 43:12f.) allowing profane slaughter for all who are distant from the cult-site which Yahweh will choose is taken very seriously, and profane slaughter is allowed only for those who are actually "distant." The notion of three-days distance was proverbial in ancient perceptions (Gen 30:36; Exod 3:18; Jonah 3:3). The insistence that anyone near enough to Jerusalem to get there and back between Sabbaths was obliged to patronize the temple and to make his slaughter sacrificial is, of course, a subtle reflex of the wording in Lev 17:3f., as the Scroll's author interpreted it.

Realistically viewed, the concern in col. 47 of the Scroll with the skins of animals has nothing directly to do with the purity of persons, notwithstanding the verbal imagery employed there. Purity terminology is being used for effect. The actual regulation appears to be an attempt to muster support for the Jerusalem temple cult by encouraging Jews who do business in Jerusalem to donate sacrifices. By prohibiting delivery of liquids and foodstuffs to Jerusalem in any except sacrificial animal skins, the Scroll was saying to the temple's purveyors that if they wished to market their goods in Jerusalem and to do business with the temple, they would have to patronize the temple!

If col. 47 is not speaking about the purity of persons, and if its terminology is unrelated to the term *ʿîr hammiqdāš* in col. 45, then what basis is there for seeing in the Scroll's provisions an extension of purity requirements to encompass the whole city of Jerusalem? There are two factors to be considered: (a) Philologically speaking, can *ʿîr* mean a complex of buildings, or a walled quarter of a city? (b) What is the frame of reference of col. 46? Does it continue the legislation of col. 45, thus referring only to the temple complex, or is it related to the whole city of Jerusalem, as is col. 47:3f.

In his study of the Zadokite Document, Louis Ginzberg (1922) presents some suggestive thoughts on the term *ʿîr hammiqdāš*. He begins by comparing it to *ʿîr dāwîd*, "the city of David," and to *ʿîr haqqôdeš*, literally "the city of the temple," i.e., Jerusalem, occurring elsewhere in the Zadokite Document (V:6; VI:12; XX:22; cf. Isa 48:2, 52:1). Further on, however, Ginzberg raised another possibility, also suggested by the comparison with *ʿîr dāwîd*, namely, that the term *ʿîr hammiqdāš* was a precursor of the term *har habbaît*, "the temple mount," frequent in Rabbinic sources. In this connection, he called attention to 2 Chr 8:11, which relates that Solomon moved Pharaoh's daughter "from the city of David (*mēʿîr dāwîd*)" to a different home he had built for her in another quarter of the city, because he felt she should not reside where the ark was deposited.

We thus see the Chronicler's own view on the graduated sanctity of the various sections of Jerusalem.

There is additional evidence which allows for the definition of *ʿîr* as a quarter of the city. In 2 Kgs 10:25 we read that Jehu ordered his guards to slay all the Baal worshippers and that they arrived at *ʿîr bêt habbaʿal*, which should be rendered "the quarter (or precinct) of the Baal temple." Several years ago in a lecture about ancient Samaria, which, interestingly, bore the Hebrew title "*ʿÎr Bêt Habbaʿal*," Yadin (1973) argued that the area referred to by this designation was situated outside the city of Samaria proper, somewhere in the province of Samaria. Whether this was the case, or whether like *bêt habbaʿal* (2 Kgs 11:18) it was located inside the city, is not our primary concern (although the usage in 2 Kgs 10:21f. seems to indicate that *ʿîr bêt habbaʿal* was roughly synonymous to *bêt habbaʿal*). The fact is that Yadin himself defined *ʿîr bêt habbaʿal* as "a kind of consecrated *temenos*, in the center of which stood the temple of Baal, and around it the dwellings of the priests and the like."[15]

Further light on usage of the term *ʿîr* as a designation of a temple complex comes from Ezek 40:2:

> In divine visions, He brought me to the land of Israel, and put me down atop a very high mountain. And upon it was something resembling the form structure of a "city" (*kĕmibnēh ʿîr*), toward the South.

From the following protracted description in Ezekiel chapters 40–43 it becomes clear that *mibnēh ʿîr* of 40:2 refers in actuality to the temple complex and should be functionally translated "the form of a walled quarter," or the like.

We must now take up the provisions of col. 46, where the terminology is admittedly perplexing, because the locations of some of the facilities enumerated are not explicit. The column deals with the following subjects, in this order: (a) preventing unclean birds from flying "over the roofs of the gates of the outermost courtyard" (lines 2–3); (b) the construction of a *rôbed*, "platform," outside the wall of the outermost courtyard, with steps in front of the gates (lines 5–8); (c) the construction of the *ḥêl*, either a rampart or a moat, 100 cubits wide; (d) construction of a complex of toilet and drainage facilities; and (e) the designation of three separate areas for lepers and unclean persons.

The relevant passages read as follows:

> You shall construct a moat (?) (*ḥêl*) *around the temple* (*sābîb lammiqdāš*), 100 cubits in width, that shall separate *between the inner temple area and the "city"* (*bên miqdaš haqqôdeš lāʿîr*), so they will not enter *inside My temple suddenly* (*balaʿ ʾel tôk miqdāšî*), etc. (lines 9–11).
>
> You shall provide for them a place of "the area" (*mĕqôm yad*) outside the "city" (*lāʿîr*), consisting of roofed buildings and cisterns, where the excrement may drain into them, so that it (i.e., the excre-

[15] See Yadin (1973:57). See also Fisher (1963).

> ment) may not be visible to anyone for a distance of 3,000 cubits from the "city" (*hāʿîr*).
>
> You shall provide three areas, east of the "city" (*lāʿîr*), separated from each other, where the lepers, and those having flux, and men who had seminal emissions [ ] (lines 13–18).

Yadin maintains that the *ḥêl*, "moat" (?), was outside the outermost wall of the temple complex. He carries this interpretation forward throughout the rest of col. 46, with the result that *ʿîr* in this column consistently refers to the whole city of Jerusalem. In his view, the *ḥêl* divided between the temple complex and the rest of Jerusalem. The toilets and drainage system were, therefore, outside the city of Jerusalem, as were the areas for lepers and unclean persons.

The only evidence on the location of the *ḥêl* is in col. 46. According to the Mishnah (*Middôt* 2:3), the *ḥêl* was located *inside* the wall of the temple mount, as Yadin notes. He insists, however, that this was not so in the Scroll's temple plan, because he claims that the orientation in col. 46 is consistently outward. Since the *ḥêl* is mentioned after the *rôbed*, "platform," which stood outside the outermost wall, it must have been the outermost extremity of the temple complex

It is not at all certain, however, that in col. 46 the orientation is consistently outward. First, we read of birds flying inward over the gates of the outermost wall. Then we read about the platform, which was, after all, an avenue of entry and is described as such. If after these two items we read about the *ḥêl*, it is entirely possible that further entry is being projected. The stated purpose of the *ḥêl* was to prevent sudden entry into the temple. If the whole case for locating the *ḥêl* outside the outermost wall rests on the orientation in col. 46, then it is a doubtful case indeed.

The crucial term is *miqdaš haqqodeš* in line 10 of the column, which has been translated "the inner temple area." The basis for this understanding of the term comes from Lev 16:33, where *miqdaš haqqodeš* refers to the innermost shrine, in contrast to *ʾohel môʿēd*, "the Tent of Meeting," which designated a larger structure (cf. Lev 16:20f.). On this basis, *ʿîr* in col. 46 refers to *ʿîr hammiqdāš*, "Temple City," as in col. 45, and *not* to the whole city of Jerusalem, as in col. 47:3f. Column 47:3f. initiates an entirely different topic, as we have seen, and is to be detached from what preceded.

If this analysis is correct, then all that is said to be outside the *ʿîr*, in col. 46, was to be outside "Temple City," not outside Jerusalem! The Scroll's plan would have thus provided for a graduated intensification of sanctity, once one entered the outermost gates. In this sense *ʿîr*, standing in contrast to *miqdaš haqqodeš*, would be synonymous with *gěbûl* in Ezek 43:12, i.e., "precinct."

The Scroll's temple plan was meant to be realistic, as Yadin repeatedly emphasizes. It is doubtful, therefore, whether its author intended all of the "encampment" (*maḥăneh*) legislation of the Pentateuch to apply to the entire city of Jerusalem. Would all the toilet facilities be outside the city of Jerusalem? Was intercourse forbidden in the entire city? After all, the Scroll's purity legislation derives directly from Scripture and is not so stringent in substance (Lev 15:16–18; Deut 23:11; and cf. Mishnah, *Kēlîm* 1:2f.). It is certainly realistic to close the markets of Jerusalem to purveyors of foodstuffs who failed to meet certain requirements, but it is quite another matter to suggest that according to the Scroll no bodily functions were permitted in the entire city. Obviously, no man could have intercourse inside the temple complex. All that the Scroll requires is that everyone exit the large temple complex projected in the Scroll, to use toilet facilities outside its walls.

If the above analysis is correct, one has much less warrant for seeing in the Scroll's provisions the sectarian asceticism or extreme rigidity which Yadin attributes to them.

The Literary Character of the Temple Scroll

The form and composition of the Scroll are no less fascinating than its contents. It is predominantly a pseudepigraphic composition. Many of its *dicta* are consciously reformulated so as to attribute them to Yahweh directly. Yahweh is often "Ego," or the first-person referent. Thus, "to Yahweh" becomes "to Me." The Scroll is likewise a nomographic document, in which a detailed plan for a temple complex and prescriptions for its attendant cult are presented as commandments and laws. These two factors hold the key to what is distinctive in the composition of the Scroll. Here our comments will be limited, for the most part, to the pseudepigraphic character of the Scroll. The substance of its nomography will have to await further investigation.

In a recent paper, Morton Smith (1971) set down certain criteria for classifying the different types of pseudepigraphic writings representative of the Israelite-Jewish tradition. These types range all the way from simple pseudepigraphic attribution to the actual alteration of an original composition so as to reinforce the fictitious authorship being claimed for it. Yadin refers to Smith's study, but in my opinion he does not use it to its best advantage.

Of considerable interest to the present discussion is Smith's view that the secondary identification of literary compositions with great persons and momentous events began quite early in ancient Israel. In a related manner Lambert (1957; 1962) compiled impressive evidence from cuneiform sources to show that the attribution of laws to gods was a well-attested literary method in ancient Mesopotamia. It lent authority to the content of the document so attributed.[16]

[16] In his studies, Lambert repeatedly notes the relevance of his findings for an understanding of literary-traditional development in ancient Israel. Of particular interest for the present discussion is the phenomenon of "notes" found on catalogues, as well as texts of incantations and hymns which refer to the contents as "the wisdom of Ea." Ea was known as the god primarily associated with exorcism. Lambert surveys considerable literature from the Ashurbanipal library, as well as from late Babylonian texts, which exhibit this attribution of exorcistic procedures to Ea.

As will become apparent, Smith's examples, which deal primarily with Scripture, are directly relevant to the textual analysis of the Scroll, and it is well worth commenting on them in detail. It is almost as if Smith anticipated the literary situation we now encounter in the Scroll itself.

Simple pseudepigraphical attribution, as regards biblical literature, may best be illustrated by the superscriptions to most of the Psalms. The Psalms themselves give no internal indications that they relate to specific events in the life of Moses, David, or others. Similar to this phenomenon, in Smith's view, are the introductory and concluding formulas in many of the priestly codes of the Pentateuch. A frequent example is the formula "As Yahweh commanded Moses." These formulas have the effect of reinforcing what is actually the secondary attribution of anonymous laws to Yahweh.[17]

A good example is provided by Leviticus chapters 1–7. Lev 1:1–2a relates that Yahweh called to Moses and commanded him to instruct the Israelites on the details of sacrifice. The same sort of caption recurs throughout these seven chapters (Lev 4:1–2a; 5:14, 20; 6:1–2a, 12, 17–18a, 22–23a, 28–29a). Finally, Lev 7:36–38 brings this unit of the book to a close by reiterating that it is Yahweh who has commanded all that preceded.

Anticipating a point to be stressed further on regarding the formulation of the Scroll's statements (see below), it is interesting that whereas chapters 1–5 are formulated casuistically, chapters 6–7 are apodictic. In both sections, however, the same method of secondary attribution is employed, except that in the apodictic chapters (6 and 7) these captions and formulas are more frequent.

After providing some examples of internal alteration, including the first two "commandments" of the Decalogue, Smith discusses the book of Deuteronomy as a whole. He considers it a forgery, in the technical and literary connotations of that word. It is "the composition of a work intended *ab initio* to be falsely attributed."[18] As regards the whole of Deuteronomy in its received form, Smith is undoubtedly correct, although it is likely that the explicit attribution of orations to Moses belongs more to the elaborate introduction and conclusion of the book, which is secondary *vis à vis* the core of Deuteronomy. As Smith himself noted, there are hardly any explicit references to Moses as the speaker in chapters 12–26 and 28. (Chapter 27 is a special problem.) Although the core of Deuteronomy is set, or projected, in the time of Moses, the identification of Moses as the speaker is only implicit. It is precisely in chapters 1–4 and 29–33 that we find frequent references to Moses. To be more accurate, therefore, it is in the introduction and conclusion to Deuteronomy that the intermediation of Moses as the teacher of Yahweh's word to the Israelites is firmly established. The compiler of the book, as we have it, stopped short only at the text of the Decalogue itself (in chapter 5), which he felt compelled to present as Yahweh's own words.

[17] See Levine (1965) for a detailed discussion of the composition of the priestly descriptions in Exodus, Leviticus, and Numbers.

[18] See Smith (1971:206).

The fact that even a pseudepigraphist senses certain limits to his license will prove significant in our detailed analysis of the Scroll.

The Scroll's author went several steps further than either the Deuteronomist or the compiler of the priestly codes of the Pentateuch. Decidedly, he went in the direction of the priestly tradition, which attributes virtually all laws and commandments to Yahweh. Moses is not the speaker in the priestly tradition. He merely bears the message in Yahweh's name. In the Scroll, the intermediation of Moses is methodically eliminated, a fact duly noted by Yadin. One immediately recalls the Passover Haggadah, which also avoids any mention of Moses, a startling fact in a collection of Midrashim on the Egyptian bondage and the Exodus.

It should be noted with respect to the question of provenance discussed earlier (see above) that the role of Moses is not at all rejected in the Zadokite Document. It is Moses who "says" that it is forbidden to approach the sister of one's mother. This further complicates the relationship of the Scroll to the Zadokite Document, with which it otherwise exhibits considerable affinity.

Yadin summarizes the evidence from the Scroll on the conversion of biblical citations from an original formulation in which Yahweh represents the third-person referent to one in which he represents "Ego." The analysis is as follows:

(a) Almost all of the citations from Deuteronomy were converted in this manner (cols. 53–55, 60–66).

(b) As a general rule, all priestly passages cited from Exodus, Leviticus, and Numbers were retained in the original biblical formulation, wherein Yahweh is the third-person referent (primarily, cols. 13–29, 39:8).

(c) In almost all of the additional Torah, Yahweh represents "Ego" (primarily cols. 29–47, 56–57).

The relatively few exceptions to the above *schema* may be instructive for probing the rules of pseudepigraphic reformulation by which the Scroll's author was guided. Let us examine them in detail:

(a) In col. 61:2–5 we find an internal quotation, whose third-person reference to Yahweh spills over into the following clause:

> Should you say in your heart: "How shall we know that this word is not one *which Yahweh spoke?*" For that which the prophet speaks *in the name of Yahweh* (not: "in My name"), but does not happen or come about—that is a word *which I have not spoken.*

(b) In col. 63:5–8, note the declaration of the elders, taken from Deut 21:7–9, with the third-person reference to Yahweh retained. This also qualifies as a kind of internal quotation.

(c) In col. 55:9 we find an infixed citation from Deut 13:2–6 containing the words *hăyiškem ʾôhăbîm ʾet YHWH ʾĕlōhê ʾăbôtêkemmāh bĕkôl lĕbabkem ûbekol napšĕkemmāh*: "Do you love Yahweh, the God of your forefathers with all your heart and with all your being," etc. The third-person reference to Yahweh was probably retained here because Deut 13:2–6 itself is citing a verse from Deut 6:5, which may have been liturgical at the time the Scroll was written.

(d) It is not entirely certain why in col. 55:9–10 the formula *kālîl lĕYHWH ʾĕlôhêkāh*, "entirely consumed by fire, to Yahweh your God," retains the third-person formulation. (See 1 Sam 7:9 for a possible clue.) Similarly, it is not clear why in col. 48:7–10 two infixes from Deut 14:1–2 are unconverted. These read: "You are children of Yahweh, your God;" and "For you are a holy people unto Yahweh your God." (Perhaps a clue may be found in Exod 19:4–6.)

We should probably assume that certain formulations were "bound" and that it was improper, even for a pseudepigraphist, to alter them.

The overall distinction, noted by Yadin, between the Scroll's treatment of the Deuteronomic material, on the one hand, and the priestly texts, on the other, is quite consistent. As regards the Deuteronomic material, it is obvious that one of the reasons for conversion to a first-person orientation was to eliminate the intermediation of Moses, as has already been noted. As regards the priestly material, however, Yadin's interpretation leaves some questions unanswered.

If, as Yadin claims, there was no need to convert the priestly material because the priestly tradition attributes its laws and commandments to Yahweh in the first place, then one may ask: How was the reader of the Scroll to "get the point," since the captions and formulas which actually identify Yahweh as the speaker in the priestly texts are never included in the Scroll? By eliminating Moses as the bearer of Yahweh's words, the Scroll's author, *ipso facto*, also removed the explicit identification of Yahweh as the speaker.

More attention must be given to the selectivity exercised by the Scroll's author in this regard. In cols. 13–29, where we find the unconverted priestly passages, *all* of the material cited exhibits an apodictic formulation. On the other hand, most of Deuteronomy's legal material, including that pertaining to the cult, was originally expressed casuistically. In other words, the various materials at the disposal of the Scroll's author were formulated differently. What is more, Deuteronomy is generally characterized by a narrative style, even in its presentation of legal material. This contrasts sharply with the rigid, formulaic style of the priestly codes or the Book of the Covenant (Exodus chapters 21–23). In Deuteronomy, Moses continually speaks about Yahweh. At times, it is he who is doing the commanding, not Yahweh!

This analysis may help to explain why in col. 48:3–10 of the Scroll the third-person formulation was retained. There we encounter originally apodictic passages from Deut 14:3f. on the matter of forbidden foods. In other words, whereas the Scroll's author had the needed biblical sources from the priestly codes in apodictic form, the required materials from Deuteronomy were almost all in casuistic form, and, except for chapter 14, had to be converted. The author felt secure in retaining the third-person formulation in the apodictic, priestly passages because his readers could hardly identify the speaker of the commandments concerning cult and ritual as any other than Yahweh. In Deuteronomy, of course, this was not the case.

This differentiation between apodictic and casuistic formulation also explains why in col. 39:8 of the Scroll the third-person reference to Yahweh was retained. There we read:

> … as the expiation for his life, a half-shekel *to Yahweh*, as an everlasting statute.

If one consults Exod 30:11–16, the overall casuistic framework of the passage becomes apparent (verses 11–12). But the citation in col. 39:8 of the Scroll is based only on verse 13, which is apodictically formulated. There is actually insufficient space in the *lacuna* preceding the word *napšô*, "his life," in the line of the Scroll to allow for any content that might have been taken from verses 11–12 of Exodus 30.

In contrast, we find in cols. 53:14–54:5 of the Scroll a priestly passage which had to be converted to a first-person formulation. It is taken from Num 30:3f., which Smith had also singled out as unusual, since it identifies Moses as the speaker or issuer of the law (cf. Lev 8:5, 9:6). In the context of our present discussion, it is most significant that this is a casuistic passage, which the author apparently needed, just as he needed similarly expressed Deuteronomic passages. (One suspects that Num 30:3f. may also be Deuteronomic.)

In still other respects, the literary character of the Scroll is determined by its pseudepigraphical nature. The Scroll's author shared the concept, basic to the priestly writings of the Bible, that all of the *minutiae* of the cult represent the express will of God, and he sought sanction for what he considered to be essential for the contemporary cult and its maintenance. He consequently cites biblical passages extensively, with varying degrees of faithfulness to their original wording. Yadin summarizes the methods this author employed in fashioning a coherent code out of diverse materials:

(a) *Juxtaposition* of originally unconnected passages and sections of Scripture so that they come together in the Scroll. This technique has most to do with the Scroll's overall composition.

(b) *Harmonizations* of passages and parts of passages from different biblical sources into a continuous formulation. This technique often results in syntactic interpenetration or the use of infixes, and it also involves some interpolation of nonbiblical syntactic elements—phrases, clauses, etc.

(c) "*Additional Torah*," whole sections of text that have no specific biblical source and are not syntactically joined to biblical citations.

It is in *b* and *c* that we find passages containing most of the new legislation incorporated in the Scroll, as well as new interpretations of old, known laws.

In source-critical terms, the Scroll's author does exactly what biblical authors and compilers had been doing all along. This is particularly true of the priestly writers of the Bible, in matters of cult and ritual; but the Deuteronomists did the same thing, in terms of the treatment of the sources they had before them.

The Scroll thus falls squarely in line with the biblical process. It represents an extension of that process. It is the most elaborate nomographic document as yet retrieved from the pre-Rabbinic period, after the Bible. Until the retrieval of the Scroll, the code preserved in the Zadokite Document IX:1–XII:22 was perhaps the most extensive nomographic text displaying a biblical, textual matrix.[19]

There is, however, a major difference between such works as the Zadokite Document and the Scroll. The code of the Zadokite Document is not pseudepigraphic; it is an original composition, which often cites biblical verses as proof texts. It is similar in form to the *pešer* and is a forerunner of later midrash. In the Scroll there is not a single instance where a biblical verse is cited as a proof text. How could there be? God is speaking to the Israelites in the first person, or, at the very least, is presumed to be the utterer of commandments.

When Yadin maintains that certain of the Scroll's statements represent contemporary interpretations, often of a polemical nature, of biblical or later law, he is inferring this from the content of the statements. In themselves, these statements give no overt indication that earlier laws or views are being reinterpreted. The Scroll is distinctive in that it is presented as a new Torah, not a commentary on the Torah. As such, the Scroll belongs with Jubilees, Enoch, and other apocryphal works which, though pseudepigraphic, are only mildly nomographic and do not remain as close to their biblical sources in the exposition of their materials as does the Scroll.

Perhaps it would be appropriate to comment on the opening section of the Scroll, as it is preserved and restored in col. 2. The author's predilection for apodictic sources, coupled with the pseudepigraphic objective of making Yahweh the identified speaker, probably helps to explain why he opened the Scroll with a citation from Exodus and not from Deuteronomy. Col. 1, which is not preserved, might have contained a passage from Deuteronomy, but in any event Exod 34:10f. proved to be very satisfactory.

First of all, it is mostly a first-person narration, and Yahweh is the speaker. In the original context, which was a dialogue between Yahweh and Moses, it is Moses who is the addressee. But, since the second-person masculine singular is often used by biblical writers in addressing the entire Israelite people, it was possible for the Scroll's author to modulate the context by merely passing over any allusion to Moses. So he begins with Exod 34:10, making many deletions but continuing to the end of verse 13. He then inserts Deut 7:25–26 between verses 13 and 14 of Exodus 34, with very little change. Finally, he resumes with Exod 34:14–16. In terms of the theme of the opening lines, the Scroll's author may have had Deut 5:2 in mind (also cf. Deut 4:10).

---

[19] See Schiffman (1975:77–131) for a new discussion of the Sabbath code of the Zadokite Document.

Conclusion

One can only speculate on the historical provenance of the Scroll. For what purpose was it written, and for which group extant in Palestine in the late 2nd century B.C.E. does it speak? The temple plan presented in the Scroll poses difficult historical problems, if one takes it as a realistic plan. This plan calls for a rectangular main temple building surrounded by three, concentric square courtyards. As such, it differs significantly from any plan known for the Jerusalem temple, either prior to the period of the Scroll or thereafter. It is certainly this temple plan, rather then any cultic prescriptions or purity regulations, which renders the Scroll so enigmatic in historical terms.

The temple portrayed in the Scroll was meant as a real temple, to be built by the Jews in accordance with God's instructions. It was to stand in Jerusalem until the time when God himself would replace it with His own future temple. The prescriptions regarding the temple cult, therefore, close quite fittingly with an eschatological statement reminiscent of Jubilees 1:15–17:

> And I shall sanctify My temple by My presence, which I shall cause to abide over it, My presence; until the day of the blessing, when I shall create My own temple, establishing it for Me all the days, in accordance with the covenant I made with Jacob at Bethel (Col. 29:8–10).[20]

Bibliography

Alon, G.
1957 *Studies in Jewish History in the time of the Second Temple, the Mishna and the Talmud*, Vol. 1. Tel-Aviv: Hakkibutz Hameuchad (Hebrew).

Ankori, Z.
1959 *The Karaites of Byzantium.* New York: Columbia.

Avigad, N.
1958 The Palaeography of the Dead Sea Scrolls and Related Documents. Pages 56–87 in *Aspects of the Dead Sea Scrolls*, eds. Ch. Rabin and Y. Yadin. ScrHier 4. Jerusalem: Magnes Press.

Baron, S.
1952 *A Social and Religious History of the Jews*, Vol. 2. New York: Columbia.

Ben-Yehudah, E.
1960 *Dictionary and Thesaurus of the Hebrew Language*, Vol. 7. New York: Thomas Yoseloff.

Cross, F. M.
1961 *The Ancient Library of Qumran and Modern Biblical Studies.* Garden City, NY: Doubleday.

---

[20] I am grateful to Morton Smith, who read the draft of this study and offered many valuable suggestions.

1965 The Development of the Jewish Scripts. Pp. 170–264 in *The Bible and the Ancient Near East: Essays in Honor of William Foxwell Albright*, ed. G. Wright. Garden City, NY: Doubleday.

Fisher, L. R.
1963 The Temple Quarter. *Journal of Semitic Studies* 8:34–41.

Fitzmyer, J.
1975 *The Dead Sea Scrolls: Major Publications and Tools for Study*. Sources for Biblical Study 8. Missoula, Montana: Society for Biblical Literature and Scholars Press.

Ginzberg, L.
1922 *Eine unbekannte jüdische Sekte*. New York: *Im selbst Vorlage des Verfassers*.

Hirschfeld, H.
1904 The Arabic Portion of the Cairo Genizah at Cambridge (Third Article): Saadyāh Fragments. *Jewish Quarterly Review* 16:98–103.

Jaubert, A.
1953 Le Calendrier des Jubilés et de la Secte de Qumran. Ses Origines Bibliques. *VT* 3:250–64.
1957 Le Calendrier des Jubilés et les Jours Liturgiques de la Semaine. *VT* 7:35–61.

Krauss, S.
1913 Die Ehe zwischen Onkel und Nichte. Pp. 165–75 in *Studies in Jewish Literature issued in Honor of Professor Kaufmann Kohler*. Berlin: Georg Reimer.

Lambert, W.
1957 Ancestors, Authors and Canonicity. *JCS* 11:1–14.
1962 A Catalogue of Texts and Authors. *JCS* 16:59–77.

Levine, B.
1965 The Descriptive Tabernacle Texts of the Pentateuch. *JAOS* 85:307–18. {*VOL 1, PP. 55–72*}
1971 *Piggûl, Piggûlîm*. Pp. 50–53 in Vol. 6 of the *Encyclopaedia Biblica*. Jerusalem: Bialik Institute (Hebrew).

Licht, J.
1972 Sectarian Calendars. Pp. 50–53 in Vol. 5 of the *Encyclopaedia Judaica*. New York: Macmillan.

Lieberman, S.
1973 *Tosefta Ki-fshuṭah: A Comprehensive Commentary on the Tosefta, Part VIII, Order Nashim*. New York: Jewish Theological Seminary of America (Hebrew).

Milgrom, J.
1972 The Alleged Wave Offering in Israel and the Ancient Near East. *IEJ* 22:33–38.

Milik, J.

1957 Le travail d'édition des manuscrits du désert de Juda. Pages 17–26 in *Volume du Congrès, Strasbourg 1956*. VTSup 4. Leiden: E. J. Brill.

1962 Description de la Jérusalem Nouvelle. Pp. 184–87 in *Les 'Petites Grottes' de Qumrân*, ed. M. Baillet et al. DJD 3. Oxford: Clarendon.

1976 *The Books of Enoch*. Oxford: Clarendon.

Neusner, J.

1974– *A History of the Mishnaic Law of Purities*. Vol. 1–. Leiden: Brill.

Rabin, C.

1957 *Qumran Studies*. Oxford: Clarendon.

Schiffman, L.

1975 *The Halakhah at Qumran*. Leiden: Brill.

Schürer, E.

1891 *A History of the Jewish People in the Time of Jesus Christ*, Vol. 2. Trans. J. Macpherson. New York: Scribners.

Smith, M.

1960–61 The Dead Sea Sect in Relation to Ancient Judaism. *New Testament Studies* 7:346–60.

1971 Pseudepigraphy in the Israelite Tradition. Pp. 191–227 in *Pseudepigrapha* 1, ed. K. von Fritz. Entretiens sur l'Antiquité Classique. Vol. 18, Fondation Hardt. Geneva: Vandoeuvres.

Strugnell, J.

1960 The Angelic Liturgy at Qumrân—4Q *Serek Šîrôt ᶜÔlat Haššabbât.* Pages 318–45 in *Congress Volume, Oxford 1959*. VTSup 7. Leiden: E. J. Brill.

Talmon, S.

1958 The Calendar Reckonings of the Sect from the Judean Desert. Pages 162–99 in *Aspects of the Dead Sea Scrolls*, eds. Ch. Rabin and Y. Yadin. ScrHier 4. Jerusalem: Magnes Press.

Yadin, Y.

1973 *ᶜÎr Bêt Habbaᶜal*. Pp. 52–56 in *The Land of Samaria*, ed. J. Aviram. Jerusalem: Israel Exploration Society (Hebrew).

Yadin, Y., ed.

1977 *The Temple Scroll*. Vol. I, *Introduction*; Vol. II, *Text and Commentary*; Vol. III, *Plates and Texts, with a Supplement*. Jerusalem: Israel Exploration Society, Institute of Archaeology of the Hebrew University of Jerusalem, and the Shrine of the Book of the Israel Museum (Hebrew).

A Further Look at the *Moᶜadim* of the Temple Scroll*

In my earlier study of the *Temple Scroll* I questioned the interpretation given to the *moᶜadim* ("annual festivals") by the late Yigael Yadin.[1] In my view, the text of the scroll failed to endorse Yadin's claim that the *moᶜadim* had been scheduled in conformity with a particular calendar associated, at least in theory, with the Qumran sect. I doubted, therefore, whether one could argue for Qumranic authorship of the scroll from the character of the *moᶜadim* and their scheduled cycles, as Yadin sought to do. My view was and continues to be that the scroll was not written initially as an expression of the views of the sect inhabiting Qumran during a specific period of history. Rather, it is a document brought to Qumran, studied there, and undoubtedly accepted by the sect.

In the intervening years, calendrical questions have been discussed in various contexts, as problems of dating the scroll and of defining its precise relationship to the book of Jubilees have been explored.[2] Quite coincidentally, we have received, in recent years, several studies initially unrelated to the scroll, that serve to elucidate the biblical sources that underlie the scroll's legislation governing the *moᶜadim*. Most notable is the investigation by H.L. Ginsberg, who has now published what some of us, his students, had learned from him verbally regarding Leviticus 23, the principal Torah source for the scroll's *moᶜadim*.[3] It is time, then, to reexamine the sectarian question as it pertains to the *moᶜadim*, and in the process to correct several oversights evident in my earlier study. Inevitably, it will be necessary to review some of what has already been stated, but the

---

* Originally published in Lawrence H. Schiffman (ed.), *Archaeology and History in The Dead Sea Scrolls: The New York University Conference In Memory Of Yigael Yadin* (Journal for the Study of the Pseudepigrapha, Supplement Studies 8; Sheffield: JSOT Press, 1990), pp. 53–66. Reprinted with permission from the Continuum International Publishing Group.

[1] B.A. Levine, "The Temple Scroll: Aspects of its Historical Provenance and Literary Character", *BASOR* 232 (1978), 3–24 {*VOL 1, PP. 171–200*}.

[2] See B.L. Wacholder, *The Dawn of Qumran* (Monographs of the Hebrew Union College 8; Cincinnati: Hebrew Union College, 1983), 53–55, and notes, 247; "The Relationship between 11 Q Torah and the Book of Jubilees(?)", *Seminar Papers* (Society of Biblical Literature, 1985), 205–16; L.H. Schiffman, "The Sacrificial System of the Temple Scroll and the Book of Jubilees", *Seminar Papers* (Society of Biblical Literature, 1985), 217–33, especially 226f.

[3] H.L. Ginsberg, "The Grain Harvest Laws of Lev. 23.26–31", *Proceedings of the American Academy for Jewish Research* 46–47 (Jubilee volume, 1979), 141–54. See also J. Tigay, "Notes on the Background of the Jewish Week", *Eretz-Israel* 14 (Ginsberg Volume, 1978), 111–21; W.W. Hallo, "New Moons and Sabbaths", *HUCA* 48 (1977), 1–18.

discussion will move rapidly to new considerations as I assess the input of the intervening studies and attempt further reflection.

Leviticus 23 in Biblical Context

Ginsberg provides us with instructive insight into the composition of Leviticus 23. I find his interpretation highly relevant. Ginsberg points out that Leviticus 23, as we have it, uses the term *šabbat* in two discrete connotations. In verses 11 and 15a, the phrase *mimmoḥŏrat ha-šabbat* means "on the morrow of the Sabbath day". But in verses 15b–16, the term *šabbat* bears an extended meaning, that of a week ending on the Sabbath day. The result is a certain confusion in terminological usage. In verse 16, the phrase *ʿad mimmoḥŏrat ha-šabbat ha-ševiʿit* means "until the morrow of the seventh 'Sabbath' of days". The term *šabbat* here designates a week, not a day. This usage is probably original to the Holiness Code, and, when compared to Lev. 25:8 reveals how the Holiness Code extended the meaning of the term *šabbat*.[4] There we read of *ševaʿ šabbetot šanim*, "seven 'Sabbaths' of years", i.e., seven septenary cycles, each ending on the sabbatical year. Interpreting Ginsberg, I see a pattern in the Holiness Code wherein the Sabbath is highlighted, so that it generates a system of reckoning time—of certain weeks during the year, and of the Jubilee cycle itself.

The words *mimmoḥŏrat ha-šabbat* in verses 11b and 15a do not accord with this pattern. I therefore accept Ginsberg's conclusion that these words were interpolated by one who sought to lock in the implications of the concept expressed by the Holiness Code. That writer took his cue from the full phrase as it appears in verse 16 and turned the phrase.

According to the original text of Lev. 23:11, 15–16, the period of counting from the initial desacralization of the new barley crop to the subsequent desacralization of the new wheat crop on the Pentecost, a period of fifty days, was to end on the day after the conclusion of the seventh sabbatical week, a Sunday.[5] But the text of Leviticus 23 had not originally fixed the starting day of the period on a Sunday, if we are correct in our analysis. This was accomplished by the interpolations, which confused the terminology in the process. Minus the interpolations, one would have understood Leviticus 23 as follows: "At the time the grain harvest begins, a sheaf of new grain is set aside, to be presented by the priest on behalf of the people". This presentation is scheduled for the first Sunday after the grain became available.

Ginsberg's reconstruction works, and its textual implications have already been explained.[6] The problem is that even in its final form, Leviticus 23 does

---

[4] In this matter, Wacholder (*The Dawn of Qumran*, 247, n. 151) is correct, and I concede the imprecision of my earlier remarks.

[5] See previous note.

[6] See J. Milgrom, "'Sabbath' and 'Temple City' in the Temple Scroll", *BASOR* 232 (1978), 25–27, wherein the precise textual implications of Ginsberg's interpretation are clarified.

not make explicit which Sabbath triggers the period of counting, whether the first Sabbath following the first day of Passover, or the first Sabbath after the conclusion of the seven-day festival. This uncertainty continued to occupy commentators and religious legislators for many centuries, and was the focus of sectarian dissent.

But there is more to the story, as Ginsberg tells it. The emphasis on the Sabbath as a factor in reckoning the period of counting did not endure in biblical, priestly circles. Surely, importance of the Sabbath continued to grow, and was expressed in creation traditions, as we know.[7] Nevertheless, priestly legislators abandoned the specific requirement of beginning and ending the counting on a Sunday, and emphasized instead the absolute number of fifty days; or to put it another way—of seven "weeks", in the sense of seven units of seven days, beginning on any day of the week.

When we, today, use the term *week* we may intend one of two meanings: Sunday-to-Saturday week, as when we say "next week"; or a unit of seven days, beginning now, as when we say "I'll see you in x number of weeks". This difference in our usage correlates with the difference between the nuance coined by the Holiness Code, *šabbat*, "a sabbatical week", and the term *šavuʿa* in biblical Hebrew. Unless further defined, *šavuʿa* never means a sabbatical week, only a unit of seven days (or of seven years, for that matter).[8]

Ginsberg learns of this abandonment of the sabbatical emphasis from Num. 28:26f., part of a cultic calendar that is decidedly subsequent to Leviticus 23. There we read:

> On the day of the first fruits, when you bring an offering of new grain to the LORD on [the completion of] your weeks (*be-šavuʿotēḵem*), you shall observe a sacred occasion....

In the language of Num. 28:26f., we read of *šavuʿot*, not *šabbatot* as in Lev. 23:15–16. In effect, Num. 28:26f. correlates with Deut. 10:9f. in its formulation of the requirement to defer the desacralization of the new wheat harvest seven weeks from the desacralization of the new barley harvest. In Deut. 10.9f. we read:

> You shall count off seven weeks (*šivʿah šavuʿot*). Start to count the seven weeks (*šivʿah šavuʿot*) when the sickle is first put to the standing grain.

Clearly, the conception of the Holiness Code has been rejected in Num. 28:26f. This attitude is also evident, in my opinion, in Josh. 5:10–12. It is a pas-

---

[7] This is brought out in Hallo's discussion (see n. 3, above), in which the singular emphasis on the Sabbath is shown to contrast with the pattern of lunar calendation in the ancient Near East.

[8] This point is explained and carefully documented by Tigay (see n. 3, above).

sage strongly influenced by priestly tradition, if not actually the work of the priestly writers of the Torah, themselves. The passage reads in part:

> The Israelites encamped at Gilgal and offered the paschal sacrifice on the fourteenth day of the month, in the evening in the plains of Jericho. They ate the crop of the land *on the morrow of the paschal sacrifice* (*mimmoḥŏrat ha-pesaḥ*) [consisting of] unleavened bread and parched grain (*qali*), on this very day (*be-ʿeṣem ha-yom ha-zeh*). The manna ceased *on the morrow as they ate* (*be-ʾoḵlam*) of the crop of the land....

In my earlier study, I failed to note that the words *mimmoḥŏrat ha-pesaḥ* also occur in Num. 33:3:

> They began the march from Ramses in the first month, on the fifteenth day of the month, *on the morrow of the paschal sacrifice* (*mimmoḥŏrat ha-pesaḥ*).

Without a doubt, Josh. 5:10–12 is modeled on Num. 33:3. Exactly forty years to the day after leaving Egypt, the Israelites entered Canaan. But Josh. 5:10–12 also echoes Lev. 23:9–22 quite clearly. Upon entering Canaan the Israelites partook of *maṣṣot we-qali*, "unleavened bread and parched grain", and they did so "on this very day" (*be-ʿeṣem ha-yom ha-zeh*). Compare Lev. 23:14:

ולחם וקלי וכרמל לא תאכלו עד-עצם היום הזה עד הביאכם את קרבן אלהיכם

> And bread and *parched grain* and fresh ears you shall not eat *until this very day*, until you have brought the offering of your God.

In Josh. 5:10–12 we find that the desacralization of the new crop (for that is surely what the passage is about) occurred as soon as possible after the paschal sacrifice. The fact that this passage seemingly ignores the first day of the festival created a problem for virtually all commentators, even the Septuagint translators, but in context it merely serves to accentuate the immediacy of desacralization.

I am not now as glib in stating that *ha-pesaḥ* is a replacement for *ha-šabbat* in Lev. 23:11 and 15a, but I still contend that both Num. 33:3 and Josh. 5:10–12 echo Lev. 23:9–22.[9] The Joshua passage has obviously parted company with the sabbatical emphasis of Leviticus 23. This further suggests a progressive turning away from the concepts of the Holiness Code, a process later to be endorsed in rabbinic tradition.

---

[9] See the interesting comment of Abraham Ibn Ezra to Lev. 23:11. He refers to "a Roman Hakham", who cited Josh. 5:10–12 as being relevant to 23:11f., even noting the occurrence in Joshua of the word *maṣṣot we-qali*, "unleavened bread and parched grain". Despite the traditional problems raised by this comparison of diction, Ibn Ezra's lengthy comment attests to an acknowledgment of the link itself. (I am grateful to my colleague, Lawrence H. Schiffman, for reminding me of this reference.)

Leviticus 23 as Subsequently Interpreted

To deal properly with the provisions of the scroll concerning the *moᶜadim* requires an analysis of how the laws of Leviticus 23 were interpreted in representative Jewish traditions of the Greco-Roman period. I shall begin with the normative rabbinic interpretations as they are concisely stated in the *Sifraʾ*, and then work back to the Septuagint translation of the Torah. It appears that the rabbinic interpretations, as we know them from later sources, are presupposed in the Septuagint renderings as well.

The *Sifraʾ* devotes considerable attention to the phrase *mimmoḥŏrat haššabbat*, as we might expect. In the section *ʾEmor*, 11:5 (on Lev. 23:11) the *Sifraʾ* comments: ממחרת השבת—ממחרת יום טוב "On the morrow of the Sabbath—on the morrow of the festival".[10]

This interpretation is repeated several times in the subsequent commentary on Lev. 23:15–16 (*ʾEmor*, ch. 12). The *Sifraʾ* inquires: Does the term *šabbat* in verses 11 and 15a refer to the Sabbath of creation, i.e., the Sabbath day itself? The response is negative, and several reasons are given: First, if the counting were to begin on a Sunday, it would often happen that more than fifty days would intervene between the conclusion of the first day of Passover and the inception of the Pentecost. This would run counter to the intent of Scripture, which stresses the span of precisely fifty days. Only when the fifteenth day of the month falls on the Sabbath itself would the literal interpretation work. Second, Deut. 16:9f. enjoins the Israelites to count off seven weeks for themselves. Now, if the term *šabbat* in Lev. 23:11, 15a referred to the Sabbath day itself, no actual reckoning would be required. The advent of the Sabbath does not need to be reckoned: it has no "date", so to speak. Third, Leviticus 23 does not specify on which Sabbath the counting was to commence, and after all, the year is replete with Sabbaths! It is assumed that the Torah would not be so indefinite in identifying "day one" of the period of counting. Fourth, comparison of verse 11 with verses 15–16 should yield a symmetrical positioning of the beginning day and the concluding day of the period of counting. Just as "until the morrow of the seventh *šabbat*" in verse 16 pinpoints a time occurring at the inception of a festival—the Pentecost—so "on the morrow of the *šabbat*" in verse 11 should designate a time at, or at least near, the inception of a festival—the first day of Passover. This would not occur if the first day of Passover fell on a Sunday or Monday, for instance, in which circumstance the counting, if it had to begin on a Sunday, would only begin during the latter days of the Passover festival.

The rabbinic interpretations presuppose a certain understanding of the intent of Scripture in ordaining a fifty-day period of counting. The overriding concern was to limit the deferral of the Pentecost to fifty days from the Passover. What

[10] *Sifraʾ*, ed. I.H. Weiss, 100b. The review presented here is not intended to be complete. Also see Onkelos: *mimmoḥŏrat yomaʾ ṭavaʾ*.

happened was that the Rabbis reinterpreted the term *šabbat* in both of its discrete connotations within Leviticus 23. As Rashi observes, they apply a generic connotation to the term *šabbat* as it designates a day. Perhaps they took it to be synonymous with *šabbaton*, "a time of cessation, rest", a term applied to sacred days other than the Sabbath (Lev. 23:24, 32, 39) as well as to the Sabbath itself (Exod. 16:23, 31; 31:15; 35:2).[11] The Rabbis further defined *šabbat* as it designates a week as merely a unit of seven days, thus reconciling Lev. 23:15–16 with Deut. 16:9, as if *šabbat* meant *šavuʿa*. They clearly favored the Deuteronomic and later priestly conception over that of the Holiness Code, in this regard.

That this policy and its supporting hermeneutic were relatively ancient is evident from the treatment of Lev. 23:9–22 in the Septuagint. In Lev. 23:11 the Septuagint renders *mimmoḥŏrat ha-šabbat* as *tē epaurion tēs prōtēs*, "on the morrow of the first [day]" (i.e., of the first day of the festival). In verses 15–16 the situation is admittedly more complex. In verse 15a the Septuagint renders *mimmoḥŏrat ha-šabbat* literally as *apo tēs epaurion tōn sabbatōn*, "on the morrow of the Sabbath day".

Why the Septuagint translated verse 15a in this way is not entirely clear. Once having made the point that Hebrew *šabbat* in verse 11 did not refer to the Sabbath day, the translators may have felt free to use the Greek term *sabbatōn* in verse 15a. We note that the Septuagint renders *šabbat*, as a term for week in verses 15–16, by Greek *hebdomas*:

> And you shall count for yourselves, from the morrow of the Sabbath (*tōn sabbatōn*), from the day on which you brought the sheaf of the presentation offering (*tou epithematos*), seven complete weeks (*hebdomadas holoklērous*), until the morrow of the last week (*tēs eschatēs hebdomados*) you count fifty days.

If we compare this translation of Lev. 23:15–16 with the Septuagint's rendering of Lev. 25:8 on the one hand, and with Deut. 16:9 on the other, we may gain some insight into the method of the translators. Deut. 16:9:

> Seven weeks (*hepta hebdomadas*) shall you count off for yourself ...

Lev. 25:8:

> And you shall count off for yourself seven "Sabbaths" of years (*anapauseis etōn*)—seven years, seven times; and they shall be for you seven "weeks" of years (*hebdomades etōn*), nine and forty years.

The Septuagint writers already operated with the concept of the Sunday-to-Saturday week, so that when they used the word *hebdomas* they could have meant what we today mean by the word "week"—either a Sunday-to-Saturday week or a unit of seven days. In Lev. 25:8, the Septuagint translators first made

[11] See the comment of Rashi to B. Menaḥot 65b, s.v. *regel u-teḥillat regel*.

the point that the seven cycles of the Jubilee were sabbatical in character; that each septenary ended on a year-long "Sabbath". This they did by translating Hebrew *šabbetot šanim*, the first time it occurred, by Greek *anapausis*, a term connoting cessation and rest. The second time around they simply employ the term *hebdomas* which, like Hebrew *šavuʿa* may also mean "septenary".

It is difficult, therefore, to know for certain how the Septuagint translators understood the term *šabbat* in Lev. 23:15b–16 as it designated a week, because of the ambiguity of Greek *hebdomas*. It could be argued that the Septuagint translators, if they had endorsed the sabbatarian interpretation of Lev. 23:9–22, would have used a term like *anapausis* to convey that meaning here, as they did in Lev. 25:8. In any event, their treatment of Lev. 23:11 seems to clinch the matter: The period of counting was to begin on the morrow of the first day of Passover, the sixteenth of the month.

The rabbinic tradition of interpretation effectively "wrote off" the sabbatarian principle endemic to the Holiness Code as it pertained to the period of counting. The Septuagint version of Leviticus 23 already reflects this policy.

In later tradition, priority was given to assuring that no more than fifty days intervened between the conclusion of the first day of Passover and the inception of the Pentecost. This consideration overrode the insistence of the Holiness Code that sabbatical weeks constitute the units of reckoning time. The Rabbis assumed a liturgical sequence in Leviticus that differed from the actual, textual sequence. *In situ*, the presentation of the sheaf (verses 9ff.) comes after the law governing the seven days of the festival (verses 4–8). For the Rabbis, it seems, the operational sequence was as follows: first the paschal sacrifice, followed by the inception of the *ḥag*, "pilgrimage festival", on the fifteenth day (verses 4–6a); then the presentation of the sheaf (verses 9ff.). This is suggested by the fact that the rabbinic discussions, summarized earlier, consistently speak of the Sabbath occurring within the seven days of the festival, so that if *šabbat* in verse 11 were to be taken literally, the counting could be delayed until the latter days of the festival.

The Evidence of the Scroll

Our objective should be to ascertain, to the degree possible, how the *moʿadim* of the *Temple Scroll* fit into the pattern of interpretation just discussed. The first problem we face is the condition of the text. Six lines, by Yadin's calculation, are missing from the top of column 18 of the scroll, and lines 1–10 in Yadin's delineation are very sparsely preserved. As a result, we cannot know for certain how the law governing "the day of presenting the sheaf" (*yom hanef/hanifat ha-ʿomer*) was formulated. Did that formulation include the critical words *mim-moḥŏrat ha-šabbat* as Yadin implies, or were they absent, as they are from the three subsequently preserved formulations?

Let us, once again, examine the three preserved formulations: first, column 18:10f.—the Pentecost, when the new wheat crop is desacralized:

> וספרתה [לכה] שבע שבתות תמימות מיום הביאכמה את העומר [תנופה תס]פורו
> עד ממוחרת השבת השביעית תספורו [חמשים] יום
>
> You shall count off for yourself seven complete *šabbatot*, from the day on which you brought the sheaf of the presentation offering you shall count. Until the morrow of the seventh *šabbat* you shall count fifty days.

Second, column 19:10f.—the *moʿed* of new wine:

> [וספר]תמה לכמה מיום הביאכמה את המנחה חדשה ליהו[ה את] לחם הבכורים
> שבעה שבועות שבע שבתות תמימות [ע]ד ממוחרת השבת השביעית תספורו
> חמשים יום
>
> You shall count off for yourselves, from the day on which you brought the offering of new grain, the bread from the first fruits, seven weeks. Seven complete *šabbatot* they shall be. Until the morrow of the seventh *šabbat* shall you count fifty days.

Third, column 21:12f.—the *moʿed* of new oil:

> וספר[ת]ה [לכ]ם מיום הזה שבעה שבעות שבע פעמים תשעה וארבעים יום שבע
> שבתות תמימות תהיינה עד ממוחרת השבת השביעית תספורו חמשים יום
>
> You shall count off for yourself from this day, seven weeks, seven times, nine and forty days: seven complete *šabbatot* they shall be. Until the morrow of the seventh *šabbat*, you shall count fifty days.

The first formulation follows Scripture quite closely. The syntax is smoother, as it is in the Septuagint, because instead of "seven *šabbatot*, they shall be complete" we have "seven complete *šabbatot*". This syntactic rearrangement diminishes the abrupt emphasis on the fullness of the seven *šabbatot* in the biblical formulation. The words *mimmoḥŏrat ha-šabbat* are, of course, absent. The singular *we-safartah*, unless it is a scribal error, which is doubtful, corresponds to the singular address in Lev. 25:8 and Deut. 16:9 (the singular probably also occurs in col. 21:12).

In the second formulation, the language of Deut. 16:9 that speaks of *šavuʿot*, "weeks", is interposed before reference is made to *šabbatot*. In the third formulation, the departure from the text of Lev. 23:15–16 is even more noticeable. Here again, reference to *šabbatot* is preceded by reference to *šavuʿot*, "weeks". Language from Lev. 25:8—"seven times, nine and forty days"—is utilized, and the Deuteronomic language persists. In both the second and the third formulations, there is no trace of the words *mimmoḥŏrat ha-šabbat*. Yadin explains this absence as follows:

> The Scroll's author omitted the words *mimmoḥŏrat ha-šabbat* in order to emphasize that the counting begins from the day of presenting

> the sheaf, the annual date (*moʿed*) of which had already been fixed previously.[12]

I consider this an insufficient response to a crucial problem of interpretation. If the author of the *Temple Scroll* had been a devotee of the calendar associated with the Qumran sect, he would not have surrendered three opportunities to lock in his sabbatarian interpretation. Furthermore, I see no logic in Yadin's point that the scroll's author sought to emphasize that the counting began on the day of presenting the sheaf. Who would have thought otherwise?

It is possible that the Torah text used by the author of the scroll did not contain the words *mimmoḥŏrat ha-šabbat*, but this is highly unlikely because the Septuagint had these words, and I maintain that the author of Josh. 5:10–12 also had them. More likely, the scroll's author undid the work of the priestly editor who interpolated the words *mimmoḥŏrat ha-šabbat* in Lev. 23:11a and 15b.

There is the further observation that the scroll's author interposed Deuteronomic language in his formulations, progressively moving away from the original formulation of Lev. 23:15–16. Living at a time when the term *šabbat*, as a term for a week, could be used more loosely, he could retain the connection with Lev. 23:15–16, while at the same time abandoning the conception of the Holiness Code, as biblical priests before him had done.

It is difficult to ascertain just how the author of the scroll understood the liturgical sequence in Leviticus 23. As has been suggested, the Rabbis understood the presentation of the sheaf to follow upon the first day of the *ḥag*. The "day of presenting the sheaf" (*yom hanef/hanifat ha-ʿomer*) is mentioned twice in the scroll: In col. 11:10 it occurs in a cultic calendar, following *ḥag ha-maṣṣot*, "the pilgrimage festival of unleavened bread", but that is only to be expected. In col. 18:9–10 it occurs at the very conclusion of the law governing the day of presenting the sheaf:

ואחר יעלו את האיל אחת פעם [אחת] ביום הניפת העומר

> And afterward, they shall offer up the single ram, once [a year] on the day of presenting the sheaf.

The ram in question is the one fortunately legible in line 2 of the same column: *la-ʾayil ha-zeh*, "for this ram".

So it is that we have no way of knowing for certain what appeared in the text where the presentation of the sheaf is prescribed. One doubts that the words *mimmoḥŏrat ha-šabbat* would be found in the missing lines.

---

[12] See Y. Yadin, *The Temple Scroll* (English edition, Jerusalem: Israel Exploration Society, 1983), II:78 to 18:11. The translation given here is, however, based on the Hebrew edition (*Megillat Ha-Miqdaš*, Jerusalem: Israel Exploration Society, 1977), II:85, and is by this author.

The Origin of the Temple Scroll's Moᶜadim

The scheduling of two *moᶜadim* subsequent to the Pentecost is part of a policy generally evident in the *Temple Scroll.* Cultic celebrations are enhanced and elaborated over and above their scriptural limits. On a similar basis, occasions are prescribed that have no biblical sanction originally.

According to my view, the process of enhancing cultic celebrations is actually evident in Leviticus 23 itself. The initial desacralization of the sheaf was a rite of presentation in which no altar offering was involved. This mode of worship, known as *tenufah*, "presentation", was widespread in the ancient Near East from early times. The presentational mode was often adapted by the biblical priesthood to the mode of burnt offerings, which progressively gained in importance within Israelite religion. This adaptation is expressed in verses 12–13, which were inserted following the primary law of verses 9–11, and which prescribe altar offerings. The same process is observable further on in Leviticus 23: The offering of first fruits was first prescribed in verses 15–17 as a rite of presentation, and then verses 18–20 were inserted where burnt offerings are ordained for it.[13]

Against this background one could say that the *Temple Scroll* carries this process further. Notwithstanding the poor state of preservation of column 18, we are able to read of a sin-offering in lines 7–8, and of the sacrifice of a ram in line 9 (cf. line 2). The theme of expiation is also expressed.

A second development is evident in the scroll. In priestly biblical usage, the term *moᶜed*, whenever it signifies an annual, sacred occasion, involves the prohibition of daily labor. As such, its usage is restricted to the major annual festivals, and once to the Sabbath, somewhat inconsistently (Lev. 23:2f.). In the scroll, the post-Pentecost celebrations are called *moᶜadim*, but there is no indication that labor was prohibited on these days. Furthermore, there is little likelihood that labor was prohibited on the day of the presentation of the sheaf. In this connection, Yadin's suggested restoration of col. 18:3 is probably incorrect. He restores: מקרא קודש יהיה [להמה] היום הזה (literally: "A sacred occasion shall it be [for them] this day").

Hebrew *miqraʾ qodeš*, "sacred occasion", connotes a day on which labor is forbidden. Yadin took this restoration from the law of the Pentecost in Lev. 23:21, and his method of restoration is therefore highly doubtful.

Structurally, the two post-Pentecost *moᶜadim* are based on the seasonal due dates of the tithes of vineyards and olive groves, a point explained by Schiffman that suggests affinities to the book of Jubilees. The triad *dagan*, *tiroš*, *we-yiṣhar*, "grain, wine, and oil", conveys the ultimate basis for the seasonal desacraliza-

---

[13] See B.A. Levine, *In the Presence of the Lord* (Leiden: E.J. Brill, 1974), 48, and now *idem*, *Leviticus* (JPS Torah Commentary; Philadelphia: The Jewish Publication Society, 1989), 157–60.

tions scheduled in the scroll. Hebrew *dagan* includes the varieties of barley and wheat, as implied by Deut. 8:8.

The triad *dagan*, *tiroš*, *we-yiṣhar* is distinctive in biblical literature and originates in Hos. 2:11 as part of a prophetic assurance of abundant produce throughout the agricultural year. In the Deuteronomic laws (Deut. 12:17; 18:14) as well as in the rubric of the book of Deuteronomy (Deut. 7:13; 28:5; cf. Jer. 31:12), it is a frequent theme associated with the duty of tithing. With great insight, Ginsberg has seen in this triad a significant link of diction joining Hosea and Deuteronomy, and pointing to the northern, or "Israelian" origin of the primary parts of Deuteronomy.[14]

This triad also occurs in the scroll (col. 43:3f.), and, as we might have expected, in the context of tithing. The two post-Pentecost *moᶜadim* correspond to the cutoff dates for presenting certain tithes. I am not certain, however, that the scroll's author invented them, as Schiffman conjectures. These *moᶜadim* may have developed quite normally over a period of time. From 2 Chron. 31:3f. we learn that in Second Temple times people from all over the land began to deliver tithes of "grain, wine, and oil" (*dagan*, *tiroš*, *we-yiṣhar*) in the third month, the month of the Pentecost, and continued to do so until the seventh month, the month of the Sukkot pilgrimage festival. We are told that these commodities were stored in bins (2 Chron. 32:28f.). Similar information is preserved in Neh. 10:38–40, and 13:5, 12. It would have been natural to schedule cultic celebrations in the Temple at the appropriate junctures of the agricultural year.

The last of the *moᶜadim*, that of new oil, is actually mentioned in a fragment from Qumran, Cave 4, cited by J.T. Milik. There it is termed *moᶜed ha-šemen*, and its date is given as the 22nd of Elul.[15] Yadin was certainly correct in concluding that the date given in this fragment could only have been based on the sectarian calendar known at Qumran. If we work back through three periods of forty-nine days, one arrives at the 26th of Nisan, the first Sunday following the seven days of Passover. This was according to the sectarian calendar that always had the 15th of Nisan occurring on a Wednesday.

This fragment is, however, external evidence when applied to the interpretation of the *Temple Scroll*. The fragment attests that this *moᶜed* was known at Qumran and celebrated by the sect on the 22nd of Elul. That is not to say, however, that the scroll computed this *moᶜed* according to the same calendar. We are back to our original problem!

---

[14] See H.L. Ginsberg, *The Israelian Heritage of Judaism* (New York: Jewish Theological Seminary of America, 1982), 19f.

[15] See J.T. Milik, "Le travail d'édition des manuscrits du désert de Juda", *Volume du Congrès: Strasbourg 1956* (VTSup 4; E.J. Brill, 1957), 25.

Conclusion

We presently know relatively little about Jewish worship in the last pre-Christian centuries. When we encounter previously unknown phenomena, we are unable to determine in most cases how narrowly or broadly they were based in the Jewish communities of the period. Lacking contemporary correlation, we logically turn to evidence from earlier or later sources, or both. This is the method employed here, with perhaps more emphasis on the biblical background than one normally finds in current studies.

This study is an attempt to argue for caution in assuming a particular sectarian provenance for the *Temple Scroll*, as though in this instance, we were certain that its provisions reflected Qumranic calendation. The scroll's formulations of the *moᶜadim* represent, on the first level, reworkings of Torah laws. Their proper interpretation should, therefore, be contingent on a thorough investigation of these particular sources, most notably the laws of Leviticus 23. Source critical analysis of Leviticus 23 is all important because it helps to chart ongoing developments in religious law. On the other hand, comparisons with the renderings of the Septuagint and with later rabbinic hermeneutic indicate that what became the normative rabbinic interpretations were known and accepted quite widely long before halakhic Midrash took final form.

How the *Temple Scroll* fits into the development of Judaism remains uncertain. For the moment, a valid argument can be made for seeing continuity in the interpretation of Lev. 23:9–22 in a direction away from the sabbatarian emphasis so prominent in the Holiness Code.

C. Phenomenology of Religion

On the Presence of God in Biblical Religion*

The late Erwin R. Goodenough devoted his best energies to the quest for meaning in graphic and glyptic representation and in ancient literary sources. He possessed great insight into the realms of both experience and doctrine, and showed considerable interest in the proper study of early Israelite religion, although that was not his primary area of inquiry. I dedicate this study to his memory, knowing his awareness of the limits of theology and his insistence on adherence to evidence in the study of ancient religions. I thus recognize my indebtedness to his intellectual leadership and to the methodology which he developed.*

"Where is God?" is the question of young children, but it constitutes as well the confrontation of mature men. Many of us have become accustomed to thinking that God is everywhere. We probably mean to convey that wherever man may find himself, the protecting God is nearby. "The Lord is near to all who call upon him" are the words of the Psalmist (Psalm 145:18). The notion of God's omnipresence would afford a great measure of assurance to man, if it were fully convincing in its emotional aspects. It has seldom sufficed, however, either for the modern believer or for his ancient predecessors; witness man's feeling that the divine being should be approached in special locales consecrated to him. Despite the many functions, other than cultic, that have always pertained to temples, it must be admitted that if men did not sense the need to build residences for deities so as to have the advantages of their proximity to the human community, the grandiose efforts devoted to temple building, and to the maintenance of elaborate cults, would have been expended on other enterprises.[1]

---

* Originally published in Jacob Neusner (ed.), *Religions in Antiquity: Essays in Memory of Erwin Ramsdell Goodenough* (Studies in the History of Religions 14; Leiden: E. J. Brill, 1968), pp. 71–87. Note that the footnote numbering here does not match that of the original publication. Reprinted with permission from Brill.

The author is indebted to the following scholars with whom he had the privilege of discussing the theme of the presence of God in biblical literature: to Profs. Yochanan Muffs, Nahum Sarna & Morton Smith. Aspects of this paper were treated in an address before the Society of Biblical Literature & Exegesis, Vanderbilt University, December, 1965.

[1] See the discussion on "The Significance of the Temple in the Ancient Near East," *The Biblical Archaeologist Reader*, I, Anchor Books, 1961, pp. 145–185, and especially the statements of G. Ernest Wright, p. 169f., where he notes the difficulties for ancient man in accepting the omnipresence of God. We note here that all translations of biblical

In reading the Hebrew Bible with the question of God's whereabouts in mind, we observe that concern with the presence of God and his nearness is a major theme. Rarely does the biblical spokesman, be he priest, prophet, or Psalmist, assume the omnipresence of God.[2] On occasion, biblical man is compelled to accept the fact that God may lay hold of him wherever he is (Psalm 139:7–9). When, however, we attempt to penetrate to the motivations underlying religious activity in ancient Israel, we perceive that prayer and lamentation express the yearning for God's nearness, and that pilgrimages are undertaken so as to be close to the deity resident in the temple. Generally speaking, the desire for God's presence in the human community seems to motivate most of the regular aspects of religious life, and we shall proceed to show to what extent this is true of biblical culture.

The desire on man's part for the nearness of divine powers reflects universal human attitudes and conceptions. We normally visualize a protector, whether father or leader, as being nearby rather than far away, and love is identified with closeness. The child often experiences anxiety when he is left alone, and the adult must also come to terms with remoteness as a factor in his relationships. Moreover, divine beings are viewed as the source of life and power. Power, in turn, is thought to be conducted from the source to that which is infused with it, and man invariably expresses concern with identifying the channels through which power is conducted. He reasons that the closer the source, the more certain and plentiful the power. It is, therefore, understandable that the presence of God becomes synonymous with the material blessings and protection afforded by his power, and the very willingness of the deity to draw near is taken as a sign of favor. This assertion is not mitigated by the prophetic critique of practical religion; a critique aimed at changing the more conventional attitudes of ancient believers by injecting certain variables into the dynamics of the divine-human encounter.

The nearness of divine power had its dangers. Wrath and punishment are also features of God's relationship to man, and he may draw near to the human

passages are the work of the author, and, where necessary, explanatory notes will be provided in justification.

[2] See Ps. 72:19, where the hope is expressed that God's *kābôd* "presence" will fill the whole earth. Isaiah 6:3 may also mean that the *kābôd* infuses everything in the world: "His presence is the fullness of the whole earth." That passage is a crux. It may also mean that the earth, itself, is God's *kābôd*. In any event, both passages relate to the notion of omnipresence. On the sense of *kābôd* as "body, person" see H. L. Ginsberg, *Mordecai Kaplan Jubilee Volume*, Jewish Theological Seminary of America, 1953, pp. 246–247. Ginsberg was concerned with other passages (*inter alia* Isaiah 10:3, 16, 17:4, 22:18, Ps. 7:6, 16:9, Gen. 49:6) bearing on the sense of the term as applied to human beings. His discussion provides a starting point for establishing the sense of the term when applied to the deity. It obviously can mean "glory, honor", but in more cases than not, we should eliminate the elements of greater abstraction, so understandably evoked by divine associations, and emphasize rather the element of real presence.

community in order to strike out at it. There are times when man may fear the nearness of God, but he normally must risk the dangers attendant on the divine presence for the blessings he hopes to receive from the divinity. It is our purpose here to explore the positive side of the relationship.

I

Where in biblical literature may we find the most fundamental expression of the desire for God's presence and nearness? The earliest indications are to be sought in biblical epic.[3] In bringing together various pre-Israelite traditions about the gods and their exploits, traditions known in Ugaritic literature and in Mesopotamian sources, biblical poets preserved for later generations the vivid memory that, on certain momentous occasions, God descended to earth and acted on behalf of Israel and its leaders. There is, of course, more than one conception embodied in biblical epic, and most often several strains have been blended into a composite description. In at least one portrayal God accomplished his act of rescue from heaven: "He sends forth (his hand) from on high and takes hold of me; he draws me up from deep waters" (Psalm 18:17//2 Samuel 22:17.[4]) The motif which becomes predominant in biblical epic is the portrayal of God as he descends to earth and approaches his people. In an early passage, which recurs with variations, God is seen approaching from the Negev and Dead Sea regions, variously Sinai, Paran, Seir, Edom, perhaps Kadesh, "the wilderness" (Hebrew *yešîmôn*) and Teman. These passages most probably refer to a particular tradition about Israel's origins and describe their first encounter with Yahweh. The approach is tremendous:

> Yahweh! When you went forth from Seir,
> When you marched from the field of Edom,
> The heavens dropped rain, even the clouds let water fall,
> Water ran down the mountainsides.
> At the approach of Yahweh!
> Yonder Sinai, at the approach of Yahweh, the God of Israel.
> (Judges 5:4–5)

> God! When you went forth before your people,
> When you marched in the wilderness, Selah;
> The earth quaked, even the heavens dropped rain.
> At the approach of God!

---

[3] See U. Cassuto, "Epic Poetry in Israel," (Hebrew), *Kenesset in Honor of H. N. Bialik*, 8, 1943–44, Pt. 3, pp. 121–142. By "epic" we mean poetic collections relating the feats of God and the exploits of heroes. By "heroic" we mean prose accounts on the same subject, with perhaps more stress on the human hero. The difference between the two genres is to some extent a matter of form.

[4] In these parallel passages it is stated that "he (God) bent the heavens descended (2 Sam. 22:10//Ps. 18:10), but it is clear from the ensuing verses that the descent did not bring God down to Earth. Also see Ps. 68:5, 34.

Yonder Sinai, at the approach of God, the God of Israel.
(Psalm 68:8–9)

A probable variant of the same description is to be found in Deuteronomy 33:2:

And he said:
Yahweh came forth from Sinai,
He shone upon them from Seir,
And appeared from the region of Mt. Paran.
He came from Ribeboth Kadesh.
To his right were waterfalls.[5]

Of similar import is the description of God as a man of war in Exodus 15, and as the swooping eagle who encircles his nest, closely guarding his young, in Deuteronomy 32. We also have the reference to the battle with the powers of the sea, which begins:

Why do you draw back your hand?
Hold back your right hand inside your bosom?[6]
My God! My king from of old!
The worker of acts of deliverance in the midst of the earth.
(Psalm 74:11–12)

Interestingly, the prophet Micah, and his contemporary Amos, invert the coin, and employ ancient images of the earth-striding deity to portray the approach of God, descending from heaven to earth, in order to devastate the idolatrous cultic centers:

For, behold! Yahweh is going forth out of his place,
And he will descend, treading on the high ridges of the earth.

---

[5] On our translation of Dt. 33:2: For *qôdeš* read *qādēš*, the place name. *Ribebôt* may be a variant of *merîbôt*, elsewhere a part of the name. See Koehler-Baumgartner, *Lexicon in Veteris Testamenti Libros*, Leiden, 1958, s.v. *qādēš*. For the problematic *ʾēšdāt* (presumably: "fire of the law") read *ʾašādôt* (or: *ʾašēdôt*) "waterfalls". See Jos. 10:40, 12:7–8. Approaching from the East, from Seir, one would have on his right two areas, one to the East and the other to the Northwest of the Jordan, which were called *ʾašēdôt*. See Y. Aharoni, *Carta Atlas of the Bible*, Jerusalem, 1964, map no. 7. The new Jewish Publication Society Torah translation tentatively suggests "lightning flashing". See E. König, *Kommentar zum alten Testament, das Deuteronomium*, Leipzig, 1917, pp. 216–218. A later echo of this epic theme is to be found in Habakkuk 3:1f.

[6] V. 11b is problematic. We follow, in principle, the rendering of H. Gunkel, *Die Psalmen, Göttinger Handkommentar Zum alten Testament*, Göttingen, 1926, s.v. Ps. 74:11. Gunkel reads *beqereb ḥêqekā tiklāʾ* "you hold back inside your bosom", for Massoretic *miqqereb ḥêqekā kallēh* which would have to mean: "draw out from inside your bosom". We do not have such a connotation attested for the Piel *kallēh*, which means "destroy, put an end to —." The word *klh* could, however, be a variant of *klʾ* "hold back" and represent the infinitive absolute, *kālôh*.

The mountains will melt underneath him,
And the valleys will be split—
As wax before fire,
As water flowing down an incline.
(Micah 1:3–4, abbreviated in Amos 4:13)

Micah and Amos achieved unusual poignancy by transposing motifs associated in the minds of the people with God's saving power into the context of the punishment of Israel. The same approach, the descent to earth, becomes for them an inevitably disastrous act, but their referent is the tradition that God's presence on earth was a situation much to be sought. In the epic selections describing God's approach to Israel, the verbs employed, especially "he came, he marched, he went forth, he will tread" serve to create a scene of earthly activity.[7] It is not only God's might that is recounted here, but his nearness.

This is the most fundamental expression of the notion, later to become basic in Israelite religion, that God's nearness is prerequisite to the blessings afforded by his great power. The exercise of that power is recounted in referring to singular occasions in the past, in projecting descriptions of the redemption to come, and in appealing to God for rescue in the present. What the cult sought to do, in a sense, was to render permanent the epic relationship of God to Israel, and thus to assure the regular availability of divine power. The cult was to routinize the singular. Whereas prophets warned the people not to rely on past indications of favor as an assurance of victory, the cultic spokesmen instituted epic recitation for the very purpose of promoting faith in God's continuously protecting power.

II

The heroic traditions of the Bible reveal still another aspect of the concern with God's nearness and presence. We are here introduced to an accepted notion (one hesitates to use the term doctrine) of early biblical religion, which we shall call "the potent presence". Simply stated, it means that God's presence in the midst of the people is the actual cause of their victory and the success of their ventures, the basis of their peace and wellbeing. Conversely, God's absence or withdrawal permits other forces to control the situation, resulting in the defeat of Israel and in its misfortune. This notion affects both the individual hero and the military band as a whole, and, as in epic, usually finds its expression in the at-

[7] In Dt. 33:2 the verb *hôpîʿa* "he appeared, he shone" (see Job 10:3) is used, as in other passages, to indicate the pose of the deity when he reveals himself. Cf. Ps. 50:2, 80:2, 94:1. The meaning "to shine" is not always used to describe sunlight. See Job 37:15, where it is said of God's protecting cloud. The verbs "come, go, shine" are elsewhere used to describe the sun, originally the sun-god. On the verb *ypʿ* in Ugaritic, and regarding personal theophoric names which incorporate this verb, see C. H. Gordon, *Ugaritic Textbook*, Rome, 1965, glossary, no. 1133. On the quaking of nature at the approach of God, see S. A. Loewenstamm, *ʿOz Ledavid*, (*Hebrew*), vol. 15, Jerusalem, 1964, pp. 508–520.

mosphere of battle. Much has been said about the "charismatic" character of the Israelite hero, stressing that the "spirit of Yahweh" alights upon him and clothes him with prowess.[8] In the context of our discussion, the concern expressed by the hero for the presence of God in the midst of the people is of primary interest. It is Gideon's encounter with the angel of God which is most revealing in this regard (Judges 6). Gideon gives direct expression to the notion of the potent presence: "Pray, oh my lord, if indeed Yahweh is with us, why has all of this overtaken us? ... For he must have abandoned us, and given us over into the hands of the Midianites" (Judges 6:13). Gideon is unwilling to take chances, and three successive signs are required to assure him of the divine presence, an absolute prerequisite to the success of the venture. That is the force of the preposition *ʿim*, which occurs four times in this passage.[9] The hero seems to understand that God may, for a time, abandon his people, but he is extremely suspicious on the question of whether God has actually returned.

Once we realize that the notion of the potent presence was an unquestioned assumption in certain biblical traditions, we can better interpret a number of accounts which are predicated upon it.[10] The book of Numbers records that after God had decreed forty years of wandering in the desert, a band of warriors attempted to advance by the direct route to Canaan and were repulsed. In warning them, Moses had said: "Do not go up, lest you be routed by your enemies, for Yahweh is not in your midst" (Numbers 14:42).[11] Significantly, the ark does not budge from its place in the camp (*Ibid.* verse 44). What is most important here is the reasoning Moses employs in pleading for Israel. Moses argues that other nations would attribute Israel's extinction in the desert to God's impotence. The reasoning is as follows: God cannot have abandoned his people, since his presence is attested by the pillars of fire and cloud that go before the Israelites on their journeys. The people, nonetheless, perish in the desert. Ergo: God is present, but he has become impotent (Numbers 14:13–16).[12]

This argument fails to consider aspects of God's relationship to Israel which figure elsewhere. It does not include the possibility that God merely refused to exercise the power of his presence, and that the decision not to exercise potency does not presuppose the actual withdrawal of the deity.

This becomes significant when we examine the account of the battle between the Israelites and the Philistines at Aphek (1 Samuel 4:3f.), and compare it with the account of the battle fought some twenty years later against the Philistines at Mizpah (1 Samuel 7:3f.). During the earlier battle, the Israelites had

---

[8] J. Pedersen, *Israel: Its Life and Culture*, Copenhagen, 1953, vol. 3, pp. 34–39. R. de Vaux, *Ancient Israel*, New York, 1961, pp. 261–262.

[9] Judges 6:12, 13, 16, 17.

[10] See de Vaux, *op. cit.*, p. 299.

[11] Cf. Exodus 32:11–12.

[12] Cf. Zeph. 1:12. The prophet attributes to the people the view that Yahweh does nothing at all, which might mean that he has no power to act.

brought the ark from Shiloh in the hope that it would afford them victory, but they were defeated, nevertheless. In the terms of that account, the potency of the ark simply failed, and no explanation is given as to why. It is only later that Samuel explains the cause of the earlier defeat. Israel had committed idolatry. They would be victorious only if they sincerely returned to the worship of God. Samuel accepts the pledge of the people and entreats God on their behalf, and they are victorious. The presence of the ark had failed, for twenty years, to relieve the Philistine oppression, but the return of the people to the worship of God was efficacious.[13]

We see the difference between the essentially heroic tradition, when unaffected by prophetic superimpositions, and the interpretation of Israelite history in terms of disobedience to God and its consequences. In the heroic tradition, the mere presence of divine power is sufficient. It is a mechanically operating pneuma, subject at times to failure.

We can thus isolate three aspects in the structure of the idea of potent presence:

1. The alternatives of presence and absence, as reflected in the Gideon account.

2. The alternatives of presence, absence, and impotence, as reflected in Numbers 14:13–16 and 1 Samuel 4:3f.

3. The alternatives of exercised and unexercised potency. In this conception, presence is generally assumed, and is not the crucial factor, and impotence is inconceivable. This conception is reflected in 1 Samuel 7:3f.

III

It has been necessary to deal with the general theme of God's presence before considering matters peculiar to the cult. Cultic notions are usually the particularized expressions of more widespread concepts operative in the culture at large, rather than the original creations of the cult itself.[14] The religious establishment tends to sanction that which the culture has accepted. The notion that God's presence is necessary for securing the blessings of life was, as we have shown, intrinsic to the early traditions of Israel. It is against this background that we must now explore its cultic applications.

We begin by inquiring into the motivations surrounding the private and local altar-building projects recorded in the Pentateuch and in the historical books of the Bible. Two complementary factors must be considered: 1) The evident presence of the deity as the determinant in establishing the sanctity of a particu-

---

[13] Cf. Jos. 7:4f.

[14] This has been clarified by our researches into biblical cultic terminology. It is possible to demonstrate that the large majority of technical terms used in cultic texts derive from other contexts. See B. Levine, "Comments on Some Technical Terms of the Biblical Cult" (Hebrew), *Leshonenu* 30, 1965, pp. 3–11.

lar site, and 2) The construction of an altar, and the offering of sacrifices, as an effort to attract the deity to the place of sacrifice; to invite him to pay a visit.

The former aspect of the sanctity of cultic locales has been duly noted and discussed. A classic example is Genesis 28, the account of Jacob's experience at Bethel. The cult is there conceived as a human response to the presence of the deity. Generally, when sanction is sought for already existing cultic centers, much is made of the fact that the deity manifested his presence at those sites in the distant past.[15]

The problem of sanctions is, however, considerably more complex. In Exodus 20:19–23, a passage containing some early regulations on the building of altars, verse 21 states: "In every place where I cause my name to be pronounced, I will come to you and bless you."[16] The point here is that God "comes" to the worshipper; he draws near to him when he is about to grant him blessings. Though a particular locale is known as a sacred site (a site where "I cause my name to be pronounced") it is not to be assumed, in the terms of this passage, that God is always present there. He must be invoked, and we are told that the deity will accept a proper invitation, and will "come." The altar must be constructed according to certain specifications, and nakedness may not be exposed in proximity to it.

The established sacredness of a site is thus subject to still another factor: the correctness of the cultic activity undertaken there. We may infer that improper rites may persuade the deity not to frequent certain sites, and he may come to despise them. This becomes a fundamental concept in prophetic literature, where it is fused with the overall prophetic critique of ritual to produce the idea that God rejects cultic sites, even places where he was present in the past, when those offering the sacrifices violate his laws of justice and love. For our discussion, it suffices to say that the tradition of Exodus 20:19–23 viewed the altar rite as an invitation, and that it is predicated on the assumption that there are acceptable and unacceptable rites, a factor crucial irrespective of locale.

In the problematic Balaam account we are brought to a consideration of those efforts aimed at attracting the deity, a more emphatic project than inviting him to an already designated site. Magic would normally be involved in ritual activities having this objective, as was the case in the Balaam episode (Numbers 22:7, 24:1). For that reason, perhaps, biblical sources would shy away from openly stating that the worshippers were attempting to attract the deity to the place of sacrifice. The writer of Numbers is aware, however, that such motives enter into ritual, and he conveys that awareness in a setting at once removed

---

[15] See de Vaux, *op. cit.*, pp. 276–277. Pederson, *op. cit.*, vol. 3, pp. 201–214. Cf. J. Lindblom, *HUCA* 32, 1961, pp. 91–106, and especially his treatment of the Gideon account on p. 103.

[16] For exegesis, see M. Noth, *The Old Testament Library: Exodus*, Philadelphia, 1962, pp. 176–177. U. Cassuto, *A Commentary on the Book of Exodus*, (Hebrew), Jerusalem, 1959, pp. 176–178.

from the normal context, and yet directly related to the God of Israel. Balaam orders that altars be built and sacrifices prepared as a means of inducing an encounter with God (Numbers 23:1–3). He had already explained that he could speak only what God put into his mouth (Numbers 22:38). The only matter to be determined was whether God would say something harmful to Israel.

The crucial term in these passages is the verb *qrh* (Numbers 23:3–4, 15–16). This root, in the Qal and Niphal, bears the connotation of establishing contact, of meeting up, and seems usually to include the nuance of a chance meeting.[17] Although the writer of this account undoubtedly shared the belief that the deity selects certain sites where he manifests his presence, he thinks of this selection in more fluid terms. The deity may be attracted to a spot, by sacrifice and magic, where he had not been present previously, and without indication that he would visit the spot again. In such cases, certain fairly obvious factors would figure in the effort to attract. Mountaintops have definite advantages. If one is to direct his words at a specific area, a spot in full view of that area is where God might logically communicate (Numbers 23:13). But, withal, methods are employed to attract the deity to a place human beings consider to be well suited for their purposes, and this is something quite different from inviting God to visit a place which he has selected. Balaam walks away a distance from the altars to encounter God, but it is clear that they provide the basic attraction in this account (Numbers 23:34).[18]

IV

We turn now to the royally sponsored cult at Jerusalem to determine in what manner the notion of the potent presence, and the effort to benefit from the nearness of God operated once a central cult was established.

1 Kings 8:12–13 is a passage quoted from an ancient collection. Verse 13 states the purpose for which the temple was built: "I have surely built a princely house for you, a dais for you to sit upon forever." Less literally, we would render: "a set place for your residence." The temple is a residence for the deity.[19]

---

[17] See Koehler-Baumgartner, *op. cit.*, s.v. *qrh*, and cf. Exodus 3:18, Numbers 11:23.

[18] Elijah's encounter with the priests of Baal (1 Kings 18) may also reflect the same objective of attracting the deity. Elijah uses magical techniques. He digs a ditch and fills it with water (18:32–35). The response to Elijah's invocation comes in the form of fire which licks up the water and consumes the sacrifice (vs. 38–39). A. Goetze has presented a Hittite ritual of attraction which he calls Evocatio (J. Pritchard, *Ancient Near Eastern Texts Relating to the Old Testament*, Princeton, 1950, pp. 351–353). Materials such as oil, wine, etc. were placed in baskets along the way to make a trail for the gods to follow on their way back to Hattiland.

[19] For exegesis, see J. A. Montgomery, H. S. Gehman, *Kings, The International Critical Commentary*, 1951, pp. 189f. V. 12 conveys the idea that the temple was meant as a place of concealment for the deity, thus reproducing his situation in the heavenly temple: "Yahweh intends to dwell in the dense cloud." See K. Baltzer, *HTR* 59, 1965, p.

Once established, the Jerusalem temple and its attending cult produce certain reflexes in the religious attitudes of the people. One such reflex is the notion that God's presence in the Jerusalem temple guarantees the security of the city and its residents, an idea extended to include the whole people of Israel and its land.

This notion is attacked by the prophet Micah, who says of the leaders of the people in Jerusalem:

> Her leaders render judgment on the basis of bribes.
> Her priests practice divination for a fee.
> And they lean on Yahweh, saying:
> Is not Yahweh in our midst?
> No evil shall come upon us!
>
> (Micah 3:11)

Jeremiah also warns the people not to trust the words of the false prophets who say:

> The temple of Yahweh! The temple of Yahweh!
>
> (Jeremiah 7:3)

Jerusalem will fall just as did Shiloh, where God also resided. Psalm 46 presents the notion which Micah and Jeremiah are criticizing:

> God is for us protection and strength.
> A most valuable source of help in trouble.
> Thus, we have no fear when the earth is overturned,
> And when mountains totter into the depths of the sea...
> A river—its tributaries bring joy to the city of God,
> The holy place of Elyon's residence. God is in her midst, she shall not fall!
> God will bestow help upon her before morning.
>
> (verses 2–3; 5–6)

In this we have applied the notion of the potent presence to the Jerusalem temple, which became God's principal headquarters, and in time the only headquarters, for the Israelite. To put it in technological terms: God's power is produced in heaven, but it is distributed from the temple. This is conveyed by the author of Psalm 68:

> Recount the might of God!
> His majesty is over Israel,
> And his might is in the heavens.
> God is awesome from your temple buildings.

263f. The notion that the deity has "a set place" for residence met with some opposition. 2 Sam. 7:1f. preserves a tradition according to which God seemed to prefer the mobility afforded by the tent (v. 6). This passage may be simply an *ad hoc* explanation of why no temple was built until the time of Solomon, or it may indeed reflect a legitimate dissent from the growing nationalization of the cult which resulted from the establishment of the monarchy. See G. Ernest Wright, *op. cit.*, p. 172f.

The God of Israel—he gives might and power to the people. Blessed is God!
(verses 35–36)

It is from heaven that God's power originates, but it is from the temple that the deity appears and gives strength to the people.[20]

Although God never ceases to answer prayers from his heavenly abode,[21] the literature of supplications seems to indicate that it was primarily the temple from whence came the divine assistance requested in prayer and sacrifice.[22] This conclusion is supported by an analysis of the anxieties and passions of the religious man with respect to the temple, as expressed in the book of Psalms.

It was felt, first of all, that to be in the sanctuary is to be under God's protection, and the temple is actually equated with the shelter of God's wings.[23] In the same way, one senses great anxiety when he is distant from the temple. The distressed supplicant, in the North or in Transjordan, recalls his joy in the cultic celebration, when he entered into the presence of God. He argues, albeit reverently, that since he remembers God from afar, God, in turn, should have him in mind when he is far from the temple (Psalm 42). The phrase *yešûʿôt panâw* "his countenance is deliverance" (or: "deliverance is effected by his countenance") in Psalm 42:6 amplifies the thought that nearness to the temple meant actual nearness to God and his protection.[24] It is in the temple that one beholds God's countenance.[25]

Just as distance from the temple can produce anxiety, so may concern over being denied entry into the temple because of unfitness. The rites of entry referred to in Psalms 15 and 24 were a means of determining fitness, and although these Psalms are a stylized formulation of religious duties, they undoubtedly go back to an actual anxiety.

Looking at the other side of things, we find passionate expressions of the desire to be in the temple, and we sense the joy experienced there by the worshipper (Psalm 63:3, 7–8).[26] It is the pilgrim who experiences the peak of elation

---

[20] Ps. 63:3.

[21] Lam. 3:44, Ps. 20:7, 123:1, 1 Kings 8:30, 32, Neh. 9:27.

[22] In Ps. 20 we find the polarity of heaven and temple. The response comes from heaven (v. 7), but the help comes from the temple in Zion (v. 3). See J. A. Montgomery, *op. cit.*, p. 194. Cf. Ps. 14:7, 53:7, 110:2, 138:1–3. In Ps. 28 it is clear, especially from v. 2, that the supplicant expects the requested help to come from the temple. Also cf. Jonah 2:8.

[23] Ps. 27:4f., 36:8–10, 61:5, 63:7, 65:2–3. The right of asylum in the sanctuary is clearly based on the concept that once in the temple a person is under God's protection, and dare not be harmed.

[24] The phrase *yešûʿôt panaî wĕʾlôhaî* in v. 12 is difficult. See H. Gunkel, *op. cit.*, s.v. 42:6. Perhaps: *yešûʿôt panâw ʾelôhaî* "My God—his countenance is deliverance!"

[25] Ps. 42:3, 63:3, 84:8, Jonah 2:5. Where the Massoretic text is vocalized *ʾērāʾeh* "I will be seen", in the Niphal stem, it is likely that the original was *ʾerʾeh* "I will behold", as is the view of Gunkel. The change was tendentious.

[26] Ps. 26, 73:27–28, 118:19–20.

in the temple. After a long journey, during which God protected him from the dangers of the road and provided for his needs, he finally stands in God's presence:

> How endearing are your habitations, Yahweh of hosts!
> My soul yearns, even becomes faint for the courtyards of Yahweh.
> My heart and my flesh—they sing forth to the living God!
> Even as the bird finds a dwelling,
> And the swallow a nest for herself,
> Where she places her young—
> So are your altars, my king and God!
> Fortunate are they who dwell in your house!
> They shall continue to praise you, Selah.
> Fortunate is the man whose strength is from you!
> As they walk on the highways,[27]
> They who pass through the valley of Bākāʾ,
> They drink from a spring.
> He (God) envelopes pools of water with rain.[28]
> They proceed from wall to wall.[29]
> He (finally) beholds God in Zion.
> Yahweh, God of hosts, hear my prayer!
> Give ear, oh God of Jacob! Selah.
> Our shield, see!
> God! Look at the face of your anointed!
> For one day in your courts is better than a thousand (outside your courts)!
> I prefer (merely) to cross the threshold[30] of the house of my God,
> Than to dwell in the tents of wickedness!
> For Yahweh, God, is a sun and shield.
> Yahweh bestows kindness and honor.
> He does not withhold goodness from those who walk in uprightness.
> Yahweh of hosts!
> Fortunate is the man who puts his trust in you!
>
> (Psalm 84:2–13)

In effect, this concern over the nearness of God produces the nexus of two factors: divine presence in the temple, and divine help. The worshipper needs

[27] In the phrase *mesillôt bilebābām* "roads in their hearts", the second word is perhaps to be read *belektām* "as they walk".

[28] For *maʿayān yešîtûhû* "they place for him a spring" read, perhaps: *yištûhû* "they drink it", or simply: *yištû* "they drink". See Gunkel, *op. cit.*, s.v. 84:7f. *Berākôt* "blessings" is to be vocalized *berēkôt* "pools".

[29] Hebrew *ḥayil* is to be vocalized *ḥêl* "wall". Cf. Ps. 48:14. We see here a description of the approaching pilgrim. He proceeds inward, into the temple, until he stands before God. An alternative is to retain the vocalization *ḥayil* in the sense of "wealth" (cf. Ps. 49:11, 73:12, etc.). It would here refer to the fact that God provided for the needs of the pilgrim during his journey.

[30] *Histôpēp* is taken as a denominative from *sap* "threshold".

the temple because he needs God's help. Note the following expressions of this nexus:

> God is in her midst she shall not fall—
> God will bestow help upon her before morning.
> (Psalm 46:6)
>
> Verily, I behold you in the sanctuary, seeing your might and glory—
> For you have been a source of help to me.
> (Psalm 63:3, 7)
>
> God is awesome from your temple buildings—
> The God of Israel—he gives might and power to the people.
> (Psalm 68:36)
>
> To you silence is praise, oh God in Zion! ...
> Oh hearer of prayer!
> All flesh approaches you—
> You have visited the land and given it water.
> You enrich it profusely...
> You have surrounded the year with your goodness.
> (Psalm 65:1–2, 10, 12)
>
> Fortunate are they who dwell in your house—
> Fortunate is the man whose strength is from you.
> (Psalm 84:5–6)

V

Another reaction to the Jerusalem temple, which testifies to its role as the locus of God's power on earth, is the anxiety over God's possible departure from the temple.[31] This anxiety, like those others we have discussed, was not born in the experience of the cult. It was far more pervasive.

The Israelites challenged the authority of Moses at a moment when they thirsted for water: "Is Yahweh present among us or not?" (Exodus 17:7). This was a legitimate concern, coming from a group of people who found themselves in the Sinai desert without water. It is significant that when God arrives on the scene (verse 6), he does not rebuke the people or strike out at them. To the contrary, he acts to save them. In the mind of the biblical writer it was a lack of faith in God's reliability which prompted the taunt, but that should not make us unmindful of the genuineness of the anxiety itself.

At other moments in his career, Moses faced similar demonstrations of Israel's tendency to lose confidence in God and in the leadership of his appointed apostle. The people required periodic reassurance: "And he (Moses) said: If I have found favor in your eyes, oh my Lord, let my Lord go in our midst; for it is a stiffnecked people" (Exodus 34:9). Here, too, God's response is

[31] Ps. 6:5, 10:1, Ps. 22, 34:19, 35:22, 38:22, 60:12//108:12, 90:13, 94:14.

not wrathful. He promises Moses that he will perform wondrous acts in full view of the people, so that they may be convinced of his presence among them. No doubt the same fear that God had abandoned his people figured in the demand put to Aaron to produce a deity "who will walk before us" (Exodus 32:1).[32]

This fear over the departure of God was understandably intensified in the near-exilic and exilic periods, and it was the task of the prophets of that time to explain the destruction of temple and land in terms other than God's withdrawal from the midst of the people. The discussion of these developments is beyond our present scope, but a brief statement, focusing on the matrix of the problem, can be attempted here.[33]

Ezekiel, pictured as residing in Babylonia, is transported to Jerusalem in a vision, and is there shown the idolatrous practices indulged by the leaders of the people within the temple itself (Ezekiel, chapter 8).[34] In the text of the vision, a view is ascribed to the sinful elders of Israel and, for that matter, to most of the people: "Yahweh does not see us; Yahweh has departed from the land" (Ezekiel 8:12).[35] In contrast, the prophetic view is presented through the words of God to Ezekiel. The idolatry of Israel and the pollution of the temple have angered God, and he issues an order for the destruction of the temple. At that point, the *kābôd*, or "presence" of God, withdraws from its position atop the cherub on the threshold of the temple, and moves into the courtyard (Ezekiel 10:4–5), a clear indication that God is departing and has consigned the temple to ruin.

May we not be a bit more objective than the prophet and suggest that there was real cause for anxiety in the years immediately preceding the final destruction and exile, and that an understandable, though not pardonable response would have been to turn to idolatrous cults in the hope that they would avail? It would be normal to conclude from the declining situation in Judea that the divine presence had actually departed. The prophet was juxtaposing cause and

---

[32] Cf. the lament that God no longer "goes forth at the head of our hosts" in Ps. 60:12//108:12.

[33] The prophets of the exile and the return further develop the notion of the potent presence (especially Ezekiel 20, 40f.), and in the post-exilic books, principally Chronicles, there is much material for consideration. Similarly, the priestly writings of the Pentateuch and the book of Deuteronomy present distinctive views on the subject of God's presence and nearness. Although it is *possible* (though we doubt it) that certain Psalms may reflect the influence of the priestly writings of the Pentateuch and the book of Deuteronomy, or of exilic and post-exilic views, we see no evidence, in the Psalms we have discussed here, of notions that clearly show such influence. It should be noted, in this connection, that God's selection of Jerusalem as the site of the temple is not, in itself, a Deuteronomic doctrine, but relates more clearly to the dynastic covenant with the House of David.

[34] As presented, the vision is set in Jerusalem in the years immediately preceding the destruction. For the purposes of our discussion it is not necessary to determine whether this was a vision or an actual experience in Jerusalem.

[35] Cf. Ezekiel 9:9.

effect. In reality, idolatry was invoked because the situation appeared hopeless. This juxtaposition served two purposes for the prophet. If accepted, it might restrain further idolatry, and, what is perhaps more important, it would establish the sinfulness of the people as the cause for the national misfortune, thus refuting the pernicious notion that God had forsaken his people. In this light we can well understand Ezekiel's statement further on: "I will be for them a small sanctuary(?) in the lands to which they have come" (Ezekiel 11:16). God had, indeed, left Jerusalem, but only so as to be close to his exiled people in Babylonia.

Ezekiel is still operating on the notion of the potent presence at this juncture, and does not really dispute the conclusion that a Jerusalem in ruins is a Jerusalem without its resident deity. In his vision, the deity departs before the destruction occurs. What the prophet does is to lend a new interpretation to the notion of the potent presence according to which the application of this notion exclusively to the Jerusalem temple is abrogated.

VI

Despite its weaknesses, the notion of the potent presence survived in biblical religion and continued to influence post-biblical Judaism as well. Prophets criticized and attacked it, and altered its force in the light of new situations. At times of crisis, even prophets betrayed their own belief, or hope, perhaps, that God's presence must surely bring deliverance. Jeremiah was audacious in his insistence that Jerusalem would fall despite the fact that the temple was God's residence, but he could not control his urge to appeal to the very belief he had attacked:

> Oh hope of Israel!
> His deliverer in time of trouble!
> Why are you like a sojourner in the land,
> Like a traveler who has turned aside (only) to spend the night?
> Why do you act like a stunned man,
> Like a warrior incapable of delivering?
> For you are in our midst, Yahweh,
> And we are called by your name!
> Do not forsake us!
>
> (Jeremiah 14:8–9)[36]

In an earlier period the Jerusalemite, Isaiah, never averse to attacking conventional reliance on the efficacy of the cult, was capable, nevertheless, of expressing great joy in the presence of the resident deity:

> Rejoice and sing, oh dweller in Zion!
> For the holy one of Israel is great in your midst.
>
> (Isaiah 12:6)

---

[36] Cf. Hosea 11:9 for similar thoughts.

Prolegomenon to G. B. Gray's *Sacrifice in the Old Testament: Its Theory and Practice*[*]

It is close to fifty years since Gray wrote his study of the Israelite cult. Most of the problems to which he addressed himself at that time have yet to receive definitive treatment. Until very recently, this area of inquiry lagged behind other aspects of biblical research; thus we probably know less today about the meaning of sacrifice in ancient Israel than we do about biblical law. So that in writing a prolegomenon to this reissue of Gray's classic work, one cannot presume to add something of value in every area of the field. Withal, we are now probably on the verge of significant breakthroughs in the reconstruction of the Israelite cult.

Gray's work is still an important research tool, for two main reasons: it established a sound methodology for the study of the cult, and it is among the last fairly comprehensive statements of the subject before the advent of the archaeological revolution which began in the mid-1920s and has not abated until this day.

George Buchanan Gray (1865–1922) was born in Blandford, England, some forty miles from Bristol. He was educated at New College and University College, London, from which he received the B.A. degree in 1886. After graduation he entered the Independent Ministry, and is listed as a Congregationalist. He continued his studies at Mansfield College, Oxford, where he served as a fellow and tutor from 1891 to 1900. He then became Professor of Hebrew and Old Testament at Mansfield College, which position he held until his death. At Oxford, Gray also served on the Faculty of Oriental Languages, and was long active in the programs of the Palestine Exploration Fund.

Gray may be classed with such scholars as S. R. Driver, A. E. Cowley, and G. A. Cooke in the British tradition of Semitic philology and biblical studies. He prepared several volumes for the International Critical Commentary series (*Numbers*; *Isaiah I–XXVII*; *Job* [with S. R. Driver]) and was attracted to problems of Hebrew epigraphy and the onomasticon. In certain respects he might be

---

[*] Originally published as a prolegomenon to Ktav's 1971 reprint of George Buchanan Gray, *Sacrifice in the Old Testament: Its Theory and Practice* (The Library of Biblical Studies; New York: KTAV Publishing House, 1971), vii–xxxvii. Gray's work was originally published by Oxford University Press in 1925. Reprinted with permission from KTAV Publishing House.

I wish to thank Professor Harry M. Orlinsky for his many helpful suggestions in the writing of this Prolegomenon.

compared to the American scholar, J. A. Montgomery. Gray maintained a lively interest in questions of religious belief. Nevertheless, one never finds any religious preconceptions in his scholarly writings. He fully realized that the character of Christian ritual could be properly understood only against the background of Israelite and Jewish practices. This interrelationship had been set down by W. Robertson Smith, with whom Gray took issue on the theory of sacrifice but whom he greatly respected. The present volume appeared in 1925, three years after Gray's death. It was published from his lecture notes, and the reader must therefore allow for a certain looseness of style and organization, which would have undoubtedly been reworked had the author lived to prepare his own manuscript.[1]

Gray treated four major aspects of the Israelite cult: sacrifice, the altar, the priesthood, and the festivals. Of these four, the section on Israelite sacrifice remains his most important contribution.

In discussing each aspect of the cult, Gray began with an examination of the technical terminology. He then proceeded to the exegesis of pertinent biblical texts and to the consideration of other data, including archaeological finds and the evidence of comparative sources. His discussions extend from what was, for him, the earliest Israelite period, until the advent of Christianity and the early Rabbinic period. Our present interests have led us to concentrate in this prolegomenon on the pre-exilic, exilic, and early postexilic periods.

In the early 1920s nothing was known of the rich literary activity of Ugarit, or the archives of Mari, Nuzi, and Alalakh—not to speak of the plentiful finds subsequently unearthed at sites previously known.[2] Progress has been more than

[1] A full bibliography of G. B. Gray appears on pp. ix–xi of the 1925 publication. For a review of the work with special reference to Gray's treatment of rabbinic materials, see L. Finkelstein, *Jewish Quarterly Review* 17 (1926), 87–91.

In the presentation of Hebrew words in Hebrew script we have noted some errors which should be corrected to assure proper use of the reissued volume. Some *corrigenda* already appear after p. xiv of the 1925 publication. In addition, note the following:

Page:	*Line:*	*Written:*	*Should read:*
22	last line	קרבנים	קָרְבָּנוֹת
23	4	″	″
26	10	″	″
75	26	נפשותיהם	נַפְשֹׁתֵיהֶם
81	11	בשובל-רצנו	בִּשְׁבִיל-רְצוֹנוֹ
149	29	ובול	זְבוּל
281	9	טב	טוֹב
327	18	אתו	אוֹתוֹ
353, n. 3	10	עבדח	עֲבוֹדַת
405, n. 3	2	שלשת	שְׁלֹשָׁה

[2] For a brief summary of activity until 1962 see Martin A. Beek, *Atlas of Mesopotamia*, 1962; the Index, pp. 153f., is especially helpful. Also, A. Leo Oppenheim, *Ancient Mesopotamia*, 1964, chapter 1, pp. 7–73.

quantitative. The methods for accurate decipherment, translation, and interpretation have also been significantly improved since that time. Palestinian archaeology was then only in its infancy.

Since Gray's time we have witnessed in biblical studies generally, and in the study of the cult particularly, two contrary tendencies. On the one hand, some biblical scholars have grasped hungrily at archaeological discoveries, and at the comparative evidence of extrabiblical sources. On the other hand, some of the best minds have resisted comparative insights. Of the two, it is our opinion that the latter tendency has constituted more of a hindrance to progress in the field. Parallelomania and superficial comparativism have led to serious distortions that tend to be accepted as fact and transmitted uncritically. The answer is not, however, to retreat from comparativism, from which there can be no real retreat, but to perfect reliable comparative methods that do not lead to distortion.

The study of Israelite religion currently suffers from two shortcomings:

1) The tendency to reach out toward generalizations in an effort to grasp the overall character of Israelite religion, without first mastering the concrete data, the terminology, etc.

2) The tendency to view religion as being different from other elements operative in Israelite society; to regard the definition of its character as less directly affected by the weight of comparative evidence and less directly related to the parallel phenomena operative in the lives of Israel's neighbors and cultural relatives in the ancient Near East.

Yehezkel Kaufmann dealt meticulously with the cult in his monumental study of Israelite religion.[3] He was the greatest of the recent systematizers, skilled in phenomenology and in the sociology of religion. He viewed the praxis of the Israelite cult as primarily symbolic in function, if not in origin. The evidence of archaeology and comparative sources, to the extent that he treated it in detail, served him as an opposite pole, which he could hold up to view so as to dramatize the basic differences between Israelite monotheism and other ancient Near Eastern religions. These other systems were mythological, and Israelite religion was not, and it therefore followed that whatever phenomena within the Israelite system appeared similar to phenomena outside its limits were not really similar. Before having been appropriated by the Israelite cult, they were divested of their original character and rendered mere symbols. Kaufmann could hardly have been oblivious to the generic character of ritual, and yet his systematic outlook so pervasively governed his methodology that parts of the whole were made to conform to a rigid framework.[4]

---

[3] Y. Kaufmann, *A History of Israelite Religion* (Hebrew), 5th ed., 1961–1962, Vol. I, Book II, and especially the chapter on the cult (pp. 522–588), which contains a treatment of the problem of sacrifice (pp. 560–514).

[4] B. A. Levine, "*Kippûrîm*" (Hebrew), *Eretz-Israel* 9 (W. F. Albright Volume, 1969), 88–95, especially pp. 93–94. Our interest was particularly Kaufmann's failure to acknowledge the presence of magical practices as an active ingredient in the Israelite cult.

Cultic activity is the stuff of which ancient religions were made. The praxis, the administration of the cultic establishments, the vested interests of the clergy, and the celebrations of the festivals were not mere functions of a systematic religious outlook, devoid of intrinsic importance. They are the index of religion as it was practiced in the life of a society.

To see ancient Israelite religion as it was, requires a methodology which proceeds from the specific to the general, and not one that imposes generalizations on the interpretation of specific data. Such a proper methodology was adopted by Gray, in his time. With all that we now know for fact, which he could not have known, the possibility of a precise reconstruction of the Israelite cult and of the accurate interpretation of biblical traditions about it is much greater than it was a half-century ago.

I

The technical terminology employed in the biblical texts relevant to the Israelite cult was the point of departure for Gray, and well it should be for all who study this field. Despite all that has been written on biblical religion, we are still unable to define some of the basic terms. We will have more to say about the problem of terminology when we discuss Gray's section on sacrifice, but at this time we should note some of the progress that has been made.

In 1934 Friedrich Blome published an extensive monograph entitled *Die Opfermaterie in Babylonien und Israel* (Rome). In it he presented a detailed catalogue of the various materials utilized in sacrificial offerings. His study is valuable for the definition of many specific terms. The title itself presupposes that data from Mesopotamian sources are relevant to the biblical cult on a comparative basis. The implications of Blome's study are that there is much to be learned about the structure of the cult from the technical terminology. Terms designating various materials often reveal how they were used and disposed of ritually, and what role they played in the celebration of sacred occasions, and in the ongoing order of the cult.

It is probable that in the Neo-Sumerian cult of the Ur III period certain patterns of ritual behavior were established which tended to persist in the ancient Near East wherever Mesopotamian cultic influences reached. One such pattern was the practice of daily sacrifices, morning and evening. On certain occasions, additional allotments were made for special sacrifices. The Mesopotamian daily sacrifices anticipated the biblical תָּמִיד, and the addition of special sacrifices for festivals anticipated the later term מוּסָף.[5]

The Septuagint has normally been used as a proper source for the study of biblical terminology. The assumption is that the renderings of the Septuagint preserve ancient traditions concerning the original meaning of Hebrew terms.

[5] B. A. Levine, "Comments on Some Technical Terms of the Biblical Cult," (Hebrew), *Leshonenu* 30 (1965–66), 3–11; A. Leo Oppenheim, *op. cit.*, 188.

Since the 1920s much work has been accomplished in Septuagint studies, and new material has been uncovered. A few years ago Suzanne Daniel published a study entitled *Recherches sur le Vocabulaire du Culte dans la Septante* (Paris, 1966).[6] It is a treatment of some of the technical terms of the biblical cultic texts as they were translated and understood variously by Septuagint writers. Daniel classifies the differing renderings of particular terms and attempts to trace trends within the Septuagint traditions.

The problematic term שְׁלָמִים may serve as an example. It has three different renderings in various Septuagint texts: 1) σωτήριος "that which saves, preserves"; 2) τελειότης, τελείωσις "complete, perfect"; 3) εἰρηνικός, εἰρηνικαί "that which concerns peace." It is Daniel's conclusion, in this instance, that the first rendering seems to have predominated in the Judeo-Hellenistic vocabulary. It conveys how the Jewish translators originally understood the term. It was the last of the three renderings, however, which finally prevailed, and which has come down through Western tradition.[7]

Accepting the essential validity of Daniel's findings, we should ask just what their relevance is. Do we have in the Septuagint actual traditions of biblical interpretation from which the translators drew for their renderings of technical terms? What are the implications of the fact that the meaning "that which saves, preserves" is earlier than the meaning "that which concerns peace?"

In this case, we cannot base our interpretation of the term שְׁלָמִים on the Septuagint without further corroboration from other sources. The primary relevance of the Septuagint seems to us to rest elsewhere. It shows how the particular renderings and their consequent ideological influences took hold in certain Jewish and Christian circles at specific periods, and thus became the received interpretations. Daniel's evidence on the variance of Septuagint renderings for any one term serves to caution scholars against accepting any single translation of a technical term without first determining the history of that definition itself.

Daniel omits the discussion of certain terms essential for a full understanding of the material she is treating. Thus, she never mentions the term כִּפֵּר "to perform an act of ritual expiation," and its reflexes, כִּפֻּרִים and כַּפֹּרֶת. This is important, in view of the fact that it is this verb which designates the process underlying the two expiatory sacrifices, the אָשָׁם and the חַטָּאת, which she discusses at considerable length.[8] One may question how it is possible to understand these sacrifices, as they were interpreted by the Septuagint writers, without knowing how these same writers conceived of the process of expiation itself.[9]

---

[6] A fairly comprehensive bibliography is presented by Mme. Daniel on pp. 417f.

[7] *Ibid.*, pp. 273–297.

[8] *Ibid.*, pp. 299–325.

[9] The discussion of the verb כִּפֵּר has been updated in our article on *Kippûrîm* (see n. 4, above), pp. 88–95, especially 90–92. We show that the basic sense of this term is "to wipe off, cleanse," hence "to purify." This is established on the basis of the Akkadian evidence. In our view, there is no basis for seeing the sense of "covering, concealing" in

II

Much of the research that has been accomplished in cultic studies during the last half-century has been encyclopaedic in character. The most noted encyclopaedist is Roland de Vaux, whose compendious work, *Ancient Israel* (1961), is a study of Israelite society, including major sections on the festivals, Israelite sanctuaries, the Jerusalem temple, the priesthood, and sacrifice. In 1964 de Vaux augmented his treatments of biblical sacrifice in a separate monograph, *Studies in Old Testament Sacrifice.*[10]

Roland de Vaux is the leader of the group centered for many years in the *École Biblique*, Jerusalem. His intellectual grasp is broad, encompassing most disciplines related to biblical studies. He is in touch with the latest findings and research in the field. He attempts to reconstruct Israelite society along institutional lines and is concerned with what actually happened, not only with the literary traditions about what happened. He presents differing views objectively, and his exposition is lucid. Yet for all its value as a reference work, *Ancient Israel* is systematic only in the formal, outward sense. Its arrangement is systematic, but there is no real synthesis or analysis. In contrast to Gray, who was by disposition a seeker after solutions, de Vaux appears content in most cases merely to present problems in their accepted formulations and to assemble new data bearing on them. He hardly ever breaks new ground, or comes up with an original point of view.

De Vaux's works may serve as an accurate summary of what is known, so long as one realizes that he frequently transmits consensus as fact. In his scholarly articles, a collection of which was recently published under the title *Bible et Orient* (Paris, 1967), de Vaux shows more of an inclination to be original, but in his encyclopaedic writing he seemingly felt the imperative to be representative. As a result, one cannot truly speak of a school of thought represented by de Vaux, except to note that the institutional approach, in and of itself, constitutes a distinctive outlook.

Menahem Haran, an Israeli scholar, may be classed with de Vaux in certain regards. Haran is a disciple of Yehezkel Kaufmann. He has followed up the logic of his master's hypothesis on the symbolic significance of the Israelite cult as portrayed in the priestly writings of the Pentateuch. His major contribution is available in an article in the *Hebrew Union College Annual*, 36 (1965), 191–226, entitled "The Priestly Image of the Tabernacle." Haran's thesis is that the cult portrayed in the priestly source was a carefully patterned presentation of

---

the biblical usages of this verb, despite the idiomatic phrase כִּפֵּר עַל which might suggest this.

[10] Extensive bibliographies are provided in de Vaux's works here cited, as well as in H. H. Rowley, *Worship in Ancient Israel*, 1967, and H. J. Kraus, *Worship in Israel*, 1965. Also see R. J. Thompson, *Penitence and Sacrifice in Early Israel outside the Levitical Law*, 1963, 256f. Additional bibliography may be found among the articles by M. Haran in *Encyclopaedia Biblica* (see n. 12 below).

symbolic acts, reflecting a graduated scale of sanctity, and described in the graphics of a tabernacle whose innermost precincts represented the most sacred of places. As one moved outward, the sanctity was systematically reduced. In a similar fashion the cultic appurtenances, the priestly vestments, the execution of the priestly office, and the sacrificial regimen all reflected this same graduation of sanctity. It was this concept that the priestly traditions were seeking to convey by the way in which they chose to describe the ancient Israelite cult. Following Kaufmann, Haran accepts the overall distinction between the priestly and the popular conceptions of the cult, a distinction which is all too convenient for the apparent resolution of real contradictions.[11]

Haran has written voluminously elsewhere on the biblical cult, especially in *Encyclopaedia Biblica* (Hebrew). In these articles he deals with many aspect of the cult, running the gamut from Israelite sanctuaries to the operation of the priesthood and sacrificial praxis. He formulates accurate, though largely conservative statements on most of the relevant questions. These many articles should be reworked into a systematic presentation.[12]

Haran is primarily an exegete, and his scope is much more limited than that of de Vaux. Whereas de Vaux utilizes the text to reconstruct the life of a society, Haran interprets the text as the expression of dominant views within that society.

III

The discoveries of archaeology, both on the soil of ancient Israel and in the Near East generally, hold the key to a fuller understanding of the Israelite cult. Certain problems relevant to the cult simply cannot be clarified without additional data, which can only come as a result of archaeological activity.

A convenient way of assessing the present relationship of archaeology to the study of the biblical cult would be to refer to Gray's section on the altar. His

---

[11] An example of the application of this alleged distinction by Haran is his treatment of the problem of the אֵפוֹד in *Tarbiẓ* 24 (1955), 380–391 (Hebrew). The אֵפוֹד is described variously as a garment and as an object that stood in the manner of a statue. These discrepancies are resolved by concluding, in effect, that the different literary sources knew of a different object by that name. A more proper method would be to investigate the origins of this object in comparative terms, and to think of it as an actual object, not merely a term! Once the distinction between priestly and popular is applied, however, there is no need to look further, and this shuts out other possible interpretations.

[12] The following articles in *Encyclopaedia Biblica* (Hebrew) by M. Haran should be consulted: Vol. IV: כְּהֻנָּה (the priesthood) 14–46; לֶחֶם הַפָּנִים (bread of display) 493–495; מַאֲכָלִים וּמַשְׁקָאוֹת (food and drink) 543–558; מִזְבֵּחַ (the altar) 763–780. Vol. V מְנוֹרָה (Menorah) 14–22; מִנְחָה (mostly as "grain offering") 23–30; מַעֲשֵׂר (the tithe) 204–212; מִקְדָּשׁ (sanctuary) 322–328, 346–360; נְדָבָה (voluntary sacrifice) 783–785; נֶדֶר (votive offering) 786–790; סֵפֶר הַקְּדוּשָּׁה (the Holiness Code) 1094–1099. See also "The Uses of Incense in the Ancient Israelite Cult," *VT* 10 (1960), 113–129. This list is not complete, but only representative.

treatment is sensitive when it comes to certain religious notions about the role of the altar in Israelite worship, but it has little value today for a reconstruction of the history of altars, cult places, and temples in ancient Israel. This is not because his methodology was unsound, but because Gray had very little to go on when he wrote his study. His discussion of the archaeological evidence actually concerns itself with dolmens and such objects as sculptured stones, situated above the ground and discovered by explorers who assumed that they had some cultic and/or funerary significance. Gray attempted to synthesize this evidence with early biblical traditions about stone altars located in the open field.[13]

It is clear, in hindsight, that before the mid-1920s Palestinian archaeology was in its infancy. Expeditions at Taᶜanak, Gezer, Jerusalem, Samaria, and at several other sites had produced important finds; but these finds, and the field techniques utilized to unearth them, cannot be compared with what was to come. The series of excavations at Megiddo, which, incidentally, yielded a four-horned altar and a well preserved pre-Israelite *bamah* installation, were initiated in 1925. The first preliminary reports on the excavation under Albright at Tell Beit-Mirsim began to appear in 1926. Albright's extended excavation is generally considered a turning point in field techniques and in the interpretation of data.[14]

In 1921, or thereabouts, very little could be said about the Israelite altar. Since that time, many cult places and their attendant artifacts have been unearthed on biblical soil. It is usually very difficult, however, to be precise in identifying such recovered objects with those described or prescribed in the Bible. It is interesting that de Vaux had very little to add to what Gray had said about the altar, although in another connection he discusses sacred locales in greater depth.[15]

Actually, the results of archaeological activity since the mid-1920s have been of mixed value in ascertaining the history of Israelite cult places. Many sites have yielded primarily pre-Israelite, or non-Israelite finds. Although such material has considerable bearing on Israelite religion because of proximity in space and time, its relevance is not the same as that of data coming from actual Israelite cultic sites. The literary, epigraphic, and glyptic yield on biblical soil has been disappointing. In other areas of the Near East, archaeologists have unearthed large archives of written records and numerous artifacts bearing inscriptions which reveal their exact provenance. On Israelite soil the scholar is limited to meager gleanings.[16]

---

[13] Gray, 96f.

[14] On Debir see n. 23 below. On Megiddo, see Y. Aharoni, *Encyclopaedia Biblica* (Hebrew), IV (1962), 614–630.

[15] R. de Vaux, *Ancient Israel*, pp. 409–414, and cf. *ibid.* 274–311.

[16] A recent chrestomathy of Palestinian epigraphy is H. Donner–W. Röllig, *Kanaanäische und Aramäische Inschriften*, 1963ff., 3 vols., sections D and E. In the quarterly of the Israel Academy of the Hebrew Language, *Leshonenu* (Hebrew), J. Naveh, epig-

Given such restrictions in available sources, it is all the more important that coordinated efforts be undertaken to create an interdisciplinary approach to the reconstruction of the Israelite cult, with the participation of specialists in several fields, and their subdivisions. These fields include: archaeology, ancient Near Eastern languages, biblical studies, history, anthropology, and environmental or ecological research. If it ever was possible for archaeologists to master all relevant disciplines necessary for the full interpretation of their data, it is impossible today. The chances for a genuine synthesis are being hindered by the failure to recognize limitations. Biblical scholars are also guilty of this oversight. What is needed is teamwork on the part of scholars with genuine interdisciplinary interests; a dialogue of specialists. Until now, almost every coordinated effort in publication has fallen short of real synthesis. Specialists are assigned separate sections in areas of their expertise, and the reader is often left with the most difficult task, that of constructing for himself a unified picture of Israelite civilization by synthesizing disparate data.[17]

There have been several "masters" who have sought, in all earnestness, to develop a proper methodology and who have achieved unusual scope in their research. The three who first come to mind are Albrecht Alt, W. F. Albright, and Benjamin Mazar. Alt's understanding of social patterns and legal institutions was exceptional, and his legacy is still very much alive in Palestinian archaeology today. As for actual work being accomplished, the students of Albright and Mazar, and their students in turn, constitute the main body of archaeologists, historical geographers, and historians contributing to the needed synthesis.[18]

As regards Israelite religion, Albright has probably come the nearest to achieving a valid methodology for the application of archaeological data to the interpretation of biblical texts. In his most recent work, *Yahweh and the Gods of Canaan* (1968), Albright included a brief discussion of the evidence for the early Israelite cult, and he conceded, in a manner not entirely typical of his usual boldness, that we know too little to allow for a reliable reconstruction. Having thus qualified himself, Albright proceeds to present some rather cogent evidence

---

raphist of the Department of Antiquities of the State of Israel, has been presenting new editions of Palestinian epigraphy, as well as new material. This series of textual studies began in 1965–66, and continues in issues of *Leshonenu*.

[17] Noteworthy as an attempt at synthesis is the series entitled *The World History of the Jewish People*, First Series: *Ancient Times*. Volume I has appeared: *At the Dawn of Civilization—A Background of Biblical History*, ed. E. A. Speiser, 1964. It is divided into three parts: The Environmental Factor, The Ethno-Linguistic Factor, and The Cultural Factor. Here one approaches a coherent presentation. Also see E. Anati, *Palestine before the Hebrews*, 1963.

[18] See A. Alt, *Kleine Schriften*, 3 vols., 1953–. For the bibliography of W. F. Albright see *The Bible and the Ancient Near East*, 1961, 363–389, and *Eretz-Israel* 9 (W. F. Albright Volume, 1969), 1–5. For B. Mazar, see *Eretz-Israel* 5 (B. Mazar Volume, 1958), and nn. 33 and 35 below. The contribution of Kurt Galling should be mentioned here; for his important works, consult the bibliographies listed in n. 10 above.

bearing on the destruction of pre-existing idolatrous cultic installations by the entering Israelites. A string of such cult centers, from Shechem to Hazor, was destroyed at about the same period. In Albright's view, the archaeological evidence synchronizes with the account in Judges 6 concerning the destruction of the Baal altar by Gideon.

According to Albright, it is possible to chart the effects of the Israelite entry into Canaan in religious terms. His view is that their attitude toward idolatrous cult places was polemical from the start. Albright also proposes a theory about the original function of the *bamah* as a type of cult installation, considering it as originally funerary in character.[19]

Albright's contribution has been primarily to revise long-held notions about Israelite religion and to demonstrate the need for a new outlook. His suggestions in this regard are quite understandably open to question, and subject to the test of new discoveries. As is usually the case, the shattering of previous constructions is more readily attainable than the erecting of new ones. Whether or not, in terms of their actual substance, Albright's proposals for the reconstruction of Israelite religion are fully acceptable, it is incontrovertible that his methodology has served as the major catalyst in the current re-examination of the Israelite way of life, in all of its ramifications.

Archaeologists cannot abandon every other field of activity and concentrate exclusively on cultic problems, but it would be of help if certain attested Israelite cult sites received immediate attention. The excavations at Shiloh (Seilun) undertaken by a Danish expedition in the 1920s, and again in the early sixties, should be continued now. Previous work on the site did not involve the acropolis to any significant extent, and yet that is where one would expect to find the cultic buildings.[20] The excavations at Gibeon (el-Jib) under J. B. Pritchard were much too limited in scope to establish the significance of that site in biblical times.[21] Bethel (Beitin), excavated in the thirties by Albright, and more recently in the late fifties by J. Kelso, has yielded impressive finds which require re-examination and further study.[22]

Albright identified Tell Beit-Mirsim, about eleven miles southwest of Hebron, as the site of biblical Debir. There has always been some doubt about this

---

[19] W. F. Albright, *Yahweh and the Gods of Canaan*, 1968, 193–207. See also M. Noth, *The Old Testament World*, 1966, 125–176, especially 173–179, for a summary of archaeological activity relative to the cult.

[20] On Shiloh see Marie-Louise Buhl and S. Holm-Nielsen, *The Danish Excavations at Tell Sailun*, in 1926, 1929, 1932, and 1963; *The Pre-Hellenistic Remains*, 1969, pp. 84 ff. and plates; also O. Eissfeldt, "Silo und Jerusalem," *Volume du Congrès, Strasbourg 1956*. VTSup 4 (1957), 138–147.

[21] On Gibeon (*el-Jib*) see the article by J. B. Pritchard in *The Interpreter's Dictionary of the Bible* (*IDB*), II, 1962, 391–393; and literature cited there.

[22] On Bethel (*Beitin*) see J. Kelso, *IDB*, I, 1962, 391–393 and literature cited there. For a more detailed treatment, see W. F. Albright and J. Kelso, *AASOR* 39, 1968.

identification because, in the same general vicinity, there are several other impressive *tells*. Recently a survey team under M. Kochavi has done surface exploration at Khirbet Rabud, raising the possibility that it is biblical Debir. Rabud should be excavated, regardless of whether or not it will prove to be the site of ancient Debir.[23]

Some recent excavations have held out new possibilities for learning about the history and character of the Israelite cult. The excavations at biblical Dan in upper Galilee, begun in 1966 under A. Biran, have already yielded impressive ramparts and structures, but until the acropolis is excavated we probably won't know what everyone would like to know about a site whose cultic history is recounted in so many biblical traditions.[24] In 1962, 1964, 1965, and again after the Six Day War in 1967, Kathleen Kenyon conducted excavations in the Ophel area of Jerusalem. In 1964 a cult installation was discovered immediately outside Hezekiah's wall, dating down to the eighth, and probably the seventh century. It contained two cultic stele (מַצֵּבוֹת) and an altar, and burial places were located in the near vicinity. Its discovery sheds light on the varieties of cultic activity extant during the late monarchy in and around Jerusalem.[25] The current excavations in Jerusalem under N. Avigad have already uncovered a massive city wall from the late first temple period, raising the hope that further activity in Jerusalem might reveal remains of importance for the study of the early cult.

In recent lectures and discussions, William G. Dever, director of the Gezer excavations, has been reporting on the future plans for that site. The expedition will concentrate on the acropolis area, and since extended occupation of the site by Israelites has been ascertained, it is likely that finds of cultic relevance for biblical studies will be forthcoming—this in addition to the pre-Israelite high place that was unearthed and recently reconstructed at Gezer.

An example of the hopefulness of the present situation was the series of excavations at Arad under Yohanan Aharoni between 1962 and 1967.[26] Arad is a town in the Beersheba region of the Negeb. The hypothesis underlying the dig at Arad was that border installations had a particular importance in ancient Israel. The quantity of epigraphic evidence from the period of the first temple was greatly increased by the discovery at Arad of a horde of ostraca. An Israelite sanctuary was unearthed on the site, one which had been in use throughout most

---

[23] On Debir, Rabud, etc., see V. R. Gold's article, "Debir," *IDB*, I, 1962, 808, and literature cited there.

[24] On biblical Dan, see the interview with A. Biran, *The New York Times*, April 3, 1970, p. 39; also his article, "In Search of the Golden Calf: Tel Dan Reveals its Secrets," *Hadassah Magazine*, May 1970, pp. 14–15, 28–29.

[25] On Jerusalem, see Kathleen Kenyon, *Palestine Exploration Quarterly*, 1963, 7–21; 1965, 9–20; 1968, 97–111.

[26] On Arad, see the most recent summary by Y. Aharoni in *New Directions in Biblical Archaeology*, ed. D. N. Freedman and J. C. Greenfield, 1969, 25–39, and literature cited there.

of the period of the first temple. The onomasticon of the ostraca reveals attested priestly and/or levitical eponyms, and indicates that the Arad sanctuary maintained close connections with the temple in Jerusalem. In effect, this means that it was a legitimate Judean sanctuary, rather than one in competition with the Jerusalem temple.

The sanctuary was housed in an enclosed building of sizable proportions, making it a veritable מִקְדָּשׁ, a cult place of greater importance than a *bamah* installation or a mere altar. In the niche of the sanctuary, one cultic stela (מַצֵּבָה) definitely—and possibly as many as three—was found *in situ*. There was also an altar for sacrifice, and several incense altars.

Aharoni has ventured some speculative historical theories on the basis of the Arad finds and, whereas one may question some of these speculations, there is no doubt that Arad represents a turning point in the study of the Israelite cult. On the theory that other border towns might yield finds of comparable importance, Aharoni reexamined Lachish very briefly in 1967, and again in 1968, and began excavations at Beersheba in the summer of 1969. He did not find any definitive evidence of an Israelite sanctuary at Lachish during the period of the first temple, and we are awaiting reports from Beersheba.[27]

The Arad excavations bring into focus some of the major questions about the Israelite cult which presently require clarification:

1) What was the relationship between the Arad sanctuary and the temple in Jerusalem? Did this border installation have specialized functions?

Aharoni discovered that the sacrificial altar in the sanctuary had not been used during the last period of the sanctuary's existence, before the destruction of the site by the Babylonians. He has tried to synchronize this abandonment of the altar with the edict of Josiah, promulgated in 622–621 B.C.E. This edict required the priests of the outlying cult places to report to Jerusalem, and apparently forbade any sacrificial activity outside the Jerusalem temple.[28]

It is risky to attempt such synchronizations. Aharoni's explanation, if substantiated, would constitute an important attestation of the effects of Josiah's reform on the religious life of Judea. It is, however, a problematic interpretation of the archaeological data. We would be left with a local cult offering incense, at a sanctuary that retained a cultic stela (מַצֵּבָה) dating from the 10th to 9th centuries B.C.E., but where altar sacrifices were no longer offered. This would not seem to be a reasonable response to Josiah's edict, based on what we know from biblical sources of its content and intent.

2) Which cultic appurtenances were considered legitimate in the Israelite cult, at various times and in different regions? Biblical traditions concerning the מַצֵּבָה are confusing. Quite a few such stele have been recovered in the last decade or so, and we may see the role and meaning of this artifact clarified in the

---

[27] On Lachish, see Y. Aharoni, *IEJ* 18 (1968), 157–170.

[28] The best discussion of the period of Josiah and his reforms is, in our opinion, the published MA thesis of the late Shalom Zemirin, *Josiah and his Period* (Hebrew), 1951.

near future. The presence of a מַצֵּבָה in an Israelite sanctuary of fairly certain legitimacy, during the late monarchy and in the region of Judea, constitutes an important link in the history of Israelite cult places.[29]

3) How was the clergy administered at regional or local sanctuaries, and what relationship did such groups bear to the Jerusalem priesthood and to the royal establishment? The correspondence recorded in the Arad ostraca merely suggests some possibilities in this connection.[30]

IV

We propose to deal only briefly with Gray's treatment of the priesthood and the festivals. The subject of the festivals has been discussed at great length by de Vaux.[31] From his summary, one has the impression that this area of inquiry has not kept up with other aspects of biblical studies. To reconstruct the character and history of early Israelite celebrations we would have to know more than we presently know, and the possibilities of securing such new information appear slim. Among the desiderata are the following: 1) The dates of the priestly codes of the Pentateuch. These are the primary sources of information on the Israelite festivals, and until we can be fairly certain as to how early or how late they are in terms of their essential content, we cannot say when the celebrations prescribed in them actually took place. 2) Information on the several calendars in use in ancient Israel. 3) The meaning of Israelite sacrifice. 4) The history and structure of the Israelite priesthood and of the other cultic groups. 5) The role of the monarchy in ordaining festivals and in determining and altering their character.

Some progress can be reported on the study of the Israelite priesthood and on the problem of the Levites. The term לֵוִי itself has been clarified considera-

---

[29] See M. Broshi, מַצֵּבָה, in *Encyclopaedia Biblica*, V, 222–225.

[30] See Aharoni's article in n. 26 above, pp. 28–30 on the Eliashib ostraca. Also see J. Liver, *Chapters in the History of the Priests and Levites* (Hebrew), 1968, pp. 39, 42, and n. 30.

[31] Of especial importance, in addition to the discussion by de Vaux, is that of J. Pedersen, *Israel: Its Life and Culture*, 1956, IV, 376–465. For the literary traditions, see S. Mowinckel, *The Psalms in Israel's Worship*, 1962, 1–41, and additional notes, 718f., and his article, "Die vermeintliche 'Passah-legende', Exodus 1–15," *Studia Theologica* V (1951), 66–88, on the Passover traditions. For a recent comprehensive treatment of the problem of dating the priestly sources see J. G. Vinck, "The Date and Origin of the Priestly Code in the Old Testament," *Oudtestamentische Studien* 15 (1969), 1–144. Vinck favors a post-exilic date, more precisely the late Persian period. Although his methodology is systematic, and his research thorough, the biblical textual evidence could lead us to entirely different conclusions. It is our view that many problems still remain with respect to the priestly source. Provisionally our view is that little, if any, of its essential content need be dated later than the destruction of the First Temple, although some redactional material may have been appended subsequently.

bly.[32] There have also been some fruitful inquiries into biblical genealogies. Building on earlier efforts, Mazar set in motion a total reexamination of the historicity of the book of Chronicles, where the important priestly and levitical genealogies occur. He showed, in several connections, that the Chronicler had before him records which the writer of Kings either did not possess or chose to ignore, for whatever reasons.[33] The hereditary question clearly hinges on the authenticity of the genealogies, as does the historicity of other historiographic traditions on the origins of the cultic groups.

The most recent investigation into the genealogies of Chronicles is that by the late Jacob Liver, *Chapters in the History of the Priests and Levites* (Hebrew; 1968). Liver regards the genealogies in 1 Chron. 23–24 as very ancient, deriving from the early days of the Israelite monarchy. He deals convincingly with their many compositional problems and apparent inconsistencies. Liver's work is more than a summary of what is known. It represents a step forward, and, like his other major studies, is form-critical in approach, but transcends the literary context in an effort to venture reliable historical conclusions.[34]

Research into the historicity of the biblical lists of levitical cities by Albright, Mazar, and Haran has strengthened the view of Alt that we have in Joshua, and in the later books, a reliable historical source.[35] If these lists actually reflect the distribution of levitical cities throughout Palestine in biblical times, then we are justified in assuming that their functionaries were united by some sort of kinship, or at least that they inhabited the same communities over long periods of time.

Our own researches into the elusive history of that group of cultic servitors known as *netinim* (נְתִינִים) have led us to the conclusion that they constituted a kind of professional guild, similar to "The Servants of Solomon" with whom they are listed in the census of returning Israelites in Ezra 2. The fact that the list of *netinim* includes a large number of foreign names had led many scholars to assume that they were temple slaves, or the descendants of such slaves. Careful investigation revealed, however, that this was not the case. The *netinim* bore the status of freemen, and were part of the economic organization which obtained in Jerusalem during Nehemiah's leadership. The fact that there is a Ugaritic list of *ytnm* suggested that this group might be quite ancient. Although there is no mention of them in Kings, or other pre-exilic sources, we had reason to accept the traditions of the Chronicler on this, and related cultic traditions as essentially authentic, and we concluded that the *netinim* probably existed in the pre-exilic period. Now, one of the eponyms in the list of *netinim* (Ezra 2.43ff. || Neh.

[32] W. F. Albright, *Archaeology and the Religion of Israel*, 1968, 109f. and n. 42.

[33] B. Mazar, *Encyclopaedia Biblica*, II, 1954, article דִּבְרֵי הַיָּמִים, 596–606.

[34] J. Liver, *op. cit.*, pp. 11–32, and English summary, viii–xi.

[35] A. Alt, *Kleine Schriften*, II, 1953, 289–305, 306–315. M. Haran, *Tarbiẕ* (Hebrew), 27 (1957–58), 421–439. B. Mazar, "The Cities of the Priests and the Levites," *Congress Volume, Oxford 1959*. VTSup 7 (1960), 193–205.

6.46ff.) has turned up in a Hebrew ostracon discovered at Arad, dating from the last years of the first temple. It is the name קֵ(י)רֹס, elsewhere unattested. We take its occurrence at Arad, in a context related to the Jerusalem temple and to matters cultic, as at least oblique evidence for the pre-exilic existence of the *netinim*, because of the extreme strangeness of the name.[36]

Applying the results of this inquiry to the problem of the Levites, it is reasonable to suppose that they constituted a similar type of professional guild. Perhaps the term "guild" is imprecise.[37] What we intend are closed groups of trained personnel, which were structured along clan lines, and which continuously inhabited certain localities. A strict hereditary principle would not have been required, because such groups occasionally adopted outsiders into their membership. This would account for the alleged intrusion of non-Levites into the levitical genealogies and, on the other hand, would explain why the Levites are classified along clan lines to begin with.[38]

V

Gray's section on sacrifice is of lasting importance. Whatever theorizing Gray permitted himself was closely linked to the textual evidence. He never allowed considerations unrelated to the text to affect his interpretation of it. He began with the theory of sacrifice, and addressed himself to the view which had been set forth by W. Robertson Smith in his pioneer work on comparative religion, *Lectures on the Religion of Semites* (1889).[38a] Robertson Smith had proposed that the predominant factor in "Semitic" sacrifice was the experience of communion actualized in the blood rites of the animal sacrifices. As Gray noted, Robertson Smith never actually denied that the notion of the sacrifice as a gift tendered to the deity figured somehow in the dynamics of Israelite ritual, but set about to refute the alleged predominance of this interpretation in favor of his conception of communion through blood. Gray never confronted the full impact of this theory, but rather attempted, purely on the evidence of the technical terminology of the cult in Biblical Hebrew, to demonstrate that many of these

---

[36] B. A. Levine, *JBL* 82 (1963), 3–11, and *IEJ* 19 (1969), 49–51.

[37] A full study of guilds in the ancient Near East is unavailable for the pre-Roman period. Karl Polnayi, *et al.* have some relevant material in *Trade and Market in the Early Empires*, 1957, especially the chapter by A. Leo Oppenheim, "A Bird's-Eye View of Mesopotamian Economic History," pp. 27–37. Also see *idem*, *Ancient Mesopotamia*, 1964, 79–81, 355–361 ("Notes to Chapter II"), and 383f. ("Bibliographical Notes to Chapter II"). See also I. Mendelsohn, "Gilds in Babylonia and Assyria," *JAOS* 60 (1940), 68–72, and the general discussion of "Social, Economic, and Legal Institutions" by H. M. Orlinsky, "Old Testament Studies," in *Religion*, ed. P. Ramsey, 1965, 86–92 (*Princeton Series*, *Humanistic Scholarship*, vol. 8).

[38] See n. 32 above.

[38a] The 3rd ed. (containing an Introduction and Notes by S. A. Cook) was reissued by KTAV (1969–70) with a Prolegomenon by James Muilenburg.

terms clearly conveyed the notion of gift or tribute, and that others were at least related to that notion.[39]

In his *Prolegomena*, written about ten years before the appearance of Robertson Smith's work, Julius Wellhausen seems to have endorsed the notion of sacrifice as gift or tribute, while noting that the extraordinary significance of the blood rites injected into the essential dynamic of Israelite sacrifice a mysterious element, reflecting the conception that blood is the life force. Wellhausen did not consider the blood rites as the essential ingredient in Israelite sacrifice, which status he reserved for the assignment of the animal as an altar offering.[40] In a sense, Robertson Smith sought to remove the sense of mystery from the blood rites. He applied to this task the findings of his earlier study of kinship patterns among the Arabs.[41]

In terms of kinship, the basic relationship between the worshipper and the deity is a function of the overall character of the community. The "Semitic" communities were united by kinship, at first in small and later in large amalgamated units. Two notions were basic in the human-divine relationship: kingship and fatherhood. Fatherhood is based on the kinship of blood. The relationship of the worshipper to the deity is thus a projection of the actual organizing principle operative in the life of the community as it was constituted. In the rituals of the community one finds the expression of what is recognized to be the basis of the group's cohesive existence.

How does the sacrifice of animals fit into this kinship pattern? Animal offerings are propitious because certain animals are considered holy. In pastoral societies, which depend on domestic animals for their sustenance, the flocks and herds predominate in this role. The animals were considered part of the religious community because they, too, bore a kinship relation to the deity. Beings related to the same father are related to each other. As Robertson Smith put it:

> The beasts are sacred and kindred beings for they are the source of life and subsistence.[42]

In very early times, so the reasoning goes, animals were eaten only in exceptional circumstances, but as time went on, a ritual pattern developed in which the meat of the animal, normally prohibited as taboo, was partially consumed in an act of communion. This was "the rite of blood brotherhood." It was a cove-

---

[39] Gray, 7f.

[40] J. Wellhausen, *Prolegomena to the History of Ancient Israel*, Meridian Books, 1961, 61f.

[41] W. R. Smith, *Kinship and Marriage in Early Arabia*, 1885. See the Introduction by S. A. Cook, xvii f., to the third edition of *Lectures on the Religion of the Semites* (cf. n. 38a above).

[42] *Op. cit.*, p. 297.

nant, "a bond of troth and life fellowship to all the effects for which kinsmen are permanently bound together."[43]

According to Robertson Smith, it is this projected kinship that became the cornerstone of Israelite sacrifice. A corollary is the prominence of the זֶבַח "slain offering" as the basic form of Israelite sacrifice, for it is the type which, by its manner of disposition, affords the opportunity for the shared, communion meal. In this framework, expiatory offerings were necessitated by the fact that, by their offenses against the deity, individuals and communities as a whole had threatened the bond with the father. Offenders were reinstated into the kinship community by a blood rite.

It is this basic formulation, with variations, that has predominated in the study of the biblical cult. René Dussaud accepted it, in principle, and most scholars have been merely repeating earlier discussions. Thus, de Vaux translates the term שְׁלָמִים as "communion sacrifice," without even bothering to explore alternatives.[44] In a recent monograph devoted entirely to the (זֶבַח-)שְׁלָמִים Rudolph Schmid accepts the prior conclusions of Robertson Smith and Dussaud, but goes on to emphasize the aspect of covenant.[45] R. J. Thompson recently published a partial, but detailed study of the fellowship theory, concluding merely that no one principle can account for the phenomenon of sacrifice in all of its aspects.[46]

As the discussion of the subject progressed, the Sinaitic covenant, as described in Exodus 24, became, for those who shared Robertson Smith's essential view, the paradigm for the use of blood in sacrificial rites.[47] According to that record of the covenant between Yahweh and Israel, half of the sacrificial blood was dashed against the altar and the other half on the entire people assembled (Exodus 24:6–8). From this procedure it is deduced that all sacrificial utilization of blood was of the same nature and for the same purpose as was the case in the covenant, i.e., to bind the worshipper and the deity in the covenantal relationship. In this sense, covenant would become the framework for ritual communion.

Robertson Smith sensed that his definition of covenant was a weak point in his argument. If the blood rite was an expression of kinship, the kinship of covenant brothers, then the covenant should, in itself, represent a kinship arrangement. He noted, however, that the covenant between Yahweh and Israel was a relationship created artificially, an adoptive relationship, if you will.[48] The fatherhood of Yahweh, like his kingship, was not based on blood kinship, but on a

[43] *Op. cit.*, pp. 314, 316, 336.

[44] Literature cited in R. de Vaux, *Studies in Old Testament Sacrifice*, 31f.

[45] R. Schmid, *Das Bundesopfer in Israel: Wesen, Ursprung, und Bedeutung der alttestamentlichen Schelamim* (Studien zum Alten und Neuen Testament 9), 1964.

[46] R. J. Thompson, *op. cit.* (see n. 10 above), 1–20; 243–249.

[47] See R. Schmid, *op. cit.*, 31f., 78, 85–86, 126.

[48] W. R. Smith, *op. cit.*, p. 319, n. 2, and additional note H (to p. 315) on pp. 479–481.

type of contract in which the terminology of kinship was proverbially metaphorical. We now know that the Israelite covenant bears affinities to ancient Near Eastern vassal treaties and royal commissions. The suzerain is obligated to protect and care for those bound to him by treaty, and his wards, in turn, bear reciprocal obligations to him. This is one of the active ingredients in the Israelite covenant.[49]

The other ingredient, discussed most profoundly by Thorkild Jacobsen, is the notion of the personal God, with whom an individual and/or his family bear a particular relationship. The covenant between Yahweh and Abraham, and between the deity and the dynasty of David, as well as that between God and the Aaronide priesthood, reflect the more individualized dimension of the relationship, whereas it is in the Sinaitic covenant that the entire people is so related to the deity.[50]

Once the artificiality of the Israelite covenant is acknowledged, we can no longer maintain that the cult, as the supposed actualization of the covenant, expresses the kinship of blood. In turn, this necessitates explaining the blood rites in another way. Even if we accept the paradigmatic status of the Sinaitic covenant, we would have to seek new explanations for the meaning of animal sacrifices. The logic of kinship would apply only where no artificial covenant existed, and where an animistic type of bond obtained between the human community and the divine powers. Once the bond is conceived of in moral, legal, and/or political terms, there is no longer an exact correspondence between the basis of the group's kindred existence and its relationship to the deity. The matter of the kinship of the group is, in itself, problematic; but that question goes beyond our present discussion.

The truth of the matter is that the nexus of covenant and cult must, in any event, be understood in a different way. The Sinaitic covenant as described in Exodus 24 cannot be accepted as the cornerstone of Israelite ritual, and cannot serve as the prototype for the use of blood in sacrificial rites. This is because the activity at Sinai represented a different phenomenon from sacrifice as such, and the blood had a different function.

The placing of sacrificial blood on persons can have the effect of binding them in a covenant, as is true in the case of the Aaronide High Priest, who is

---

[49] See primarily D. S. McCarthy, *Treaty and Covenant*, 1963; also D. R. Hillers, *Covenant: The History of a Biblical Idea*, 1969; M. Weinfeld, "The Covenant of Grant in the Old Testament and in the Ancient Near East," *JAOS* 90 (1970), 184–203. Weinfeld distinguishes between the obligatory type of covenant, such as the one enacted at Sinai, and the covenant of grant, such as the ones enacted with Abraham and David.

[50] See n. 62 below for references. Prof. Jacobsen has yet to publish a full statement of his views on this subject, which he has discussed in great detail in several scholarly addresses and colloquia during the last few years. Also see H. M. Orlinsky, *Ancient Israel* 1954, pp. 27–29 and 39–40 for a discussion on the relationship of personal to national covenants.

invested in this manner (Lev. 18:22–24). According to the priestly source, a covenant obtained between Yahweh and the Aaronide house (Num. 25:12–13). The blood placed on the person of the High Priest was from the ram of investiture. In such rites, the persons upon whom blood was placed did not have the status of worshippers, and it was not by virtue of the act of sacrifice itself that the blood was disposed of in this manner. In such rites, the altar represented one party to the covenant, i.e., the Deity. As the binding agent, blood was placed on both parties. In sacrificial rites, blood is not placed on the worshippers, and its use is governed by other considerations entirely.[51]

The efficacy of blood, however we conceive of its uses in ritual and however we interpret the prohibitions against its consumption, is predicated on the notion of its potency as the life force, an idea explicitly conveyed in the cultic codes of the Pentateuch (Leviticus 17:10f.), and fundamental to the entire structure of the Israelite cult. Because it is the life force, blood can substitute for a life, *pars pro toto*. This is how we understand Leviticus 17:11:

> For the life of the flesh is in the blood, and I have assigned it to you to serve as expiation for your lives on the altar; for the blood may expiate according to the value of life.

The technical idiom -לְכַפֵּר עַל נֶפֶשׁ means "to serve as ransom for a life." The final part of the verse is crucial, and expresses the notion of ritual substitution: כִּי הַדָּם הוּא בַּנֶּפֶשׁ יְכַפֵּר. The preposition *Beth* in the word בַּנֶּפֶשׁ is *Beth pretii*, "of price." The sense is that blood can substitute for life to the extent required to redeem it, to ransom it. Deities, like demons, accept blood in lieu of human life, and do the bidding of those who offer it to them. The efficacy of blood is a result of its potent properties. This is what has led us to the hypothesis that the uses of blood in the Israelite cult were magical, and not primarily ritual.

We distinguish between two types of use:

1) The blood libation, originally intended for the chthonic deities, and adopted by the Israelite cult as an apotropaic means for appeasing Yahweh and for preventing his wrath. Yahweh accepts the blood and does not allow his wrath to be destructive of his worshippers when they stand in his presence, as occasionally happened. This is the purpose of the dashing of the blood against the altar, which was prescribed for sacrifices generally. It is this use of blood that Leviticus speaks of in specifically employing the phrase -לְכַפֵּר עַל נֶפֶשׁ.[52]

---

[51] M. Noth, *Exodus* (in *The Old Testament Library*), 1962, 194–197, to Exodus 24:1–11.

[52] On the phrase: לְכַפֵּר עַל נֶפֶשׁ see Levine, *Eretz-Israel* 9 (W. F. Albright Volume, 1969), 90 and n. 16. Besides Lev. 17:11, this phrase occurs only in two other passages of cultic provenance: Ex. 30:16 and Num. 31:50. Both are related to the census and have nothing to do with blood rites. The sense of the phrase is established by Ex. 30:12: "… each shall pay the Lord a ransom for himself (literally: for his life) …"

2) The use of blood in expiatory sacrifices. Such use is always designated by the verb כִּפֶּר "to perform an act of ritual expiation," and never by the phrase לְכַפֵּר עַל נֶפֶשׁ-. Such use of blood was also apotropaic, but the force of the blood was not directed at the deity being worshipped but at demonic powers which threatened him. The offenses, which had necessitated the expiatory sacrifices in the first instance, had unleashed these demonic powers, and had allowed them to penetrate the Israelite community where the deity resided. They threatened the purity of his sanctuary residence, and had to be driven out. They accepted the blood offered to them and withdrew. This is the purpose of the dabbing of sacrificial blood on the horns of the altar of incense, and on other cultic furnishings, which stood on the route of entry into the innermost precincts of the sanctuary. The defilement of these inner precincts might endanger the purity of the resident deity and induce him to withdraw.[53]

If this interpretation of the blood rites is correct, and the derivation of the sacrificial blood rites from the binding power of blood in the enactment of covenants incorrect, there would be further reason to reject Robertson Smith's view of sacrifice as communion.

If kinship cannot account for the basic cultic relationship between the Israelite worshippers and their deity, what was the underlying factor in that relationship? All that has been said above as to the nexus of covenant and cult points to one answer: The worshipper is the servant of the deity. He brings his requests before his master, thanks him for his kindnesses, tries to expiate for any offenses committed against him, praises him, does his will, and attempts to provide proper hospitality for the resident deity, so as to retain his abiding presence in the midst of the community.

What the worshipper wants from the deity is that power, in the form of life and sustenance—one may call it fertility—which the gods grant to those who find favor in their eyes. He wants protection from the ravages of nature and from human enemies. He wants a good future for his land and his people. To worship is to serve, expressed by the verb עבד, and ritual celebration is עֲבֹדָה "service." This verb also connotes the fulfillment of the duties of vassaldom.[54] To offend the deity or to fail in serving him properly is conveyed, *inter alia*, by the verbs

[53] Gray included an interesting discussion of the verb כִּפֶּר on p. 67f. See also n. 9 above.

[54] The verb עבד clearly connotes vassaldom in 2 Ki. 18:7; Isa. 19:23; Jer. 25:11, 27:11, 17, 28:14, 40:9, and most probably also in Gen. 15:13–14. It connotes service to a king in many passages, including Jud. 9:28 and 1 Ki. 12:7. The performance of cultic service is a well-attested sense of this verb. Cf. in the Decalogue (Ex. 20:5//Deut. 5:9), Mal. 3:18, and frequently in Deuteronomy. Cf. also Ex. 13:5, 2 Sam. 15:8, etc. The Akkadian verb *palāḫu* shares the range and most of the nuances of Hebrew עבד; see W. von Soden, *AHw*, 812–813, s.v. *palāḫu* and its derivatives.

חטא and פשע, and the offenses are termed חֵטְא, חַטָּאת and פֶּשַׁע. These same verbs refer to improper treaty relations.[55]

Now we can appreciate the semantics involved in such terms as מִנְחָה "tribute", as well as בְּרָכָה and מַשְׂאֵת. They are all predicated on the sense of something remitted or granted, depending on the point of view. Thus the מִנְחָה is usually presented to the one possessing the power in a particular situation. The term בְּרָכָה usually connotes that which is granted by the one possessing the power, but it can also mean tribute.[56] Even the term תָּמִיד "daily sacrifice" is related to the notion of a payment. In its original administrative context it meant "regular, daily ration," and designated the ration granted by kings to their retainers.[57] In this dimension, sacrifice had as its most immediate objective the care and feeding of the gods, to borrow a phrase from A. Leo Oppenheim's discussion of cultic procedures in Mesopotamia.[58]

Gray glossed over the problematic term שְׁלָמִים, not even summarizing prior discussions of the term. He neither referred to the evidence of the Carthaginian tariffs available to him, nor to the discussion of this evidence by Robertson Smith.[59] This term is pivotal for an understanding of the Israelite cult. In a forthcoming monograph on the technical terminology of biblical sacrifice we hope to show that it, too, fits in well with the gift theory advocated by Gray.

This is the overall importance of the technical terminology in ascertaining the meaning of biblical sacrifice. It is Gray's emphasis on terminology which rendered his methodology sound. It becomes apparent that the lexicon of the cultic texts consisted largely of a shared vocabulary, and in many cases a derivative one. In studying the variations in usage we learn something about the meaning of sacrifice, observing more clearly how the cultic establishment interacted with other elements in Israelite society.

The terminology thus suggests the servant-lord relationship as that which underlies the sense of sacrifice as gift or tribute. It is the orientation of needs, relative to power, which explains the dynamics of cultic activity. This basic outlook was adopted by Johannes Pedersen.[60] G. van der Leeuw was troubled by

---

[55] The terms חֵטְא and פֶּשַׁע require an extended treatment which lies beyond the scope of this discussion. Suffice it to call attention here to the Akkadian evidence bearing on the cognate root *ḫaṭû*. See *CAD Ḫ*, 156–158, s.v. *ḫaṭû*, verb; 158–159, s.v. *ḫāṭû*, adj.; 208–210, s.v. *ḫiṭīṭu*, noun; 210–212, s.v. *ḫīṭu*, noun; 212, s.v. *ḫīṭu*, in *bēl ḫīṭu*. These forms frequently connote offenses relevant to treaty obligations.

[56] As with respect to terms for offenses (see n. 55 preceding), a full treatment of terms connoting "gift, offering," etc., is beyond our present scope. Provisionally, see B. A. Levine and W. W. Hallo, "Offerings to the Temple Gates at Ur," *HUCA* 38 (1967), 46, n. 21. The term מַשְׂאֵת figures prominently in the Carthaginian tariffs, for which see H. Donner-W. Röllig, *op. cit.*, I, nos. 69 and 74.

[57] B. A. Levine, *Leshonenu* 30 (1965–66), 5–8.

[58] A. Leo Oppenheim, *op. cit.*, 183f.

[59] W. R. Smith, *op. cit.*, 237, and n. 1.

[60] J. Pedersen, *op. cit.*, IV, 1956, 330–334.

the notion that sacrifice should be thought of as little more than bartering with the gods. Although his orientation was clearly dynamistic, he spoke of a higher type of giving, and of the bond created between worshipper and deity through offering something of one's own, which is akin to giving of one's self. Van der Leeuw tried to reconcile his basic outlook with that of Robertson Smith, and saw in the latter's concept of communion an expansive idea. His interpretation of Robertson Smith was hardly accurate in this regard.[61]

Our own thinking has been influenced considerably by the studies of Thorkild Jacobsen into the character of Mesopotamian religion. By an analysis of the mythology, of the literature of hymns and prayers, and of the actual records of the great establishments of ancient Mesopotamia, Jacobsen has shown how the central concerns of each age dominated the attitudes toward the gods. Each millennium or other definitive age in Mesopotamian history characterized divine power in terms of its most vital concerns. Until increased food production reduced the chronic threat of famine, it was this critical need which was projected onto the personality of the chief gods.[62] When one stops to inquire what it was that most vitally concerned a people, what its greatest anxiety was, he will come close to identifying the main thrust of its religious outlook.[63]

The above considerations seem to be predicated on the idea that sacrifice, as the primary means of petitioning the gods, of seeking their assistance, was a gift, either obligatory or voluntary. In mythological religions, gods are usually pictured as requiring sustenance, and the supplying of food and other energizing substances to them was thought to increase their potency, thus rendering them more capable of assisting their worshippers. Some of this dynamic was still operative in the Israelite cult.

When comparative evidence is employed in the study of Israelite religion, as has been done here, one opens himself to the challenge that Israelite religion was different, *sui generis*, and that such evidence does not apply to its ritual practices. It is our view that from the more abundant evidence of other Near Eastern societies we can learn something of the generic character of religion in that area, in ancient times. This should not preclude the drawing of legitimate distinctions between one way of life and another, against the background of broad acquaintance and knowledge.

Gray came closest to theorizing when he presented two important arguments that support the gift theory of sacrifice:

[61] G. van der Leeuw, *Religion in Essence and Manifestation*, 1938, 350–360.

[62] T. Jacobsen, "Ancient Mesopotamian Religion: The Central Concerns," *Proceedings of the American Philosophical Society* 107, 1963, 473–484, and literature cited there.

[63] This was the theoretical point of departure in our study, "On the Presence of God in Biblical Religion," *Religions in Antiquity: Essays in Memory of Erwin Ramsdell Goodenough*), 1968, 71–87 {*VOL 1, PP. 215–29*}.

1) The dynamics of the נֶדֶר, the votive offering, and the formulary employed in pronouncing the vow, clearly reflect the contractual relationship. The worshipper pledges a gift to the deity in an effort to secure his assistance. That gift was to be remitted, usually in the form of a sacrifice or a donation to the cultic establishment, when the deity fulfilled his part of the contract. This presupposes that the sacrifice was a gift.[64]

2) Deductive proof that the sacrifices were conceived as a presentation to the deity comes from the prophetic critique of the cult. The prime target of that critique was the belief, apparently widely held at the time, that the God of Israel desires and/or requires sacrifices. In the context of the covenant between God and Israel, God requires sacrifices as the partial fulfillment of the duties imposed by that covenant. In a more general sense, the deity desires sacrifices and is appeased and entreated by them, and grants the requests of those who worship him in this manner. All of this presupposes that the sacrifice was essentially the presentation of objects to the deity, and militates against the notion that the primary significance of the sacrifice was the mystical experience of the blood rite.[65]

The evidence is mounting in support of the gift theory. That is not to say that any unitary conception can account for all the phenomena, for the entire gamut of experiences that were embodied in Israelite ritual. What we are discussing is an organizing principle, on the basis of which we can accurately view all the diverse factors involved in cultic activity in their proper perspective. As an organizing principle, the proposition that the God of Israel desired the sacrifices of his people as a form of tribute to him as their sovereign, in return for which he would grant them the blessings of life, seems to convey the theory of Israelite sacrifice more accurately than the proposition that Israel, as a community bound together and bound to its deity by blood, sacrificed to that deity sacred animals, which shared with it, and with the deity, a triangular blood kinship.

Some of the import of the above comments on the theory of sacrifice will become apparent in the following remarks on some specific types and modes of sacrifice discussed by Gray.

1) The slain offering (זֶבַח). Gray was troubled by the fact that the larger part of the זֶבַח was not assigned to the deity on the altar, but rather consumed by the officiants and/or donors. He correctly sensed that this type of sacrifice had other significance than merely the presentation of a gift to the deity. However, he need not have concerned himself with questions of relative quantities. The fatty portions of the sacrificial victim (חֵלֶב), which were assigned to the deity, were considered the choicest portions of the animal, from a cultic point of view. This

[64] Gray, 7, 36, 38f.; G. van der Leeuw, "Die *do-ut-des* Formel in der Opfertheorie," *Archiv für Religionswissenschaft* 20 (1920–21), 241–253; and M. Haran, *Encyclopaedia Biblica*, s.v. נֶדֶר, V, 1968, 786–790.

[65] Gray, 41–54. For bibliography see R. de Vaux, *Ancient Israel*, 549; H. M. Orlinsky, "Who is the Ideal Jew: the Biblical View," *Judaism* 13 (1964), 19–28.

notion is attested in biblical sources, quite independently of the priestly codes. Since it was thought that the deity especially desired these sections of the animals, they would constitute a fitting gift to him.[66]

The edible portions of the sacrificial victim were consumed by the donors and the priests, with the share of the priests increasing, as time went on. From Lev. 7:31–34 it is clear that sections of the animals originally assigned to the donors were subsequently allotted to the priests. Perhaps a further stage in the appropriation of sacrificial flesh by the priests is to be seen in the provisions of the Carthaginian tariffs, usually dated to the fourth or third centuries B.C.E. According to those provisions, the donors of a זֶבַח received what was left over after the priests had taken a fixed quantity of flesh, computed by weight in amounts relative to the class of animal involved. The routine provision was that the donor received the hides, the feet, and other portions of uncertain identification, which could not have constituted choice, edible sections of the animal.[67]

The meat to be eaten was boiled in pots. An exception was the paschal זֶבַח, as ordained in Ex. 12:9, which was to be broiled. In Deut. 16:7 this regulation is rescinded, and the paschal זֶבַח is treated in the same way as all others.[68]

The most elaborate description of a זֶבַח is the account in 1 Sam. 9. Samuel ascends the *bamah* at Ramah to bless the offering, and to partake of it, together with קְרֻאִים "those called," his invited guests (cf. 1 Ki. 1:41, 49; Zeph. 1:7). He orders the cook to give Saul his own share (מָנָה) from the slain offering.[69]

---

[66] The New Jewish Version (NJPS) of the Torah (1962) renders Gen. 4:4 as a hendiadys: "and Abel, for his part, brought the choicest of the firstlings of his flock." Our rendering was purposely more literal. Also note the reservations of H. M. Orlinsky, *Notes on the New Translation of the Torah*, 1969, 67. Although we cannot be certain about the manner in which Abel executed his sacrifice, there is no reason to conclude that it was not a burnt offering. Biblical evidence, generally considered, makes it doubtful that animals were offered up in any other way (see our discussion below on modes of sacrifice). On the burning of the fatty portions see, in addition to the priestly codes of the Pentateuch, 1 Samuel 2:15–16.

[67] On the Punic tariffs see H. Donner and W. Röllig, *op. cit.*, I, nos. 69, 74, and commentary II, 84f. For topical treatment of biblical sacrifice see T. H. Gaster, "Sacrifices and Offerings, O.T.," *IDB*, I, 1962, 147–159, and bibliography cited.

[68] See Ex. 29:31; Jud. 6:19; 1 Sam. 2:13; Isa. 65:4; Ezek. 46:20, 24; 2 Chron. 35:13. Also consider the prohibition against boiling a kid in its mother's milk. Ex. 23:19; 34:26, Deut. 14:21.

[69] See 1 Sam. 9:24: אֶת-הַשּׁוֹק וְהֶעָלֶיהָ, "the flank and that which covers it (i.e., the fatty portions)." The flank was one of the sections reserved for the priests according to Lev. 7:32, and is called the מָנָה of the priest, as here in 1 Sam. 9:23, and also in Ex. 29:26 and Lev. 8:29. This is a relatively rare term, the more normal one being חק "statutory allotment" (Lev. 7:34). In Lev. 7:35 we have the term מִשְׁחָה "measure," an apparent Aramaism. The point is that there is an affinity between the traditions of Samuel and what is probably the oldest stratum in the priestly writings of the Pentateuch. But see H. M. Orlinsky, *Notes on the New Translation of the Torah*, 1969, 211, for problems related to this term.

If the sequence of events described in 1 Sam. 9 is accurate, the meal was partaken of in a bureau (Hebrew לִשְׁכָּה), which was within the *bamah* installation, located outside the city. This is what was meant by the designation לִפְנֵי ה׳, "in the presence of Yahweh." The meal was conducted in the sacred precincts of a sanctuary, or high place.[70] Although it is not clear from this account, it is probable that the presence of the deity was manifested in the altar fire, which consumed the fatty portions of the זֶבַח.[71]

The meal described in 1 Sam. 9 can be characterized as an experience of fellowship, so long as we intend by this term primarily the social aspect of the sacrificial meal, and not any particular effects of the blood rites associated with it. Such an experience undoubtedly possessed a numinous quality, deriving from the presence of Yahweh, and from the partaking of sacrificial flesh as part of a select group of participants, within sacred precincts. One felt the nearness of the deity, as well as sensing the fellowship of fellow Israelites.

2) Gray's method in classifying the various sacrifices by their graduated relation to the altar is suggestive. He projects a scale ranging from the holocaust, given over entirely to the altar fire, to the offerings of first fruits and the bread of display, of which no part ascended the altar.[72]

From a comparative Near Eastern perspective, we may go beyond the distinctions formulated by Gray. Two operating principles were involved in Israelite modes of sacrifice:

a) The practice of placing offerings before the deity, so as to be viewed by him. His seeing the offering constituted either its actual consumption, or, at the least, its acceptance by him. When the deity had been afforded ample opportunity to view the offerings, they were removed from his presence and assigned to human consumers, usually the priests.[73]

b) The practice of burning parts of sacrifices, or whole sacrifices, on the altar. The principle here was that the deity consumed the sacrifice after it had been transformed into smoke, which the deity breathed in.[74]

The former principle was normal for most areas of the ancient Near East, whereas the latter principle seems to be peculiar to the Northwest-Semitic sphere in the second and early first millennium B.C.E.

---

[70] The precise sense of this term requires further study. It is doubtful whether it refers consistently to the same precinct or location. See provisionally N. Rabban, לפני ה׳ (Hebrew) *Tarbiẕ* 23 (1942), 1–8.

[71] Cf. Lev. 9:24, and see B. A. Levine, "On the Presence of God," etc. (see n. 63 above), 71–87 {*VOL 1, PP. 215–29*}.

[72] Gray, 27f.

[73] On the Mesopotamian practice of placing offerings before the gods, see Oppenheim, *op. cit.*, 188f.

[74] *Ibid.*, 192, and 365, n. 17. The notion that Yahweh breathes in the smoke of the sacrifice is conveyed in Gen. 8:21; 1 Sam. 26:19; Amos 5:21; also cf. Lev. 26:31; Deut. 4:28; Psa. 115:6.

The account of Gideon's theophany at Ophrah (Jud. 6) may be an etiology, explaining the superimposition of one principle on the other. Gideon at first prepared a sacred meal and set it before the angel, the divine manifestation. The key verb is הניח "to set down" (v. 18), also employed in Deut. 26:10 in prescribing the offering of the first fruits. The angel thereupon instructed Gideon to make of the animal a burnt offering, and it was subsequently offered up on a rock altar. The angel ascended heavenward in the altar flames, which may be a way of defining the term עֹלָה as "an ascending offering," i.e., one in which the substance of the sacrifice ascends heavenward in fire and smoke.[75]

Judging from this folkloristic account, it was once the custom to set offerings before the deity, and Israelites would have supposed this to be the usual procedure, in the early periods. The episode explains the change to burnt offerings. The difference in procedure results from a different conception of how Yahweh consumes sacrifices.

From Ugaritic ritual texts we have clear evidence of the widespread use of burnt offerings in pre-Israelite times. It is primarily this evidence which helps to classify the geographic distribution of burnt offerings as a primarily Northwest-Semitic ritual. Elsewhere in the Near East, burnt offerings were exceedingly rare in the early periods. Whereas fire was often used in magical rites associated with the cult, it was not generally employed in actual sacrifices.[76]

The Ugaritic term *šrp* "burnt offerings" occurs in ritual texts in association with *šlmm*, biblical שְׁלָמִים, the most prominent type of Israelite slain offering.[77] The presence in the Ugaritic cult of burnt offerings, and of counterparts to biblical arrangements of sacrificial offerings, is further indication of the intimate connections between the practices of the Israelites and those of the Northwest-Semitic sphere. On the other hand, the Gideon account, as an example, would suggest that the Israelites introduced distinctive practices into Canaan proper, which were not necessarily native to that particular area. A distinction thus emerges between Syrian and Canaanite attitudes, one which is readily overlooked by lumping together the entire region of Palestine-Syria indiscriminately.

---

[75] The sense of "ascending" can have three possible referents: a) The ascent of the offering to heaven in smoke, fire, and aroma. b) The ascent of sacrifice onto the altar. c) The ascent of the officiants to a high place, tower, wall, or the like for the purpose of offering it up. C. Schaeffer, *Syria* 23 (1942–1943), 39–41, has suggested, on the basis of Ugaritic evidence, that the עֹלָה was a tower offering. Keret ascends the ramparts of his city wall to offer sacrifice to El, and the verb *šʿly* (= Hebrew הַעֲלָה) is there used. See H. L. Ginsberg, *The Legend of King Keret* (*BASOR*, *Supplementary Studies* 2–3), 1946, 15, line 73f. *et passim*, and 37, note to lines 70f.).

[76] *CAD I/J*, 229f., s.v. *išātu*, 2.

[77] B. A. Levine, "Ugaritic Descriptive Rituals," *JCS* 17 (1963), 105–11 {*VOL 1, PP. 45–54*}; C. H. Gordon, *Ugaritic Textbook*, 1965, glossary, 2489, and text 1:4: *dqt šrp wšlmm* "a female head of small cattle for the burnt offerings and the *shelamim* offering." In text 52: 31, 38–39, 41, *et passim*, burnt offerings are described in detail. This text is a ritual drama of the birth of gods.

In the biblical cult, the more widely attested Near Eastern practice of placing offerings before the deity, so as to be viewed by him, is a mode of sacrifice that is on its way out. It is retained in certain instances as a sufficient means of sacrifice, and in other cases it is employed as a preliminary act to the burnt offering. Deut. 26:1–11 prescribes the presentation of the first fruits, and we have already noted the technical terminology characteristic of that code. The substances were merely set before the deity, probably to be removed after an appropriate interval. Another instance of this method is the placing of the bread of display (לֶחֶם הַפָּנִים) on a table in the sanctuary, located outside the screen (פָּרֹכֶת), near the altar of incense (Ex. 25:30; Lev. 24:5–9; 1 Sam. 21:7; 1 Ki. 7:48; 2 Chron. 4:19; and cf. Num. 4:7). Each week, the twelve loaves were removed from the table and eaten by priests in a sacred place. The fact that the bread of display is mentioned in a story from the early career of David, and that it is included in the description of Solomon's temple, attests to the antiquity of the practice.[78]

A burnt offering actually accompanied the bread of display. Pure frankincense was offered up on the altar when the bread was set on the table. This was a substitute for the אַזְכָּרָה, a part of the מִנְחָה "grain offering," that was normally burnt on the altar (Lev. 24:7).[79] The requirement of an accompanying burnt offering points up the tendency to adapt the one mode of sacrifice to the other. The mode of sacrifice known as תְּנוּפָה, "wave offering," is further evidence of this tendency. The term תְּנוּפָה occurs only in the priestly sources.[80] The waving of the offering was for the purpose of showing it to the deity. It was originally an independent mode of sacrifice, and even remained a sufficient act of sacrifice in the case of some grain offerings, such as the sheaf of fresh grain (עֹמֶר) (Lev. 23:11–15). It is interesting to note that the grain offering which accompanied the עֹמֶר, called מִנְחַת בִּכֻּרִים (*ibid.*, 23:17), could be made of leavened bread, since no part of it ascended the altar. In contrast, the animal sacrifice which accompanied the עֹמֶר was waved only as a preliminary act to its subsequent disposition on the altar fire (*ibid.*, 23:18–20).[81]

---

[78] On the first fruits see A. S. Hartom, *Encyclopaedia Biblica*, II, 1954, 126–128, s.v. בִּכּוּרִים, On the bread of display see M. Haran, *ibid.*, IV, 1962, 494–495, s.v. לֶחֶם הַפָּנִים.

[79] The אַזְכָּרָה is prescribed in Lev. 2:2, 9, 16; 5:12; 6:8; Num. 5:26. The priest took a fistful of the dough from the מִנְחָה and cast it into the altar fire as a "reminder." Cf. Isa. 66:3 where the Hiphil participle מַזְכִּיר represents a denominative from אַזְכָּרָה, i.e., "he offers up an אַזְכָּרָה of frankincense." But see NJPS to Lev: 2:2, "token portion," and H. M. Orlinsky, *Notes on the New Translation of the Torah*, 1969, 205–206. There is still some doubt as to the precise sense of this term.

[80] On the wave offering see A. Vincent, *Mélanges Syriens offerts à M. René Dussaud* I, 1939, 267–272, and G. R. Driver, *Journal of Semitic Studies* 1 (1956), 97–105. The term תְּנוּפָה may have the sense of a levy or tax "raised" (Ex. 35:22; 38:24, 29).

[81] The only possible instance where an animal was actually presented to Yahweh not for the purpose of offering it up on the altar is the scapegoat (Lev. 16). Two goats were

Perhaps some further light on the practice of setting offerings before the deity as a mode of sacrifice can be shed by the provisions of Num. 7, where we have a record of the contributions to the tabernacle brought by the chiefs of the tribes of Israel. Even though the articles so donated by the chiefs—vessels, beasts for transport, wagons, etc.—were clearly not intended for the sacrificial altar, they are designated קָרְבָּן, a term which, in all other occurrences, refers directly to substances of which at least a part was intended for the altar. Elsewhere in the priestly sources, such contributions would undoubtedly be designated by the term תְּרוּמָה. In Num. 7, we have a different vocabulary, one less adjusted, perhaps, to the normative priestly conception of sacrifice as an altar offering.[82]

There is much more that could be noted about Gray's treatment of biblical sacrifice. In hindsight, it is clear that he came close to establishing the precise distinction between the two types of expiatory sacrifices, the אָשָׁם and the חַטָּאת. He found the key to the problem of these confusing terms in a better understanding of the procedures of commutation, whereby contributions to temples were recorded and computed according to standards of exchange, usually silver or gold. This subject has more recently been discussed by the late E. A. Speiser, on the basis of comparative evidence. In our proposed monograph, we hope to clarify the problem of the expiatory sacrifices.[83]

The reissue of G. B. Gray's classic work exhorts students of biblical religion to remain faithful to sound philological methodology in treating a subject which, somehow, tends to draw us away from precise data, and attracts us, almost irresistibly, toward theory and abstraction. It is hoped that the foregoing remarks helped to characterize the present state of biblical cultic studies, and to emphasize, as well, the most pressing requirements of the field.

---

secured and presented, or stationed, לִפְנֵי ה׳ "in the presence of Yahweh" (v. 7). Lots were cast, and one was designated a חַטָּאת sacrifice (vv. 8–9). The other goat was then again stationed, or presented in the presence of Yahweh before being dispatched into the wilderness (v. 10). We have attempted to deal with this problematic verse in *Eretz-Israel* 9 (W. F. Albright Volume), 1969, 93, and n. 38 (Hebrew section). The point is that the animal is displayed to the deity, but not as part of the *sacrificial* offerings associated with the purification of the sanctuary. See also T. H. Gaster, "Azazel," *IDB*, I, 1962, 325f.

[82] See Gray's discussion of the term קָרְבָּן, on, 4f., 13f., 17f., and 22f. In a later source we have קָרְבַּן הָעֵצִים, "the contribution of wood" (Neh. 10:35; 13:31). The term קָרְבָּן is predominantly limited to the priestly sources of the Pentateuch, and to Ezek. 20:28; 40:43. In every case except Num. 7, the reference is to substances of which at least a part ascended the altar, in one form or another. On the other hand, the term תְּרוּמָה connotes objects for sanctuary use in the priestly source (Ex. 25:2; etc.). It can also designate priestly gifts. See B. A. Levine, *JAOS* 85 (1965), 307–318 {*VOL 1, PP. 55–72*}.

[83] See E. A. Speiser, "Leviticus and the Critics," *Yehezkel Kaufmann Jubilee Volume*, ed. M. Haran, 1960, 30–33; R. de Vaux, *Studies in Old Testament Sacrifice*, 90f.

Lpny YHWH—Phenomenology of the Open-Air-Altar in Biblical Israel[*]

Phenomenology is the crossroad at which biblical cult studies intersect with biblical archaeology. Phenomenology is the study of essence and manifestation of meaning and expression. The phenomenologist of religion seeks to clarify the meanings or significance underlying the overt acts involved in cultic praxis such as sacrifice, celebration, processions and purifications. Most activity of this kind takes place in sacred precincts. In consequence, the phenomenologist must also consider the architecture and iconography of cult installations, which range from simple altars located in open-air courtyards to elaborate temple complexes. To put it simply, the phenomenologist cannot be content to study textual descriptions of cult installations and rituals but must also deal with the meanings behind the discrete use of space, dimension and form, as aspects of material culture.

During the last couple of decades, archaeological excavations in Israel and in neighboring countries, such as Jordan, have yielded many new examples of cult-installations of both Israelite and non-Israelite provenience.[1] What is more, archaeologists have shown greater sensitivity to phenomenological concerns in their excavation reports. They regularly pose questions concerning the relation of form to function. Biblical scholars, on the other hand, have been much less forthcoming in relation to the archaeological evidence.

A paradigm of phenomenological analysis in the area of biblical studies is Menahem Haran's early work on the symbolic significance of the priestly Tabernacle as depicted in Torah literature.[2] The fact is, however, that Haran's work

---

[*] Originally published in Avraham Biran and Joseph Aviram (eds.), *Biblical Archaeology Today, 1990: Proceedings of the Second International Congress on Biblical Archaeology, Jerusalem, June-July 1990* (Jerusalem: Israel Exploration Society, 1993), pp. 196–205. Reprinted with permission from the Israel Exploration Society.

[1] As an example of an open-court sanctuary in Transjordan, referred to by several Israeli archaeologists, see K. Yassine, "The Open-Court Sanctuary of the Iron-Age. Tell-el-Mazar, Mound A," *ZDPV* 100 (1984):108–118. Unfortunately, Yassine does not provide drawings of the building, which dominates the site, although he describes it and the objects and installations of the courtyard inconsiderable detail. The building dates from the 11th to the 10th centuries B.C.E. and was destroyed in the 5th century B.C.E. There is ample evidence of cultic activity.

[2] See M. Haran, *Temple and Temple Service in Ancient Israel* (Oxford, 1978), chaps. 8–9, "The Priestly Image of the Tabernacle" and "Grades of Sanctity in the Tabernacle," pp. 149–187. Haran's phenomenological study first appeared in 1960. On p. 26, n. 24

analyzes a textual tradition, not artifacts and structures actually discovered in what was ancient Israel or in neighboring areas. A paradigm of synthesis, in which textual evidence and actual archaeological material are brought to bear on one another, is Thorkild Jacobsen's recent contribution, "The Mesopotamian Temple Plan and the *Kitîtum* Temple" in the *Yadin Memorial Volume.*[3] Jacobsen is able to identify technical terms of reference used in temple records, and even in other types of literature, with actual structures and artifacts uncovered in excavations—such as gates, buildings, *temenos* areas, etc. A major problem in biblical studies is confusion over the identification of artifacts with biblical terms, such as *bāmāh*, for instance, whose functional definition will be discussed further on.

In discussing the phenomenology of open-air altars, we proceed on the assumption of certain positions. It would be of value to formulate them at the outset so that the relevance of the discussion which follows will be understood as intended.[4]

Proposition 1.

The phenomenology or meaning of open-air courtyards and their altars is not religion-specific; they do not necessarily express concepts particular to Israelite monotheism. Chronologically, open-air courtyards take us back to the Early Bronze period and the Megiddo altar. Other examples carry us through the Middle Bronze and Late Bronze periods into the Iron Age. This subject was recently summarized clearly by Amihai Mazar in the valuable compendium, *The Architecture of Ancient Israel.*[5] It is, therefore, both valid and necessary to include non-Israelite sites, both contemporary and pre-Israelite, in an attempt to understand the importance through time of the open-air courtyards evident in Israelite sanctuaries of diverse types. We are dealing with a typology which was widely employed in the ancient Near East, a fact brought out clearly in the reports submitted after the Hebrew Union College colloquium of March 1977, "Temples and High Places in Biblical Times." Of particular relevance to the present discussion is Ruth Amiran's attempt to determine to what extent conti-

---

Haran offers his interpretation of the idiom *lpny* YHWH, which differs in some respects from that presented here.

[3] See T. Jacobsen, "The Mesopotamian Temple Plan and the Kitîtum Temple," *Eretz-Israel* 20 (Y. Yadin Volume, 1989):79–91.

[4] This format was employed by J.M. Lundquist, "What Is A Temple? A Preliminary Typology," in H.B. Huffmon, et al. (eds.), *The Quest for the Kingdom of God, Studies in Honor of George E. Mendenhall* (Winona Lake, 1983), pp. 205–219.

[5] See A. Mazar, "Sanctuaries in the Middle and Late Bronze Periods and in the Iron Age," in *Architecture of Ancient Israel* (Jerusalem, 1987), pp. 136–160. (Hebrew)

nuity in design and form reflected cultic continuity and the actual survival of the same pantheons and religions at Canaanite sites through successive periods.[6]

Proposition 2.

Although there is an obvious incremental factor evident in the structural development from fairly simple, delimited, open-air cult-installations to roofed sanctuary buildings, it is also significant that unroofed courtyards were usually retained in elaborate temple complexes, with altars often placed in such courtyards. The tendency to dismiss unroofed environments in sanctuaries as being representative of an earlier stage in religious development masks the meaning of openness. The significance attached to open courtyards and their altars remained relevant throughout the course of structural development, so that the diachronic approach is insufficient to explain the phenomenon.

Proposition 3.

Admittedly, the Hebrew Bible is disappointing insofar as the information it yields concerning material culture is limited. We lack the data to accomplish Jacobsen's brand of terminological identifications because of the scarcity of written evidence from the biblical period deriving from Canaan and neighboring areas. On the other hand, the Hebrew Bible is rich in phenomenological insights once we know where to look for them and provided that a framework exists within which to discuss them. The method recommending itself is elaboration on perceptions of the sacred expressed in biblical literature. In this way we may lend graphic realism to the biblical idiom: *lpny YHWH*, "in the presence of YHWH."

A glance at the Edomite cult complex at Qitmit, a Negev site, may set the stage for our discussion of the phenomenology of the open courtyard and its altars. I. Beit-Arieh, the site's excavator, dates this ephemeral complex to the late 7th-early 6th century B.C.E. More elaborate sanctuaries have been excavated, of course, but few, if any, afford the clarity and definition of Qitmit. Notwithstanding its Edomite, non-Israelite origin, Qitmit seems most appropriate as a basis for discussion.[7]

The cult complex at Qitmit sits on a bed of chalk-like rock on an isolated hill. Beit-Arieh identifies two configurations and after describing them architecturally, proceeds to itemize the objects found in each area. In the lower area we find a complex comprising three principal components: a three-chambered building, which we would designate a *liškāh* "bureau" (1 Samuel 9:22); an altar and its accompanying water channel and cistern; and a *bāmāh*-platform, so clas-

[6] See R. Amiran, "Some Observations on Chalcolithic and Early Bronze Age Sanctuaries and Religion," in *Temples and High Places in Biblical Times* (Jerusalem, 1977), pp. 47–54.

[7] See I. Beit-Arieh, "An Edomite Shrine at Horvat Qitmit," *Eretz-Israel* 20 (Y. Yadin Volume, 1989):135–146 (Hebrew). See Illustration 3, p. 136 for plan.

sified by Beit-Arieh himself. The objects found in each area further clarify its functions. The building we have called *liškāh* contained three sections, with openings facing southward. One of the rooms contained a bench along one of its walls, and all three contained stone ledges of a sort, with flat tops. Assuming these ledges had no structural function, it is reasonable to regard them as furniture on which food and other items may have been placed for distribution. The contents of these rooms consisted largely of wheel-turned ceramic vessels, crude hand-made ceramics, statuettes, and bones of sheep and goats.

The *bāmāh* was made of medium-sized field stones and was enclosed on three sides by a stone wall, with the northern side, which faced the *liškāh*, exposed. Found in the area of the *bāmāh* were large caches of objects, including cult objects of considerable interest, some decorated with anthropomorphic and zoomorphic forms. These objects have been the subject of a special study by P. Beck.[8] The quantity and quality of the finds in the area of the *bāmāh* clearly indicate that votives and other offerings were presented in this part of the cult-complex.

About 15 m. north of this tripartite complex of *bāmāh*, altar, and the building we have called *liškāh*, stood yet another building, partially roofed and containing several interior rooms, and partly open, as a courtyard. Some animal bones and a considerable number of ceramic vessels were found in various parts of this building. At the southern edge of the building, near the southern wall of Room 108, a large flint stone, probably to be regarded as a *maṣṣēbāh*, was found standing in the open. In front of the *maṣṣēbāh*, on its northern side, was a stone-paved floor with a stone border. Most probably worshippers stood on this paved floor, in front of the *maṣṣēbāh*, and assumed postures of devotion in front of it. Beit-Arieh suggests that priests may have been housed in this building. The name of the Edomite deity Qôs is attested on an inscription. As regards orientation, Beit-Arieh notes that the *bāmāh* at Qitmit is quite closely oriented to the four winds and that there is an overall southern orientation toward the land of Edom.

Combining both complexes, we emerge with four principal components at Qitmit: 1) a building and court where a *maṣṣēbāh* stood, 2) a *liškāh* with three rooms, 3) an altar with cistern and water channel, 4) a *bāmāh*. Anticipating further discussions, we provisionally suggest that the cult installation at Qitmit, situated on a hill away from any settlement, is of the type mentioned in the narrative of Samuel and Saul, preserved in 1 Samuel 9. With this in mind, we return to our discussion of phenomenology.

The essential phenomenology of open-air altars in courtyards, whether or not they relate functionally to roofed buildings, expresses a two-dimensional, or bi-directional dynamic. The vertical orientation is towards the heavens, where God, or the gods in polytheistic pantheons, is perceived as normally residing. The sun, moon, and stars, usually personified or synthesized in some way, are

---

[8] See P. Beck's article in this volume.

also found in the heavens, of course. At times, mountain peaks also express the vertical dimension.

In the earliest performances of cultic rites associated with outdoor altars, it was assumed that the deity was not automatically to be found at the site of worship. It was necessary to invite or attract him to the site. Only when the rites of invocation had been performed in an efficacious manner, was the deity assumed to be present at the site, either sitting on an outdoor platform, a *bāmāh*, or housed in a roofed building, perceived as a residence. At that point, the dynamics of spatial orientation turned horizontal, even though we often find some angle of ascent evident in the architectural design. Rites were then directed toward a present, or resident deity, who had descended to earth, arriving at the site in response to his worshippers. Biblical literature then describes the worshippers as being *lpny* YHWH, an essential horizontal image in its cultic applications.

More is known and more has been said about the horizontal phenomenology. Careful investigation of the designation *lpny* YHWH in biblical usage shows that it also occurs in narratives which tell of human-divine encounters where a vertical orientation is projected. In Genesis 18, we read of divine messengers, perceived as manifestations of God, who visit Abraham and announce Isaac's birth. At a certain point in the narrative the theme of the wickedness of Sodom and Gomorrah is introduced. The angels are assigned the mission of inspecting those towns. In verses 21–22 God speaks as follows:

> I will descend (אֵרֲדָה נָּא) to observe whether its outcry, which has reached me, corresponds to what they have committed irreversibly; and if this is not so—I will know that, as well. The men then changed course, proceeding to Sodom, while Abraham was still standing in the presence of the LORD (וְאַבְרָהָם עוֹדֶנּוּ עֹמֵד, לִפְנֵי ה').

In this narrative, God is perceived as having descended to earth, in angelic manifestation, and Abraham can be regarded as standing in his presence. The descent of God, conveyed by the verb *yārad*, is a major theme in the biblical epic tradition. It sheds light on the meaning and function of the *bāmāh*. Outside biblical literature, a cognate of the term *bāmāh* occurs in the Moabite Mesha inscription, where we also find the cognate of the composite term *bêt bāmôt* "a house for *bāmāh*-platforms" (cf. 1 Kings 12:31). Hebrew *bāmāh* exhibits a Ugaritic cognate, *bmt*, referring to the back, or shoulders of a pack animal. In the Amarna letters one usually encounters the formal salutation in which a subordinate affirms that from afar he has prostrated himself before his lord: *i-na pa-an-te-e ù ṣi-ru-ma*, which probably means: "from the top of the body all the way down to the back," if, indeed, we are dealing with the same noun.[9]

---

[9] See B.A. Levine, "Cult Places, Israelite," in *Encylopaedia Judaica*, vol. 5 (New York, 1971), pp. 1165–67. For the Ugaritic cognate, see M. Dietrich, et al., *Die keilalphabetischen Texte aus Ugarit* (Neukirchen-Vluyn, 1976) (AOAT 24), texts numbered 1.4, col. IV, lines 19–20 and 1.19, col. II, line 10, for *bmt pḥl* "The back of a mare." For

Parts of the body, human and animal, but especially human, are applied to the natural, topographical and geographical features of heaven and earth. As a result, *kitpê hārîm*, literally shoulders of the mountains," means "mountain ridges," and *bāmôtê ʾāreṣ*; means "the back-parts, shoulders of the earth," hence "the plateaus" or "high-points of the earth." A corollary to the semantic transfer from body to natural world is another semantic shift from man-made structures to parts of the body. Thus, we have: *ṣelaʿ hammiškān*, literally "the rib of the Tabernacle."

Thus with respect to the term *bāmāh* we can postulate that the structural *bāmāh* represented the high-places of the earth. It was the platform on which the deity touched down after his descent. Micah 1:3 refers to this:

> Behold, the LORD is exiting His place, He will descend, treading on the high-points of the earth. וְיָרַד וְדָרַךְ עַל-בָּמוֹתֵי-אָרֶץ

The structural *bāmāh*, like the raised *temenos* in Mesopotamia and elsewhere, realized the separation of the holy from the profane vertically, a point stressed by Jacobsen, just as the delineation of zones and gradated exclusion and heightened purity accomplished this objective in the horizontal perspective, a point emphasized so precisely by Haran.

The cache of objects discovered in the area of the *bāmāh* at Qitmit suggests that it might have been a pedestal for one or more deities, or that symbolic cult objects were placed on or near the *bāmāh*.

What happens, of course, is that once a term like *bāmāh* enters into use, it can assume further, less precise connotations and refer to the complete cult installation, which seems to be the case in 1 Samuel 9. Once a *bāmāh* is moved indoors, it becomes a veritable *mākôn* ("dais"), a term also reflected in Ugaritic. Thus in Exodus 15, *mākôn lĕšibtĕkā* indicates the function of the artifact: "a dais for you to sit upon." The *bāmāh* is essentially the platform on which the deity sits, or it may be manifest in some graphic form after arriving at the cult-site. It is possible, of course, to place an altar on a large *bāmāh*-platform, but more often than not, the altar was a separate artifact, located near the *bāmāh*, as at Qitmit.

With respect to the altar itself, there remains a degree of uncertainty as to whether the verb *d/z-b-ḥ* in West Semitic languages necessarily involves slaughter of animals, or whether, like Akkadian *zîbu*, "meal, food offering," the West

---

bmt and *bt bmt* in Moabite, see J. Gibson, *Textbook of Syrian Semitic Inscriptions*, vol. 1 (Oxford, 1971), pp. 74–75, in the Mesha inscription. The singular: *hbmt zʾt* "this *bāmāh*-platform" occurs in line 3, and *bt bmt*, usually understood as a toponym, is in line 27. In *CAD B*, 78–79, s.v. *bamtu* B "rib chest," hence: "thorax of an animal," is differentiated lexically from pl. tantum: *bamâtu* (*ibid.* 76–77) "open country, plain," But, this predication of two unrelated vocables is questionable, since in the Izbu Commentary 1935, cited by *CAD B*, s.v. *bamâtu*, a synonym of *ba-ma-a-tum* is given as *ṣe-e-rum*, thus connecting the two components of the epistolary formula.

Semitic verbal root realized in the term *mizbēaḥ/mdbḥ* would be appropriate for presentational offerings not involving slaughter, such as first-fruits, cakes, etc.[10] Even archaeologically, there is some vagueness concerning what altars were used for in actual practice. Altars have been found with blood smeared on their sides, or with grooves cut into the stone top, presumably for blood to drain, as well as with ash and evidence of actual burning on their tops. Where burned-out pits are discovered adjacent to altars, it seems that sacrifices were first roasted near the altar, and only then placed upon it. The disposition of most sacrifices prescribed in the Bible, where parts of the sacrifice were burned on the altar and the rest prepared separately, also defines the function of the sacrificial altar. 1 Samuel 2 speaks of pots and forks for cooking parts of sacrifices. In any event, the location of the altar in an open courtyard reflects both the vertical and the horizontal directioning discussed above. This is most clearly evident in the phenomenology of the burnt offering, variously called *iššeh*, "offering of fire" *ʿôlāh* "burnt offering," and also: *kālîl*, "holocaust".

In Judges 13, we find what seems to be an etiology of the burnt, altar offering and of the altar as the point from which it ascends. (The most persuasive etymology of Hebrew *ʿôlāh*, based on the verb *ʿālāh*, is that the flames and smoke "ascend" from the altar.)

> And it happened that as the flame arose from atop the altar heavenward (*haššāmaymāh*), the angel of YHWH ascended in the altar flame... (Judges 13:20)

Movement in the reverse direction is to be found in the narrative of Elijah's encounter with the Baʿal priests, as recounted in 1 Kings 18. In verse 24 we read: "The deity who responds in the form of fire, he is the true deity:" and, in verse 38:

> The fire of YHWH fell and consumed the *ʿôlāh* and the wood and the stones, and the dirt, and the water in the channel it lapped up.

As noted above, a water channel was found at the altar at Qitmit, and an elaborate channel for water was discovered by A. Biran at Tel Dan.[11] These discoveries prompt a different reading of the Elijah narrative.

The immediate context, highlighting the need for rain, may cause us to ignore the more general significance of the water channel depicted in 1 Kings 18. That text refers to stone and dirt, and indicates what altars were *usually* made of. The water channel should also be understood as a common feature at the altar, for sacrificial material often had to be washed and water libations were more common than the biblical reader might assume.

---

[10] See the discussion of this problem by B.A. Levine, *In the Presence of the Lord* (Leiden, 1974), Appendix 1, pp. 115–117.

[11] See A. Biran, "The Temenos at Dan," *Eretz-Israel* 16 (H. M. Orlinsky Volume, 1982):15–43.

At this point, it would be well to discuss Exodus 20 where we find pre-Deuteronomic legislation regarding altar building. This legislation prohibits the use of hewn stone (*gāzît*) in altars, for the reason that metal instruments would have been utilized in dressing the stones. Although a remarkable example of an altar of hewn stone, reconstructed to be sure, was reassembled by Y. Aharoni at Beersheba, it is noteworthy that most reported altars (with the exception of sculpted, stone incense altars like those found at Tel Miqne), were made of unworked stones, occasionally with stone slabs serving as the altar tops.[12] This fact is carefully documented in Amihai Mazar's report on Tell Qasile and suggests the need for further investigation of attitudes toward the use of metals in the cult. This theme seems to correlate with the evidence for natural rocks used as altars.[13] Also relevant in the provisions of Exodus 20, is the theme of divine arrival at the altar site:

This statement is best rendered:

בְּכָל-הַמָּקוֹם אֲשֶׁר אַזְכִּיר אֶת-שְׁמִי אָבוֹא אֵלֶיךָ וּבֵרַכְתִּיךָ

> At whichever cult-place I allow My name to be pronounced, I shall come to you and grant you blessing.

More should be said of the horizontal phenomenology. Some years ago, we noted that the *ʿôlāh* ("holocaust") consistently preceded the *šĕlāmîm* ("sacred gifts of greeting") in composite sacrificial rites.[14] To us, this meant that the deity had first to be attracted to the site and to indicate his readiness to descend and respond before humans could bring their petitions before him. It occurs to me that attraction may have been the function of incense offerings, as well. What may have happened in Israelite cults (and conceivably, in other cults, as well), was that as burnt, altar offerings assumed more prominence, they appropriated the functions of incense. The pleasing aroma of the burnt, altar offering rose heavenward, taking over the vertical dimension, while incense was moved indoors (or nearer the cult object representing the deity outdoors) and its function was horizontalized, so to speak. Incense now pleased the deity who had already arrived at the site!

What we learned further from Jacobsen's study is that gifts of greeting were offered in the courtyards of Mesopotamian temples, prior to entry. We had related the Hebrew term *šĕlāmîm*, with cognates in Ugaritic epic and ritual texts, to Akkadian *šulmânû*, the very term designating the "gifts of greeting" offered in temple courtyards. So, if the *ʿôlāh*-holocaust reflects the vertical phenome-

---

[12] Stone incense altars have been found in significant numbers at Tel Nagila, and are discussed in detail, with comparative data, by S. Gitin, "Incense Altars from Ekron, Israel and Judah: Context and Typology," in *Eretz-Israel* 20 (Y. Yadin Volume, 1989):52–67.

[13] See A. Mazar, *Excavations at Tell Qasile* (*Qedem* 12) (Jerusalem, 1980), Table 15: "Sacrificial Altars in the Levant and in Cyprus," p. 72. Also see Table 13: "Raised Platforms in Temples of the Levant," p. 69.

[14] See Levine, *In the Presence* (see note 10), pp. 26–27.

nology, the attractive rite directed heavenward, the *šĕlāmîm* initiated the horizontal phenomenology. The deity had arrived in response to the holocaust and was now being greeted by his worshippers who, like those in attendance upon the lord in his manor-house, waited in the main courtyard before being admitted. As Jacobsen explains, pursuant to Frankfort's insight, the courtyard was reserved for the more menial tasks, like cooking, and was secondary to the house itself. All of this analysis is predicated on the reasonable assumption that temples are domiciles, and indeed, during many periods of history and in diverse areas, temples have been modeled after residences.

What has been discussed above is relevant for explaining why altars were located in the courtyards of temple buildings. What can be said, however, of the persisting pattern of locating altars in open courtyards where there were no roofed structures and no buildings at all standing in an architectural relationship to the altar? It is difficult to imagine that altars were built to stand alone, with no visible, physical cult object, such as a *maṣṣēbāh, in situ*. Sacrificial worship takes place, after all, in spatial relationship to a deity, or deities, who must be represented in some way. Possible exceptions may be peak cult-sites where a topographical proximity to celestial deities was presumed to be sufficient evidence of a divine presence, or altars placed adjacent to natural sites perceived as divine, such as rivers. For the most part, however, one assumes that even in Israelite religion, with its aniconic conception of divinity, a physical sign of divine presence was required. Ultimately, this function was assumed in biblical Israel by the Ark of the Covenant. Before the objection to *maṣṣēbôt* and Asherah representations became pronounced, we are to assume that it was normal to have a *maṣṣēbāh* at Israelite cult sites (and at others, of course). There was at least one operative *maṣṣēbāh* at Arad; probably two, at certain periods. This conclusion is suggested by Hosea 3:4, which H. L. Ginsberg assigns to the 9th century B.C.E.:

כִּי יָמִים רַבִּים יֵשְׁבוּ בְּנֵי יִשְׂרָאֵל אֵין מֶלֶךְ וְאֵין שָׂר וְאֵין זֶבַח וְאֵין מַצֵּבָה וְאֵין אֵפוֹד וּתְרָפִים

> For a long time, the Israelite people shall live without kings or princes, without offerings or *maṣṣēbôt*, without *ʾēpôd* or *terāpîm*.

This statement is to be taken as a projection of societal well-being, the very quality lost by the northern Israelite kingdom as punishment for its infidelity. If there is any doubt as to the initial legitimacy of the *maṣṣēbāh*, Genesis 28 will dispel it. That northern-Israelite narrative, a *hieros-logos* of Bethel, incorporates most of the ingredients of a phenomenology of cult-stelae, and of open-air cult sites generally.

Consider the following features of this narrative:

1) In Jacob's dream theophany, angels are ascending and descending a ladder to heaven. This scene surely expresses the vertical dynamic, whether or not we accept the view that Jacob's ladder represented the ziggurat typology.

2) Jacob's reaction to the descent of the divinity envisioned in the dream is worth noting:

אָכֵן יֵשׁ יְהוָה בַּמָּקוֹם הַזֶּה וְאָנֹכִי לֹא יָדָעְתִּי

Assuredly, YHWH is present at this cult-site, but I was unaware of it.

3) Most telling is the projected function of the *maṣṣēbāh*, anointed and dedicated by Jacob. I regard this scene as basic for our overall understanding of the role of the *maṣṣēbāh*. A *maṣṣēbāh* commemorates; it marks the spirit of a significant event or experience in the life of the religious group. A *maṣṣēbāh* may mark a grave, of course, or the place of a victory; or, as in our case, the sanctity of a site selected by a deity, where a theophany had occurred. A later word for *maṣṣēbāh* is *ṣiyyûn* "marker" (2 Kings 23:17, Ezekiel 39:15). As a matter of fact, Jacob raised more than one stela in his career!

So, Bethel is a site fit for a temple, *bêt ʾelohîm*, a gateway to heaven, *šaʿar haššāmāyîm*, both terms expressing the vertical phenomenology. In verse 22, which concludes the narrative, the *maṣṣēbāh*, it is said, will become a temple, thus suggesting the growth of the cult-site from an open-air courtyard to a roofed temple.

To one who reasonably inquires why it is that in biblical narratives about altar building we do not consistently read of a *maṣṣēbāh* or Asherah, I would answer the following: perhaps such information was suppressed, or left out of certain biblical narratives as a result of the eventual condemnation of such artifacts. They may have not been discredited in and of themselves, but precisely because they were an integral component of an altar-based cult system. As Ginsberg has proposed, the movement toward cult centralization, highlighted in Deuteronomy, actually originated in northern Israel and was related to Second Hosea's 8th century polemic against the many altars which had been erected under royal sponsorship in northern Israel. It is in Deuteronomy, after all, where we read the most vocal prohibitions of the *maṣṣēbāh*.[15]

Recalling the two complexes at Qitmit—the one with the *maṣṣēbāh* and the other with the *bāmāh*, we are prompted to attempt an explanation of the relationship between these two components of the overall complex. We propose that a cult complex such as that at Qitmit was structured so as to afford worshippers and celebrants an experience in two dimensions. The visitor worshipped at Qitmit in front of the *maṣṣēbāh* which commemorated the historic presence of the deity, a theophany signifying the selection of the site by the deity as sacred space. The *bāmāh* provided another experience, the dramatic appearance of the deity in response to sacrificial worship, a phenomenon which occurs anew each

---

[15] See H.L. Ginsberg, *The Israelian Heritage of Judaism* (New York, 1982), pp. 19–24.

time the deity is ritually invoked, or attracted. This is what it meant to say that a worshipper stood *lpny YHWH* “in the presence of YHWH.”[16]

---

[16] The author wishes to thank P. Beck and I. Beit-Arieh for personally discussing the excavations at Ḥorvat Qitmit and the cultic finds at the site with him.

Ritual as Symbol: Modes of Sacrifice in Israelite Religion*

In the Land of Israel of biblical times, as elsewhere in the ancient Near East and the Mediterranean world, temples and other cult installations were built with established cultic rites in mind or with the purpose of instituting new or revised rites. The result was that the architectural plans of ancient temples and the placement of installed artifacts within their sacred space expressed or reflected intended functions. Conversely, the choreography of cultic celebrations was itself conditioned by certain notions of space and location deriving from customary building methods and designs and from the relationship of human construction to the natural environment—to mountains and rivers. It would be of great value, therefore, were we able to choreograph the celebration of the biblical sacrificial rites so as to link function to form, in the same way that plans of excavated ancient temples are redrawn so that we can now visualize how they might have looked.

Ultimately, both art and architecture, as well as the choreography of performance, hark back to phenomenology, to the perceived meaning of ritual in its various forms. We need to understand how differing modes of sacrifice signified the different meanings attributed to various ritual celebrations.

A basic question poses itself at the outset: Where was the deity presumed to be, in spatial terms, when the sacrifice was initiated? Essentially, temples and other cult installations were conceived as divine residences or as visitation sites of the gods. Basic to the phenomenology of worship is the perception that the deity must be invited, often attracted to the cult-site; that we cannot presume, as a generalization, that the deity is always present or in residence at the site before the worship sequence begins. In other words, we should seek to determine from analyzing the mode of a particular sacrificial rite where the deity is perceived as being when the rite was about to commence. If the mode indicates that the deity is, indeed, perceived to be present at that point, it remains to explain how he got there. I have discussed this subject in an essay entitled "Phenomenology of the Open-Air-Altar in Biblical Israel"[1] and in scholarly lectures.

---

* Originally published in B. M. Gittlen (ed.), *Sacred Time, Sacred Space* (Winona Lake, IN: Eisenbrauns, 2002), pp. 125–135. Reprinted with permission from Eisenbrauns.

[1] B. A. Levine, "*Lpny YHWH*—Phenomenology of the Open-Air-Altar in Biblical Israel," in *Biblical Archaeology Today: Proceedings of the Second International Congress on Biblical Archaeology, Jerusalem, June 1990* (Jerusalem: Israel Exploration Society, 1993) 196–205 {*VOL 1, PP. 259–69*}.

Corollary to the question of divine whereabouts is the zoning of sacred space within cult edifices and their courtyards, including the process of enclosure and the raising of terrain. The demarcation of zones on the basis of gradated sanctity, as Menahem Haran has shown, not only served to restrict and control human access but to lend a particular character to certain, more sacred areas, those in which the deity (or deities) resided, or sat, when they were present. This process was clearly expressed in architectural design and the planned use of space, and it correlates with the purificatory rites associated with temples. The requirements of purity also affected the stationing of cultic personnel and the storing of *Opfermaterie*, in addition to limiting the access of worshippers. Purity requirements thus determined to a large degree what took place in various sectors of the temple and its environs and how the temple plan was executed.

To clarify the methodology I will employ in the present inquiry I will first state how I read Priestly sources, such as those preserved in Exodus, Leviticus, and Numbers, that speak of a portable Sanctuary (variously termed *miškān*, *ʾōhel môʿēd*). I take them to be projections of the *ritus* of the Jerusalem Temple at various periods of biblical history. What is more, it is my view that the Holiness School and the authors of the *Priesterschrift* were operating with the Deuteronomic requirement of a single, central temple. Consequently, such Priestly sources, notwithstanding their wilderness scenery and nomadic terminology, should be interpreted against the reality of a stationary temple edifice, with gates and courtyards.

With considerations of form and space in mind, an attempt will be made here to discuss the modes of biblical sacrifice, factoring in several variables as we proceed. These variables include:

1. The manner of disposing of an offering—whether or not an altar was used and whether the offering, in whole or in part, was burned on an altar and turned into smoke.
2. The primary location where the offering was presented within sacred space, whether inside a covered edifice or under the open sky, as in a courtyard.
3. The basic state of the offering, whether prepared and/or processed or whether offered in unprocessed form—as it was harvested, for example.
4. The materials or substances used in comprising or concocting the offering: the recipe.

At the risk of oversimplification, I would state at the outset that Israelite sacrifice was realized in three primary modes: (a) The mode of presentation and display before the deity. The deity was perceived as viewing the offering—favorably, it was hoped. Once accepted or received in this way by the deity, the offering would be consumed by priests and in some cases by donors. The substance of the offering may or may not have been prepared for consumption before presentation. In ancient Near Eastern perspective, the modes of presentation and display were the most pervasive. (b) The mode of offering prepared food, intended for a sacred meal in the company of the deity, with the deity variously perceived as host or as guest. This mode is exemplified by the *zebaḥ*, a term that I take to be cognate with Akkadian *zibū* ('meal') and that does not, in the first instance, mean 'slain offering' or the like, although it was often realized in that way. Ugaritic temple rituals often describe the *zebaḥ* mode (*dbḥ*, in Ugaritic), and in fact this term was generalized to connote any major celebration, including a sacred feast. (c) The mode of the burnt altar offering. The rising, aromatic smoke of the offering is thought to be inhaled by the deity and in this way ingested, or consumed, by him. The ultimate logic of this mode is realized in the holocaust, which feeds the deity food in its most extremely reduced form. At times, incense was utilized in this mode, although it also had other functions.

In actual practice, most biblical sacrifices were realized in mixed modes and methods of disposition, representing adaptations and combinations of the primary modes. Thus, parts of them might be cooked and other parts burned on the altar, as was the case with most prescribed forms of the *zebaḥ* and *ḥaṭṭāʾt* ('sin offering'). Or most of the offering might be presented, with only a small part of it burned on the altar. Methodologically, it would be useful to trace certain sacrifices back to their original form, to the extent that this is possible, so as to be able to consider the development of Israelite sacrifice.

In the course of writing the Leviticus commentary, I became aware of a pattern of development in the disposition of the grain offering, or *minḥâ*, that clearly illustrates a process of modal adaptation and that may serve as a model. I hope to go a bit further here in analyzing the presentational mode by focusing on forms of the *minḥâ* in particular, making reference to other modes by contrast.

Both etymologically and in terms of its known character, the *minḥâ* of biblical worship is best viewed as a presentation offering, most often but not exclusively in baked or other prepared form. The verb *nāḥâ* means 'to conduct, to lead', so that nominal *minḥâ* bears the sense of something brought. The term *minḥâ*, like many others designating cultic gifts, comes from the administrative vocabulary. It means 'tribute, gift' and is so used in the Hebrew Bible itself, without reference to ritual. The locus classicus is 2 Kgs 3:4: "Mesha, king of Moab, was a herder, and he remitted (*hēšîb*) to the king of Israel as tribute (*minḥâ*) 100,000 fattened lambs and the wool of 100,000 rams."

In the cultic vocabulary, the term *minḥâ* came to designate a grain offering, whereas it may have been a generic term for any kind of sacrificial offering. In Gen 4:3–4, both the animals of Abel and the produce of Cain are referred to as *minḥâ*, but it remains an open question whether animals and fowl were ever actually offered in ancient Israel in the purely presentational mode. It seems more likely that in relatively early times they may have been disposed of in the *zebaḥ* mode but without recourse to an altar of burnt offerings, much in the way of the paschal *zebaḥ* of Exodus 12–13, originally a domestic sacrifice. We must also bear in mind that an altar was conceived as a table and that not every altar was an altar of burnt offerings. Altars were also used for presentation, just as they served as a locus for gods to join in meals with their devotees. Archaeologists have found very early altars in Canaan of pre-Israelite times, their sides spattered with blood, but with no evidence of burning on them. The enigmatic account of 1 Sam 14:32–35 may reflect the same practice in ancient Israel of desacralizing the *zebaḥ* by offering its blood on the altar before roasting a sacrifice or cooking it in pots. So, we should not conclude that the utilization of an altar, on the one hand, and presentation, on the other, are mutually exclusive modes of sacrifice, although the preponderance of the biblical evidence might suggest this conclusion. What we do not know about the early development of Israelite ritual far exceeds what we do know.

Let us begin with a careful analysis of Leviticus 23, the festival calendar representative of the Holiness School, for information on the presentational mode in biblical worship at a rather late stage in its overall development. Leviticus 23 shows evidence of the adaptation of the *minḥâ* from a presentation offering to an expanded rite that included burnt offerings. The section beginning in Lev 23:16–17 is most relevant to our discussion. Israelites are to bring from their settlements *minḥâ ḥădāšâ lYHWH* ('an offering of new grain to YHWH'). It is to consist of two loaves classified as *tĕnûpâ* ('raised, elevated offering') made of a specified quantity of semolina flour. These loaves are then designated *bikkûrîm lYHWH* ('offerings of firstfruits to YHWH'). This is to occur annually, seven sabbatical weeks after the first sheaf (*ʿōmer*) of new barley grain had been brought to the priest by the Israelites, likewise 'raised' by him (the verb *hēnîp*) in the presence of YHWH (Lev 23:10–11). With the passage of seven weeks, wheat from the new harvest had become available, hence the prescribed semolina. The *minḥâ* of *bikkûrîm* was to be baked in a *tannûr* of unleavened dough, *ḥāmēṣ*.

There can be little doubt that what has just been described constituted a complete, or sufficient, rite in and of itself—one expressive of presentation and display. This description contrasts with what we read immediately following, in Lev 23:18–20. There we are told what was to accompany the *bikkûrîm* offering. The relevant formula is: *wĕhiqrabtem ʿal halleḥem* 'You shall offer in addition to the bread' or 'together with the bread', thereby implying what the essential *bikkûrîm* offering had consisted of. An entire regimen of animal sacrifices is now prescribed as accompaniment, even including additional grain offerings and libations. I take Lev 23:18–20 to be redactional, introduced by a subsequent Priestly legislator who knew of the adapted grain offerings of Leviticus 2, for instance where we also encounter a *minḥâ* of first-fruits (Lev 2:14–16). The same redactional pattern is evident earlier on in vv. 12–13, where the *ʿōmer* was to be accompanied by a similar, though less elaborate, regimen of sacrifices.

However, the primary presentational mode of the *minḥâ* of firstfruits of Leviticus 23 had not initially involved any use of the altar of burnt offerings whatsoever. The standard Priestly adaptations, such as those prescribed in Leviticus 2, differ in this regard; they effect an internal change in the disposition of the *minḥâ* itself with the result that some part of it went into the altar fire, thereby satisfying the superimposed requirement of burnt offerings. In Leviticus 23, the presentation offering was expanded by combination with other rites that themselves make use of the altar while remaining unchanged.

On the face of it, I would conclude that the redactors of the Priestly School, when working with an ancient and honorable offering, may have felt constrained not to alter its internal character. But, when prescribing their own regimen of rituals, as in Leviticus 2, they felt free to structure them so as to incorporate the requirement of a burnt altar offering. We shall see below how they did this.

Against Israel Knohl (and others who hold similar views), who has recently analyzed Leviticus 23 with an eye to demonstrating that the Priestly Torah (PT) antedates the writings of the Holiness School (H), of which the core of Leviticus 23 is a salient part, the above analysis may be offered as partial rebuttal. Knohl does not give sufficient weight to the redaction of Lev 23:9–23, or he may not acknowledge this redaction. Surely in structural terms, or in terms of mode, it is arguable that the primary *bikkûrîm* offering of Leviticus 23, representing the Holiness School, was entirely presentational and for display and that its adaptation in the direction of the burnt offering is secondary and hence subsequent. A reverse process would appear to be less arguable.[2]

That offerings of firstfruits were characteristically presentational may be inferred from Deuteronomy 26, which informs us how one kind of offering of firstfruits, presumably in the harvested state rather than having been prepared as food, was presented. An Israelite was to take of the 'first' or 'prime' fruits (Hebrew *rēʾšît*) of the earth, place it in a covered basket of some sort, and proceed to the central Temple. He was to hand the basket of firstfruits over to the priest, who would then set it down (the verb *hēnîaḥ*) in front of the altar. The offerant declared that he had settled n the land in fulfillment of God's promise, and in gratitude, was now desacralizing the firstfruits of the land. Presumably, *mizbaḥ Yhwh ʾĕlōhêkā* ('the altar of YHWH, your God') of Deut 26:4 refers to the altar of burnt offerings that stood in the Temple courtyard, and yet no subsequent use of that altar is indicated in the performance of the rite. Now, this rite is not designated *minḥâ*, truth be told, although it qualifies as such. It is cited here to exemplify the presentational mode applicable to offerings of the firstfruits of the earth. I would conclude that Deuteronomy 26 is speaking of an earlier from of the *minḥâ* of firstfruits ultimately legislated in Leviticus 23.

We should now trace other adaptations of the presentational *minḥâ* in the direction of the burnt offering. One step is represented by the 'bread of display' (*leḥem happānîm*) as ordained in Lev 24:5–8. The sense of *pānîm* in this terminology relates to being in the divine presence or purview. Twelve loaves are baked from semolina flour and placed on two purified tables constructed for that purpose. Other biblical sources, while giving evidence of the relative antiquity of the Bread of Display, also indicate that the one or two tables, as the case may

---

[2] See I. Knohl, "The Priestly Torah Versus the Holiness School: Sabbath and the Festivals," *HUCA* 58 (1987) 65–117; and now *idem*, *The Sanctuary of Silence* (Minneapolis: Fortress, 1995).

be, stood inside the Sanctuary building; actually, near the altar of incense (see 1 Samuel 27; 1 Kings 7; Exod 35:13, 39:36; Num 4:7). Although the text of Lev 24:5–8 is not explicit in calling the bread of display *ḥāmēṣ*, it was, like the *minḥâ* of firstfruits, not baked as *maṣṣôt*, a point whose significance will become apparent below.

The adaptation of *leḥem happānîm* was realized by placing containers of pure frankincense on the set tables. The frankincense was lit, with the aroma ascending as a burnt offering. It served as an *ʾazkārâ* ('token') of the presentational *minḥâ*, thereby satisfying the requirement of a burnt, altar offering in the process.

The method of utilizing a substance pinched off from the offering in place of the whole offering, as a token representing the offering, called *ʾazkārâ*, is first encountered in the types of *minḥâ* ordained in Leviticus 2. The suggested sense of Hebrew *ʾazkārâ* as 'token' comes from the Akkadian cognate *zikru* 'effigy', an explanation first proposed by G. R. Driver. This, then, is a significant adaptation: a fistful of the dough of the *minḥâ*, now unleavened in accordance with Priestly law, is burned on the altar, and the rest of the dough is baked, fried, and so forth. The ultimate adaptation of the *minḥâ* was realized in the *minḥâ* holocaust (*kālîl*), also ordained in Leviticus 2.

Leviticus 24 shows what pains were taken to preserve the presentational character of a relatively ancient offering, the Bread of Display. We observe how a device routinely employed by legislators of the Priestly school, the *ʾazkārâ* is, itself, adapted to the needs of *leḥem happānîm*. No part of the loaves ever reached any altar, inside or outside the Sanctuary building—frankincense was just placed near the loaves and lit to give its aroma.

To understand modes of presentation and their adaptation requires, of course, reviewing the substances used in the offerings themselves and the way these substances were prepared. The most significant fact pertaining to the primary *minḥâ* of firstfruits of Leviticus 23 is that it was baked of leavened dough, of *ḥāmēṣ*, not in the form of *maṣṣôt* ('unleavened cakes'). There were several offerings made of leavened dough, additional to the ones already reviewed, and in all of them recourse to the altar was either limited or absent entirely.

The *tôdâ* ('thanksgiving offering') was made of *ḥāmēṣ*, as we learn from Lev 7:12–15. The code of Lev 7:11–27 details the various types of *zebaḥ šĕlāmîm* ('sacred offerings of greeting'). It stipulates, *ʾim tôdâ yaqrîbennû* ('If one offers it [namely, a *šĕlāmîm*] to serve as, or for, a thanksgiving offering'), the following specifications apply. The main offering under discussion, the *šĕlāmîm*, is partially an altar offering, consisting of both animals and a grain offering, variously prepared. Then we read: *ʿal ḥallōt leḥem ḥāmēṣ yaqrîb qorbānô* ('with loaves of leavened bread added shall he make his offering'), namely, his *šĕlāmîm* offering of thanksgiving (Lev 7:13). Reference to the loaves of the thanksgiving offering is introduced almost as an aside, as an accompaniment to the *šĕlāmîm*. This is the reverse of what we saw in Leviticus 23, where it was the *zebaḥ* component that was introduced as an accompaniment.

There is, however, good reason to believe that the grain offering of *tôdâ*, made of *ḥāmēṣ* ('unleavened dough'), originated as a separate and sufficient sacrifice, one whose independent origin is submerged in Leviticus 7. This is intimated by the provision of Lev 22:29–30, where the composite *tôdâ*, as known to us from Lev 7:11–15, is prescribed separately from the other types of *zebaḥ* stipulated immediately preceding: those serving as payment of vows and as free-will offerings. The *tôdâ* is not one of a bound group of three, as was true in Leviticus 7.

More specifically, it is from Amos 4:4–5 that the distinctiveness of the *tôdâ* becomes apparent. The prophet castigates the worshippers of Bethel:

> Come to Bethel and transgress;
> To Gilgal and transgress even more:
> Present your sacred meals (*zibḥêkem*) the next morning
> And your titles on the third day;
> Burn a thanksgiving offering (*tôdâ*) from leavened dough,
> And proclaim free will offerings loudly,
> For you love that sort of thing, O Israelites.

The prophetic criticism voiced in the above passage hardly pertains to modes of sacrifice but, rather, to Israel's tendency to mistake the purpose of worship generally. There is, however, the problem of burning the *tôdâ*, which is what the Piel form, *qiṭṭēr*, must necessarily mean. After all, in Priestly ritual law, *ḥāmēṣ* could not be burned on the altar, and what is more, it is doubtful whether the *tôdâ* was ever intended as a holocaust. Either the *ʾazkārâ* method was in practice in Amos's day or, as is much more likely, incense was offered in conjunction with the *tôdâ*, which was itself baked and eaten by priests, thereby making the disposition of the *tôdâ* similar to that of the Bread of Display. Generally, usage of *qiṭṭēr* refers to the burning of incense. So the problematic Amos passage does not contradict the definition of the *tôdâ* offering as presentational.

To summarize up to this point, I would say that there is ample biblical evidence for projecting a development in the mode of the *minḥâ* and other offerings of the fruits of the earth, however classified, from a presentation offering to a burnt, altar offering. This development reflects the rising importance of the burnt offering, whose phenomenology will be discussed as we proceed.

It would now be well to identify the venue of the several primarily presentational offerings that have been discussed thus far. The Bread of Display (*leḥem happānîm*) was presented inside the Sanctuary, with the pure frankincense set down next to the loaves serving as a burnt offering. We note that the altar of incense was located inside the Sanctuary. As has just been suggested, the *tôdâ* referred to by Amos may have also been accompanied by an incense offering and would have also been brought inside the Sanctuary. It is likely, however, that the *tôdâ* of Leviticus 7 was part of a larger rite performed near the altar of burnt offerings in the Sanctuary courtyard, and the same was true of the *minḥâ* of firstfruits, as prescribed in Leviticus 23. This may be inferred from Deuteronomy 26, where the offering of firstfruits was set down in front of the altar of burnt offerings in the courtyard. The conclusion is that the presentational mode was characteristic of offerings brought both inside the Sanctuary and in the courtyard. We should not dismiss the likelihood, however, that an offering may have been presented initially inside the Sanctuary, shown to the deity, and then taken out to the courtyard for disposition. This pattern is evident in Ugaritic descriptive rituals and, effectively, all over the ancient Near East. After all, few ancient ritual texts fully choreograph the sacrificial rites that they describe.

We note in passing that, practically speaking, the only type of burnt offering that could be performed inside the covered Sanctuary was an incense offering; offerings of which any part was burned in the altar fire were performed in the open-air courtyard on the altar of burnt offerings. In extreme cases, burning could take place outside the encampment when total destruction was the objective.

Passing mention was made above of the offering designated *tĕnûpâ* ('raised, elevated offering') and of the verb *hēnîp* ('to raise, elevate'). The priest raised the *ʿōmer* in this manner (Lev 23:11), and seven weeks later, the essential *minḥâ* of firstfruits is called *leḥem tĕnûpâ* ('the bread of the raised offering'). In addition, the accompanying offerings, consisting of animals, were raised over the bread of the firstfruits.

The character of *tĕnûpâ* has been most concisely discussed by Jacob Milgrom, who presents graphic depictions of this mode taken from Egyptian wall paintings.[3] It is the display offering par excellence, and in its essential form, no part of it ascends the altar. *M. Menaḥot* 5:6 provides a postbiblical description of how such offerings were displayed, one that may, for all we know, be a continuation of more ancient practice. The offering was carried to and fro and shown to the deity. Most often, this mode served in biblical rites as a prelude to other forms of disposition; first the offering was shown to the deity and then was disposed of on the altar or in some other way. It is of interest that, whereas the *minḥâ* is set down before the deity, the *tĕnûpâ* is raised to show to him, but essentially the mode is the same.

A remarkable application of the *tĕnûpâ* pertains to the dedication of the Levites, prescribed in Numbers 8. The *tĕnûpâ* is there projected as a multi-phased rite, performed in the courtyard of the Sanctuary, there referred to as *ʾōhel môʿēd* ('the Tent of Assembly'). More precisely, it took place in the area of the courtyard outward of the altar. The display character of the dedication was realized by having the Levites stand near the altar as the Israelites, most likely their representatives, laid their hands on the heads of the Levites. This was a rite of assignment used in any number of sacrificial offerings, and discussed most clearly

---

[3] J. Milgrom, "The Alleged Wave-Offering in Israel and the Ancient Near East," *IEJ* 22 (1972) 33–38; repr. in *Studies in Cultic Theology and Terminology* (Leiden: Brill, 1983) 133–38.

by David Wright.[4] At this point, Aaron raised the Levites as a *tĕnûpâ* in the presence of YHWH. The Levites were an offering given by the Israelite people. They then brought their own offering of atonement, after which the text repeats that Aaron and this sons displayed the Levites as *tĕnûpâ*. What we learn from this application of the *tĕnûpâ* is that its acceptance by the deity was conceived as visual.

It remains to discuss the posture, or venue, of the deity while all of this sacrificing has been going on inside and outside the Temple building. Logically, presentation and display, aimed at having the deity view the offering and hopefully view it with favor, presume that the deity is already present inside the Sanctuary, his residence; or, at less elaborate cult-sites, he is outside on a platform (*bāmâ*) or the like, situated near the altar. In a fully built cult installation, where the altar of burnt offerings is oriented toward the entrance of a building, we may presume that the deity was thought to be able to view what was set down near the courtyard altar, or displayed there, from within the depths of the building.

Elsewhere, I speak of this as the horizontal phenomenology—the contact established once the deity has arrived at the cult site. The realization of the *zebaḥ*, in its various forms, would also seem to presume the near presence of the deity, although the matter is more complex because in its primary form the *zebaḥ* may not have been associated with the altar, or with sanctuaries, as such.

In utter contrast, it would seem that the burnt offering, the offering of fire (*ʾiššeh*), expresses the vertical phenomenology. In my 1974 work, *In the Presence of the Lord*, I first put forth the hypothesis that the *ʿôlâ*, routinely the opening sacrifice in a fixed series, was offered for the purpose of invoking the deity, of attracting him to the cult site.[5] This emerged from an analysis of the Elijah encounter, from the etiological narrative of Judges 6, and from the utilization of *ʿôlôt* by Balaam in his peregrinations (Numbers 22–24). Now I have added to this body of textual evidence an analysis of the open-air cult installation at Edomite Qitmit, whose plan and features I discussed in *Biblical Archaeology Today*.[6] Problems remain of course, but it would seem, as has been suggested thus far, that the growing importance of the burnt altar offering accounts for most of the adaptations of horizontally oriented presentation and display offerings in biblical Israel.

The subject of burnt, altar offerings requires much more study. It is not the typical Near Eastern mode, which is presentation or display, and outside of temples probably the *zebaḥ*. Nor is there solid evidence for its early use in Canaan

[4] D. P. Wright, "The Gesture of Hand Placement in the Hebrew Bible and in Hittite Literature," *JAOS* 106 (1986) 433–46.

[5] B. A. Levine, *In the Presence of the Lord: A Study of the Cult and Some Cultic Terms in Ancient Israel* (Studies in Judaism of Late Antiquity 5; Leiden: E. J. Brill, 1974).

[6] *Idem*, "*Lpny YHWH*—Phenomenology of the Open-Air-Altar" {VOL 1, PP. 259–69}.

of pre-Israelite times. We are now able to trace its path from Eblaite *śarapātu* to Ugaritic *šrp* to biblical *miśrāpâ*, attested only in the plural construct, *miśrĕpôt* (Jer 34:5). The verb *śārap* is, however, frequent in biblical cultic texts.

It is my sense that the introduction of burnt, altar offerings into Canaan comes from Syria and that it may have been introduced by the Israelites, suggesting that they too came from Syria. In other words, the history of burnt offerings in biblical Israel may argue for the Syrian origin of the Israelites themselves. Putting this aside for the moment, suffice it to say that the mode of burnt, altar offerings projects the process of reaching the deity in heaven or far away atop high mountains, by perceiving the deity as inhaling the ascending column of aromatic smoke. Its message is "Come down!" Of course, once the burnt, altar offering more or less took over in the disposition of Israelite sacrifices, it was expressed in those offerings brought before the present deity in horizontal perspective as well. Whereas relatively early biblical accounts speak of the altar fire coming down from heaven, it is likely that Lev 9:24 had fire emitting from within the Sanctuary at the initiation of the altar of burnt offerings and igniting the first sacrifices offered on it.

Having suggested where the deity was during the performance of certain rites, we must similarly locate the worshippers and priests. We have probably tended to underestimate how much was going on in the courtyards of ancient temples. As Thorkild Jacobsen has shown, the courtyard was the venue for many presentations before the deity. In Mesopotamian temples, the *šulmānu* ('sacred gift of greeting') was presented in the courtyard, and in biblical temples of a certain period the same was true of its cognate, the *šĕlāmîm*. Generally, notions of strict purity prevented the entry of ordinary worshippers into the temple building itself; this was even true of priests. These restrictions inevitably shifted a good deal of ritual activity to the courtyard. As temples grew in size, more courtyards were added.[7] It would be interesting to summarize all of the activities consigned to the *ḥāṣēr* of the Temple and to review biblical references to *ḥaṣrôt bêt Yhwh* ('the courtyards of YHWH's Temple').

The phenomenology of the presentational mode directs our attention to both human and divine processionals. The deity, or deities, having alighted on earth in response to invocation or having arrived as inspectors and masters of their domain or to celebrate scheduled rites such as festivals, entered the temple edifice, circumambulated it, and so forth. It was obviously a matter of great significance to know that God was in his holy temple, present and ready to accept the offerings of his people, to hear their petitions, and to bless them. Would that biblical literature afforded more information on the processionals of the God of Israel. There are a few allusions, but the clearest reference is in Psalm 24, as is well known. This psalm is of three parts, which bear analysis. The psalm opens with a statement of God's status as creator of the world, thereby reflecting the

---

[7] T. Jacobsen, "The Mesopotamian Temple Plan and the Kititum Temple," *Eretz-Israel* 20 (Yadin Volume; 1989) 79–91.

perception of the physical Temple compound as *axis mundi*. It continues with a rite of entry, rhetorically asking who may ascend the mount of the Lord and replying with an ethical modulation of the requirement of purity, defined as clean hands and a pure heart (compare Isaiah 1). The last part of the psalm achieves the meeting of man and God. The worthy worshippers have entered, and now God enters:

> O gates, lift up your heads!
> Up high, you everlasting doors,
> So the King of Glory may enter!

Now, the presentation offerings may proceed.

The Cultic Scene in Biblical Religion: Hebrew ʿAL PĀNÂI (על פני) and the Ban on Divine Images*

In the Jewish tradition, it is the second commandment of the Decalogue (Exod 20:3–6; Deut 5:7–10) that prohibits the worship of "other gods." There are, of course, many additional biblical statements to this effect (in Exodus alone, see 22:19, 23:24, 34:14, 17). The exclusive worship of YHWH (usually written out as "Yahweh") is the principal mandate of biblical religion, a mandate variously fulfilled and unrealized by the ancient Israelites. The commandment begins: לא יהיה לך אלהים אחרים על פני, "There shall not be for you (= You shall not have) other gods in my presence."[1] It is the aim of the present study to define the physical environment projected by the Hebrew expression על פני, the functional connotation of which changed in the course of the biblical period. Where was one if said to be "facing" God, in terms of the literal meaning? It is argued that in the second commandment, the environment originally envisioned was limited to the sacred space at Israelite cultic sites. In the course of time, the scope of the expression על פני became territorial, so that it spanned the whole land inhabited by the Israelites. This amounted to the prohibition of pagan worship throughout the Land of Israel, by non-Israelites as well as Israelites. As it is said of the Promised Land in Deut 11:12, in what may have been the parting words of the Deuteronomist, "[It is] a land which YHWH, your God, attends to. At all times the eyes of YHWH, your God, are (fixed) on it, from year's beginning to year's end."

Tracing the changing meanings of Hebrew על פני raises a second question, which has occupied modern scholarship in its own right. Is the ban on divine images directed at images intended to represent the God of Israel or at images of the "other gods," whose worship is forbidden? To put it another way, does the *second commandment* prohibit cultic images of YHWH? There is no question that images of YHWH would have been prohibited; the question is whether the second commandment prohibits them. It is my sense, contrary to the prevailing view, that the issue consistently addressed by the second commandment is the worship of other gods, not the idolatrous worship of YHWH himself. This

---

* Originally published in Sidnie White Crawford et al. (eds.) *"Up to the Gates of Ekron": Essays on the Archaeology and History of the Eastern Mediterranean in Honor of Seymour Gitin* (Jerusalem: The W. F. Albright Institute of Archaeological Research; The Israel Exploration Society, 2007), pp. 358–369. Reprinted with permission from the W. F. Albright Institute of Archaeological Research and the Israel Exploration Society.

[1] All translations from the Hebrew Bible are original to the author

judgment is based on an analysis of the formulation of the second commandment, which is, in turn, dependent on how we understand the Hebrew expression על פני in immediate context. It is my understanding that the cult of YHWH was aniconic from the start, so that prohibiting images of YHWH was not of central concern to the authors of the second commandment. Their concern was eliminating the worship of *other* gods.

Some may question the appropriateness of an apparently theological inquiry in a volume dedicated to an archaeologist, but it is the focus on the phenomenology of sacred space that would allow for its inclusion. Seymour Gitin has shown particular interest in cultic sites and their artifacts throughout his many years of archaeological activity, and we owe him a great debt for his contribution to our understanding of their significance and function. A salient example is his penetrating analysis of the altars found at Ekron (1989; 1992; 2002), which clashed with the views of Menachem Haran (1993), a prominent scholar of biblical literature and religion. In that ongoing debate, it became evident that Gitin's perspective had contributed to deepening our understanding of biblical religion, not only in interpreting the archaeological evidence from a prominent Philistine site. Dialogue between those who uncover sites and their artifacts and those who study texts advances our knowledge of both.

Facing the God of Israel

The present investigation was triggered by Noth's comments on the second commandment, where he speaks of its cultic context (1962:162, on Exod 20:3):

> The expression which is rendered in the RSV "before me," probably points to the cultic sphere, in so far as it contains the concept of the 'face' of God ('before' in Hebrew is literally 'before my face'), which frequently describes the presence of God which is encountered in the worship of him.

It should be clarified that in classical Hebrew, as in many languages, parts of the human body are used to generate prepositional constructions. Thus, the Hebrew expression על פני contains two elements: the preposition על, "on, over," and the substantive פנים, "face," yielding the normalized meaning "facing me, in my presence." It is the challenge of translators and commentators to determine in each case just how graphic or, in contrast, how "leveled" the usage of this fairly frequent prepositional construction was intended to be. Noth sensed that in referring to the God of Israel, the expression על פני was "charged," one might say, because YHWH is described as having a face. We would translate על פני literally as "in front of my face, opposite my countenance." In a parallel way, as Noth points out, the frequent construction לפני יהוה is best translated as "in the presence of YHWH, before YHWH's face." It often designates delimited sacred space, a location where the deity is perceived to be present for purposes of worship. As such, it is a technical term, not merely a general expression.

Building on Noth's insight, although not in the direction he pursued, I understand the second commandment of the Decalogue to project a cultic scene. As such, the expression על פני formulates a prohibition against installing images of other gods in YHWH's "space." This is precisely what the commandment proceeds to specify (Exod 20:4–5):

> You shall not fashion for yourself a sculptured image; nor any likeness of what is in the heavens above or of what is on the earth below, or of what is in the waters under the earth. You shall not bow down to them in worship, for I am YHWH, your God, an impassioned god (אל קנא)...

Images of more than one god, often of a god and his consort and of lesser deities, were normally installed at cultic sites and temples, where worshippers would bow down to them. Worship of a national god, for example, of Qaus (consonantal *qws*) by the Edomites or of Kemosh by the Moabites, did not essentially alter this pattern. These peoples and others like them worshiped additional deities alongside their national god. This is exactly what the second commandment was aimed at precluding. One contemporary non-Israelite site illustrates this critical distinction. The archaeological report on Ḥorvat Qitmit, edited by the principal excavator, Itzhaq Beit-Arieh (1995), includes an annotated catalogue of cultic objects found at this late Iron Age site prepared by Pirhiya Beck (1995). In a previous study on the open-air cultic installation (Levine 1993), I explored the phenomenological relevance of Ḥorvat Qitmit, with its altar, *bamah*, and roofed structure, for charting patterns of worship in biblical Israel. For the purpose of this study, my interest is in the artifactual finds at Qitmit, which include statues of unidentified deities and other forms of iconography, as well as representations of priests and worshippers; actually a wide variety of objects. Beck tentatively concluded that Qaus, whose name occurs in some of the few inscriptions from Qitmit, was depicted as a bull, images of which were found at the site, whereas the unnamed chief goddess, perhaps a fusion of Astarte/Ishtar, was depicted as a female anthropomorphic figurine in various poses (1995:187–89).

The message of the second commandment is precisely that Israelites should not furnish their cultic sites in this customary way, because YHWH, their God, has strong feelings about his unique status and will not "share the stage" with any other deity. He will not "countenance" the presence of other gods (or goddesses) within his purview, a cultic scene that would offend him grievously. For Israelites, there is only one god deserving of worship, namely, YHWH, the deity who has identified himself as Israel's liberator: אנכי יהוה אלהיך "I am YHWH, your God" (see further below). Practically speaking, since most deities were manifested in the form of images, a prohibition against fashioning images, if obeyed, would be an effective means of preventing pagan worship altogether.

As the above interpretation of the second commandment indicates, I would dispute Noth's interpretation of the Decalogue's prohibition against fashioning images. He states (1962:162):

> As the strict prohibition of other gods has already been expressed previously, the prohibition of images is hardly concerned with the images of strange gods but with any images which might possibly be made for the legitimate worship of Israel.

This is also the view of de Vaux (1978:464–66) and many other scholars. I respectfully dissent, for two interrelated reasons. In the first place the style of the second commandment, which may appear to be repetitive, is rather to be taken as rhetorically elaborative. In Rabbinic parlance, such elaboration in biblical style is conveyed by the Aramaic/Hebrew verb פרש in the Aramaic Paᶜᶜel (= *pārēš*), "to express clearly, state specifically" and in the Rabbinic Hebrew Piᶜᶜel (= *pērēš* [see examples in Levy 1963 IV:141–42; Sokoloff 1990:450–51; 2002:939–40]). Once this stylistic feature is acknowledged, we can see how adopting the prevalent interpretation would "load" the second commandment, the agenda of which is actually unitary and consistent; it is speaking only of pagan worship. The verses that comprise the second commandment, Exod. 20:3 and 20:4–6, are not prohibiting two separate things, respectively—worship of other gods (v. 3) and iconic representation of the God of Israel (vv. 4–6)—but only one thing: worship of other gods, which translates into a ban on images of *other* gods. This is also how nearby Exod 20:19b–20 should be understood:

> You have experienced ("seen") for yourselves how I spoke with you from heaven. Therefore, you shall not fashion gods of silver with me (אתי), nor shall you fashion gods of gold for yourselves.

This verse is saying that once the identity of YHWH had been made known to the Israelites, they should understand that no other deity may be worshiped. Once again, we can picture a cultic scene in which no images of other gods were installed. Subsequent verses (Exod 20:22–26) present additional rules applicable to Israelite cultic sites regarding the construction of altars and the character of the rites performed thereon.

Another statement of similar import is Exod 34:10–17. It resonates with the second commandment, but it shows the intervening influence of the Deuteronomist. Within this passage, v. 14 reads: "For you shall not bow down to any other god, for YHWH is named 'the impassioned one' (קנא שמו); he is truly an impassioned god (אל קנא הוא)." A few verses later, Exod 34:17 reads: "You shall not fashion for yourselves molten gods (אלהי מסכה)." Here, too, the context indicates that the reference is to images of other gods. In fact, it can be argued that within Exodus 34, vv. 15–16 were interpolated, and that v. 17 originally followed directly upon v. 14. A close reading reveals that v. 15 amplifies vv. 12–13, and that v. 16 takes its cue from v. 12. On this basis, the antecedent of "molten images" would more clearly be "any other god."

This interpretation accords with a long-standing Jewish exegetical tradition in which the second commandment has taken on the force of an ontological statement, fully monotheistic in its exclusivity. The reference to "other gods" is seen as merely reflecting contemporary idiom: it echoes the pagan gentiles, who erroneously suppose that there are indeed other gods. In its original context, however, the second commandment should be seen as a more limited, henotheistic statement that does not deny the existence of "other gods"; it merely prohibits their worship. And yet, there appears to be a confluence of critical and traditional interpretation on the meaning of the prohibition against cultic images.

In their comments on the second commandment, the authors of the principal Tannaitic Midrash on Exodus, the Mekhilta of Rabbi Yishmaᶜel, assumed that the second commandment is speaking of the worship of other gods throughout. Consider the following passage from Pareshah 6 of the tractate "In the third month" (ed. Meir Ish-Shalom [Friedman] 1948:68a):

> "*You shall not bow down to them nor worship them.*" Why was it stated? It is because (elsewhere) he states: "*So that he went about worshiping other gods and bowing down to them*" (Deut 17:3). It was to assign culpability for worship in and of itself, and for prostration in and of itself. Is this what you mean, or is it that one is not culpable until he both worships and bows down? Learn to cite (the text): "*You shall not bow down to them nor worship them.*" It was to assign culpability for each individual act, in and of itself. Another interpretation: "*You shall not bow down to them.*" Why was it stated? It is because (elsewhere) he states: "*One who offers sacrifice to any deity shall be proscribed, except to YHWH, alone*" (Exod 22:10). We are (here) taught the penalty; but whence the admonition? Learn to cite (the text): "*Do not bow down to them.*" And he similarly states: "*For you shall not bow down to any other god*" (Exod 34:14).

In their own way, the authors of the Mekhilta performed the same exercise in intertextual comparison that has been attempted here, albeit with a different question in mind. Their concern was to define the culpability imposed by the second commandment and to itemize the acts covered by it; they never questioned that it referred to the worship of other gods.

To return to the analysis of the second commandment in its original context, we can add a further refinement. It was directed at Israelite cultic sites specifically, and its intent was to prevent Israelites from combining the worship of YHWH with the worship of other gods at the same sites. In graphic terms, the second commandment is saying that only images that YHWH would have seen facing him fall under the prohibition, not those at pagan cultic sites, which undoubtedly continued to operate in Canaan, but where YHWH was not thought to be present. This conclusion is supported by Exod 20:21b: "At every cult place where I pronounce my name I will come to you and grant you blessings." When properly invoked at a cultic site consecrated to him, the God of Israel would draw near and be "present." He would not be present at illegitimate cultic sites. Therefore, the second commandment would not prohibit non-Israelites, such as Canaanites and foreigners, from worshiping pagan gods in the Land of Israel. At this point, the ban was not territorial, although it would become so in time; it could be characterized as ethnic.

An Intriguing Question

The proposed interpretation of the second commandment raises an unexpected question. If the Decalogue is not addressing the issue of the iconic representation of YHWH, the God of Israel, but only images of other gods, where in Scripture is the fundamental, aniconic principle of the cult of YHWH set forth? Where is it stated explicitly that Israelites are prohibited from fashioning images of YHWH?

As a first response, one could say that the second commandment is categorical in its prohibition of images, so that its ban would apply to images of the God of Israel as well. If I understand van der Toorn (2001) correctly, this is how he reads the second commandment; but it is difficult to be certain of this because he poses different alternatives from those being considered here. He differentiates between practice within the official cult and outside of it, for example, a distinction often enlisted to explain phenomena that do not seem to fit into preestablished definitions. In his exchange with Sasson (2001), the latter correctly challenges him on this point and offers us a broad, comparative view on Israelite religious perceptions. For his part, van der Toorn produces valid evidence of idolatry, to be sure; but much of what he cites actually pertains to the worship of other gods, as we will attempt to show, rather than to the idolatrous worship of YHWH. I do not question that Israelites were often heterodox in their religiosity, especially in pre-exilic times, but the precise nature of this behavior remains to be clarified.

As tempting as the inclusive interpretation is, I find it problematic. It seems to me that opposition to the iconic representation of YHWH, if it had been intended, would have been stated emphatically and unmistakably, not left to inference. I also question whether YHWH's disposition as an impassioned deity, zealous about his uniqueness, would be invoked to rationalize his opposition to images of himself! I prefer, therefore, to explore whether the iconic representation of YHWH was an issue at all for those who authored the second commandment and similar statements, such as those discussed above. Perhaps the cult of YHWH was thought to be inherently aniconic, so that this feature was self-evident and not a central concern requiring specific legislation. This is not to deny that some Israelites may have worshiped YHWH idolatrously along with worshiping other gods, although one is hard pressed to find specific evidence of this. My analysis merely intends to define the frame of reference of the relevant biblical authors.

The Narrative of the Golden Bull-Calf and the Second Commandment

Some have pointed to the narrative of the golden bull-calf (Exodus 32; see also Deut 9:16) and to chronistic references to the bull-calves installed at Dan and Bethel by Jeroboam I (1 Kgs 12:28–33, 2 Kgs 10:29, 2 Chron 11:15, 13:8) as indications that in various periods, some Israelites made a practice of depicting YHWH in the form of a bull. If such an interpretation could be sustained, it might lend support to the views of Noth and others on the import of the second commandment. As Noth understood it, the worship of the golden bull-calf would have constituted a direct violation of the second commandment in that it constituted the worship of an image intended to represent YHWH (1962:248). In like manner, the sin of Jeroboam and of those northern Israelites who installed images of bull-calves would not have amounted to the worship of another god as such, but rather to the idolatrous worship of YHWH. The narrative of the golden bull-calf is best regarded as etiological; it lays the foundation for discrediting those very cults at Dan and Bethel in northern Israel. There are also cryptic references to a northern Israelite bull cult in Hos 8:5 and 10:5

Exodus 32 has always presented difficulties in interpretation, if for no other reason than because of its redactional complexities. In its composite form, it gives out mixed messages. On the one hand, Aaron proclaims a festival to YHWH after the bull-calf is installed (Exod 32:5), implying that the bull-calf represented YHWH. On the other hand, the narrative suggests that Aaron was acting to replace YHWH with another god—thus Exod 32:4: "This is your god (אלה אלהיך), oh Israelites, who brought you up out of the land of Egypt." This theme is repeated in Exod 32:8.

Deconstructing the overall narrative leads me to conclude that the Hebrew pronoun אלה ("these" in Hebrew; functionally, "this") expresses contrast. It is as if to say: it was not YHWH who liberated you, but rather this bull-calf that you now see before you. This pronouncement has the effect of undoing the second commandment. The stated basis for the anxieties expressed by the people was, after all, the invisibility of Moses' God, paralleled by the prolonged absence of Moses, the one who spoke in his name. The resonance of the term עגל מסכה, "a molten bull-calf" (Exod 32:4), with אלהי מסכה, "molten gods," of the prohibition in Exod 34:17 suggests pagan worship, not the idolatrous worship of YHWH himself.

De Vaux was on the right track in calling attention to the El cult in connection with Exodus 32 (1978:456–59), but in my opinion, he became increasingly entangled in the subtleties of the so-called "El-Yahweh synthesis." I discussed this phenomenon at length in my Anchor Bible commentary on Numbers 21–36 (2000:217–34), with special reference to the Balaam orations (Numbers 23–24), to which de Vaux also calls attention. I owe to de Vaux the insight that the narrative of the golden bull-calf resonates with the Balaam orations. A reasoned and well documented summary discussion of the El background of Israelite religion is provided by M. Smith in his discussion of the origins of Israelite religion (2001:45, 135–48).

Briefly stated, there is a strong biblical tradition that the Patriarchs worshiped the Syro-Canaanite deity El, who appeared to them and to whom they dedicated stelae, *inter alia*. El was later synthesized with YHWH, rather than being rejected, as Baal was, so that Hebrew אל more often than not functions as a common noun meaning "deity, god," and not as a proper noun representing the name of a known deity. As such, it continued to be used in Hebrew personal names, even in the name of the people, ישראל. This semantic process is widespread and is not limited to Hebrew אל and its cognates. Yet there are texts, mostly poetic in form, that are unaffected by this synthesis (probably because they preceded it), in which אל represents the proper name of the West-Semitic deity. In my view, this is true of the Balaam orations, *inter alia*, which know of YHWH as Israel's national God (Num 23:21b), but which, as I read them, credit El, not YHWH, with the formative liberation from Egypt—thus "El, who liberated him from Egypt, has horns like a wild ox" (Num 23:22, cf. 24:8).

The El-Yahweh synthesis itself is most clearly pronounced in Exod 6:2–9, which explains, as it were, that it was really YHWH, not El, who had appeared to the Patriarchs and who in the future will liberate Israel from Egypt and bring them to their land. This transparent reinterpretation, so critical in the history of modern biblical research, reverberates in the second commandment's opening declaration: "I am YHWH, your God, who brought you out of the land of Egypt." The 1st person formulation recalls Gen 31:13, אנכי האל בית-אל, best rendered, "I am El of Bethel" (cf. Gen 35:11), as well as many other 1st person addresses by YHWH in the Hebrew Bible. It is a formula also known in Neo-Assyrian prophecies, for example, where the goddess Ishtar "introduces" herself to Esarhaddon, king of Assyria, by saying: "I am Ishtar of [Arbela]" (Parpola 1997:7, s.v. 1.6, line 7). Weippert (2001) has presented other fascinating comparisons of Neo-Assyrian with biblical statements of this order. Such conventions, apart from their dramatic directness and the reassurance they offer to the addressee, reflect the perception that the deity appearing in a theophany wished to identify himself/herself conclusively. In the same vein, the frequent references to the liberation from Egypt in YHWH's pronouncements about himself serve to highlight the centrality of this event in identifying Israel's God, post-synthesis, lest Israelites mistakenly identify their liberator as El or some other member of the West-Semitic regional pantheon.

El is associated with the bull in Ugaritic myth, in which Baal's father is named *ṯr il*, "Bull-El" (for sources, see M. Smith 2001:45). There is also archaeological evidence for this association. It must be borne in mind, however, that ancient West-Semitic deities often had both anthropomorphic and zoomorphic representations, a factor discussed by Stadelmann with respect to the iconography of Baal (1967:31) and, more recently, by Watson and Wyatt with respect to El (1999:587, 593). Furthermore, the same form might represent different deities. Mazar (1982) excavated what appears to be an Iron I Israelite cultic site near Dothan in northern Samaria, where he found a statuette of a young bull. In their discussion of bull cults, King and Stager relate this find both to the report about Jeroboam I in 1 Kings 12 and to the narrative of the golden bull-calf in Exodus 32 (2001:322–23). For our purposes, the mere fact that Num 23:22 describes El as having horns like a wild ox is a clue that Aaron's choice of a bull-calf to replace YHWH was not coincidental.

Enter Exodus 32. The people, who had a background of worshiping El and who, in terms of the narrative, had just experienced the revelation of YHWH were regressing; to use the old terminology, "backsliding." They were demanding of Aaron that he reinstate the earlier regime, having lost confidence in Moses' assurances that YHWH would "walk before" them. Similarly, the sin of Jeroboam I and of those Israelites who worshiped the golden bull-calf consisted of cultic regression from the point of view of the Book of Kings. In the narrative of the golden bull-calf and in the relevant passages from Kings we may have rare biblical polemics against the cult of El. The above-mentioned passages in Hos 8:5 and 10:5 should be viewed in the same way. The narrative of the golden bull-calf does not, however, attest to the use of images in the worship of YHWH. At most, it indicates that Israelites were particularly attracted to the familiar bull image of the El cult.

It is significant that none of the Patriarchs—of whom it is recorded in the Hebrew Bible that they worshiped El and built altars and dedicated cultic stelae to him—are reported to have utilized cultic images in the process. This portrayal may well reflect psychological denial on the part of the biblical authors, the suppression of what actually occurred. It is highly unlikely that those who worshiped El did not have recourse to images in doing so. It is just that it was not "politically correct" for any biblical author to admit as much, especially as regards the Patriarchs.

Another source that has been cited as indicating the utilization of images in the cult of YHWH is the incident of Micaiah from the Ephraimite hill country reported in Judg 17:1–6. It is an introduction that was probably added to a larger, etiological narrative (Judges 17–18), also aimed at discrediting the northern Israelite cult of Dan. The narrative recounts the internal migration of the tribe of Dan northwards and the establishment of its cult. We read that Micaiah's mother had two idols fashioned for him, which he kept in his house. The combination פסל ומסכה, "sculptured image and molten image," in Judg 17:3–4 resonates with Deut 27:15, "Cursed be the person who fashions an idol or molten image (פסל ומסכה), abhorred by YHWH, a craftsman's work, and stores it away in a secret place." These are the only two biblical attestations of this specific combination, strongly suggesting that Judg 17:1–6 is a reflex of Deut 27:15; actually, of Deuteronomy 27 in its entirety. It is a telling detail that Micaiah kept his images at home and did not install them in the local temple that he himself owned. After all, he was doing exactly what Deut 27:15 forbade—he was storing images of a pagan god or gods in secret! No information is provided as to the form of the images, and all we are told is that they were made of silver.

It is doubtful that Judg 17:1–6 reflects some quaint, realistic version of the cult of YHWH practiced at an early time when every man did as he pleased. The blatant Yahwism of both Micaiah and his mother, who bless in the name of YHWH and install an ephod (and make use of teraphim!), merely provides local color. Once we acknowledge that Micaiah's idols represented pagan deities, *à la* Deut 27:15, this passage cannot be said to attest to the utilization of images in the worship of YHWH. At most, it shares with Exodus 32 the role of illustrating cultic regression.

On the Phenomenology of Cult Images

One finds in biblical literature a pervasive antipathy to cult images in general, but I have yet to find an explicit statement specifically prohibiting cultic images of YHWH. The derisive invective that we encounter in Deutero-Isaiah (Isa 44:9–20) and in Psalms (Ps 135:15–18), to name only two of the most poignant sources, is directed at images of other gods, at eliminating pagan worship, not at some form of idolatrous worship of YHWH. The closest we come to that phenomenon is precisely in the narrative of the golden bull-calf and related biblical sources, which, if I am correct, denounce El worship.

I concede that I cannot fully explain the palpable aversion to divine images in biblical literature. I regard it as primarily an aspect of the protracted struggle within the Israelite religious leadership, first in the northern Kingdom of Israel and then in Judah, to break free of the overarching West-Semitic regional pantheon shared by Israel and its neighbors. Prophets and pious priests sought to unseat El and Baal, as well as Asherah, Ashtoreth, and Dagon, and to establish the exclusive sovereignty of YHWH. This movement undoubtedly spoke for an ethos or mentality operative within elements of the society at large, and it would be misleading merely to call it "official." The most observable feature of religious worship among Israel's neighbors and among the Canaanite inhabitants of the land was, after all, the cultic image. It would be a case of aniconism in the service of exclusivity, and it is this anomalous exclusivity that most eludes explanation.

Our understanding of the phenomenology of cultic images in the ancient Near East has been greatly advanced by the recent publication of a long-awaited work by Walker and Dick, *The Induction of the Cult Image in Ancient Mesopotamia: The Mesopotamian* Mīs pî *Ritual* (2001). This work has been reviewed with great insight by Hurowitz (2003). Earlier on, S. Smith (1925) and Jacobsen (1987) had each dealt with this subject in depth. Hurowitz emphasizes that the governing principle of divine image phenomenology in Mesopotamia is "the idea that the divine statue is a god created by gods and not by humans"; human manufacture is merely "a rehearsal of the mythological moment," when the god now being manifested in the cult image had created himself, a phenomenon known as autogenesis (2003:150, 154).

It is interesting that Hurowitz sees in the narrative of the golden bull-calf a possible allusion to the mythological and ritual notions that underlie divine image phenomenology in Mesopotamia and elsewhere. To be sure, we read in Exod 32:4 that Aaron crafted a "molten bull-calf" (עגל מסכה) from the gold supplied to him by the people, but in reporting to Moses what had occurred, he says (in Hurowitz's translation): "I cast it (= the gold) into the fire, and out came this calf" (Exod 32:24). Stated as an excuse, Aaron's words actually correspond to reports of image sanctification in Mesopotamia, examples of which are cited by Hurowitz. Thus, Sennacherib reports that he had a divine image fashioned, and virtually in the same breath, he confirms that the image was divinely created. Similarly, Aaron manufactures the molten image and then states that it had emerged from the fire as if by magic. The authors of Exodus 32, like most biblical spokesmen, would have clearly disavowed this phenomenology, but it may nevertheless have been known to them.

For the most part, the Hebrew Bible offers no indication that YHWH desired to be represented iconically. There may be an allusion to such a divine desire in the creation narrative of Genesis (1:26–28), but it was addressed in a very different way. Instead of commanding that images of himself be erected, Elohim set about creating the first male and female humans in his own image (Hebrew צלם) and likeness (Hebrew דמות). This suggests that the human creature was to serve in the capacity of an avatar, reminding all of the creator.

However we interpret the notion that humans were created in the image of God, it is clear that as the object of worship, YHWH was perceived as a hidden God, most often invisible even when thought to be present. Apart from metaphorical anthropomorphism and from materialized manifestations, such as fire, or from angels who appeared as humans, YHWH in the cultic traditions was thought to possess something like a human form. Thus in the vision of Ezekiel (1:26): "Above the expanse over their heads was the form of a throne, having the appearance of sapphire, and above the form of a throne, on top of it, was a form having the appearance of a human being (דמות כמראה אדם)." Even Moses, however, was able to see only YHWH's back as he passed by. This reassured Moses that YHWH was "real," even if he was not permitted to see YHWH's face (Exod 33:12–25). Another tradition has it that Moses, alone among all the earthly members of YHWH's household, was able to see "the likeness of YHWH (תמונת יהוה)" while speaking to him directly (Num 12:6–8). Biblical traditions—epic and priestly—that speak of a cloud envelope reinforce the idea of YHWH's obscurity. YHWH had an audible voice, which provided a degree of sensory presence, and his stupendous acts, beheld by multitudes, gave evidence of his power, as did the forces of nature acting on his command.

I could continue to survey other biblical texts of similar import, including the visions of Moses and the elders of Israel (Exod 24:9–11), of Isaiah (Isa 6:1–7), and especially of Ezekiel (Chapter 1, already noted in part), but the point should by now be clear. Based on what we know about the origin and provenance of the cult of YHWH—and admittedly, our knowledge is severely limited—the cult of YHWH was inherently imageless. In time, even utilization of the cultic stela (Hebrew מצבה) and the Asherah tree (or post) was prohibited (Deut 16:21; see also the etiological narrative in Judg 6:25–32).

Much has been written about the putative relevance of religious developments in Egypt during the Amarna period for understanding biblical religion. Without engaging in the complex historical, cultural, political, and religious issues that come into play whenever this subject is broached (a subject discussed in a summary way most recently by Hornung [2002]), it must be acknowledged that in phenomenological terms, certain features of the religion of Pharaoh Akhenaten (Amenhotep IV) invite comparison with biblical cult and religion. As an example, a comparison of Psalm 104 with the Great Hymn to the Aten (Lichtheim 1997) is highly suggestive in this regard. Most relevant to the present discussion is the aniconism of the cult of Aten, no less enigmatic for Egyptologists than is the corresponding phenomenon for students of biblical religion.

In the "House of the Aten," the Great Temple at Akhetaten (Tell el-Amarna), there were no cultic images, only a stela standing behind an altar. It was an icon of the king and queen as worshippers of the Aten, not a sacred object of worship—nor was the oft-mentioned sun disc of the Aten, with its emanating rays. The object of worship was the sun in the heavens, which accounts for the fact that temples of Aten were open to the sky. This cultic environment is described by Aldred in his comprehensive essay on the Amarna period (1975:50–58). In one respect, the absence of cultic images in Aten temples is explicable as a means of ensuring that the sun itself would be worshiped, to the exclusion of other possible objects of worship.[2] Such reasoning cannot be fully applied to biblical religion, however. In Egypt, the heavenly sun shone brightly, and no one could possibly doubt its existence. There is no comparable referent for YHWH, the hidden God; his existence was regularly doubted!

In summary, the original context of the second commandment projects the scene orchestrated at cultic sites where images of gods were normally installed. The God of Israel forbade the installation of images of other gods at such Israelite sites, images that would be facing him, insisting that he alone be worshiped. This spatial scope of the prohibition is defined by the expression על פני. The narrative of the golden bull-calf serves to reinforce the second commandment on the matter of cultic images, making certain that its prohibition against worshiping other gods was properly interpreted. It was meant to exclude images of El, notwithstanding the earlier acceptability of El worship. The agenda of the second commandment is pagan worship, not the prohibition of images of YHWH, which is unaddressed by the Decalogue. The aniconic character of the cult of YHWH itself, however, remains to be adequately explained.

The God of Israel Has the Whole Land in His Sights

By tracing the nuances of the expression על פני, we can observe how the prohibition of pagan worship ultimately became territorial. In the prophecies of Jeremiah, the threat of exile and destruction is sometimes expressed as "casting out" the people of Israel from YHWH's presence. After predicting the destruction of the Jerusalem Temple by reference to the earlier destruction of the northern Israelite temple at Shiloh, the prophet proclaims: "I shall cast you out from my presence just as I cast out all of your kinsmen, all of the seed of Ephraim" (Jer 7:15). In other words, Judah will be exiled as northern Israel had been. The same rhetoric is used in another of Jeremiah's tirades against the people of Jerusalem and Judah: "Then YHWH said to me: Even if Moses and Samuel were to stand

[2] This insight was communicated to me by my colleague Ogden Goelet of New York University in a recent conversation.

before me (as intercessors), I would not empathize with this people. Dismiss (them) from my presence (מעל פני) and let them depart!" (Jer 15:1).

In two further instances, the target of prophetic denunciation is Jerusalem, perceived as epitomizing YHWH's anger against the whole people. Playing on the derivation of the term משא, "burden (= what is carried), prophetic oration," Jer 23:39 states: "Therefore, I will surely *carry you away* (read: ונשאתי), and I will cast you out, together with this town which I granted to you and to your ancestors, from before my presence (מעל פני)." Finally, in Jer 32:31–32: "This town has aroused my rage and my wrath since the day it was built and until now, so that it must be removed from before my presence (מעל פני), because of all of the evil of the Israelites and Judeans, which they committed in order to anger me—they, their kings, their officials, their priests and their prophets, and the men of Judah and the residents of Jerusalem."

It should not surprise us to find similar rhetoric in two redactional passages in the Book of Kings that interpret the tragic downfall of the kingdom of Judah *ex eventu*. Thus, 1 Kgs 9:1–10 predicts, as it were, the destruction of Jerusalem and its temple as a punishment for Judah's waywardness. Most pertinent is 1 Kgs 9:7: "And I will cut Israel off from the face of the land (מעל פני האדמה) which I granted to them, and the temple which I dedicated to my name I shall dismiss from my presence (מעל פני), so that Israel will become a taunt and a by-word among the nations." The parallelism of the Hebrew והכרתי, "And I will cut off," and אשלח "I will dismiss" (= Piʿʿel *ʾašallaḥ*; or perhaps read: אשליך "I will cast off," as in 2 Chron 7:20), together with the interface of מעל פני האדמה <> מעל פני, serve to reinforce the graphics of destruction and exile, and to extend YHWH's purview to the entire land.

Similarly, 2 Kgs 23:27, within a larger passage comprising 2 Kgs 23:24–27, is a prediction—or more likely, a reflection in hindsight—of destruction and exile, presented against the backdrop of pagan worship: "Then YHWH said: Judah, as well, will I remove (אסיר) from before my presence (מעל פני), just as I removed Israel, and I will abandon (ומאסתי) this town which I had selected, Jerusalem, and the Temple where I commanded: 'Let my name be there!'." In a recent study, I cite this passage in support of my argument that the Hebrew verb מאס, usually translated "to despise, reject," often conveyed movement, with actual physical effects (2004).

A final illustration of our theme comes in Isa 65:2–3a, within an oracle lamenting the destruction of the land and people and attributing these misfortunes to Israel's cultic disobedience:

> I stretched out my arms all day long to a rebellious people,
> Who pursue the path that is not good; following their designs.
> The people who anger me (המכעיסים אותי) in my very presence (על פני) continuously.

As is indicated in the continuation of the oracle, the reference is to the sinfulness of the people who engaged in pagan practices throughout the land—in graveyards and gardens, in secret places and on hilltops (Isa 65:3b–7).

All of the above passages from Jeremiah and Kings—and from Trito-Isaiah—exhibit certain features in common. They all reflect a cultic matrix, and in various ways focus the divine purview on the temple of Jerusalem. But they all go beyond the temple as the horizon of God's purview to encompass the town of Jerusalem as Judah's capital and the land and people as a whole. The organizing theme is exile from the land, presented either as an imminent catastrophe or as a poignant memory. The horizon of the expression על פני has become territorial, expanding from the cultic scene to the land, so that being removed from God's sight now means being exiled to a foreign land.

An important corollary of this development in the connotation of the expression על פני is the prohibition of all pagan worship, no matter by whom, within the territorial limits of the Land of Israel. This objective was a major thrust of the Deuteronomic school. In recasting the prohibitions of idolatrous worship stated in the Decalogue and in Exodus 20 as a whole, Exod 34:11–17 adds a significant requirement missing from those earlier statements. It is the demand that all pagan cultic accoutrements—altars, cultic stelae, and Asherah-pillars—be demolished. Actually, this theme is first evident in Exod 23:20–33, where we also encounter polemical statements. All of these pronouncements correlate with core-Deuteronomy (12:2–3), which mandates that all pagan cultic sites in the land be destroyed. This requirement is further amplified by the subsequent Deuteronomist who authored Deut 7:1–5, and who, like the authors of Exod 23:20–33 and 34:11, 15–16, speaks of the deportation of the Canaanite peoples and of the ban on intermarriage or covenant with them. The same agenda informs additional redactional passages in the Book of Kings. Thus, 1 Kgs 11:13 explains the breakaway of northern Israel as God's punishment for Solomon's heterodoxy. In words reminiscent of Deuteronomy 17 and of the Deuteronomist, we are told that Solomon improperly married many foreign wives, for whom he built cultic platforms where, presumably, these wives worshiped their native gods. This was an affront to the God of Israel.

Conclusion

Jonah sought to escape his prophetic assignment in Nineveh by sailing off to Tarshish, a far-off coastal town, perhaps to be identified as a site in southern Sardinia (Baker 1992). Of interest to the present discussion is the manner in which the narrator characterizes Jonah's flight (Jonah 1:2–3):

> Jonah set out to flee to Tarshish from the presence of YHWH (מלפני יהוה). So, he went down to Jaffa and found a ship going to Tarshish... He boarded it to go with the others to Tarshish away from the presence of YHWH (מלפני יהוה).

It has often been suggested that the narrative of Jonah's fugue is predicated on the notion that one was thought to be in the presence of the God of Israel only within the Land of Israel, a corollary of the territorial outlook. By escaping to a far-off land across the sea, Jonah would no longer be under the control of his God, presumably because he was outside his purview. One of the messages of the tale of Jonah is precisely that this predicate is untrue. It would require much further study, however, to trace the progressive expansion of the purview of the God of Israel during the exilic and post-exilic periods of biblical history and beyond.

References

Aldred, C.

1975 Egypt: The Amarna Period and the End of the Eighteenth Dynasty. Pp. 49–97 in *The Cambridge Ancient History* (3rd ed.) 11/2: *The Middle East and the Aegean Region ca. 1380–1000 B.C.*, ed. I.E.S. Edwards, et al. Cambridge: Cambridge University.

Baker, D.W.

1992 Tarshish (Place). *ABD* 6:331–33.

Beck, P.

1995 Catalogue of Cult Objects and Study of the Iconography. Pp. 27–197 in *Ḥorvat Qitmit: An Edomite Shrine in the Biblical Negev*, ed. I. Beit-Arieh. Monograph Series of the Institute of Archaeology 11. Tel Aviv: Tel Aviv University.

Beit-Arieh, I., ed.

1995 *Ḥorvat Qitmit: An Edomite Shrine in the Biblical Negev*. Monograph Series of the Institute of Archaeology 11. Tel Aviv: Tel Aviv University.

Gitin, S.

1989 Incense Altars from Ekron, Israel, and Judah: Context and Typology. *Eretz-Israel* 20 (Yigael Yadin Volume): 52–67.

1992 New Incense Altars from Ekron: Context, Typology and Function. *Eretz-Israel* 23 (Avraham Biran Volume): 42–49.

2002 The Four-Horned Altar and Sacred Space. Pp. 95–123 in *Sacred Time, Sacred Space: Archaeology and the Religion of Israel*, ed. B.M. Gittlen. Winona Lake, IN: Eisenbrauns.

Haran, M.

1993 Incense Altars—Are They? Pp. 237–47 in *Biblical Archaeology Today, 1990: Proceedings of the Second International Congress on Biblical Archaeology, Jerusalem, June–July, 1990*, ed. A. Biran and J. Aviram. Jerusalem: Israel Exploration Society.

Hurowitz, V.

2003 The Mesopotamian God Image, from Womb to Tomb. *JAOS* 123:147–57.

Hornung, E.

2002 Das Denken des Einem im alten Ägypten. Pp. 21–32 in *Polytheismus und Monotheismus in den Religionen des Vorderen Orients*, ed. M. Krebernik and J. van Ourschot. AOAT 298. Münster: Ugarit-Verlag.

Jacobsen, T.
1987 The Graven Image. Pp. 15–32 in *Ancient Israelite Religion: Essays in Honor of Frank Moore Cross*, ed. P.D. Miller, P.D. Hanson, and S.D. McBride. Philadelphia: Fortress.

King, P.J., and Stager, L.E.
2001 *Life in Biblical Israel*. Library of Ancient Israel. Louisville, KY: Westminster John Knox.

Levine, B.A.
1993 *Lpny YHWH*—Phenomenology of the Open-Air Altar in Biblical Israel. Pp. 196–205 in *Biblical Archaeology Today, 1990: Proceedings of the Second International Congress on Biblical Archaeology, Jerusalem, June–July, 1990*, ed. A. Biran and J. Aviram. Jerusalem: Israel Exploration Society. {*VOL 1, PP. 259–69*}
2000 *Numbers 21–36*. AB 4A. New York: Doubleday.
2004 When the God of Israel "Acts-Out" His Anger: On the Language of Divine Rejection in Biblical Literature. Pp. 111–29 in *Inspired Speech—Prophecy in the Ancient Near East: Essays in Honor of Herbert B. Huffmon*, ed. J. Kaltner and L. Stulman. London: T&T Clark. {*VOL 1, PP. 365–84*}

Levy, J.
1963 *Wörterbuch über die Talmudim und Midraschim* I–IV. Darmstadt: Wissenschaftliche Buchgesellschaft (reprint of first edition, Berlin and Vienna: Harz, 1924).

Lichtheim, M.
1997 The Great Hymn to the Aten. Pp. 44–46 in *The Context of Scripture I*, ed. W.W. Hallo and K.L. Younger. Leiden: Brill.

Mazar, A.
1982 The Bull Site: An Iron Age I Open Cult Place. *BASOR* 247:27–42.

Meir Ish-Shalom (Friedman), ed.
1948 *Mekhilta of Rabbi Yishmaᶜel*. New York: OM (reprint of first edition, Vienna, 1870).

Noth, M.
1962 *Exodus: A Commentary*. Old Testament Library. Philadelphia: Westminster.

Parpola. S.
1997 *Assyrian Prophecies*. SAA 9. Helsinki: Helsinki University Press.

Sasson, J.M.
2001 On the Use of Images in Israel and the Ancient Near East: A Response to Karel van der Toorn. Pp. 63–70 in *Sacred Time, Sacred Space: Archaeology and the Religion of Israel*, ed. B.M. Gittlen. Winona Lake, IN: Eisenbrauns.

Smith, M.S.
2001 *The Origins of Biblical Monotheism*. Oxford: Oxford University.

Smith, S.

1925 The Babylonian Ritual for the Consecration and Induction of a Divine Statue. *Journal of the Royal Asiatic Society of Great Britain and Ireland* 1925:37–60.

Sokoloff, M.

1990 *A Dictionary of Jewish Palestinian Aramaic of the Byzantine Period*. Ramat-Gan: Bar Ilan University.

2002 *A Dictionary of Jewish Babylonian Aramaic of the Talmudic and Geonic Periods*. Ramat-Gan: Bar Ilan University.

Stadelmann, R.

1967 *Syrisch-Palästinensische Gottheiten in Ägypten*. Leiden: Brill.

Toorn, K. van der

2001 Israelite Figurines: A View from the Texts. Pp. 45–62 in *Sacred Time, Sacred Space: Archaeology and the Religion of Israel*, ed. B.M. Gittlen. Winona Lake, IN: Eisenbrauns.

Vaux, R. de

1978 *The Early History of Israel*. Philadelphia: Westminster.

Walker, C., and Dick, M.

2001 *The Induction of the Cult Image in Mesopotamia: The Mesopotamian* Mīs pî *Ritual*. State Archives of Assyria Literary Texts I. Helsinki: Neo-Assyrian Text Corpus Project.

Watson, W.G.E., and Wyatt, N., eds.

1999 *Handbook of Ugaritic Studies*. Leiden: Brill.

Weippert, M.

2001 "Ich bin Jahwe"—"Ich bin Ištar von Arbela": Deuterojesaja im Lichte der neuassyrischen Prophetie. Pp. 31–59 in *Prophetie und Psalmen*, ed. B. Huwyler, H.-P. Mathys, and B. Weber. AOAT 280. Münster: Ugarit-Verlag.

An Essay on Prophetic Attitudes toward Temple and Cult in Biblical Israel*

The ethical message of the biblical prophets may be formulated simply: in the eyes of the God of Israel, it is more important that Israelites follow the dictates of morality and justice, commanded by him, than that they offer sacrifices to him and celebrate sacred festivals. Furthermore, no amount of ritual purification will expiate wrongdoing between one human being and another, or atone for an unjust and corrupt society.

Nevertheless, different prophetic statements of this essential doctrine differ in their emphasis and perspective, and are set in different historical situations. They often leave us unclear as to the proper role of temple, cult and worship in the ideal Israelite society, in which justice would prevail.

Here I will examine this prophetic message in three principal dimensions. I begin with Jeremiah 7, a relatively late, but powerful, statement of the view that the presence of the temple and the performance of the cult do not guarantee divine favor or ensure national security. I will then take up Micah 6 and Isaiah 1, earlier prophetic statements on the same theme, with primary attention being given to Isaiah 1. This opening chapter of the book of Isaiah is informed by deep perceptions of Israel's culpability, and it presents a universal vision of Jerusalem's role as a reconstituted temple city. I will conclude with a discussion of the tension between prophetic and other biblical views on cultic efficacy, and the extent of their integration within the Israelite ethos.

In a volume of studies honoring our colleague and teacher Nahum Sarna, a discussion of biblical religion is certainly appropriate. The present discussion will be presented in the form of an essay, with a minimum of annotation.

1. The Prophetic Definition of Obedience

No prophet of the classical period, from First Hosea of the ninth century B.C.E. to Jeremiah of the late seventh century B.C.E., ever explicitly advocated suspension of the formal, sacred worship of the God of Israel.[1] The classical prophets

---

* Originally published in Marc Brettler and Michael Fishbane (eds.), *Minḥah le-Naḥum: Biblical and Other Studies Presented to Nahum M. Sarna in Honour of his 70th Birthday* (JSOTSup 154; Sheffield: JSOT Press, 1993), pp. 202–225. Reprinted with permission from the Continuum International Publishing Group. Note that the footnote numbering here does not match that of the original publication.

[1] The view that there are two Hoseas, First Hosea of the ninth century B.C.E. (Hosea 1–3) and Second Hosea of the eighth century, was most convincingly advanced by H.L.

acknowledged an ongoing cult, or cults at various temples, and surely appreciated the meaning of worship and celebration. First Hosea prophesied the suspension of Israel's joyous pilgrimage festivals, new moons and Sabbaths as God's punishment of his people (Hos. 2:13). He describes Israel rejected as a society devoid of a proper cult and undermined by political anarchy both as consequences of divine abandonment (Hos. 3:4).

It is relevant to observe, nevertheless, that prior to the advocacy of Sabbath observance in Jer. 17:19–27, we do not find a single explicit prophetic exhortation to the Israelites to be more pious or ritually observant, in the usual sense.[2] Prophetic statements on the subject of cult and ritual in the classical period show concern for maintaining strict monotheism in worship, condemning all forms of paganism. While criticizing the pollution of contemporary religiosity through idolatrous practices, and insisting on ethical behavior as a precondition of divine favor, the prophets did not at the same time urge the people to be present at temples more often, or to increase their dedications and offerings, for example.

Indeed, only when the prospect of national destruction and exile was imminent do we find prophets stressing the importance of the Sabbath (Jer. 17:19–27), or deploring cultic impurity in the selection of sacrificial materials (Ezek. 4:13–14). This emphasis was to endure throughout the exile and the period of the return, and may reflect a sense of collective guilt, what we would call an identity crisis. Later prophetic endorsements of cultic correctness require a separate study, and were not representative of the prophetic agenda for almost the entire pre-exilic period. Prior to the deportations preceding the final destruction of Jerusalem and Judah in 586 B.C.E., Jeremiah was still echoing the thoughts of earlier prophets:

> Thus says YHWH, God of the heavenly hosts, the God of Israel: Add your burnt offerings to your other sacrifices and eat meat. Verily, I did not speak with your ancestors nor did I command them, at the time I brought them out of the land of Egypt, on matters of burnt offerings and sacred feasts. Rather, it is this oracle that I commanded them, saying: Heed my voice; then I will be your God and you shall be my people. You must traverse the entire path that I direct you in order that things will be well with you (Jer. 7:21–23).

It is this message of obedience and loyalty that the people had failed to comprehend, pursuant to repeated and reinforced prophetic admonitions, not the essential obligation to offer sacrifice as participants in the cult of the Jerusalem temple. The message of Jeremiah is that obedience to the God of Israel and the pursuit of his path require both a just society and strict monotheism in the cult. In

---

Ginsberg ("Studies in Hosea", in M. Haran (ed.) *Yehezkel Kaufmann Jubilee Volume* [Jerusalem: Magnes Press, 1960], pp. 50–69).

[2] For an awareness of the problem, see H.L. Ginsberg, *The Israelian Heritage of Judaism* (New York: Jewish Theological Seminary, 1982), p. 7 n. 8. As noted by Ginsberg, Jer. 17:19–27 sound very much like Neh. 13:19–21.

the negative dimension, social sins balance with pagan worship as abomination (*tôᶜēbāh*), and provoke God's wrath. One seeking to make sense out of impending disaster must understand this dynamic, so Jeremiah would insist.

Nevertheless, Jeremiah's characterization of what God had and had not commanded Israel at the exodus is somewhat puzzling. It is part of a larger prophecy, declaimed at the gate of the Jerusalem temple, in which the sanction of the temple is declared to be conditional and revocable, not eternal. God had brought about the earlier destruction of Shiloh and the northern Israelite kingdom, and he would do the same with respect to the temple of Jerusalem and the kingdom of Judah. Those who proclaimed, "The temple of YHWH! The temple of YHWH! The temple of YHWH" (Jer. 7:4) would be severely disappointed. Jeremiah goes on to describe the horrific situation that obtained in Jerusalem and its environs, with the deadly Tophet and the improper *bāmôt*, and he reiterates God's firm intention to abandon "the generation of his wrath", who had defiled the temple.

How can the prophet maintain, however, that the God of Israel had not commanded the Israelites of the exodus to worship him through sacrifice? Which sources, records or policies could Jeremiah have had in mind when he made this assertion? Was he merely indulging in hyperbole (an unlikely conclusion), or was he, perhaps, recasting the traditions of the exodus and Sinai? Surely, he was not conforming to the priestly traditions of Exod. 24:15–31:18 and chs. 35–40, which effectively join the Tabernacle cult, with all of its specifications, to the Sinaitic revelation of laws and commandments. Nor, as a matter of fact, could he have been thinking of early laws preserved in the Book of the Covenant, for these also enjoin sacrifices, though with less specification. Even the primary statement of the Passover law in Exodus 12–13 calls for a *ḥag*, "pilgrimage festival", to celebrate the exodus; and the Decalogue, for its part, enjoins the observance of the Sabbath.

To satisfy our curiosity we must, first of all, elucidate Jeremiah's own viewpoint on the issue of obedience to God. By further tracing the diction of Jeremiah's statement we may then be able to align his views with other biblical traditions on this question. The main components of Jeremiah's statement are his emphasis on heeding God's voice, expressed by the idiom *šāmaᶜ beqôl*, coupled with the notion of a path, *derek*, commanded by God and to be walked or traversed, an action expressed by the verb *hālak*. There is also the theme of Israel's becoming YHWH's own people, expressed by the idiom *hāyāh leᶜām*.

We should note that Jeremiah himself uses similar diction elsewhere. Most enlightening for the present discussion are the prophet's statements in Jer. 11:3–7, also referring to what God had commanded the Israelites at the exodus. Thus:

> Say to them: Thus says YHWH, God of Israel: Cursed be the person who will not heed the terms of this covenant, which I commanded your ancestors on the day I brought them out of the Land of Egypt, from the iron crucible, as follows: Heed my voice, and observe them, in accordance with all I have commanded you, that you may become my people and I may be your God (Jer. 11:3–4).

Here we find expressed two of the three themes contained in Jeremiah's temple prophecy: the command to heed God and God's election of Israel.[3] With respect to the notion of the "path" to be followed or traversed, we find in Jeremiah only a few occurrences of the precise idiom *hālak bederek* (Jer. 6:16, 42:3, occurring not long before Jer. 42:13, the reference noted above to heeding God's voice). More dominant in Jeremiah's thinking is the general theme of a proper path, YHWH's path. The prophet searches the markets of Jerusalem in vain for any of the common folk who know this path (Jer. 5:1–4), and then in disappointment rationalizes that the wealthy might understand what the poor did not: "So I will go to the wealthy and speak with them, for they surely know (*yādeᶜû*) the path of YHWH (*derek YHWH*)—but they as well had broken the yoke, had snapped the bonds" (Jer. 5:5).

As Jeremiah sees the world, every nation follows its *derek*, adhering to a particular pattern of belief and behavior (Jer. 10:2), but Israel is admonished against following the "way" of other nations. The wicked among Israel likewise pursue an evil *derek* (Jer. 2:33, 36; 3:21; 12:1; 22:21; 31:20), whereas there is a proper path, the path of life (Jer. 21:6), the just path of obedience to YHWH (Jer. 32:39). It seems, however, that only in Jer. 7:23 does the prophet combine all three components—the themes of heeding God's voice, God's election of Israel and the ordained, right path—in a single statement.

When we look beyond the book of Jeremiah in our effort to identify and align Jeremiah's views we are led first to the Deuteronomist's recounting of the exodus, in which the themes of "heeding", conveyed by the verb *šāmaᶜ*, and of "the way", as well as of Israel's becoming YHWH's people, figure prominently.

The Deuteronomist repeatedly calls upon the Israelites to listen, heed, and perhaps also learn, what YHWH speaks and commands, a complex of ideas expressed by the verb *šāmaᶜ* (Deut. 5:1; 6:3–4; 7:12; 11:13). As if to verify that God is the source of the commandments attributed to him, the Israelites are reminded that they have actually heard God's voice (Deut. 4:12, 33; 5:19–20, 22–23). The precise idiom *šāmaᶜ beqôl* characterizes the diction of the Deuteronomist.[4] On the theme of the path to be traversed, we find in Deut. 5:30 a partial paraphrase of Jer. 7:23: "You must traverse the entire path which YHWH, your God, has commanded you so that you may live, and that it go well for you, and you long endure in the land which you shall possess".

Just as Israel has literally heard God's voice and is now commanded to heed it, so Israel has been led by God on a path to its promised land (Deut. 1:22, 31, 33; 8:2) and is now commanded to follow God's path, and is admonished

---

[3] Cf. Jer. 3:13, 25; 18:10; 22:21; 42:13; 13:11; 24:7; 30:22; 31:1.

[4] Deut. 3:20; 28:1, 15, 45, 62; 30:8, and cf. 1 Kgs 20:36, 2 Kgs 18:12. It is probable that most of the occurrences of the idiom *šāmaᶜ beqôl* in Deuteronomy are, in fact, attributable to the work of the Deuteronomist, not to the core of Deuteronomy. This is especially likely in those statements which speak of YHWH's commandments (*miṣwôt*), such as Deut. 13:5, 15:5.

against departing from it (cf. Deut. 9:12, 16; 11:28; 31:29; 2 Kgs 21:22). Actually, the notion of following a path, in the sense of persisting in the behavior of a predecessor, typifies the diction of the books of Kings in their condemnation of wicked rulers (cf. 1 Kgs 15:26, 34; 22:43, 53; 2 Kgs 8:18; 16:3; 22.2).

The theme of becoming YHWH's people also links Jeremiah to the Deuteronomic school. The idiom *hāyāh le*ᶜ*ām* is frequent in the writings of the Deuteronomist (Deut. 4:20; 7:6; 26:18; 27:9; 28:9; 29:12), and is echoed in 2 Kgs 11:17. These correlations should hardly surprise us, since they merely confirm the close association of Jeremiah with the so-called Deuteronomic school active at the end of the seventh century B.C.E. and at the beginning of the sixth century.

It would be inaccurate, however, to view Jeremiah's themes as being primarily of contemporary origin. The notion of obedience expressed as *šāma*ᶜ *beqôl* "to heed the voice", harks back to both the Yahwist and the Elohist in Torah tradition, and to narratives preserved in Judges and Samuel.

The general principle to be applied to the dictional analysis of biblical Hebrew idioms for "heeding" is that sources which normally use the idiom *šāma*ᶜ *beqôl* will more specifically express obedience to God in this way. Although such diction is not specific to northern Israelite literature, it seems to be prominent there. This emerges most clearly from the cycle of Samuel narratives, which are largely of northern Israelite provenance. Samuel is instructed by God to heed the people in their demand for a king (1 Sam. 8:7; 9:22), while the people refuse to heed Samuel in doing without a king (1 Sam. 8:19), both actions being conveyed by the use of the idiom *šāma*ᶜ *beqôl*. Similarly, Samuel admonishes the people to heed God's voice, warning them of the consequences of refusing to heed (1 Sam. 12:14–15). Most enlightening is the sequence of statements centering on the notion of obedience in 1 Sam. 15:17–23.

We first hear Samuel castigating Saul for not heeding YHWH's voice in failing to proscribe the spoils of the Amalekite war. Then, we hear Saul protesting that he had, by his understanding, heeded YHWH's voice, and had even "walked in the path in which YHWH sent me", echoing another of the three themes under discussion. Finally we have Samuel's classic statement of the prophetic view on the subject of obedience to God, weighed against cultic devotion:

> Does YHWH have desire of burnt offerings and sacred feasts as much as heeding the voice of YHWH (*kišmô*ᶜ*a beqôl YHWH*)? Surely, heeding (*šemô*ᶜ*a*) is preferable to sacred feasts; to obey—more than the fat of rams. For recalcitrance amounts to the sin of divination; obstinacy—to iniquitous teraphim (1 Sam. 15:22–23a).

Obedience expressed as *šāma*ᶜ *beqôl* figures in the narrative of Judges 13 recounting episodes in the southern Shephelah. We first read that the angel heeded Manoah's voice (Judg. 13:9), and later that God had allowed Manoah and his wife to "hear" great tidings (Judg. 13:23). In the northern narrative of Judges 20 we read that the Benjaminites refused to heed the charge of their kinsmen from the other Israelite tribes (Judg. 20:13). The same theme informs the ideological review of Israelite history in Judges 2, which, however, actually sounds like the work of a student of the Deuteronomist!

The Elohist in Genesis likes to speak of heeding God's voice. Abraham will be blessed by all the nations of the earth because he has heeded God's voice (Gen. 22:18), while Rachel is grateful that God has heeded her request for a child (Gen. 30:6). Note, however, that the Yahwist in Gen. 26:5 matches the Elohist of Gen. 22:18 in crediting Abraham's obedience to YHWH as the basis for the blessing of his seed. The Yahwist also employs the idiom *šāmaᶜ beqôl* freely in Gen. 27:8, 13, 43 in human contexts, as he does with respect to obedience to the divine will in Exod. 4:1 and Num. 14:22.

Of particular interest is the theme of obedience in Exodus 18–19, the former being primarily the work of the Elohist and the latter primarily that of the Yahwist. Both compositions are set in the timeframe immediately following the exodus from Egypt, and their relevance to Jeremiah's utterances is, therefore, direct and significant.

In Exodus 18 the Elohist presents us with a complex of transactions on the theme of hearing, expressed by the verb *šāmaᶜ*. Jethro "hears" of God's great acts of providence (18:1), and, upon observing the extent of Moses' burden as arbiter of the people's grievances, urges him to heed his advice (18:19), using the idiom, *šāmaᶜ beqôl*. Thereupon Moses in fact heeds his father-in-law's counsel (18:24), appointing subordinates to assist him. Along the way, Jethro opines that a better system of leadership would enable Moses to show the people the path in which they were to walk (18:20), thereby giving expression to another of the three themes of Jeremiah.

In Exodus 19, the Yahwist similarly emphasizes the importance of heeding YHWH's voice, using the idiom *šāmaᶜ beqôl*. Most dramatic are the words of Exod. 19:5–6a: "And now, if you will heed my voice and observe my covenant, you shall be my possession from among all the peoples, for all the earth is mine. You shall be my kingdom of priests and holy nation."

This theme is resumed by the Elohist in Exod. 20:19 after the presentation of the Decalogue, when the people say to Moses, "You speak with us and we will heed (*wenišmāᶜāh*), but let not God speak with us lest we die!" Even further, the theme of obedience is dramatized in Exod. 23:20–27, a passage of probable northern Israelite derivation, in which Israel is admonished against disobeying the angel whom God will dispatch to lead the people to its land, and to accomplish the defeat of the Canaanite peoples.

If we apply the same method to tracing the theme of the path (*derek*), we immediately perceive that this is a major motif of biblical Wisdom literature, just as we would expect. It also informs early narrative and classical prophecy, even though it hardly predominates in those contexts. It would be reasonable to assume that prophets and other biblical writers knew Wisdom, and often formulated their teachings and writings didactically. When doing so, they would employ Wisdom categories and the notion of the right path was one of them. This motif could be explored further, and with great profit, but to do so here would carry us far afield.

The theme of the divine election of Israel, expressed by the idiom *hāyāh* (*lî*/*lô*) *leʿām*, and variations of the same, clearly harks back further than the Deuteronomist.[5] The Yahwist of Exod. 6:2–9 features this motif, expressed quite similarly: "I will acquire (*welāqaḥtî*) you for myself as a people, and I will become your God" (Exod. 6:7a; cf. Exod. 19:5–6).

It should not surprise us that Samuel, in his parting words, reassures the Israelite people as follows: "For YHWH will not abandon his people (*ʿammô*) on account of his great name, for YHWH has agree to make you his people (*laʿásôt* *ʾetkem lô leʿām*)" (1 Sam. 12:22, and cf. 2 Sam. 7:23–24).

What was the context of Jeremiah's writing? Jeremiah studied Torah literature, particularly the works of the Elohist and Yahwist in their respective presentations of the exodus saga, where the commandment of obedience figures prominently. This very idea informs the narratives in 1 Samuel 8:12 and 15, especially the prophetic interpretation of the Amalekite war in 1 Samuel 15. That account provides a twofold etiology: it explains the rejection of Saul's dynasty, albeit in a less than fully credible way, and it makes a prophetic pronouncement on the priority of obedience to God over cultic devotion.

The ironic position of an Israelite king claiming, sincerely or hypocritically (one can hardly tell), that he had sought to please God precisely in a manner involving disobedience to God's command makes the statement that the God of Israel will reject the sacrifices of those who disobey him. The dictional links between Jeremiah's pronouncements and the Samuel narratives are what suggest the interpretation, epitomized both in the narratives of the exodus and in those of the conquest of Canaan, that the first duty of the Israelites and their leaders is to obey God, not simply to worship him in accepted or expected ways. According to Jeremiah, this is what the Judeans and Jerusalemites of his day had failed to understand. The presence of the temple of Jerusalem was not unconditional evidence of divine favor, nor was performance of the cult a guarantee of security.

2. The City of God

One of the earliest statements of prophetic doctrine on the primacy of ethical behavior appears in Mic. 6:6–8, a passage of Israelian, or north-Israelite provenance. H.L. Ginsberg has dated Micah 6–7 to the early part of the reign of Jeroboam II, during the third quarter of the eighth century B.C.E.[6] The relevant passage appears in a group of oracles in which denunciation is followed by a vision of Israel's restoration. The prophet refers to a law-suit between YHWH and his people, in which the God of Israel acts both as prosecutor and judge:

> For YHWH has a case (*rîb*) against his people,
> He is pressing a verdict (*yitwakkāḥ*) against Israel (Mic. 6:2b)

---

[5] See S.-T. Sohn, *The Divine Election of Israel* (Grand Rapids, MI: Eerdmans, 1991), pp. 123–82, for a discussion of how the idea of Israel's election developed.

[6] See Ginsberg, *The Israelian Heritage*, pp. 25–27.

After recounting how God had liberated Israel from Egyptian bondage, had sent Moses, Aaron and Miriam to lead his people and had accomplished triumphs on behalf of his people, the prophet poses the quintessential question of biblical religion:

> With what shall I come into the presence of YHWH,
> Do homage to the celestial God?
> Shall I come into his presence with burnt offerings,
> With yearling calves?
> Would YHWH be pleased by thousands of rams,
> By myriad streams of oil?
> Should I offer my firstborn for my sin,
> The fruit of my loins for my own transgression?
> It has been told to you, O man, what is proper;
> What YHWH requires of you:
> Only to administer justice,
> To love kindness,
> To deport yourself modestly when close to your God.
> Then will your name experience wisdom.[7]

The comparison of cultic and ethical behavior is somewhat overdrawn, to be sure, but that seems to be the point. The dictum *haṣnēᶜa leket ᶜim ᵓelōhêkā* is translated in a different way from its usual rendering, because it is our sense that the issue being addressed is, precisely, the profusion of cultic activity in northern Israel. Hence, *ᶜim ᵓelōhêkā* should refer to what is performed in sacred space, in the presence of the LORD. The prophet is decrying the elaborate cult of Samaria, operating in an unjust society. He foresees what was to be the Assyrian conquest of northern Israel, and his references and allusions resemble what we read in Hosea, another northern prophet of the period.[8]

As we shall observe, several of Micah's themes also inform the opening prophecy of Isaiah, a dramatic statement on the primacy of ethical behavior. One is hardly surprised to find Isaiah and Micah employing the same diction and expressing the same themes. Isaiah 1 is set in the period when Jerusalem and Judah, rather than the northern kingdom, were threatened by Neo-Assyrian power. There has always been a question, however, as to the position of Isaiah 1 in the chronological sequence of the prophet's speeches, since the prophet's initiation does not come until Isaiah 6. It is not certain, therefore, that Isaiah 1 marks the beginning of Isaiah's ministry, and it is entirely possible that Isaiah 1–5, in

---

[7] See NJPS to Mic. 6:8–9. The suggested translation excerpts from v. 9 the words *wetûšîyyāh yirᵓeh šemekâ*, which seem to be out of place, and inserts them at the end of v. 8, so that the anticipated result of deporting oneself properly is the acquisition of wisdom.

[8] See B.A. Levine's review of Ginsberg, *The Israelian Heritage*, in *AJS Review* 12 (1987), pp. 143–157 {*VOL 1, PP. 101–12*}. There, Hosea's objection to the proliferation of altars and to the elaborate royally sponsored cult of the northern Israelite kingdom in the period before the Assyrian onslaught is discussed.

part or in whole, are out of sequence and originate from later phases of the prophet's career.

Isaiah 1 might well refer to the situation during the third campaign of Sennacherib to Judah in 701 B.C.E. The prophet describes Jerusalem as a besieged city, and speaks of few survivors in Judah. The towns of Judah are laid waste, with foreigners consuming the produce of the land; many are wounded. The prophet wonders why the people persist in offending their God since such behavior would only invite further suffering (Isa. 1:5–9). What is more, Isaiah predicts a restoration, which makes sense because, in fact Jerusalem was spared destruction in 701 B.C.E. and the Assyrian siege was withdrawn.

In any event, the argument advanced in Isaiah 1, like those informing Micah 6–7 and Jeremiah 7, is only understandable in the context of a national disaster, imminent or already in progress. The prophet offers his interpretation of "knowing" (the verb *yādaʿ*) as he denounces a sinful Israel, whose failure to acknowledge God's role in history accounts for its continuing disobedience. If Israel possessed knowledge it would understand the causes of its adversity, depicted by Isaiah in considerable detail. But Israel persists in offending God because it lacks such knowledge:

> An ox knows its owner,
> An ass its owner's crib;
> *Yisrāʾēl lôʾ yādaʿ*
> Israel does not acknowledge,
> My people does not realize (*lôʾ hitbônān*) (Isa. 1:3).

What Israel fails to realize is that God is enraged by the injustice and corruption of Jerusalem and Judah, and will not be appeased by the glorification of his name in the cult of Jerusalem's temple. Jeremiah had spoken of 'the generation of my wrath', whereas Isaiah gives verbal definition to divine wrath, having God speak in the first person. But in Isa. 1:10–23, the most dramatic of all prophetic critiques of cultic correctness, there is no mention of paganism, as was true in Jeremiah 7, only of societal evil. In all of Isaiah 1 the only reference to paganism comes in v. 29, where the prophet predicts that when Jerusalem recovers from its wickedness, the sinful of Israel will abandon in disgrace the groves and gardens where they had engaged in idolatrous practices. For the rest, Isaiah seems to be concerned exclusively with the people's reliance on the temple cult at the same time that their hands are filled with blood:

> Hear the word of YHWH
> You chieftains of Sodom;
> Give ear to the teaching of our God, People of Gomorrah!
> What need have I of all your sacrifices?
> —says YHWH.
> I am sated with burnt offerings of rams,
> And suet of fatlings,
> And blood of bulls;
> I take no delight

in lambs and he-goats.
When you make an appearance before me—
Who asked such from your hand?
Trample my courts no more!
Bringing grain offerings is futile;
Incense is an abomination to me!
New Moon and Sabbath,
The proclamation of a convocation,
Fast day and assembly—
I cannot abide
Your New Moons and annual feasts
My feelings despise;
They have become burdensome to me,
I cannot bear them.
When you raise your palms,
I will turn my eyes away from you.
Though you pray at length,
I am not listening.
Your hands are filled with blood! (Isa. 1:10–15)

The God of Israel is annoyed with the cult of the Jerusalem temple, though it was undoubtedly being performed properly. Its continuance, under existing conditions of societal evil, is the brunt of prophetic ridicule. The chieftains and people of Jerusalem were presiding over, and living in a wicked and perverse city, being compared to Sodom and Gomorrah, and to be spared the fate of those towns only through God's mercy (v. 9). In such circumstances, not only are sacrifices futile, even loathsome, and Sabbaths and festivals unbearable to God, but prayer is not efficacious either. The reason is simple: "Your hands are filled with blood (*yedêkem dāmîm mālēʾû*)".

The nuances of the Hebrew term *dāmîm*, "blood", have led some to translate it as "crime", because in legal contexts *dāmîm* connotes capital crime. In an example of inner-biblical exegesis, Ezek. 7:23 understands the passage in this way: "For the land is filled with bloody crimes (*mišpaṭ dāmîm*), and the city is full of lawlessness". This sense is expressed in the characterization *ʿîr haddāmîm*, "the city of murder", used elsewhere by Ezekiel in speaking of Jerusalem (Ezek. 22:2; 24:6, 9).

And yet, one senses a cultic, along with a legal, nuance in the reference to bloodied hands in Isa. 1:15. In the continuation of Isaiah's oracle we read that the blood of guilt must be washed away, and v. 18 speaks of sins red as crimson, another allusion to blood. One is immediately reminded of the ritual of the heifer prescribed in Deuteronomy 21. That unusual ceremony, which combines ritual, magical, and legal acts, also has as its referent the responsibilities of a city. In Deuteronomy, we encounter a town seeking to acquit itself of guilt for an unsolved murder that has occurred near its municipal limits.

The town's elders wash their hands over a heifer whose neck has been severed, as its blood runs into the stream, and they declare, "Our hands did not spill this blood nor did our eyes see. Grant expiation to your people, Israel, whom you redeemed (*ʾašer pādîtā*) YHWH" (Deut. 21:7–8). The prayer goes on to express the hope that guilt for the blood of the innocent will be removed from among the people of Israel. Isaiah also urges cleansing:

> Wash yourselves, be purified (*hizzakkû*).
> Remove your evil deeds from my purview.
> Cease to do evil; learn to do good.
> Promote justice,
> Support the oppressed,
> Take up the case of the orphan,
> Plead the cause of the widow (Isa. 1:16–17).

The Hebrew form *hizzakkû* has been variously analyzed, some deriving it from *zkh*, "to merit acquittal, clearance" as a byform of the *hithpael hitzakkū*, and others from *zkk*, 'to be pure', as a *niphal* imperative.[9] Actually, *zkh* is probably just another realization of geminate *zkk*, whose specialized meaning is more appropriate here. Initially, one is cleansed or purified by washing, and only exonerated as a result of this. We know, of course, of the transactions attendant upon terms for cleansing and purification, whereby they signify legal clearance, acquittal and innocence, and such a transaction is certainly at work in Isa. 1:16. The implication is that a pure or proper temple cult will not save Jerusalem, only the re-establishment of justice within the city's jurisdiction. The purification required of the people is not ritual but rather ethical, legal and social. The two images which express the required transformation are the washing away of blood and the purging of alloys to produce pure metals, the well-known image of the crucible. Of the two, the image of blood as guilt and of its cleansing with water is closer to cultic phenomena and yet does not reflect a standard means of ritual purification.

The responsibility of a good city to prosecute justice informs Isaiah's prophecy, as it does the law of Deuteronomy 21. This is borne out by Isa. 1:21:

> Alas, she has become a harlot,
> The faithful city
> That was filled with justice.
> Where righteousness dwelt—
> But now murderers!

Unlike the good judges, elders, and Levitical priests of the Deuteronomic city, who are concerned with murders committed even outside their city limits, the Jerusalemites have forsaken the pursuit of justice within their city proper. The verb *pādāh*, "to redeem", used in the Deuteronomic prayer cited above (Deut. 21:7–8) further links Isaiah 1 to Deuteronomy, for in Isa. 1:27 we read,

> Zion shall be redeemed (*tippādeh*) through justice,
> And her restored people (*wešābêhā*) through righteousness.

---

[9] Cf. the *niphal* imperfect *yissabbû*, "they rotate", from *sbb* in Ezek. 1:9.

Of course, others have translated this verse differently, interpreting it to mean that in the judgment to come, Zion will be redeemed, and her "penitents" will be redeemed with her.[10] It is argued that Isaiah 1 nowhere projects Jerusalem's destruction and the exile of its populace, so that it would be imprecise to understand *wešābêhā* in the sense of "her returnees". And yet, Isaiah is actually envisioning a rebirth of the city and its citizenry. Though Jerusalem will not "fall" in the usual way of being conquered and razed, it will be struck down in the way that a revolution brings about the fall of an entrenched government. This revolution will be mounted by God himself, who regards the rulers, judges and the corrupt of the citizenry as his foes:

> Ah, I will get satisfaction from my foes,
> I will wreak vengeance on my enemies (Isa. 1:24b).

One should definitely allow for the likelihood of double entendre in the usage of the Hebrew form *mišpāṭ*, "justice/judgment" and participial *šābêhā*, "those restored to her/her penitents". And yet, the primary image seems to be that of the restoration of a city through the reestablishment of justice and righteousness within its limits. This is at least a logical way of understanding the sequence of (1) Zion's lapse from justice, described dramatically in Isa. 1:21–23, followed by (2) Zion's purging and reconstitution as a just municipality in vv. 24–27. As *double entendre*, participial *šābêhā* may connote the "return" or the penitence of the sinful, but the diction of the preceding verses more clearly suggests the dynamics of restoration:

> 25 I will bring down my arm (*weʾāšîbāh yādî*) upon you.
> 26 I will restore (*weʾāšîbāh*) your judges as formerly.

The author is playing on the nuances of the verb *šûb*, "to return", *hiphil hēšîb*, "to restore, bring down (the arm)". Idiomatic *hēšîb* + *yād* + *ʿal* means "to strike down", by an action of lowering one's arm with force (Ezek. 38:12; Amos 1:8; Ps. 81:15). First, the God of Israel will strike down the corrupt of Jerusalem, the dregs and dross, and eventually they will perish like tow hit by a spark (Isa. 1:28–31). God will then restore Jerusalem's proper judges, and following that Jerusalem itself will be redeemed and acquitted of its guilt, and its populace reconstituted within a righteous city. When all of this has happened, a new role will begin for Jerusalem and its temple, as predicted in Isa. 2:1–4.

Before leaving Isaiah 1 to take up the vision of Isa. 2:2–4 which follows, we should comment on Isa. 1:18–20, which speaks of the lawsuit brought against Jerusalem by the God of Israel. In legal language, one could say that Jerusalem is found guilty, but will be spared destruction and be placed on probation:

---

[10] Thus the NJPS, but see S.D. Luzzatto, *Il Profeta Isaia* (Padova, 1867; repr. Jerusalem: Akademon, AM 5727), Isa. 1:27, and Luzzatto's Hebrew commentary, pp. 42–43. Luzzatto strongly objects to the sense of "penitents" for Hebrew *šābêhā*, an interpretation actually endorsed by Rashi and Ibn Ezra.

Come, now, let us reach a verdict (*weniwwākeḥāh*),
Says YHWH.
Be your sins like crimson,
They can turn snow-white;
They can become like fleece.
If you consent and pay heed,
You will eat the bounty of the land.
But if you refuse and disobey,
You will be devoured by the sword,
For it was YHWH who spoke (Isa. 1:18–20).

The student of the Bible is aware of the ambiguity of this passage. The suggested translation, "reach a verdict", represents an attempt to make sense out of the *niphal* form *weniwwākeḥāh*. Etymologically, the English word "verdict" harks back to the Latin *vere dictum*, words "truly said", thereby conveying the sense of "proof, demonstration" associated with the Hebrew verb *w-k-ḥ*. The English "verdict" also conveys the nuance in the closure of this passage: "For it was YHWH who spoke", that is, it was YHWH who issued the verdict. What is more, Isa. 2:4 states that in the restored Jerusalem the God of Israel "will arbitrate, render verdicts" (Hebrew *wehôkîaḥ*) between disputing nations, further echoing *weniwwākeḥāh* in Isa. 1:18. Earlier I noted that Mic. 6:2b uses the *hithpael* form *yitwakkāḥ* ("He [= God] is pressing a verdict") against Israel in a law-suit. We are not far from the mark in proposing that Isaiah 1 be understood as a law-suit brought by the God of Israel against his people.

The theme of obedience, so prominent in Jeremiah's prophecy, is delivered by Isaiah in a binary statement. The entire future of Jerusalem is made contingent on Israel's obedience, and Isaiah has defined obedience primarily in judicial and ethical terms.

Now it becomes possible to comprehend Isaiah's vision of days to come, of a restored Jerusalem, that is projected in Isa. 2:4. A temple will stand on Mount Zion, to be sure, but it will be more than a house of worship. It will serve as an international court of justice, where disputes among nations will be settled through verdicts issued oracularly by the God of Israel himself.

In the days to come,
YHWH's temple mount
Shall stand firm above the mountains,
And be raised higher than the hills.
All the nations shall look brightly upon it.
Many peoples shall set out [for it], saying:
Come, let us ascend the mountain of YHWH,
To the temple of the God of Jacob;
That he may instruct us of his ways,
So that we will walk in his paths.
For rulings are issued from Zion,
YHWH's oracle from Jerusalem.
Thus he shall adjudicate between the nations,
And render verdicts to many peoples.

They shall beat their swords into plowshares,
Their spears into pruning hooks.
One nation shall not raise the sword
against another nation,
They shall never again train for war.

This passage can be interpreted from many different perspectives. Here we are concerned with Isaiah's attitude toward the temple of Jerusalem and its cult, and my comments will consequently focus on this aspect. Several relevant themes inform the prophecy. We should note, first of all, the figure of firmness associated with the temple: it will be *nākôn*, "standing firm", unshakeable. We will have occasion further on to discuss the typology of temples in ancient Near Eastern literature. By saying that the temple of Jerusalem will stand firm Isaiah means to say that it is a temple of righteousness, for a temple of wickedness would not endure.

Several terms of reference also require comment. God's verdicts are to be rendered as *dābār* and *tôrāh*. In the present context, *dābār* is best translated "oracle", and *tôrāh*, "ruling". The Hebrew term *tôrāh* is actually of priestly provenance, referring primarily to the rulings issued by priests on questions of law in their role as judges. This priestly function is most specifically expressed in Deuteronomy 17 which sounds as though it is related to Isaiah's prophecy:

> If a case is too deep for you to adjudicate, be it a dispute over homicide, civil damages, or assault, matters of dispute in your gates, you must promptly ascend to the cult-site (*māqôm*) which YHWH your God will have selected. You must approach the Levitical priests and the judge (*šôpēṭ*) presiding at that time, and request a decision. They will announce to you the verdict/oracle in the case (*debar hammišpāṭ*), and you must act in accordance with the verdict/oracle (*haddābār*) they announce to you at that cult-site which YHWH will have selected. You must carefully carry out all that they instruct you. In accordance with the ruling (*tôrāh*) they instruct you and in accordance with the judgment they inform you, you must act (Deut. 17:8–11a).

Here we have all of the terms of reference featured in Isaiah's prophecy, and it is a moot point whether to translate *dābār* in Deuteronomy 17 as "verdict" or "oracle".

The use of *dābār* in Isaiah's prophecy clearly expresses the function of the Jerusalem temple as an *oraculum*, a function epitomized in early traditions by the Tent of Meeting mentioned by the Elohist in Exod. 33:7–11; 34:34–35. One knowing *tôrāh* and in receipt of *dābār* would find YHWH's "path", *derek* (and *ʾôraḥ*), a theme already discussed in the treatment of Jeremiah 7.

It is improbable that Isaiah envisioned a temple in Jerusalem that would no longer serve as a house of worship of the God of Israel. What he seems to be saying is that Jerusalem has a role as the seat of justice and, conforming to the pervasive ancient Near Eastern pattern, the court would be located adjacent to the temple in an acropolis complex.

The court on Mount Zion, standing near the temple, would settle the wars of Assyrian conquest and domination through the rule of divinely revealed law. This process would end the direct threat to Jerusalem and Judah, and bring peace to other nations as well. But before Judah and Jerusalem could assume a role in international affairs, and before the God of Israel could enlighten the nations by revealing just settlements of international conflicts, the existing Jerusalem, with its injustice and corruption, must be reconstituted into a Jerusalem of righteousness.

In Isaiah's eyes, the persistence of a wicked society in Jerusalem, capital of Judah, was in reality preventing the fulfillment of YHWH's plan for his people and for the world. Could this be the reason for divine wrath over the profusion of cultic activity in the temple of a corrupt Jerusalem? What an irony! The Judeans delude themselves that they are glorifying YHWH in the temple, whereas in truth they are delaying YHWH's exaltation as God of all nations!

3. The Offerings of the Wicked

The reference to Shiloh in Jeremiah 7 is linked by diction and theme to the oracle of Ahijah the Shilonite in 1 Kings 14. There, as in Jeremiah 7, we read of doing evil. Thus in 1 Kgs 14:9 the verb *wattāraʿ* "You (= Jeroboam) have done evil" recalls Jer. 7:12, where we read that YHWH destroyed Shiloh "because of the evil of my people Israel (*mippenê rāʿat ʿammî Yiśrāʾēl*)". The Israelites "anger" YHWH (the verb *hikʿîs*) in 1 Kgs 14:9, as in Jer. 7:18–19. The result is that the God of Israel will "cast off" his people (the verb *hišlîk*) from his presence, namely from the land (Jer. 7:15), just as in 1 Kgs 14:9 Jeroboam had cast YHWH off, discarded him over his shoulder!

Jeremiah's reference to Shiloh as a symbol of the northern Israelite kingdom recalls Psalm 78, a Zion psalm that epitomizes the selection of Jerusalem and the rejection of Shiloh, God's abandonment of the northern Israelite kingdom and his election of the Davidic dynasty. There is, however, a salient difference in viewpoint between Jeremiah 7 and Psalm 78. In his lengthy review of Israelite history, the Psalmist endorses the essentials of the prophetic outlook, but when he speaks of the more recently chosen temple of Jerusalem (Ps. 78:60–72), his tone changes: "He built his sanctuary like the heavens; like the earth that he established forever" (Ps. 78:69).

For the Psalmist, the dynastic covenant with David and the divine selection of Mount Zion as the site of the temple are eternal. These critical acts on the part of the God of Israel mark a break with the prior dynamic of Israelite history, and with the chronic shifts from divine favor to punishment that had characterized Israel's experience since Egypt. What had happened to Shiloh and northern Israel would not recur with respect to Jerusalem and Judah. Although the Psalmist hardly disputes the doctrine that Israel's historic misfortunes, most notably the loss of the northern kingdom, were the consequences of its persistent sinfulness, he voices the doctrine basic to cultic religion that the presence of the deity in the Jerusalem temple guarantees the security of city and kingdom. In this respect he belongs with the authors of other psalms who give expression to the same doctrine. Thus Psalm 46:

> God is our refuge and stronghold,
> A help in trouble; very near.
> Therefore, we are not afraid
> Though the earth reels,
> Though mountains topple into the sea …
> There is a river whose streams gladden God's city,
> The dwelling place of the Most High.
> God is in its midst, it will not be toppled;
> By daybreak God will come to its aid.
> Nations rage, kingdoms topple;
> At the sound of his thunder the earth dissolves.
> YHWH of Hosts is with us;
> The God of Jacob is our haven.

Similarly, Ps. 48:9 states that the city of God will remain firm forever, just as in his prayer Solomon refers to the eternity of the temple of Jerusalem as God's seat (1 Kgs 8:13). This concept is common to the literature of the ancient Near East. Best known, perhaps, is the epilogue to the Code of Hammurabi, where it is stated that the king has erected a stela bearing his laws in the temple. He refers to Babylon and to Esagila, its main temple, as follows;

> In Babylon, the city whose head Anum and Enlil raised aloft,
> In Esagila, the temple whose foundations stand firm like heaven and earth
> I wrote my precious words on my stela.[11]

Such expressions are of course hopeful, even wishful, but they represent the essential belief of the cultic establishment which the priesthood undoubtedly encouraged the people to accept. Ironically, this is the very notion denounced by Jeremiah as a falsehood (Jer. 7:4, 8), because it affords the unwarranted sense of security that the Israelite people attribute to the presence of God in his holy temple in Jerusalem.

Just as the author of Psalm 78 was familiar with prophetic teaching, so Jeremiah was familiar with the promise of an everlasting temple and kingdom. Only if the people fulfill the requirements of strict monotheism and uphold the moral code will YHWH "allow you to dwell in this place, in the land that I gave to your fathers for all time" (Jer. 7:7). Otherwise "I will do to the House which bears my name, on which you rely, and to the cult-place which I gave you and your fathers, just what I did to Shiloh: (Jer. 7:14).

---

[11] See *ANET*, p. 178, lines 63–67, in the Epilogue to the Code of Hammurabi (trans. by T. Meek).

We should not, therefore, take the view that the policy of priests, kings and Psalmists was diametrically opposed to that of the prophets. Legitimate Israelite priests did not teach that moral behavior had no bearing on the efficacy of the cult nor that the offerings of the wicked were acceptable. We are dealing with differences in emphasis and values not with mutually exclusive doctrines. Furthermore, we are dealing with aspects of religion and culture that derive from different sources. The cultic view of the human-divine relationship was rooted in very ancient cosmic and mythological notions about temples and sacred space, about theophanies and sanctifications, whereas the moral view came from other sources—from Wisdom literature, from oracles and prophecy, and from law and political doctrine. The question that should occupy us is the extent to which these two outlooks were compatible with each other in biblical culture, as opposed to the extent to which there was tension and conflict between them.

For insight, we turn to Jeremiah 5 where, as in Isaiah 1, it is the verb *yādaʿ*, with all of its subtleties and nuances, that informs the prophet's evaluation of the Israelite people of his day. Jeremiah suggests that there is a message or teaching which the Israelites fail to acknowledge, a notion of a moral order which they persist in doubting, notwithstanding the lessons of their past history and the danger of their current predicament. Their mind-set vis-à-vis the conditionality of cultic efficacy and its dependence on upholding the divinely ordained moral order parallels their thinking on the question of paganism in the cult. They do not accept the idea that compromising strict monotheism in worship invalidates the efficacy of the cult, just as they fail to face up to the fact that God will reject the offerings of the wicked.

There seems to be an ironic difference, however, between the two failures of the Israelite people. Although historically the prophetic insistence on strict monotheistic worship represents an innovation, and hardly reflects a consensus in the Israelite societies of pre-exilic times, the very notion of the indispensability of correct cultic procedures was hardly novel in ancient Near Eastern religions. The gods had ordained fixed and regular codes of cultic procedure, a notion expressed in Akkadian by the term *parṣu*. When the people reject the prophetic definition of the proper *parṣu*, so to speak, they act in disobedience of a code with which they may disagree in substance but whose attribution to divine will they understand. In other words the people believe that God, or the gods, eternally command the order of the cult and its specific components. One might say that the priestly traditions of the Hebrew Bible, especially those preserved in Torah literature, corresponded more closely to what the people understood religion to be about. The problem lay in the exclusivist character of Israelite monotheism, as defined by the prophets. Was this the true *parṣu*?

A different dynamic is at work in the prophetic insistence on obedience to the moral code as a condition of cultic efficacy. Culturally there is nothing new in the notion that moral behavior is requisite for divine approval. The ancient Egyptians, in protesting their guiltlessness at the time of death, insisted along with their declarations of piety that they had lived their lives in a moral and compassionate manner. In effect, they insisted that they had followed the wise teachings of the sages. A perusal of the list of these declarations reveals a certain quantitative balance between ethical and ritual attainments, and even shows a pattern of regularity in the alternation of the two categories in their sequence.[12] In ancient Near Eastern royal inscriptions kings and leaders declare that they have established justice in their realms, and boast that the gods regularly accept their sacrifices because they are pleased with their social and ethical behavior as well as with their devotion to and respect for the cult. The pantheons of the major ancient Near Eastern societies all include divine judges, who weigh the hearts of men according to standards of justice and goodness.

Internal Israelite sources yield the same information, namely that the God of Israel demands justice and kindness. This idea is basic to early formulations of the covenant between Israel and YHWH, and is implicit in the notion that the legal norms by which Israel was to be governed were revealed by YHWH and bore the sanction of divine commands. Unless one maintains that literary prophecy antedated the earliest statements of law as revelation in biblical Israel, hardly a tenable hypothesis, one is led to the conclusion that the Israelites of the ninth to the seventh century should have had no illusions on the subject of morality as a precondition of divine approval.

It would be inaccurate to conclude, therefore, that the classical prophets of Israel first introduced into Israelite religion the notion that the efficacy of the cult was conditional upon upholding the moral order. What does it mean, then, to say that Israel does not "know"? Perhaps it means that the notion of cultic indispensability was objectionable not for itself, but because its monotheistic restriction had not been acknowledged by king and people. For its part, the notion that the cult is conditional on obedience to the moral order was resisted because Israelites, like other human beings, often lacked moral fiber and were deluded into believing that they could deceive God.

It is probable nonetheless that in Israelite culture the integration of the moral and the cultic agenda had gone beyond what was typical of contemporary polytheistic cultures. This is evident from the biblical Wisdom tradition. If we compare the lament of the so-called "Babylonian Job" in the composition entitled *Ludlul Bēl Nēmeqi* ("I will Praise the Lord of Wisdom") with the protestations of the biblical Job, such a difference in ethos is clarified. The similarities between the two compositions are compelling on many levels, as is their relative contemporaneity and their common attribution to the Wisdom tradition. Most striking is the similarity between the unfortunate conditions which each lamenter describes, and the sense of disappointment each experiences. There is also common ground in the sense expressed by both of being confounded by the seemingly irrational actions of the gods, or of God in the case of Job. It is significant, therefore, that in his complaint over his misfortune, the Babylonian appeals entirely to his piety and cultic devotion. He claims that he is being treated as one who has not performed all of the rites that he insists he has performed

[12] See *ANET*, pp. 34–36, "The Protestation of Guiltlessness" (trans. J.A. Wilson).

dutifully; that he has been treated by gods of various ranks as though he were a callously irreverent person:

> Like one who has not made libations to his god,
> Nor invoked the goddess when he ate,
> Does not make prostrations nor recognize [the necessity of] bowing down …
> Who has even neglected holy days, and ignored festivals,
> Who was negligent and did not observe the gods' rites,
> Did not teach his people reverence and worship …
> [Like such a one] do I appear.[13]

We observe a citizen or leader of some stature, not unlike the biblical Job, who characterizes himself as a dutifully religious man. One searches in vain for a similar emphasis on cultic devotion in biblical Wisdom, more particularly in the book of Job. In fact the biblical Job never appeals to his cultic correctness in pressing his case before God, whom he holds responsible for his suffering and for the loss of his former status and well-being. What he consistently cites as deserving of divine favor is his social responsibility, his probity and integrity, his compassion for the unfortunate and his civic leadership.

Those who would dispute the above conclusion by citing the piety ascribed to Job in the Prologue (Job 1–2) are on weak ground. The Prologue and Epilogue, where Job is indeed portrayed as a reverent man, are not made of the same cloth as the dialogues and speeches of the book of Job proper. These compositions not only differ in diction and literary character, but also serve to define the problem of Job within the context of traditional Jewish religion and culture by rationalizing Job's predicament as a divine test of faith. The dialogues proper never advance such a resolution. In fact the Prologue and Epilogue correlate more closely with the Babylonian Job's perspective on his suffering and eventual recovery. It appears, therefore, that in the Israelite Wisdom tradition cultic correctness counted for much less in the human-divine equation than it did in Babylonian Wisdom. Proverbs has the following to say on the subject:

> Honor YHWH from your wealth,
> and from the first of all your crop.
> And your barns will be filled with grain,
> Your vats will burst with new wine (Prov. 3:9–10).

Indeed, God will bless those who make offerings to him. Be it known, however, that God's favor is conditional:

> The sacrifice of the wicked is an abomination to YHWH.
> But the prayer of the upright secures his favor
> (Prov. 15:8; cf. Prov. 21:27).

---

[13] See *ANET*, p. 597, "I will Praise the Lord of Wisdom", lines 13–23 (trans. R.D. Biggs).

The Language of Holiness: Perceptions of the Sacred in the Hebrew Bible*

One cannot speak of God or of religious experience without coming face to face with the theme of holiness. As a concept, holiness relates to a complex of elusive phenomena that retain an aura of mystery and resist definition. The phenomenologist of religion seeks to uncover the mysterious dimensions of human experience by penetrating the interior mentality which is reflected in the manifest phenomena. The purpose of this essay is to illustrate one of the methods available to us in our quest for the meaning of biblical religion, the study of language and diction. A semantic treatment of the words used in the Hebrew Bible to express perceptions of the sacred will test the proposition that language may serve as a fruitful point of departure. The language of holiness will lead us to a consideration of the *idea* of the holy.

There are questions that go beyond what a study of language can reveal. Theologians seek to formulate the relationship between holiness and the "nature" of God. Phenomenologists want to know more about human responses to the holy. Students of cult and ritual search for evidence bearing on forms of celebration and on the role of religious institutions in the life of a society. Historians of literature trace the transmission of themes and the modulation of concepts attributable to different schools of biblical writers. None of these tasks is at odds with the approach being exemplified here. The question is: Where do we begin? Here we will begin with language and diction!

The Hebrew verb which most precisely expresses the concept of holiness is *qādaš*, "to be, become, remain holy." The nominal and adjectival derivatives of this verb, and various relevant syntactic structures, condition our understanding of the phenomena associated with holiness. In the course of analyzing the functions of the verb *qādaš* and its derivatives, we will pursue some of the phenomenological implications of our analysis beyond the limits of diction. Though the analysis of language does sometimes appear atomistic, the student does not operate in a vacuum. The true challenge is to employ models in such a way as to place the detailed findings of our analysis in perspective, rather than allowing models to control the analysis from the outset.

* Originally published in Michael P. O'Connor and David N. Freedman (eds.), *Backgrounds for the Bible* (Winona Lake, IN: Eisenbrauns, 1987), pp. 241–255. Reprinted with permission from Eisenbrauns.

I

The Biblical Hebrew vocabulary of holiness is based on the root *q-d-š*. Thus, what is "holy" is designated by the adjective *qādôš*. "Holiness" is designated by the noun *qodeš*. A temple or shrine is called *miqdāš*. The processes whereby sanctity is attributed to persons, places, objects, and the like are usually expressed by forms of the verb *qādaš*.

The Semitic root *q-d-š* has a history which considerably antedates the biblical period. Most significant are cognates in Akkadian and Ugaritic, languages related to Hebrew and attested in the same ancient Near Eastern milieu. The etymology of *q-d-š* remains uncertain. The ancient lexical texts from Mesopotamia provide Sumerian equivalents for Akkadian words; these give an indication of relevant senses. The Akkadian verb *qadāšu* is only one of the equivalents listed for Sumerian UD, a word which exhibits a broad semantic range. Other Akkadian equivalents of UD include *ellu*, "pure, clean, clear," *ebbu*, "clean," and *namru*, "bright," as well as related verb forms. It might be of interest to note that the word UD also has as an equivalent Akkadian *urru*, "light, daylight," as well as *umu*, "day, daytime."

The intensive form of the Akkadian verb is *quddušu*, "to purify, consecrate," and normally describes the processes of ritual and magical sanctification. These did not differ in procedure from similar rites performed within the Israelite cult and conveyed by the cognate Hebrew form, *qiddēš*. Sanctification was accomplished by means of sacrifice, unction, the recitation of prayers and incantations, and by the investiture of priests, the dedications of statues, etc. In short, Akkadian *quddušu* describes the whole array of activities usually connected with the attribution of holiness.

Some cultic personnel are identified by forms derived from the verb *qadāšu*. We find titles such as *qadištu*, literally "consecrated woman," the title of a class of priestesses, well known in the Old Babylonian period (the early second millennium B.C.E.). We also find forms exhibiting metathesis, such as *qašdu* (instead of *qadšu*), "holy," and *qašdatu* (instead of *qadšatu*), "priestess; consecrated woman." We even have the abstract noun, *qadšūtu*, "holiness, the status of a priest." These terms, seen in the light of the verb-forms, point us in the direction of the cult—its consecrated personnel, its sacred spaces, and its sacral rites.

It is true that Akkadian *qadāšu* is linked to other equivalents of Sumerian UD which sometimes connote physical properties, as for example, *ellu*, "pure." Nevertheless, the general impression is that the attested forms of Akkadian *qadāšu* connote effects or processes. They describe the brilliance or aura surrounding gods and kings, or characterize processes relevant to cleansing and purification. These forms do not signify an inherent *mana*. This is an important point, because further on we will have occasion to suggest that monotheistic writers in ancient Israel found the root *q-d-š* particularly appropriate for characterizing the God of Israel, for the very reason, perhaps, that it did not inevitably denote physical properties.

The next historical link is provided by the Ugaritic documents, dating from the second half of the second millennium B.C.E. In Ugaritic a finite form of the root *q-d-š* may be attested once or twice, but for the most part we find nominal forms. (1) *qdšt* means "goddess, holy one"; this occurs in a personal name: *bn qdšt*, "son of a priestess," or possibly "son of a goddess." (2) *qdšm*, "priests" are listed together with *khnm* (compare the Hebrew cognate, *kohānîm*, "priests"). (3) *mqdšt* is a plural form, meaning "temples," a cognate of Hebrew *miqdāš*. There is also a place name built on the root *q-d-š*, just as in Hebrew we find place names such as Qadesh and Qedesh.

Most commonly, however, we find in Ugaritic the nominal form *qdš*, comparable to Hebrew *qodeš*. As in Hebrew, the most frequent sense of Ugaritic *qdš* is "holy place, sanctuary." Again as in Hebrew, Ugaritic *qdš* may have adjectival force, meaning "holy," rather than "holiness." For example, a *ks qdš*, "holy cup," is one from which a goddess drinks! Similarly, *bn qdš*, literally "holy sons," are simply "young gods." There is also a goddess named Qudshu.

When we combine the evidence of Akkadian and Ugaritic, we can consider the background of the later uses of the *q-d-š* root. Akkadian supplies some of what is missing from Ugaritic, i.e., finite verb-forms that describe the processes of consecration. Ugaritic, on the other hand, emphasizes the intimate connection between holiness and divinity. In Ugaritic, the nominal form *qdš* seems never to connote an abstract state of holiness, as its morphology might suggest, but only some "thing" or "being" characterized as holy. We will have occasion to observe that a similar, though somewhat more complex, usage is characteristic of Hebrew, where there is little expressed in the way of abstract holiness.

As is true in Semitic lexicography generally, synonyms of the root *q-d-š* point to differences in usage among the several Semitic languages, differences probably determined by mentality. For example, an Akkadian writer may say of gods that they are "pure" (*ellu* or *ebbu*), but in the Hebrew Bible one never finds the God of Israel described as *ṭāhôr*, "pure," the Hebrew equivalent of the Akkadian adjectives. The closest we come to this perception is in Habakkuk 1:13, where God is said to be "pure of vision," which means simply that He countenances no injustice. We cannot be entirely certain why the adjective *ṭāhôr*, "pure," never describes the God of Israel in the Hebrew Bible. This may be merely a "coincidence," that is, a fact of distribution with no conceptual implications. In Ugaritic, gods are likewise never described as *ẓhr* or *ṭhr*, but these words are so rarely attested in Ugaritic that we must, once again, reserve judgment. The difference in usage evident between Akkadian and Hebrew may be significant, for one would hardly expect the God of Israel to be described in terms which suggest that He shares an innate property of metals and stones! The property of purity is elsewhere conveyed by the Hebrew adjective *ṭāhôr*; note, for example, that in Exodus 24:10 there was visible under God's feet "something like the whiteness of sapphire and the essence of the heavens in purity (*lāṭohar*)." This was not how God himself appeared, but only how the aura near Him shone! It may be that what makes the verb *qādaš*, in distinction to *ṭāhôr*, so appropriate is that it does not compromise God's transcendence, a notion basic to Israelite monotheism. Thus, despite the close connection between "purity" and "holiness," there is a significant difference between them in the biblical perception.

II

In Hebrew the simple verb-form *qādaš* focuses attention on the pivotal change that occurs when the "not-holy" becomes "holy." This relatively uncommon form conveys the atmosphere of *tabu*, the negative dimension of holiness—its dangers, its restrictiveness, and its insulation from the profane. Perhaps the most direct statement on the change from the "not-holy" to the "holy" occurs in Deuteronomy 22:9, within a legal context:

> You may not sow your vineyard with a second variety of seed, lest the fresh crop from the seed you have sown, as well as the yield of the vineyard itself, become holy (*tiqdaš*).

It is forbidden to plant grain or vegetables in proximity to vines. If, in violation of the law, such planting occurs, the produce yielded thereby, along with the fruit of the vines, becomes *tabu*. In his classic study of the phenomenology of religion, G. van der Leeuw explains that the term *tabu* (or *tapu*), of Melanesian origin, means "what is expressly named, exceptional"; the verb *tapui* means "to make holy." In the law of Deuteronomy 22:9, the change to the status of *tabu* is legally determined. The law declares the total yield to be holy. We are not told, however, what was to be done with the produce—What did it mean in practical terms that it had become "holy"?

In this law, the nexus of holiness and prohibition is clearly expressed. Here the verb *qādaš* has a rare negative connotation. A later sage translated *tiqdaš* in this verse as *tēʾāsēr*, "it shall be prohibited." Other Rabbinic traditions construed it as a contraction of two words, *TûQaD* + *ʾēŠ*, "it shall be burned in fire." In the exegetical process of *notarikon* exemplified here, the consonants of a single verb-form are vocalized differently, and the syllables divided to form two words. Notwithstanding its precious ingenuity, this play on sound may be correct about the procedures operative in biblical times. The most spontaneous reaction to *tabu* is avoidance, which often requires elimination. Destruction was one of the methods for disposing of proscribed or condemned materials.

If this is what Deuteronomy 22:9 intended, an account in Numbers 16–17 clearly indicates an alternative method, *restriction of use*. In that account, we read that a group of Levites sought to unseat the Aaronide clan from its hegemony over the Israelite priesthood. This challenge aroused God's wrath. According to one version of the story, the entire dissident faction perished in a conflagration; this happened as the two-hundred-and-fifty men were standing near the entrance to the Tent of Meeting, bearing copper firepans filled with incense. Aaron was also present. This scene was orchestrated at God's command as an ordeal of sorts. God's acceptance of the offerings presented by the dissidents would have indicated divine endorsement of their suit. God rejected those offerings, favoring Aaron instead, and all who stood for the ordeal, except Aaron, met with death. The biblical account continues with God's instructions to Aaron:

> Let him remove the firepans from the remains of the conflagration and throw the incense away. The firepans borne by those who lost their lives *have become holy* (*qādēšû*), so let them be hammered into sheets as plating for the altar. For once having been offered in the presence of the LORD, they had become holy (*wa-yiqdāšû*). (Numbers 17:2b–3)

As I understand this passage (and others understand it differently), it was the prior assignment of the firepans for use in a specific rite, albeit in an offering subsequently rejected by God, that rendered them *tabu*. They had become God's property, so to speak, at the moment of their assignment, an act that was irreversible. The copper, like the incense, could no longer be used for ordinary purposes. The incense was thrown away, but the copper was used for refurbishing the altar of burnt offerings, which was initially fashioned with overlaid copper.

The two cases just discussed represent alternate methods for dealing with materials that had become holy. Comparable modern procedures are the laws that authorize the government to condemn private property, often used to permit its confiscation for roads, public buildings, etc.; this right extends to the demolition of unsafe buildings, for instance, when they become a danger to public safety. Ultimately, such legal instrumentalities hark back to ancient notions of *tabu*.

In biblical literature, condemnation is also expressed by the term *ḥērem* "*tabu*, proscription." The verb *ḥāram* means "to set aside, declare sacred, condemn." In Biblical Hebrew it bears a one-sided relation to the verb *qādaš*, expressing solely the negative aspect of sanctification. It never connotes a sought-after condition or a procedure undertaken voluntarily. (In some other Semitic languages, cognates of Hebrew *ḥāram* share the entire range of associations, positive as well as negative, of sanctification.)

What becomes *ḥērem* is either to be destroyed or restricted in its utilization. Biblical laws seem to drift between these alternatives. Common to what is holy and what is *ḥērem* is the element of danger. In the Hebrew Bible that danger is perceived as coming from God and is manifested in His wrath. It is not thought to derive from any immanent feature or property of the substances which are *tabu*. The "reason" for God's wrath is disobedience to His will.

The simple form of the verb *qādaš* does more than describe the change from the "not-holy" to the "holy." it also expresses the retention of holiness, since holiness is a volatile state. Defilement may virtually undo the effects of sanctification. To protect what is holy requires that the clergy be consecrated, because to handle sacred objects or stand in holy places one must be holy. This is expressed in Exodus 29:37 (cf. 30:29) where we find a basic regulation relevant to the sanctuary altar: "Whoever comes in contact (*ha-nogēaʿ*) with the altar *must be in a holy state* (*yiqdaš*)." This translation is predicated on a particular understanding of this enigmatic and rather abrupt statement. It is assumed that the governing concern is with protecting the altar from defilement; only a consecrated person, a priest, may have contact with it. Others have interpreted this verse as expressing a result: "Whoever comes in contact with the altar *will become holy*." This rendering of the simple form of the verb expresses the notion that sanctity is contagious; that one who touches something holy becomes holy as a consequence, or "contracts" holiness, if you will. This interpretation is unlikely, and there is actually little evidence for the theory of contagious holiness. In two related passages, Leviticus 6:11 and 6:20, we find the formula: "Whoever would come in contact *ʾăšer yiggaʿ*) with them (= with sacrifices) *must be in a holy state* (*yiqdāš*)." In that context, concern is definitely with the consecration of the priests, not with any possible aftereffects of contact with sacrificial *materiel*.

A distinction must be made: There is no question that the simple verb *qādaš* sometimes connotes result and means "to become holy." For example, in Exodus 29:21 we read that upon his consecration Aaron "became holy" (*wĕqādaš*), and this was true of his vestments and those of his sons. This does not, however, indicate contagion! In fact, there is an instance where *qādaš* clearly means "to become holy," and yet the context demonstrates that sanctity is *not* transferrable through physical contact alone. In Haggai 2:11–13 we have a remarkable inquiry addressed to the priesthood on questions of purity and defilement.

> Thus said the LORD of Hosts: Seek a ruling from the priests as follows: If a man is carrying sacrificial flesh in a fold of his garment, and with that fold touches bread, stew, wine, oil, or any other food, will the latter *become holy* (*yiqdaš*)? In reply, the priests said: "No." Haggai went on: If someone defiled by a corpse touches any of these, will it be defiled? And the priests responded: "Yes."

The point of this dialogue is that holiness can be lost more easily than it can be acquired.

A similar point about defilement is made in 1 Samuel 21:2–7. We read that David confirms to the priest of Nob that his fighting men and their vessels are in a state of purity. He insists that it is permissible for them to partake of the consecrated bread of display kept in the sanctuary: "In reply to the priest, David said: 'Most assuredly, women are [now] being kept from us, as formerly, whenever I sallied forth. The vessels of the fighting men are, (therefore), holy, though the mission is a common one. At this time, it [= the bread] would surely retain its sanctity (*yiqdaš*) in the vessels." This last reference exhausts the biblical attestations of the simple form of the verb.

The intensive verb form *qiddēš*, "to sanctify, devote," and other derived verb-forms describe the ritual means consciously undertaken for the purpose of attributing holiness. The biblical texts which use these forms most precisely and specify the ritual processes involved in consecration are the Priestly law codes and ritual descriptions of the Torah; although these sources are generally of late date, they are valuable because they outline religious celebrations in detail. We may analyze two of these texts here: Leviticus 8 and Exodus 29:1–37, a later text derived from the Leviticus passage.

In chapter 8 of Leviticus, a number of rites are described by use of the verb *qiddēš*, "to sanctify." (1) *Unction.* The sanctuary and its interior appurtenances, most of all the altar of sacrifice, are anointed with a specially mixed oil; in this way, they are consecrated (vv. 10–11). The same oil is poured over the head of Aaron, the chief priest; this process constitutes his consecration (v. 15). (2) *Investiture of the priests.* A mixture of sacrificial blood and the special oil of unction is sprinkled on the persons of Aaron and his sons as they stand clad in their priestly vestments; this, too, constitutes an act of consecration (v. 30).

In Exodus 29:1–37 the verb *qiddēš* describes some kinds of eating as processes of consecration. Partaking of the unleavened bread (*maṣṣāh*) offered on the occasion of the investiture is required to complete the consecration of the priests (v. 33). Portions of the "ram of investiture," a sacrifice offered in celebration of the event, are "consecrated" and designated as the share of Aaron and his sons from the sacrifice (v. 27). In this last case, the verb *qiddēš* connotes a declaration to the effect that sections of the animal were "devoted" to the priests. This connotation is significant because it means that the verb *qiddēš* expresses the power of the word. Sacred dicta consecrate!

Though we lack the actual declarations, there is no doubt that formulas of consecration were used in biblical times. Many have been preserved in post-biblical Jewish sources. Hebrew usage subtly implies as much, since the verb *qiddēš* is occasionally parallel with *qārāʾ* "to declare, proclaim" (Joel 1:14, 2:15, 4:9).

The Sabbath laws illustrate the power of the word in accomplishing consecration. Dicta were usually combined with other acts, but they had an efficacy of their own. Thus God had declared the seventh day holy: *wayĕqaddĕšēhû* "He declared it holy" (Genesis 2:3, Exodus 20:11, etc.). On the other side of the coin, the people of Israel is to declare the Sabbath holy (Exodus 20:8, Deuteronomy 5:12, etc.). In the commandment, "Remember the Sabbath," the verb rendered "remember," Hebrew *zāḵar*, essentially means "pronounce." Its mnemonic connotation derives from the act of pronouncing or speaking; thus the commandment to "remember" the Sabbath day required one to declare its sanctity. In the course of time, liturgies were composed in fulfillment of this requirement. In addition to declarations of sanctity, the consecration of the Sabbath necessitated certain performances. Just as God rested on the seventh day, Israel, for its part, was commanded to celebrate the Sabbath by cessation from assigned daily labors, and by ritual and worship. Similarly, the Jubilee year, which was modeled after the Sabbath, is to be formally proclaimed: it is to be heralded by the blast of the ram's horn (Leviticus 25:9–10).

In light of our discussion of the forms of the verb *qādaš*, we can consider the relationship between holiness and power, for sanctification is essentially a quest for power. The Dutch phenomenologist G. van der Leeuw states the matter with clarity:

> The sacredness of life is a matter of either what is given or possibility: two viewpoints which must be distinguished, even though

> they seldom appear in practice in their pure forms. The first of them asserts that, together with life itself and as such, power is given. The expansion and expression of life are the development of Power; potencies lie in the given life.
>
> But this in no means implies that man has ever accepted life simply as sacred.... For, apart from some criticisms of life, no religion whatsoever is possible. Religion means precisely that we do not simply accept life; it is directed always to "the other," and although it has sprung from human life, religion cannot orient itself to this life as such. But it can bring into prominence special aspects of this existence as "sacred" and give emphasis to certain phenomena in life as being potent.

At some point in early antiquity, animism and dynamism were fused in the notion of god, a latecomer in the history of religious ideas. As time passed, the god-idea, having become the focus of power concepts, began to transcend its immanent conceptualization, with the result that power itself could be perceived as transcendent. Based on what is known of ancient Near Eastern civilizations, we can say that the conception of divine power as transcendent was first formulated within the context of Israelite monotheism and expressed in the Hebrew Bible; there we learn that power comes from the God of Israel, who is all-powerful. It is a moot question as to whether Israelite monotheism, in any of its phases, allowed for the reality of power that did not come from the God of Israel, but it is quite certain that it advocated exclusive reliance on God's power and thoroughly condemned reliance on any other presumed source.

The difference between the biblical attitude toward power and the attitude characteristic of Mesopotamian religion has been stated most clearly by Thorkild Jacobsen. His view is presented in a discussion of a biblical theophany, the episode of the "burning bush" in Exodus 3:1–5:

> The story makes it clear that God is totally distinct from the bush out of which he chose to speak to Moses. God happened, as it were, to sojourn there; but he is altogether transcendent, and there is nothing but a purely situational, ephemeral relation with the bush. An ancient Mesopotamian would have experienced such a confrontation very differently. He too would have seen and heard numinous power, but power of, not just in, the bush, power at the center of its being, the vital force causing it to be and making it thrive and flourish. He would have experienced the numinous as immanent.

The Mesopotamian view was common to ancient Near Eastern religions generally. Israelite monotheism, as reflected even in early biblical narrative, operated with a predominantly transcendent conception of God, whereas the polytheistic religions, even those that may have been on the road to monotheism, like Egyptian Atonism, the religion of Akhenaton, functioned with a predominantly immanent conception.

We can now pose the question of power in a new perspective: How, in a transcendent frame of reference, does the holy interact with divine power? Because power is viewed as transcendent, not immanent, its presence or availability cannot be taken for granted. For power to be present, God must be present. To a limited degree, the same dynamic operates even within the framework of immanence, but when access to power is restricted to one, transcendent being, there is bound to be more anxiety about securing it! From the perspective of the divine, holiness is God's preferred way of relating to the religious community. To the extent that the community does things "God's way," so to speak, its benefits increase. In contrast, God is alienated by unholiness, such as is generated by the failure to sanctify what stands in an intimate relation to Him. In such an event, God becomes enraged and either abandons the community or punishes it severely, even to the point of destroying it; in other words, He denies it power.

Holiness thus becomes a necessity if the community is to receive the power it wants or needs. Holiness is the *way* to deal with God's power. One of the functions of an organized religion is, therefore, to identify what should be sanctified; in other words, to set down procedures for dealing with God's power. This sort of activity encourages God to be "present" in the human community and enhances the "potent"-ialities of the human-divine encounter. This is the import of Leviticus 19:2, one of the best-known biblical statements on the subject of holiness: "You must be holy, for I, the LORD, your God, am holy."

III

Thus far we have treated verb-forms which describe the change from the "not-holy" to the "holy," as well as the active means undertaken to attribute holiness. The noun *qodeš* and the adjective *qādôš*, usually rendered "holiness" and "holy," respectively, must now be discussed. The sense of both forms is subject to the effects of syntax, which inject a degree of ambiguity into the proper interpretation of the biblical passages in which these forms occur.

The noun *qodeš* belongs to a class of nouns common to the Semitic languages; as we have seen, Ugaritic cognates of Hebrew *qodeš* occur frequently. The form of the class (technically known as the *qutl* form) usually signifies an abstract sense. In dealing with ancient texts, however, we must guard against reading in our own notions of abstraction. Hebrew *qodeš* most often connotes something identifiable, even concrete; what is more, it often has an adjectival sense. In fact, there are only a few contexts in which it bears an abstract connotation, and then only partially so!

One common meaning of *qodeš* is "holy place, sanctuary." In many biblical passages this meaning is immediately perceived, e.g., Psalm 134:2: "Lift up your hands toward the sanctuary (*qodeš*), and bless the LORD." In other instances, however, the meaning of *qodeš* is ambiguous, as, for example, in Psalm 96:9:

> Bow down to the LORD *bĕhadrat qodeš*
> Tremble in His presence, all the earth

The Hebrew of the first stich is usually rendered, "in the majesty of holiness." The sense would be that an atmosphere of majestic holiness invests the temple, where one prostrates himself before God. Yet we could just as well render v 9a: "Bow down to the LORD in the majesty of the *sanctuary*." Ugaritic has amplified our understanding of the theophanic force of the rare word *hadrat*, but the ambiguity of *qodeš* persists.

To show how significant the interpretation of *qodeš* may be, I turn now to Exodus 15:11, a verse from the "Song of the Sea," an epic biblical poem which has become part of Jewish liturgy. The verse reads:

> Who is comparable to You among the gods, LORD?
> Who is comparable to You, *neʾdār baqodeš*,
> Venerated in hymns of praise, worker of wonders!

Hebrew *neʾdār baqodeš* may be rendered so as to yield the sense of "mighty by virtue of being holy; *sacredly* mighty." This interpretation is suggested by v 6 of the same poem:

> Your right arm, LORD, is *powerfully mighty* (*neʾdārî bakōaḥ*);
> Your right arm crushed the foe!

One could reason that just as *neʾdārî bakōaḥ* means "*powerfully* mighty," which is unambiguous, so *neʾdār baqodeš* means "sacredly mighty." The parallelism in the immediate context of v 11, however, suggests a different rendering, one which involves a slight emendation of the text. It has been proposed that we read *neʾdār baqĕdôšîm* "mightiest among the divinities." As we shall observe further on, the adjective *qādoš* does not only mean "holy," but may also represent a substantive, having the sense "holy being." In this sense, Hebrew *qādoš* is used in parallel to *ʾēl* "god," and other terms for deity such as *ʾĕlôah*. The proposed interpretation would yield a more precise parallelism in Exodus 15:11:

> Who is comparable to You among the gods, LORD?
> Who is comparable to You, mightiest among the divinities
> Venerated in hymns of praise, worker of wonders!

In Psalm 77, which consistently echoes the themes of the Song of the Sea, there is also sufficient ambiguity to allow for the conclusion that no abstract notion of "holiness" is expressed. Psalm 77:14) is usually translated as follows:

> O God, *Your way is holiness* (*baqodeš darkēḵā*);
> What god is as great as God?

One of the ancient translators understood *qodeš* in a less than abstract sense, rendering: "Your ways are holy ways." If we allow the same emendation made in Exodus 15:11, we might render:

> O God, Your dominion is over the divinities (*baqĕdôšîm*);
> What god is as great as God?

We here interpret Hebrew *dereḵ*, which usually means "path, road," to mean "power, dominion," a meaning which has been recognized on the basis of Ugaritic evidence.

These ambiguous passages illustrate the subtlety of textual interpretation and caution against generalizations regarding the nature of the holy. An exhaustive survey of the occurrences of *qodeš* in the Hebrew Bible indicates that there is only one context in which we find abstract connotations, the context of oaths which God himself takes. In Amos 4:2 we read: "The LORD, God, has sworn by His *holiness* (*beqodšô*)." This is effectively identical to Amos 6:8: "The LORD, God, has sworn by His life (*bĕnapšô*)." The interchangeability of "holiness" and "life" is echoed elsewhere: in Psalm 89:36 we read, "Once and for all I have sworn *by My holiness*," whereas in Jeremiah 51:14 we read, "The LORD, God, has sworn *by His life*." In these passages, the Bible speaks of God's holiness as a way of referring to what is most intimately associated with Him, just as God may swear by His faithfulness (Psalm 89:50). God may also swear "By Myself," as human beings do (Genesis 22:16, Jeremiah 22:5, 49:13). One might define this usage of *qodeš* as qualitatively rather than genuinely abstract.

Other usages of *qodeš* take us away from abstract notions. The term *qodeš* often designates a sacred offering, as in the frequent formula *qodeš lYHWH*, "a sacred offering to the LORD." Syntax plays a clear role in making *qodeš* have adjectival rather than abstract force. When *qodeš* occurs in juxtaposed (construct) formations, it is to be understood adjectivally: for example, *šēm qodšô* means "His holy name" (*not* "the name of His holiness"); it is the name that is holy. The frequency of this formation effectively eliminates most of the abstract ideas one might associate with the form *qodeš*.

Just as nominal *qodeš* may have adjectival force, so, too, primarily adjectival *qādôš* evidences nominal meanings. The word class to which the word belongs (the *qātôl* form) actually represents more than just one linguistic phenomenon, and it is not surprising that *qādôš* should function both as noun and adjective. The fluctuating nominal and adjectival functions reflect the fact that the Semitic languages have few purely adjectival forms.

As an adjective, *qādôš* may serve in direct attribution, e.g., *gôy qādôš*, "a holy nation," or *māqôm qādôš*, "a holy site." It may also serve as a predicate adjective: *qĕdôšîm tihyû kî qādôš ʾanî*, "You must be holy, for I am holy" (Leviticus 19:2). Such functions require little comment. Of greater complexity are instances where *qādôš* means "a holy being; a deity." This meaning is not restricted to Hebrew; the comparable adjectival form in Aramaic, *qaddîš*, has the same sense; *bĕʿēl qaddîšîn* in the story of Ahiqar means "chief of the gods," a clear attestation of an adjectival form serving as a noun.

There are more biblical instances of *qādôš* in the meanings "deity, angel, holy person than are normally recognized. Consider the following examples:

> (1) God (*ʾĕlôah*) approached from Teiman;
> The Holy One (*wĕqādôš*) from the Paran range.
> (Habakkuk 3:3)

(2) For I am a god (*ʾēl*), not a mortal man;
A Holy One (*qādôš*) in your midst. (Hosea 11:9)

Most frequent is the epithet of the God of Israel, *qĕdôš yiśrāʾēl* "the Holy One of Israel." This epithet is known primarily from the various prophetic writings subsumed in the Book of Isaiah.

Though the substantive function of Hebrew *qadoš* is generally recognized, its implications for biblical interpretation have not been fully grasped. This function leads me to propose an interpretation of the trisagion of Isaiah 6:3, a well-known biblical dictum bearing on the idea of the holy, a declaration which has entered both Jewish and Christian liturgy:

qādôš, qādôš, qādôš, YHWH ṣĕbhāʾôt
The whole earth is filled by His presence.

The first line of the trisagion is usually rendered: "Holy, Holy, Holy; the LORD of Hosts," or "Holy, Holy, Holy is the LORD of Hosts." But S. D. Luzzatto (1800–1865) came closer to a correct understanding of this verse in his Italian rendering of Isaiah 6:3:

Santo, Santo, Santo, egli è il Signore Sabaot.
Holy One, Holy One, Holy One; He is the LORD Sabaot.

Clearly, Luzzatto understood that *qādôš* can mean "Holy One," since in his rendition of Isaiah 40:25 he translates *yōʾmar qādôš* "*dice il Santo*," "The Holy One says." Luzzatto's version of the Isaiah 6 phrase can be refined if we reconsider what is happening. The *mis-en-scène* is not one of direct address. Rather, a third-person orientation predominates: the God of Israel is being announced. The seraphim are His heralds; they are not addressing God as worshippers. The LORD has entered His throne room and taken His seat. The angels proclaim to all present that He is enthroned:

The Holy One, the Holy One, the Holy One!
The LORD of [the heavenly] Hosts!
The whole earth is filled by His presence!

The throne room is an integral part of Isaiah's experience, and its protocols are a shaping feature of what he hears and sees.

IV

The term "community" has been used here occasionally, and I have continually referred to the people of Israel. This orientation reflects a principle of phenomenology, most clearly stated by van der Leeuw: "In its relation to power … human life is first of all not the life of the individual, but that of the community." In the Hebrew Bible, the community is the Israelite people, variously named and described, but always clearly identified. Holiness was to be realized, as an objective of the religious life, through the historic unfolding of Israel's collective experience. What is more, it could not be achieved by individuals alone, except insofar as they act as part of the group or on its behalf.

The biblical God is god of a community. Even in the moments of extreme wrath when God threatened to destroy Israel and to spare Moses, the plan was to make Moses leader of another nation (Exodus 32:9–10). According to the dominant biblical traditions, God's purpose could not be realized through royal dynasties and chosen leaders, or through personal covenants. The covenants with the Patriarchs and the dynastic covenant with the House of David are based on the concept that fulfillment of the promise depends on the character of collective life, not on the virtues of illustrious individuals.

The historic experience of the Israelite people was ultimately meant to serve as a model for all nations, but initially a unique relationship was declared to exist between God and the Israelite people, one not shared by any other nation. This relationship allowed the Israelites to approach a transcendent god more intimately than one would have expected. In a sense, the idea of *chosenness*, with its emphasis on the holy as a goal of collective existence, to be pursued by all Israelites, took up the slack created by notions of transcendence. God's transcendence was not compromised by the holy relationship, and maintaining this relationship was the way to experience the same closeness to transcendent power that the polytheist was able to experience with respect to immanent power.

In time, Israelite monotheism came to differ from other ancient Near Eastern religions not only in terms of its concept of transcendence, but also because of its insistence on covenantal peoplehood. Though the "otherness" of *tabu* was represented in biblical religion, there are indications that the gulf separating the sacred from the profane was meant to be bridged, not perpetuated. That gulf was, perhaps, ephemerally unavoidable, but it was not to endure forever. For Israel there is a revealed way to unify the experience of divine power: it is for all Israelites, working in consort, to form a holy nation: "You shall become My kingdom of priests and holy nation" (Exodus 19:6).

Bibliographical Note

On the phenomenology of religion, see the still basic work of G. van der Leeuw, *Religion in Essence and Manifestation* (trans. J. E. Turner; London: RKP, 1938). Mesopotamian religion is treated in Thorkild Jacobsen, *The Treasures of Darkness* (New Haven: Yale University Press, 1976); there is unfortunately no comparable work on biblical religion. I am indebted to Thorkild Jacobsen and Jacob Neusner for reading the manuscript of this essay, and to H. L. Ginsberg for discussing aspects of it with me.

Silence, Sound, and the Phenomenology of Mourning in Biblical Israel*

As a scholar for whom words are all important, Yochanan Muffs has surely experienced the insouciance of the philologian. In addition to seeking out new evidence that might extend the range of possible meanings, the philologian must also generate new associations. Thus it is that after completing a commentary on the book of Leviticus, I was able to learn more about certain words than I had known previously. In tribute to Yochanan Muffs, a master of Semitic semantics, I would like to share an illustrative example of review and reconsideration, taken from the text of Leviticus.

I. Wayyiddōm ʾAhărōn (Lev. 10:3b)

The accepted interpretation of Lev. 10:3b is that Aaron remained silent, or was stunned, upon learning of the sudden death of his two sons, Nadab and Abihu. Thus, Onkelos renders *wayyiddōm ʾAhărōn* as *ûšĕtēq ʾAhărōn*, "and Aaron remained silent," and the Septuagint has *kai katenukhthê Aarôn*, "and Aaron was stunned; kept silent."[1] Whereas the rendering of the Septuagint suggests a shocked response, one we might associate with extreme depression, the rendering of Onkelos allows us to see a stoic attitude, a courageous acceptance of the divine decree.

The Masoretic pointing, *wayyiddōm*, predicates a geminate root, *d-m-m* (cf. *wayyissôb*, "he turned," from *s-b-b*). The verbal root *d-m-m*, "to be still" (here to be classified as *d-m-m* I for reference), is morphologically indicated in Biblical Hebrew, so that initially, there is no problem in reading Lev. 10:3b in the accepted way.

Both the comparative and the inner-biblical evidence to be adduced presently will, however, suggest an alternative rendering: "—and Aaron *mourned*." This rendering identifies in Lev. 10:3b a homonymous Hebrew root, here to be classified as *d-m-m* II, "to moan, mourn." Understood in this way, Lev. 10:3b

---

* Originally published in *JANES* 22 (*Comparative Studies in Honor of Yochanan Muffs*; 1993), pp. 89–106. Reprinted with permission from the Journal of the Ancient Near Eastern Society.

I am grateful to my former student, Dr. Amina Serour (Gomaa), for assisting me on questions of Arabic lexicography, and to my colleagues in the Columbia University Seminar for the Study of the Hebrew Bible for their learned responses.

[1] See Liddell-Scott, *Greek Lexicon* 903 s.v. *kara-nuktikos*, passive: *kata-nugêsomai*.

means that Aaron reacted in the customary manner; he moaned or wailed and was about to initiate formal mourning and lamentation for his two lost sons.

Once this line of interpretation is considered, the commentator will read the remainder of Leviticus 10 differently. Immediately after the bodies of the two dead sons of Aaron had been taken outside the encampment for burial (vv. 4–5), Moses issued instructions to Aaron and his two remaining sons not to engage in formal mourning, by baring their heads and rending their garments, lest they meet death and arouse God's wrath against the Israelite community. Rather, the entire house of Israel was to act in their stead, and mourn (the verb *b-k-y*, "to weep") the untimely death of the two priests (vv. 6–7). Mourning, even over a son or brother, would have defiled Aaron and his two remaining priestly sons at a time when their purification was just taking hold. Read in this way, Leviticus 10 actually achieves a higher degree of symmetry.

II. Biblical Hebrew d-m-m II, "to mourn, moan"

The late Mitchell Dahood revived an earlier suggestion that several biblical passages would be better understood as expressing *d-m-m* II, "to mourn, moan," rather than *d-m-m* I, "to be still." Earlier, Friedrich Delitzsch and Paul Haupt had noted the cognate Akkadian verb, *damāmu*, "to mourn, moan," and, after the Ugaritic evidence became known, C. H. Gordon and J. Blau, together with Dahood, pointed out a Ugaritic verb, *d-m-m*, clearly cognate with Akkadian *damāmu* and used in parallelism with *b-k-y*, "to weep."[2] As will be shown here, the recent Ebla discoveries have yielded further cognates of proposed Hebrew *d-m-m* II.

The association of *wayyiddôm* in Lev. 10:3b with proposed *d-m-m* II, "to mourn," has not been adequately discussed in modern scholarship. In his recent commentary on Amos, S. M. Paul lists, in his notes to Amos 5:13, a number of biblical verses attesting the proposed *d-m-m* II, including Lev. 10:3, but he offers no comment on this reference.[3] Haupt had also referred in his study to Lev. 10:3b, but he suggested vocalizing consonantal *wydm* as *wayyādûm*, from the root *d-w-m*. He took the statement to mean: "Aaron was stunned, petrified." Hebrew *d-w-m*, "to stay, be silent," and its suggested Arabic cognate *d-w-m*, "to endure, continue; to be still, await," have been discussed in the literature.[4] It was

---

[2] See M. Dahood, "Textual Problems in Isaia," *Catholic Bibilical Quarterly* 22 (1960) 400–9; cf. F. Delitzsch, *Prolegomena eines nëuen hebräisch-aramäischen Wörterbuchs zum Alten Testament* (Leipzig, 1886) 64, n. 2; P. Haupt, "Some Assyrian Etymologies," *AJSL* 26 (1909), 1–26; J. Blau, "Über Homonyme und Angeblich Homonyme Wurzeln," *VT* 6 (1956), 242–48, at 243; C. H. Gordon, *Ugaritic Textbook*, 385, Glossary, no. 674.

[3] S. M. Paul, *Amos*, Hermeneia (Memphis, 1991), 175–76 with n. 169, to Amos 5:13.

[4] See A. Guillaume, *Hebrew and Arabic Lexicography* (Leiden, 1965), 8 with nn. 21–22, s.v. *d-w-m* and *d-m-m*, summarizes the question. The association of Hebrew *d-w-m* with Arabic *d-w-m* is not without problems. The connotation "still" in Arabic develops

Haupt's view that in Biblical Hebrew the geminate root *d-m-m* never means "to be silent" and that this meaning is always conveyed in Hebrew by forms of the middle-weak root *d-w-m*. Hebrew *d-m-m*, according to Haupt, means only what Akkadian and Ugaritic *d-m-m* do, namely, to "moan, mutter." In effect, Haupt concluded that in the case under discussion two lexemes, with their respective sets of meanings, were morphologically differentiated in Biblical Hebrew.

Throughout the present discussion, it should be borne in mind that movement is a function of sound, that what is silent is still, and that what moves produces sound. It is our view that stillness and silence, on the one hand, and moaning and similar sounds, on the other, are indeed distinguished from each other in Biblical Hebrew, but on a different basis. We will review here a series of Hebrew forms meaning "to be still, immobile, silent" and morphologically derived from a geminate root, *d-m-m*, based on their Masoretic vocalization. To deny these forms to *d-m-m* I one would have to revocalize all of these on the model of the middle-weak root *d-w-m*, assuming this to be possible, thereby reading *d-m-m* I out of existence entirely. One doubts that such a process would yield credible results. The reality of *d-m-m* I in Biblical Hebrew should be acknowledged.

We prefer to classify the evidence as follows. On the one hand is *d-m-m* II, cognate with Eblaic, Akkadian, and Ugaritic lexemes, and bearing the primary sense of mourning and the emission of sounds associated with mourning. On the other hand are three morphological realizations of a lexeme which connotes stillness and immobility as well as silence: (a) a homonymous geminate form, to be registered as *d-m-m* I; (b) a middle-weak form *d-w-m*; and (c) a third-weak form, homonymous with *d-m-y* I, "to be equal, similar," but to be registered as *d-m-y* II. The meanings attendant upon these three realizations seem to be semantically compatible.

For his part, Blau likewise postulated three realizations of an originally distinct lexeme connoting shock, stillness, and silence. Furthermore, he acknowledged an originally homonymous geminate form, with cognates in Akkadian and Ugaritic, that connoted moaning and mourning. But Blau concluded that *d-m-m* I and *d-m-m* II no longer functioned as genuine, distinguishable homonyms in Biblical Hebrew. These are his words:

> Eine klare Scheidung zwischen diesen beiden Wurzeln durchzuführen ist dagegen unmöglich, denn die Bedeutungen "schweigen > (vor schmerz) erstarren" und "wehklagen" berühren sich und wurden naturgemäss kontaminiert.

---

from the notion of remaining in place, lasting, enduring, not from that of ceasing to move, being frozen in place, or the like. To attempt to restrict the cognate connotations of Arabic *d-w-m* to a single one of the three Hebrew realizations—*d-m-m*, *d-w-m*, or *d-m-y*, respectively—is misleading. The Arabic root *d-w-m* can shed light on all three realizations in Hebrew, in varying contexts. And yet, one suspects that some contamination may have occurred in Arabic so that more than one lexeme is represented by Arabic *d-w-m*.

As a consequence of the assumed compatibility of the two sets of connotations we are to conclude, according to Blau, that original homonyms, whose existence is indicated by Akkadian and Ugaritic, eventually blended or interpenetrated so that in Biblical Hebrew they were no longer distinguishable in their usage.

Although the process of "contamination" that Blau describes is well attested in its own right, we must dispute his judgment on the matter of semantic fields. Anticipating the results of our detailed review of both the comparative and the biblical evidence, it is clear that the notion of "mourning, moaning" is differentiated in biblical usage from "stillness, silence, cessation" and that it operates in different contexts.

Whereas the two sets of meanings are hardly compatible with each other, it is admittedly difficult in certain instances to determine which lexeme is being expressed by a given form in Biblical Hebrew. This is so, however, not because the two sets of meanings are compatible and have become indistinguishable in their usage but because they are realized in forms which are, in the Masoretic vocalization, usually homophonous as well as homographic. We must also remain sensitive to plays on words, to the phenomenon of *double entendre*. It is quite possible that in certain instances, biblical writers intended that the reader associate both sets of meanings homophonously in a given verse. Nevertheless, the biblical writers undoubtedly knew the difference between what we are here calling *d-m-m* I and what we are calling *d-m-m* II, and it is their meaning, after all, that we wish to decode.[5]

Dahood pointed to several likely attestations of *d-m-m* II in Biblical Hebrew that will be taken up here; but, as mentioned, he never applied his insight to Lev. 10:3b. As will be shown, some of Dahood's suggested attestations of Hebrew *d-m-m* II stand up under scrutiny, whereas others will be questioned. In a similar way, we shall suggest additional biblical attestations of *d-m-m* II.

III. Comparative Indications

It would be well to begin by surveying the comparative evidence bearing on cognates of proposed *d-m-m* II in Biblical Hebrew. Akkadian *damāmu*, "to mourn," and nominal *dimmatu*, "moaning" (and similar nominal forms such as *dimmu* and *dummu*, *damāmu* and *dumāmu*), attest clear connotations in context. In the lexical series as in literary sources verbal *damāmu* is synonymous with *bakû*, "to weep," and we read of humans and animals, as well as objects such as swamp reeds emitting sounds akin to moaning. Especially interesting is the use of this verb with respect to the cooing of doves, as we shall observe further on, in the analysis of Hebrew diction. The occurrence of Š-stem *šudmumu*, "to order another to mourn," in Akkadian, in parallelism with *šubkū*, "to cause to weep,"

[5] The recovery of lost forms that had been masked by Masoretic vocalizations was discussed incisively by H. L. Ginsberg, "Behind the Masoretic Text," *Tarbiz* 5 (1933–34), 208–23; *Tarbiz* 6 (1934–35), 543 [in Hebrew].

also serves to reinforce the sense conveyed by the Akkadian verb. Thus we read in the seventh part of the Gilgamesh epic:

> [*ušabk*]*akka nišī ša Uruk; ušadmamakka* [*šamḫāti*]
> He will order the people of Uruk to perform the mourning (ritual) for you, and the courtesans to mourn for you.[6]

Recently, evidence from Eblaic texts has added to our knowledge of the cognate Semitic root which would be expressed by Biblical Hebrew *d-m-m* II. I have referred elsewhere to Eblaic texts, originally edited by G. Pettinato, wherein ideographic SI.DÙ is a term meaning "lament." In a bilingual lexicon, also edited by Pettinato, ideographic SI.DÙ is rendered by the Eblaic noun *t/di-mu-mu*, "lament."[7]

To be more specific, royal records from the reign of Ibbi-Zikir, the last king of Ebla in the early period, list various sacrifices to be offered during the month of the Ishtar festival by the king of Ebla and his family and court. Among these are: SI.DÙ.SI.DÙ EN.EN, "the laments for the kings." These rituals were apparently part of the royal cult of dead kings at Ebla.

An actual derivative of *d-m-m*, "to mourn, lament" (possibly realized as *d-m-y*) occurs in a collection of administrative texts from Ebla, recently re-edited by A. Archi. There we read of a deposit of textiles designated: *in da-ma-ti* KI.SUR, "for the lament of the catacomb."[8] The Eblaic lexicon thus yields two cognate terms meaning "lament," *ti/di-mu-mu* and *da-ma-tu*, thereby indicating a provenience for this lexeme in the West Semitic languages prior to the Old Babylonian period in which Akkadian *damāmu* is first attested.

We agree with Dahood, who finds *d-m-m* II in the Ugaritic Keret epic, where *d-m-m*, "to mourn," parallels *b-k-y*, "to weep":

bn. al tbkn.	Son, weep not,
al / tdm. ly.	Lament not for me;
al tkl. bn / qr. ʿnk.	Exhaust not, son, the well of your eye,
mḫ. rišk / udmʿt.	The marrow of your head with tears.
ṣḥ. aḫtk / ṯtmnt.	Speak to your sister, Thitmanat,
bt. ḥmḥh / dnn.	A young woman whose *passion* is strong;
tbkn. wtdm. ly	Let her weep and lament for me.

6 See Thompson, *Gilgamesh*, VII, iii:45, and *CAD D*, 60–61, s.v. *damāmu*; and 143, s.v. *dimmatu*.

7 G. Pettinato, *Culto ufficiale ad Ebla durante il regno di Ibbi-Šipiš* (Rome, 1979), 47, text 1, rev. ii:24–iii:12; 84, text 3, rev. xii:21–26. Further: G. Pettinato, *Testi lessicali bilingui della Biblioteca L.2769* (Naples, 1982), 320, entry no. 1116. Also see B. A. Levine, "The Impure Dead and the Cult of the Dead: Polarization and Opposition in Israelite Religion," *Bitzaron*, Jubilee Issue (1990–91), 80–89 [in Hebrew].

8 A. Archi, *Archivi reali di Ebla, Testi I, Testi amministrativi: Asseganzioni di Tessuti (Archivo L.2769)* (Rome, 1985), 126, text 13, rev. iv:5–7. The same document had been edited earlier by G. Pettinato, *Testi Amministrativi della Biblioteca L.2769* (Naples, 1980), 60, text 7, rev. iii: 15–iv:7, and see comments, 68.

[*ǵzr*]. *al. trgm. laḫtk*	[Hero], truly speak to your sister.
[*t*]*tr*[*gm*] *l*[*h. t*]*dm*	Spe[ak to] her [and let her] lament.
aḫtk / ydᶜ krḥmt	Your sister—I know she is compassionate.[9]

Not only does parallelism reinforce the conclusion that here we have *d-m-m* II and not *d-w-m*, but poetic context considerably clarifies Ugaritic usage of the verb *d-m-m*, for we read, in words reminiscent of biblical verse, of eye-wells gone dry from excessive weeping.[10]

What has not been given adequate notice is the fact that in the same Keret epic, the root *d-w-m* occurs twice and means "to stay put, tarry." In the theophany, El instructed Keret at one point:

dm ym wṯn	Tarry a day and a second;
ṯlṯ rbᶜ ym	A third, a fourth day;
ḫ(!)*mš ṯdṯ ym*	A fifth, a sixth day.
ḥẓk al tšᶜl qrth	Thine arrows shoot not into the city,
abn ydk mšdpt	(Nor) thy hand-stones *flung headlong.*

We have presented the translation by H. L. Ginsberg which is preferable to Gibson's rendering: "Stay quiet a day and a second."[11] Here we have the singular, masculine imperative of *d-w-m*, "to remain in place, stay," expressing the very connotation that characterizes the Arabic cognate, *d-w-m*. That the morphological root is, indeed, *d-w-m*, emerges from the second occurrence, in the chronicle of Keret's expedition:

d[*m*] *ym wṯn*	He tarr[ied] a day and a second.[12]

Notwithstanding the need to restore *mem*, it is virtually certain that here we have the 3rd masculine perfect form of *d-w-m* since in the Keret epic the fulfillment of what has been predicted carefully follows the predictive formulation. What we learn from Ugaritic usage is, therefore, that the notion of immobility is clearly differentiated from that of moaning and mourning and is expressed by a separate word.

The common denominator unifying all of the cognate evidence relevant to *d-m-m* II is a complex of sounds associated with mourning and death and, by extension, of sounds akin to moaning, like the cooing of doves and sounds emitted by certain other animals, as well as by the rustling of reeds.

---

[9] J. C. L. Gibson, *Canaanite Myths and Legends* (Edinburgh, 1977), 95, no. 16:25–33 [hereafter: *CML*]. Gibson's translation has been adapted.

[10] See Jer. 8:23; Lam. 1:16; 3:47–48, 51.

[11] Text and translation in Gibson, *CML*, 85, no. 14, iii:114–18. Preferred translation by H. L. Ginsberg in *ANET*, 144, ll. 116–18.

[12] See Gibson, *CML*, 88, no. 14, v:218.

IV. Biblical Attestations of Hebrew d-m-m II

Now that comparative evidence has been reviewed, it would be well to establish the occurrence of *d-m-m* II in Biblical Hebrew, independent of its proposed attestation in Lev. 10:3b. The first passage to be examined is Isa. 23:1–2:

maśśāʾ Ṣôr hêlîlû ʾoniyyôt Taršîš
kî šuddad mibbayit
mibbôʾ mēʾereṣ Kittîm niglāh lāmô
dōmmû yôšěbê ʾî
sôḥer Ṣîdôn
ʿôbēr yām milʾûk

The vision of Tyre:
Howl, you ships of Tarshish!
For havoc has been wrought, not a house is left;
As they came from the land of Kittim.
This was revealed to them,
"*Moan*, you coastal dwellers,
You traders of Sidon,
Once thronged by seafarers."

The above translation, taken from NJPS, highlights the parallelism of *hêlîlû*, "Howl" (or "wail"), and *dōmmû*, "Moan." The meaning "be still, silent" is possible, of course, since the B colon does not always reiterate the sense of the A colon in poetic parallelism. And yet, there is something irresistible about the striking parallelism that is produced by proposed *d-m-m* II in this verse, which was central to Dahood's analysis, and was first so understood by Delitzsch.

A second attestation of *d-m-m* II is probably to be found in Lam. 2:10:

yēšěbû lāʾāreṣ yidděmû
ziqnê bat-Ṣiyyôn

They sit on the ground; they *mourn*,
The elders of Daughter-Zion;
They have placed dirt over their head,
Wrapping themselves in sackcloth.
The young women of Jerusalem
Have lowered their head to the ground.

The context is demonstrably one of formal mourning. As noted by Dahood, it was customary in ancient Israel as at Ugarit to mourn sitting on the ground.[13]

One could argue, however, that in the doublet, *yēšēb bādād wěyiddōm* (Lam. 3:28), the form *yiddōm* clearly derives from *d-m-m* I, "to be still, silent," as we emphasize further on (in section IV). As D. Marcus has observed, this is

---

[13] See Jon. 3:6; and in the Ugaritic Baal cycle, see Gibson, *CML*, 73, no. 5, vi:11–13ff. There we read that Latipan descended from his throne and sat on the ground when mourning over Baal, who had died.

one of the many non-recurring doublets in Lamentations, and one might have expected *yiddĕmû* in our verse to share this meaning.[14]

Each occurrence must be judged independently nevertheless. In Lam. 3:28, adverbial *bādād* alters the situation and suggests the stillness of solitude. What is more, the single sufferer is not mourning, as are the gathered elders of Lam. 2:10. These differences suggest that the link between doublets is, perhaps, not as hard and fast as some suppose.

Furthermore, if we were to translate: "Silent sit on the ground / The elders of Fair Zion" (thus NJPS), we would be implying that it was customary to mourn in silence. Does this correlate with what is known about the phenomenology of mourning in ancient Israel? Was it, in fact, customary to maintain silence while sitting on the ground, garbed in sackcloth or with garments rent, with dirt or ashes on one's head? Or, is that very depiction largely the result of taking the verbal root *d-m-m* to connote stillness and silence in passages related to mourning?

Some have pointed to the dire circumstances depicted in Job 2:11–13, part of the prologue, as suggesting that silence was a customary aspect of mourning in biblical times. There we are told that Job's companions arrived to comfort him after hearing of his misfortunes, including the awful news that Job's children had died in a storm. Verse 13 reads: "They sat with him on the ground for seven days and seven nights, and no one would speak a word to him, for they perceived how great the pain had become."

It should be noted, however, that when the companions first arrived and saw that Job's visage had altered beyond recognition, they did what mourners usually did—they wept aloud, rent their garments, and tossed dirt upward so that it fell on their heads (Job 2:12). They subsequently refrained from addressing Job only as a reaction to his state of shock. No one questions the reality of shock as part of the mourning experience. This does not imply, however, that maintaining silence was a formal aspect of mourning, either by the bereaved or on the part of their comforters, which is the claim being challenged in the present discussion.

If we were to exclude all forms of the verbal root *d-m-m* I, of *d-m-y* II, "to come to an end," and of *d-w-m*, "to be still, silent; to await," from consideration, we would find little further indication that silence was actually a customary feature of mourning in biblical Israel. We would find wailing, bitter weeping, sighing, sobbing, and moaning—outcries of woe and grief, and liturgical words of lamentation. It is difficult to isolate each of these emotions in the biblical texts because such reactions are, by their very nature, complex and are reported and described in different ways.

If a mourner remained silent, it was most likely out of gloomy depression, often expressed by Hebrew *qôdēr* and related forms,[15] or because one was

---

[14] D. Marcus, "Non-Recurring Couplets in Lamentations," *HAR* 10 (1986), 177–95, esp. 179, 188.

[15] Cf. Isa. 50:3; Jer. 8:21; Mal. 3:14; Ps. 35:14; 38:7; 42:10; 43:2; Job 5:11; 30:28.

stunned by shock, a state sometimes conveyed by Hebrew *šômēm* (Lam. 1:13, 16; 3:11). It was not because it was customary to stifle one's cries, or because Israelites were expected to accept death stoically. As a rule we should not, therefore, assume that forms which predicate a geminate root *d-m-m* necessarily characterize the phenomenology of mourning as one of shock or silence. It is this thinking, of course, that led in the first place to the interpretation of *wayyiddōm ʾAhărōn* in Lev. 10:3b as: "Aaron kept silent; was stunned."

Once we free ourselves of the notion of stillness, we are led to consider other probable attestations of *d-m-m* II in Biblical Hebrew, where we previously assumed derivation from *d-m-m* I—or from *d-m-y* or *d-w-m* for that matter.

One such verse that possibly attests *d-m-m* II is Amos 5:13:

> *lakēn hammaśkîl bāʿēt hahîʾ yiddōm kî ʿēt rāʿāh hîʾ*
>
> Therefore, the prudent person at such a time *mourns*,
> for it is [decidedly] a time of disaster.

The usual rendering "keeps silent" does not jibe with the prophet's call to his people, expressed in the oracle of Amos 5:4–15 as a whole. Amos urges Israel to seek the LORD sincerely, by acts of righteousness and equity, not through their usual sacrifices at sites such as Bethel, Gilgal, and Beer-sheba, shrines about to be destroyed. The operative term of reference in this passage is the verb *dāraš* (vv. 4, 5, 6, 14), whose nuances are suggestively evoked by the prophet. The people are urged to "seek" good, not evil (v. 14), as well as to "seek" the LORD. In such contexts, the verb *dāraš* often refers to oracular inquiry, or to similar acts intended to receive divine guidance.[16] This is suggested by the exhortation of the prophet that the people are to cease "seeking" at the improper, condemned cult sites. So, it is far from obvious that the prudent should be silent in the face of impending disaster. Knowing the truth about the consequences of the evil they observe all around them, the prudent grieve, rather than enjoy their current prosperity in complacency (Amos 6:1).[17]

It is true, of course, that one experiencing the full impact of death and disaster might be shocked into silence. *In extremis*, one would be cautioned to hold his tongue and refrain from pronouncing God's name (Amos 6:10), probably out of a fearfulness best explained as demonic. After all, the calamity was brought about by God. One could, therefore, detect in Amos 5:13 a resonance of the same anxiety, so that we find the prudent person holding one's tongue when disaster is imminent so as not to invite further misfortune. From Amos 8:3 we learn that both reactions—wailing and shock—may be present in the same situation, although they are described in different language:

> And the singing women of the palace shall howl (*wĕhêlîlû*) on that day—
> declares my LORD, God:

---

[16] Cf. Gen. 25:22; Exod. 18:15; Deut. 18:11; Isa. 19:3; Jer. 8:2; Ezek. 20:1.

[17] Cf. Paul, *Amos* (see n. 3 above).

> So many corpses
> Left lying everywhere!
> Hush!

A balanced view would give preference to immediate context, and interpret Amos 5:13 to mean that the prudent grieve over social ills and gross injustice, knowing these will hasten ultimate disaster. There would be no virtue to their silence in such circumstances, nor were they already in reactive shock.

Common to all of the above passages is the context of mourning or disaster. But, as we have seen, the sense of *d-m-m* II as "moaning," a sense which originates in the context of mourning, also describes sounds akin to moaning in other contexts. This fact allows us to consider Ps. 4:5, whose context may not be entirely devoid of grieving after all:

> *rigzû wĕʾal teḥĕṭāʾû*
> *ʾimrû bilbabkem ʿal miškabkem*
> *wĕdōmmû, Selah.*

> So, tremble and sin no more;
> ponder it on your bed,
> and *sigh*, Selah.

This is the translation of NJPS, where it is noted that an alternative rendering is "be still." The reference to a bed is resumed in v. 9, at the conclusion of this Psalm, in which the worshipper had been entreating God to hear his prayer:

> Safe and sound I lie down and sleep,
> for You alone, O LORD, keep me secure.

The worshipper can sleep peacefully at night in the knowledge that God protects him, whereas his antagonists will experience anxiety on their beds, in fear of God's punishment. What recommends "sighing" rather than "silence" is the observable association of trembling (the verb *r-g-z*) with moaning or the emission of other sounds brought about by fear or pain. As has been shown, the notion of silence attendant upon *d-m-m* I derives from the primary sense of "stillness, immobility" so that one would hardly tremble and be still simultaneously.

And yet, the rendering "be silent" might make sense if the man suffering mockery at the hands of others is, in this verse, adjuring his tormentors to be silent, to cease maligning him, in his confidence that God will ultimately vindicate him.

On balance, the former interpretation is preferable, however, since the one afflicted complains not of forensic abuse, in particular, but of suffering fraud and shame. There is no specific emphasis on the speech of the worshipper's enemies, which would counterbalance a call for their silence. Rather, the devotee calls upon his tormentors to cease their offenses against him, and, in effect, to repent.

We may, therefore, have a further attestation of *d-m-m* II in Biblical Hebrew. This is also the view of Dahood, who notes that the Ugaritic Keret epic affords a description of weeping on one's bed, as does Psalm 6, which projects the same anxiety over one's enemies.

Dahood suggested that in Isa. 38:10 Hebrew *bidmî yāmây* expresses *d-m-m* II, "to mourn, moan." This suggestion is, in our opinion, off the mark and must be rejected. Nevertheless, a discussion of it will enlighten us in other respects.

Since Dahood cites the RSV translation of Isa. 38:10, we will do the same:

> *ʾāni ʾāmartî—bidmî yāmây ʾēlēkāh;*
> *bĕšaʿărê šĕʾôl pūqqadtî, yeter šĕnôtây*
>
> I said in the noontide of my days I must depart,
> I am consigned to Sheol for the rest of my years.

The implication of the RSV is that *dĕmî* means "half," hence: "midday." For his part, Dahood questions whether nominal *dĕmî* can mean "half," but in fact, there is a semantic bridge between the concept of "half" and that of "equal, like," the sense of *d-m-y* I, "to be similar, like, equal." One "half" is equal to the other. As noted in *KB* 217, s.v. *dĕmî*, Hebrew *dĕmî* is to be compared with Akkadian *mišlu* (from the verb *mašālu*), which means "half, midpoint, midday, midyear." One notes, as well, nominal *mašlu* in the idioms *ūm mašil*, "midday," and *mūšu māšil*, midnight.[18] The cognate Hebrew root *m-š-l* is surely relevant to our discussion. Cf. Isa. 46:5:

> *lĕmî tĕdammĕyûnî wĕtašwû; wĕtamšîlûnî wĕnidmeh*
>
> To whom can you compare Me
> Or declare Me similar?
> To whom can you liken Me,
> So that we seem comparable? (NJPS)

That *d-m-y*, *m-š-l*, and *š-w-y* are synonyms also emerges from Isa. 40:25:

> *wĕʾel mî tĕdammĕyûnî wĕʾešweh yōʾmar qādôš*
>
> To whom, then, can you liken Me,
> To whom can I be compared—says the Holy One. (NJPS)

The root *š-w-y* has the specific connotation "be of equal value" in Prov. 3:15 and 8:11, in variations of the same dictum:

> She (wisdom) is more precious than rubies,
> All of your goods cannot equal her (*lôʾ yišwû bāh*). (Prov. 3:15; NJPS)

Quite clearly, unique *dĕmî* in Isa. 38:10 derives from *d-m-y* I, "to be similar, equal." But Dahood also questions the phrasing, a point which I fail to understand. As formatted above, the Hebrew verse may be analyzed as 2+3/3+2, which is a common pattern. In any event, Dahood's suggested rephrasing, which would yield the pattern 3+2/3+2, runs into difficulty:

---

[18] See Gibson, *CML*, 83, no. 14, i:26–30.

ʾanî ʾāmartî bĕdōmmî	*yāmây ʾēlēkāh*
bĕšaʿărêi šĕʾôl pūqqadtî	*yeter šĕnôtây*
I said *in my sorrow*:	*I have marched my days*.
I have been consigned to Sheol	for the rest of my years.

The problem is that the postulated idiom *hālak yāmîm* would mean "to march for X number of days," with *yāmây* used adverbially. This is the sense in the Ugaritic idiom cited by Dahood: *ylk ym wṯn*, "He marched for a day and a second."[19] To regard *yāmây* as an accusative of duration would, in any event, yield the sense: "I have marched, walked during my days," telling us what the person in question had done during one's lifetime. It would not mean what Dahood proposes—"I have marched my days"—which is to say, "I have reached the end of my days; I have traversed the duration of my life." In fact, the verb *hālak* itself, in certain contexts, may mean "to depart" from the land of the living, from life. This is most clearly expressed in Qoh. 1:4: *dôr hôlēk wĕdôr bāʾ*, "One generation departs and the next arrives."[20] Most revealing, perhaps, are Job 10:20–21 and 16:22.

> My days are few, so desist!
> Leave me alone, let me be diverted awhile;
> Before I depart—never to return (*bĕṭerem ʾēlēk wĕlôʾ ʾāšûb*)—
> For the land of deepest gloom.
> For a few more years will come [to pass] (*yeʾĕtāyû*)
> And I shall go (*ʾehĕlôk*) the path of no return.

In conclusion, Dahood's suggestion that nominal *dĕmî* in Isa. 38:10 derives from *d-m-m* II, "to mourn," must be rejected, and his corollary rephrasing is unnecessary and, in any event, reflects an incorrect understanding of the connotation of *hālak*, "to go," in this verse.

An additional passage is attractive to the philologian for what it may tell us about usage of *d-m-m* II in Biblical Hebrew, even though it presents complex semantic problems. Reference is to Ezek. 24:16–17, where a possible attestation of *d-m-m* II occurs. We first present the rendering of NJPS:

> O mortal, I am about to take away the delight of your eyes [the prophet's wife] through pestilence; but you shall not lament or weep or let your tears flow. Moan softly; observe no mourning for the dead [*heʾānēq dōm*; *mētîm ʾēbel lôʾ taʿăśeh*]. Put on your turban and put your sandals on your feet; do not cover your upper lip, and do not eat the bread of comforters.

Although the syntax of *mētîm ʾēbel lôʾ taʿăśeh* remains awkward, it is acceptable.[21] In effect, the rendering of these words by NJPS requires us to understand the Hebrew in the following way: "As for the dead—mourning do not perform."

[19] See *CAD M*/II, 126–29, s.v. *mišlu*; and *CAD M*/I, 379, s.v. *mašlu*.

[20] See Gibson, *CML*, 88, no. 14, iv:207.

[21] Cf. Qoh. 3:20; 6:6; 12:5; and also Josh. 23:14 = 1 Kgs. 2:2; 1 Chr. 17:11.

Or, the sequence of the wording may be a case of *hysteron proteron*, the reversal of usual syntactic order, and should be understood as *ʾēbel mētîm*, "mourning over the dead."

More important is the question of whether "softly" is what Hebrew *dōm* means, or whether *d-m-m* I connotes complete stillness and silence. This question will occupy us considerably as the present discussion unfolds, and it will be argued that the connotations attendant upon *d-m-m* I are uncompromising.

An alternative rendering would derive *dōm* from *d-m-m* II, "to moan." Such a derivation could express itself in two ways:

a. One could analyze *dōm* as a substantive, yielding the composite term *dōm mētîm*, "the lament over the dead." If one allows for haplography, it is even possible to reconstruct the consonantal text as: *dm*[*m*] *mtym* (= *dĕmām mētîm*), "the lament over the dead," thereby producing a geminate form similar to Eblaic *dimūmu*, "lament." On this basis, we would translate verse 17a as follows:

> *hēʾānēq! dōm/dĕmām mētîm, ʾēbel lôʾ taʿăśeh*
>
> Groan! But the lament over the dead, (and) mourning do not perform, etc.

This rendering would at once remove the awkwardness of the Masoretic syntax and resolve, as well, the apparent contradiction between moaning and silence.

> b. *hēʾānēq! dōm! ʾēbel mētîm lôʾ taʿăśeh*
>
> Groan! Moan! But do not perform mourning over the dead.

Taken either way, v. 17a would parallel v. 23b, thereby forming an *inclusio*, as the prophet repeats God's instructions, now applying them to the people collective: "You shall be heartsick because of your iniquities and shall moan (*ûnĕhamtem*) to one another."

The depictions of verses 17a and 23b, however we interpret *dōm* in v. 17a, mean that only primal feelings are to be expressed: the irrepressible groaning and moaning over the dead. Formal mourning is eschewed because the envisioned disaster represents deserved punishment for iniquity. One should not mourn over God's punishment, which is just, nor would it do any good. Here, a more subtle distinction is suggested between sounds like groans and moaning, which are virtually involuntary, and the more formal and intentional acts that comprised mourning in ancient Israel, such as words of eulogy and those traditional formulas uttered while weeping (Jer. 22:18; 34:5), prescribed radical changes in attire, and the donning of a mask to cover the lower part of one's face.

Whereas the dynamics of the prophet's statement in Ezek. 24:16–23 are understandable, the particulars of the phenomenology hinge on the precise semantic ranges of *d-m-m* I and proposed *d-m-m* II, respectively. Does the semantic range of *d-m-m* I extend in Biblical Hebrew to such connotations as "speaking softly, murmuring," and the like, as J. Blau maintained, or is it less flexible, always connoting utter stillness? If the semantic range of *d-m-m* I is taken to be flexible, then *hēʾānēq dōm*, "Moan softly," is acceptable. If, however, *d-m-m* I contrasts with any audible sound, just as it does with any perceptible motion, then to render *hēʾānēq dōm*, a unique biblical locution, as "Moan softly," produces an oxymoron. One would have to translate: "Moan in silence."

The same issue informs our determinations regarding the nominal form *dĕmāmāh*, which surely reflects a geminate root. In fact, it is only by means of an analysis of the semantic range of the form *dĕmāmāh* that we can hope to demonstrate that *d-m-m* I and *d-m-m* II are genuinely distinguishable homonyms in Biblical Hebrew. One suspects that the oft-suggested rendering of *d-m-m* I as "speak softly" derives from an imprecise understanding of the nominal form *dĕmāmāh*, which occurs three times in the Hebrew Bible (1 Kgs. 19:12; Ps. 107:29; Job 4:16).

It would be best to begin with Job 4:16, more precisely with Job 4:12–16, so as to comprehend the context:

> A spoken message came to me in stealth,
> Terror gripped me when I heard it.
> In thought-filled visions of the night,
> When deep sleep falls on men,
> Fear and trembling came upon me,
> Causing all my bones to quake with fright.
> A wind passed by me,
> Making the hair of my flesh bristle.
> *wayyaʿămôd wĕlōʾ ʾakkîr marʾēhû*
> *tĕmûnāh lĕneged ʿênāy*
> Something stood up, whose appearance I did not recognize;
> A form [loomed] before my eyes;
> I heard a *droning* voice (*dĕmāmāh wāqôl*).

Our translation is based on NJPS, but with significant changes, some of which were suggested by H. L. Ginsberg's insightful reading of this passage.[22] The semantics are, indeed, subtle. Does Hebrew *rûaḥ* mean "wind," which a comparison with the scene described in 1 Kgs. 19:12, the Elijah episode, would suggest? Or, does *rûaḥ* refer to the "spirit," the apparition beheld, as Ginsberg understood it? Does *dĕmāmāh* express the oft-experienced stillness after the storm, in which case a derivation from *d-m-m* I would be acceptable? Or is *dĕmāmāh* produced by the voice of the apparition, or by the wind, so that *dĕmāmāh* refers to sound and movement—which is also Ginsberg's view? Even if the Septuagint's reading is upheld, so that *dĕmāmāh* is a sound made by the wind, albeit greatly reduced, we are still dealing with sound, not absolute stillness. In these events, a derivation from *d-m-m* II might be more accurate. After all, Akkadian *dĕmāmāh* is used to describe sounds in nature, like the rustling of reeds when the wind blows.

Reference to Ps. 107:29–30 further focuses the question. NJPS translates as follows:

---

[22] See A. B. Ehrlich, *Mikrâ ki-Pheschutô* (Ktav reprint: New York, 1969), 3:336.

He reduced the storm to a whisper (*yāqēm śĕʿārāh lidmāmāh*),
the waves were stilled (*wayyeḥĕšû gallêhem*).
They rejoiced when all was quiet (*kî yištôqû*).
and He brought them to the port they desired.

It would seem that NJPS took *dĕmāmāh* to represent what we are calling *d-m-m* II. All motion did not stop at once; there was a breeze that was audible, after which the waves fell silent. Such an interpretation, actually adopted in the Septuagint, would help to clarify the sense of 1 Kgs. 19:12. There we read that Elijah first heard a tumultuous, crashing wind, then an earthquake, then a fire raging. God was not discernible in these intensely audible phenomena, however. Then came *qôl dĕmāmāh daqqāh*, which, as v. 13 informs us, was likewise audible to Elijah. NJPS translates: "And after the fire—a soft murmuring sound." It would seem that here, too, the NJPS translation derives *dĕmāmāh* from *d-m-m* II "to moan, sigh, mourn," and we, too, opt for this derivation. If this choice is correct, there would be no clear evidence in Biblical Hebrew of the connotation "speak softly, murmur" for *d-m-m* I.

The fact that Akkadian *damāmu*, which we take as a cognate of Hebrew *d-m-m* II, is used to describe the cooing of doves (Akkadian *summātu*) suggests a comparison of the semantic range of Hebrew *d-m-m* II with the semantic ranges of the verbs *h-g-y* and *h-m-y*, which both describe the sounds emitted by doves, among other things.

The Hebrew verb *h-g-y* describes the cooing of doves (Isa. 38:14; 59:11), and in Isa. 16:7 refers to mourning, together with *hêlîl*, "to howl":

lākēn yĕyêlîl Môʾāb; lĕMôʾāb kūllôh yĕyêlîl;
laʾăšîšê Qîr-Ḥarāšet tehgû nĕkāʾîm

Ah, let Moab howl;
Let all in Moab howl!
For the men of Kir-haresheth
You shall moan most pitifully.

But, Hebrew *h-g-y* can also describe the sound made by a lion (Isa. 31:4), just as Akkadian *damāmu* is said of the sounds emitted by donkeys, and other animals.

Turning to Hebrew *h-m-y*, we note its use to describe the cooing of doves (Ezek. 7:16) and also with respect to sounds emitted by other animals like bears (Isa. 59:11) and dogs (Ps. 59:7, 15). Further subtlety emerges from the usage of *h-m-y* to describe the shrill sound emitted by a recorder (*ḥâlîl*) (Jer. 48:36) and the sound of a lyre (Isa. 16:11). As regards context, we note that *h-m-y* also describes mournful moaning, at least by implication (Ps. 42:6, 12; 43:5). Most telling perhaps is the decibel range of Hebrew *h-m-y*; it may refer to the roaring of the waves and the tumult of a crowd, very loud sounds expressed by the form *hāmôn*, for example.[23]

[23] See H. L. Ginsberg, "Job the Patient and Job the Impatient," *Congress Volume, Rome 1968* (VTSup 17; Leiden: E. J. Brill, 1969), 88–111, esp. 105–6.

The foregoing discussion argues for taking the nominal form *dĕmāmāh* from *d-m-m* II, "to moan, mourn," and for restricting derivation from *d-m-m* I, "to be still, silent," to usages and meanings that contrast with motion and sound altogether.

To test this hypothesis, it is necessary to examine all clear biblical attestations of *d-m-m* I, "to be still, silent," and its derivatives. In this way, it should be possible to differentiate more precisely between the two homographic vocables and the forms related to each. We must also take up the matter of the roots usually listed as *d-m-y*, "to be still, come to an end, cease to be," and as *d-w-m*, "to be silent, to await." We know that Biblical Hebrew morphology is sufficiently fluid to allow for three realizations of the same lexeme when expressed by weak verbs: (a) a middle weak form, in our case *d-w-m*, (b) a 3rd weak form, in our case *d-m-y*, and (c) a geminate form, in our case *d-m-m*. It is our contention that all three of these realizations are distinguishable from proposed *d-m-m* II.

V. Biblical Hebrew d-m-m I, and Its Alternative Realizations, d-m-y and d-w-m

There can be little question that in Josh. 10:12–13 the sun and moon were ordered to stop in their paths, and that there imperative *dōm* means "stand still," as is confirmed by the parallel word, *ʿāmad* "halted." The same is true of 1 Sam. 14:9, where the response to imperative *dōmmû*, "stay put," is *wĕʿāmadnû taḥtēnû*, "We will stand in place." The precise sense of *d-m-m* I is further clarified by Jer. 47:6:

> O sword of the LORD,
> When will you will be quiet (*lôʾ tišqōṭî*) at last?
> Withdraw into your sheath,
> Rest and be still (*hĕrāgĕʿî wādōmmî*)!

In all of the above, the primary concept underlying the usage of *d-m-m* I is immobility, or inertness, in contexts that describe motion or refer to it.

In Lam. 3:28 *yiddōm* describes how one remains solitary and immobile because one is somehow compelled to do so. That *yiddōm* in this verse means "to stay put," and not primarily "to be silent," is indicated by what precedes, in v. 26: "It is best that he await without stirring (*wĕdûmām*) / For rescue by the LORD." The same can be said of usage of *d-m-m* I in Job. 31:34, where one is said to remain indoors, and stay put. The notion of patient, immobile waiting or expectation is also conveyed by forms of *d-m-m* I in Ps. 37:7; 62:6; 131:2–3; and Job. 29:21.

Seldom do we find that *d-m-m* I connotes specifically silence in contrast to sound. One could interpret Ps. 30:13 precisely in this way:

> *lĕmaʿan yĕzammerkā kābôd wĕlôʾ yiddōm*
> *YHWH ʾĕlôhây lĕʿôlām ʾôdēkkā*

> That [my] whole being may sing hymns to You and not be silent;
> O LORD, my God. I will praise you forever.

But one could just as easily translate *wĕlōʾ yiddōm* "without end, endlessly" (thus NJPS). The sense of silence is clearly present, however, in Ps. 31:18–19:

> O LORD, let me not be disappointed when I call You;
> Let the wicked be disappointed;
> Let them be silenced (read: *yiddammû*) in Sheol;
> Let lying lips be stilled (*tēʾālamnāh*).
> That speak haughtily against the righteous,
> With arrogance and contempt.

Having referred above to the occurrence of the form *dûmām*, "in an inert state," in Lam. 3:26, it is now time to consider a suggestive occurrence of the same form in Hab. 2:19:

> *Hôy ʾômēr lāʿēṣ hāqîṣāh; ʿûrî lĕʾeben dûmām*
>
> Ah, you who say, "Wake up" to wood,
> "Awaken" to inert stone (NJPS).

The form *dûmām* appears to derive from *d-w-m*, with the affix *–ām* having adverbial force: *dûm* + *ām* = *dûmām* "in an inert state silently" (cf. *yômām*, "by day"). For the postulated form *dûm*, "silence," compare *ḥûg* "ellipse, circle" (Isa. 40:22; Job 26:10, 14; Prov. 8:27). Of course, *d-w-m* is simply an alternative realization of *d-m-m*, and the identification of the root as alternatively middle-weak or geminate is often merely a function of the phonetic determinations made by the Masoretes. In any event, the imagery of petrification is also expressed in Exod. 15:16:

> *bigdōl zĕrôʿakā yiddĕmû kāʾāben*
>
> When Your arm was extended,
> They became inert as stone,
> Until Your people would pass through, LORD,
> Until the people would pass through—
> Whom you brought into being.

Whether we take Exod. 15:16 to refer to the Egyptians who plummeted to the bottom of the sea, to the waters which froze up, or to the neighboring peoples who were seized with dread, the imagery of utter stillness is the same.

To summarize: there is no indication of motion or sound in any occurrences of *d-m-m* I, or in those expressions of *d-w-m* that have been surveyed up to this point. Most likely, the forms *dûmāh* (also: *dūmmāh*); *dûmiyyāh* (also: *dūmmîyyāh*), all connoting stillness and silence, also derive from middle-weak *d-w-m*, although derivation from geminate *d-m-m* I or from 3rd-weak *d-m-y* II, "to cease, come to an end," is not impossible. The same can be said of the form *dŏmî* (דֳּמִי) in Isa. 62:6–7; Ps. 83:2, which may be analyzed as a masculine alternative to *dûmiyyāh*.

We proceed, therefore, to consider *d-m-y* II for what it informs us. Surely to be classified under *d-m-y* II is the usage in Jer. 14:17:

> Let my eyes run with tears,
> Day and night let them not cease (*wĕʾal tidmênāh*).

The same is true of Lam. 3:49 (cf. 2:18): "My eyes shall flow without cease (*wĕlôʾ tidmeh*), / Without respite." Note similar imagery conveyed by a form Masoretically pointed as deriving from *d-m-m* I, in Job 30:27: "My bowels are in turmoil (*rūttĕḥû*) without respite (*wĕlôʾ dammû*)."

It is a Niphal form of *d-m-y* II that is most probably reflected in Isa. 6:5:

> Woe is me; I am undone (*kî nidmêtî*),
> For I am a man of impure lips,
> And I live among a people
> Of impure lips.

The sense is that the prophet feels unable to perform his role by speaking to his people because he has sinned by impious speech. Until he is purified, he cannot continue. One could even translate: "Woe is me, for I am *struck dumb*!"

Whereas Isa. 6:4 occurs in a forensic context, which refers to impure speech, the lexicographer faces a more difficult decision with respect to Hos. 4:5–6:

> So you shall stumble by day,
> And by night the prophet shall stumble with you,
> And I will destroy (read: *dimmîtî*) your mother.
> My people are destroyed (*nidmû ʿammî*) for lack of knowledge.[24]

At this point the lexicographer is compelled to decide whether we need to posit a form *d-m-y* III or, for that matter, whether we need to posit a form *d-m-m* III, both of which are registered in *KBL*. What we find are biblical passages in which Niphal forms, and others connoting destruction and ruin are vocalized as derivatives of *d-m-y*. Thus, forms like *nidmāh* (from *d-m-y*) are paralleled by *nišmĕdû*, "they were in ruin," and *nikrĕtû*, "they were cut off," or by *šôdēd*, "ravaging," and Pual *šūddād*, "was ravaged," just as in Hos. 4:5–6 there is reference to stumbling (the verb *k-š-l*).[25]

The same is true with respect to forms derived from *d-m-m*. Thus, we read in 1 Sam. 2:9 that the wicked "will perish in darkness" (*baḥōšek yiddammû*), and we find similar forms derivative of proposed *d-m-m* III in Jer. 25:36–37; 48:2, all in the context of destruction. May such contexts and meanings be legitimately subsumed under *d-m-y* II and *d-m-m* I so that the separate entries, *d-m-m* III and *d-m-y* III, may be regarded as superfluous?

---

[24] For the usage of the verb *h-m-y* to describe the roaring of waves, see Isa. 17:12; 31:35; 51:15; Jer. 5:22; 6:23; 31:35; 50:42; 51:55; Ps. 46:4.

[25] The Masoretic pointing, Qal-stem *wĕdāmîtî*, in Hos. 4:5 yields no acceptable meaning, and it has been suggested that taking this verb as a Piel form would yield the sense of bringing to an end, to ruination, and would lead into v. 6.

Perhaps a comparison of the connotations attested for *d-m-y* II and of *d-m-m* I with the observable semantic range of the Hebrew verb *š-m-m*, "to be desolate, in ruin," will shed some light on the problem. This verb, in various contexts and expressed in its various forms, connotes both (a) the stillness of devastation and ruin and (b) the numbness and dumbness of shock. Common to all of its predications is the concept of stillness. We would, therefore, endorse a semantic range for *d-m-m* I and *d-m-y* II that extends all the way to desolation and ruin, although this extension is far from certain.

VI. Conclusions

We have found a home in Biblical Hebrew for *d-m-m* II, "to mourn, moan," in contexts of mourning and sadness, as well as in describing the sounds of animals and of nature itself—sounds which are reminiscent of mourning.

As we understand Lev. 10:3, it tells us that Aaron began to mourn Nadab and Abihu, and would have continued to do so had he not been instructed to refrain from such activity. Mourning would have rendered him and his remaining sons impure through contact with the dead. They were, instead, to give precedence to their purification as the priests of the Israelite community.

Leviticus 10 may, however, secrete an additional, phenomenological nuance. In our earlier discussion of the depictions of mourning in Ezek. 24:16–23 we found a distinction drawn between the irrepressible moaning and sobbing of bereavement, which could not be stifled or effectively prohibited, and formal mourning, which could be authoritatively forbidden. The involuntary sounds were there expressed by the verbs *hēʾānēq*, "Groan!" (v. 17), and *ûnĕḥamtem*, "You shall moan" (v. 23). If our reading is correct, Ezek. 24:17 also attests a form of *d-m-m* II, either the imperative *dōm*, "Moan!", or a substantive form, *dom* (possibly *dĕmām*), "a lament." In either case, the distinction between the irrepressible and the intentional is clearly evident.

Could not the same dynamic inform Leviticus 10? Aaron was not able to repress his emotions, and he moaned (*wayyiddōm*), just as one would have expected him to do. But neither he nor his remaining sons were permitted to initiate formal mourning. In fact, the prohibited forms of mourning stipulated in Lev. 10:6–7 for Aaron and his remaining sons bear the same function as those prohibited in Ezek. 24:16–17, 22–23 with respect to the prophet in his personal grief, and the people of Israel in their collective exile. To dramatize the justice of God's punishment, one ought not perform rituals of mourning for those whose death at God's hand was brought about by their disobedience of His will.[26]

---

[26] See Isa. 15:1; Hos. 4:6; 10:7; Obad. 5; Zeph. 1:11; and cf. Jer. 47:5; Ezek. 32:2; Hos. 10:15.

Offerings Rejected by God: Numbers 16:15 in Comparative Perspective*

Introduction

In the course of preparing the Anchor Bible Commentary to the book of Numbers, I encountered two suggestive themes capsulized in a single verse. Each of the themes led me to extensive evidence, and together they clarified the nexus of source criticism and the comparative method. Far from being incompatible or unrelated, these methodologies often nourish one another. The verse in question is Num 16:15:

(15a) *ʾal tēpen ʾel minḥātām*
(15b) *lōʾ ḥămôr ʾehād mēhem nāśāʾtî wělōʾ hărēʿōtî et ʾaḥad mēhem*
(15a) Do not turn toward their offering(s);
(15b) I have never misappropriated the mule of even one of them,
nor have I ever harmed a single one of them.

This verse occurs within a discernible textual unit of the book of Numbers, chaps. 16–17, which are comprised of several literary strands. Their composite character allows us to explore the interaction of source criticism and the comparative method. Comparative insights shed light on the cultural provenance of their components, the building blocks of historiographic narrative, whereas source analysis enables the scholar to trace phases in the formation of the biblical text.

The latter part of v. 15 (labeled 15b) has received more attention than the former part (labeled 15a). Verse 15b has been correctly compared to the *apologia* of the cult-prophet Samuel preserved in 1 Samuel 12, especially the statement of 1 Sam 12:3. In almost the same words as those in Num 16:15b, Samuel

---

* Originally published in J. E. Coleson and V. H. Matthews (eds.), *Go to the Land I will Show You: Studies in Honor of Dwight W. Young* (Winona Lake, IN: Eisenbrauns, 1996), pp. 107–116. Reprinted with permission from Eisenbrauns.

Author's note: The discussion following is offered in tribute to my learned teacher, Dwight W. Young, who impressed upon all of his students the importance of linguistic competence for the proper interpretation of ancient Near Eastern literature. The student of the Hebrew Bible never ceases to be amazed at the close affinity of biblical literature to the themes and diction of ancient Near Eastern creativity preserved in any number of languages.

This article is based on a paper delivered at the annual meeting of the American Oriental Society in Atlanta, Georgia, in March, 1990. I am grateful to D. O. Edzard, T. Frymer-Kensky, and W. W. Hallo for their helpful comments I received there.

asserts his integrity before the assembled Israelites. Analogues to the negative confession have been identified in ancient Near Eastern literature. A classic example from the Egyptian mortuary texts is entitled by its translator, John A. Wilson, "The Protestation of Guiltlessness" and is taken from the *Book of the Dead*.[1] In the Amarna correspondence we find the following statement of a vassal to his suzerain, which rhetorically recalls the protestations of both Moses and Samuel: "Furthermore: Let the king, my lord, inquire if I have misappropriated a single human, or if a single ox, or if a single mule from him!"[2] To these examples, we may add the biblical rite of entry into sacred precincts, formulated most clearly in Psalm 15. The diction of the negative confession was appropriate in diverse situations.

It is Num 16:15a which will concern us here, however. We shall investigate two of its aspects: theme and diction. Viewed as a theme, v. 15a pronounces a curse of sorts. Moses calls upon God to reject the offerings of those who were his enemies, thereby punishing them for having opposed him. In terms of diction, that is, the choice of *how* to express the intended thought, v. 15a reflects the idiom of liturgy and resembles a petition to a deity. The subtle interaction of theme and diction will lead us to differing, though related, genres of ancient Near Eastern literature.

Source Criticism

The immediate context of Numbers 16–17 pertains to an insurrection against Moses and Aaron, the divinely endorsed leaders of the Israelite people. The words of v. 15 are addressed to God by Moses in fear and anger after two leaders of the rebellion, Dathan and Abiram, had defied Moses' authority.

Now, anyone who reads chaps. 16–17 holistically, as a unified literary composition, would tend to understand 16:15a in relation to what follows in vv. 16–24 of the same chapter. In vv. 16–24 we read that the leaders of the rebellion were commanded to present themselves for a cultic ordeal, in the course of which they would offer incense at the entrance to the Tent of Meeting. The ordeal would settle the issue of Israelite leadership. By rejecting the offerings of the insurgents, God would announce his will in the matter, and once again he would endorse Moses and Aaron as his chosen ones. Interpreted in this way, Moses' angry plea that God reject the *minḥâ* of the enemies referred to the imminent *minḥâ* of the cultic ordeal, the very one projected in vv. 16–24 of the same chapter. Usage of the term *minḥâ* seals the link.

This reading of chap. 16 is valid, to be sure, and represents one of the views expressed in medieval Jewish exegesis, which poses the logical question of

[1] See the introduction and translation by John A. Wilson, "The Protestation of Guiltlessness," *ANET*, 34–36.

[2] See J. A. Knudtzon, *Die El-Amarna Tafeln* (reprinted, Aalen: Zeller, 1964) 1.849, no. 280, lines 24–29.

which *minḥâ* is intended in v. 15a.[3] The structuralist, ever intent upon bringing out the inner coherence of the final literary product, might be content to inquire no further. For the source critic, however, the textual make-up of chap. 16 (and of chaps. 16–17, taken together) is both problematic and promising. Source analysis shows that Numbers 16–17 exhibit the blending, or "braiding" of a least two literary strands, the JE and the P narratives, respectively. Most source-critics would assume a diachronic relationship between the JE and P sources, according to which JE represents an earlier strand, available to the narrators of P, who modulate its content and expand upon its themes.

"JE" is the siglum given to a composite Pentateuchal source comprised primarily of J (= *Jahwist*, in German), presumed to be of Judean origin, and E (= Elohist), presumed to be of northern Israelite origin. Most scholars date the completion of JE to the seventh century B.C.E., with its primary sources, J and E, traceable to earlier centuries. P (= *Priesterschrift*, in German) is the siglum given to the writings of the priestly school of biblical Israel, undoubtedly produced in more than one stage. Although there is disagreement on the dating of P, we may regard it as subsequent to JE for purposes of this discussion.[4]

It is possible to identify the respective input of JE and P in chaps. 16–17. In effect we have two principal happenings. (1) There is a rebellion instigated by Dathan and Abiram and a third, largely unknown Reubenite, against Moses. The JE material is concentrated in 16:12–15, 25–34. (2) There also is an internecine conflict within the Levitical clans led by Korah, a leader of the clan of Kohath. The issue in this priestly version was the sole right granted to the Aaronides, of the Amramite clan of Levites, to the Israelite priesthood. This determination relegated the other Levitical clans to a considerably lower status. The P material is concentrated in 16:3–11, 16–24, 35, and all of chap. 17.[5]

In order to blend these two narratives, the priestly writers reworked 16:1–2 so as to recast the rebellion in conformity with their agenda, thereby obscuring its original basis. Priestly writers likewise inserted the name of Korah into several JE passages, to maintain a modicum of consistency. In effect, P superimposed its agenda, namely, the endorsement of the uniquely legitimate Aaronide priesthood, upon one of a series of challenges to Moses' leadership, one that initially had nothing to do with Aaron or the status of the Levites.

---

[3] See J. Milgrom, *Numbers* (JPS Torah Commentary; Philadelphia: Jewish Publication Society, 1989) 134 sub Num 16:15; and 313, in the notes for chap. 16, numbered nn. 35–39. Milgrom refers to traditional Jewish commentators who discuss the frame of reference intended in this verse.

[4] For a discussion of the priestly source and its relation to the other components of Torah literature, see my commentary, *Leviticus* (JPS Torah Commentary; Philadelphia: Jewish Publication Society, 1989) xxv–xxx.

[5] Chapter 17 exhibits internal literary problems that need not concern us here. Most likely, the ordeal of the tribal "staffs" (17:16–24) represents a separate, priestly tale.

Bearing in mind that v. 15 is part of the JE narratives (vv. 12–25), the source critic realizes that at one stage in the formation of the biblical text, v. 15 was not followed by vv. 16–24, but most likely by vv. 25–34. When JE resumes in v. 25, it tells of an act of divine punishment wherein the insurgents and their households were swallowed up alive. Pursuant to a horrendous suggestion by Moses, God created a fissure in the earth. Not to be outdone, P has the insurgents meet their death in a conflagration (16:35).

The upshot of the above source analysis is that Moses' curse stated in 16:15a did not originally refer to a cultic ordeal involving an offering, but was intended to suggest something else to the reader.

The Theme of Cultic Rejection

Moses' petition in 16:15a recalls statements in the curse sections of ancient Near Eastern treaties and royal inscriptions. After all, insurrection was an offense often stipulated in treaties and royal inscriptions as incurring the punishment of the gods. Before citing comparative evidence on the theme of cultic rejection, we should note several innerbiblical reflexes of this theme.

In terms of diction, the only other biblical source that employs the precise idiom *pānâ ʾel ... minḥâ* "to turn toward ... an offering" is Mal 2:13, although the theme itself is expressed through other images quite frequently in biblical literature.

Malachi, the anonymous postexilic prophet, decried the corruption of the Levitical priesthood serving in the restored temple of Jerusalem:

> And this you must do, in addition: You must cover the altar of the LORD with weeping and moaning, because there will be no further turning toward the offerings (*mēʾên ʿôd pĕnôt ʾel hamminḥâ*), nor their favorable acceptance from your hand (*wĕlāqaḥat rāṣôn miyyedkem*).

In addition to restating the theme of cultic rejection, which was the punishment Moses wished upon his enemies, Mal 2:13 significantly extends the diction of acceptance and rejection to include the idiom: *lāqaḥ min yād* "to receive from one's hand". This will prove to be a link to the comparative evidence soon to be discussed.

The theme of cultic rejection recalls the disposition of the diverse sacrifices offered by Cain and Abel according to Gen 4:4b–5a:

> *wayiššaʿ YHWH ʾel Hebel wĕ ʾel minḥātô, wĕʾel Qayin wĕ ʾel minḥātô loʾ šaʿâ*
>
> The LORD turned toward Abel and toward his sacrifice, but toward Cain and toward his sacrifice He did not turn.

In this statement, the verb *šaʿâ*, rather than *pānâ*, expresses this "turning" of the neck or the face toward a person or away from him, or by extension, toward or away from one's prayer or sacrifice.

"Receiving from one's hand" expresses acceptance of gifts in several biblical contexts: in Gen 33:10–11 the reference is to Jacob's gift to Esau and in 1 Sam 25:35–36 to Abigail's gift to David. Most instructive are the words of Manoah's wife, Samson's mother-to-be. She understood the phenomenology of sacrifice better than her husband. Reacting to a theophany that terrified her husband, she said:

> Had the LORD indeed sought to cause our death, he would hardly have received from our hand (*lōʾ lāqaḥ miyyādēnû*) burnt offerings and offerings of grain, nor would he have announced all of these things to us at this time.

Following leads of theme and diction brought me to the recently discovered inscriptions from Tell Fekherye, in which similar statements of cultic rejection occur. These royal inscriptions, found in the area of Gozan across the Ḫabur River from Tell Ḫalaf, preserve parallel Aramaic and Assyrian versions. They have been dated to the ninth century B.C.E., albeit with a degree of uncertainty.

Adad-itʾi, governor of Gozan and its constituent towns, admonished in the following words any person who would efface his name from the appurtenances of the Adad temple:

> *mrʾy hdd lḥmh wmwh ʾl ylqḥ mn ydh*
>
> May my lord, Hadad, his food and his water not receive from his hand.

In the Assyrian text we read as follows:

> dIŠKUR *be-li* NINDA-*šú* A-*šú la i-ma-ḫar-šú*
>
> Adad, my lord, his food and his water, may he not accept it.

This curse is repeated with reference to the goddess Šala, Adad's consort.[6]

A similar curse is expressed in the inscription of Panammuwa I, found at Zinjirli and dated to the first half of the eighth century B.C.E. It is written in the so-called Yaudian dialect and preserves both the ideal, positive formulation of acceptance and the negative, maledictory formulation of rejection.

First, we present a positive statement, in which the king speaks of his own special relationship with the gods:

> *wbymy ḥlbṫ*[*y*]-*ḋṫ-ʾhb*
> *lʾlhy wmt yqḥw mn ydʿy*
> *wmh ʾšʾl mn ʾlhy*
> *mt yt*[*n*]*w ly*
>
> And during the days of my succession (?) x[= gifts, offerings] I proffered

[6] See H. Abou-Assaf, P. Bordreuil, and A. R. Millard, *La Statue de Tell Fekherye, Études Assyriologiques* (Cahier 7; Paris: Recherche sur les Civilisations, 1982) 23 (the Aramaic version, lines 17–18), and 14 (the Assyrian version, lines 28–29). Also see the alignment of the two versions on p. 65.

to the gods (or: "to my gods"), and they always received them from my hand(s).
And whatever I asked of the gods (or: "of my gods"),
they always granted me.[7]

Contrast the above with what Panammuwa has to say concerning any of his successors who fail to honor him in the future:

wyz[bḥ. hdd. zn. wlʾ. yzk]
r ʾšm. pnmw. . . . . . . -zbḥh.
wʾl. yrqy. bh. wmz. yšʾl. ʾl.
ytn. lh. etc.

and he offers sacrifice to this same Hadad, but does not pronounce the name of Panammuwa—[may Hadad not receive] his sacrifice, nor view it with favor; and whatever he asks, may he (=Hadad) not grant to him.[8]

Notwithstanding the fragmentary condition of the text, we are able to observe in the above citations expressions of the theme under discussion. When we combine the preserved contents of both citations, the positive and negative reflexes, we emerge with a binary projection of considerable impact.

The Panammuwa inscription brings us face to face with the interaction of theme and diction of which we spoke earlier. The positive formulation is liturgical in its diction, expressing the language of prayer and incantations, which speak of the acceptance of prayer and sacrifice from worshippers favored by the gods. The negative formulation, on the other hand, calls one's attention to the curse sections of treaties and royal inscriptions. Based on an admittedly partial search, we have the impression that the theme of cultic rejection is relatively rare among the punishments that the gods are called upon to impose. For the most part, treaties and royal inscriptions threaten disease and devastation, the denial of progeny or their extinction. I have not found the theme of cultic rejection in the Aramaic Sefire treaties or in the Neo-Assyrian treaties, either.

Denial of Cultic Access

Related to the theme of the rejection of sacrifice and prayer is the denial of cultic access, most often expressed as exclusion from entry into the presence of the gods, in a temple. This theme is evident in some of the Neo-Assyrian treaties. The so-called "Esarhaddon's Succession Treaty" enables us to define the

---

[7] See J. C. L. Gibson, *Textbook of Syrian Semitic Inscriptions* (3 vols.; Oxford: Clarendon, 1975) 2.66, no. 13, lines 12–13. My translation differs from Gibson's in some respects, and the same is true of the following citations in n. 8.

[8] Again in Gibson, *op. cit.*, 2.67–68, parts of lines 21–23. The restorations in the text are virtually certain, because the full formulas are evident elsewhere. The bracketed insertion in the translation is, however, merely an educated guess as to what the missing text said.

implications of the denial of cultic access in treaty curses. There is a series of curses pronounced against any who violate the terms of the treaty:

> ^{d}30 *na-an-nar* AN-*e u* KI.TIM *ina* SAḪAR.ŠUB-*pu li-ḫal-lip-ku-nu ina* IGI DINGIR.MEŠ *u* LUGAL *e-rab-ku-nu a-a iq-bi ki-i sír-ri-me* MAŠ.DA *(ina)* EDIN *ru-up-da*
>
> May Sin, the brightness of heaven and earth, clothe you with *skin disease*, and forbid your entry into the presence of the gods or king. Roam the desert like the wild ass and the gazelle![9]

It is clear that being denied entry into the presence of the gods and the king was part of a more extensive set of punishments. What links this type of curse logically to the theme of cultic rejection is precisely the reference to the presence of the gods: being barred from the temple would make it impossible to participate in sacrificial worship, to petition the gods, initially.

Liturgical Diction

What renders liturgical diction so appropriate for treaties and royal inscriptions is the direct involvement of the gods. Functionally, ancient Near Eastern curses are petitions to gods urging them to do certain things. This dynamic encourages the appropriation of liturgical diction by the ancient scribes in formulating their curses.

A good illustration of this process occurs as part of a lengthy oration attributed to Esarhaddon in what is known as a *Gottesbrief*, a letter addressed to the god Aššur, Esarhaddon's patron. The letter reports on the activities of Esarhaddon with respect to the king of Shupria, with whom he had problems. The latter was begging Esarhaddon to forgive him for offenses he had committed. Esarhaddon is informing Aššur that he had flatly rejected these entreaties. Historically, the reference is to the situation following the Assyrian subjugation of Shupria in 673 B.C.E. Shupria was a region lying in the northwest reaches of the Tigris, west of Lake Van and almost due north of Tell Ḫalaf.

In his letter to the god Aššur, Esarhaddon berates the king of Shupria for his treaty violations. Esarhaddon refuses to forgive the king of Shupria, a policy he is certain will please Aššur:

> [*ṣu*]-*ul-le-šú ul áš-me*
> *un-ni-ni-šú ul al-qí*
> *ul am-ḫu-ra šu-up-pi-šú*
> [*š*]*ab-šu ki-šá-di ul ú-tir-raš-šum*-[*m*]*a*
> [*u*]*l ip-šah-šú ez-ze-tú ka-ba-ti*
> [*a*]*g-gu lìb-bi ul i-nu-uḫ-ma*

9 See S. Parpola and K. Watanabe, *Neo-Assyrian Treaties and Loyalty Oaths* (SAA 2; Helsinki University Press, 1988) 45, no. 6, lines 419–21. Also see the restored text on p. 22, no. 4, lines 16–17, which relates to the same theme.

re-e-mu ul ar-ši-šú-ma
ul aq-bi-šú a-ḫu-la[*p*]

His request, I did not hear;
His supplication I did not receive;
I did not accept his prayer;
My averted neck I did not turn back toward him;
I did not assuage for him my angry feelings;
My raging heart did not rest;
Friendship I did not show him;
I did not say to him: "Forgiven."[10]

Arrogating to himself the right to speak as a god would speak, Esarhaddon (more accurately, the author of the *Gottesbrief*) appropriates liturgical diction. A literary commentary on Esarhaddon's speech would cite the literature of prayer and incantations. Exclamatory *aḫulap* "Forgive! Help! Redress!" as well as idioms referring to assuaging the angry heart and to turning the neck toward and away from another are typically liturgical and are frequent in the genre of prayers known as ŠU.IL.LÁ "the lifting of the hands". What is rashly denied by Esarhaddon to his enemy is precisely what a prayerful worshipper seeks.[11]

Conclusions

The suggestiveness of Num 16:15a might have been missed had we been content to interpret Numbers 16–17 in purely holistic terms. Responding to questions raised by source analysis, we have been able to pursue comparative leads of considerable interest.

Having disassembled the text, broken it down into its component sources, it now behooves us to inquire what the priestly elaboration of the JE narrative contributes to our understanding of that earlier source itself. Apart from superimposing the priestly agenda, may we view the priestly source as a commentary on the JE narrative, as a particular interpretation of it?

For one thing, the priestly writers inform us how they understood cultic rejection phenomenologically: though Moses called upon God to reject the sacrifices of his enemies in the JE narrative, in the priestly narrative it is God who

---

[10] See R. Borger, *Die Inschriften Asarhaddons Königs von Assyrien* (AfO Beiheft 9; Osnabruck: Biblio-Verlag, 1976) 104, lines 33–35.

[11] See E. Reiner and H. G. Güterbock, "The Great Prayer to Ishtar and Its Two Versions from Boğasköy," *JCS* 21 (1967) 255–66, esp. 256 n. 6 for bibliography. On p. 260, lines 27–30 of the Neo-Babylonian version of the prayer to Ishtar have a litany wherein four successive entreaties begin with the invocation *a-ḫu-lap-ki be-let* AN-*e u* KI.TIM "Have mercy, Lady of heaven and earth!" For examples of petitions in ŠU.IL.LÁ prayers, see S. Langdon, *Babylonian Penitential Psalms* (Paris: Geuthner, 1927) 16–17, "The Psalm to Enlil" (reverse, K.5098 and K.4898), lines 23–24; p. 29, "Penitential Prayer to Aya" (K.4623), lines 17–26; pp. 80–81, "Penitential Psalm to a Goddess" (K.101, reverse), lines 3–9.

acts out that rejection by rendering his verdict in the cultic ordeal. He convicts those who had opposed his chosen leaders of the people, imposing a death sentence on those whose offering he rejects.

A curious interaction becomes evident: JE's reference to cultic rejection is suggestive, if somewhat metaphorical. Cultic rejection is one way of expressing divine wrath that results in destruction. The priestly writers took this threat literally! All biblical traditions enunciate the ideal state, the sought-after response from God: *raṣôn* "favorable acceptance".

When the God of Israel “Acts-Out” His Anger: On the Language of Divine Rejection in Biblical Literature*

In an earlier study, written in honor of my teacher, Dwight W. Young, I explored the biblical doctrine that the sacrificial offerings of the unworthy are rejected by God, a theme suggested by Num. 16:15a. In the heat of the Korah insurrection, an angry Moses implored God to reject the offerings of those who were then rebelling against him: אל-תפן אל-מנחתם (“Do not turn toward their offering”) (Levine 1993a: 414, 426–28; 1996). The only other biblical source that replicates the precise formula פנה אל מנחה (“to turn toward an offering”) is Mal. 2:13, where the pronouncement is similarly negative: the Temple altar is covered with tears, because God does not “turn toward” the sacrifices of the people and refuses to accept them. This theme is, however, one of broad currency in biblical literature, and the Epilogue to the Holiness Code, in its blessings, says that YHWH will turn toward his people (Lev. 26.9; cf. Ezek. 36:9). Anticipating the forthcoming discussion of Jer. 14:17–22, which will serve as our core text, we may cite 14:11–12, which precedes that very prophetic oration: “Then YHWH said to me: Do not pray on behalf of this people for good things. When they fast, I will not listen to their chanting, and when they raise up burnt offerings and grain offerings, I will not accept them. Rather, will I do away with them by sword, and by famine, and by pestilence.” This pronouncement resonates most clearly with Isa. 1:10–15, and reflects the belief that one of the penalties inflicted upon evildoers by God (in polytheistic religions, by the gods) is the denial of cultic access and efficacy to those who are out of favor. Such cultic rejection foreshadows disastrous consequences on the ground. On this basis, a person might curse his enemies by wishing this upon them, as Moses had done.

Here, I would like to carry the inquiry further by discussing other ways of expressing divine rejection in biblical literature. It is surely more heartening, and less painful, to focus on the positive aspects of the human-divine encounter, on covenant promises, and on blessing and reward. But, truth be told, biblical literature as a whole is replete with denunciations and admonitions, sanctions and dire predictions, and with other expressions of divine anger. This aspect of biblical religion is every bit as revealing as are biblical visions of redemption and tri-

---

* Originally published in John Kaltner and Louis Stulman (eds.), *Inspired Speech: Prophecy in the Ancient Near East, Essays In Honor Of Herbert B. Huffmon* (JSOTSup 406; London; New York: T&T Clark, 2004), pp. 111–129. Reprinted with permission from the Continuum International Publishing Group.

umph, and of God's love and favor—phenomena that cannot be appreciated fully without a clear understanding of their opposites.

Methodology

A basic element of my approach to religious phenomenology has been to examine in depth the semantics of Hebrew idioms and formulas, rather than to assume that their meanings are transparent and obvious. In this vein, I have investigated "The Language of Holiness: Perceptions of the Sacred in the Hebrew Bible" (Levine 1987b); "Silence, Sound, and the Phenomenology of Mourning in Biblical Israel" (Levine 1993b); "The Semantics of Loss: Two Exercises in Biblical Hebrew Lexicography" (Levine 1995) and other themes. Regarding expressions of emotion, in particular, it is noteworthy that they are often predicated on graphic, sometimes physical acts and responses, even if they become figurative or metaphorical through extended usage. One will say that he is "desolate", in French *desolé*, when being distressed, or that he is "crushed", or "overwhelmed" by circumstances. In Biblical Hebrew, one who is in shock may be characterized as *šōmēm* ("desolate", 2 Sam. 13:20; Lev. 26:32), which is a graphic description in the first instance (Lam. 1:4, 16).[1]

Translators and lexicographers seem to favor "leveled" definitions, which are more functional, and produce a smoother reading. And yet, *Grundbedeutung* and the analysis of semantic fields remain essential, and we inevitably miss something when we try to bypass them. In the context of the present discussion, this judgment aptly applies to the English verb "reject". It is derived from Latin *reicio* and related forms, "to throw back, throw off, fling aside", and, by extension, "to disdain, reject with scorn" (Simpson 1971:510). An ancient Latin author would normally employ the verb *reicio* to express physical acts, and even in contemporary English usage, the verb "reject" occasionally describes physical action, or reaction. Thus, one who received a transplanted organ may be said to "reject" it subsequently. In my estimation, most of the Biblical Hebrew terms for divine rejection retain more of their graphic or physical connotations than is true of the English verb "reject" in contemporary usage.

The task of the lexicographer and the exegete is, therefore, to determine in each specific case how verbs expressing divine rejection are being used. This will entail analysis of immediate context so as not to miss references to physical effects. Here I will study two verbs that characteristically connote divine rejection. They are known parallels, and both occur together in Jer. 14:17–22, which will serve as our core text. These are *māʾas*, usually translated "to reject, despise", and *gāʿal*, usually translated "to spurn, reject". I have previously discussed these verbs as they figure in the Epilogue to the Holiness Code (Lev.

[1] An interesting treatment of emotional expression in biblical literature is that of Grushkin (2000). It was my privilege to direct this dissertation, which also benefited from the assistance of the psychology faculty.

26.3–46), making brief reference to Jeremiah 14 in the process (Levine 1987a, 1989). In those studies, my concern centered on the functions of these verbs in the overall composition of the Epilogue as it progressed from one stage of national crisis to another. Here it will be shown, on grounds of semantics and context, that these verbs, and others like them, convey physical or graphic effects so that their connotations are not limited to the emotional or relational dimension. Their accurate definition affects our understanding of the human-divine encounter as conceived by the many biblical authors who employed them.

A corollary consideration of a more formal nature is the syntactic environment in which the two verbs under discussion occur. We have to do with two constructions: (1) a direct-object construction, and (2) an indirect-object construction with prepositional *beth*. It will be my task to show that syntax affects the sense of verbs in discrete ways and is not simply a matter of alternative options or different ways of saying the same thing. As an example, I maintain that the construction *gāʿal* + direct object means something different from *gāʿal* + prepositional *beth*, and that the same is generally true with respect to the verb *māʾas*, whose analysis is admittedly more complex. Of the two principal verbs under discussion, Hebrew *māʾas* attests a cognate in Akkadian (possibly even two cognates), whose usage will prove to be relevant to our understanding of the Hebrew.

Jeremiah 14:17–22. A Prophecy of Divine Rejection

With these considerations in mind, we turn to the interpretation of Jer. 14:17–22, which will serve as our core text. Anticipating the discussion to follow, I translate this oration as follows:

> 17 May my eyes run with tears,
> day and night, let them not be still!
> For my people, the maiden daughter, has suffered
> a grievous injury, a very critical wound.
> 18 If I go out to the open country, (I) behold those slain by the sword;
> if I enter the town, (I) behold those made sick by famine;
> for both priest and prophet travel about in the land,
> at a loss to understand.[2]
> 19 Have you utterly cast off Judah (המאס מאסת את-יהודה)?[3]

---

[2] The syntax of the Hebrew is somewhat strange. We normally expect that the verb *sāḥar* ("to encircle, move around") would take an accusative. As written, the sense is either that the priests and prophets roam "to" an unknown land, or that they don't know what has happened as they wander about their own land. That is how the verse has been translated here, giving weight to the *waw* of ולא ידעו, as if to say, "with the result that they failed to know". Cf. the discussions in Bright 1962:101–102; and Lundbom 1999:713.

[3] I am happy to agree with Bright (1962:99), against many other commentators. He aptly translates, "Have you utterly cast aside Judah?"

Have you become nauseated over Zion (אם-בציון געלה נפשך)?
Why have you struck us down,
leaving us without healing;
Left hoping for wholeness, but without wellbeing;
for a time of healing, but, instead, facing terror?
20We acknowledge our wickedness, YHWH,
the sins of our forefathers,
for we have offended you.
21Do not spurn (אל-תנאץ), for your (own) name's sake;[4]
do not dishonor your glorious throne.
Remember, do not breach your covenant with us!
22Are there any among the false gods of the nations who can bring rain?
Can the heavens (of themselves) bring showers?
Are you not the one, YHWH, our God?
So (it is, that) we hope in you!
For it is you who have made all of these things.

This poetic oration follows upon a prose section that warns the people of disaster (Jer. 14:10–16) in which the prophet is reassured that those who speak falsely in YHWH's name, promising wellbeing, are not his true messengers. In reality, the dead will be left unburied in the streets of Jerusalem! It is at this point that we encounter, in Jer. 14:17–22, the prophet's lament and supplication over the impending fulfillment of this dire prediction.

We begin with the verb *māʾas* in Jer. 14:19, whose parallel is *gāʿal*. This parallelism is well established in Biblical Hebrew, but whereas the etymology of the verb *gāʿal* is known, the same is not true for the verb *māʾas*. We know what *gāʿal* "means". It starts out as a physical act, and then appropriates an extended or figurative meaning. We cannot be sure that the same is true for the verb *māʾas*, which, for all we know, may begin by describing a state of mind, or emotional disposition, and then go on to connote physical and graphic acts. Translating Hebrew *māʾas* accurately requires, therefore, that we study its usage in con-

[4] As it stands, the verse either uses the verb *nāʾaṣ* without an object, or intends that both verbs *nāʾaṣ* ("to spurn"), and *nibbēl* ("to dishonor") share the same direct object, namely, כסא כבודך ("your glorious throne"). Lundbom (1999:716) cites an earlier suggestion by Dahood that we read: *limeʾon šemekā* ("the abode of your name"), written defectively with accusative *lamedh*. Thus, "Do not spurn the abode of your name". This would produce excellent parallelism. However, the pointing *lᵉmaʿan* may be correct after all; it resonates with the earlier statement of Jer. 14:7 עשה למען שמך ("Act for your own name's sake"). That the verb *nāʾaṣ* does not always take an object may be suggested by Deut. 32:19: "Then YHWH saw, and he spurned (וינאץ), because of the anger (ignited by) his sons and daughters (מכעס בניו ובנותיו)". Of course, *mikkaʿas* may have the same adverbial sense as *bekaʿas* ("out of anger"), in which case we would have a direct object: "Then YHWH saw, and angrily spurned his sons and daughters". On balance, I would retain the Masoretic pointing in Jer. 14:21. Actually, Jer. 14:17–22 and Deut. 32 resonate with each other. One notes, in this regard, that the verb *nibbēl* ("to dishonor") also occurs in Deut. 32:15.

crete contexts, and then proceed to the role of this verb in the human-divine encounter, where the God of Israel is variously subject and object. My first observation is that *mā'as* serves as a replacement for *hišlîk* ("to cast off, throw away"). This can be learned from a comparison of Isa. 2:20 with Isa. 31:7:

> On that day, each person will throw away (ישליך) his silver idols and his golden idols, which he fashioned for himself (as objects of) worship.
> On that day, they shall cast off (ימאסון), each person, his silver idols and his golden idols, which your (own) hands fashioned for yourselves in sinfulness.[5]

The scene is one of removing idols from cult-sites or from one's home, an act usually conveyed by the verb *hēsîr*, as in 1 Sam. 7:3–4. Clearly, Isa. 31:7 is a cognizant restatement of Isa. 2:20; its author seized upon the verb *mā'as* to convey the same action as did *hišlîk* in the typological source known to him. One is reminded of the parable of the Nazirite-locks in Jer. 7:29. Addressing the Israelite people, the prophet says:

> Shear your Nazirite-locks and throw them away (והשליכי)!
> Take up a lament on the foothills!
> For YHWH has cast off in abandonment (כי מאס יהוה ויטש)
> the generation of his wrath.

I hasten to cite this passage here, because it again illustrates that the verbs *hišlîk* and *mā'as* are synonymous in that they express reciprocal actions. The Israelites may just as well throw away their Nazirite-locks because YHWH has cast them off!

Several biblical attestations of the verb *mā'as* describe actual changes in physical condition. We note usage of the verb *mā'as* in an enigmatic passage, Ezek. 21:14–16, which describes the sharpened sword of YHWH:

> 14O mortal, prophesy and declare:
> The Lord spoke as follows, Say:
> O sword, sword! Sharpened and also burnished,
> 15to wreak slaughter has it been sharpened,
> to have a flashing blade has it been burnished...
> It can fell any tree (מאסת כל-עץ)!
> 16It has been given over for sharpening;
> to be held in the palm of the hand.
> That sword has been sharpened and burnished,
> to be put into the hand of a killer.

A thorough, recent treatment of this problematic passage is presented by M. Greenberg (1997:422–23). I agree with Greenberg that the bracketed Hebrew

[5] The force of *ḥēṭ* would seem to be adverbial, hence, "in sinfulness", or perhaps "as a sin".

words in v. 15 are probably extraneous—although one is at a loss to know how they crept in here—or that they reflect corruption in the transmission of the text. However, Greenberg's judgment that "the notion of a whetted sword being wielded against a tree is unlikely" may be mistaken. After all, what follows in Ezek. 21:23–25 speaks of the "sword" of the king of Babylon advancing against Rabbat Ammon, Judah and Jerusalem: "And clear a place (ויד ברא) at the crossroad (leading into) the town" (Ezek. 21:24). As Greenberg notes, this is what the verb ברא (Piel *bārēʾ*) means in Josh. 17:18, speaking of cutting down trees in a forest. That this action can be accomplished with a sword is revealed in, of all places, Ezek. 23:47: "They shall pelt them with crowd-stones, and cleave them with their swords (וברא אותהן בחרבותם)". What interests us is the concreteness of the imagery, whereby a sword is said to be so sharp that it can cut down any tree.

Also indicative of physical condition is Lam. 3:45—"You have made us refuse and filth (סחי ומאס) in the midst of the nations" (cf. Isa. 5:25)—where there is an actual play on the meaning of *māʾas*, carrying us from the physical to the emotional in Jer. 6:29–30:

> 29The bellows puff; lead is consumed by fire;[6]
> yet the smelter smelts to no purpose.
> The base elements have not been purged.
> 30They are called "base silver" (כסף נמאס),
> because YHWH has base feelings toward them (כי מאס ה׳ בהם).

The context is blatantly physical, in the first instance. The prophet is employing the known metaphor of the purging fire, except that in this instance the process is ineffectual. As the previous verses tell us, Israel failed the test and has not been purged of the evildoers in its midst. In a single verse we find both the Niphal and an active, indirect-object construction. The Niphal is physically descriptive of low-grade silver, whereas the indirect-object construction would seem to convey YHWH's disposition. Of the latter, more is to follow.

A blending of motifs characterizes a complex description of devastation in Isa. 33:7–9:

> 7Hark! The Arielites cry out aloud,
> Shalom's (= Jerusalem's) messengers weep bitterly.[7]
> 8Highways are desolate, wayfarers have ceased.
> He has broken the covenant (הפר ברית),
> he has ruined towns (מאס ערים);
> he has not shown regard for people.

---

[6] Most read מאשתם as מאש תתם (*meʾeš tittōm*, "by fire, it will be finished/consumed"), assuming haplography.

[7] Read *ʾerʾelîm*, the plural form, as suggested in NJPS, and see Isa. 29:1, where *ʾărîʾēl* is a poetic name for Jerusalem. This is the key to understanding *šālôm* as a veiled reference to Jerusalem, known as *šālēm* (Ps. 76:3).

[9]The land is wilted and withered (אבל אמללה),
Lebanon is paled (החפיר) and moldering;
Sharon has become like a desert,
and Bashan and Carmel are stripped bare.

By way of background, Isaiah 33 concludes a series of prophecies (chs. 28–33) that open with the exclamation הוי ("Hark!") and pertain to the Assyrian crisis. The prophet begins by railing against the Assyrian king, and by metonymy against the Assyrian Empire, predicting that he will meet a disastrous end (33:1). He proceeds to petition the God of Israel for deliverance, praising him as a powerful redeemer (33:2–6). Then comes the depiction of a ravaged land that was just cited (33:7–9), followed in turn by a resumption of the theme of deliverance. In poetry of unusual force and beauty, the prophet foresees YHWH arising in power to strike down the enemy. He portrays a redeemed Zion, a secure city governed in justice (33:10–24).

Our concern is with the connotation of the verb *māʾas* in v. 8, part of the accusation against the elliptical, unnamed enemy. He has broken his treaty, which harks back to the characterization of him in v. 1 as "betrayer", and he is also referred to as a "ravager". Some have taken the reference to a covenant as their cue, and have accordingly followed up with emotional and legal translations. Thus, החפיר would mean "disgraced", and ערים ("towns") might even be emended to עדים ("testimonies"), intended as a parallel word for ברית ("covenant"). It is preferable, however, to sustain the graphic imagery. After all, the verb *ḥāpar* only bears the sense of disgrace because it means "to turn white, pale". Curiously, both אבל and אמלל exhibit a semantic field that reaches from the graphic sense "to wilt, dry up, wither", to the emotional sense "to mourn, grieve, be saddened, miserable" (cf. Hos. 4:3). Furthermore, the verbs *hēpēr* and *māʾas* are acknowledged parallels, and the verb *hēpēr* means "to break up, breach" from the root *p-r-r* (*HALAT*, 916–17). Hence, we once again take *māʾas* in its physical, graphic sense; the towns were not merely "despised", they were ruined, or perhaps emptied of their populations. Further on, we will have occasion to discuss 2 Kgs 23:27, where Hebrew *ʿîr* ("town"), a reference to Jerusalem, is likewise the direct object of the verb *māʾas*.

One recalls the words of the psalmist (Ps. 118:22), "The stone which the builders discarded (אבן מאסו הבונים) has become the primary cornerstone". We observe masons removing a stone from the site because they regarded it as unsuitable for use. Returning to the site we find, to our amazement, that the same stone had been used as a cornerstone. A sense of movement is also conveyed in Isa. 8:6, "Because this people has forsaken (מאס) the waters of Siloam that flow slowly". In Ps. 89:39, *māʾas* is synonymous with *zānaḥ* ("to abandon"), and the Niphal of the former in Isa. 54:6, within a metaphor of divorce, is similar in meaning:

For, as an abandoned wife, and one sad of spirit,
has YHWH called you back.
Can the wife of one's youth be cast off (כי תמאס)?

We may now proceed to the human-divine encounter, where we find the God of Israel is the subject of the verb *māʾas*, but let me first clarify the usage of the verb in Hos. 9-16–17:

> [16]Ephraim has been struck down,
> its root is dried up;
> they cannot bear fruit.
> Even if they do bear children,
> I will slay their cherished offspring.
> [17]My God casts them off (ימאסם אלהי)
> because they have not heeded him;
> and they shall be wanderers among the nations.

In effect, this is a prophecy of exile and ethnic extinction, the punishments for disobedience to God, in which the verb *māʾas* conveys the expulsion of a beleaguered population into foreign lands, where they will not be able to settle down. To render the verb *māʾas* as merely expressive of God's rejection or dislike, in the emotional sense, ignores the graphic depictions conveyed in these oracles of doom.

That the verb *māʾas* conveys a sense of movement is subtly expressed in the beautiful prophecy of Isa. 41:8–10a, where *māʾas* serves as an antonym of *bāḥar* ("to choose, select"):

> [8]But you, Israel my servant,
> Jacob, you whom I have selected (אשר בחרתיך);
> the seed of Abraham, my dear friend.
> [9]You, whom I pulled in from the ends of the earth,
> you, whom I summoned from its far recesses.
> To whom I declared: "You are my servant!
> I have selected you (בחרתיך), I have not cast you off (ולא מאסתיך)."
> [10a]Fear not, for I am with you.

The contrast that informs this prophecy of restoration is one of remote exile vs. nearness to God, to be regained through the ingathering of exiles. One recalls the statement of 2 Kgs 23:27, "Then YHWH declared: Judah, as well, will I remove from my presence, just as I removed Israel. And I will abandon this town which I had selected (ומאסתי את-העיר הזאת אשר-בחרתי), Jerusalem, and the temple where I commanded: "Let my name be there!"

There are very few instances in all of Hebrew Scripture where the God of Israel is the direct object of the verb *māʾas*. The first occurs in Num. 11:20. Numbers 11 is part of the JE narrative, which relates a dramatic challenge to the leadership of Moses on the part of the Israelites in the wilderness after the Exodus from Egypt. It records a change in governance whereby seventy of the elders, selected by Moses, are endowed with God's spirit and designated to share in the burdensome tasks of leadership. The people had demanded meat in the wilderness, finding the manna-bread nauseating, and were expressing regret over having left Egypt, where there was better food to eat. YHWH comes to Moses' aid, and angrily acquiesces to the demands of the people:

> You shall eat it (i.e. meat) not for one or two days, or for five or ten days, or even for twenty days; rather, up to a whole month of days, until it comes out of your nostrils, and is loathsome to you. For you have overthrown YHWH (כי-מאסתם את-יהוה) who is present in your midst by complaining to him, saying: "Why did we ever leave Egypt?"

That Numbers 11 originated in northern Israel as part of the Elohist tradition is suggested by the second instance. We find similar language in 1 Sam. 8:7, part of the account of Israel's demand for a king, which is likewise presented as a challenge to God's authority. Thus, YHWH instructs Samuel, "Heed the voice of the people in all that they say to you, for it is not you whom they have overthrown (כי לא אתך מאסו), but rather me whom they have overthrown (כי אתי מאסו) as their king". To this, compare 1 Sam. 10:19a: "But you, this very day, have overthrown your God (מאסתם את אלהיכם), who rescues you from all of your calamities and troubles, and have demanded, "We insist (לא כי)! Appoint a king over us!"

In both of these passages from 1 Samuel there is poignant reference to the earlier, rebellious behavior of the Israelites in the wilderness after the Exodus from Egypt. It would appear, therefore, that in two, related contexts YHWH/God can be the direct object of the verb *māʾas*: (a) when Israel renounces God's plan to make them his people and bring them to the land, in effect, attempting to undo the Exodus and the Sinai covenant, and (b) when Israel renounces God's kingship in favor of a human king. For the rest, the direct-object construction is used most often to say that humans "cast off" God's "word, command" (*dābār*, 1 Sam. 15:23, 26), "judgments" (*mišpāṭîm*, Ezek. 20:13), "teaching" (*tôrâ*, Amos 2:4), and the like.

Is Israel, the people, or any individual Israelite ever the direct-object of the verb *māʾas*? This is so in the rhetorical question posed in the core text at Jer. 14:19. One could say that this relationship is expressed in Jer. 7:29, already cited above, where we read, "For YHWH has cast off in abandonment (כי מאס יהוה ויטש) the generation of his wrath". In contrast, the God of Israel elsewhere denies that he would ever do this:

> Thus spoke YHWH: "Only if my covenant with day and night, the boundaries of heaven and earth I had not established, only then would I cast off (אמאס) the seed of Jacob, and David my servant, not selecting any of his seed as rulers over Abraham, Isaac, and Jacob, for I will surely restore their repatriates, and have compassion for them." (Jer. 33:25–26)

King Saul is the direct object of this verb (1 Sam. 15:23; 16:1) as are other potential candidates for kingship over Israel (1 Sam. 16:7–10), whereas an unnamed priest who rejected knowledge is told that he will be accordingly disqualified (Hos. 4:6). And, of course, we have Lam. 5:20–22:

> [20]Why have you forgotten us forever,
> abandoned us (תעזבנו) for so long!

> [21]Bring us back, YHWH, to you, and we will return;
> Renew our days as they were in the past,
> [22]For you have utterly cast us off (כי מאס מאסתנו),
> You have become exceedingly enraged at us.

The plea to be restored more or less confirms that the verb *māʾas* is synonymous with *ʿāzab* ("to abandon"). There is, however, one instance where the meaning of the verb *māʾas*, with the God of Israel as subject, is ambiguous. Amos 5:21 reads, "I hate, I reject/brush aside (שנאתי מאסתי) your pilgrimage festival offerings, and I will not breathe in the aroma of your solemn assembly offerings".

One could say that the offerings keep coming, but God does not accept them, thereby rendering them ineffective. Alternatively, one could assign a more active sense to the verb *māʾas* and say that the deity brushes the offerings aside, as the prophet Malachi (2:3) put it quite graphically: "And I will strew dung on your faces, the dung of your pilgrimage festival offerings".

The Wisdom tradition affords any number of examples where the construction *māʾas* + direct-object conveys something between an emotional disposition and an overt act. True to the distinctive vocabulary of wisdom, such usage, as subtle as it is, adds to our understanding of how this verb is used in specific contexts. A basic principle of wisdom is that we are to pursue truth and virtue, and submit to rebuke and discipline. We are to repudiate evil and sinfulness, and keep ourselves far from them. Such acts and dispositions may be expressed by the verb *māʾas* + direct object. Consider the following:

1. Psalm 15:4, speaking of the virtuous person: "One who is contemptible in his eyes he repudiates (ימאס), but he honors those who fear YHWH".[8]
2. Psalm 36:5, speaking of the wicked person: "He plots iniquity on his bedstead, he stations himself on a course of doing no good; he does not repudiate evil (ורע לא ימאס)".
3. Proverbs 3:11 and 15:32 both employ the Wisdom terms *mûsār* ("discipline") and *tôkaḥat* ("rebuke") in parallelism: "YHWH's discipline do not repudiate (אל-תמאס), my son; do not abhor his rebuke" (Prov. 3:11); "One who breaks loose from discipline diminishes his capacity (מואס נפשו), but one who heeds rebuke, acquires understanding" (Prov. 15:32). Akin to this is Job 5:17, "Behold, fortunate is the man whom the deity rebukes; do not repudiate (אל-תמאס) the discipline of Shadday".

In the book of Job, God is at times the subject of the verb *māʾas*, as are humans such as Job, and such passages yield interesting connotations. At one point, Job appeals to God not to convict him: "Does it benefit you to defraud, so that you repudiate (כי-תמאס) the work of your hands, while approving of the designs of the wicked?" At another point Job affirms God's justice when he says, "For El does not repudiate the innocent (לא ימאס-תם), and he will not give support to

[8] It is suggested that we read ימאס instead of MT Niphal נמאס to accord with the parallel יכבד, also an imperfect form.

evildoers" (Job 8:20). Just as Job appeals to God's justice, he also affirms his own in 31:13. "Did I ever brush aside (אם-אמאס) the case of my servant or maid servant?" Job feels he cannot win his suit against God despite his innocence (Job 9:20–21):

> Though I were right, my words would convict me.
> Though I were innocent, he would declare me crooked.
> I am innocent! But I am out of my mind! I repudiate my life (אמאס חיי).

In a moment of bitterness over his downfall, Job says, "But now, those younger than me in years mock me, whose ancestors I so shunned (אשר-מאסתי אבותם) as to put them with my sheep dogs!" (Job 30:1)

In the book of Job there are instances where we encounter the syntax *māʾas* + Ø-object, with the direct object being implied (cf. Ps. 89:39). Thus, Job 36:5: "For El is mighty, he would not condemn (ולא ימאס); he is mighty in strength and mind". In other words, he would not condemn the just. Elsewhere, Elihu poses a poignant question to Job that uses the same construction: "Does he (God) repay men's deeds by your say-so, that you have denounced (כי מאסת)?" (Job 34:33).[9] That is to say, you have denounced the deity. The most dramatic, and the most subtle, instance of the syntax *māʾas* + Ø-object comes in Job's final statement to God, in which he concedes that after seeing God revealed in the storm, he realizes that he is in no position to challenge him. "For this reason, I give up (אמאס), and reconcile myself over being (only) earth and ashes". In other words, Job withdraws his suit (cf. the sense of *māʾas* in Job 31:13).

There is Akkadian evidence bearing on the Hebrew verb *māʾas*. A sure cognate of the Hebrew is Akkadian *mêšu* ("to despise, to have contempt for, to disregard", hence, "to disregard sins, to forgive", *CAD M*/II, 41–42). It is frequently found in Wisdom texts of a religious character that are not too different from biblical prophecy. A second possible cognate is Akkadian *mêsu* ("to crush, squash, to trample, destroy, overwhelm", *CAD M*/II, 35–36). It is said of crushing soft stone, trampling on grass and plants, and the effects of destructive weaponry. In certain of their respective realizations these two verbs, which may be totally unrelated, are homophonous and homographic, with some drifting of the /*s*/ and /*š*/ sounds. They exhibit different lexical equivalents, and are used in different contexts, and yet they share a synonym in common, Akkadian *kabāsu* ("to trample"). In the case of *mêsu* ("to crush"), this is attested only in a lexical series, but as regards *mêšu* ("to despise") we have parallelism in a literary source. Thus, in the Babylonian Theodicy (Lambert 1960:78, line 135) we read: *pilludē ili lumēš* // *parṣi lukabbis* ("I will cast off [my] god's regulations // I will surely trample on [his] rites"—normalized *apud CAD*). Lambert translated "ig-

[9] The Hebrew is difficult and translates literally as "Is it from you that he repays it?" The verb *šillem* ("to repay"), is often used in reference to the rewards and punishments that God metes out. The "it" undoubtedly refers to people's deeds, what they do to incur punishment; hence, our free translation "men's deeds".

nore", but I prefer a higher degree of semantic parallelism, and therefore I render *mêšu* as "to cast off". In the same way, I favor a physical translation in an inscription of Esarhaddon, where *mêšu* is parallel with *abāku* ("to overturn"; cf. *CAD A*/I, 8–10, s.v. *abāku* B): *ilīšina ībukama i-me-šá ištaršin* ("They overthrew their gods // they cast off their goddesses", *CAD M*/II, 41–42). There are additional parallel verbs that indicate physical action.

It is relevant at this point to mention the verb *nāʾaṣ* ("to spurn") which occurs in Jer. 14:21. It also attests an Akkadian cognate, *nâṣu* ("to scorn", *CAD N*/II, 53), a rare verb from the West Semitic, peripheral tradition. Its synonyms are *nadû* ("to castoff, forsake") and *ṭarādu* ("to expel"), and, like Akkadian *mêšu*, this verb also occurs in Wisdom Literature Thus, in the Babylonian Theodicy (Lambert 1960:76, line 79, in my translation):

> *kitta tattadûma // uṣurti ili ta-na-ṣu*
>
> Rectitude—you have cast off; the designs of your god—you spurn.

Compare Ps 107:11:

> כי המרו אמרי אל ועצת עליון נאצו
>
> For they disobeyed the teachings of El, and spurned the designs of Elyon.

I would, therefore, apply the same reservations to the translations of Akkadian *mêšu* (and *nâṣu*) provided in the *Chicago Assyrian Dictionary* as I have to the usual translations of Biblical Hebrew *māʾas*. In many instances Akkadian *mêšu*, whose usage parallels that of Biblical Hebrew *māʾas* to a substantial degree, would be better rendered "to cast off", rather than "to despise". It is significant that Akkadian *mêšu* (and *nâṣu*, for that matter) appears never to describe the actions or dispositions of gods and those in authority, but only of those who disrespect those in authority. The matter is further complicated by bringing Akkadian *mêsu* ("to crush") into the discussion. Whether *mêšu* and *mêsu* represent, respectively, two specialized offshoots of a common root, or whether they have no etymological connection whatsoever, they may have interpenetrated in Akkadian. Another possibility not to be ignored is that *mêsu* ("to crush") may be reflected in certain usages of Hebrew *māʾas*. The best candidate is the expression מאסת כל עץ ("It can fell any tree") in Ezek. 21:15. Another is מאס ערים ("He has ruined towns") in Isa. 33.8. If this analysis is warranted, the Akkadian evidence has contributed indispensably to our understanding of at least two biblical passages, and in a general way to usage of the verb *māʾas*. Conversely, the fairly extensive use of the verb *māʾas* in Biblical Hebrew can enhance our understanding of its Akkadian cognate, *mêšu*.

I now turn to the verb *gāʿal*, usually translated "to spurn, reject" which occurs in Jer. 14:19 in the verbal idiom *gāʿ*[a]*lâ nepeš* ("the stomach/esophagus vomits, ejects; becomes nauseous"), and the nominal idiom *gōʿal nepeš* ("vomit of the stomach/esophagus", Ezek. 16:5). It may be that these idioms were so well known that it became unnecessary to state the subject (*nepeš*) in every case. A comparable abbreviation is the Hiphil *hibʾîš* ("to make foul"), short for *hibʾîš rêaḥ* ("to make the odor foul"). By extension, this was a way of saying "to give another person a bad name, to ruin a reputation" (Exod. 5:21). Thus, in Gen. 34:30 we hear Jacob saying to his two reckless sons, Simeon and Levi, "You have sullied me, to make me foul (להבאישני) in the eyes of the inhabitants of the land, the Canaanites and Perizites" (cf. 1 Sam. 27:12). On this basis, one would similarly use the verb *gāʿal*, without adding *nepeš*, to mean "to vomit, eject, spew out".

Except for Jer. 14:19, in the core text, remaining occurrences of this verbal root are limited to Ezek. 16:3, 45, and Lev. 26:11, 15, 30, 42, 44, in the epilogue to the Holiness Code. Ezekiel 16 is a composite text, and my parsing of it differs in some respects from most previous suggestions:

1. The caption (16:1).
2. The Hittite-Amorite *māšāl*, wherein Jerusalem is cast, in the lineage of her mother (and father), and like her sisters, Samaria and Sodom, as a wife committing תועבות ("abominations") who "expels" or "ejects" (the verb *gāʿal*) her husband and children (16:2–3, 43b–58).
3. The metaphor of infidelity, expressed by forms of the verb *zānâ*, wherein Jerusalem is cast as the wanton harlot who gave away all of the gifts bestowed upon her by her true covenant-partner, the God of Israel, including her children, to false lovers (Ezek. 16:4–43a). Within this section, we are told that at her birth the harlot had been exposed and left to die, but was rescued, reared and cared for by God (16:4–7).
4. YHWH remains true to his covenant despite Jerusalem's violations of it, forgiving her so as to teach her the rewards of loyalty (Ezek. 16:59–63).

By way of explanation, the theme of *tôʿēbôt* ("abominations") is introduced in 16:2, and explained in terms of foreign birth in v. 3. These motifs reappear only in 16:43b, where the Amorite-Hittite metaphor resumes, whereas from 16:4–43a they are entirely absent. Ezekiel 16:4 accomplishes the switch by means of a semantic transaction on the word *mōlᵉdōtayik*, which in v. 3 had meant "place of your birth", or perhaps "lineage". In v. 4, which begins the harlot metaphor, it means "the event of your birth, the time of your birth", as Ezek. 6:4 clarifies. Whereas there are two repetitive attestations of verbal *gāʿal* in the Hittite-Amorite *māšāl* (16:45), there is only a single attestation of the nominal idiom *gōʿal nepeš* in the depiction of exposure within the extended harlot metaphor (16:5). What is more, no matter how we interpret the nominal idiom in Ezek. 16:5, it refers to Jerusalem as the helpless victim of exposure, whereas in Ezek. 16:45 it refers to Jerusalem as the perpetrator. With this analysis in mind, let me begin by examining Ezek. 16:5, "No one cared enough for you to do even one of these things for you, out of compassion for you. You were exposed upon the open field, in the vomit/spewing of your innards (בגעל נפשך), on the day of your birth."

Jerusalem is cast as a female infant, exposed at birth and left to die, until God later rescues her and lovingly cares for her. The question is whether *gōʿal nepeš* either (a) describes the physical condition of the infant, herself, namely, that she is unwashed and lying in the vomit of her innards, in her own filth, or (b) whether it refers to her as the target of riddance and exposure, so that we would alternatively translate the Hebrew בגעל נפשך ("in the spurning of your person"). Each of these interpretations has a tradition in scholarship.[10] I favor the more concrete interpretation whereby the referent of the verbal noun *gōʿal* is the infant herself, not the action of whoever had spurned the child. Throughout, the child is addressed in the second person feminine, in very graphic terms describing the horrible state of her body, with umbilical chord still uncut, and without swaddling clothes. It would disrupt the powerful graphics of this description to switch suddenly to an elliptical subject, never precisely identified. Furthermore, in the few attestations of the idiom *gāʿălâ nepeš*, the term *nepeš* consistently refers to the actor, or subject, whether human or divine; it is that actor's "stomach, esophagus" that does the regurgitating, or does whatever it is that the verb connotes, in an extended sense. If this analysis is correct, we are dealing with a set of physical actions and reactions characteristic of nausea, whereby the *nepeš* rids itself of ingested content; it ejects something unwanted.

This analysis leads us directly to Ezek. 16:43b–45, where the *māšāl* of the abominable wife resumes:

> Have you not committed depravity on top of all your (other) abominations (תועבותיך)? Why, everyone who composes a *māšāl* about you, will compose the *māšāl* as follows, "Like mother, like daughter!" You are (indeed) your mother's daughter, (one who) expels (געלת) her husband and children; and you are the sister of your sisters, who have expelled (אשר געלו) their husbands and children. For your mother was a Hittite and your father an Amorite.

The subject of the metaphor is Jerusalem, who has violated the covenant with her husband, the God of Israel. In so doing, Jerusalem has followed the precedent of her foreign mother and her two ethnic sisters, Samaria, the Northern Kingdom of Israel, and Sodom, representing Judah. The verb that connotes covenant breach is *gāʿal*. The wife has "expelled" her husband, driven him away in anger, which in turn has brought about the exile of her children, their "ejection" from the land. It is curious that the verb *qāʾâ* ("to vomit, regurgitate") in its extended usage also expresses the expulsion of sinful nations by their own lands, personified; they are said to "cough them up" (Lev. 18:25, 28; 20:22). More will be said about the force of the *gāʿal* + direct-object in Leviticus 26 as part of the discussion of syntax. Before doing so, it might be well to examine two unusual

[10] For a brief review of scholarly interpretation, see Greenberg 1983:275. I note that in principle, my interpretation is in agreement with the medieval commentator, David Kimḥi (Radaq) on Ezek. 16.5. He notes that Hebrew *nepeš* means "body, self", and suggests that *gōʿal* refers to the blood of parturition, more generally, to the condition of the infant on the day of her birth.

usages of the verb *gāʿal*, whose proper interpretation follows from our analysis of Ezek. 16:5:

1. The Niphal form *nigʿal* in 2 Sam. 1:21: "For there was the shield of heroes sullied (נגעל), the shield of Saul, no longer polished with oil". The force of the Niphal is denominative, as if to say, "made into *gōʿal*, filth". In the context of David's lament over Saul and Jonathan, which graphically depicts a mountainous battleground after the awful defeat of the Israelites, it would be abstract to translate Hebrew *nigʿal* as "rejected". The sword of the victor is polished with oil, but that of the vanquished is sullied with blood! This connotation supports the suggestion that the form with *ʿayin* and the form with *ʾaleph*, Hebrew *gāʾal* ("to pollute, contaminate, defile", Mal. 1:7, 12, and elsewhere), are phonetic variants (*HALAT*, 162–63, *s.v.* *gāʾal* II). The form with *ʾaleph* elsewhere describes objects sullied with blood (Isa. 59:3, Lam. 4:14).
2. The Hiphil form *yagʿil* in Job 21:10: "His bull impregnates (עבר) without making a mess (ולא יגעל) (of its seed); his cow gives birth without losing her young". That is to say, the bull inserts his sperm inside the cow, rather than letting it go to waste, which is precisely what happened to Onan's seed (Gen. 38:9). This is also a denominative "to make into *gōʿal*, filth". This verse is part of a cynical reflection on the injustice of life, which takes up all of Job 21. In a word, everything goes well for the wicked! The present Hiphil form is reminiscent of the anomalous and likewise causative-factitive ʾEphal form of *gāʾal* II in Isa. 63:3: "And I sullied (אגאלתי) all of my garments".

It bears mention that although we possess little, if any, contemporary cognate evidence bearing on the verb *gāʿal*, Rabbinic Hebrew provides useful information relevant to it. The Hiphil *higʿîl* conveys a privative-denominative sense, "to remove the *gōʿal*, filth; to cleanse". This form is used to describe the scouring of kitchen utensils so as to render them ritually fit. Similarly, the Piel *giʿûl* and the Hiphil *hagʿālâ* conjugations refer to this cleansing process (Levy 1963, I:350–51, *s.v.*). Such later usage is predicated, therefore, on the concrete, physical sense of the biblical Hebrew verb *gāʿal* adopted here.

The Interaction of Semantics and Syntax

Thus far, we have limited ourselves to a discussion of direct-object constructions, where physical and graphic meanings are in evidence, along with figurative connotations that express emotions. However, both *māʾas* and *gāʿal* occur in indirect-object constructions with prepositional *beth*, as was true of the verb *gāʿal* in Jer. 14:19. The preposition *beth* exhibits a variety of meanings and effects, many of them subtle in character. It will be argued here that recourse to the indirect-object syntax in the cases of *gāʿal* and *māʾas* was purposeful, and that, allowing for some drift, it modulates the meaning of the verb in question.

Let us begin with the verb *gāʿal*, and idiomatic *gāʿ*^{a}*lâ nepeš*. In my analysis of Ezekiel 16, I have shown that the direct-object construction has active-transitive force. That is to say, the *nepeš*, as subject, regurgitates the object, either actually or figuratively. Thus, the infant wallows in the vomit that her innards have coughed up (16:5), just as, figuratively, Jerusalem ejects her husband and children who inhabited her (16:44–45). Does the indirect-object construction have a different meaning?

It is important to clarify the *Sitz im Leben* of the author by identifying the situation in Judah and Jerusalem presupposed in the prophecy of Jeremiah 14. Judah had already been stricken beyond healing, and it seemed that God had, indeed, abandoned it and ravaged it—all the things that the verb *māʾas*, in the direct-object construction, connotes. Only Zion and the temple remained. Accordingly, the prophet was pleading for the glorious throne of YHWH to be spared. Had he asked אם את ציון געלה נפשך it would have meant, "Has your stomach ejected Zion?" In other words, "Has God exiled the inhabitants of Zion?" At that point in time, this had not happened. Jerusalem was in a threatened state because God had become sickened by the sins of the people and its leaders. His *nepeš* had reacted to Zion in revulsion, but had not yet ejected it, so to speak; the prophet could still plead for Zion to be spared, he could still ask that God's throne not be defiled, and that God not breach his covenant for his own name's sake.

This analysis can be confirmed by studying the syntax of the verb *gāʿal* in Leviticus 26, the epilogue to the Holiness Code. In fact, Leviticus 26 resonates with Jer. 14:17–22 in a clear way. In the promise of blessing, the reward for Israel's adherence to the covenant, God declares, "I will place my sanctuary in your midst, and I will not expel you (ולא תגעל נפשי אתכם; literally, 'my stomach will not eject you'). Rather, will I walk about in your midst and be your God, and you shall be my people" (Lev. 26:11–12).

Contrast the words of the execration in Lev. 26:30–33, which vividly project what happens when the God of Israel finally "ejects" Israel, the direct object of his wrath:

> And I will destroy your cult-platforms, and cut down your *ḥammānîm*, and heap your carcasses on the lifeless forms of your idols. My stomach shall eject you (וגעלה נפשי אתכם), and I will lay your towns in ruin, and make your sanctuaries desolate, and I will not savor your pleasing aromas. I will make the land desolate so that your enemies who dwell in it shall be desolate over it. And I will scatter you among the nations, and I will unsheathe the sword against you. Your land shall become a desolation, and your towns will be in ruin.

Leviticus 26:3–45 resonates as well with Ezekiel 16. This can be seen by comparing Ezek. 16:59–63 with Lev. 26:42–45. The common theme is God's faithfulness to his covenant with Israel; he remembers the covenant after Israel repents of its violation of it. Of particular interest is how this relationship is portrayed in Lev. 26:44–45:

> Yet even then, when they are in the land of their enemies, I will not cast them off and I will not eject them (ולא מאסתים ולא געלתים) to de-

> stroy them, breaching my covenant with them, for I am YHWH, their God. And I will remember in their favor the covenant with the ancients, whom I brought out of the land of Egypt in the sight of the nations to be their God. I am YHWH.

The difference between *gāʿal* + direct object and *gāʿal* + *beth* is that the former connotes the ejection of the direct object by the subject's *nepeš*, whereas the latter describes the subject's attitude toward the indirect object. In other words, it conveys the experience or reaction of the subject to the indirect object. The force of prepositional *beth* is close to that of *beth instrumentii* (*GKC* §119q). Thus, in Jeremiah 14, Zion (= Israel) is the cause of God's nausea. It is because of Zion's deeds that God has become nauseous. In Leviticus 26, God is said either to eject or not to eject Israel and this is conveyed by the direct-object construction, and the same is true in Ezekiel 16. God's anger cannot be contained.

The human-divine relationships that are conveyed by the verb *gāʿal* are not reciprocal, however, as are those conveyed by the verb *māʾas*, soon to be discussed. The God of Israel both "ejects" Israel, with Israel as the direct object of the verb, and experiences nausea at Israel's behavior, or at Zion, which is conveyed by the indirect-object construction. As for Israel's behavior and responses, nowhere in the Hebrew Bible is the God of Israel the direct object of the verb *gāʿal*. Israel can only "eject, cough up" God's judgments and statutes (Lev. 26:15, 43), but not God himself. As a matter of fact, God is nowhere the indirect-object of the verb *gāʿal* either. In other words, Israel never experiences nausea over God.

This asymmetry is not easily explained. One could say that the verb *gāʿal* can be used only when speaking of something that has been ingested, or in an extended sense, has been taken in, enveloped; in a word, something that is in the *nepeš* and is now to be ejected from it. One can vomit food, of course, and figuratively, a land can cough up its inhabitants, or a city its children. God can eject a people whom he has brought into his land, or experience revulsion in response to the actions of a people who are near to him, whom he has embraced. But precisely because the verb *gāʿal* never loses its innate physicality, the Hebrew Bible will not say that humans can be rid of God. They lack the power to eject him; he is not theirs to eject. Their deeds may induce God to depart, he may become angry and abandon his people, and there is much more that humans can do to distance themselves from God, but God cannot be ejected!

So much for the syntax of the verb *gāʿal*. What of the verb *māʾas*, whose usage is more complex, its semantic range broader, and its etymology unclear? We cannot be certain, but it is reasonable to conclude that the primary meanings of *māʾas* are "to cast off, discard, overthrow, ruin", and that its attitudinal connotations, such as "despise, reject" are predicated upon them. In fact, one could say that the progression in meaning observable in the case of Hebrew *māʾas* resembles that of Latin *reicio* ("to throw back, throw off"), an example of semantic development from the graphic to the figurative that was cited at the outset. General usage may be stated as follows: with respect to the verb *māʾas*, there are certain graphic and physical connotations that are consistently expressed by the direct-object construction. One could say that in such instances semantics govern syntax. This is illustrated by the very passages that have been studied above, all of which exemplify the direct-object construction. We are bound to ask, nevertheless, whether the same connotations are ever conveyed by the indirect-object construction.

A test case is the prophetic admonition in 2 Kgs 17:13–23. It opens with a review of the failure of northern Israel to heed prophetic calls for repentance. They have forsaken (וימאסו) God's statues and his covenant, and pursued false ways (cf. Jer. 2:5), worshipping idols and Baal, and doing everything to anger God. YHWH became enraged at northern Israel, and removed them from his presence, so that only the tribe of Judah remained. A redactor most likely added v. 19, which states that Judah, too, eventually followed the precedent of northern Israel. 2 Kings 17:20 recapitulates, "Then YHWH felt hatred toward all of the seed of Israel (וימאס יהוה בכל-זרע ישראל), and he reduced them to subjugation, and handed them over to ravagers, until he cast them off (עד אשר השליכם) from his presence".

I began the discussion by citing passages wherein the verbs *māʾas* and *hišlîk*, in the direct-object construction, are synonymous (Isa. 20:26//31:7; Jer. 7:29). But here, in 2 Kgs 17:20, we observe three stages: (1) God feels hatred toward northern Israel; (2) he then hands them over to conquerors; and (3) he finally casts them out from his presence into exile. It is my view that here the indirect-object construction focuses on the subject; it informs us of God's emotional state before anything actually happens to the indirect object. His emotions prompt his acts, but the *māʾas* + *beth* construction does not connote the acts themselves. In this respect, as discussed above, the force of *māʾas* resembles that of the verb *gāʿal* in the indirect-object construction. Here, however, the force of prepositional *beth* is spatial and relational; it expresses the notion of contact. It can be translated as "at, toward", and even "against".

And yet, it seems that *māʾas* + direct object and *māʾas* + indirect object have drifted together, and that in some instances they appear to be interchangeable, with no real difference in meaning intended. This may be so in Isa. 30:12, where the people of Israel are said to show disregard for (*māʾas* + *b*–) God's word. In Ps. 78:59–60, 67–68, 70–72, we have repeated interactions between the verbs *māʾas* and *bāḥar*, with God as the subject, where there are shifts from direct- to indirect-object constructions. A perusal of usage of the verb *māʾas* in Ezek. 5:6; 20:13, 16 (cf. Lev. 26:15, 43), shows that there, too, syntax of the verb *māʾas* is fluid. For the rest, usage of the indirect-object construction seems to focus attention on the mental disposition of the subject rather than on the effects upon the object. Thus, God will punish the people for the fruits of their designs (פרי המחשבותם) because they failed to heed God's words, "and as regards my teaching (ותורתי), they have shown disregard for it" (וימאסו בה, Jer. 6:19). Similarly, in Jer. 2:37 Israel's reliance on foreign powers will not succeed "because YHWH disapproves of those in whom you trust (כי מאס יהוה במבטחיך), you will not prosper through them". On the human level, this may be the meaning of Job

19:18, "Even youngsters have shown contempt toward me (מאסו הי)". And of the Israelites in the wilderness it is said, "They turned against the desirable land (וימאסו בארץ חמדה), and put no faith in his promise" (Ps. 106:24).

Conclusion

I have attempted to show that Hebrew verbs expressing rejection retain their graphic, physical meanings. By translating such verbs only as expressions of emotion or disposition we are missing an important ingredient in the biblical message. Like his human creatures, the God of Israel acts out his anger, and other negative feelings, quite graphically, often physically. His reaction to the misdeeds of his people can be visceral, and in punishing them he casts them off, ejects them, ravages them, ruins them and abandons them. An examination of the verbs *māʾas* and *gāʿal* thus reveals something specific about the biblical agenda: the prophets who used these locutions to characterize God's relationship to Israel, or Israel's relationship to God, were deeply concerned about the prospect of defeat and exile, the loss of the land and its devastation, and the loss of collective identity in foreign lands after deportation. The same is true of Torah authors, biblical narrators, chroniclers and historiographers.

In contrast, the negation of divine rejection (לא מאס, לא געל), namely, God's affirmation of his covenant and his promise of reward, are often projected as the restoration of the people to the land and the conferral of blessings upon them. Hebrew *māʾas* ("to cast off") and *bāḥar* ("to select, choose") are frequent antonyms.

Bibliography

Bright, John
1962 *Jeremiah*. AB 21. New York: Doubleday.

Greenberg, Moshe
1983 *Ezekiel 1–20*. AB 22. New York: Doubleday.
1997 *Ezekiel 21–37*. AB 22A. New York: Doubleday.

Grushkin, Esther
2000 *Emotions and their Effect on the Human Body as Depicted in the Hebrew Bible*. New York University PhD. Dissertation.

Lambert, Wilfred G.
1960 *Babylonian Wisdom Literature*. Oxford: Clarendon Press.

Levine, Baruch A.
1987a The Epilogue to the Holiness Code: A Priestly Statement on the Destiny of Israel. Pages 9–34 in J. Neusner *et al.* (eds.), *Judaic Perspectives on Ancient Israel*. Philadelphia: Fortress Press.
1987b The Language of Holiness: Perceptions of the Sacred in the Holy Bible. Pages 241–55 in M.P. O'Connor and D.N. Freedman (eds.), *Backgrounds for the Bible*. Winona Lake, IN: Eisenbrauns. {*VOL 1, PP. 321–33*}

1989 *Leviticus: JPS Torah Commentary*. Philadelphia: Jewish Publication Society of America.

1993a *Numbers 1–20*. AB 4. New York: Doubleday.

1993b Silence, Sound, and the Phenomenology of Mourning in Biblical Israel. *JANES* 22:89–106. {*VOL 1, PP. 335–53*}

1995 The Semantics of Loss: Two Exercises in Biblical Hebrew Lexicography. Pages 137–58 in Z. Zevit *et al.* (eds.), *Solving Riddles and Untying Knots: Biblical, Epigraphic, and Semitic Studies in Honor of Jonas C. Greenfield.* Winona Lake, IN: Eisenbrauns. {*VOL 2. PP. 281–99*}

1996 Offerings Rejected by God: Numbers 16:15 in Comparative Perspective. Pages 107–16 in J.A. Coleson and V.H. Matthews (eds.), *Go to the Land I Will Show You: Studies in Honor of Dwight W. Young*. Winona Lake, IN: Eisenbrauns. {*VOL 1, PP. 355–63*}

Lundbom, Jack R.

1999 *Jeremiah 1–20*. AB 21. New York: Doubleday.

Simpson, D. P. (ed.)

1971 *Cassell's New Latin-English, English-Latin Dictionary*. London: Cassell & Co.

D. Religious Themes

Comparative Perspectives on Jewish and Christian History*

In the first of three volumes of collected studies by Elias Bickerman, ten articles are reproduced with some updating in the notes, and appendices. Critical comment will center around three studies having direct bearing on the ancient Near East, and the Judaic tradition. They are "Couper une Alliance," a comparative study of covenant enactment; "The Edict of Cyrus in Ezra I," in which Bickerman defends the essential authenticity of the Hebrew version of the edict; and "Two Legal Interpretations of the Septuagint," in which Bickerman shows how specific Greek renderings of Hebrew terms and passages reflect conditions in the Hellenistic world. Especial attention will be paid to the Greek rendering of the Hebrew term *môhar* "bride price" as *pherne* "dowry," and its implications for the institution of the dowry in later Judaism.

We now have the first of three volumes of collected studies by the eminent classicist and historian, Elias Bickerman. The Table of Contents lists the studies to be included in the second and third volumes, as well. In all, thirty-eight pieces will be republished, with ten of these appearing in Part One. Some revisions and appendices are presented for the first time.

In the Preface, Bickerman explains his interest in Jewish and Christian history as follows: "First, it is more fun to work on a question one is not familiar with. … Secondly, my classical studies again and again led me into the neighboring fields." Bickerman succeeds in communicating his fascination for comparative studies to the reader. His parallels are real, and he poses questions of broad scope, whose proper investigation requires going beyond the confines of the traditional disciplines. He is most interested in the character of the great societies of antiquity, and he seeks to clarify just how their dominant patterns affected all who came within their orbit. Most of all, perhaps, Bickerman shows us, in these exercises, how his mind works in approaching specific problems; and this object lesson is well worth the learning!

Because of their scope, Bickerman's studies could be reviewed from any number of perspectives. There is much in them that this reviewer is not compe-

---

* Originally published in *JAOS* 99 (1979), pp. 81–86. Reprinted with permission from the American Oriental Society.

This is a review article of Elias Bickerman's *Studies in Jewish and Christian History*, Part One (Arbeiten zur Geschichte des Antiken Judentums und des Urchristentums, Band IX). Pp. x + 288. Leiden: E. J. Brill. 1976. Gld. 110.00.

tent to discuss. Critical comment, will, therefore, be reserved for three studies which relate significantly to the biblical and Judaic traditions, and to aspects of ancient Near Eastern cultures, in the pre-Hellenistic period: "Couper une alliance" (1950), "The Edict of Cyrus in Ezra I" (1946), and "Two Legal Interpretations of the Septuagint" (1956).

The other seven studies in Part One will be described only in the briefest terms. Two studies relate specifically to the Greek version of the book of Esther: "The Colophon of the Greek Book of Esther" (1944), and "Notes on the Greek Book of Esther" (1951). The former is a total interpretation of the unique colophon, in which the *Sitz-im-Leben* of the author is deduced from specific wording. In the latter, Bickerman analyzes the distinctive features of the Greek version of Esther, itself. Two further studies treat specific questions of dating and textual transmission: "*Zur Datierung des Pseudo-Aristeas*" (1930), and "The Date of Fourth Maccabees" (1945). Here, again, Bickerman uses clues provided by the authors to identify the actual, rather than the projected, environment reflected in these works. The Septuagint to the Pentateuch is discussed in two, related works: "Some Notes on the Transmission of the Septuagint" (1950), and "The Septuagint as a Translation" (1959). Whereas the former study deals primarily with questions of recension and textual transmission, the latter addresses itself to several pivotal issues regarding the character of the Septuagint to the Pentateuch: 1) Why was this translation undertaken? 2) What type of Greek is employed in it? 3) What can be said of it in terms of: a) literalness vs. free translation, and b) reflections of contemporary ideas and institutions in the translation? Briefly summarized, Bickerman's view is that the Septuagint to the Pentateuch, which has an independent history, was, as tradition has it, a project sponsored by Ptolemy II, so as to provide "the authoritative image of the living Jewish past" (p. 175). In this respect, it is comparable to Manetho's history of the Pharaohs, also sponsored by Ptolemy II, and to Berossus' history of Babylonia, dedicated to Antiochus I of Syria.

The point is that the Septuagint to the Pentateuch was *not* written, in the first instance, for the Synagogue, for Jews "who no longer knew enough Hebrew to satisfy their religious needs" (p. 171). The Greek of the Septuagint is the spoken Greek of the period, not some kind of Judeo-Greek. The translation was accomplished by those trained in the skills of the dragomans, who usually were called upon to render legal documents, business records and official correspondence into another language. The art of translation, as we know it, was not highly developed in the third pre-Christian century.

Finally, Bickerman provides a remarkable example of *Traditionsgeschichte* in his study: "Les Deux Erreurs du Prophète Jonas" (1965). He guides the reader on an intellectual tour through Jewish, Christian, Muslim, and more modern secular literature, in order to show how all of these traditions reacted to the main problems of interpretation arising from this ancient tale.

I.

"Couper une Alliance" is an elaborate comparative study on the theme of covenant enactment.[1] Bickerman begins with an analysis of the biblical formula: *kāraṯ b^e rîṯ* "to cut a covenant," and concludes, quite correctly, that it originally designated a complex of physical acts whereby animals, and other living beings were actually "cut" or "split," in a manner resembling what is portrayed in Genesis 15, and referred to in Jeremiah 34:18–20. Passage through the sections of the animals was a means of binding the covenant.

Drawing on many relevant parallels (Hittite, Greek, etc.), Bickerman proposes a dynamistic phenomenology. The passage through the sectioned animals allowed those undergoing the ceremony to absorb the vital force of the animals which was released by the exposure of their internal organs and the letting of their blood. Power moved from the animals to the persons, just as elsewhere it was transferred from persons to animals. This explains the relationship between purification, one frequent purpose of such rites, and the covenant promise, so important in the biblical covenants. In purification, the newly acquired power strengthens its recipients, and is effective in warding off impurity and evil. This power also stands behind the covenant promise, and renders it binding (p. 26). Corollary to this analysis is Bickerman's contention that the curse, or execration, so often associated with covenants, is a secondary element, not intrinsic to the phenomenology of the covenant, itself.

This dynamistic interpretation might work better in explaining rites whose purpose was purification than it does with respect to the binding force of the covenant promise; but even as regards purification, it raises problems.

The Hittite Ritual of Tunnawi describes, *inter alia*, how power, conceived as fertility, is transferred from an animal to a woman. In the course of a purification rite, a woman who seeks to become fertile, seizes the horn of a fertile cow and makes the following declaration:

> Sun-god, my lord, as this cow is fertile, and she (is) in a fertile pen, and she is filling the pen with bulls (and) cows, just so let this sacrificer be fertile; let her just so fill her house with sons and daughters, etc.[2]

The fertile cow is then driven back into the pen. Just prior to making this declaration, the woman in question had taken hold of a tree covered with fruit, and had said something of a similar nature. In this Hittite ritual, power is being magically transferred from the fertile cow (and the fruit-bearing tree) to a person in need of power. Power comes from a living fertile animal; and from the cowpen, a fertile environment.

---

[1] Since this study is written in French, certain passages have been translated into English by the reviewer, who bears responsibility for the translations.

[2] A. Goetze, *The Hittite Ritual of Tunnawi*, *American Oriental Series*, 14, New Haven, 1938, 21–23 (§34).

In other rites, amply attested throughout the world, the power of an animal can be absorbed by eating its vitals, especially its heart, or by drinking its blood. Power can also be transmitted by various forms of tactile contact with the blood or vitals of an animal, as is true in some of the composite rituals cited by Bickerman, himself. The point is that when power is conceived of being conducted in one direction or another, actual contact or intermixing of sorts should occur. On the other hand, in a rite characterized as *bên beṯārim* "between ... sections" (Jer. 34:18–19) we are dealing with a different phenomenology. The principal acts are: the sectioning of living beings, and passage through the sections. It is almost inescapable to conclude that such procedures were meant to dramatize destruction, *per se*. This is certainly the interpretation to be assumed from the following passage, Jer. 34:20. The symbolism is actually two-fold: cut-up animals are destroyed, and rapidly spoiling. Passing through such split sections further enhances the awareness of destruction, because one is caught between the parts of something that was once whole, but is now rent asunder.

In the principal Hittite ritual cited by Bickerman (pp. 9–10) we encounter a series of performances undertaken by a defeated army upon its return to the city. The soldiers pass under a ritual gateway, flanked by two burning fires. Behind the gateway, the split sections of a man and some animals have been lined up in two rows, and it is likely that the soldiers continued past the gateway, filing between the sectioned creatures. Finally, living water from a river is sprinkled over the soldiers.

Now, the actions of the fire and the water are blatantly purificatory, in some form. Bickerman further explains that passing under the gate was symbolic of subjugation, and served to relieve the humiliation of defeat. At this point, Bickerman introduces his interpretation of the passage through the sections:

> Just as the magical gateway and the purifying fire had as their purpose the exorcism of defeat, the effective life properties (French: *la vertu de vie*) of the immolated animals restored vigor to the battered troops by re-establishing their normal state (pp. 9–10).

An alternative interpretation is possible: Just as subjugation was symbolized by passing under the gateway, the passage between sectioned creatures was also of a cathartic character. Both may be viewed as re-enactments of defeat, which purge the soldiers of the real experience, for good. In Polybius' description of how the Macedonian soldiers prepared for battle, also cited by Bickerman (p. 10), we find the same catharsis, in anticipation of battle, rather than following upon defeat. Soldiers pass through the sections of split dog (a widely known symbol of ferocity), and also engage in mock combat. Both of these performances anticipated the destruction characteristic of battle. By facing the tragic fate of the fighter in advance, the soldiers experience a catharsis which alleviates their fears. The phenomenology is similar to that underlying the dirge, chanted while marching to battle.

In Bickerman's analysis, timing seems to be a governing factor. Thus, the Arabs of Moab pass through sectioned animals so as to protect themselves from an epidemic. Bickerman emphasizes the fact that at the time this was performed, the persons in question were healthy. *Ergo*: This rite cannot be purificatory (p. 10). It is, however, an apotropaic rite. The sectioned animals symbolize disease and death, and those passing through the sectioned animals were protected against that fate.

Another example of the importance attached to timing in Bickerman's analysis can also be interpreted differently. Bickerman states:

> In order that the victim offered represent the violation of an oath, it is necessary that the pre-figurative identification take place before (or during) the immolation (p. 16).

Ergo: The sectioned animals in a covenant enactment cannot symbolize the consequences of violating the covenant oath, because nothing was said in advance to identify them as such.

This insistence on the prior identification, or assignment, of the victim would be crucial if the performance we are discussing were actually as cultic or sacrificial as Bickerman assumes. Perhaps it is a methodological error to apply cultic criteria so specifically to the dynamics of covenant enactment. Were the sectioned animals actually sacrifices, in the usual sense? To whom are they being offered? Perhaps the sectioned animals should be viewed in the context of sympathetic magic. The animals are sectioned so as to show what will happen if the covenant is violated. One experiences the passage through the sections, observes the destroyed animals, and gets the message!

The inhabitants of Jabesh Gilead were besieged by the Ammonites, and needed relief, but the other tribes had not come to their aid. Learning of this, Saul "took a pair of oxen and cut them in pieces, and sent messengers with the pieces all through Israel to proclaim that the same would be done to the oxen of any man who did not follow Saul and Samuel into battle. The fear of the Lord fell upon the people, and they came out, to a man" (1 Sam. 11:7, translation in NEB). In the book of Judges we read that a man whose concubine had been raped and killed by the men of Gibeah, in the territory of Benjamin, "cut her up, limb by limb, into twelve pieces; and he sent them through the length and breadth of Israel" (Jud. 19:29, translation in NEB). Upon seeing this awful thing, the tribes were stirred to join in battle against the Benjamites.

This interpretation of the sectioning of animals is further supported by three observations: 1) The two terms, *berîṯ* "covenant" and *ʾālāh* "curse, execration" are probably not as differentiated as Bickerman claims (p. 18). The mere fact, cited by Bickerman, that in the Arslan-Tash inscription we find the formula *krt ... ʾlt*, as a parallel to biblical *kāraṯ berîṯ*, indicates a degree of synonymity, as does the fact that *berîṯ* and *ʾālāh* (as well as *šeḇûʿāh* "oath") are so often used together (Deut. 29:11, 13; Ezek. 16:59f., 17:18; Hosea 10:4; Ps. 105:9). In Deut. 29:20 we have the composite term *ʾālôṯ habberîṯ* "the sanctions of the covenant" (NJPS) (NEB renders: "the denunciations of the covenant"). This suggests that such combinations as *habberîṯ wehāʾālāh* represent hendiadys, rather than the differentiation of two phenomena. 2) The relationship of sacrifice to covenant enactment is also problematic. Not all biblical covenants were accompanied by sacrifice, and when they were, the sacrifice may have served as a celebration of the enactment, rather than as the instrumentality of enactment.[3] 3) In biblical imagery, the devastation of herds and flocks is one of the ways God punishes those who disobey his commands and violate his covenant (Deut. 28:30f.; Isaiah 34; Jer. 5:10f., 12:4, 25:32f., 51:40; Amos 3:11f.; Zech. 11:4).

If the above considerations are valid, the execration is basic to the covenant, in that the sectioning of the animals conveys a warning.[4]

II.

Bickerman's study "The Edict of Cyrus in Ezra I," taken together with Roland de Vaux's similar treatment of the Aramaic edicts of Cyrus and Darius, add up to a convincing demonstration that the book of Ezra contains authentic information on the period of the return, in the late sixth century B.C.E.[5] Both Bickerman and de Vaux agree that the Hebrew and Aramaic edicts of Cyrus do not derive from the same source, and the authenticity of each must be considered independently. There are really two questions regarding the Hebrew decree in Ezra I: 1) Is the received version based on an authentic proclamation of Cyrus? 2) Does the received version give evidence of significant alteration in content by the Chronicler, or another later compiler? Bickerman leaves little room for doubt on the former, but to answer the latter question, one must examine the literary composition of Ezra 1:1–6 in a slightly different way, but with results similar to those reached by Bickerman. The following *schema* may be proposed:

Ezra 1:1	Superscription.
1:2–4a	The edict.
4b–6	Recapitulation.

Most likely, vv. 1 and 4b–6 are not part of the edict, proper. They appear to be the work of the Chronicler.[6] This analysis is based on the following considerations:

1) Aside from the fact that superscriptions by later authors and compilers are commonplace in the Hebrew Bible, v. 1 betrays the hand of the Chronicler. The idiom *hēʿîr rûaḥ* "to arouse the spirit" is rather distinctive in biblical Hebrew usage. In another connection Bickerman states that the text of the edict

[3] See my discussion in *In the Presence of the Lord,* Leiden, 1974, 35–41.

[4] Note the comment to Gen. 15:9 in E. A. Speiser, *Genesis*, Anchor Bible, Garden City, NY, 1964, 112.

[5] R. de Vaux, "The Decrees of Cyrus and Darius on the Rebuilding of the Temple," originally published in *RB* 46, 1937, and now in *The Bible and the Ancient Near East,* Garden City, NY, 1971, 63–96.

[6] It is not necessary, for our present purposes, to discuss the question of whether Ezra-Nehemiah is the work of the Chronicler, or of some other later writer, as maintained by S. Japhet. See S. Japhet, "Chronicles, Book of," in *Encyclopaedia Judaica* 3:517–534.

"was not composed by a Hebrew writer, but drafted by Cyrus' multilingual scribes and, then, rendered into Hebrew" (p. 87). Now, the idiom *hēʿîr rûaḥ* occurs in Jer. 51:11, a reference to the kings of Medea, and in Haggai 1:14, a reference to Zerubabel and Joshua, the High priest, whose spirits were "aroused" to complete the construction of the temple. The verb *hēʿîr* "to arouse" is a code word of II Isaiah (Isa. 41:2, 45:13), who uses it with specific reference to Cyrus. The Chronicler borrowed the idiom *hēʿîr rûaḥ* from the earlier sources and used it to refer to Tiglath-Pileser III (called Pul), who was aroused to act as God's agent in punishing Israel (1 Chron. 5:26). Here, and in 2 Chron. 36:22 the same Chronicler used this idiom to refer to Cyrus, rendering II Isaiah's code explicit. Although Cyrus' scribes certainly knew the ideology underlying this usage, it is less certain that they knew this distinctive way of expressing it. 2) A more important consideration relates to v. 4b, which introduces an element absent from the Aramaic edict, and, in fact, from any biblical source known to be representative of what may be termed the early Persian period (538 B.C.E.—the Cyrus edict, to 444 B.C.E.—the death of Artaxerxes I). This element is the *nedāḇāh* "voluntary contribution" of the people as a whole. The notion that the people as a whole bore a responsibility to provide for the temple and cult is a doctrine favored by the Chronicler, who artificially synthesizes two distinct methods of temple funding in his recasting of Israelite history: a) royal sponsorship, and b) popular funding. The priestly tradition (Exod. 25:1f., 30:11–16, 35:21; Num. 7, etc.) endorses popular funding, and the Chronicler piously blends this Torah tradition with the realities of royal sponsorship, epitomized in 2 Kings, chapters 12 and 22. He reads popular funding into the early monarchy, so that David and Jehoshaphat, both devout Yahwists, are identified with it (1 Chron. 29; 2 Chron. 24).

At times, popular funding became a necessity in the later Persian period (from 444 B.C.E. to the conquests of Alexander), which encompasses the period of the Chronicler. We learn this from Nehemiah 10 (especially vv. 33–34). Poor economic conditions in the provinces of the empire undoubtedly account for the fact that in an Aramaic papyrus from Elephantine, dated 419 B.C.E., we read of extensive popular donations to the local Jewish temple. These were emergency measures, however. The principle of royal funding actually remained in force well into the Seleucid period. This subject is addressed in one of Bickerman's studies scheduled for the second volume: "Hélidore au Temple de Jerusalem."

The popular *nedāḇāh* is mentioned in other Ezra passages (Ezra 3:5, 8:25f.). Ezra 3 is patently the work of the Chronicler. It bears all the earmarks of the Chronicler's penchant for the details of ritual, even to the inclusion of a hymnodic excerpt in the narrative, a feature characteristic of the Chronicler (cf. Ezra 3:11 with 1 Chron. 16).

Ezra 3:7 is a special problem. It mentions that the Tyreans and Sidonians transported cedars from the Lebanon into the port of Jaffa under the authorization of "Cyrus, King of Persia," the same title used in Ezra 1:1, which Bickerman claims could have been applied to Cyrus at the time of his edict (p. 77f.).

Ezra 3:7 does not, however, contradict the general rule that references to the *nedāḇāh* in the book of Ezra reflect a later ideology.

Now, Jaffa was a Sidonian port in the late fifth and fourth centuries, and thereafter, as shown by J. Kaplan's excavations at Jaffa. We also have the evidence of fourth-century Pseudo-Scylax, a manual for seamen, which mentions Jaffa in this connection. Kaplan now reports that he has found remains of a structure at Jaffa from the late sixth century. Furthermore, the inscription of Eshmunazor II, king of Sidon, reliably dated by M. Dunand to ca. 500 B.C.E., or soon thereafter, mentions Dor and Jaffa as Sidonian ports. It is possible, therefore, to argue that Ezra 3:7 echoes the realities of the latter years of the reign of Darius I (523/2–486), but one seriously hesitates to agree with E. Stern that Jaffa became a Sidonian colony ca. 525, during the reign of Cambyses![7]

In any event, the epigraphic evidence speaks of the Sidonians, whereas the author of Ezra 3 brings Tyreans into the picture, as well. One could maintain that Ezra 3:7 is merely a later, historiographic statement, similar to 2 Chron. 2:15, which aims at blending the data of 1 Kings 5, with the realities of the Chronicler's own period. This would explain the inclusion of the Tyreans in Ezra 3:7, because according to 1 Kings 5, the Tyreans did the shipping, whereas Hiram says that the Sidonians were the experts at *felling* the cedar trees (1 Kings 5:20)! 1 Kings fails to specify where the cedars were delivered, whereas both Ezra 3:7 and 2 Chron. 2:15 have them being unloaded at Jaffa! Like 2 Chron. 2:15, Ezra 3:7 is probably a case of modeling: The Phoenicians had a prominent role in building the Solomonic temple, so Ezra 3 has them shipping cedars from the Lebanon for the second temple, as well.

As regards Ezra 1:4b–6, it is clear that they derive from a different hand. This is indicated by the parallel vocabulary. Contrast *yennaśśeʾûhû* "Let them support him" in v. 4a with *ḥizzeqû bîydêhem* "They supported them" in v. 5. Also contrast *ʾanšê meqômô* "the residents of his locality" in v. 4a with *weḵol seḇîḇôṯêhem* "all who reside in their environs" in v. 5.

III.

In the study entitled "Two Legal Interpretations of the Septuagint" Bickerman discusses two Greek renderings of legal passages in the Torah. One case, that of Exod. 22:4, concerns liability for damages to another's field. Bickerman shows how the translation, and the addition of several words absent from the Hebrew original, served to bring biblical law into accord with prevailing agrarian admin-

---

[7] For relevant source materials see M. Broshi, *Encyclopaedia Biblica* (Hebrew), "*Yāpô*," vol. 3, 1958, 738–743, and H. and J. Kaplan, "Jaffa," in *Encyclopaedia of Archaeological Excavations in the Holy Land*, ed. M. Avi-Yonah, 1976, vol. II, 532–541. Also see M. Dunand, "Nouvelles Inscriptions Phéniciennes du Temple D'Echmoun à Bostan Ech-Cheikh, près de Sidon," *Bulletin du Musée de Beyrouth* 18, 1965, 105–109, and E. Stern, *The Material Culture of the Land of the Bible in the Persian Period* (Hebrew), Jerusalem, 1973, 22, and note 69; and the chronological chart, 282.

istration in Ptolemaic Egypt. The second case deals with the history of the dowry in Jewish law, a subject which this reviewer has treated from another perspective.[8]

The starting point of Bickerman's discussion is a datum: In Gen. 34:12 and Exod. 22:16 the Septuagint renders Hebrew *môhar* as *pherne* "dowry." This translation is very suggestive, since the Hebrew term *môhar*, however we define it legally, designated a transfer of property from the groom or his family to the bride's father and/or family: whereas Greek *pherne*, however we define it legally, clearly designates a transfer from the bride's family to the newly married couple. The burden of Bickerman's study is to account for this change of direction, so to speak. He concludes that the dowry of post-biblical Judaism "is an extraneous and intrusive element in the Jewish matrimonial system, where it is superimposed on the bride price" (p. 205). He further states as follows:

> In biblical law, the principle of separate property governed matrimonial property relations ... Thus, the *môhar* was the sole financial link between families related by marriage (p. 203).

As for the evidence of dowry-type financial relations provided by the fifth century B.C.E. Aramaic contracts from Elephantine, Bickerman states:

> These documents, however, though the parties are Jewish, follow the common law of the Aramaic scribes and notaries, and do not necessarily represent the development of Jewish law (pp. 205–206).

According to Bickerman, the dowry "entered the Jewish marriage contract in the Greek age, as a borrowing from Greek law" (p. 213). This happened sometime between 400 and 200 B.C.E., and is epitomized in the Septuagint rendering of *môhar* as *pherne*. This development was brought about "by the use of money as a medium of exchange in the Greek age" (p. 212). In earlier periods, wealth was measured in terms of real property, cattle, etc., and a Hebrew father could hardly "alienate land from his sons by settling it on a daughter" (p. 212).

This reconstruction raises several questions of a methodological nature. There is, first of all, the problem of definition. It is not clear precisely what Bickerman means by the term "dowry." At one point he speaks of settling property on a daughter (p. 212), but at other points he seems to be construing the term "dowry" more strictly, as property conveyed, in the legal sense, to the husband. It would have helped matters if Bickerman had provided a precise, operative definition of "dowry" to start with, because there is warrant, historically speaking, for adopting a broad definition, which would embrace various types of financial arrangements connected with marriage. Bickerman, himself, stresses the fluidity of legal terminology (p. 202).

---

[8] B. A. Levine, "*Mulūgu*/*Melûg*: The Origins of a Talmudic Legal Institution," *JAOS* 88 (1968), 271–285 {*VOL 2, PP. 103–25*}. Prof. Bickerman was kind enough to cite this study in his updated notes.

Mosaic law contains no definitive statement of marriage, to parallel its statement on the essential legalities of divorce (Deut. 24:1–4). As a result we do not find the explicit requirement of a marriage contract, comparable to the requirement of a bill of divorce. As Bickerman notes, this fact created a problem in later Jewish law. In view of this situation, Bickerman's contention that the only financial link between families related by marriage was the *môhar* sounds a little like *argumentum ex silentio*. To comprehend the actual practice in biblical times will necessarily require utilizing material from the non-legal sources of the Bible. In terms of custom, the granting of a fief by Caleb to his daughter after her marriage to Othniel is perhaps more significant than Bickerman assumes. Caleb's daughter, Akhsah, coaxes this gift from her father, and there is the strong implication that in so doing she was demanding a customary right that her father could not refuse (Josh. 15:16–19; Jud. 1:12–15). This grant of land is termed *berāḵāh*, which elsewhere may designate a share of the family estate (Gen. 27:35–37).

Rather than dwell on the biblical period, which is admittedly problematic, it might be preferable to concentrate on another aspect of Bickerman's argument, i.e., the status of the Aramaic contracts from Elephantine. At one point Bickerman questions the relevance of these sources to the later development of Jewish law (pp. 205–206), but elsewhere he stresses the contribution of the Aramaic scribes to Jewish legal institutions (pp. 214–215).

In a sense, Bickerman is begging the question. If a Jewish community in fifth century B.C.E. Egypt adopted certain Near Eastern legal practices and regarded them as material to marriage and inheritance, is not that fact relevant to the subsequent development of Jewish law? After all, the biblical *môhar* was not exclusively an Israelite institution, either. We actually find the term *mhr* in a Ugaritic myth describing the divine marriage of Yariḫ and Nikkal, and a comparable term *terḫatum*, also designating a payment initially made to the bride's father, is known from cuneiform sources.[9]

There have been some important studies of Aramaic legal terminology and formulation which demonstrate the significant similarity between the Elephantine documents and Rabbinic texts, including the *ketûbāh* "writ of marriage." About seventy years ago, J. N. Epstein reacted to the initial publication of some of the Elephantine papyri by citing evidence of continuity and development, not only as regards the substance of legal institutions, but also with respect to terminology and formulation; and since that time, more evidence has become available.[10] Now, one cannot prove absolutely that this appropriation process began in

---

[9] See Levine, *ibid.* 273, and note 11, and 274, n. 19 {*VOL. 2, PP. 106, 108*}.

[10] J. N. Epstein, "Notizen zu den jüdisch-aramäische Papyri von Assuan," *Jahrbuch der jüdisch-literarischen Gesellschaft* 6, 1908, 359–373. More recently, R. Yaron, Y. Muffs and B. Porten, whose works are noted by Bickerman in other connections, have further documented this continuity, which is evident in later Syriac culture as well. See J.

the pre-Hellenistic period, but neither can that likelihood be dismissed. In any event, the later tradition drew heavily on non-Hellenistic factors. Much of what became standard in the Rabbinic *ketûbāh*, such as a) the requirement that dowry property be inherited by the wife's sons, and not by sons of other wives married to the same man, and b) restrictions on the sale of property acquired as dowry, is anticipated in the Elephantine contracts.

It would perhaps be more accurate to state that the progressive limitation of the wife's rights over dowry property, evident in Rabbinic law, reflects conditions under Roman domination, and may have represented the adaptation of certain Roman legal concepts. We refer specifically to the rule that the husband's control over the person of his wife extended to control over her property, as well (Mishnah, *Ketubôt* 8:1). As regards the institution of the dowry itself, there is a strong comparative argument for concluding that, despite the quiescence of biblical law on the subject, it has a long history in Israelite-Jewish practice.

It is also questionable whether the institution of the dowry necessarily reflects the expanded use of currency, in and of itself. In very ancient societies, objects of value—precious metals and jewelry, as well as real property, cattle, and slaves, were conveyed as dowry. Conversely, real property (Hebrew: *qarqaʿ*) continued to be the standard of wealth in guaranteeing legal transactions, including the *ketûbāh*, within Rabbinic law.

Bickerman's studies are models of comparative analysis, regardless of whether or not one finds himself in agreement with all of his particular conclusions. Now that these studies are more accessible, added interest will undoubtedly be generated by their remarkable statements, and by the questions posed in them. "The question posed by the Sage is, in itself, half the answer!"

A. Goldstein, "The Syriac Bill of Sale from Dura-Europos," *JNES* 25, 1966, 1f., and especially 12, and notes 60–61. Also see E. Y. Kutscher, "On the Terminology of Writs in the Talmud" (Hebrew), *Tarbiz* 17, 1945–46, 125–127; *Tarbiz* 19, 1948, 53–59, 125–128. Also note literature cited in B. A. Levine, "On the Origins of the Aramaic Legal Formulary at Elephantine," *Christianity, Judaism, and other Greco-Roman Cults (Studies for Morton Smith at Sixty)*, ed. J. Neusner, Leiden, 1975, vol. III, 37–54 {*VOL. 2, PP. 57–71*}.

The Place of Jonah in the History of Biblical Ideas*

Each year, the entire Book of Jonah is read aloud in Jewish synagogues as part of the afternoon service of the Day of Atonement, Yom Kippur. The story of Jonah epitomizes the power of repentance, and serves to reassure the worshippers that God's arm is extended to receive them. Even the cruelest of Israel's ancient enemies, the Assyrians of Nineveh, were spared by God when they and their king heeded the admonitions of the Israelite prophet, Jonah, and turned back from their evil ways.

Since late antiquity, certain questions about the story of Jonah have puzzled commentators, who, like George Landes, the persistent scholar being honored here, have struggled to find the key to its interpretation.[1] What will follow are some reflections on certain themes in the book of Jonah that have crystallized in my thinking over many Days of Atonement and semesters of teaching, and through dialogue with learned colleagues. Recent studies have reawakened interest in this fascinating composition, replete as it is with wisdom themes, and brimming with intertextual allusions.[2]

I. The Education of a Prophet

Among the several themes informing the Book of Jonah there is a pedagogic, or therapeutic message directed to the reader (or listener), one of psychological and moral import. The tale of Jonah dramatizes the contrast between self-awareness and self-denial. The role of God is that of the divine pedagogue, one often attributed to him in biblical literature and even more so in post-biblical Midrash. God's actions become meaningful not only for themselves, but because they teach humans his ways; they serve as object-lessons. God's behavior, al-

---

* Originally published in Stephen L. Cook and S. C. Winter (eds.), *On the Way to Nineveh: Studies in Honor of George M. Landes* (ASOR Books 4; Atlanta: Scholars Press, 1999), pp. 201–217. Reprinted with permission from the American Schools of Oriental Research.

[1] I have profited greatly from George Landes' scholarly work on Jonah, especially his careful examination of linguistic criteria published in the H. M. Orlinsky Volume (Landes 1976). It is a source of personal pleasure to me that the two of us were "bound together" in that volume, where one of my Hebrew studies deals with similar linguistic criteria used in dating the priestly source of the Pentateuch. Over the years, George's addresses to the Columbia Seminar on the Hebrew Bible dealing with the interpretation of Jonah have been particularly enlightening to me.

[2] The reader is referred to the expansive commentary by Sasson (1990) for a recent discussion.

ways to be emulated, emerges as a model of the highest capacities of the human spirit, the best that is in us. For humans to be aware of the best in themselves requires, however, overcoming what we, these days, refer to simply as "denial." So long as we continue to deny that we have done wrong, repentance is impossible. But we must also cease to deny our innate goodness, our capacity to change for the better. It is this capacity to change that makes repentance at all possible. To promote such self-awareness, to jog humans out of their complex denials, biblical wisdom literature places God in the role of the experimental mentor who subjects certain of his creatures to intense, often painful experiences that force them to confront their inner feelings. This is what happened to Jonah, and recounting his experience is intended to encourage us to see in ourselves the capacity for love and human kindness that makes it possible to change course, to return to the right path. We are to learn from Jonah's experience.

The central enigma of the story comes at the end of chapter three, where we read that God spared Nineveh, relenting about the destruction he had decreed for the city. Inevitably, the key to the Jonah story is to account for the prophet's overwhelming distress at this news. This is, in fact, the burden of the fourth chapter, whose literary analysis is admittedly complicated. Notwithstanding, there can be no misreading Jonah's own interpretation of his distress as the author attributes it to his leading character. Jon 4:2 paraphrases Exod 34:6–7 on the subject of God's attributes of mercy and forbearance, a resonance already present in Jon 3:9–10, and which strongly recalls Joel 2:13–14. God is *ḥannûn wĕraḥûm ʾerek ʾappayim wĕrab-ḥesed wĕniḥām ʿal-hārāʿâ* ("gracious and merciful, slow to anger and abundant in lovingkindness, who relents of doing harm"). Being aware of these attributes of God, the prophet becomes incredibly angry and depressed, wishing for his own death. What he had always known had now been realized: Because the God of Israel is merciful and forgiving he had allowed Nineveh to be spared.

One of several, traditional Jewish interpretations explains that Jonah foresaw what the Assyrians would do to his own people, Israel, in days to come and was distressed that he was making God's mercy available to these potential enemies through the fulfillment of his prophetic mission. This apprehension would account for his attempted flight in the first instance: He could not bear to bring a message of repentance to perhaps the cruelest of Israel's future enemies.[3]

This interpretation bears the stamp of homiletical hindsight, and would require us to assign an unrealistically early date to the book of Jonah, one which I doubt can withstand critical examination. In a related manner, Yehezkel Kaufmann's modern espousal of an early date for the composition of Jonah, one preceding the rise of the Neo-Assyrian Empire, and before its threat to northern Israel and Judah became real, is contradicted by linguistic and cultural considerations (Kaufmann 1967:279–87). But, leaving aside the predictive theme in the traditional interpretation we must admit that its major thrust is symmetrical. It is

[3] See Ginzberg (1928:349 n. 27), for the relevant Midrashic sources.

an effort to answer both of the reader's (or listener's) queries on the same basis, and it reinforces the statement of Jon 4:2 that from the outset Jonah knew what to expect and for this reason had sought flight to Tarshish. That Jonah should have been distressed at the sparing of Israel's enemies is taken by the later tradition as an indication of his love for his people and his land. The prophet was angry with God for failing to prevent an outcome devastating to his own people by mercifully allowing the Assyrians to avert divine punishment.

In such terms, how are we to understand the lesson of the gourd (Jon 4:6–11)? The final didactic words of the book of Jonah make the point that just as human beings are innately compassionate so is God, and that the prophet was wrong to have been distressed over the sparing of Nineveh. The lesson of the gourd teaches that the people of Nineveh are also God's creatures, men, women and small children too young to know their right hand from their left, and that the gates of repentance are open to them. Proverbially, the most wicked of humans are capable of changing for the better. That being so, it would not have been insightful, or morally proper for the prophet to have evaded his mission even out of concern for his own people. Jonah's attitude had been based on a misunderstanding of God's true posture with respect to his creatures, and on a misunderstanding of human nature, as well. He required painful education, and this would not be long in coming.

Despite the persuasiveness of this traditional interpretation in illuminating Jonah's lesson, a hypothetical argument against it can still be raised along the following lines. If, indeed, the Assyrians had repented at an early period, they might never have become an evil empire and would not have later constituted a danger to Israel. Should not the prophet have hoped, therefore, in anticipation, that his admonitions would be effective? But, the Jewish sages may have been more skeptical than we realize. Perhaps their message was, precisely, that the message of the book of Jonah is naive; that repentance may work for a time under immediate threats, but that people who are wicked at the core usually revert to their former state once they are spared, that the lasting lessons of experience are not easily learned or applied. In fact, a Midrashic tradition has it that after forty days the people of Nineveh actually reverted to their wicked ways (see Ginzberg 1913:246–53). It was typical of the Jewish sages to doubt the sincerity of repentance. To quote their own words: "One who says: 'I will sin and then repent, sin and then repent,' is never afforded sufficient opportunity to achieve repentance" (see the Babylonian Talmud, *Yômāʾ* 85b). Moreover, such skepticism is not limited to post-biblical thinking. Ezekiel also speaks of similar recidivism (Ezek 3:20–21; 18:21–23). Nevertheless, such attitudes directly clash with the tenor of the book of Jonah, itself, which, whether we judge it to be naive or not, clearly thinks well of people, including non-Israelite people. And so, we are left with our original queries.

In the search for answers we return to the scene on the ship, narrated in the first chapter. This scene has more to do with the message of repentance than has usually been assumed. I have found no comparable set of human attitudes expressed anywhere in the Hebrew Bible. Here we have people of diverse nationalities who are literally "in the same boat." They share a common belief in divine power, which overrides their differing religious and national identities. They do not doubt that the deity worshipped by any of them had the power to cause a storm at sea. Their initial complaint against Jonah was, precisely, that he was not doing his part in appeasing his god, who might, for all they knew, be the one responsible for their perilous situation. When prayer failed, those aboard turned to an acknowledged strategy of ancient peoples: The expiation of an offense through the surrender of the offender to the proper divine power. There can be no expiation until the offender has been punished and the deity appeased. The offender was identified, or trapped, if you will, by casting lots, and the lot revealed that Jonah was the offender, and that his God had whipped up the storm.

Some of what happened next is unusual to find in a biblical tale. True, it is not unusual in the biblical literary tradition for gentiles to acknowledge the awesome power of Israel's God, *in extremis* (though their pronouncement of sacrificial vows stretches matters a bit!), but it is exceptional to find people of different nations making such efforts to save a Hebrew from death, at great risk to themselves, after his guilt had been established, and after he, himself, had come clean in acknowledging it. The reader is impressed that these are good people; the author of Jonah leaves no doubt on that score. One could even say that the people on the ship, by hesitating to act on the result of their oracular determinations, were deviating from the accepted predicates of religious behavior. After all, they weren't pleading for the life of an innocent man, and yet, in Jon 1:14, they say that his death at their hands would constitute *dām nāqîʾ* "innocent blood," a characterization elsewhere reserved for the death of the truly innocent. Could it be that the author of Jonah wants the reader (or listener), at this early point in the story, to regard Jonah's confession of his own guilt and his acknowledgment of God's power (Jon 1:9, 12) as acts of repentance that should have entitled him to be spared? And further: Could this be Jonah's first lesson by the divine pedagogue; was the prophet supposed to learn something about himself from the extraordinary demonstration of human compassion by those aboard ship? Did he learn something from this experience, after all?

A piece of Jewish folklore I first heard in my youth, and for which I do not know the source, goes something like this: "What a strange story Jonah is! Throughout our history, the nations of the world have repeatedly caused us suffering on account of our religious beliefs and our national identity; they have expelled us from many lands and cast us into the sea. We pleaded with them to spare us, but they would not heed our voice. But listen to Jonah and consider his gentile shipmates! He identifies himself as a Hebrew who worships the God of heaven, fully acknowledges his guilt, and pleads with the passengers and crew to cast him overboard so as to save themselves. What do these gentiles do? They call upon Jonah's God to spare him, try bravely to reach the shore, and finally, in desperation, ask forgiveness for doing what they had to do!"

Jonah is spared for the while; God assigns the great fish the task of swallowing him. One could say that God spared Jonah because his job was not done, because words pronounced by God do not return unless they have attained their mark (Isa 55:11). Or, without opposing this notion, one could suggest that God had accepted Jonah's repentance. But, did Jonah understand the power of human repentance at this point in the story?

Whoever deserves our thanks for composing the psalm of chapter two, or for inserting it as an available psalm, or for adapting the same, left us subtle clues: Jonah had sought to flee from God's presence (Jon 1:3), but now, crying out to God from the belly of the fish, he longed for that very presence (Jon 2:5). So, the prophet did learn something about God from his near-death experience: He now realized that escape from God's reach was impossible. As one who had tried to get beyond the range of God's voice he now hoped that God would hear his voice from Sheol (Jon 2:3). Significantly missing from the psalm, however, is any clue that Jonah had learned something about the power of human repentance, or that his perception of his role as a prophet had changed. He had been spared by a merciful God for reasons unclear to him, so that when God reiterated his charge, Jonah knew better than to disobey a second time.

Although we are left up in the air as the story of Jonah ends, it seems that its author wanted us to conclude that the parable of the gourd got through to Jonah. It is often the case that biblical narratives conclude with an unanswered query, or leave a situation unresolved. The absence of any indication to the contrary is taken to imply that the closing statement was meant to stand. A classic example is the dialogue between Moses and his Midianite father-in-law, Hobab (Num 10:29–36). Moses urged his father-in-law to join up with the Israelites on their journey to Canaan, stressing his need of Hobab's familiarity with the desert, and promising to deal generously with him in the new land. Hobab declines, but Moses persists, repeating his offer in Num 10:32. But the very next verse, Num 10:33, merely relates that "they" journeyed on for three days, leaving it unresolved whether or not Hobab had, indeed, decided to join up with them. The reader is to assume that this is what occurred, although nothing that follows makes this outcome explicit.

Jonah was now a different man. He had failed to respond to the kindness of others, or to God's kindness, but he finally responded to his own inner feelings of compassion. But, we are getting ahead of the story!

Had Jonah indeed responded on the first two counts, he would not have been so upset at the expectation of Nineveh's repentance; he would have rather welcomed it. It is clear, therefore, that as chapter three of Jonah begins, Jonah is the same man that he was before, except that he is now more realistic about his own position. He knows that he must carry out his prophetic charge. In Jon 4:3 we read that the prophet beseeches God to take his life, for it would be better to be dead. The key verb is Hebrew *ḥ-r-h* (v. 1), which may be merely an alternate realization of geminate *ḥ-r-r* "to be heated, to flare up." Idiomatic *lāmmâ ḥārâ lĕkā*, "Why have you become so agitated?," and variations of the same occur several times outside of Jonah (Gen 4:6; 2 Sam 19:43; 22:8 // Ps 18:8, and so forth). The image seems to be that of flared nostrils, as indicated by the frequent idiom *ḥārâ ʾap* "the nostrils flared up." This idiom describes reactions to a complex of related emotions, though rejection seems to be at the core of them. Thus, Cain felt severely rejected after his offerings had been rejected by God (Gen 4:5–6). Rejection also accounts for the angry response of the northern Israelites when they felt that David and the Judeans had slighted them (2 Sam 19:21–44). David speculates that Saul might become enraged at the thought that he was plotting against him, and for this reason failed to appear at the New Moon feast (1 Sam 20:5–8).

If rejection, or abandonment by God was Jonah's dominant response as he monitored the actions of the people of Nineveh and their king, then we may characterize his understanding of his prophetic role and of his relationship to God in the following terms: The true prophet is one sent by God bearing a reliable message, and when what he or she has predicted actually happens, all recognize the legitimacy of the prophet through whom God has spoken, and all acknowledge God's power. If, however, a prophet was disproved by unfolding events, it is a sign either that the spirit of prophecy had left him or her, or that the person claiming to be a true prophet was a charlatan. A Midrashic tradition has it that Jonah actually suffered from a bad reputation; that he had once predicted the destruction of Jerusalem only to be discredited by the people after Jerusalem's repentance. He then became known as "the false prophet" (Ginzberg 1913:246–53). In effect, this Midrash imputes to the people the same perception as it does to Jonah, himself.

This view of prophecy is not unknown in biblical thinking. Thus, Deut 18:21–22 states: "And should you say to yourself: 'How shall we recognize the oracle (as one) which YHWH has not spoken?' What the prophet speaks in the name of YHWH but does not happen, nor does it come about, that is the oracle that YHWH has not spoken. The prophet spoke it brazenly; you need not be in fear of him." Beyond this pragmatic test, meant to apply between the Israelites and their would-be prophets, there is the further consideration that Jonah was sent to a foreign city as a prophet of doom. This might explain how it is that as chapter four begins, we find Jonah dejected and angry as he observes the people of Nineveh acting effectively to avert God's decree. The fact that his unreliability had been exposed among a gentile population might have added to his depression, as well as the likelihood that he may have been less willing to save the Ninevites than he would have been to be of help to his own people. To put it bluntly: Jonah felt that God had "set him up."

This raises the question as to whether we ever encounter in biblical literature, in the genre usually referred to as "oracles against the nations," an Israelite prophet of doom who holds forth the prospect of repentance to foreign nations and peoples, those whose sins and crimes, and often their acts against Israel, specifically, would have expectedly sealed their doom. One searches hard for such mitigation of the divine decree in oracles against the nations. It would, therefore, be reasonable for an Israelite prophet to be angry over a rescue mission to Nineveh. In fact, there were occasions when Israelite prophets were angry even when called upon to offer rescue to their own people! Moses initially resisted the mission of liberating the Israelites from Egypt with repeated objections (Exod 3:10–11, 13; 4:13), and he was subsequently distressed over it (Exod 5:22–23). Jeremiah was very frightened initially when called, so that strong assurances were necessary (Jer 1:6–9, 17–19). What is more, he cried out continually, accusing God of haying seduced him into submission, rendering him unable to resist the fire burning within him (Jer 20:7–10). He cursed the day of his birth (Jer 20:14–18).

In this connection, it is striking how dramatically the oration against Nineveh preserved in Nahum, chapter 1, contrasts in tone with the story of Jonah. There, the God of Israel is characterized as wrathful and destructive, and there is no thought of his ever forgiving Nineveh. What is most suggestive is the resonance of Exod 34:6–7 in Nah 1:2–3. Above, we saw how Jon 4:2 had resonated the same version of divine attributes so as to dramatize God's willingness to forgive. In contrast, Nahum's horrendous oracle of doom is construed to produce the opposite characterization: "A passionate and vengeful deity is YHWH (*ʾēl qannôʾ wĕnōqēm YHWH*); YHWH is vengeful and possessed of wrath (*ûbaʿal ḥēmâ*); YHWH is vengeful towards his foes and he retains his anger towards his enemies. YHWH is slow to anger and forbearing in power (*YHWH ʾerek ʾappayim ûgĕdol kōaḥ*), but he will surely not exonerate (*wĕnaqqēh lōʾ yĕnaqqeh*).

To put it bluntly: God allowed the Assyrians to gain enormous power and domination; he took his time bringing them down, being, as we know, long forbearing. But now, the time had finally come, and at this point, there was no escaping God's terrible punishment. The deferral of punishment, viewed as a sign of divine mercy in Exodus, here becomes a liability. Seizing on the "down side" of Exod 34:6–7, and picking up the theme of passion from the continuation of Exod 34:14, the author of Nahum rather invidiously turned on the attribute of divine patience, which, as regards Nineveh, worked to the ultimate ruin of that imperial capital. Whereas the inevitable consequence expressed as *wĕnaqqēh lōʾ yĕnaqqeh* in Exod 34:7 meant, originally, that notwithstanding God's mercifulness, there could be no escape from accountability for transgression, the author of Nahum voiced that caveat with extreme emphasis. Although extreme even for an oracle against the nations, Nahum, chapter 1, produces more of what we would expect in terms of likely attitudes toward the Neo-Assyrian Empire in biblical literature.

Perhaps the closest we come to the vision of penitent gentiles is in the late prophecies preserved in Isaiah 19. This chapter presents several interpretive and historical problems, and yet its oracles progress in a recognizable pattern: Egypt's doom is predicted (Isa 19:1–15), as is the hegemony of Israel over Egypt, and the acknowledgment of the power of Israel's God among the Egyptians (Isa 19:16–21). Among other things, Egyptians will worship the God of Israel sacrificially and pronounce vows that they will duly fulfill. After the Egyptians will be alternately battered by Israel's God and granted respite by him (an echo of the saga of the ten plagues), they will finally "turn back to YHWH" (*wĕšābû ʿad-YHWH*), who will hear their entreaty and bring them well being (Isa 19:22). Then we read the following:

> On that day, there will be a highway leading from Egypt to Assyria; Assyrians will come into Egypt, and Egyptians into Assyria, but the Egyptians will be tributary to Assyria.
>
> On that day, Israel will constitute the third party alongside Egypt and Assyria. A blessing shall be pronounced by YHWH of the Heavenly Hosts in the midst of the earth, as follows: "Blessed is my people, Egypt, and the work of my hands, the Assyrians, and my possession, Israel" (Isa 19:23–25).

Without attempting to identify the *Sitz-im-Leben* of these oracles precisely, which, even if it were possible, would take us far afield, it is obvious that they have something in common with the perceptions that inform the book of Jonah. The Egyptians will repent sincerely only after many beatings, whereas the people of Nineveh will repent as an immediate response to Jonah's oracle of doom. A telling link with Jonah comes in the characterization: *ûmaʿăśēh yāday ʾaššûr*, "and my creatures, the Assyrians" (Isa 19:25), which recalls God's explanation of the parable of the gourd: "You would have spared (*ʾattâ ḥastā ʿal-*) the gourd, over which you did not toil (*ʾăšer lōʾ-ʿāmaltā bô*), nor did you raise it; which came into being in a night and perished in a night. Should I not spare Nineveh, that populous town where many more then twelve myriads of human beings reside, who cannot tell between their right arm and their left, and much cattle?" (Jon 4:10–11).

It is precisely the factor of repentance, so dominant in the late prophecies in Isaiah 19, which helps explain why Jonah would not have understood initially how an Israelite prophet might be the instrument of rescue for the gentiles. Jonah's conversion to a belief in repentance occurred only after the lesson of the gourd, as we shall see presently. When he arrived at Nineveh, Jonah was still the traditional prophet of doom, so that when his prediction of Nineveh's destruction did not come true, he was devastated.

The divine pedagogue then staged a situation that aroused in Jonah strong feelings of loss. The gourd that had given him shade from the scorching sun and brought him pleasure withered away as fast as it had grown. His pain at this loss was too real to deny. In the mode of a caring teacher, God verbalized Jonah's own feelings. The care that others, probably strangers, had shown toward him aboard the ship, and the care that God had shown toward him in the depths of the sea had failed to induce compassion in Jonah. What did get through to Jonah was the awareness that he, himself, had felt intense loss, and he was given to understand that God also experiences loss at the death of his creatures. The choice of a withering plant by the author of Jonah to epitomize the transitory character of human life was not incidental; it is a frequent simile in biblical wisdom literature. Like grass and aftergrowth, the human creature withers away before we know it, as if in a single day (Pss 37:2; 90:5; 103:15). Jonah's gourd vanished in a single night!

This is as much as can be said for now about Jonah's education as a prophet, about his inner development. I realize that I have not adequately accounted for the issues at stake in his relationship with God. This will require us to explore the premises of biblical prophecy further, and to examine the theme of repentance itself. Beyond both human and divine compassion is the dynamism of human behavior and its effect on God.

II. Repentance as Empowerment: A Variable in the Human-Divine Relationship

Yehezkel Kaufmann (1967:279–87), whose literary-historical assignment of the book of Jonah to an early date must be rejected on critical grounds, is the very scholar who has clarified for me how consequentially the theme of repentance functions in certain biblical sources, while it is conspicuously absent from others. He does so, in the first instance, by contrasting the story of Jonah with the narrative preserved in Gen 18:20–32 on the overturning of Sodom and Gomorrah. In utter contrast to Jonah, who seeks to evade a mission of mercy, Abraham, unsolicited, petitions God to spare the twin towns of wickedness if only a few righteous citizens could be found residing in them.

The dictional link between the two narratives is localized in the verb *h-p-k* "to overturn." Significantly, destruction depicted as "overturning" (Hebrew *hăpēkâ*, *mahpēkâ*) and conveyed by forms of the verb *h-p-k* is said chiefly with reference to Sodom and Gomorrah (Gen 19:25, 29; Deut 29:22; Isa 1:6–7; 13:19; Jer 49:18; 50:40; Amos 4:11) and Nineveh: "Forty days from now Nineveh is to be overturned (*wĕnînĕwēh nehpāket*)" (Jonah 3:4).[4] By innuendo, Sodom and Gomorrah are probably the indefinite referents in Jer 20:16, as well. The thematic, or intertextual link between the Book of Jonah and Genesis 18 is in the expression *kî-ʿālĕtâ rāʿātām lĕpānāy*, "for their evildoing has ascended to me" (Jon 1:2). Compare Gen 18:20–21: "Then YHWH said: 'The outcry of Sodom and Gomorrah has truly become great, and their offense is grievous. I must descend in order to ascertain whether they have irreversibly committed what their outcry reaching me (*habbāʾâ ʾēlay*) [indicates they have], and if not, I will know [that as well].'" (Also see Gen 19:13.)

What this means is that the wickedness of Nineveh, like that of Sodom and Gomorrah, was an internal matter primarily affecting the people of these towns themselves. There is no indication of hostility on the part of the Ninevites toward Israel; in fact, no relationship with Israel is ever intimated. As is the case with the oracle of Nahum, in the book of Jonah the people of Nineveh are never identified as Assyrians, nor is Nineveh ever referred to as the capital of the Assyrian state, or empire, although in Nahum there are clear allusions to conquest and imperial domination that are suggestive in this regard. In a similar vein, there is no indication in the narratives of Sodom and Gomorrah of hostility between the Canaanites of these towns and the clan of Abraham, who was actually allied with their kings in the war against the invading forces (Genesis 14). The

[4] The verb *h-p-k* is used with reference to a destruction but without obvious reference to Sodom and Gomorrah in 2 Sam 10:3; 1 Chr 19:3; Prov 12:7; and Hag 2:22.

aggressive xenophobia exhibited by the Sodomites toward strangers, like that of the residents of Gibeah (Judges 19), was clearly a reflection of the perverseness and demoralization of their own community, and the same was undoubtedly true of the crimes of the Ninevites.

In this connection, it is significant that the greatest crime of all that a king can commit is one against his own land and people. In the dramatic *māšāl* against the king of Babylon (Isa 14:3–20), historically the king of Assyria, of course, he is charged with vast destruction of other lands, of turning the known world into a desert. But his most horrendous crime is what he brought upon his own land and people: "You shall not be united with them (= with all the kings of the earth) in burial for you have destroyed your own land; you have slain your own people" (Isa 14:20). Once again, we are talking about Assyrians.

Kaufmann notes two differences between the story of Jonah and the narratives of Sodom and Gomorrah. The first may be referred to as the "terms of engagement" between the human and the divine, and the second as the presence, or absence of repentance as a dynamic factor. According to Kaufmann, Abraham appealed to God's justice when the latter was moved by wrath, whereas Jonah demanded justice from God when the latter was moved by compassion. Thus Abraham: "Shall the judge of all the earth fail to act justly?" (Gen 18:25). And thus Jonah: "For I know that you are a gracious and compassionate God, slow to anger and abundant in steadfast love, who relents of doing harm" (Jon 4:2).

But this difference, in and of itself, falls short of yielding an understanding of the story of Jonah as it is told, and is mild compared with the second difference discussed by Kaufmann. He correctly focuses on repentance as the crucial variable in the human-divine relationship. The Sodom and Gomorrah narratives project only limited human options. They belong with a genre of encounter narratives where the disposition of the appeal is left to God. Humans may beseech God for mercy on any number of grounds, or outdo themselves in appeasing him by prayer and sacrifice. They may appeal to his justice, as did Abraham, or, like Moses on several occasions, they may appeal to God's good name, to his wish to be acknowledged by the nations as reliable and all powerful, or as merciful and forgiving. But there is no suggestion that the people of Sodom and Gomorrah might be spared if they repented and turned back from evil. It is never suggested that humans are empowered with the means to annul a divine decree in this way, and if sincerely repentant, that they could count on God's merciful response. Even the "call" of Jonah to the people of Nineveh (Jon 2:4) merely announces a prediction of doom, but says nothing about a way to avert such an outcome through repentance. The reader may be a little surprised to read that the wicked people of Nineveh placed credence in the prediction, but one is even less prepared for the surprise of their repentance.

The author of Jonah introduces the theme of repentance through three key words that define the human-divine relationship. The first is the noun *rāʿâ*, which enjoys a range of connotations including "evildoing, harm, suffering." The second is the verb *šûb*, "to return, turn back." The third applies only to God and is conveyed by the verb *n-ḥ-m*, "to relent, have a change of heart." As the story begins, the *rāʿâ* "evildoing" of the Ninevites had reached God (Jon 1:2). Later, they were to renounce their *rāʿâ* and "turn back" (*šûb*) to the true path: The text of Jon 3:5–4:1 warrants a close reading:

> The citizens of Nineveh placed their trust in God, and proclaimed a fast, and donned sackcloth from their smallest to their greatest. The matter reached the king of Nineveh, who arose from his throne and removed his robe, and covered himself with sackcloth and he sat upon ashes. He issued a loud call in Nineveh by order of the king and his lords as follows: 'Neither man nor beast, herds or flocks may eat anything; they may not graze or drink. Let them cover themselves with sackcloth and call out to God vociferously. Let them turn back (*wĕyāšūbû*), each one, from his evil path (*middarkô hārāʿâ*) and from the violence that is in their palms. Who knows but that God will turn back (*yāšûb*) and relent (*wĕniḥḥam*), and turn back (*wĕšāb*) from his rage, so that we shall not perish.' Then God observed their deeds, that they had turned back (*kî-šābû*) from their evil path, and God relented of the harm (*wayyinnāḥem hāʾĕlōhîm ʿal-hārāʿâ*) that he had commanded to do to them, and did not do it. Then Jonah experienced great suffering (*wayyēraʿ ʾel-yônâ rāʿâ gĕdôlâ*), and he became agitated.

As represented, the people of Nineveh and their king were experimenting with God; they were uncertain, initially, whether their contrite acknowledgment of wrongdoing and their return to the true path would induce God to relent but it did. This is a way of saying that humans can rely on the efficacy of repentance. The author of Jonah undoubtedly regarded repentance as a dispensation deriving from God's love for his creatures and for the world he created. It is a function of divine mercy, but it goes beyond that. When humans repent they become entitled to divine mercy and forgiveness. Repentance is an empowerment of humankind. In its dynamic, repentance shares the binding force of vows and of the covenantal relationship. It is a type of contractual assurance offered by God through his spokesmen, the prophets, that if humans return to the true path, God has undertaken to cancel their liabilities.

It is not difficult to trace the diction of repentance as expressed in the passage from Jonah cited above. In addition to the themes already noted, we have the frequent image of the "path" (Hebrew *derek*). Life is a path, and people often stray from the right path, or choose the wrong road on which to continue their journey through life. If, however, at any point they turn back to the right path, they are again headed in the right direction, and will avert the punishments meted out to those who have left the right path but who fail to return to it.

The idiom *šûb midderek rāʿâ*, "turn back from an evil path," is characteristic of Jeremiah (18:11; 25:5; 35:15; 36:3, 7), and it is picked up by Ezekiel (3:18; 13:22; 33:8–9, 11) and First Zechariah (1:4). (Compare 1 Kgs 13:33; 2 Kgs 17:13, both late redactional passages.) It would not be inaccurate to conclude that it was introduced in the near-exilic or early-exilic period. The role in which Jonah is eventually instructed, and which he initially had failed to comprehend, is very close to that projected for the true prophet in Ezek 3:17–19, where the factor of repentance is likewise crucial:

> Son of man, I have appointed you as a lookout for the House of Israel. When you hear a word from my mouth, you must forewarn them on my behalf. When I announce to the wicked person: 'You shall surely die!'—but you do not forewarn him, and do not speak in order to warn the wicked person away from his wicked path and thereby enable him to live—he, as a wicked person, shall die as punishment for his own sin, but I will requite his blood from you. But, if you did forewarn the wicked person, and yet he did not turn back from his wickedness and from his wicked path, he shall die as punishment for his sin, and you will have saved your own life.

The crucial power of repentance, of true and lasting repentance without reversion to sinfulness, is repeated in Ezekiel 18 in a similar manner. Whereas Ezekiel is defining the role of the Israelite prophet sent by God to his own people, the author of Jonah extends the same prophetic responsibility to prophets on a mission to the nations. This means, among other things, that God was being exceptionally merciful in granting Jonah a second chance, and it also means that God strongly sought to avoid the destruction of Nineveh. Abraham's God was not as compassionate!

III. Conclusion

The inner agenda of Jonah, and its most insightful idea is that repentance and denial cannot co-exist in human experience. Beyond that, we learn that repentance requires the belief that just as God is capable of overcoming his anger, human beings can do the same; that like God, humans can relent of the harm they intended to do, and if they succeed in this, God will answer "Amen." In a sense, all that happened to Nineveh happened to Jonah, and all that happened to both Nineveh and Jonah happened to God, or, shall we say, with respect to the conception of God as presented by the author of the book of Jonah.

That Nineveh should be the object of divine compassion is hardly incidental. Again one is reminded of the utopian visions of Isaiah 19, canonically attributed to the Isaiah of eighth-century B.C.E. Jerusalem, but which actually derive from a later time. That earlier prophet, Isaiah of Jerusalem, had been most concerned with the role of Jerusalem in an age of world peace. Perhaps the author of Jonah, not unlike those who gave us the late prophecies of Isaiah 19, understood how important would be the role of Nineveh, the capital of the gentiles, in a redeemed world.

References

Ginzberg, L.
1913 *The Legends of the Jews*. Vol. IV. Philadelphia: Jewish Publication Society.

1928 *The Legends of the Jews*. Vol. VI. Philadelphia: Jewish Publication Society.

Kaufmann, Y.

1967 *History of the Religion of Israel*. Vol. 2. Jerusalem: Bialik Institute, and Tel-Aviv: Dvir.

Landes, G. M.

1976 Linguistic Criteria and the Date of the Book of Jonah. Pp. 147–70 in *H. M. Orlinsky Volume*. Eretz-Israel 16. Jerusalem: Israel Exploration Society.

Sasson, J. M.

1990 *Jonah: A New Translation with Introduction, Commentary, and Interpretations*. AB 24B. New York: Doubleday.

René Girard on Job: The Question of the Scapegoat*

ABSTRACT

The book of Job must be studied within the context of biblical literature, culture and society, with attention to the role of languages in the interpretation of ancient classics, and to literary motifs in ancient Near Eastern perspective. Biblical applications of the scapegoat phenomenon to humans is quite different from what we find in Job, as we shall see with reference to Lev 16 and other "riddance" rites. The servant song of Isa 52–53 tells how the human scapegoat was conceptualized in the early post-exilic period and shows how the scapegoat differed from other sufferers. There is no connection between the well-being of the community and the sufferings of Job, whose laments admit of a psychological explanation. His heroic dissidence is not a scapegoat phenomenon.

René Girard calls Job a scapegoat. He arrives at this definition through an analysis of several important poetic passages in the dialogues of Job in which our fallen hero bemoans his social isolation, his economic plight, and the rejection of his kinsfolk. He is *déclassé*. His position in society has suddenly plummeted, leaving him in a state of shock, angry and depressed. In Girard's view, it is not God who is Job's real enemy, the cause of his troubles, but rather his society. His community has made Job, the innocent victim, its scapegoat.

Girard's interest in the scapegoat is intense. He has devoted one work, *Le Bouc émissaire*, to this subject, and he utilizes the scapegoat theme to interpret ancient myths, to explain the role of society in ritual sacrifice, and to characterize social and political movements.

It is not my purpose to argue for or against Girard's many applications of the scapegoat phenomenon, a task surely beyond my competence. I'm reasonably sure I could agree with some of these applications. My question is whether Job can legitimately be called a scapegoat, in context. As much as usage undoubtedly changed from Leviticus, chapter 16, to Job, I do not think that one who speaks as Job does, or whose dialoguers confront him in the terms they do, can qualify as a scapegoat.

As I intend to show, we have biblical applications of the scapegoat phenomenon to humans. The conceptualization of the human scapegoat that emerges is quite different from what we find in Job. All innocent victims (or, to be more

* Originally published in *Semeia* 33 (*René Girard and Biblical Studies*; 1985), pp. 125–133. Reprinted with permission from the Society of Biblical Literature.

precise: all victims who claim to be innocent), share much in common, but the scapegoat differs in certain critical respects, at least within the context of biblical literature, culture, and society, to the extent that we know them. It is this context that must be clarified, and which must delimit our definition of the scapegoat, as it might or might not apply to Job.

In one matter, I agree with Girard quite definitely: The prose-tale of Job (the Prologue and Epilogue) is not integral to the book in literary terms. It is, indeed, an error to allow the more traditional tone of these chapters to determine the parameter of the dialogues themselves. Professor Avi Hurvitz has made a useful contribution to this problem by showing, through diachronic analysis of the language of the prose-tale, that it is probably later than the dialogues. In any event, I feel confident in regarding these chapters as a rubric, written expressly so as to interpret the startling dialectic of the dialogues in a manner more readily understandable to the ancient reader.

Girard focuses attention on social issues and has, at least for me, posed a question I had failed to confront in my own reading of the dialogues of Job: Why is it that societies react as they do to the victims of misfortune in their midst? How are we to understand the often-endorsed rationalization that such victims have only themselves to blame, that they are responsible for their own plight? To put it in the words of Job himself, who cites an ancient proverb:

lappîd bûz lᵉʿaštût šaʾᵃnān
nāḵôn lᵉmôʿᵃdê rāgel

Disaster strikes the despised—
so the reasoning of the complacent;
It readily awaits stumblers! (12:5)

I must, however, object to Girard's disdainful attitude toward the role of languages in the interpretation of ancient classics. Our present understanding of Job is admittedly inadequate, but it is also true that whatever progress has been made in the recent past has resulted from the careful study of the text of Job, with its strong Aramaic substratum, through an investigation of literary motifs in ancient Near Eastern perspective, and against the background of biblical literature itself.

I

In the first instance, the dialogues of Job should be studied within the context of biblical literature, culture, and society. But here we encounter a degree of uncertainty: The dialogues of Job are creations of the post-exilic period, perhaps of the fourth century B.C.E., or later. It is not entirely clear, however, for whom the dialogues speak. (The prose tale speaks for post-exilic Judaism, in a general sense.) Some doubt that the dialogues were written by Jews, or that they were composed within the Jewish society of their time. Ultimately, the book of Job was canonized by Jewish synods, not without resistance, because, at some later time, Jewish religious leadership responded positively to its message, as they understood it. Some Talmudic sages conceded that Job was not an historical person, but felt that his life experience could serve as a *māšāl*, an object lesson (Ginzberg, II:223–24, V:381, n. 3).

The authors of the dialogues were intimately familiar with earlier biblical literature, as was shown most incisively by M. Z. Segal in his study of the literary parallels in Job (Segal 1949–50). If we allow for the influx of non-Jewish ideas, there is no reason to doubt the Jewish provenience of the dialogues. In fact, they may well serve to indicate how broad was the post-exilic Jewish universe.

The scapegoat ritual of Leviticus, chapter 16, should be our starting point in any discussion of the scapegoat phenomenon. This is not to say that the question of Job's definition should be engaged within this context alone, but only to insist that it cannot be discussed without reference to the dynamics of the scapegoat ritual. Biblical phenomena never completely lose their moorings!

The ritual of Leviticus chapter 16 has many dimensions. Explicitly, the religious community acts to contain impurity by extracting it from places, objects and persons contaminated by it. Then the impurity is transferred to an animal—a goat—(Hebrew: *śaʿîr*) who is promptly removed from the settlement, and whose return is prevented. By certain traditions, the goat meets its death in the wilderness.

Thus far the phenomenology is eminently clear: To eliminate dangerous impurity, we must localize it, pin-point it, thus reducing its area and volume, so that it can be eliminated without destroying everyone and everything in the process. We do this today when we grow viruses in laboratories, or try to contain the area of oil slicks, pumping the oil from a reduced area. This process is basic to rituals of "riddance," as they are called.

The goat was not a fortuitous choice, however. It represented the demonic powers of the wilderness, an idea suggested in Isaiah 13:21, and 14:14, both late passages which speak of *śᵉʿîrîm* in the wilderness. From Leviticus 17:7 we learn that the Israelites had once worshipped such *śᵉʿîrîm*, and they continued to serve as the most frequent animal in sin-offerings.

These observations lead to the more implicit dimension of the scapegoat ritual: The sin-laden goat comes to be identified with sinfulness and impurity to start with, even before it was burdened. It is as if a goat had brought impurity into the community, initially, from the wilderness, its domain. The dispatch of the goat sent impurity back whence it had come! It is this sense of the scapegoat ritual that holds the most obvious applications for the psycho-social phenomenon we call "scapegoating."

Caught between the alternatives of worshipping the powers of impurity or of combating them, the priests of ancient Israel opted for the latter course. This decision was understood by several Medieval Jewish sages and exegetes, including Nachmanides and Abraham Ibn-Ezra.

What is established by the above analysis is the nexus of riddance and the future well-being of the community. What is done to the scapegoat is explained by the belief that its disposition was essential, prerequisite to the well-being of the group. A cause and effect relationship between the two is pronounced. In the most basic sense, the scapegoat *substituted* for the group; it suffered what the entire community would have suffered had the goat not been laden with the collective impurity. It spared the group! This phenomenology is common to the rites of riddance found in the priestly codes of the Torah.

The most dramatic application of the scapegoat phenomenon to humans is expressed in the so-called "servant of the Lord" oracles, preserved in Isaiah, chapters 52–53. In themselves, these poems are cryptic, and have generated widely diverse interpretations throughout the centuries, since late antiquity. They have been associated with Christology in complex ways. For the purposes of our present discussion, they are most interesting because of what they have to say about different perceptions of suffering. I add my proposed translation to the many and worthy efforts already available:

A.

52:13) Behold, My servant shall prosper;
He shall be uplifted, raised to great height!
14) Just as the public had been aghast at him,
So much had his human appearance deteriorated,
His form from that of human beings—
15) Just so shall he cast down nations;
Because of him, kings shall hold their speech.
What was not foretold to them, they shall see;
What they never heard, they shall observe!

B.

53:1) Who would have believed what we heard?
Upon whom was the Lord's arm thus revealed?
2) For he grew like a tree-crown in His presence,
Like a trunk from arid soil.
3) His form was not majestic that we would prefer him,
No such appearance that we would want him.
4) He was despised and dehumanized,
Suffering pain, experiencing sickness;
One others turned away from,
Despised, so that we gave him no heed.
In fact, he was suffering the effects of our sickness;
He was bearing the burden of our pain.
Whereas we had regarded him as one stricken,
Smitten by God and tortured—
5) He was, in fact, stabbed for our failures,
Because of our errors.
The chastisement [required] for our well-being
was [laid] upon him;
Through his wound we were healed!
6) All of us strayed like sheep,
Each of us went his own way;
While the Lord made him the target

Of our collective punishment.
7) Though beaten, he remained submissive;
He did not open his mouth.
Like a lamb brought to the slaughter,
Like a ewe dumb before its shearers,
He did not open his mouth.
8) Through miscarriage of justice
He was taken away;
Who can describe his abode?
For he was cut off from the land of the living;
Because of the failure of My people,
Who deserved to be smitten!
9) His grave was set among the wicked,
With evildoers his funerary platform.
Though he had done no violence,
Had spoken no falsehood.
10) But the Lord chose to crush him with sickness!
- - - - - - -
Once his life *is declared* sacrosanct,
He will see descendants,
He will live a long life;
So that the Lord's purpose may succeed through him!
11) Out of his torment he shall see [this],
He shall enjoy [it] to the full,
Out of his devotion.
My Servant shall bring vindication to the public
By bearing the punishment for their error.
12) Therefore, I will allow him to share with the public;
With the multitudes share in the spoils;
In return for exposing himself to death,
For being numbered among the sinful.
For he bore the penalty for the public's offense,
He substituted as a target for the sinful.[1]

These passages tell us how a human scapegoat was conceptualized in the early, post-exilic period, and they highlight the difference between the scapegoat and other sufferers. They are clearly related in diction and concept to the scapegoat ritual of Leviticus 16, and to other riddance rituals. The priestly vocabulary is represented by the terms for sinfulness, *ᶜᵃwôn* and *pešaᶜ*, and by forms of the verb *nāgaᶜ* literally: "to touch," connoting the disabling touch of the gods. The

[1] My translation is influenced by the NJPS. It is, however, an independent translation, for which I am responsible. The only emendation reflected in it that is crucial for our discussion (translations based on emendations are italicized), is in 53:10, where Masoretic *tāśîm* "You shall place, make" is revocalized: *tuśśām* "shall be made, declared." No change of consonants is required. The subject of the passive verb, as now vocalized, is *nepeš* "life," a feminine noun.

formulas *nāśāʾ ḥēṭʾ* "to bear the punishment for transgression" in 53:12, and *sābal ʿᵃwôn* "to bear the burden of error" in 53:11 recall the priestly formula: *nāśāʾ ʿᵃwôn* "to bear the punishment for error." Most telling is the clause: *kî nigzar mēʾereṣ ḥayyîm* "For he was cut off from the land of the living," which recalls: *ʾel ʾereṣ gᵉzērāh* "to the land cut off," in Leviticus 16:22, the destination of the scapegoat. Finally, we have the term *ʾāšām* in 53:10, usually rendered in one of two ways: "guilt," a state, or "guilt offering."

I sense a different connotation in Isaiah 53:10, however. God had crushed the servant with sickness. Then—the turning point: The servant's life is declared sacrosanct! Here, Hebrew *ʾāšām* possesses a positive rather than a negative connotation, known from 2 Chronicles 28:10 where we have the masculine plural: *ʾᵃšāmôt* in the sense of "devoted persons." There we read that the Ephraimites, who had defeated the Judeans in battle, thus arousing God's wrath, were told that they dare not take Judean captives as slaves. They were protected by God, sacrosanct!

This interpretation of the passage in 2 Chronicles was discussed elsewhere (Levine 1974:130). Its application to the special meaning of *ʾāšām* in Isaiah 53:10 did not occur to me until later. In our verse, the rescue of the servant is signaled. He is saved at the brink of death. In some way, his suffering symbolizes that of the Judean exiles in Babylonia, who speak of themselves as being "cut off" (Ezekiel 37:11; Lamentations 3:54).

In terms of our present discussion, the most significant subtlety comes in Isaiah 53:4–5. The people recognize that they had been mistaken about the sufferings of the servant. They had regarded him as one being punished for his own sins, and they consequently paid him no heed. The descriptions of his deteriorated form belong with this perception of him, and they are the ones which remind us of Job. The servant was: *nāgûʿa mukkēh ʾᵉlôhîm ûmᵉʿunneh* "stricken, smitten by God and tortured." Similarly Job (19:21) states: "For the hand of God struck at me (*nāgeʿāh bî*)."

As it turns out, the servant of Isaiah, chapters 52–53 is a different type of victim. He suffers for the sins of others, truly a human scapegoat! (The goat has become a lamb, however.) The rescue of the scapegoat was a most unusual occurrence. How many human scapegoats have actually been rescued? Even more remarkable is the compassion shown him by his own people, or at least by some of them. They recognize their debt to him. Most often, a society seeks to banish or destroy what it cruelly and incorrectly identifies as the carrier of impurity, the cause of its troubles!

There is not a single indication in the speeches of Job, or in those of his dialoguers, of a connection between the suffering of Job and the wellbeing of the community. The authors of the dialogues were simply not thinking in such terms, either compassionately or cruelly. Otherwise, the argumentation would have been very different.

II

In the dialogues of Job we find a challenge to the doctrine that the unfortunate must have offended God, who is just and does not punish the innocent. We also find lengthy, almost tiresome laments. In ancient Near Eastern literature other similar laments have come to light. The best known is that of the so-called "Babylonian Job".[2] The main difference between Job's laments and those of the Babylonian sufferers is in the terms of the complaint. The Babylonian sufferer appeals from his cultic piety, his munificence in contributing sacrifices, his participation in public celebration. Why was someone so pious treated so cruelly, in a manner which only the impious deserve?

Job doesn't mention any such factors. He cites his uprightness, his goodness to others, his innocence of any injustice. In the late biblical tradition a sufferer who claimed cultic piety as his foremost virtue would be open to the challenge that such was not sufficient in God's eyes. In a sense, the prose-tale places Job's sufferings in a more popular perspective. There, Job's piety is highlighted, a theme which continues in the post-biblical Jewish tradition.

Job persists in his hope that God will redeem him by vindicating him. In this respect, he more closely resembles the speaker in one of the earlier servant passages of Isaiah (50:4f.); if, indeed, that speaker is to be associated at all with the servant of chapters 52–53. In chapter 50 we have a first-person statement by a leader who is repudiated by his people, but who is confident nevertheless of his eventual vindication:

> 50:5) The Lord-God has opened my ears;
> I did not rebel, nor did I retreat!
> 6) My back I offered to floggers,
> My cheek to pluckers;
> I did not turn away
> From shaming and spittle.
> 7) For the Lord-God will come to my aid.
> For this reason I am not shamed;
> For this reason I made my face strong as flint!
> For I know I shall not be disgraced.
> 8) My vindicator is near;
> Who dares to dispute with me?
> Let us appear together!
> Whosoever would be my antagonist—
> Let him approach me!
> 9) Behold, the Lord-God comes to my aid—
> Who can convict me?
> May they all wear thin like a garment;
> Be consumed by moths!

---

[2] See Robert D. Biggs, translator, "I Will Praise the Lord of Wisdom," and "The Babylonian Theodicy," in *ANET*, pp. 596–604.

The authors of the dialogues of Job may well have taken their cue from this passage. Sylvia Scholnick, a former student of mine, has stressed the importance of the legal language we find in the dialogues of Job. She has investigated the *rîḇ*, the legal dispute, and specific connotations of the verb *šāpaṭ* "to judge," and *ṣādaq* in the sense of "vindication." These locutions are common to Isaiah, chapter 50 and to the dialogues of Job. The speaker of Isaiah chapter 50 claims God as his defense attorney, who will plead his case in court. Job would have settled for an appearance in court by God, to answer for His treatment of one of His creatures!

God is very real in the dialogues of Job. For the sake of argument I am prepared, however, to accept a humanistic equation: God = reality, fate, the human condition, etc. Let's assume that all that Job charges God with—indifference, injustice—is an ancient way of saying that one's community, family, or the impersonal realities of one's life are the cause. Even in such terms, we do not have a scapegoat in Job. What we find is the rationalization that the "loser" has only himself to blame. People tend to shun losers. This attitude can best be explained psychologically: The loser makes us uneasy, even frightens us by identification. What happened to him may happen to us! I have often observed wealthy persons, in particular, who are morbidly fascinated by tales of those of their group who suddenly lost their fortunes!

Job is shunned because of *what had already become of him*, and what had become of him did not result from any effort to eliminate him from society, initially, so that society would be spared through his riddance.

III

René Girard extracts from the dialogues of Job those passages which epitomize his own concerns: How do the many treat the few, the mob the individual, the strong the weak? I insist, however, that Job is no scapegoat. He is an heroic dissident! God's answer to Job may be a hard pill to swallow, but Job exacted an answer nonetheless, showing that God is reachable if we don't despair of the effort to communicate with Him. Leaving God out of the picture, we learn from the dialogues of Job that consensus is not truth. In this I find much common ground with René Girard.

Bibliography

Ginzberg, Louis

19a09–38 *The Legends of the Jews*. 7 vols. Philadelphia: The Jewish Publication Society of America.

Levine, B. A.

1974 *In the Presence of the Lord: A Study of Cult and Some Cultic Terms in Ancient Israel*. Studies in Judaism in Late Antiquity 5. Leiden: E. J. Brill.

Segal, M. Z.

1949–50 Parallels between Job and other Books of the Bible (Hebrew). *Tarbiz* 20:35–48.

The Four Private Persons Who Lost Their Share in the World to Come: The Judgment of m. *Sanh.* 10:2*

I have always been intrigued by the 10th chapter of *m. Sanhedrin*, which is devoted to the subject of the World to Come; in Hebrew, עולם הבא. Specifically, I would like to understand the basis for the Mishnah's exclusion of four biblical personalities—Balaam, son of Beor; Doeg the Edomite; Ahithophel; and Gehazi—from the share in the World to Come that is granted to all Israelites collectively (*m. Sanh.* 10:2). What was it that that these four persons had done that was so exceptionally heinous? What lines did they cross and which principles did they compromise so as to be singled out for damnation among so many obvious biblical candidates?

When we review the rabbinic profiles of the four exceptions listed by the Mishnah, along the lines of Louis Ginzberg in his classic work, *Legends of the Jews*,[1] we encounter reconfigured personalities, often playing different roles and seen through later eyes. This raises an important question: when the authors of the Mishnah designated these four persons as unworthy, were they reflecting primarily on the biblical narratives, or were they looking instead at rabbinic reconfigurations of these individuals? To explore this question, I have analyzed the biblical narratives in search of a common denominator in this group of four. The Jerusalem Talmud, in the Aggadic material presented on *m. Sanhedrin* 10, begins by posing the same question that is being asked here, namely, what had these biblical personalities done? This analysis will take up most of this essay, with only minimal annotation. It will be followed by a review of the rabbinic profiles of the same four individuals.

The Sages read the Hebrew Bible in multiple ways and respected the original context of passages. This is what is meant by the canon: אין מקרא יוצא מידי פשוטו "The biblical text never disconnects from its direct meaning" (*b. Šabb.* 63a). It will be observed that, in the present case, the rabbinic reconfigurations tend, if anything, to reinforce the essential message of the biblical portrayals

---

* Originally published in Nili Sacher Fox et al. (eds.), *Mishneh Todah: Studies in Deuteronomy and Its Cultural Environment in Honor of Jeffery H. Tigay* (Winona Lake, IN: Eisenbrauns, 2009), pp. 487–508. Reprinted with permission from Eisenbrauns.

Author's note: I present this study in tribute to a colleague of long standing, Jeffrey Tigay, who combines in his scholarly work the comparative study of the Hebrew Bible in its ancient Near Eastern context with a deep interest in the great Judaic tradition of post-biblical exegesis.

[1] Louis Ginzberg, *The Legends of the Jews* (7 vols. with notes by Boaz Cohen; Philadelphia: Jewish Publication Society, 1909–38).

themselves. In effect, they dramatize the seriousness of the offenses committed by the biblical personalities by assigning to their perpetrators roles that are more in consonance with contemporary rabbinic prototypes of leadership and authority. Thus, even as Doeg the Edomite is depicted as an eminent Torah scholar rather than the chief shepherd that he was in the biblical narrative, he is condemned for the same essential offenses. This turns out to be true as well for the three other excluded persons. It is my sense, therefore, that the way to understand why these four private persons, specifically, were denied a share in the World to Come according to the Mishnah is by probing the biblical narratives and then examining how the later tradition reconfigured them.

Background for an Understanding of m. Sanh. 10:2

M. Sanh. 10:1 opens as follows:

> כל ישראל יש להם חלק לעולם הבא. All Israelites have a share in the world to come. As it is said (Isa 60:21): "And your people, all of them are righteous; forever (לעולם) shall they possess the land (ארץ). They are the shoot of my plantings, my handiwork in whom I glory."

In its original context, the cited biblical verse is part of a prophecy of restoration: as a nation loved by God, Israel will possess its land forever. In the manner of Midrash, the Mishnah interprets adverbial לעולם "forever" as alluding to that other "world," which is inhabited by the departed. Most probably, the author of this Mishnah saw in the word ארץ "land, earth" a further spatial allusion to another world. A similar homily on adverbial לעולם occurs in the very next mishnah, 10:3, where we read that the generation of the flood will have no share in the World to Come. There, the Mishnah cites Gen 6:3: "Then YHWH said: My spirit shall not abide in humankind forever (לעולם), being that he is only flesh. His days shall be limited to one hundred twenty years." This is taken to mean not only that the human life span would thenceforth be limited but also that the generation of the flood will be denied an afterlife because of their corruption.

Chapter 10 comes at a special point in the sequence of tractate Sanhedrin, and we hold to the rule that the arrangement of the Mishnah (סדר המשנה) is significant (b. ʿErub. 54b). Chapter 10 interrupts a systematic review of "the four methods of capital punishment imposed by the court" (ארבע מיתות בית דין). This review began in chap. 7 and is resumed in chap. 11. Sequence suggests, therefore, that there is a thematic link between the death penalty and the entitlement to the World to Come. We are to understand, in the first place, that persons sentenced to death by the court did not, solely as a consequence of their crimes and conviction, lose their share in the World to Come. Denial of this entitlement comes from another sphere; it is a divine judgment. In this regard, it may be significant that chap. 9 concludes with a statement regarding the punishment to be imposed on an "alien" (זר) who enters the sacred precincts of the temple, an act calling for the death penalty and forbidden in the Torah (Num 1:51; 3:10, 38; 18:7). Whereas Rabbi Akiba decreed that the offender must be executed, it was the view of the sages that his punishment should be "death at the hands of heaven" (מיתה בידי שמים).

Enter chap. 10. After a general statement, the Mishnah proceeds to specify exceptions to the rule, enumerating individuals and categories of persons who have lost their shares in the World to Come as a consequence of particularly heinous acts. The pattern of beginning with a blanket statement and then listing exceptions is frequent in the composition of the Mishnah, and we more or less expect it. And so 10:1 continues as follows:

> ואלו שאין להם חלק לעולם הבא However, these are the ones who do not have a share in the World to Come.

The first series of exceptions includes persons who deny basic religious tenets, such as the doctrine that the resurrection of the dead is derived from the Torah and that the Torah is divinely revealed (one who denies that there is another world can hardly expect a share in it!). Also included is the *epicurus*, an ambiguous term that seems to indicate an individual who actively disrespects the commandments and teachings of the Torah, as would a Hellenizing Jew. Individual sages add further exceptions, such as one who reads "the external books" or who invokes God's name in magical incantations during the process of healing. An early sage, Abba Shaul, denied the share to anyone "who pronounces the name of God according to its consonants" (ההוגה את השם באותיותיו), a cryptic prohibition that has been variously interpreted. Individuals such as these have no share in the World to Come, for by showing flagrant disregard for fundamental norms of rabbinic Jewish belief, they had effectively divorced themselves from the religious community. It is interesting to find in the Mishnah so great an emphasis on theological issues.

There is much more to be said about these exceptions, but it is the second Mishnah of chap. 10 that will be the focus of the present study. It reads as follows:

> Three kings and four private persons (הדיוטות) have no share in the World to Come. The three kings are: Jeroboam, Ahab, and Manasseh. Rabbi Judah says: Manasseh does, indeed, have a share in the World to Come, as it is written (2 Chron 33:13): "Then he prayed to him [= to God] and he responded to his entreaty and listened to his supplication, and restored him to Jerusalem, to his kingship." But they [= the sages] said to him: To his kingship he restored him, but he did not restore him to the life of the World to Come. The four private persons are: Balaam, Doeg, Ahithophel, and Gehazi.

The Mishnah continues in this vein, enumerating others who have no share in the World to Come; whole generations of humans, residents of entire towns, and classes of sinners.

The exclusion of the three kings is readily explicable though not without its own subtleties. The difference of opinion regarding the Judean king, Manasseh, reflects differing attitudes toward the tradition of the Chronicler regarding Manasseh's repentance, whether or not it had completely reversed the condemnatory tradition of 2 Kings.

The term הדיוט is an Aramaic-Hebrew rendition of the Greek *idiotēs*, a nuanced term that bears many meanings. As used in the Mishnah, it contrasts with public figures, for example, civilian judges in contrast to professional judges, ordinary priests in contrast to the High Priest, and here, private individuals in contrast to kings.

The selection of the four is immediately problematic in that it poses a problem of identity. Balaam was not an Israelite; Num 23:7 states that he was summoned, or invited, from Aram. This anomaly did not go unnoticed, of course. Bartenura, the classic commentary on the Mishnah, echoes rabbinic interpretations by explaining that Balaam might have qualified for a share in the World to Come as one of "the righteous of the Gentiles" (חסידי אומות העולם).[2] Balaam at first acknowledged the sovereignty of the God of Israel and pronounced blessings over his people, Israel. However, because he later conspired to harm Israel, he was denied a share in the World to Come. This "slide" in Balaam's persona will be discussed in due course.

Rabbinic tradition surely identified the other three commoners as Israelites, else the exceptions would be out of sync with the rule! The personal name, גיחזי (also written defectively as גחזי), may well be non-Hebraic, even non-Semitic. No acceptable etymology has been found for it, and its morphology is highly unusual in Semitic personal names. Rabbinic tradition, which I will discuss further below, undoubtedly took this name as Semitic, based on a derivation from the verb חזי "to see, envision", expressive of the clairvoyance they attributed to this prophet's apprentice. This is, however, an Aggadic interpretation. Doeg is called "the Edomite" (האדומי), but this gentilic can also indicate place of residence rather than nationality, as is true of the gentilic הגילוני "the Gilonite", which identifies Ahithophel, David's counselor, as one who hailed from Giloh. We shall see how later tradition derived the gentilic האדומי in a way that obviates the identity problem.

And yet, one cannot escape the impression that there is something odd about the specific selection of these four individuals. Can it be that the authors of the Mishnah were aware of the identity problem, not only in the obvious case of Balaam but also with respect to Doeg and Gehazi, at the very least? After all, the kings of Israel and Judah employed non-Israelite mercenaries and other personnel, just as practitioners of prophetic and cultic arts were often transnational. In fact, some modern scholars have speculated that even Ahithophel was of non-Israelite origin. Benjamin Mazar has suggested that he was a Canaanite in David's service.[3] Worth noting in this regard is the fact that in the narrative of Ahi-

---

[2] See משניות תפארת ישראל (vol. 1; New York: Pardes, 1952–53) 249, leaf 125a, comment of Bartenura ad loc. *m. Sanhedrin* 10:2.

[3] See B. Mazar, "Ahitophel the Gilonite" (Hebrew), *Encyclopaedia Biblica* 1:226–27.

thophel's betrayal of David we encounter repeated references to the Cherethites and Pelethites, David's foreign mercenaries, and to soldiers from Philistine Gath, as well as mention of Ittai the Gittite and Hushai the Archite, all intensely loyal to David. It would not strike us as strange, therefore, if Saul's chief shepherd, Doeg, was of Edomite origin or if Elisha's apprentice, Gehazi, was a foreign practitioner or even if Ahithophel, David's erstwhile counselor, turned out to be of non-Israelite origin. For their part, the sages may be insinuating that these integrated, shall we say, "naturalized," individuals were capable of perfidies that born Israelites could not bring themselves to commit. This seems to be implied most noticeably in the narrative about Doeg the Edomite, as we shall see. In sum, I remain mystified by the identity factor.

The Four Private Persons in the Biblical Narratives

Gehazi

The case that first attracted my interest is the last in the list, Gehazi, apprentice (Heb. נער) of the prophet Elisha. The part of the Elisha cycle that is specifically relevant to our discussion is the incident involving Naaman, the Aramean general, as recounted in 2 Kings 5. The prophet Elisha was continually involved in ongoing relations between Northern Israel and the Arameans, who posed an ongoing threat to Israel. Now, the king of Israel (in fact, Jehoram—see 2 Kgs 3:1) received a request from the king of the Arameans (the Ben-Hadad of 2 Kgs 6:24, passim). He asked that the prophet of YHWH in Samaria, namely Elisha, cure his general, Naaman, from an acute skin ailment, inaccurately identified in modern times with leprosy. Naaman had learned about the prophet's unusual healing powers from an Israelite girl, captured during a raid across the Jordan. She felt compassion for her master and informed her mistress about Elisha. Jehoram was alarmed by this request, suspecting that the Aramean king was entrapping him by presenting him with an uncertain task. If he failed to come through, the Arameans would have a pretext to attack Israel. Elisha reassured the king of Israel: "Why have you torn your garments? Let him come to me, so he may know that there is a prophet in Israel" (2 Kgs 5:8).

Elisha sent a messenger to Naaman, instructing him to bathe seven times in the waters of the Jordan. After first scoffing at the prophet's prescribed treatment and feeling slighted, Naaman was persuaded by his entourage to do as instructed, and behold—he was immediately cured! At that point Naaman became a believer:

> Then he returned to the man of God, he and his entire corps. He arrived, and stood in attendance before him, and said: "Behold, I truly realize that there is no god in all the earth except in Israel. Now, then, please accept a gift from your servant." Then he [= Elisha] said: "As Yahweh lives, before whom I have stood in attendance, if I ever accept." Though he pressed him, he refused to accept. Then Naaman said: "Even if not, let your servant be given two mule-loads of earth,

> for your servant will never again offer up either burnt sacrifices or sacred meals to other gods, only to YHWH." (2 Kgs 5:15–17)

Naaman quickly amended his statement, however, asking Elisha to pardon him for bowing down before Rimon, god of the Arameans, whenever it was his duty to escort the Aramean king into the pagan temple. Elisha then wished Naaman a good journey.

What happens next is unexpected. Gehazi was disappointed that his master, Elisha, had refused the gifts that Naaman, "that Aramean" (note the ethnic slur) had brought with him. He caught up with Naaman and fabricated a story to secure the gifts.

> Then he [Gehazi] said: "Be well! My master [Elisha] sent me (with a message), as follows: 'Behold, just now two members of the prophets' guild have come to me from the hill country of Ephraim. Give them a talent of silver and two suits of clothing.'" (2 Kgs 5:22)

Naaman doubled the amount of silver, which Gehazi stashed away together with the garments. Gehazi then returned to stand in attendance once again before his master, Elisha:

> Then Elisha said: "Where have you been, Gehazi?" He answered: "Your servant has not gone (לא הלך) anywhere in particular." Then he said to him: "Did not my thoughts go along (לא לבי הלך), when a man got down from his chariot to meet you? Is this a time to accept the silver, and to accept clothing; and olive groves and vineyards and sheep and cattle and male and female slaves? May the leprosy of Naaman cling to you and to your descendants forever!" He [Gehazi] departed from his presence, leprous as white as snow. (2 Kgs 5:25–27)

Gehazi was guilty of at least two acts of betrayal. He lied to Elisha about his whereabouts and activity, and he lied to Naaman in a way that cast his master Elisha in a less favorable light. Elisha had not dispatched him to Naaman to ask for gifts. Gehazi disguised his request by saying that the gifts were for someone else, not for his master. This subterfuge was intended to make Elisha's change of heart more understandable, but it was a further lie, nonetheless, because Gehazi clearly coveted the gifts for himself. But there is much more to the story, which epitomizes the incremental consequences of deceit.

Ironically, it was customary for prophets and "men of God" (at times, one and the same person) to receive gifts from people whom they had helped. Thus, Saul was concerned that he had nothing left to offer the man of God as a gift (Heb. תשורה) when appearing before him in need of his clairvoyance (1 Sam 9:7). It was not at all improper, therefore, for Naaman to offer gifts to Elisha. From all that we read about this prophet, he lived modestly and depended on the support and hospitality of others, which he readily accepted. In this instance, his insistent refusal to accept gifts from Naaman had more to do with the particular status of the client, an Aramean general close to the Aramean king. We must remember that Elisha had taken the initiative in offering his services in order to protect his people and his land from Aramean attack by dramatizing the power of Israel's God. For Elisha to be rewarded materially would detract from his stature.

This dynamic emerges from the narrative itself. In his statement of refusal, Elisha interjected a parenthetical remark to the effect that he stood in attendance before YHWH, God of Israel, a relationship conveyed by idiomatic עמד לפני-. As counterpoint, Naaman "stands in attendance" before Elisha in a reverent manner when he declares his faith in YHWH as the true God. He swears off sacrificing "to other gods" (לאלהים אחרים), using language that resonates with the Decalogue. Finally, Naaman desired to take with him some earth from the land of Israel, presumably for constructing an earthen altar in his native land on which to offer sacrifices to the God of Israel. How sensitive is the observation of the medieval commentator, Joseph Kaspi, who, in commenting on this passage, cites Exod 20:24: "And should you construct an earthen altar (מזבח אדמה) to me."[4]

It would help to delve further into the special role of Gehazi and his relationship with his master, Elisha. We are first introduced to Gehazi in 2 Kings 4, in the context of Elisha's relationship with a Shunamite woman who had been hospitable to him and whose son he later revived. Gehazi is repeatedly sent out to greet her or to fetch her. In one instance, he pushed her away from Elisha when she had grasped the prophet's feet. Apparently, Gehazi considered it improper, or even dangerous, for a petitioner to get that close to the prophet. In another encounter, Elisha dispatched Gehazi with his staff to revive the woman's son, which suggests that the apprentice was, indeed, a capable healer able to act independently. But Gehazi's actions were ineffectual in that instance, so that Elisha himself had to undertake the task. Finally, in 2 Kgs 8:4–6, we find Gehazi conversing with none other than the king of Israel about the exploits of his master, while making representations on behalf of the woman whose son Elisha had revived but who now had other troubles. These tales give the impression that Gehazi was greatly trusted by Elisha and that he enjoyed high status. Gehazi's betrayal of this trust in the case of Naaman was, therefore, more than a personal affront to Elisha; it threatened the prophet's international stature and effectiveness and hence the fortunes of all Israelites.

Doeg the Edomite

We first encounter Doeg, second in the list, in 1 Samuel 21. We read that David, fleeing Saul's rage, arrived alone and bedraggled at the town of priests, Nob. There he was warmly welcomed by its head priest, Ahimelech, who was unaware, according to the story, that Saul was seeking David's death. David concocted a story to explain to the priest of Nob why he had come without his

---

[4] *Mikraʾot Gedolot Ha-Keter: 1 & 2 Kings* (ed. Menahem Cohen; Ramat-Gan: Bar-Ilan University Press, 1995) s.v. 2 Kgs 5:17.

men, and he requested food for himself and his men and a worthy sword. After forswearing Ahimelech to secrecy and assuring him that his men were ritually pure and not on a military mission, David was provided with consecrated bread and given Goliath's sword.

It is at this point that we read an aside, almost a stage whisper:

> Present there was a man, one of Saul's courtiers, at that time confined in the presence of YHWH, and his name was Doeg, the Edomite, chief of the shepherds in Saul's service. (1 Sam 21:8)

Doeg next appears in 1 Sam 22:6–23. Saul is holding court in Ramah, having just been informed that David and his men had been located and that Jonathan was in their company, giving aid and comfort to David. Saul complained that no one of his inner circle had revealed these goings on to him. At that point, Doeg spoke out:

> Doeg, the Edomite, then spoke up, as he was standing among Saul's courtiers: He said: "I saw the son of Jesse arriving at Nob, with Ahimelech, son of Ahitub. He made oracular inquiry of YHWH on his behalf, and gave him provisions, and the sword of Goliath, the Philistine, he also gave him." (1 Sam 22:9–10)

We note that the earlier narrative in 1 Samuel 21 had made no mention of oracular inquiry. Accepting Doeg's version, however, Saul summoned Ahimelech and his entire clan and accused them of disloyalty, including undertaking oracular inquiry on David's behalf as Doeg had reported (1 Sam 22:12–13). Most interesting is Ahimelech's protesting response:

> Who among all of your courtiers is as trusted as David, the king's son-in-law; who acts under your orders, and is honored in your household? *But would I now commence* to undertake oracular inquiry of God on his behalf? God forbid that I do so! Let the king not find fault with his servant or with any of my father's house; for your servant knew nothing whatever about all this. (1 Sam 22:14– 15; emphasis mine)

The formulation of these statements is admittedly difficult. Samuel Meier suggests that the interpretation of 1 Sam 22:15 could go either way; it could be either a denial of the charge of undertaking oracular inquiry on David's behalf or an admission to the charge, following up the priest's tacit confession that he had given aid and comfort to David.[5] The crux of the matter is the Hebrew היום החלותי, which lends itself to several interpretations. The NEB has "Is this the first time?" whereas the NJPS has "This is the first time". Both of these translations agree with Meier's analysis, in principle. The translation of the Hebrew given here (in italics) accepts the interrogative mode but understands the priest's response quite differently. This response was of two parts: in the first instance,

[5] S. A. Meier, "The Heading of Psalm 52," *HAR* 14 (1994) 149–50.

Ahimelech admits to giving succor to David but insists that he should not be blamed for doing so. He claims that he only knew David as the king's intimate and was unaware of the enmity between Saul and David. In contrast, he emphatically denies the serious charge that he undertook oracular inquiry on David's behalf. This was something he would not do, God forbid!

I take the view here that Doeg's accusation was a fabrication, a clever lie. He began with a true report of the priest's aid and comfort to David and his men but invidiously attached a false charge of a much more serious nature. We should clarify the phenomenon of oracular inquiry itself, how and when it was utilized and by whom and why it was so serious an exercise. Doeg's accusation, if believed by Saul, would be guaranteed to incriminate Ahimelech. The priest's alleged undertaking of oracular inquiry on David's behalf could not be excused on the pretext that he did not know that David had fallen out of Saul's favor. This would have made no difference, because oracular access was a guarded right, an indicator of divine favor and a portent of victory. When, later on, we read that YHWH did not respond to Saul's oracular inquiry (1 Sam 28:6), we understand that the denial of oracular access was a signal that Saul was about to be rejected as the anointed of YHWH and lose his kingdom to David. Turning to a medium in desperation, Saul conjured up the prophet Samuel, who revealed this to him in no uncertain terms (1 Sam 28:15–17). In contrast, David, the chosen of God, persisted in successful oracular inquiries of God (1 Sam 23:2, 30:8). In our view, Ahimelech was being truthful in his denial and was a tragic victim, along with all the slain, of those who opposed God's plan of divine selection.

Doeg emerges as an evildoer who played on Saul's rage against David. In an effort to ingratiate himself to Saul, he incited an atrocity, carried out by his own hand. Saul ordered his elite guard to slay the priests, but "they were unwilling to raise their hand to strike down the priests of YHWH" (1 Sam 22:17). Unhesitatingly, Doeg carried out Saul's savage order, slaying not only the priests but the entire population of Nob. The fact that Doeg is identified as an Edomite renders his extreme brutality more comprehensible. There is the implication that no true Israelite would have obeyed Saul or even exceeded his order.

Of particular interest in this regard is the epilogue to the story. A lone survivor named Abiathar managed to escape to David and report to him on the massacre at Nob:

> Then David said to Abiathar: "I was aware on that day that Doeg, the Edomite, was present, and that he would surely report to Saul. It is I who has caused the loss of life of your entire clan. Reside with me; have no fear! For whoever seeks your life must seek mine, as well. For it will be my duty to protect you." (1 Sam 22:22–23)

David's feelings of guilt further corroborate the interpretation that Doeg was a suspicious character who should have been watched more carefully. The caption to Psalm 52 also attests to a negative judgment of Doeg's character: "When Doeg, the Edomite, came to inform Saul, saying to him: 'David has arrived at the home of Ahimelech.'" When we proceed to read the psalm itself, we see that it is of the didactic-wisdom genre, verbose in characterizing the deceitful and false, whom God will duly punish. Once again, we observe how the conduct of individuals who served leaders, prophets, and kings and were close to the centers of power figured in the ongoing, biblical narrative of Israel's history.

Ahithophel

Biblical references to Ahithophel, third in the list of commoners, are bracketed in 2 Samuel 15–17 and appear in the context of Absalom's rebellion against his father, David, king of all Israel. Ahithophel's name also appears in a genealogical reference to his son, one of David's elite warriors (2 Sam 23:34). We first encounter Ahithophel out of the blue, in 2 Sam 15:12, and are told that Absalom was at that time in Hebron, fulfilling a vow to sacrifice to YHWH. This was his pretext for being there; in fact, he was plotting rebellion against David and had proclaimed himself king. We read that he had won over large numbers of Israelites to his side.

Absalom sent for Ahithophel, David's premier counselor (יועץ), who hailed from Giloh, near Jerusalem (see 1 Chr 27:33–34). We are to understand that Ahithophel promptly defected to Absalom, although the text does not make this explicit at this point. We next encounter Ahithophel at Absalom's side in Jerusalem (2 Sam 16:15), where he is holding court after David had already fled. A lot had transpired between the first mention of Ahithophel and the later scene in Jerusalem. In the interim, David used his wits to survive, with the help of old friends and allies. However, those events do not relate to Ahithophel directly and need not concern us here. Suffice it to cite David's entreaty to YHWH on the Mount of Olives as he was fleeing from Jerusalem: "Please, YHWH, frustrate Ahithophel's counsel" (2 Sam 15:31).

Ahithophel's defection had presented David with an added challenge at a particularly dangerous time. He must thwart the designs of his former counselor, whose sagacity was well known to him. We are never told what motivated Ahithophel to change sides, but personal ambition must have surely been part of the story. To understand what made Ahithophel's defection so worrisome to David requires insight into the intimacy that normally obtained between a royal counselor and his king. We read of Ahithophel's credibility and high status in 2 Sam 16:23, which reads like an explanatory gloss:

> The counsel given by Ahithophel in those days was received like an oracle sought from God; such was all of the counsel of Ahithophel, both for David and for Absalom.

Would that we knew more about the role of the יועץ "counselor" in biblical Israel, but the Ahithophel episode provides virtually the only biblical narrative that sheds light on the specific functions of a royal counselor, distinct from prophets and men of God. In the unfolding story, we encounter complicated intrigue, as Absalom, like David, faced critical decisions that risked death and defeat. In Jerusalem, Ahithophel was invited by Absalom to offer his עצה "counsel, design" (2 Sam 16:20). His first bit of advice was to suggest to Absalom that he have intercourse with his father's concubines, left to guard the palace, in view of all of the people (2 Sam 16:21–22). This was a brazen act of arrogance, reminiscent of Reuben's defilement of his father Jacob's concubines, for which he was later cursed (Gen 35:22, 49:3–4). Ahithophel reasoned that this sort of behavior would harden the resolve of Absalom's forces, but it may have shocked many of the people in Jerusalem. In any event, the biblical narrator undoubtedly meant for this outrageous act to presage the undoing of both Ahithophel and Absalom. By their own excesses, the wicked bring themselves down!

David's tactical challenge was to get to Transjordan, where he had reliable allies and where he could better position himself for a decisive battle against Absalom's forces in the open field. So long as he still remained west of the Jordan he was vulnerable. The question facing Absalom was, therefore, whether he should seize the moment and attack David immediately or take the time to amass a much larger army. Now, David had cleverly assigned Hushai, the Archite, a foreigner in his loyal service, to operate as a double agent who would work his way into Absalom's confidence, and so it was. In Absalom's council of war, Ahithophel laid out his plan. He would assemble a force of 12,000 men, which he would command, and pursue David's weary forces at night. If he should be able to slay David himself, the rest of David's forces would flee in disarray and would eventually come over to Absalom's side.

At first, this plan appealed to Absalom, but, as was often the case, the king sought "a second opinion" from Hushai, who argued that, if David's forces, known for their bravery, scored an initial success, the reaction would be that Absalom had failed altogether. Hushai emphasized that David knew better than to spend the night in proximity to his forces and would be hard to locate. It would be better to recruit a large army, from Dan to Beersheba, and carry out an overwhelming attack on David. This plan was acceptable to Absalom and there was unanimous agreement to reject Ahithophel's counsel, at which point the biblical narrator comments:

> YHWH had decreed that Ahithophel's good advice be nullified in order that YHWH might bring ruin on Absalom. (2 Sam 17:14b)

Herein is the irony: Ahithophel's plan was sound and would have, indeed, led to David's defeat, as we gather from the message Hushai secretly dispatched in haste to David through priests loyal to him:

> Do not spend the night at the fords of the wilderness, but cross over at once, otherwise the king and all the troops with him will be annihilated. (2 Sam 17:16; see further vv. 21–22)

It is fascinating to contemplate how the ambitions of Ahithophel and of Absalom collided. In outlining his plan, Ahithophel speaks consistently in the first person: "I shall recruit," "I shall actively pursue," "I shall come upon him," "I shall restore" (2 Sam 17:1–3). In contrast, Hushai's plan called for Absalom himself to command the forces and claim the victory, a scenario that played to the usurper's vanity.

Ahithophel's acumen is never questioned; only his evil intentions are decried. It took divine intervention to undermine Ahithophel's counsel, because it was offered in support of an enemy of David, the chosen of God. Ultimately, David returned to Jerusalem, Absalom was slain, and David was overcome with grief. As for Ahithophel, he committed suicide (2 Sam 17:23), unable to bear his rejection. A prominent individual, an actor in the succession narratives that carry into 1 Kings, Ahithophel met a bad end because he used his abilities to the potential detriment of all Israel.

Balaam, Son of Beor

I have saved Balaam, first in the list, for last because of the elaborateness of the biblical sources and of the rabbinic-midrashic interpretations associated with him and also because the biblical view of him is dynamic in itself. Balaam is heroic in the earliest, poetic sources, the Balaam orations, but less so in the primary prose narrative; he is actually insidious in the later, Priestly tradition. I have devoted considerable scholarly effort to interpreting the Balaam orations, as well as the entire Balaam pericope preserved in Numbers 22–24. The reader can find an extensive treatment of these themes, including discussion of the Balaam texts from Deir ʿAlla, in my Anchor Bible commentary to Numbers 21–36.[6]

What emerges from a critical reading of the Balaam pericope is that the poetic orations and the prose narrative of Numbers differ from each other significantly in their respective evaluations of Balaam. In the poems, Balaam sees himself, to be sure, as subservient to the will of YHWH (and of El and Shadday and Elyon). He recognizes that the Israelites had been irreversibly blessed and that he was powerless to curse them. At the same time, Balaam is personally impressed by what he observes. He extols Israel's heroism and special relation to its God. He is perceptive and responds to his own sensations. In the prose narrative, however, Balaam pronounces blessings instead of the expected curses only because he is totally controlled by the God of Israel, leaving the reader to infer that, for his own part, he was prepared to curse Israel but was constrained from doing so. He comes across as a mechanical practitioner of his arts, who does nothing to harm Israel only because he cannot.

The prose narrative of Numbers 22–24 lines up with the statement in Deut 23:5–6 mandating the permanent exclusion of Ammonites and Moabites from the community of YHWH:

> because they did not greet you with bread and water when you were leaving Egypt, and because he hired Balaam, son of Beor against you.

[6] B. A. Levine, *Numbers 21–36* (AB 4A; New York: Doubleday, 2000) 137–275.

> But YHWH, your God, refused to listen to Balaam, and YHWH, your God, overturned the curse into a blessing for you, because YHWH, your God, loved you. (Deut 23:5–6; compare with Neh 13:2)

In contrast, the earlier, heroic tradition of the Balaam orations correlates with the prophetic endorsement in Mic 6:5:

> My people! Remember what Balak, king of Moab plotted,
> And what Balaam, son of Beor answered him,
> [As you marched] from Shittim to Gilgal,
> So that the triumphs of YHWH may be known.

In Micah's prophecy, Balaam is credited with refusing to do Balak's bidding on his own, without reference to a divine command, thereby implying a degree of courage on his part. Balaam's spurning of Balak's design helped to make known the triumphs of YHWH. In contrast, it is only one step from Deuteronomy 23 to Numbers 31, a Priestly chronicle of the Midianite war, in which we find two references to Balaam:

> And they slew the kings of Midian, along with their other victims; Evi, Reqem, Zur, Hur, and Reba, the five kings of Midian. They also put Balaam, son of Beor, to the sword. (Num 31:8)
> They [= the Midianite women] were the very ones who were detrimental to the Israelites in the Balaam affair (בדבר בלעם) by instigating sacrilegious rebellion against YHWH in the Peor incident (על דבר פעור), so that a plague struck the community of YHWH. (Num 31:16)

Num 31:8 is repeated, with some changes, in Josh 13:21–22, where Balaam is labeled הקוסם "the diviner", hardly a complimentary title in the biblical view. Thus, the Priestly tradition links Balaam to the Baal Peor incident in Numbers 25, especially the Priestly component in 25:6–18, which triggered the Midianite war of Numbers 31. It is interesting that one of the lookouts that Balaam visited was "the summit of Peor, which overlooked the wilderness" (Num 23:28). In effect, the sinful incident at Baal Peor occurred in the same immediate area, already alluding to a possible connection between Balaam and Baal Peor. As a result of this sort of inner-biblical exegesis, Balaam is exposed in Numbers 31 as the one who came up with the idea of employing Midianite women to lure the Israelites into pagan worship, with its disastrous consequences. In fact, NJPS translates Num 31:16, admittedly a difficult verse, to say this: "Yet they were the very ones who, at the bidding of Balaam (בדבר בלעם) induced the Israelites to trespass," and so on. Either way, the link between Balaam and Baal Peor is clearly established.

This leaves two questions to be explored. (1) Why the radical shift in the evaluation of Balaam? (2) What made the Baal Peor incident so important? We can only speculate as to the historical situation that occasioned the hostility against Balaam that animates the Priestly writings. His earlier, heroic depiction is more understandable; it is shared by the recently discovered Balaam texts from Deir ʿAlla, dated to ca. 800 B.C.E.[7]

As noted, Numbers 31 is a Priestly text that reports on a war with the Midianites, and it is there that the negative judgment on Balaam is explicitly expressed by its record that he was slain along with the kings of Midian.[8] We must distinguish, however, between the Midianites of the historical books of the Bible (see Judges 6–8; compare with Isa 9:3), who were foreign enemies with whom the Israelites did battle in the course of securing the promised land, and the Midianites of Numbers 25 and 31. Noting that some of the names of the five kings of Midian are identical with stations on the Nabatean trade route, we can probably identify the Midianites of Numbers 25 and 31 as early Arabs, the precursors of the Nabateans. Perhaps they were in reality the Qedarite Arabs ruled by Geshem the Arab of Neh 2:19, 6:1–2, who is also known from external sources.[9]

Simply put, Priestly writers retrojected the hostility from contemporary Arabs, experienced by Nehemiah during the period of the return under the Achaemenids, into the much earlier period of the Israelite settlement of Canaan. These same authors cast Balaam as the evil seer who did Israel harm. Based on the views of other scholars, I came to this resolution in my Anchor Bible commentary on Numbers.

Something should be said about the special significance of the Baal Peor incident. The Hebrew Bible never allows the reader to forget what happened at Baal Peor, which was, after all, only one of several episodes of "backsliding" that brought plague and death upon the Israelites. In recalling the incident, Hosea has the God of Israel saying the following:

> I found Israel [as pleasing]
> As grapes in the wilderness;
> Your forefathers seemed to me
> Like the first fig to ripen on a fig-tree.
> But when they arrived at Baal Peor,
> They became devotees of a shameful idol,
> Then they became just as detested
> As they had been loved. (Hos 9:10)

---

[7] These texts commemorate the exploits of one *blʿm brbʿr*, who saved his land and people in Transjordan from a calamity announced by celestial omens.

[8] For its part, Deut 23:5–6 associates Balaam with the Ammonites and Moabites, not with the Midianites, but shifts of this sort in identifying the Transjordanian peoples are frequent in the Hebrew Bible.

[9] An inscription mentioning Geshem was discovered at Dedan (el-ʿOula) and an inscription mentioning Qainu son of Geshem the Qedarite was discovered at Tell el-Maskhuta in Egypt (E. Stern, *The Archaeology of the Land of the Bible*, vol. 2: *The Assyrian, Babylonian, and Persian Periods [732–332 B.C.E .]* [New York: Doubleday, 2001] 420).

Subsequently, the Deuteronomist (4:3–4) admonishes the Israelites to remember what happened in the wake of the Baal Peor episode, when the sinful perished but all who adhered to YHWH remained alive and well. The contrast is dramatic and suggests that the Baal Peor incident was a crisis that threatened the continued existence of the Israelites as a people, and their successful settlement of Canaan. Finally, Psalm 106, in its review of Israel's long list of sins, recalls the disloyalty of the people at Baal Peor (v. 28).

What made the Baal Peor incident so crucial is that it was the first major sin of the new generation of Israelites, heroic fighters who conquered the towns of Transjordan (Numbers 21). It seems that no sooner had God granted them great victories and brought them near to the Jordan, than the new generation of Israelites, who had not known Egypt, replicated the disloyalty of their forebears. This was particularly discouraging, and that Balaam was behind this unfortunate lapse was sufficient to condemn him.

Rabbinic Profiles

The Jerusalem Talmud at *m. Sanh.* 10:2 provides an Aggadic treatment of the four commoners. It is more structured than the same section of the Babylonian Talmud, which is, however, more profuse (the Babylonian Talmud registers פרק חלק "the Chapter of the 'Share'" as the 11th chapter of tractate *Sanhedrin*, not the 10th chapter). I will, therefore, draw on the Jerusalem Talmud, which takes up the case of each of the four excluded private persons and clarifies his particular offense.[10] With Louis Ginzberg's *Legends of the Jews* in hand, I will then proceed to round out the profiles. Here, the order of the Mishnah's list will be followed.

Balaam, Son of Beor

The relevant passage in the Jerusalem Talmud opens with the fundamental question:

> וכי מה עשה בלעם הרשע What is it that Balaam, the wicked, had done? It is because he provided Balak, son of Zippor, with a plan to defeat Israel by the sword. He said to him: "The God of this people despises harlotry; therefore, station your daughters in a licentious manner, and you will gain dominance over them." (*y. Sanh.* 28d; 1321–22)

This attribution of conspiracy to Balaam amplifies the Priestly view of him, epitomized in Numbers 25 and 31. As seen by the sages, Balaam had found a way to harm Israel insidiously after being unable to do so through the practice of his prophetic and magical arts. He succeeded in bringing down God's wrath on the Israelites, so that the Moabites (and Midianites) ultimately achieved what they

---

[10] Citations are from *Talmud Yerushalmi* (Jerusalem: Academy of the Hebrew Language, 2001).

had been unable to by warfare. The Talmud weaves an elaborate tale of how Midianite young women lured Israelites into their latticed booths, presumably to buy linen garments, and then step by step seduced the Israelites, amidst imbibing heady wine, to have sexual relations with them. These harlots insisted, however, that they would indulge their Israelite visitors only if the Israelites first worshiped Baal Peor, represented by a small figurine. In time, large numbers of Israelite men succumbed to the attraction of pagan, cultic immorality. In effect, Balaam exploited the services of Moses himself. He created a situation whereby Moses was compelled to order the Israelite chieftains to slay people who had worshiped Baal Peor. This was followed, in the Priestly version, by a plague unleashed by God, in which thousands of Israelites perished. In this way, one could say that Balaam exploited the God of Israel as well! The Talmud concludes with a colorful dialogue between Phinehas, the avenging priest, and Balaam:

> When the Israelites set about to exact the vengeance of the Lord against the Midianites, they found Balaam there. What had he come to do? He had come to collect the reward for the twenty-four thousand of the Israelites who died by his doing at Shittim (Num 25:9). Phinehas said to him: "Neither your own orders have you carried out, nor have you carried out those of Balak. You have not carried out your own orders, for he (= God) said to you: 'Do not go with the messengers of Balak,' yet you went. You did not carry out those of Balak, who said to you: 'Go, curse the Israelites,' instead you blessed them. Nevertheless, I will not cheat you of your reward." This explains what is written (Josh 13:22): "And also Balaam, the diviner, the Israelites slew, in addition to the other they had slain." What does "in addition to the others they had slain" mean? [It means] that he was of equivalent weight to all of their slain. (*y. Sanh.* 29a)

Ginzberg's rabbinic profile of Balaam (*Legends* 3:354–82) goes beyond the Baal Peor incident to include Balaam's role as the one who pronounced the orations. Even these beautiful words are interpreted in a manner that makes them harmful to Israel, in effect turning Balaam's blessings into curses! The involvement of Balaam with the Israelites was his own undoing. He is depicted as a tragic figure who, before he turned against Israel, had rivaled Moses among the nations of the world. In the end, he was slain along with the kings of Midian and also lost the share in the World to Come that might have been his. He had said that he would share the heroic fate of Israel's fallen warriors, but instead he ended up sharing the ignominious fate of Israel's enemies. It is interesting that Balaam remains in the role given to him in the biblical narrative, whereas the sin of Baal Peor, which is attributed to him, is recast in the spirit of the orgiastic cults of the Greco-Roman period.

Doeg

In the case of Doeg the Edomite, the Jerusalem Talmud at *m. Sanh.* 10:2 provides only a limited profile:

> דואג אדם גדול בתורה היה Doeg was a great Torah scholar. The Israelites came and inquired of David: "As regards the Bread of Display: What is the ruling as to whether it overrides the Sabbath?" He said to them: "Its arrangement overrides the Sabbath, but neither its kneading nor its preparation overrides the Sabbath." Now, Doeg was there, and he said: "Who is this person who presumes to issue rulings of law in my presence?" They said to him: "It is David, son of Jesse." Whereupon he immediately went and counseled Saul, King of Israel, to put Nob, the town of priests, to death. (*y. Sanh.* 29a; 1323)

The key to decoding this tale lies in the halakhic ruling pertaining to the Bread of Display. In the biblical narrative, one of Ahimelech's offenses was that he gave David and his hungry men some of last week's sanctified bread, which had been removed from the offering table, a ritual performed each Sabbath. Reconfigured as a leading authority on the law, Doeg resented David's presumption, and this is how his enmity toward David originated.

In his composite profile, Ginzberg (*Legends* 4:74–76) emphasizes the significance of Doeg's false report to the effect that Ahimelech had made oracular inquiry on David's behalf. He refers to the play on the gentilic האדומי, derived by the sages from the adjective אדום "red", with redness taken as a sign of embarrassment. It is as though it says that Doeg put other scholars to shame by his great learning. Doeg, reconfigured in some of the sources as president of the Sanhedrin, misused his acumen to misconstrue the legal ruling (הלכה) on the matter of oracular inquiry through the Urim and Thummim. Doeg maintained that the Urim and Thummim could only be employed on behalf of a king, thus making Ahimelech's inquiry on David's behalf treasonous, because it implied that he, not Saul, was the true king. Understood in this way, Doeg's murder of Ahimelech merely constituted the imposition of the death penalty on one guilty of treason. The dominant view was that oracular inquiry through the Urim and Thummim was sanctioned whenever the common good could be served thereby, a requirement surely met by acting to save David and his men. The rabbinic sources contain many more midrashic spins on themes taken from the biblical narrative of Doeg, now in his reconfigured role—his jealousy, his mendacity, and his misuse of his great learning. These later sources effectively resonate with the biblical narratives by focusing on Doeg's lie in accusing Ahimelech of treasonous acts.

Ahithophel

The passage in the Jerusalem Talmud (*y. Sanh.* 29a; 1323–24) opens with the following description of Ahithophel: אחיתופל אדם גדול בתורה היה "Ahithophel was a great Torah scholar". It goes on to relate instances when his powers were effective. Most interesting, perhaps, is the following passage:

> What did Ahithophel customarily do? When a person set about taking counsel of him on a matter, he would say to him: "Go, do this or that. But if you don't trust me, go and inquire of the Urim and Thummim." So, he would go and make inquiry, and discover that it was right. This explains what is written: "And the counsel given by Ahithophel in those days was accepted like an oracle sought from God." (2 Sam 16:23)

It appears from the larger passage in *y. Sanh.* 29a that David had not appointed Ahithophel as one of his many elders, a perceived insult that generated intense antagonism between them. When subsequently David was in need of his counsel after all, to attend to something that had gone wrong with the ark during transport, Ahithophel refused to assist him, saying sarcastically: "Send word to inquire of those wise men whom you appointed!" To this David replied: "One who knows how to resolve a problem, but fails to resolve it will ultimately be hanged." Ahithophel was refusing to use his skills on behalf of his king and people; he was insincere and unreliable. This was not because his counsel was unsound but because his intentions were objectionable.

Reading Ginzberg's profile (*Legends* 4:94–97), we see that, just as in the case of Balaam, Ahithophel's role was not reconfigured in the manner of Doeg. The Ahithophel of Midrash remains a counselor, albeit with magical powers and with associations not present in the biblical narrative. Reasons are given for his antagonism toward David, thereby explaining his defection to Absalom. For the most part, however, what is implicit in the biblical narrative about Ahithophel's ambitions is made explicit. He calculated that Absalom, although he would be victorious under his recommended plan, would ultimately be condemned to death for rebelling against his father. When that happened, and with David gone, Ahithophel could ascend to the throne of Israel without objection.

Yet another thematic link between Balaam and Ahithophel is the fear of falling prey to false counsel, the apprehension that leaders of the people, in particular, would arrive at disastrous decisions and embrace the wrong policies. This is a prevalent theme in wisdom literature and is part of the mystery of ascertaining the true will of God.

Gehazi

Thus, the Jerusalem Talmud states,

> גיחזי אדם גבור בתורה היה Gehazi was a great master of the Torah—except that he had three faults: He was begrudging of others, and he was given over to sexual license, and he did not acknowledge the resurrection of the dead. (*y. Sanh.* 29b; 1324)

In effect, the Jerusalem Talmud (*y. Sanh.* 29b–c; 1324–25) strengthens the biblical case against Gehazi, in his reconfigured role. The talmudic text documents Gehazi's three faults, relating that, out of envy, he blocked the students' access to Elisha when the master was studying. When he moved away from the entrance, throngs of students came to learn from Elisha. His disbelief in the resurrection of the dead is epitomized by his failure to follow Elisha's instructions when he was sent to resurrect the Shunamite woman's son, a misbehavior that caused his master's staff to be ineffectual. Gehazi was admonished not to greet anyone on the way or stop to converse with anyone, but he disobeyed, ridiculing his mission to resurrect the dead. Gehazi had broken the numinous chain from prophet to client, realized in his master's staff. How different was the relationship between Moses and Aaron, whose casting of the staff was effective. As for sexual misconduct, we read further that Gehazi did not simply push the woman away from Elisha when she had grasped his feet, but groped her between her breasts. So, we are led to believe that there were lapses on the part of Gehazi even prior to the Naaman episode.

The retelling of this episode in the Jerusalem Talmud represents a veritable Aramaic paraphrase of the biblical narrative but adds a significant explanation absent from the original: Elisha says to Gehazi: מיאנתה מתן שכרן שלצדיקין "You have forfeited the granting of the reward of the righteous". This reward is granted only in the World to Come, as we read in *m. ʾAbot* 2:16: ודע מתן שכרן שלצדיקים לעתיד לבוא "And know [this]: The granting of the reward of the righteous is in the future (life) to come". We are not allowed to profit from righteous acts in this life. In this way, the Jerusalem Talmud links denial of the World to Come to Gehazi's own greed, as exhibited in the Naaman incident.

Still another aspect of Gehazi's activities is portrayed in the Jerusalem Talmud, namely, his situation after his dismissal by Elisha and after having been stricken by the same ailment that had afflicted Naaman. Elisha eventually regretted that he had sent Gehazi away, because Gehazi, who possessed exceptional powers, proceeded to employ them in promoting idolatry. By using his magical arts, Gehazi fashioned a talking idol, which he represented as the God of Israel (shades of Aaron's fashioning of the golden bull-calf). In an effort to redeem Gehazi and bring him back to the true faith, Elisha betook himself to Damascus (as we read in 2 Kgs 8:7), where Gehazi had fled. But Gehazi was too far gone, in the language of the Jerusalem Talmud: מוחלט "irretrievable". On this account, Elisha is criticized for his harsh treatment of Gehazi. One should temper rejection with acceptance; when the right arm pushes away, the left arm should draw a person near. Elisha had pushed Gehazi away with both arms! Once again, Ginzberg's rabbinic profile of Gehazi (*Legends* 4:244–46) rounds out the picture.

Summary

It was mentioned earlier that Psalm 52, the caption of which refers to Doeg the Edomite, is a classic didactic composition of the wisdom genre. The meaning of the Mishnah's focus on the four private individuals is precisely the meaning found in the biblical wisdom tradition. Wisdom and skill must be informed by fear of the Lord, else they may be used for evil. "The fear of the Lord is the best part of wisdom" (Prov 1:7). Never is the actual skill of any of the four individuals who are singled out by the Mishnah doubted. To the contrary, all four are depicted in rabbinic literature as eminently capable, and the same is true in the biblical narratives. But they were villains! On the individual level, their acts are demonstrations of betrayal, of intrigue and deception, of giving in to baser instincts, such as greed and ambition. In the rabbinic profiles, these character defects are given a more religious tenor.

Both the biblical narratives and the rabbinic profiles show primary concern with the consequences of individual behavior for the future of entire peoples. The four individuals singled out by the Mishnah—Balaam son of Beor, Doeg the Edomite, Ahithophel, and Gehazi—all served leaders of nations. Balaam served the king of Moab (in the Priestly tradition, also the Midianites and their kings) against Israel, led by Moses. Doeg the Edomite served Saul, the rejected king of Israel, thereby acting against David, the chosen of God. Ahithophel served the pretender, Absalom, against David. Gehazi served Elisha, prophet of the God of Israel, who, in turn, served kings of Northern Israel and who had an important role in relations with the Arameans.

Thus, the denial of a share in the World to Come to the four private persons is based not only on the acts they committed, heinous as they were, but also on the roles they played in their relations with leaders. This is what made the stories of the four worthy of saga. They caused great harm to the entire people of Israel and were hardly entitled to a share in the World to Come, when God will right the wrongs of history.